History and Religion
of the
Egyptians, Assyrians, Babylonians, Medes, Persians, Greeks and Romans

History and Religion
of the
Egyptians, Assyrians, Babylonians, Medes, Persians, Greeks, and Romans

By
George Smith, F.A.S.

Athens ✢ Manchester

The History and Religion of the Egyptians, Assyrians, Babylonians, Medes, Persians, Greeks and Romans

Published by: Old Book Publishing Ltd

Book Cover Design: Old Book Publishing Ltd

Copyright © 2012 Old Book Publishing Ltd
All rights reserved.

Title of original: The Gentile Nations: or, The History and Religion of the Egyptians, Assyrians, Babylonians, Medes, Persians, Greeks and Romans.
Originally published in 1853

Cover image: Babylonian, about **700-500 BC**. Probably from Sippar, southern Iraq, (British Museum). A unique ancient map of the Mesopotamian world. This tablet contains both a cuneiform inscription and a unique map of the Mesopotamian world. Babylon is shown in the centre (the rectangle in the top half of the circle), and Assyria, Elam and other places are also named. The central area is ringed by a circular waterway labelled "Salt-Sea". The outer rim of the sea is surrounded by what were probably originally eight regions, each indicated by a triangle, labelled "Region" or "Island", and marked with the distance in between. The cuneiform text describes these regions, and it seems that strange and mythical beasts as well as great heroes lived there, although the text is far from complete. The regions are shown as triangles since that was how it was visualized that they first would look when approached by water.

ISBN–10: 1-78107-111-X
ISBN–13: 978-1-78107-111-3

EDITOR'S NOTE

Old Book Publishing Ltd takes care in preserving the wording and images of the original books. For this reason we have invested in technology that enables us to enhance the quality of such reproduction. This investment helps overcome problems encountered when reproducing old books, such as stains, coloured paper, discolouration of ink, yellowed pages, see-through and onion skin type paper. This reproduction book, produced from digital images of the original, may contain occasional defects such as missing pages or blemishes due to the original source content or were introduced by the scanning process.
These are scanned pages and the quality of print represents accurately the print quality of the original book, though we may have been able to enhance it.
As this book has been scanned and/or reformatted from the original we cannot guarantee that it is error-free or contains the full content of the original.
However, we believe that this work is culturally important, and despite its imperfections, have elected to bring it back into print as part of our commitment to the preservation of printed works.

Old Book Publishing

THE GENTILE NATIONS:

OR,

The History and Religion

OF THE

EGYPTIANS, ASSYRIANS, BABYLONIANS, MEDES, PERSIANS, GREEKS, AND ROMANS;

COLLECTED FROM ANCIENT AUTHORS AND HOLY SCRIPTURE, AND INCLUDING THE RECENT DISCOVERIES IN EGYPTIAN, PERSIAN, AND ASSYRIAN INSCRIPTIONS:

FORMING A COMPLETE

CONNEXION OF SACRED AND PROFANE HISTORY,

AND SHOWING

THE FULFILMENT OF SACRED PROPHECY.

BY GEORGE SMITH, F. A. S.,

MEMBER OF THE ROYAL ASIATIC SOCIETY OF GREAT BRITAIN AND IRELAND, OF THE ROYAL SOCIETY OF LITERATURE, OF THE IRISH ARCHÆOLOGICAL SOCIETY, ETC.

FOURTH EDITION.

New York:
PUBLISHED BY CARLTON & PORTER,
200 MULBERRY-STREET.

PREFACE.

IN presenting the third and concluding part of the "Sacred Annals" to the public, the author feels called upon to apologize for the delay which has taken place in its publication. In the Preface to "The Hebrew People," he announced that, so long since as 1849, he had made considerable preparation for the composition of this portion; but, notwithstanding this preparation, and his most diligent exertions, it has not been found possible to complete it at an earlier period. This has been in part the result of unexpected demands which have been made on the author's time; but the principal cause has been his anxious wish to avail himself to the utmost of the recent important discoveries in the East, and to incorporate their result, as far as practicable, in his account of the annals and faith of the earlier of the four great empires.

This has been done; and the history and religion of these ancient Gentile nations are now placed before the reader, with the full advantage of the additions, corrections, and corroborations, which have been obtained by the disinterment of Assyrian and Babylonish sculptures, and the translations of the inscriptions which have been found in those countries, and in Persia.

In this part of the work, as well as in the preceding, it has been the author's unvarying aim to exhibit an intelligible view of the history and religion of these ancient monarchies. From the size of the book, the historical part can hardly be expected to extend beyond a mere sketch of each of the great empires. Yet, even in this limited compass, scarcely a single difficulty or an important event has escaped notice and elucidation. Especial attention has been given to chronology; and this, which has been aptly termed "the soul of history," has, in respect of the early portion of the annals of every nation, been very carefully investigated, and, it is hoped, accurately ascertained.

But the ruling element of this volume, and, in fact, of the whole work, is its religious character. The maintenance of this throughout the series of researches comprised in the "Gentile Nations," has been a labour attended with very great difficulty. To pass beyond the ritualism and ceremonial externalism everywhere prevalent, to penetrate into the nature and genius of the various forms which idolatry assumed, and to form a sound judgment respecting the religious doctrines, practices, and morals of Egypt, Assyria, and Babylon, of Persia, Greece, and Rome, has been a most arduous task. But it has been honestly and earnestly attempted; and the result is now submitted to the candid consideration of the Christian public.

If the author has succeeded in these efforts, it will have been made plain, that, in every one of these far-famed nations, God left himself not without an efficient witness. Everywhere is seen demonstrative evidence of the existence and operation of divine truth, and of divine influence, in ancient days; and ample proof is afforded, that the soul-destroying and mind-debasing idolatry of those nations was not an accident, or an error, but a crime induced by Satanic agency.

The author ventures to hope, that more than this has been effected by these researches; and that the field of ancient history has been wrested from the power of infidelity and scepticism, and made subservient to the interests of revealed truth. It has at least been shown, that an honest and candid examination of the annals of the primitive nations, not only does not produce any facts in opposition to the records of Holy Writ, but actually furnishes the most important illustrations and corroborations of their teaching: and, what is yet more remarkable, it has been clearly shown, that the foul and false systems of doctrine and worship, which Satanic energy fastened at length on every part of the Gentile world, in all their darkness and enormity, bear witness to the light from which men had departed, and the truth which they had forsaken: so that, in future, the history and religion of the ancient heathen world may be numbered among the most important of the external evidences of the verity of divine revelation.

At all events, the author has filled up his plan in accordance with his first announcement. More than ten years ago he formed the purpose of writing "An Epitome of the History and Religion of the World, from the Creation to the Birth of Christ." By a steady and continued course of exertion, amid the pressure of many important avocations, he has at length, by the good providence of God, completed his task; and, with feelings of unaffected thanksgiving to the Author of all good, he consecrates the result of his toil to the cause of evangelical godliness, for the advancement of Scriptural knowledge.

Trevu, Camborne,
  October 13th, 1853.

CONTENTS.

PRELIMINARY DISSERTATION.

THE ORIGIN, CHARACTER, MYSTERIES AND ORACLES OF PAGAN IDOLATRY.

KNOWLEDGE of this Subject necessary—False Religion attests the Religious Tendency of Man—Heathen Idolatry must be studied with a distinct Recognition of Satanic Influence—Necessity of admitting the Evidence of Revelation—ORIGIN OF IDOLATRY—Idolatry in Postdiluvian Times arose before the Dispersion—And emanated from Babel—Was not at first a violent Introduction of Error, but a fatal Perversion of Truth—Elements of Truth liable to this Perversion—Plurality of Persons in one Deity—Promised Incarnation—Rites of Patriarchal Worship—Man's primitive Purity and Fall—Similarity of the Adamic and Noachic Families—Hero-Worship considered as arising out of the promised Incarnation, and taking the Form of a Triad from the Great Father and his three Sons—Peculiar Case of Egypt—Animal-Worship—Folly of many Attempts to account for it—Originated in the Cherubim—Worship of material Elements—The Agency under which all this Error was evolved made apparent by the universal Worship of the Serpent Form—THE RELIGIOUS CHARACTER OF THIS SYSTEM—It practically obliterated the essential Principle of the Divine Unity—Banished all Idea of Divine Purity—And destroyed at once the Knowledge of God, and Confidence in him—Character of Idolatrous Worship—General Admission—But the Being to whom this Worship was offered was not God—And the Service, although often grand and imposing, was generally associated with foul and filthy Abominations—THE MYSTERIES—The Theory of Warburton refuted by Leland—Conflicting Theories as to the Origin of the Mysteries—Their Object equally contested—Their Origin defined—Their Object explained—Essential Elements of Heathen Mysteries—THE ORACLES of Heathen Worship—An undoubted Privilege of Patriarchal Times to have Access unto God, and to obtain special and important Instruction by this Means—Contest between the Learned as to whether Heathen Oracles were sustained by Satanic Influence—Testimony of Scripture—Judgment of the Learned on the Character and Credit of the Oracles—Case of Crœsus, King of Lydia, from Herodotus—The Result of the Inquiry establishes the Operation of Satanic Influence—General Observations in Conclusion....... Page 15

CHAPTER I.

EGYPT: ITS HISTORY.

GENERAL View of Egypt—Difficulties which oppose our Acquaintance with its Early History—Undoubted Evidence of High Civilization in the most Remote Times—Prowess and Reign of Amosis—EIGHTEENTH DYNASTY—Death of Jacob—Wonderful Perfection of Mechanical Art—Death of Joseph—Moses—The Exodus—Canaanitish Nations weakened by Egyptian Invasion before the Israelites crossed the Jordan—Sesostris—NINETEENTH DYNASTY—Sethos—His Conquests—The Absence of further

Allusion to Canaan on the Monuments, a striking Proof of the Truth of Scripture—TWENTIETH DYNASTY—TWENTY-FIRST DYNASTY—Effect of the Commercial Policy of the Hebrews on Egypt—TWENTY-SECOND DYNASTY—Shishak—His Invasion of Judea—TWENTY-THIRD DYNASTY—Decline of Egyptian Power—TWENTY-FOURTH DYNASTY—Bocchoris—TWENTY-FIFTH DYNASTY—Tarkus—TWENTY-SIXTH DYNASTY—The Dodecarchy—Triumph and Reign of Psammiticus—Pharaoh-Necho—His Victory over the Hebrews—Apries, the Pharaoh-Hophra of Scripture—Defeated and put to death by Amosis—Conquest of Egypt by a Persian Army—TWENTY-SEVENTH DYNASTY—Era of Persian Rule—Successful Government of Darius—Gallant Effort of Inaros—His Defeat and Death—Herodotus—TWENTY-EIGHTH DYNASTY—Amyrtœus—TWENTY-NINTH DYNASTY—THIRTIETH DYNASTY—Chronological Difficulties—Persian Invasion defeated—Slothful Habits and Ultimate Energy of Darius Ochus—THIRTY-FIRST DYNASTY—Persian Rule reëstablished—THIRTY-SECOND DYNASTY—Conquest of Egypt by Alexander the Great—His profound and successful Political and Commercial Policy—Alexandria built—Ruin of the Macedonian House—THIRTY-THIRD DYNASTY—The Ptolemies—Lagus—His Successful Rule—Power and Cultivation of Egypt under Philadelphus—Euergetes successful in War—Intercourse between Egypt and Rome—Gradual Decline of Egyptian Power—Excessive Vices of the ruling Princes—Cleopatra, Cæsar, and Antony—Egypt a Roman Province.. Page 53

CHAPTER II.

THE RELIGION OF THE EGYPTIANS.

REFERENCE to this Subject in "the Patriarchal Age"—The Importance of THEOLOGY to Religion—Egyptian Triads, their Relation to primitive Promise and Noah—The probable Identity of these Triads—Animal-Worship originated in the Cherubim, and carried out to an infamous Extent—General View of Egyptian Mythology—The MORALS of Egypt, recognised in Jurisprudence—Prominence given to Truth and Justice—Illustrations—The Doctrine of THE IMMORTALITY OF THE SOUL—Curious Corruptions associated with this Doctrine—Object of Embalming—The Doctrine of a future Judgment—The Opinions held by this People exhibited—Important Light imparted thereby on the Subject of Morals—The Hall of Judgment and forty-two Assessors—All resulting in everlasting Happiness or Punishment—Providence—General Accuracy of Doctrine, but neutralized by Polytheism—General Character and Influence of this Religion—Morals—Divine Sanction—Future Retribution—Spiritual Character—Remarkable Juxtaposition of Truth and Error... 128

CHAPTER III.

THE HISTORY OF THE ASSYRIANS

HISTORY of Assyria resumed with the Reign of BELOCUUS—Absence of precise Information respecting this and succeeding Reigns—Probability that even in this Age the Power of Egypt was felt on the Banks of the Euphrates—Interference of Assyria in the Trojan War—Fragmentary Notices of ancient Reigns recovered from Inscriptions by Colonel Rawlinson—Connected Assyrian History begins about the Tenth Century, B. C.—ADRAMMELECH I.—SARDANAPALUS I.—His military Career and Successes—DIVANUBARA—The Annals of his Reign from the Black Obelisk and other Sculptures—SHEMAS ADAR—ADRAMMELECH II. or THONOS CONCOLEROS—The Termination of the Old Imperial Dynasty—ARBACES the Mede on the Throne of Assyria—The Mission of Jonah, and its Results—The Assyrians recover their Sovereignty—PUL obtains the sceptre—Menahem, King of Israel, destroys Tiphsah—Pul invades Israel, and extorts a thousand Talents of Silver from Menahem—Tiglath-Pileser succeeds to the Throne—At the Solicitation of Ahaz, he invades Syria and Israel, and carries the trans-Jordanic Tribes and the Inhabitants of Galilee into Captivity—Colonel Rawlinson's Arrangement of the Information obtained from the Sculptures of Khorsabad and Kouyunjik—Sargina usurps the Throne—His Annals and public Works—Sennacherib—His Campaigns from the Inscriptions—Remarkable Accordance between their Account of his War with Hezekiah, and that given in the Scriptures—The Destruction of his Army—His subsequent Reign—Esarhaddon—The Ruin of Samaria, and final Subversion of the Kingdom of Israel—The Captivity and Restoration of Manasseh—Nabuchodonoson—His Wars in the East—Defeat and Death of Phraortes—An Army under Holofernes sent into Western Asia—The General slain by Judith, and the Army surprised and routed—Sarac, or Sardanapalus II.—Alliance of Media and Babylon against Assyria—Nineveh besieged and taken—The Assyrian Empire subverted..Page 148

CHAPTER IV.

THE HISTORY OF THE BABYLONIANS.

Babylon the Seat of the first Postdiluvian Sovereignty—Conquered and subjected to Assyria—Policy of Assyria toward subject Countries—Nabonassar—The Era bearing his Name—He was independent—Nadius, Chinzirus, Porus, and Jugæus, successively reign—Mardocempadus or Merodach-Baladan—His Embassage to Hezekiah—Archianus—Hagisa—Maradach Baldanes—Belibus defeated by Assyria—Asordanes—Nabopolassar—Babylon asserts its Independence—Coalition of Babylon and Media against Nineveh—Scythian Invasion—Nineveh destroyed—The King of Egypt defeated at Carchemish—Nebuchadnezzar—Takes Jerusalem—Carries away the principal Inhabitants into Captivity—Makes Zedekiah King—He rebels—Jerusalem again taken, and destroyed—Tyre taken, after a Siege of Thirteen Years—Egypt conquered—Nebuchadnezzar greatly improves Babylon by many Splendid Erections—Nebuchadnezzar's Dream of the Great Image—Explained by Daniel—Its wonderful Revelations—The Golden Image—Extraordinary Measures adopted for its Dedication—Heroism of the Three Hebrews—Glorious Revelation of the Son of God—Important Results of this Divine Interposition—The Dream of a Great Tree—Its Interpretation and Accomplishment—Noble Acknowledgment of the King—His Prophecy and Death—Evil-Merodach King—Liberates Jehoiachin from Prison—Neriglissar reigns—Forms a Combination against Media—He is slain in Battle—Laborosarchod reigns—The Belshazzar of the Book of Daniel—His Youth and Cruelty—He profanes the Sacred Vessels—Is slain—Darius takes the Kingdom, and appoints Labynetus Viceroy of Babylon—He rules subject to Media—Declares himself independent—Is defeated in Battle—Babylon taken by Cyrus—Labynetus taken at Borsippa, and sent into Carmania—Termination of the Babylonian Monarchy.. 181

CHAPTER V.

THE RELIGION OF THE ASSYRIANS AND BABYLONIANS.

Babylon the seat of the first post-diluvian Apostacy—Peculiar Religious Position of Babylon and Assyria—Epiphanius on the Early Declension of Religion—Information contained in his Statement—Fragment of Damascius—Its Important Teaching—The Chaldæan Oracles exhibit the same Fact—A Triad consisting of the Great Mother, Father, and Only-begotten Son—Further Development of Chaldæan Mythology—Chaldæan Deities—Their Origin and Peculiarities—Worship of the Heavenly Bodies, and of Fire—Chaldæan and Assyrian Idolatry began with Hero and Demon Worship in the Form of Triads—Mr. Faber on this Subject—Symbolical Representation of the Great Triad—Other Symbols—Assarac—Cherubic Figures—The Sacred Tree—A Garden called "Paradise" attached to each Royal Palace—The Palace itself a Sacred Temple—Doubts of Layard—Elaborate Proof of Fergusson—The King revered as a Divine Person—Proof of this—Manner in which the Kings evinced their Claim to this Character—This Idea shown to pervade the whole System—Remarkable Identity of Character which the Religion of Assyria and Babylon maintained through so many Ages—General Views—Gradual Declension in Theology—Worship of Fire—The Results of Hebrew Intercourse and Divine Interposition on the Religion of these Countries—Sabæanism not the Primitive Religion of Assyria—A large Amount of Patriarchal History and Religious Knowledge must have remained in the Primitive Nations long after the Dispersion—Patriarchal Longevity designed to prevent a Deterioration in Religion—Connexion with the Hebrews—Divine Interposition more likely on this Ground to be effective—Assyrian Intercourse with Egypt—Assyrian Knowledge of Hebrew History—The Mission of Jonah—Its Religious Results—The Destruction of the Assyrian Emigrants in Samaria by Lions—A Hebrew Priest sent to teach them the Law of the Lord—Babylon elated by the Ruin of Jerusalem—The King humbled, and all the People taught Divine Truth, on the Plains of Dura—Nebuchadnezzar's Insanity, Restoration, and Proclamation.......................... Page 202

CHAPTER VI.

THE HISTORY OF THE MEDES.

LINEAGE and Country of the Medes—Ecbatana, the Capital—Revolt of the Medes against Assyria—They recover their Independence—A Season of Anarchy—Public Spirit and judicial Efforts of DEJOCES—He is raised to the Sovereignty of Media—Establishes a regular Government and greatly improves the Country—PHRAORTES, a martial Prince, subdues Persia, and extends the Median Power over other neighbouring Nations—Invades Assyria, is defeated and slain—Ecbatana stormed and spoiled by the Assyrian King—CYAXARES invades Assyria—Defeats the Imperial Army, and besieges Nineveh—The Scythian Invasion—The Medes defeated—The Scythians overrun Asia—Their Massacre and Expulsion—The Lydian War—It is suspended, and Nineveh besieged a second Time, and taken—The Lydian War renewed—Terminated by the Eclipse of Thales—ASTYAGES reigns—Prosecutes various Wars—Belshazzar slain—The Kingdom of Babylon reverts to Astyages—Media conquered, and the Kingdom subverted by Cyrus 243

CHAPTER VII.

THE PERSIANS AND THE MEDO-PERSIAN EMPIRE.

PERSIA a Province of the Assyrian Empire—Peculiar Interest attaching to this Part of Persian History—The Spirit and Prowess of the Blacksmith Kawah obtain the Independence of his Country—FERIDOON placed on the Throne—His long and just Reign—He divides his Kingdom between his Sons, SELM, TOOR, and ERIJ—Erij slain by his Brothers—The Assassins defeated and slain by MANUCHEHER, who reigns with great Celebrity—Sam, Prime Minister—Roostum, his Grandson, the great Persian Hero, born—NOUZEN succeeds to the Throne—His cruel Reign—He is slain—Zoo expels the Enemy—His Son KERSHASP raised to the Throne, and afterward deposed—End of the Peshdadian Dynasty—The Kaianian Dynasty—The Median Ascendency concealed by imaginary Kings, KAI KOBAD representing Dejoces and Phraortes, and KAI KOOS Cyax-

CONTENTS. 9

ares and Astyages—Reference to the Eclipse of Thales—KAI KHOSRU, or CYRUS, succeeds to the Throne—The Account of Ctesias respecting his Parentage—The probable Career of this Warrior, until he defeats and deposes Astyages—Cyrus marries the Daughter of Astyages—The Death of the deposed King—Cyrus conquers Lydia—Takes Babylon, and establishes a universal Empire—His Conduct toward the Hebrews—The Restoration of Jerusalem begun—Extent of the Persian Empire—The Death of Cyrus—CAMBYSES—He prohibits the Progress of Building at Jerusalem—Invades and conquers Egypt—His impolitic Cruelty and Impiety—Usurpation of Smerdis the Magian—Death of Cambyses—Smerdis destroyed by a Conspiracy of Nobles—DARIUS raised to the Throne—His improved Mode of Government—The Case of Democedes, the Greek Physician—Makes an Edict in favour of the Hebrews—Reduces Samos—Babylon rebels—The Self-sacrifice of Zopyrus—Babylon is taken—Conquests in the East—A Body of Greek Troops wage War in Asia Minor, and burn Sardis—Darius contemplates the Invasion of Greece—Failure of the first Expedition under Mardonius—Battle of Marathon, and Ruin of the second Persian Invasion—Death of Darius—Persepolis—Behistun Sculptures—XERXES—Subdues Egypt—Makes vast Preparations for the Invasion of Greece—Crosses the Hellespont—Battle at Thermopylæ—The Persian Fleet defeated at Salamis, and their Army destroyed at Platæa—The Remnant of the Persian Fleet and Army destroyed at Mycale—Horrible Crime and Cruelty perpetrated in the royal Court—Xerxes assassinated—ARTAXERXES I. established on the Throne—Marries Esther—Ezra and Nehemiah sent to Judea—Revolt of Egypt—Peace with Athens—XERXES II.—SOGDIANUS—DARIUS NOTHUS subdues his Rivals—Demoralization of the Persian Court—ARTAXERXES II.—Revolt of Cyrus—He marches into the East—Is slain, and the Army dispersed, at Cunaxa—Retreat of the Ten Thousand Greeks—Continued Iniquity of the Court—Revolt and Death of the Heir-apparent—ARTAXERXES III. murders the royal Family—Restores Persian Authority in Egypt, Phenicia, and Cyprus—DARIUS III. undertakes the Government—Alexander invades the Empire—Triumph of the Macedonian...................... Page 251

CHAPTER VIII.

THE RELIGION OF THE PERSIANS.

IMPORTANCE and Difficulties of the Subject—Great Aid supplied by ancient Inscriptions—The Religion of Persia identical in its original Elements with that of Assyria and Babylon—Opinion of Jacob Bryant on the first Zoroaster—Its probable Import—The Magi—General Elements of the Persian Faith—Deity of the King—Palace-Temples—Paradises—Sacred Tree—Cherubic Figures—Divine Triad—Persian Peculiarities in this Symbol—The supreme Deity in Persia represented with the Head of a Bird—The Religious System of Zoroaster—The first Triad: Cronus, Ormuzd, Ahriman—This changed to Ormuzd, Mithras, Ahriman—Their respective Character and Position—The Antagonism and Creations of Ormuzd and Ahriman—The Worship of Fire, its probable Origin—The System of Zoroaster professed to rest on Divine Revelation—The Creation of Angels, the World, and Mankind—General Accordance with Holy Scripture—The Fall of Man—The Prevalence of Evil—The Flood—Continuance of Depravity—Mission of Zoroaster—The Spiritual Nature of Man—Future Judgment—Resurrection—Doctrine of universal Restoration—Wicked Men, and even Ahriman, raised to Heaven—The Priesthood—Their Three Orders: Herboods, Mobeds, and the Dustoor—Altars and Temples—Perpetual Fire—Public Worship—Sacred Rites—Holy Water—Morals—Sound Principles mingled with much that is puerile and superstitious—The Faith of Persia formed a perfect Type of Papal Superstition—Observations on the Manner in which this Inquiry has been conducted—Folly of forming an Opinion on this Subject under the Influence of Grecian Mythology—Necessity of recognising the Founders of the Nation as Members of the great patriarchal Family—General View of the System.. 287

CHAPTER IX.

THE HISTORY OF THE GRECIAN STATES.

ALTHOUGH occupying a small Country, and not possessing early Civilization, the Greeks arose to superlative Distinction in History—The Geography of Greece—The Origin of the Greeks—Pelasgians and Hellenes kindred Races—Legendary History—The Argonautic Expedition—The Theban Legends—The Trojan War—The Return of the Heracleids—State of the Grecian States in the Time of Lycurgus—Division into numerous independent Communities—Their Unity of Blood, Manners, and Religion—The Political and Civil Institutions of Lycurgus—Sparta subdues the Messenians—The State of Athens—Prevalent and long-continued Disorder—Solon—He regains Possession of Salamis—Succeeds in the Sacred War against Cirrha—Fearful State of Society—Solon invested with Supreme Power—His Reforming Measures, and new Political Constitution, established—Pisistratus obtains the Chief Authority—The Tyrant expelled, and Democracy established, by the Aid of Sparta—The smaller Grecian States—The Islands and Colonies—Causes which led to the First Persian Invasion—It utterly fails—A Second prepared, and disembarked at the Bay of Marathon—Completely defeated by the Athenians under Miltiades—Further Persian Preparations for the Conquest of Greece—Suspended by the Death of Darius—Xerxes at length determines on another Invasion—His immense Preparations and Vast Army—Checked at Thermopylæ—His Fleet defeated at Artemisium—Athens destroyed—The Persian Fleet ruined at Salamis—Xerxes retreats—Returns to Asia—Mardonius makes the most flattering Overtures to the Athenians—Which they nobly reject—Apathy of Sparta—Attica ravaged a Second Time—A United Greek Army at length opposes the Foe—The Persian Force is annihilated at Platæa—On the same day the Persian Fleet is destroyed at Mycale—Successful Prosecution of the War, followed by Peace with Persia—The Period, Causes, and Progress of Grecian Civilization and Advancement—Thales—Pythagoras—Greece attains her Highest Intellectual Elevation—Great Wealth and Power of Athens—First Peloponnesian War—Mischievous Policy of Alcibiades—Second Peloponnesian War—Ruin of Athens—Sparta tyrannizes over the other Grecian States—Restoration of Athens to Independence—Xenophon and the Ten Thousand—Thebes—Pelopidas and Epaminondas—Philip of Macedon—His Improved Military Tactics—Takes advantage of the Disunion and Rivalry of the Greek States to make himself Master of the Country—Alexander succeeds his Father—Prepares for the Invasion of Persia—Battle of the Granicus—His uninterrupted Success—In Three Years he extends his Sway from the Mediterranean to India—His Death—State of Greece during the Victorious Career of Alexander—Aggression of Sparta on Macedon—Repelled—Tumults on the Death of Alexander, repressed by Antipater—Cassander—His Government—Interference of Rome—Progress of her Power—Greece a Roman Province.......................... Page 313

CHAPTER X.

THE RELIGION OF GREECE.

THE earliest Religion of this People appears to have been a strange Compound of the Adoration of the material Elements and Powers of Nature; united with a sacred Regard for Mythic Legends, which had been traditionally preserved—Expansion of this Scheme after the Return of the Heracleids, and the Establishment of the Dorian Power—Outline of Grecian Theology and Cosmogony—The Grecian Deities—Zeus—Hera—Apollon—Artemis—Hermes—Hephaistos—Aphrodite—Ares—Eros, and other minor Divinities—The Greek Triad—Evident Connexion of the whole Scheme with Scriptural Tradition—The Temples—Priests—Worship—Divination—Oracles and Mysteries—The Influence of Philosophy examined—THALES—His Doctrines, and the Ionic

School—PYTHAGORAS—His System—Failure in Greece, and wonderful Success in Sicily—The Character of his Teaching—SOCRATES—His Mode of Instruction—Doctrines—He claims a Divine Mission—The important Character and Influence of his Teaching—PLATO—General View of his Object—His Doctrines—Grand Intellectual Development evinced in his Philosophy—But his Efforts unfavourable to Morals and Religion—ARISTOTLE—His brilliant Intellectual Efforts—Inefficient in respect of Religion—ZENO and the Stoics—Physical and Moral Doctrines—Unsatisfactory Result—EPICURUS—His System—Its pernicious Effects—General View of Grecian Faith—Importance of Divine Influence, and a recognition of its Power—The Effect of these four Schools of Philosophy fatal to the Religion of Greece—Utter Failure of every Influence to correct the Effects of a vitiated Theology.. Page 360

CHAPTER XI.

THE HISTORY OF ROME.

IMPORTANCE of Roman History—Unusual Extent of its Legendary Portion—Arrival of Æneas on the Banks of the Tiber—Lavinium—Alba—Romulus and Remus—Rome—Death of Remus—Rape of the Sabine Virgins—Sabine War—Political Constitution of the first Romans—Numa—Tullus Hostilius—Albans removed to Rome—Ancus Martius—The Reigns of the Tarquins and of Servius Tullius—Tragic Fate of Lucretia—Abolition of Royalty—Junius Brutus—War with Porsenna—Destruction of Veii—Invasion of the Gauls—Distress of the Romans—Oppressive Character of the Laws respecting the Poor—Legislative Reform—Renewed aggressive War—All Italy subdued by the Romans—War with Carthage—The First Punic War—Sicily added to Rome as a Province—Further Extension of Territory on the Continent procured by the Romans—Sardinia seized—Hannibal—His deadly Enmity to Rome—His Measures in Spain—The Second Punic War—Hannibal invades Italy—His wonderful Success—Repeated Defeat of the Roman Armies—Scipio leads a Roman Army into Africa—Obtains successive Victories—Hannibal recalled to Carthage, and defeated—Peace between Rome and Carthage, on Terms dictated by Rome—War with Macedon, in which Rome is triumphant, Philip reduced to Submission, and Liberty proclaimed to Greece—Antiochus of Syria makes War on Rome—Is entirely defeated—War between Rome and Perseus, King of Macedon—He is completely subdued—Rapid Increase and vast Extent of the Roman Dominions—The Third Punic War—Destruction of Carthage—Continued Progress of Roman Power—Results of these successive and immense military Operations on the Parent State—Isolation of the Ruling Class from the People—Great Distress of the latter—Tiberius Gracchus endeavours to effect legislative Reforms for correcting these Evils—Is circumvented, and murdered—Caius Gracchus succeeds his Brother in his Efforts to redress the Grievances of the People—Carries several Measures—Loses his election on being proposed a third Time for the Tribuneship—Determines on armed Resistance—Is defeated, and slain—Progress of Patrician Power, and the Demoralization of Roman Governments—Jugurthine War—Marius Consul—Termination of the War, and Captivity and cruel Death of Jugurtha—War with the Cimbri—The Romans sustain several Defeats, but the Enemy is ultimately routed and destroyed by Marius—Civil Wars in Sicily and Italy—Italians incorporated as Roman Citizens—Factious Rivalry between Marius and Sylla—The former in a Tumult expels his rival, and makes himself Master of Rome—Sylla at the Head of an Army marches to Rome, and takes Possession of the City—He removes his Enemies from Power, and proceeds to conduct the War against Mithridates—The King of Pontus completely defeated—Rome subjected to fearful Carnage and Disorder by Marius and Cinna—Sylla grants Mithridates Terms of Peace, and, uniting the Army of Fimbria to his own, returns to Rome—Sylla defeats the Troops of the Consuls, and makes himself absolute Master of Rome—Fearful Extent of his Proscriptions, and consequent Slaughter of Soldiers and Citizens—His Death—Pompey defeats a Marian Faction in Spain—Destroys the Cilician Pirates—

Defeats Mithridates, and annexes his Dominions to Rome—Conspiracy of Catiline at Rome—Defeated by Cicero—The First Triumvirate—Pompey, Crassus, and Julius Cæsar—Crassus slain in the Parthian War—Cæsar, commanded by the Senate to disband his Army, marches on Rome—Pompey retires to Greece—Is followed by Cæsar, and defeated—Flies to Egypt, and is slain there—Julius Cæsar sole Ruler of the Roman Dominions—Cæsar slain by Conspirators—Strange Irresolution and want of Unity evinced by the Conspirators after the Death of Cæsar—The selfish Policy, Peculation, and Ambition of Antony—Prudent Conduct of the young Octavius—He is elected Consul—Flight of Brutus and Cassius—The Second Triumvirate—Antony, Lepidus, and Octavius—Defeat and Death of Brutus and Cassius—Antony's disgraceful Residence in Egypt—Lepidus banished—Defeat of Antony at Actium—He commits suicide in Egypt—Octavius, as Augustus, supreme Ruler at Rome...................... Page 406

CHAPTER XII.

THE RELIGION OF ROME.

MISTAKEN Notion which obtains of this Religion—Rome greatly indebted to Etruria—The Religious Institutions of the Etruscans—Importance of the Establishment of these Religious Institutions in Italy, before the Rise of Rome to Power—The Etruscan Religion exhibited much important Truth and Divine Influence—Considerable Reference to Primitive Traditions, and the Recognition of a Future State and Judgment—The Founders of Rome educated in these Doctrines—All the Primitive Arrangement and Organization of Rome formed on an Etruscan Basis—Sabine and Latin Deities introduced by the Union of these Tribes—Numa and his Institutions—Reign of Tarquin—Servius Tullius—Corruptions in Theology and Image-Worship introduced—The Gods of Rome—*Dii majorum*—*Dii selecti*—*Dii minorum*—Sacred Persons—Priests—Augurs—*Fetiales*—Flamens—The Sacred Places and Rites of this Religion—Temples—Prayers—Vows—Sacrifices—Festivals—*Lupercalia*—*Bacchanalia*—*Saturnalia*—General View of the Roman Religion—Remarkable Unity maintained, notwithstanding so much Extension and Addition—Completeness of the Ecclesiastical Economy—It answered its Design so far as to pervade the public Mind with its Influence—Originally identified with many important Religious Truths—Inquiry into the Effect of this System on the People—The Knowledge of God which it gave to the People—The Opinions of Deity entertained by Philosophers—Analysis of the Religious Works of Cicero—The Result—The Philosophy of Rome afforded nothing better than Epicurean or Stoical Views of Deity—Knowledge possessed by the Romans of the Immortality of the Soul, and of Future Rewards and Punishments—Effect of this Destitution of Truth upon Roman Morals—The Description given by St. Paul—State of Domestic Manners—Condition of Slaves, and their Cruel Treatment—Horrid Cruelty displayed toward the Children of Sejanus—Awful Prevalence of Licentiousness and unnatural Impurity. 459

CHAPTER XIII.

A GENERAL REVIEW OF THE HISTORY AND RELIGION OF THE GENTILE NATIONS.

MISTAKEN Notions respecting the Accordance of ancient History with Holy Scripture—The Elevation of Man in his primitive State—Remarkable Corroboration of Scripture by Facts in Ancient History—Gentile Religion an important Development of Mosaic Teaching—It contains wonderful Revelations of the Power and Providence of God—Ancient History, as a Fulfilment of Prophecy, a remarkable Attestation of revealed Truth—Relation of Revelation to the Teaching of Science—The Testimony of ancient History in Respect of Religion in remarkable Accordance with the Bible—Proofs of the Existence and Power of Satanic Influence—Infinite Absurdity of Idolatry—Yet it was universal—False Theories devised for the Purpose of accounting for the Existence of Idolatry, considered and refuted—Satanic Aggression on the Purposes of God and Happiness of Man—The Deluge one of its Results—Corruption of the patriarchal Faith —Attempt to frustrate the divinely-appointed Dispersion—Miraculously defeated—The Call of Abraham, and Election of the Hebrew People, still further show the Violence of Satanic Aggression on the Purpose of God—The Succession of great ruling Empires displays the Power of diabolical Influence—The World prepared for the Introduction of the Kingdom of God.. Page 505

NOTES.

ANTEDILUVIAN Idolatry, p. 525.—Was the Doctrine of the Trinity known to the early Patriarchs? p. 526.—The Worship of Man, p. 528.—The Geography and Population of Egypt, p. 530.—The Chronology of Ancient Egypt, p. 531.—The Monumental Names of Kings, p. 534.—Sir Gardiner Wilkinson on the Date of the Exodus, p. 535.—The Providential Preparation for the Israelitish Invasion of Canaan, p. 535.—The Martial Career of Sesostris, p. 535.—The Cruelty exhibited in Egyptian Sculptures, p. 536.— The Fulfilment of Sacred Prophecy in the History of Egypt, p. 537.—The progressive Development of this Idolatry, p. 541.—The Changes made in the Egyptian Triad, p. 542. —Glass sent as an Article of Tribute from Assyria and Babylon to Egypt, p. 543.—The Army sent from Assyria, under the Command of Memnon, to assist Priam during the Trojan War, p. 543.—The Remarkable Means by which the Reading of ancient Monumental Inscriptions has been recovered, p. 544.—The peculiar Difficulty of identifying Assyrian proper Names, p. 545.—The proper chronological Succession of the Reigns exhibited in the Assyrian Sculptures, p. 546—The chronological Position of the lower Line of Assyrian Kings, and their Relation to the Median Revolt, p. 547.—Evidence of Sargina's Wars with Egypt, and the Kind of Tribute sent thence to Assyria, p. 549. —The Fulfilment of Sacred Prophecy in the History of Assyria, p. 549.—The Era of Nabonassar, p. 553.—Probable State of the Political Relation of Babylon to Assyria, prior to the Reign of Nabopolassar, p. 553.—The Punishment of Zedekiah, p. 554.—The Median Princess whom Nebuchadnezzar married,—the Queen Nitocris, p. 555.—The Magnitude and Splendour of Babylon, p. 555.—The chronological Succession of Babylonian Kings after Nebuchadnezzar, p. 556.—The Geography of Borsippa, where Labynetus took Refuge, p. 560.—The Fulfilment of Sacred Prophecy in the History of Babylon, p. 561.—The Testimony of Herodotus respecting the Temple of Mylitta at Babylon, p. 565.—What was the true Principle and Meaning of Sabæan Worship? p. 566.—The Assyrian Triad, p. 567.—The Cherubim of Ezekiel, and their Relation to the compound Figures of the Assyrian Sculptures, p. 568.—Imitations of Paradise attached to the royal Palaces of the Assyrian Kings, p. 569.—Babylon the Type of Papal Antichrist, p. 570.— The Time of Anarchy, and the Accession of Dejoces, p. 572.—The Period of Scythian Domination over Asia, p. 573.—Chronology of the Eclipse of Thales, p. 573.—Who was the "Darius the Mede" of the Book of Daniel? p. 573.—The Fulfilment of Sacred Prophecy in the History of Media, p. 575.—The personal History of Cyrus, p. 576.—Was Cyrus made acquainted with the Prophecies of Daniel? p. 577.—The successful Opposition of the Governors of Syria and others to the Building of Jerusalem, and the Evidence thereby afforded of the Integrity and Perfection of the national Records at the Court of Persia, p. 579.—The Deliberations of the Conspirators as to the future Government of Persia, and the appointment of Darius Hystaspes to be King, p. 580.—The Succession of Xerxes to the Throne of Persia, p. 581.—The Behistun Inscriptions, containing Darius's own Account of his Wars, p. 582.—Did the Jews fight in the Army of Xerxes? p. 590.—The Inscriptions relating to the Reign of Xerxes, p. 591.—The Inscriptions relating to the Reign of Artaxerxes, p. 592.—The Fulfilment of Sacred Prophecy in the

History of Persia, p. 592.—The conflicting Opinions and Controversy respecting Zoroaster and his Doctrines, p. 595.—Probable Theology of Persia before Zoroaster, p. 596.—The Origin of Fire-Worship, p. 599.—The Rewards of Heaven, and the Punishments of Hell, according to Zoroaster, p. 600.—The Argonautic Expedition, p. 603.—The Theban Legends, p. 606.—The Trojan Wars, p. 609.—The Return of the Heraclidæ, p. 612.—The Seven Wise Men of Greece, p. 615.—The Amphictyonic Council, p. 616.—Mortgage Pillars, p. 617.—The Judicial Court of Areopagus, p. 617.—Banishment by Ostracism, p. 617.—The curious Mode employed to count the Army of Xerxes, p. 618.—The Rebuilding of the City of Athens and its Fortifications, p. 618.—The Fulfilment of Scripture Prophecy in the History of Greece, p. 619.—The Grecian Theogony, a poetic and corrupted Version of primitive History and of the Scenes of Babel, p. 621.—The Divine Inspiration of Gentile Prophets, p. 622.—The certain Presence of Satanic Energy in Grecian Soothsaying and Oracles, p. 624.—The sacred nocturnal Scenes of the Eleusinian Mysteries, p. 625.—The Doctrines of Plato respecting the Soul and its Transmigration, p. 628.—The Credibility of the earliest Roman Historians, p. 630.—The Legend of Æneas, p. 633.—The Legend of Alba, p. 634.—The Legends of Romulus and Remus, p. 634.—The Legend of Tarpeia, p. 635.—The Etruscan Origin of Roman Power and Civilization, p. 635.—The Origin and Character of the Dictatorship, p. 636.—The first standing Army of Rome, p. 636.—A general View of the legendary History of Remus, to the Capture of the City by the Gauls, p. 637.—The oppressive Laws of ancient Rome respecting the Poor, p. 637.—The Fulfilment of Sacred Prophecy in the History of Rome, p. 638.

PRELIMINARY DISSERTATION.

THE ORIGIN, CHARACTER, MYSTERIES AND ORACLES OF PAGAN IDOLATRY.

KNOWLEDGE of this Subject necessary—False Religion attests the Religious Tendency of Man—Heathen Idolatry must be studied with a distinct Recognition of Satanic Influence—Necessity of admitting the Evidence of Revelation—ORIGIN OF IDOLATRY—Idolatry in postdiluvian Times arose before the Dispersion—And emanated from Babel—Was not at first a violent Introduction of Error, but a fatal Perversion of Truth—Elements of Truth liable to this Perversion—Plurality of Persons in one Deity—Promised Incarnation—Rites of Patriarchal Worship—Man's primitive Purity and Fall—Similarity of the Adamic and Noachic Families—Hero-Worship considered as arising out of the promised Incarnation, and taking the Form of a Triad from the Great Father and his three Sons—Peculiar Case of Egypt—Animal-Worship—Folly of many Attempts to account for it—Originated in the Cherubim—Worship of material Elements—The Agency under which all this Error was evolved made apparent by the universal Worship of the Serpent Form—THE RELIGIOUS CHARACTER OF THIS SYSTEM—It practically obliterated the essential Principle of the Divine Unity—Banished all Idea of Divine Purity—And destroyed at once the Knowledge of God, and Confidence in him—Character of Idolatrous Worship—General Admission—But the Being to whom this Worship was offered was not God—And the Service, although often grand and imposing, was generally associated with foul and filthy Abominations—THE MYSTERIES—The Theory of Warburton refuted by Leland—Conflicting Theories as to the Origin of the Mysteries—Their Object equally contested—Their Origin defined—Their Object explained—Essential Elements of Heathen Mysteries—THE ORACLES of Heathen Worship—An undoubted Privilege of Patriarchal Times to have Access unto God, and to obtain special and important Instruction by this Means—Contest between the Learned as to whether Heathen Oracles were sustained by Satanic Influence—Testimony of Scripture—Judgment of the Learned on the Character and Credit of the Oracles—Case of Crœsus, King of Lydia, from Herodotus—The Result of the Inquiry establishes the Operation of Satanic Influence—General Observations in Conclusion.

A KNOWLEDGE of the religion of the ancient heathens is essential to a correct acquaintance with the history, the character, and the condition of this immense and interesting portion of the population of our world.

The attainment of this knowledge is, however, as difficult as it is desirable. Not only do the remoteness of the period whence the information is to be obtained, and its recondite nature, offer formidable obstacles to the prosecution of this inquiry; but, in addition to these, we have the disadvantage of exploring an almost untrodden path. The philosophy of the ancients has been laboriously investigated; the mythologies of the several primitive nations have been elaborately detailed; early history and chronology come before us, elucidated by the labour, learning, and genius of the greatest authors of ancient and modern times: but no writer of eminence with whose works I am acquainted, has done more than make a passing allusion, or give an incidental reference, to the *religion* of the ancient world, in the sense in which the term is here used.

Before entering on this investigation, it may be observed, that the religion of the heathen world is not to be regarded as any invention or wayward aberration of the human mind; much less can it be considered as the result of any combination of human circumstances. Viewed in connexion with man's fall and its consequences, it is rather the substitution of an evil which the human mind, in its darkness and obliquity, and in its unextinguished aspirations after happiness, has chosen, instead of embracing that which God has prescribed as its satisfying portion. The worship of idols attests man's capacity for the worship of God. The adoration even of material elements is one of the collateral proofs of the possession and perversion of a noble attribute, which allies man with the spiritual world, and speaks his intended intercourse with Deity. Idolatry, in the nature of things, could not have been the original exercise of the human mind in respect of worship. While, therefore, this adoration, perverted from its divine object, tends to prove the primitive purity of man, his devotional access to God, and his spiritual ruin through sin; its existence in human history exactly harmonizes with all these elements of man's early condition, and is utterly incompatible with any other supposed commencement of his subsequently devious career.

Again: the origin of idolatry will never be understood while the investigation is confined to the character of the human mind or the history of the human race, without a distinct recognition of man's exposure to Satanic influence and aggression. It might as reasonably be attempted to write a history of England while ignoring the Norman Conquest, or a system of physics without reference to gravitation, as to give a consistent and rational account of the origin of idolatry in the absence of all reference to Satan, its real author and object. It may be said, "This is unscientific and unphilosophical." But is it not in perfect accordance with the purest science, and the soundest philosophy, to apply all truth to useful purposes, and, by the judicious adaptation of ascertained principles to cognate subjects, to solve apparent mysteries, unravel difficulties, and make that clear and plain which was before confused and obscure? Why, then, should this mode of proceeding be prohibited in respect to the truths of the Holy Scriptures by those who admit their divine origin? Sceptics and infidels may decline such a method: it is their consistent habit so to do. But why should those who make the undoubted verity of God's holy word the basis of their highest hopes and dearest interests, hesitate to apply its teaching to the great problems presented by all the aspects of the world's religion?

In the investigation of the origin and character of idolatry, this aid is essential. The moment we enter on this study, we are met by such questions as these:—"What were the origin and design of bloody sacrifices? Why were they universal, when the most profound sages were ignorant of their origin and object? Why was the form of the serpent, above every other, consecrated to supreme elevation and honour?" These and many other queries cannot be solved by any study of human nature or human history. No recondite researches into ancient mythology, no laboured exploration into the poetry or religion of the primitive nations, will afford a satisfactory answer. To understand the origin, object, and character of idolatry, we must pass beyond the twilight of mere human intelligence and induction, and, standing in the full glory of revealed truth, contemplate the primitive condition and early history of mankind. Here we learn our glorious origin, and the mighty agencies with which our nature, in the outset of its career, was brought into contact; mark the fearful change wrought in man's moral nature, and watch its terrible results, until we see him turn away from the God of his life, and bow in profane adoration before the most filthy impersonations of his foul destroyer.

In this light we see that the relentless foe of God and man did not quit his prey when covered with guilt, and involved in condemnation. It may be fairly questioned whether any crisis in the affairs of the human race stands invested with more terrible grandeur than this. Here we see that as Divine Mercy interposed the scheme of redemption for the salvation of man, the arch-foe not only opposed its principles and its progress by a wide range of malignant effort, but, in a manner at once daring and insidious, he devised idolatry, and succeeded in introducing it into the world, as a means of wresting the spiritual dominion of mankind from the Mediator-Deity, and establishing himself as "the god of this world." This was the agency under which idolatry was introduced, and rose into influence and power; and throughout its almost infinite range of development, the evil and debasing character of its author is legibly imprinted upon all its numerous deities, doctrines, rites, and religious observances.

Our limits forbid any extended proof of these statements. It may, however, be necessary to observe that the primitive progress of man in purity and religion is an undoubted doctrine of the Bible. Learned men may, indeed, persist in asserting that "fetichism, or the worship of the material elements, was the universal religion of the earliest inhabitants of the earth:" and this has been done so frequently and so confidently, that it has to a great extent been admitted by incautious and inconsiderate readers. Nothing, however, can be more opposed to the history of every primitive nation, as well as to the explicit declarations of holy writ, than this notion. It has been already shown, that all ancient testimony proves the condition of man in the outset of his career to have been one of religion, happiness, and moral elevation. The word of God fully confirms this view, and assures us that idolatry did not arise in a season of ignorance, but when men "knew God;"—that it could not, therefore, have been a primitive religion of man, but a superinduced corruption;—that it arose not so much from intellectual obliquity as from spiritual unfaithfulness,—not so much from the influence of a debased mind as from an affectation of wisdom: for it was when men "knew God" that "they glorified him not as God, neither were thankful, but became vain in their imaginations, and their foolish heart was darkened. Professing themselves to be wise, they became fools; and changed the glory of the incorruptible God into an image made like to corruptible man, and to birds, and four-footed beasts, and creeping things." Rom. i, 21–23. It is also declared with equal explicitness that in ancient times the heathen offered "their sacrifices unto devils." Lev. xvii, 7.

Clearly as these points are ascertained, it is not so easy to state when, and under what circumstances, this abomination arose. It has been already shown that Jewish tradition ascribes the introduction of idolatry to the days of Enos in the antediluvian period. (Patriarchal Age, pp. 235, 236.) Whatever doubt may rest on the statement of Maimonides, it must be admitted that it is so consistent in all its parts, and in such exact accordance with the general teaching of antiquity on the subject, as to stand invested with a high degree of probability of its being, at least in its main particulars, an approximation to the truth. (See *Appendix*, note 1.)

But whatever was the religious condition of the human race before the Deluge, it is certain that there must have been a commencement of idolatry subsequent to that event. Here we meet with one fact nearly amounting to a demonstration, that the postdiluvian origin of this evil is restricted to a comparatively short period: idolatry must have arisen before the Dispersion. "The various systems of pagan idolatry in different parts of the world correspond so closely, both in their evident purport and in numerous points of arbitrary resemblance, that they cannot have been struck out independently in the several countries where they have been established, and must all have originated from a common source. But if they all originated from a common source, then either one nation must have communicated its peculiar theology to every other people in the way of peaceful and voluntary imitation; or that same nation must have communicated it to every other people through the medium of conquest and violence; or, lastly, all nations must, in the infancy of the world, have been assembled together in a single region and in a single community,—must, at that period and in that state, have agreed to adopt the theology in question, and must thence, as from a common centre, have carried it to all quarters of the globe.

"These are the only three modes in which the universal accordance of the Gentiles in their religious speculations can be accounted for. But as the incredibility of the first, and the equal incredibility and impossibility of the second, may be shown without much difficulty, the third alone remains to be adopted."—*Faber's Origin of Pagan Idolatry.* The assertion, therefore, that idolatry arose before the Dispersion, is justified.

This fact is, moreover, sustained by explicit proof from the inspired records. Babel, or Babylon, is well known to have been the seat of the world's population prior to the Dispersion. This locality is rendered infamous in the Bible as the place whence this foul evil arose, and radiated to poison the nations. "Babylon hath been a golden cup in the Lord's hand, that made all the earth drunken: the nations have drunken of her wine; therefore the nations are mad. Every man is brutish by his knowledge; every founder is confounded by the graven image: for his molten image is falsehood, and there is no breath in them." Jer. li, 7, 17. The New Testament affords similar evidence. Without at all impugning the application of the Apocalyptic prophecies to the Roman Antichrist, we hold that the terms in which they are couched derive point and power only from their previous connexion and import. Hence, when we read of "Babylon the great, the MOTHER of harlots and abominations of the earth;" (Rev. xvii, 5;) and, "Babylon the great is fallen:—for all nations have drunk of the wine of the wrath of her fornication;" (Rev. xviii, 2, 3;) we have marked intimations of the primitive scene, and principal seat, of idolatry, the greatest invasion of the prerogatives of Heaven.

Having thus ascertained by undoubted induction, confirmed as it is by Scripture proof, the period and place whence idolatry originated, we may proceed another step, and elicit from the great and common principles of all heathen mythology some notion of the ruling elements of unhallowed feeling and corrupt imagination, which generated the evil of which we speak. In this effort it will be of consequence for us to recognise the important fact, that in all ages Satanic error has been most successful when presented to the human mind as *a perversion of truth.* Faber justly observes: "The human mind rarely tolerates any great changes if they be violent and sudden, particularly in matters of religion. It seems natural to suppose that this great apostasy was not a violent and abrupt setting aside of true religion; that it was not a sudden plunge from the worship of Jehovah into the grossness of rank idolatry. I should rather apprehend that it must have commenced with a specious perversion of sound doctrine, and with an affectedly devout adoption of authorized rites and ceremonies and phraseology."—*Faber's Origin of Pagan Idolatry,* vol. i, p. 100. This judgment of an experienced and learned writer, who had carefully investigated the subject, may be safely admitted as sound.

What, then, were those prominent elements of patriarchal religion which were most likely, being generally known and partially obscure in their character, to lead to speculation, corruption, and ultimately to idolatry? Here it may be necessary to remind the reader, that our first parents must have had peculiar means of obtaining an acquaintance with God. Who can tell the knowledge of Deity which Adam enjoyed in his state of innocence? Nor can the form of language used throughout the patriarchal age in respect of God be accounted for, except on the supposition that man, at the commencement of his career, obtained a knowledge of the divine nature and character which has never been fully explained, and probably never will be, in this world. We have always spoken guardedly (Patriarchal Age, pp. 266–271) of the knowledge which in præ-Christian times obtained concerning the Divine Trinity: but the more the subject is studied, the more clearly does it appear that, whatever doubt may exist as to the acquaintance of the later heathens with this doctrine, there can be little as to the prevalence of an opinion of this kind among the early patriarchs. (See *Appendix*, note 2.)

Further, it is certain that, from the first family downward, the hope of the world was centred in the birth and actions of a superhuman Being,— in other words, in the work of an incarnate Saviour. There might have been much vagueness of view and opinion in respect of this subject: but we greatly err if we suppose that all the information possessed by the first family and their descendants, in respect of this doctrine, was merely that which is contained in the primitive promise. Gen. iii, 15. Of the various revelations which Adam received from God we have scarcely any information. It is certain that sufficient knowledge on this subject was revealed to afford a basis for an enlightened, operative, saving faith in the mind of Abel and others: and if so, it must have been sufficiently complete and defined to afford to other men an intelligible acquaintance with the subject. (See *Appendix*, note 3.)

Again: in addition to these elements of religious knowledge, the early races of mankind had a prescribed mode of worship. Enough has been already said in the preceding volumes of this work to warrant the conclusion of Faber, that the worship of the Israelites " was no other than Patriarchism, by various additions and special institutions, adapted to the peculiar situation of a people which had been selected by Jehovah." There was, therefore, a special place where God was worshipped by sacrifice before the cherubim. Of the nature and character of the rites performed in this primitive worship it is difficult to speak with any precision; but it is evident that there must have been a person (in those days generally the father of the family) to offer the sacrifice; and in all probability there was, in the pure patriarchal period, some visible fire, or glory, representing the presence of Deity. (See Faber's Pagan Idolatry, vol. i, p. 425, and note to p. 424.)

Besides these doctrines, there were facts in the early history of the world which must have been traditionally known, and which, from their character, would more or less influence the opinions and the views of the people.

There was, in the first place, the paradisiacal scene of man's primitive glory and fall, which, with all its circumstances, would certainly have been preserved in memory. The temptation, the serpent, the trees in the midst of the garden, the judgment of the offenders, their expulsion from Eden,—all these prominent particulars would have been narrated by father to son continually, until they had perfectly imbued the mind and memory of mankind.

The Deluge introduced another element into the religious traditions of the new race of mankind. For, while they would preserve and cherish the knowledge of all the religious doctrines, rites, and facts with which man had been endued in the outset of his being, and which had been evolved in the course of his career, it could not escape observation that the beginning of the postdiluvian race bore a remarkable similarity to that of the primitive family. In each case there was a patriarchal father, with his wife. In each case this father had three sons: and in both instances one of these sons exposed himself to divine malediction.

With these elements of religious knowledge, and facts popularly known and pervading the public mind, we have to contemplate the postdiluvian population of the world under the aspect in which they are presented to us in the pages of holy writ. We are told that they "*knew God.*" They had sufficient acquaintance with the being, attributes, and providence of God. Yet in those circumstances, this people did not glorify God, nor evince gratitude toward him: and with these sins of the heart, there existed in active operation a strong tendency to refined speculation. They "became vain in their imaginations," indulging in unworthy expositions of established truth, and adding to it according to the dictates of their corrupted fancy. The consequence of this conduct produced its natural result:—it darkened their mind, and introduced death into the religious affections of their hearts; and thus, "professing themselves to be wise, they became fools." The consequence of all this was the introduction and practice of the vilest idolatry. Rom. i, 21-23.

Were we able to detail with certainty and precision the progress of this declension, it would form a very important branch of the early history of our race. But this is more than can be expected. When we have placed the *result* in connexion with the *cause*, we shall have furnished materials from which to form some idea of the steps by which mankind descended downwards to the lowest estate of moral degradation.

In the first instance, it may be observed that a ruling element in the idolatry of heathenism is the deification of human nature. Man has been everywhere invested with divine attributes, and honoured with divine worship. What could have originated such extravagant and unreasonable conduct? With all the bodily weakness incident to his constitution,—exposed to casualty, disorder, disease, and death,—utterly unable to ward off mental or physical evil, or to sustain the mind in peace, or to provide for the wants of the body by any inherent power,— what could have originated the idea of investing poor perishing humanity with the attributes of Divinity? It is not wonderful that, after the practice had been introduced, a martial hero like Alexander should have aspired to such a vain and monstrous distinction. The question is, What could have led to the introduction of the absurd and proud assumption?

After carefully considering all the professed solutions of this problem which ancient or modern times have supplied, we can receive none as satisfactory but that which refers its origin to the promised incarnation. Ill-understood and imperfectly-transmitted traditions of the primitive promise of an incarnate Redeemer naturally induced expectation and inquiry. When any man obtained more than usual celebrity, or arose into great prominence under very extraordinary circumstances, there would always be a motive for inquiring whether he was *the Incarnate One* who had been promised. This would of course incline any man of a daring, ambitious mind, who aspired to great elevation and power, to claim this divine character, and put himself forward as the expected incarnation. It is more than probable that Nimrod acted thus, in order to persuade all the people to remain under his government at Babel, rather than to disperse themselves over the world in obedience to the command of Heaven.

The whole practice of heathen demonolatry, however, proves that whatever influence the promised incarnation might have had on the origin of the evil, other agencies must have operated to mould and form it into a system. No fact is more evident than that the earliest human objects of worship are almost always presented to us in triads. Mr. Faber attributes this singular circumstance entirely to the fact that Adam, as the great father, and his three sons, were regarded as reappearing in the persons of Noah and his sons. Indeed, every part of the heathen world affords ample evidence that the three sons of Noah were the popular triad of Gentile idolatry. Yet this does not, in my judgment, include the opinion that the hope of the promised incarnation was the sole origin of this human deification.

In the case of Egypt, for instance, we have, in the researches of Champollion, a very curious exception to this rule. According to this erudite writer, " the primary form or antitype of the entire mythology (of Egypt) is a triad of divinities, composed of Amoun, the father, Mout, the mother, and Chons, the infant son." On this curious fact I quite agree with a learned Egyptologist, who observes, "It does not appear probable that men to whom the doctrine of the triunity of God was unknown, could have framed such a system as this."—*Osburn's Antiquities of Egypt*, p. 138. It is not to be imagined that these persons had refined and elevated views and clear conceptions of this doctrine, like those who have the Christian Scriptures in their hands; but that they had a vague and imperfect notion of the triune personality of Deity. Taking the Egyptian triad in connexion with the triads of other countries, it does not seem possible to avoid the induction, that the general system of human deification arose out of a combination of influences, arising from a corrupted tradition of the promised incarnation, a vague notion of the doctrine of the Trinity, and a speculative fancy of the application of these to the sons of the first great father, as reproduced in the offspring of Noah. And this induction, be it observed, is justified by numerous instances in the history and mythology of the ancient world.

Idolatry, however, was not confined to the worship of eminent living men, and their revered ancestors: it extended to the animal creation. If this practice had not been all but universal, and as such attested by indubitable evidence, it would appear utterly incredible. That man should bow down in lowly adoration, and worship the image or person of his fellow-man appears passing strange; but that he should stoop to ascribe divinity to a brute, and prostrate himself in religious reverence before it, seems too much for belief. Yet so it was, and in heathen lands is even now. What could have originated such gratuitous debasement and profanation? This question has been frequently asked both in ancient and modern times, but has seldom obtained a satisfactory solution. The obscurity which rested on this subject in respect to the learned among the heathen, we may see finely illustrated in the false and foolish answers which they vainly offered.

One reason assigned for this practice, according to Diodorus Siculus, is, that the gods, in the early ages of the world, being in fear of the numbers and wickedness of mankind, assumed the form of animals, in order to avoid their cruelty and oppression; but that, having afterward brought the world under their government, the gods decreed that the forms under which they had obtained security should be regarded with religious veneration. A second reason assigned is, that the ancient inhabitants of Egypt, having suffered many defeats from their enemies in consequence of confusion and want of discipline in their army, devised the plan of carrying standards, and for this purpose selected the figures of animals. These serving as a rallying-point for the several divisions of the troops, they obtained a victory, and ever afterward treated these figures with religious respect. A third reason given is, that this worship arose out of gratitude for the benefits conferred by them on mankind. But when it is remembered that the lion and the eagle were prominent in the early stages of animal-worship, this answer will sink down to a level with the preceding. Other notions, equally ridiculous and absurd, have been handed down to us; but this diversity of opinion, and this laboured effort to devise any plausible origin for so strange a practice, only prove the darkness which rested on the subject. Porphyry, who though a clever writer was a bitter enemy to revelation, has inadvertently on this point given us an important suggestion. In propounding his theory on this subject, he attributes the origin of animal-worship to the operation of the principle that the Deity permeates other beings, as well as man; that, in fact, "nearly the same spiritual essence pervades all the tribes of living creatures." On this account, he adds, "in fashioning images of the gods, they have adopted the forms of *all* animals; sometimes joining the human figure with those of beasts; at others, combining the shapes of men and of birds," &c.—*Porphyrius de Abstin.*, lib. iv, cap. 9.

It it always important in investigations of this kind to distinguish between fact and philosophical speculation. In this instance the learned heathen, I have no doubt, gives us an important fact, namely, that animal-worship originated in a practice which had grown up, of combining portions of the figures of animals, or of birds, with parts of the human figure. If we may rely on this statement, which is open to no reasonable doubt, we find that, unlike almost every other part of heathen idolatry, the worship of animals was not the first form of this error. The veneration of images preceded that of the real animals. Nor were these images representations of complete animal forms, but of compound figures, exhibiting different combinations of the cherubic elements—man, lion, ox, and eagle.

Here, then, we have an account of the origin of animal-worship which meets all the difficulties of the case. The cherubic figures, we are sure, were copied in the sculptures of the ancients in almost every diversity of form and combination. These, like the teraphim of the Hebrews, became, in process of time, objects of superstitious regard, and ultimately of idolatrous reverence. The next step produced images of animals as meriting similar devotion; and living brutes succeeded as objects of worship.

Beneath this depth of human abasement, folly, and sin, there is yet a lower deep. Men not only condescended to worship brute beasts, and birds, and creeping things; they proceeded even to reverence and adore the different parts of inanimate creation. Reference has been already made to the causes which led to an early reception of the false dogma of an endless succession of worlds. This opinion, however, when once accepted, induced a belief of the principle involved in it, namely, the eternity of matter: and, eternity being clearly recognised as a divine attribute, the entire natural creation was regarded as divine; and both notions were extensively propagated. In the progress of this error, however, the speculative perversity of the men who, professing to be wise, sunk into such folly, encountered a serious difficulty. While admitting the eternity of matter, they could not repudiate the eternity of the great father, the belief of whose reappearance, at the commencement of each cycle of the world's existence, lay at the foundation of the whole system of error. But then they found themselves stumbling between the idea of two *eternals:* one occasionally, and at great intervals of time, appearing in human form; the other infinitely diversified throughout the whole material world.

This difficulty was solved, or rather the Gordian knot cut, by supposing the first of these to represent the mind or soul—the second, the material body—of the world. "As it was observed that man consisted of two parts intimately associated, the circumstance was analogically extended to the world at large. The spirit of man for a season animated a body; and when that body was worn out, and its component particles were resolved into their original substance, the spirit occupied another tenement; and again, at a stated interval, quitted it for a new one. In a similar manner, the intellectual great father for a season animated his body the world; and when that body at each great catastrophe was resolved into the primeval crude matter out of which it had been formed, the soul soon formed to itself another body in a new world, which it again occupied, and again quitted, at the close of the new period."—*Faber's Pagan Idolatry,* vol. i, p. 163.

Thus the foundation was laid for the most extended system of idolatry, in which every part of nature might be regarded as divine. The modifications of this notion, and the inferences derived from it, were numberless. This mystic union of spirit and matter was frequently exhibited under the notion of a conjugal union, in which the pervading spirit is spoken of as the great father, and the material world as the great mother. Another representation exhibited the heavenly bodies as embodiments, or residences, of the pervading and ruling spirit; while the terrestrial world was regarded as the body of the universal deity.

Another modification of this error, which arose afterward, taught that the intellectual principle was light and goodness, and the material principle darkness and evil. And thus was exhibited the idea of two independent and rival deities: one, the patron of purity and light; the other, of evil and darkness. It can scarcely be doubted that this latter inflexion of the error was greatly modified under the influence of a tradition respecting the grand tempter and the fallen angels.

Thus, by these several means, the great elements of a universal idolatry were established in the world. If it had been judged necessary, the several particulars which have been noticed might have been amply sustained by learned references: but the best, as well as the most ample and convincing proof which can be given in their support will be afforded by the various developments of them which will be found in the chapters exhibiting in detail the religion of the several nations which have to come under our notice. Enough has been said to indicate, in outline at least, the more prominent of those speculations by which men, even while knowing the true God, and "professing themselves to be wise, became fools."

In proceeding to notice the object and character of idolatry, it may be first observed, that, regarded in the united light of reason and Scripture, it stands before us as a grand effort to defeat or neutralize the great scheme of redemption. I freely confess, I know of no subject that has been treated so unworthily as this. According to established usage, the youth in our best schools—the readers of our most erudite manuals and educational works—are all introduced to an acquaintance with this subject as a curious development of human ingenuity and speculation,—as a science mainly consisting of the actions, character, and worship of certain imaginary mythological personages. With these it is thought an accomplishment to have some acquaintance; and no one can doubt that this is essential to any intelligent study of classic authors. But does all this present to the mind any consistent idea of the object and character of idolatry? We teach the rising generation, and all inquiring minds, the great elements of man's primeval history from the sacred record. They are instructed respecting man's innocency and temptation, his expulsion from Paradise, and the promise of a Redeemer. But when they are called to study the history of our race, to mark the progress of a fearful moral and mental deterioration, which covered the world with gross darkness, and rendered the isolation of the elected Hebrew people necessary to the maintenance of the knowledge of God in the world, all this fearful system of error and evil is exhibited as totally unconnected with spiritual agencies and moral ends. Is this reasonable or consistent? Is it not certain that the same agency which effected the fall, and thus spoiled the purity of man, induced the whole scheme of idolatry, in order to defeat the promised redemption, and to frustrate the purpose of God in the promised mission of his Son? Can there be a doubt in any reasonable mind on this important point? Evidence from Scripture has been briefly adduced, and might be extended: but this is not necessary; the whole tenor of holy writ is decidedly in favour of my argument. I wish, however, to call more particular attention to one important point—the worship of the serpent.

That the malign foe should repeat his assault on human happiness after the promise of redemption, is not wonderful. That he should have persevered in his aggression, might be inferred from his subtilty and malice. But it will scarcely be believed, that even Satan should not only have aimed so high as to supplant the adorable and eternal God as the object of human worship, but should also have aspired to put himself forth as the object of supreme worship, and challenge the adoration of the world, under the precise form in which he had succeeded in effecting the ruin of the race. Yet so it was. The serpent form has in all probability approached nearer to universal adoration than any other.

A learned author, who has investigated this subject with great labour and research, assures us that he has "traced the worship of the serpent from Babylonia, east and west, through Persia, Hindûstan, China, Mexico, Britain, Scandinavia, Italy, Illyricum, Thrace, Greece, Asia Minor, and Phenicia. Again, we have observed the same idolatry prevailing north and south, through Scythia on the one hand, and Africa on the other. THE WORSHIP OF THE SERPENT WAS THEREFORE UNIVERSAL. For not only did the sacred serpent enter into the symbolical and ritual service of every religion which recognised THE SUN, but we even find him in countries where solar worship was altogether unknown,—as in Sarmatia, Scandinavia, and the Gold Coast of Africa. In every known country of the ancient world, the serpent formed a prominent feature in the ordinary worship, and made no inconsiderable figure in their Hagiographa, entering alike into legendary and astronomical mythology.

"Whence, then, did this ONLY UNIVERSAL idolatry originate? That it preceded polytheism, is indicated by the attribution of the title OPS, and the consecration of the symbolical serpent, to so many of the heathen deities. The title OPS was conferred upon Terra, Vesta, Rhea, Cybele, Juno, Diana; and even Vulcan is called by Cicero *Opas.*

"In Grecian mythology the symbolical serpent was sacred to Saturn, Jupiter, Apollo, Bacchus, Mars, Æsculapius, Rhea, Juno, Minerva, Diana, Ceres, and Proserpine:—that is, the serpent was a sacred emblem *of nearly all the gods and goddesses.*

"The same remark may be extended to the theogonies of Egypt, Hindûstan, and Mexico,—in all of which we find the serpent emblematic, not of *one* deity, but of *many.*

"What, then, is the inference? *That the serpent was the most ancient of the* heathen *gods.*"—*Deane's Worship of the Serpent,* pp. 441-443.

So the great and terrible truth stands clearly attested, not only by the word of God, but by authentic records of every ancient nation, that the old serpent, the devil, who seduced our first parents from their allegiance, succeeded in establishing himself, under the very figure in which he wrought his first fatal triumph, as the almost universal object of human worship,—"the god of this world." Yes, and as the corrupt fancy and bewildered speculations diversified modes of worship, and multiplied forms and objects of adoration, this malign spirit, as if to assert his universal supremacy, and perpetuate his name and influence over the wide world of human nature, stamped the serpent name on every deity, and the serpent form on every ritual. To use the elegant language of the author already cited, "The mystic serpent entered into the mythology of every nation; consecrated almost every temple; symbolized almost every deity; was imagined in the heavens, stamped upon the earth, and ruled in the realms of everlasting sorrow. His *subtilty* raised him into an emblem of *wisdom;* he was therefore pictured upon the ægis of Minerva, and crowned her helmet. *The knowledge of futurity* which he displayed in Paradise exalted him into a symbol of vaticination; he was therefore oracular, and reigned at Delphi. The '*opening of the eyes*' of our deluded first parents obtained him an altar in the temple of the god of *healing;* he is therefore the constant companion of Æsculapius. In the distribution of his qualities the genius of mythology did not even gloss over his malignant attributes. The fascination with which he intoxicated the souls of the first sinners, depriving them at once of purity and immortality, of the image of God and the life of angels, was symbolically remembered and fatally celebrated in the orgies of Bacchus, where serpents crowned the heads of the Bacchantes, and the *poculum boni dæmonis* circulated under the auspices of the ophite hierogram, chased upon the rim. But the most remarkable remembrance of the paradisiacal serpent is displayed in the position which he retains in Tartarus. A cunodracontic Cerberus guards the gates; serpents are coiled about the chariot wheels of Proserpine; serpents pave the abyss of torment; and even serpents constitute the caduceus of Mercury, the talisman which he holds when he conveys the soul to Tartarus. The image of the serpent is stamped upon every mythological fable connected with the realms of Pluto."—*Deane's Worship of the Serpent*, pp. 443, 444.

To such a fearful extent is the presence and image of Satan the destroyer impressed on the wide range of idolatry! Nor is the character with which he has imbued it less dubious than the symbolism under which it is exhibited to the world. The genius of heathen idolatry is throughout diabolical. It would be easy to exhibit this with the most ample proofs, if our limits would allow the insertion of a wide range of evidence. But this is impossible. All, therefore, that is permitted us is, to cite a proof or two under a few leading particulars, which may confirm and illustrate this strong assertion.

I. One great object, then, of religion is to make known to man the nature and character of God. How does the idolatry of the heathen world, sustained as it has been by science, intellect, and genius of the highest order, meet this grand requirement? The only answer which can be given is this,—With utter and unmitigated disappointment. The first law of revelation, and the first dictate of reason respecting God, clearly assert the divine unity. To this truth all idolatry stands directly opposed; for it exhibits "lords many and gods many." I am well aware that it has been boldly asserted, that this apparent multiplication of deities and images is ideal; that these poetic and material representations were only intended to shadow forth the attributes of Deity, and to bring him vividly before the mind. Do the persons who make these assertions know that in the best days of Greece the philosopher Stilpho was banished from Athens, by a decree of the Areopagus, for affirming that the *statue* of Minerva was not a god? (Diogenes Laertius, lib. ii, segm. 116.) Is it not notorious that a form of invocation was long preserved in the ritual of the supreme pontiff, which was used by the Romans for the purpose of coaxing the tutelary deity of a place with which they were at war, by the promise of more costly offerings than he had been accustomed to receive, to come over to them? (Valerius Maximus, cited by Pliny, lib. ii, cap. 7.) Yes, and although the Greeks and Romans sometimes affected to despise this superstition, they could themselves descend to the absurdity of chaining the images of gods to their pedestals. (Plutarchus, De Iside et Osiride, Opera, tom. iii, p. 397.) No sarcasms of satirists or maxims of philosophers can be poised, for a moment, against the weight of this practical evidence.

Next to the unity of God, religion should exhibit his purity. For all the moral ends of religion this is unquestionably essential. What heathen idolatry has done to manifest this attribute of God to mankind, scarcely need be detailed. Let all mythology be examined, the Pantheon of every heathen nation be investigated, and where can one prominent deity be found whose moral character, as exhibited by his worshippers, would not expel any living individual from any civilized society? What crimes did not one or another of these celestials commit? Murder, adultery, incest, —all that lust could suggest, that rage could induce, that ambition and jealousy could inspire,—abundantly stained the conduct of these imaginary beings. There is no point in the whole system of idolatry more affecting than this. Here the fountain is polluted at its source. Can man be expected to present a purer character than his God? Yet here the teeming multitudes of heathendom have a concentration of every vice presented to their view as their model of character. Yet our best *literati* speak as if this idolatry was innocuous, and only presented the divine character under another name. Witness the famous stanza of Pope, which has been so often placed in the hands of our children :—

> "Father of all, in every age,
> In every clime adored,
> By saint, by savage, and by sage,
> Jehovah, Jove, or Lord."

Is it true, then, that the person and character of the great Jehovah were exhibited of old by the foul and filthy impersonations of Olympus?

Above all, are we to be told *now* that this was the case? No: the purity of God was unknown to idolatry. That offspring of Satanic influence and human depravity produced ideas of Deity in direct accordance with the temper and spirit of the mind of the poet.

Nor was the evil resulting from this polytheism and impurity merely notional and speculative: it directly tended to destroy all real knowledge of God, and practical confidence in him. How could God be known, when only seen through the medium of heathen divinities? Or if these were taken as exhibiting the divine character, who could confide in such a manifestation of Deity? How, in fact, could such confidence be exercised, when the recognised deities were divided into factions always disunited, and frequently decidedly hostile? He who sought the favour of Venus excited the anger of Juno: he who sacrificed on the altar of Jove, rather displeased than propitiated Neptune. Realms and kingdoms, as well as individuals, were exposed to this evil: every nation had its natural patrons and foes in the council of Olympus; and its prosperity or decline did not so much depend on its virtue or piety, as on celestial favour fortuitously gained, or celestial enmity unknowingly and undeservedly provoked.

It may, indeed, be objected that these were the sentiments thrown out in the poetry, and adopted by the people, of heathen lands, but that the philosophers and the learned knew better. If this argument could be admitted, it would but very slightly improve the case. For, in a religious aspect, who are they that compose the masses of nations, and involve their dearest interests and final destiny? Are they not the people? If, therefore, the *literati* and philosophers had entertained higher or clearer views, it would be saying little in the favour of this religious system if it required them to keep the people in ignorance. But, notwithstanding all these allegations, there is no satisfactory proof that either learning or philosophy presented an efficient antidote to the evils of idolatry.

I may cite here the summary of a learned author who has carefully studied this subject:—

"On three points the theological discords of the ancient schools were softened into unusual harmony. 1. All the philosophers, excepting the atheistical sects, agreed in admitting a plurality of gods. If some of them occasionally speak of deity in the singular number, they speedily lapse into the error of the popular faith, and avow persuasions which sufficiently prove they had no conception of the unity of the Divine Being. Socrates and Plato, the best and purest of the philosophical theologists, were scarcely less devoted than the plebeian disciples of the popular creed to the dogmas of polytheism. 2. The ancient philosophers also agreed in limiting the attributes of their gods. The deity was said neither to exercise nor to possess creative energy. Matter, uncreated, eternal, and self-existent, might be shaped into diversity of form by divine skill, but it existed independently of divine power. It was thus invested with the fundamental qualities of Deity. 3. The popular creed of Greece and Rome was an extravagant Manicheism, in which demoniacal powers were mingled with divine. The philosophers adopted, but modified the doctrine. An eternal and disorderly principle was supposed to interfere perpetually in the government of the world. The existence of moral evil, not to be accounted for, as was thought, under the sole dominion of a benevolent deity, was thus explained; and the wisdom and goodness of the ruling god were subjected to a counteracting and malignant power."—*Alley's Vindiciæ Christianæ*, pp. 30, 31.

It is, therefore, certain that the direct tendency of idolatry, as established in the most civilized and refined nations of the earth, effectually concealed the knowledge of God from almost all classes of society; and at the same time not only spread over the whole surface of religion unmistakable emblems of the evil principle, but actually recognised *the evil one* as a real divinity, counteracting the designs, and frustrating the purposes of the beneficent God.

II. We next turn our attention to the general character of idolatrous worship.

Of all the exercises of the human mind, the worship of God is the most noble, and most intimately allies man to the heavenly world. If ever the best affections of human nature are called into lively action, and the highest attributes of the human mind are likely to be employed under the highest influence, it must be when man, under a sense of weakness and want, comes in an acceptable manner to God, as the Author and Giver of all good, to receive those blessings of which he feels the need. In this devotional duty the mind, when rightly directed, apprehends the infinite majesty and mercy of God, humbly offers its penitence and prayer, and earnestly implores a visitation of grace. How did the most refined systems of idolatry meet this requirement, and lead man into intercourse with God?

It cannot be denied that this idolatrous worship, in highly cultivated countries,—in Greece, for instance,—" often afforded a beautiful and interesting spectacle. The extensive area before the temple, and the noble porticoes which generally surrounded it, were crowded by a devout and zealous multitude. The priests or priestesses, in splendid garbs, appeared at a little distance, in the vestibule, at the foot of the altar. After a solemn pause, one of the subordinate ministers, in order to excite the attention of the people, demanded, 'Who are those that compose this assembly?' and a universal response was returned, 'Upright and pious citizens.' The officiating priest then slowly advanced, and, in distinct and awful voice, exhorted the congregation 'to offer up their prayers, and to suppli-

cate the gods.' Prayers adapted to the occasion were next recited by the priest; or hymns, in which the divine genius of the poet had celebrated the majesty of the gods, were chanted by a chorus of youths and virgins."
—*Alley's Vindiciæ*, p. 151.

Yet notwithstanding the pleasing order and affecting character of these ceremonies, it must not be forgotten that the being to whom all this was addressed was not God, but a creature of the imagination. In most instances these deities were not only imaginary, and therefore imperfect, but highly criminal, cruel, or licentious. In those cases the absurdity and wickedness of the worship would be in proportion to the ignorant zeal of the worshippers. Nothing, indeed, can be more certain than that, so far as the great mass of the people were concerned, this worship was mere ceremony. The multiplicity of deities,—the confusion of ideas arising from their manifold and conflicting attributes,—the minute ceremonial connected with the offering of sacrifice,—would effectually prevent any *real* worship of God, except under circumstances the most extraordinary.

But the irreligious character of this worship is one of its most favourable features. It was frequently degraded by the vilest cruelty and ferocity. Human beings—not unfrequently women—were savagely butchered, and offered upon the altars of these sanguinary deities. In other cases this service became a mere purchase and sale of sinful licence. The sacrifice was not an expression of contrition and a means of pardon for sin, but a means of exemption from its punishment by the presentation of a costly bribe to the divinity supposed to have been aggrieved. At other times filthier, if not fouler consequences resulted from this adoration. The deity was, in many instances, an embodiment of licentiousness; and then the worship would be of a corresponding character. Bands of courtezans, armed with every blandishment of beauty, music, and dancing, by a thousand arts inflamed the excited worshippers, until they were prepared to wallow in pollution from which the mind turns away with infinite disgust.

The cause of truth demands that it should be distinctly stated that these abominations are not accidental circumstances, arising in some particular age or country. No; they are the natural results of idolatry. Wherever this fearful error has reigned, in ancient or modern times, it has produced similar effects. Carnal, unmeaning ceremony,—cruelty and blood,—licentious impurity, to an extent forbidding all description,—have always been the natural fruits of this evil.

When exhibiting the religion of the several Gentile nations, it will be necessary to present these subjects in greater detail. Enough has here been said to give a general idea of the spirit and genius of idolatry; and to show that, as a standing rule, it has banished all just and worthy views of God from the minds of men, and has substituted, for that divine worship which was appointed by God as the great means of raising the mind and renewing the character of man, a system of creature-worship which has debased mankind, and become a fruitful cause of the blackest crimes, and of the most filthy impurities.

If, therefore, an investigation of the origin of this compound of wickedness and folly led to the opinion that it arose in the world through the direct agency and influence of Satan, all that we have seen of its results, in respect of man's knowledge and worship of God, fully confirms this view. In all its character, spirit, tendency, and resulting circumstances, idolatry presents itself to the mind as the work of Satanic guile, and of a powerful influence exercised on the depraved hearts of unfaithful men.

Notwithstanding the overwhelming amount of evidence by which these views of the origin and character of pagan idolatry are supported and attested, a disposition has been evinced by some men of learning—especially by those among them who have not carefully studied the sacred Scriptures, or the Christian religion—to endeavour to show that the moral impurity and intellectual perversion, which obviously resulted in a fearful torrent from this source, were not universal; that among certain classes or sections of heathen society the doctrines of a pure theism were plainly taught, and the precepts of a sound morality carefully enforced. And, strange as it may appear, an eminent Christian divine and English bishop has mightily promoted these (in our judgment) erroneous views.

Bishop Warburton, in his "Divine Legation of Moses," strongly asserts that in the heathen mysteries all the errors of polytheism were explained and neutralized; that here the initiated were taught, "that Jupiter, Mercury, Bacchus, Venus, Mars, and the whole rabble of licentious deities, were only DEAD MORTALS; subject in life to the same passions and infirmities with themselves; but having been on other accounts benefactors to mankind, grateful posterity had deified them, and with their virtues had indiscreetly canonized their vices. The fabulous gods being thus routed, the Supreme Cause of all things naturally took their place. Him they were taught to consider as the Creator of the universe, who pervaded all things by his virtue, and governed all things by his providence." But, according to the judgment of this learned prelate, not only were prevalent errors repudiated, and sterling truth enforced; a religious change of heart, and a life of unblemished purity and virtue, were also enjoined. He says, "The mysteries openly proclaimed it as their chief business to restore the soul to its original purity,"—"taught the necessity of a strict and holy life." Hence, "those that were initiated, were obliged by solemn engagements to commence a new life of the strictest purity and virtue: nor was a less degree of purity required of the initiated for their future conduct." —*Divine Legation*, book ii, sec. 4.

If these strange assertions had been sustained by reasonable proof, although it might not necessarily impugn what has been said respecting the Satanic origin, character, and influence of heathen idolatry, it would certainly compel us to admit that some gracious interference had infused into the centre of this corrupt mass a counteracting influence of truth and righteousness. It would, therefore, be most cheering to find the speculations of the learned prelate of Gloucester on this subject abundantly verified. It is with sincere regret that we are compelled to affirm that, although they are supported with all his energy and learning, his reasoning is inconclusive, and his inferences are unsatisfactory. A careful and extended inquiry completely dissipates the hopeful scheme which his ingenuity had raised. Leland, (Christian Revelation, part i, chap. viii,) by an elaborate and learned investigation, showed very clearly that the bishop's conjecture is entirely unsupported, and falls to the ground in the absence of proof.

It does not comport with the plan of this work to give even a sketch of this controversy, or of the various opinions which have been promulgated on this important and interesting subject. It will, however, be necessary to furnish some distinct idea of these heathen mysteries, and to state our opinion of their origin, object, and progressive character.

Entering upon this needful, but very difficult, part of our undertaking, it may be proper to premise, that while our space forbids great amplification, and restrains the exhibition of our views, and the production of evidence, to a limited compass; it will, nevertheless, be attempted to state the case so clearly, and to exhibit such an amount of proof, that in future this stronghold of scepticism may be deprived of its power to counteract the teaching of God's holy truth. And, as the subject is very obscure, it will be our aim to be particularly explicit.

The term "mysteries," by which in our language these sacred services and rites are designated, comes from the Greek μυστήριον, and, in its modern acceptation, imports something above human intelligence; something awfully obscure and enigmatical; anything artfully made difficult; the secret of any business or profession. This term is frequently used in the New Testament Scriptures; and, when thus employed, generally signifies those doctrines of the gospel which the Jews in preceding times did not understand, in consequence of the darkness of their religious dispensation; or those profound truths—such as the Trinity in Unity, the Incarnation, &c.—which the weakness of human reason can never adequately comprehend.

In the application of this term, however, to the sacred and occult rites of the heathen, its meaning is not so obvious. Many ingenious and conflicting conjectures, on the etymology of the term, and its application to this subject, have been offered by learned writers; but that seems most probable which derives the word from the Hebrew מסתר—which means "any place or thing hidden or concealed." As there can be little doubt that the occult rites to which this term was applied, were imported into Greece from Egypt and the East, and as in those regions names and distinctive terms possess a peculiar significancy and force, this sense of the word may be safely received.

On a subject so recondite and obscure as the origin of these religious rites, it might be expected that great difference of opinion would be found among the learned. This is the case in a more than ordinary degree.

One able writer insists that "the mysteries were the offspring of bigotry and priestcraft; they originated in Egypt, the native land of idolatry." "They were instituted with a view to aggrandize that order of men," (the priesthood,) "to extend their influence, and enlarge their revenues. To accomplish these selfish projects, they applied every engine toward besotting the multitude with superstition and enthusiasm. They taught them to believe that themselves were the distinguished favourites of Heaven; and that celestial doctrines had been revealed to them, too holy to be communicated to the profane rabble, and too sublime to be comprehended by vulgar capacities.

"All the orientals, but more especially the Egyptians, delighted in mysterious and allegorical doctrines. Every maxim of morality, every tenet of theology, every dogma of philosophy was wrapped up in the veil of allegory and mysticism. This propensity, no doubt, conspired with avarice and ambition to dispose them to a dark and mysterious system of religion."—*Ency. Brit.*, art. *Mysteries*.

Another and very opposite opinion respecting the origin of the heathen mysteries is given by Warburton. Instead of regarding them as invented and brought into use to promote the objects of the priesthood, he considers "that the mysteries were invented, established, and supported by lawgivers." He argues this, "1. From the place of their original; which was Egypt. This Herodotus, Diodorus, and Plutarch, who collect from ancient testimonies, expressly affirm; and in this all antiquity concurs. Now, in Egypt, all religious worship being planned and established by statesmen, and directed to the ends of civil policy, we must conclude that the mysteries were originally invented by LEGISLATORS."

2. Secondly, it is urged that "the sages who brought them out of Egypt, and propagated them in Asia, in Greece, and Britain, were all kings or lawgivers; such as Zoroaster, Inachus, Orpheus, Melampus, Trophonius, Minos, Cinyras, Erechtheus, and the Druids.

"3. They were under the superintendence of the state. A magistrate entitled ΒΑΣΙΛΕΥΣ, a 'king,' presided in the *Eleusinian mysteries*. Lysias informs us, that this king was to offer up the public prayers, according to their country rites; and to see that nothing impious or immoral crept into their celebration. This title given to the president of the *mysteries* was, doubtless, in memory of the first founder; to whom were joined four officers, chosen by the people, called 'ΕΠΙΜΕΛΗΤΑΙ, or 'curators;' the priests being only under-officers to these, and had no share in the direction: for, this being the legislator's favourite institution, he took all possible care for its support, which could not be done more effectually than by his watching over it himself.

"4. But this original is still further seen from the qualities required in the aspirants to the mysteries. According to their original institution, neither slaves nor foreigners were to be admitted into them. Now, if the *mysteries* were instituted, primarily, for the sake of teaching religious truths, there can be no reason given why every man with the proper qualifications should not be admitted: but supposing them instituted by the state for civil purposes, a very good one may be assigned; for slaves and foreigners have there neither property nor country.

"5. Another proof of this original may be adduced from what was taught promiscuously to all the initiated; which was, *the necessity of a virtuous and holy life, to obtain a happy immortality*. Now this, we know, could not come from the sacerdotal warehouses: the priests could afford a better pennyworth of their Elysium, at the easy expense of oblations and sacrifices.

"6. Another strong presumption of this original is the great use of the mysteries to the state; so amply confessed by the wisest writers of antiquity, and so clearly seen from the nature of the thing itself.

"7. But, lastly, we have the testimony of the knowing Plutarch for this original; who, in his treatise 'Of Isis and Osiris,' expressly tells us, that it was 'a most ancient opinion, delivered down from legislators and divines to poets and philosophers, the author of it entirely unknown, but the belief of it indelibly established, not only in tradition, and the talk of the vulgar, but in the MYSTERIES and in the sacred offices of religion, both among Greeks and barbarians, spread all over the face of the globe, that the universe was not upheld fortuitously, without mind, reason, or a governor to preside over its revolutions.' "—*Divine Legation*, book ii, sec. 4.

These conflicting views of the origin of the mysteries are sufficiently startling; but it will be necessary to add to their number before proceeding to investigate the subject. We are told in a modern work of great merit, "That the ancient mysteries were nothing but the impositions of priests, who played upon the superstitious and ignorant, is an opinion which, although entertained by Limburgh-Brouwer, the latest writer on the subject, certainly cannot satisfy those who are accustomed to seek a more solid and vital principle in all religious institutions that have ever had any lasting influence upon mankind. The persons united and initiated to celebrate the mysteries in Greece were neither all priests, nor did they belong to the ignorant and superstitious classes of society; but they were, on the contrary, frequently the most distinguished statesmen and philosophers. It has been remarked, that it is far more probable that the mysteries of the various parts of Greece were remains of the ancient Pelasgian religion. The associations of persons for the purpose of celebrating them must, therefore, have been formed at the time when the overwhelming influence of the Hellenic religion began to gain the upper hand in Greece, and when persons who still entertained a reverence for the worship of former times united together, with the intention of preserving and upholding among themselves as much as possible of the religion of their forefathers. It is natural enough that they formed themselves for this purpose into societies, analogous to the brotherhood of the Church of Rome, and endeavoured to preserve against the profanation of the multitude that which was most dear to them. Hence the secrecy of all the Greek mysteries, and hence the fact that the Greek mysteries were almost invariably connected with the worship of the old Pelasgian divinities."—*Smith's Dict. of Greek and Roman Antiquities*, art. *Mysteries*.

Again: a different solution of this difficult subject is given by Mr. Faber. He first identifies the mysteries, notwithstanding the diversity of deities and names under which they were celebrated; and, having established their common origin, he proceeds: "Bishop Warburton, agreeably to his system of deducing everything from Egypt, contends that they were first invented in that country; whence, in process of time, they were carried into Greece, Persia, Cyprus, Crete, Samothrace, Lemnos, Asia Minor, Britain, Hindostan, and all those barbarous nations, wherever situated, among which we find them established.

"This theory seems to me so utterly incredible, that I feel myself altogether unable to adopt it. Whatever was the origin of the mysteries, such also must have been the origin of the whole fabric of the pagan mythology: for the two are so intimately connected, that it is impossible to separate them from each other and to derive them from different sources. If, then, we subscribe to the hypothesis of Warburton, we must prepare ourselves to believe that the whole frame-work of Gentile idolatry, with the sacred mysteries attached to it, was the exclusive contrivance of the Egyptian priesthood; and that the entire human race were but servile copyists of one single nation. We must believe, not only that the neighbouring Greeks and Phenicians borrowed from Egypt, but that the most remote communities, the British Celts, the Pelasgic Scythians, the Magi of Persia, the Chaldeans of Babylon, and even the Brahmins of Hindostan, were all content to receive their theology from the same country. We must believe, too, that this universal obligation to Egypt was incurred in the very earliest ages: for, not to enter into a discussion respecting the antiquity of Babylon, or Persia, or Hindostan, we find the orgies of Adonis, or Baal-peor, and of Astartè, or Lida, completely established in

Palestine prior to the time of the Exodus; and we observe the Greeks acknowledging that they had already received from the northern Pelasgi, or Thracians, those very mysteries which were again imported by the southern settlers from Egypt.

"The whole of this appears to me perfectly incredible. Egypt, no doubt, was a civilized and well-regulated state at a very remote period; and its established idolatry was, I believe, coeval with its very existence as a nation: but, neither was it the only civilized community; nor, even if it were, would this satisfactorily account for the universal adoption of its mysteries, as well by its more immediate neighbours, as by the far-distant colonies of the extreme east, and north, and north-east. When the earth was once peopled by the descendants of Noah, and when his children had once formed distinct states in regions widely separated from each other, I can never bring myself to believe, that any single nation could communicate its own peculiar religious system to the whole world; I can never persuade myself, that all mankind with one consent forsook the worship of their fathers, merely that they might adopt the fantastic inventions of Egypt.

"How, then, are we to account for the general prevalence and identity of the pagan mysteries? and from what common origin are we to suppose them to have sprung? I undoubtedly account for the matter precisely as I account for the identity of the various systems of pagan mythology. So remarkable and exact accordance of sentiments and institutions, which may be distinctly traced in every part of the world, leads inevitably to the belief that, in the infancy of society, when as yet mankind were but few in number, all the children of Noah were associated together in one community; that, while they thus formed but one empire, a great apostasy from the worship of the true God took place; that at that period the original system of idolatrous mythology and the sacred mysteries attached to it were first contrived; and that afterward these, by the Dispersion, were spread over the world."—*Pagan Idolatry*, vol. iii, p. 106.

If it had been my object to exhibit to the utmost the discordance which obtains among the learned respecting this subject, I should next quote the opinion of Dr. Hales, who believes the mysteries to have had their origin in the Hebrew feast of tabernacles, and then adds some equally strange notions from other authors: but my limits forbid an exposure of the eccentricities of scholars, which can yield no practical advantage.

It may appear a Utopian undertaking to attempt to reconcile these conflicting opinions; although it may be candidly acknowledged that elements of truth may be found in each of them. The prevalent error into which these and other eminent men have fallen seems to be that they have not only studied the subject each under different aspects, but they have also confounded changes introduced into the institution of which they speak, in different ages and countries; and, consequently, that which ought only to be regarded as a peculiar and local feature, has been spoken of as a general and prevailing characteristic.

It will, however, now be necessary for us to give the view of the origin, object, and character of these institutions, which we have formed after a careful consideration of all these opinions.

1. As to their origin, the argument of Mr. Faber appears to be irresistible. The learned writer in Dr. Smith's Dictionary may as reasonably contend for the origin of the mysteries in Greece,—although it is notorious that they previously existed in Egypt,—as Warburton can for their Egyptian origin, when their early prevalence and general identity cannot be denied. Whatever precise period, therefore, may be fixed on as having produced these strange ceremonies, it must be placed before the Dispersion, in order to account for their general prevalence.

2. The most curious and important section of the inquiry, however, respects the object or design which led to the establishment of a religious ceremonial, that spread so widely, and exercised such an immense influence over the world throughout succeeding ages. On this point it does not become me to speak positively; yet it seems probable that, by carefully reviewing a few particulars, some definite information may be obtained even on this recondite topic.

It appears that in all these mysteries there is mention made of a certain sacred ark. "Apuleius mentions the ark of Isis; and describes it as containing the sacred symbols which were used in the mysteries: he also exhibits Psychè as deprecating Ceres by the silent orgies of the ark of that goddess. Plutarch, in treating of the rites of Osiris, speaks of the sacred ark which his long-robed priests were wont to carry, and which contained within it a small golden *boat*. Pausanias notices an ancient ark which was said to have been brought by Eurypylus from Troy, and within which the sacred image or symbol of Bacchus Esymnetes was enclosed: he likewise mentions certain arks as being ordinarily dedicated to Ceres, who was worshipped in conjunction with Bacchus, just as Isis was in conjunction with Osiris. Eusebius informs us, that, in celebrating the mysteries of the Cabiri, the Phenicians used a consecrated ark. Clemens says that a similar ark was employed in the orgies of the same Corybantic Cabiri, who were venerated in Mount Olympus; that it contained an indecorous symbol of Bacchus; and that it was conveyed by the Cabiric brethren themselves into Etruria, where the mystic use of it was likewise adopted. This author speaks also of the ark of the Eleusinian Ceres, and is very particular in noticing its contents. Theocritus, in describing the mysteries of Bacchus as celebrated by the three Lenæ,—Ino, Autonoë, and Agavè, the three representatives of the triplicated great mother,—fails not to specify the sacred ark, out of which they take the hidden symbols that were used in the orgies."—*Faber's Pagan Idolatry*, vol. iii, p. 119.

Further proof to the same effect might be produced respecting the use of the ark for these sacred purposes in Greece, Rome, Babylon, India, and Britain. This important element may, therefore, be considered as fully established.

"The question, then, is," as Mr. Faber very pertinently puts it, "What are we to understand by this so generally reverenced ark?" This learned writer supplies an elaborate answer, in accordance with his theory of heathen idolatry; and satisfactorily establishes the fact, that this sacred ark, as used in the mysteries, was employed in significant reference to the Deluge, and the great father and mother who were there preserved. On one point, however, I think it necessary to suggest an extension or emendation of this learned author's views. I cannot divest myself of the belief that the ark devised for the purpose of this idolatry and these heathen mysteries, was the original or first sacred ark. If it has been established that the cherubim of Eden were appointed for a purpose similar to that to which the cherubim were applied in the Mosaic sanctuary; (Patriarchal Age, pp. 143-148;) and that, throughout all patriarchal times, the faithful had a place of worship, a seat of the divine presence, a depository for sacred emblems of the patriarchal faith, and an oracle; (Hebrew People, pp. 525, 526, 528, 529;) then it is, to say the least, extremely probable that the origin of the mysteries, in the outset of postdiluvian idolatry, was not the invention of a new ceremonial of sacred things, but a perversion of an old and pure service.

Intimations of this may be discovered in the evidence which has been already given. For instance, in the extract from Plutarch's description of the rites of Osiris, he speaks of the "sacred ark:" but this is not, as in many other instances, the symbol of the ark of Noah; on the contrary, it contained *a small golden boat*, which was evidently intended to serve that purpose.

It seems, therefore, that the measure which led to the establishment of the mysteries was a virtual repudiation of the old pure patriarchal faith, and the adoption of a scheme of idolatry which deified the great father and mother, as reappearing in Noah and his wife, and then triplicated in the persons of their children; and that the mysteries were an adaptation of the sacred patriarchal worship to this idolatry.

It is not to be expected that any particular solution of this difficult subject will be received with favour, or commend itself to general acceptance; especially as the most ample collection of evidence which could be exhibited, must, from the nature of the subject and the character of the testimony, fail to furnish that absolute proof which the mind requires, in order to rest with implicit reliance on the certainty of the thing.

All, therefore, that can be hoped, and which, indeed, the nature of the subject seems to admit, is, to supply such a solution as shall meet all the requirements and difficulties of the case. It has been already shown that none of the schemes to which we have alluded, although propounded by men of eminence, have done this. It is, for instance, vain to furnish the most plausible account of the origin of the mysteries derived from the relative influence of Hellenic and Pelasgian doctrines in Greece, when it is an incontestable fact, that essentially the same ceremonies previously obtained in Egypt. It is equally futile to argue, with Warburton, for their Egyptian origin, when, from their prevalence in such remote countries as India and Britain, it must be seen that they could not have emanated from any single nation, but must have originated prior to the Dispersion. No arguments can be satisfactory which ascribe these sacred services to any particular class, whether priests or statesmen, when it is undeniable that both these classes, as well as the most profound philosophers, took a deep interest, and felt a vital concern in the maintenance of their sacred character. Nor is it possible to make the more correct theory of Faber meet all the requirements of the case. To suppose the ark of the mysteries to have had no other prototype than the ark of Noah, is irreconcilable, not only with the fact that in some instances the symbols of the ark of the Deluge are found separate and distinct from the sacred chest of the mysteries, but also with this most important circumstance,—that the sacred ark of the Hebrew tabernacle, which could have had no reference to the Deluge, was almost identical with those found in ancient Egyptian sculptures of religious ceremonies.

I am desirous to subject to the same test which I have applied to other schemes, the solution which I have suggested.

1. We find a sacred ark used in the mysteries of almost every (if not every) ancient people. This ark not only is, in many instances, shaped like a ship, a boat, or a lunar crescent,—but, in many others, has additional figures and emblems of this kind, while the body of the ark itself is almost an exact copy of the Hebrew ark of the tabernacle. (Kitto's Cyc. of Bib. Lit., art. Ark.) Again: let the population of the world at the time of the Dispersion be fairly considered, and whether we refer to the evidence afforded by the general identity of all heathenism, or the Scriptural account of the patriarchal times, it must be believed that the service and worship of God were conducted publicly, intelligently, and by the offering of sacrifice in or before a place sacredly set apart as the dwelling of God. To ascribe the origin of the mysteries to a corruption of this service, is, therefore, to obtain the countenance of all antiquity to the probability of our theory.

2. It is not intended here to expand the hints which have been given respecting the sin of Nimrod in his effort to make himself the religious, as

well as the political, head of the new world. It can, however, scarcely be doubted by any who will carefully peruse the voluminous evidence collected by Faber, that the establishment of postdiluvian idolatry was effected by the deification of Noah and his sons, as reappearances of the great father, to the end that the aspirant himself might also claim divinity as a descendant from them, most probably in the character of the promised Seed. If such was the fact, what means could have more certainly carried out such a project successfully, (and carried out we know it was,) than making those sacred services of patriarchal worship which, from the rapid increase of population, must have become select, accessible only to a few, who had entered into the ambitious and profane purpose; and then ingrafting on all its sacred things, doctrines, and rites, a refined and elaborate, but corrupt and debasing idolatry?

3. It will be obvious that the ascription of special sacredness to these religious rites would allow ample opportunities for the changes sought, and at the same time would have invested these new rites and doctrines with peculiar and important influence. Nor is it easy to conceive how else a whole people could be led into such serious errors. It is, however, certain, that in all ages the introduction of fatal errors respecting religion has been covered with combined prescriptions of secrecy and mystery.

4. It must be admitted that this idea of the origin of the mysteries perfectly accounts for the essential identity, and, at the same time, national diversity, which they exhibit. Having had one common origin, they were all framed on the same principle and pattern: but alterations in the detail of names, rites, and ceremonies, would be afterward introduced, harmonizing them severally with the diverse peculiarities of national mythology.

5. This theory of these sacred heathen rites is no less important in respect of their object than with reference to their origin. If it had been desirable here to quote detailed particulars, both these points might be amply sustained and illustrated. This will, however, be more suitably done when we come to consider the religion of the several nations in separate chapters. Still it may be proper to remark, that much confusion has been introduced into the subject by learned writers speaking of the origin and object of the mysteries from the aspects which they present in a particular nation. It is very conceivable that they might have been introduced into Greece in a very different manner from that in which they were first produced at Babel; and that priests and legislators might, in different countries and ages, have made them subservient to their own purposes. The view we have taken, therefore, corrects what is erroneous, and harmonizes what is sound, in the several conflicting theories which have been propounded under limited and local impressions of the subject.

6. Yet although this is not the place to insert in detail the various

ceremonies which were incorporated into the mysteries of ancient nations, it is necessary to give some idea of the general character which they exhibited, and of the ruling elements which everywhere distinguished them.

The mysteries were sacred sacrifices and ceremonies which took place at night, or in secret, within some sanctuary, into which the uninitiated were not permitted to enter.

There were several particulars essential to these religious services, and common to them in all countries.

(1.) There were always objects of worship. The mysteries were, in fact, always a secret worship of some particular deity or deities. In Egypt, Isis and Osiris were adored; in the Grecian Eleusinian mysteries, Demeter and Persephone; in those of Thebes, Bacchus; and in other places other divinities were the centres and objects of these select and secret rites. In each and every case, these orgies were celebrated in honour of some deity whose praises were the special business of the officiating hierophant. This precisely harmonizes with our view of their origin in the deification of Noah and Nimrod.

(2.) Another essential to the celebration of the mysteries was, the use of sacred utensils. We have already observed, the principal of these was an ark or chest, containing sacred articles which, it seems, were generally exhibited in the mysteries. Apuleius mentions the ark of Isis as containing secret symbols. Plutarch, treating of the rites of Osiris, says that the ark contained a golden boat. Pausanias notices an ancient ark, within which the sacred image or symbol of Bacchus Esymnetes was enclosed. Clemens says, that a similar ark was employed in the orgies of the Corybantic Cabiri, and that it contained an indecorous symbol of Bacchus. Numerous other instances might be cited from classic authors; but these are sufficient to show that sacred arks, containing religious symbols, were common in different countries in the celebration of the mysteries.

(3.) A third requisite for these secret services was a recital, by the hierophant, of ancient traditions, with their interpretation.

Warburton has employed his mighty genius and learning to show that the doctrines taught in the mysteries were the human origin, death, and sepulture of the heathen gods,—the real unity of the Deity,—and the necessity of a holy life.

The sense in which the learned prelate understands these points, and the consequences which he has drawn from them, have been ably controverted by Leland and Faber. Yet, to a great extent, these writers are obliged to admit the accuracy of the *data* upon which the bishop reasons, however successfully they have overturned his inductions.

It seems, then, to be an undoubted fact, that the mysteries taught the origin of the hero-divinities of postdiluvian idolatry. Whether, as Warburton conjectures, the fragment of Phenician history preserved by Sanchoniatho was the very account read to the initiated or not, the constant reference to the mutilation of Osiris and other deities, combined with other circumstances, identifies this teaching with the story of Noah beyond any chance of mistake. Nor does it appear at all improbable, notwithstanding the objections of Faber, that, in the origin of this hero-worship, there was a recognition of the unity of the supreme God, and that this was verbally proclaimed in these sacred rites, even when in practice unbounded polytheism prevailed. In like manner, it is very conceivable that the introduction of this system of idolatry, and the establishment of these sacred rites for its promulgation, were connected with large professions of purity and moral improvement : and this may account for the existence of many passages in classic authors on which much reliance has been placed. But if this was the case at first, it soon gave way to the prevailing spirit which imbued the whole idolatrous system, until at length, as Cicero says, the mysteries became synonymous with "abomination."

On the whole, then, it may be regarded as an established fact: that the mysteries originated in a series of grand, but secret or covert efforts to establish polytheism, and to secure the great rebellion against the purposes of God in the days of Nimrod; that in the progress of these efforts the pure patriarchal religion was corrupted, and hero-worship established; that the means used in effecting the alteration were afterward continued with a view to sustain it, and the sacred patriarchal symbols were retained, but with considerable modifications and additions; and that, in harmony with the whole design and object, these mysteries were open only to the initiated, who were bound not to divulge any of the privileged communications which they had received.

III. We now direct attention to THE SACRED ORACLES of the heathen. These were everywhere regarded as means of obtaining from the Deity some solution of difficult cases, or information respecting events in distant places, or at future times, beyond that which merely human wisdom could possibly furnish. The fact of their institution and prevalence is, therefore, a testimony borne by all antiquity to the fact of the divine omniscience, and to the certain existence of a primitive revelation.

If, as some would-be philosophers are anxious to make us believe, mankind began their career in a semi-bestial state, and by gradual and successive improvements worked their way up to their present elevated intellectual position, whence could possibly have originated a belief in the divinity of oracles? We might as reasonably calculate on a herd of baboons seeking such illumination, as that man would do so in such circumstances. No; it stands confessed, that heathen oracles, however vain, or false, or guileful, were but corruptions of a true and real revelation from God to man.

It was, indeed, the crowning glory of the pious in patriarchal times, that they had access unto God. The few elements of information which have reached us respecting this period, do not explain, as fully as could be desired, the manner and means by which this boon was realized: but it speaks to the fact in such a way as to place it beyond all doubt. When Rebekah was driven by her distress to seek divine succour, she was at no loss for the means of obtaining it: *"She went to inquire of the Lord."* The puerile exposition of commentators, that this was an appeal to some patriarch, or a simple exercise of prayer, is altogether inadmissible: the clear, ample, explicit, and prophetic answer which she received, decides the case, and proves that she had access to *an oracle of God*. Gen. xxv, 22, 23.

When, therefore, Satanic guile and power had succeeded in diverting the minds of men from the only true object of worship to deified men, and brutes, and elements, it became necessary that the false, idolatrous religion thus introduced should possess a real or pretended power, equivalent to that afforded by the oracle of Jehovah in patriarchal times. Hence we find everywhere, among the cultivated heathen nations of antiquity, oracles established which professed to give responses dictated by Deity in answer to the inquiries of the worshippers; and, as the learned Banier affirms, " every nation where idolatry prevailed had its oracles." Egypt, Greece, Rome, and other countries, afford abundant evidence in proof of this assertion.

The important question is then suggested, What was the real character of these oracles? Were they the result of combined fraud and ingenious contrivance? or did they in any measure emanate from, and were sustained by, Satanic influence? In the solution of this question, the learned of our own as well as of other countries are much at variance with each other. Bishop Sherlock is so confident of the Satanic character of the heathen oracles, that he does not hesitate to state that he regards those who deny that *the devil* gave out the oracles to the heathen world, as evincing "a degree of unbelief" which deprives them of all right to debate questions of this kind. (Works, vol. iv, p. 49. London. 1830.) While, on the other hand, Dr. Middleton pleads guilty to this degree of unbelief, and maintains that these oracles were " all mere impostures, wholly invented and supported by human craft, without any supernatural aid or interposition whatever." (Miscel. Works, vol. v, p. 262. Lon., 1755.) When such divines stand thus opposed to each other, nothing can be hoped for in respect of authority. Our only resource is, therefore, to investigate the subject for ourselves, under the guidance of such aids as its nature affords.

It may be observed *in limine*, that an objection has been taken to supernatural interposition in respect of oracles, which appears to be most unsound and unreasonable. It has been asserted that numerous proofs exist of fraud, deceit, and corruption, in the agency by which they were administered: and hence it is argued, that they could not have emanated from diabolical influence. It is difficult to conceive of a more inconsequential conclusion. If it had been alleged that these oracles were the result of divine prescience, then the proof of positive guile and wickedness in the agents might be held sufficient to disprove the claim. But surely there is no such obvious antagonism between Satanic influence, and fraud, guile, and wickedness, that the presence of the one must necessarily prove the absence of the other. On the other hand, I am free to confess, that this asserted guile and fraud, instead of disproving the presence of Satanic influence, rather inclines me to infer the operation of such agency.

In the investigation of this subject, then, it appears to me, we have to decide on these important questions:—First, have we any certain knowledge that a fallen spirit, at any time, or under any circumstances, has been permitted to dictate superhuman knowledge to mankind? And, secondly, if this has been done, is the case of heathen oracles one which reasonably justifies the belief that such influence was exerted in respect of them?

1. Passing by other and more doubtful cases, I call attention here to a clear and indubitable instance of the communication of superhuman knowledge by a diabolical agency. The case I refer to has been noticed for another purpose in a note; it is that of the Pythoness of Philippi. We have here (Acts xvi, 16–19) an unquestionable proof of such a communication of superhuman knowledge. It may be first observed, that the term used by the sacred writer to describe this woman's occupation, μαντεύομαι, and which our translators have rendered "soothsaying," signifies "to *foretell*, *divine*, *prophesy*, DELIVER AN ORACLE." It is precisely the same word which is used by Herodotus when referring to the divination of the Scythians, (Lib. iv, cap. 67,) and which is also employed by him when speaking of the famous oracle at Delphi. (Lib. vi, cap. 76; *et* lib. viii, cap. 38.) The case is, therefore, strictly in point.

In this instance, then, it is clear that an evil spirit gave to the woman the power of making superhuman, or *oracular*, communications. The presence and power of this spirit were absolutely necessary to the production of these results: for, when the demon was expelled, her masters "saw that the hope of their gains was gone," and their chagrin and rage led to a fierce persecution. It is vain to urge that this was a mere mercenary affair; and that it is not to be supposed that Satanic influence would be permitted in such a case. The Holy Ghost has declared it to be a fact. Whatever fraud or wickedness might have been employed in connexion with this business, it is, therefore, an acknowledged truth by every believer in revelation, that oracular answers, communicating superhuman knowledge, were in this case given by diabolical agency.

2. We have to inquire, in the second place, whether the case of the heathen oracles is such as to justify the opinion that this diabolical influence was sometimes used in respect of them.

(1.) It seems reasonable to suppose, that if such Satanic influence was employed in what appears to have been merely a private and mercenary effort, it might surely be expected in those great national institutions which stood associated with idolatrous delusions, and which had all been brought into operation by the same infernal power.

(2.) It is important to consider the fact, that these oracles were sustained in high credit, and trusted with implicit confidence, by the wisest statesmen and sovereigns of the nations of antiquity most celebrated for their high state of civilization. Not only did this continue under particular circumstances and for a season or an age, but it lasted throughout successive centuries. This is an argument which all candid minds have felt. Hence the learned Banier asks, "Is it, then, credible, that if the oracles had been nothing but the offspring of priestcraft, whatever artful methods they may be thought to have used, and however successful in pumping out the secrets and schemes of those who came to consult them;—is it credible, I say, that those oracles would have lasted so long, and supported themselves with so much splendour and reputation, had they been merely owing to the forgery of the priests? Imposture betrays itself, falsehood never holds out. Besides, there were too many witnesses, too many curious spies, too many people whose interest it was not to be deluded. One may put a cheat for a time upon a few private persons, who are overrun with credulity, but by no means upon whole nations for several ages. Some princes who had been played upon by ambiguous responses,—a trick once discovered,—the bare curiosity of a free-thinker,— any of these, in short, was sufficient to blow up the whole mystery, and at once to make the credit of the oracles fall to the ground. How many people, deluded by hateful responses, were concerned to examine if it was really the priests by whom they were seduced! But why? Was it so hard a matter to find one of the priests themselves, capable of being bribed to betray the cause of his accomplices, by the fair promises and more substantial gifts of those who omitted no means of being thoroughly informed in a subject of such concern?"—*Mythology*, vol. i, p. 328.

Lempriere echoes the same argument, and says, "Imposture and forgery cannot long flourish, and falsehood becomes its own destroyer."—*Dictionary, s. v. Oraculum.* Yet it is an undeniable fact that, "during the best period of their history, the Greeks, generally speaking, had undoubtedly a sincere faith in the oracle, its counsels and directions."—*Smith's Dict. of Greek and Roman Antiq.*, p. 670. Hence Lucan, who wrote his *Pharsalia* scarcely thirty years after our Lord's crucifixion, laments as one of the greatest evils of the age, that the Delphic oracle was become silent. From the general credit which the oracles maintained in an enlightened age, and during a very lengthened period, it is extremely improbable that they should have been nothing more than the base results of fraud and fiction.

(3.) The nature of the communications given forth by these oracles is strongly confirmatory of the existence of Satanic agency. Our reference must be confined to one remarkable instance; but shall be a case of such public notoriety as to form a fair example of the general character of the institution.

I refer to the case of Crœsus, King of Lydia, and the Pythian oracle. Herodotus informs us that this sovereign, alarmed at the growing power of Cyrus, King of Persia, and meditating an attack on his dominions, was anxious first to consult the most celebrated oracles as to the issue of such an important enterprise, before he committed himself to it. Prior, however, to his submitting to the oracle the important question upon which his fate depended, he was determined to propound one which should enable him, as he thought, to test the prescience of the oracle. He accordingly sent messengers to Delphi; and having carefully considered the period required for the journey, and allowed them ample time, he commanded them at the appointed hour to present themselves before the Pythoness, and propose this question; "What is Crœsus, son of Alyattes, now doing?" They were to write the answer carefully down, and send it to him. The answer was to this effect:—

> "I count the sand, I measure out the sea;
> The silent and the dumb are heard by me.
> E'en now the odours to my sense that rise
> A tortoise boiling with a lamb supplies,
> Where brass below and brass above it lies."

The fact was, that Crœsus, determined to be occupied in the most unlikely and unkingly manner, was engaged at that time in boiling the flesh of a tortoise and a lamb together in a covered vessel of brass.

Crœsus was so impressed with the exactness of this response, that he determined to do all in his power to propitiate this oracle, and to trust himself to its direction. He accordingly sent to Delphi the most costly presents in gold and silver,—amounting altogether, according to the computation of the Abbé Barthelemy, to £879,547,—with orders to make the following inquiry: "Crœsus, sovereign of Lydia and of various nations, esteems these the only genuine oracles. In return for the sagacity which has marked your declarations, he sends these proofs of his liberality. He finally desires to know whether he may proceed against the Persians, and whether he shall require the assistance of any allies." The answer was, that if Crœsus carried his arms against the Persians, he would overthrow a great empire; and that he would do well to make alliances with the most powerful states of Greece. Interpreting this reply to his own advantage, but anxious to put the case in another aspect before the oracle, he sent a third time, to inquire as to the duration of his empire. The answer on that occasion was,—

> "When o'er the Medes a mule shall sit on high,
> O'er pebbly Hermus then, soft Lydian, fly,
> Fly with all haste; for safety scorn thy fame,
> Nor scruple to deserve a coward's name."

Still giving to the answers of the oracle the interpretation most favourable to himself, Crœsus regarded the reign of a mule over Media as an impossibility, and thence inferred the stability of his own power. Under this impression he made war on Persia, and, as is well known, was soon vanquished, stripped of his dominions, condemned to death, but ultimately preserved and supported as a captive by Cyrus.

Reference will be elsewhere made to the history of these events. In this place I have simply to investigate these oracular responses, with a view to ascertain their character. First, then, it cannot be denied that the first answer, which referred to the strange occupation of Crœsus at the time, exhibits remarkable accuracy. We may think ourselves very wise in dismissing such a case with the cry of "jugglery and cheating;" but it is doubtful whether by such conduct we do not evince great folly. The King of Lydia was a man of great energy and intellectual power: he was therefore competent to judge of the chances of imposition, and to guard against them, much better than we can now imagine. Yet he, by the presentation of gifts to the value of nearly one million sterling, gave ample proof that he regarded the whole as a *bona fide* transaction. Is it not, then, reasonable to ask, "By what means could the Pythoness have given such a reply? By what means could the priestess at Delphi have ascertained what the King of Lydia was doing at a given hour, in his palace at Sardis, hundreds of miles away, when he had determined to exercise his utmost care and ingenuity in order to test her ability?" Neither captious querulousness nor unmeaning sneering will meet the case. Here is an undoubted historical incident, which, I am bold to say, admits of no satisfactory solution, except on the principle of diabolical agency. But on this principle all is plain: the difficulty, otherwise insurmountable, immediately vanishes.

But then it is asked in the most triumphant tone, "Why were not all the responses given in language equally distinct and intelligible? Why the double meaning and equivocation of the other replies?" It is truly astonishing to see the confidence with which this objection is urged, when it is open to a very simple and rational solution. It is easy to conceive, that diabolical agency might enable the Pythoness to give a clear and distinct answer as to what was transpiring at the moment in a distant place, which to all merely human intelligence would have been wholly inscrutable; but it is far from certain that this agency could unravel the mystery of future contingent events. This is the exclusive attribute of Jehovah: he challenges this power to himself alone: "I am God, and there is none else; I am God, and there is none like me, declaring the end from the beginning;" (Isa. xlvi, 9, 10;) while to the idols and their worshippers he says, "Produce your cause, saith the Lord; bring forth your strong reasons, saith the King of Jacob. Let them bring them forth, and show us what shall happen: let them show the former things, what they be, that we may consider them, and know the latter end of them; or declare us things for to come. Show the things that are to come hereafter, that we may know that ye are gods." Isa. xli, 21–23. Diabolical aid, therefore, although it might give superhuman knowledge in respect of passing events, and afford a means of conjecture beyond all human wisdom as to the future, could not communicate the power of foretelling future contingencies. Obscure, conjectural, and enigmatical expressions, in the communication of oracles, would consequently be as necessary under this agency as without it.

The result of our inquiry, then, is,—

1. That we find the heathen oracles maintaining a high character and general confidence, to an extent, and for a period, beyond that which would be likely to result from continued and unaided human fraud and falsehood.

2. The accredited declarations of these oracles exhibit a measure of knowledge respecting passing events, and a sagacity in respect of futurity, far above all that merely human ingenuity or contrivance could produce.

3. Yet all this is found in such combined operation with wickedness, fraud and corruption, as clearly to prove that if superhuman knowledge was connected with the oracles, it must have been diabolical.

4. It is a certain fact, based on the authority of New-Testament revelation, that diabolical agency was used in ancient times for the purpose of giving forth superhuman oracular responses.

From all these premises we conclude that the sagacity and general credit of heathen oracles was in some instances owing to diabolical agency.

It only remains to offer a few brief observations on the entire system.

1. We see its unity of character. It did not set itself in positive collision with primitive truth; but, incorporating important elements of this truth into the system, it fell back on these for support and defence. It was by this means that a common ground of union was established between the old idolatrous nations. The truths which they had incorporated and perverted were at the same time so many links in the chain by which, notwithstanding the diverse names of their deities, they were united, and plates of the armour by which they were defended.

2. It will be seen how directly all the parts of this idolatrous system were pointed against the actual sovereignty of God, and his divinely appointed scheme of redemption. Whether we look to the origin, character, mysteries, or oracles of this idolatry, we find it specially hostile to the unity, providence, and religion of God. Moral truth, on some occasions, might be admitted; the fact of a future judgment could be conceded; a general but vague notion of providence might be taught: BUT GOD MUST BE DETHRONED; men, or beasts, or material elements, or heavenly bodies, or the foul serpent-form, MUST rule supreme, and receive divine adoration. Is not this a deeply instructive fact? It is the common badge of the system, the unmistakable evidence of the presence and power of the arch-destroyer.

I cannot close this chapter without placing on record my strong and decided opinion, that this subject has been usually treated in such a manner as to palliate or conceal the enormous sinfulness of idolatry. I contemplate with the deepest regret the results flowing to the religion of our country from the tone of teaching imparted by men of the most respectable character. Let any enlightened Christian mind contemplate the learning of our colleges and academies, our treatises and manuals, on this subject. Charmed as we must be with the glitter of genius and heroism, the philosophy and learning, of classic times and persons, are we justified in allowing our children to rise up into life with merely sufficient instruction to enable them to infer that idolatry is an absurdity, when they ought to be distinctly taught that it is the most enormous sin?

With unfeigned and deep veneration for the learned of our land, I feel bound, at any hazard, to assert my strong conviction, that the honour due alone to the Triune Jehovah, as the God and Governor of this world, is not made sufficiently prominent; and that the heinous evil and fearful sin of idolatry, as such, is not adequately enforced.

On this point we cannot be too jealous—we cannot go beyond the requirements of our Bible—for the honour of our God. It was idolatry which, as a master-evil, blasted, and withered, and ruined the ancient world, despite all its learning, genius, arts, and arms: and it can only be by a general and devoted fidelity to the truth on the part of Christians that the kingdoms of this world can ever "become the kingdoms of our God and of his Christ."

THE HISTORY AND RELIGION OF THE GENTILE NATIONS.

CHAPTER I.

EGYPT: ITS HISTORY.

General View of Egypt—Difficulties which oppose our Acquaintance with its Early History—Undoubted Evidence of High Civilization in the most Remote Times—Prowess and Reign of Amosis—Eighteenth Dynasty—Death of Jacob—Wonderful Perfection of Mechanical Art—Death of Joseph—Moses—The Exodus—Canaanitish Nations weakened by Egyptian Invasion before the Israelites crossed the Jordan—Sesostris—Nineteenth Dynasty—Sethos—His Conquests—The Absence of further Allusion to Canaan on the Monuments, a striking Proof of the Truth of Scripture—Twentieth Dynasty—Twenty-first Dynasty—Effect of the Commercial Policy of the Hebrews on Egypt—Twenty-second Dynasty—Shishak—His Invasion of Judea—Twenty-third Dynasty—Decline of Egyptian Power—Twenty-fourth Dynasty—Bocchoris—Twenty-fifth Dynasty—Tarkus—Twenty-sixth Dynasty—The Dodecarchy—Triumph and Reign of Psammiticus—Pharaoh-Necho—His Victory over the Hebrews—Apries, the Pharaoh-Hophra of Scripture—Defeated and put to death by Amosis—Conquest of Egypt by a Persian Army—Twenty-seventh Dynasty—Era of Persian Rule—Successful Government of Darius—Gallant Effort of Inaros—His Defeat and Death—Herodotus—Twenty-eighth Dynasty—Amyrtæus—Twenty-ninth Dynasty—Thirtieth Dynasty—Chronological Difficulties—Persian Invasion defeated—Slothful Habits and Ultimate Energy of Darius Ochus—Thirty-first Dynasty—Persian Rule reëstablished—Thirty-second Dynasty—Conquest of Egypt by Alexander the Great—His profound and successful Political and Commercial Policy—Alexandria built—Ruin of the Macedonian House—Thirty-third Dynasty—The Ptolemies—Lagus—His Successful Rule—Power and Cultivation of Egypt under Philadelphus—Euergetes successful in War—Intercourse between Egypt and Rome—Gradual Decline of Egyptian Power—Excessive Vices of the ruling Princes—Cleopatra, Cæsar, and Antony—Egypt a Roman Province.

Egypt must always hold a position of special prominence and interest in any investigation into the history and religion of ancient nations.

In the earliest ages we find this country under a powerful political government, and possessed of all the advantages resulting from a knowledge of the arts and sciences, and consequent civilization. The colossal prowess, gorgeous magnificence, immense wealth, and extensive learning of Egypt, stand out in the dim haze of remote antiquity, like her own pyramids, with a grandeur of outline, and a substantiality of character, which shame all scepticism as to their existence, and indubitably attest their magnitude and power; although no traces remain of their rise and progress, and none can tell us what wise and potent agencies produced these grand results.

Egypt, unlike Rome and other ancient empires, was not an association of different tribes, alien from each other in blood, language, and habits. It was, on the contrary, in the strict sense of the terms, *a great nation*. "We here see," as an eloquent writer observes, "a single people of pure unmixed race, and limited both as to numbers and territory, (see *Appendix*, note 4,) preserving, during" many centuries, "the most rigid union of character, custom, and social polity. We see them maintaining, during that long period, an indomitable spirit of political independence, often in the midst of the severest disasters and discouragements. We see them consolidating a power which, while its very essence was incompatible with such an extension of frontier as formed the boast of their rivals, rendered them more than a match for the mightiest among them."—*Edinburgh Review*, 1845, p. 392.

But while ancient Egypt presents to our view a fabric of civilization more complete in itself, and surpassing, in many essential points of excellence, what more highly-gifted races have since been able to accomplish, it has not left us a history of the nation, nor indeed materials for a history. This great defect is not to be attributed to the inability or indisposition of this people to record events. On the contrary, the Egyptians were "the most zealous race of scribes that ever existed. Their temples, their houses, their tombs, their idols, their portraits, their domestic furniture,—almost every tangible object they possessed, was covered with writing."—*Wilkinson's Ancient Egyptians*, vol, ii, pp. 12, 13. It is probable that the peculiar character used in these inscriptions may account for the unsatisfactory amount of information which, when regarded as historical records, they are found to communicate. As far as can be now ascertained, the use of hieroglyphics was the only mode which the ancient Egyptians possessed of recording events, or of communicating ideas to posterity. But this mode was so exceedingly complex and difficult, that it appears as if adapted to conceal, quite as much as to communicate, knowledge. The great body of the Egyptian people were, as might be expected, ignorant of the art of reading these strange symbols; and—what is of more importance, as accounting for the scant information respecting ancient Egypt to be found even in neighbouring countries—stran-

gers were universally unacquainted with the import of the Egyptian
language and character. There is no evidence which warrants
the opinion, that any of the Greeks who visited Egypt, and wrote
on its history, understood either the language or the hieroglyphics
of that country. They were consequently entirely dependent on the
priestly or learned caste for all the information which they acquired.
This must have opposed mighty obstacles to the attainment of any
correct and extensive knowledge of early Egyptian history; especially as the attention of these Greek sages was directed to the
study of the antiquities and history of this land only when the glory
of Egypt had passed away, and her priests had ample reasons for
magnifying and mystifying their national annals. Even these
inquiries were conducted by literati, whose only native historical
authorities were Homer and Hesiod, and who were, therefore, but ill
qualified to test with critical acumen the authenticity of the communications and claims of the Egyptian priesthood.

These circumstances are amply sufficient to account for the admitted fact, that ancient Egypt has been for centuries an enigma,—
a mystery to modern Europe. But it is said, "Now the enigma is
solved, the mystery unravelled. Now, as the genius and learning
of the present age have mastered the reading of the recondite hieroglyphics, ancient Egypt stands revealed to our vision; and we can
see the progress of her great career, and trace her wonderful history,
in the hitherto unreadable monuments which her departed glory has
bequeathed to us." It is important that the great advantages of this
discovery be neither under-estimated nor over-rated. Imperfect,
even yet, as is the art of deciphering hieroglyphics, it has cast great
light upon the early condition and history of Egypt. We can now not
only see in the remaining monuments of this primitive nation an almost
endless range of public events recorded, but also a pictorial exhibition, the most elaborate and minute, of their manufactures, sports,
domestic habits, social manners, private employments, with the battles, sieges, exploits, and public works which distinguish the national
progress. As, by the recovery of the knowledge of hieroglyphics,
these several records can now be at least tolerably understood, and
the several sculptures identified as to their subject, design, and the
reign of the prince under whose government they were executed,
valuable means are placed within our reach for acquainting ourselves
with Egyptian affairs, and for ascertaining the measure of civilization of the country, and the state of its manners, science, and art, in
different ages.

But notwithstanding all these advantages, and this profusion of
information, neither the monumental inscriptions, the accounts fur-

nished by Greek visitors, nor the fragments of native authors which have been preserved, give us any history of ancient Egypt. We find, for instance, numerous dynasties of kings; and the monumental inscriptions prove that some of these were contemporaneous, while others were successive: but no friendly hand has given an arrangement of these classes; nor do the monuments, or any other authority, afford an intelligible and consistent chronology of the different reigns.

Yet with all this lack of precise information on important points, enough is given to prove that the state of Egypt, at the period when we have to resume its history, was one of great power, science, civilization, and refinement. Whatever difference of opinion may exist as to the chronological arrangement of dynasties and reigns, it is certain that at the death of Isaac Egypt exhibited indubitable proofs of mighty genius, abundant wealth, and great cultivation. At this period Thebes was the capital of a district to which it gave its name. The great temple of Karnak or El-Usquor stood in all its majesty and glory. The caves of Beni-Hassan, with their beautiful and elegant catacombs, displaying even to this day the most perfect architectural symmetry and arrangement, and ornamented throughout with coloured figures and devices, had been excavated and finished. Heliopolis was also founded about, or prior to, this period; and its splendid obelisk, made out of a single block of granite, and covered with the most exquisitely sculptured hieroglyphics, had already been raised. Such works prove the power, wealth, and energy of Egypt, and attest the existence of art and science in great perfection.

A learned lady-traveller has, from the monumental sculptures still existing, given the following vivid description of Egyptian life and manners at the early period to which we refer: "We have here the art of writing, as a familiar practice, in the scribes who are numbering stores on every hand. There are ships which would look handsome in Southampton Water, any sunny day. There are glass-blowers who might be from Newcastle, but for their dress and complexion. There are flax-dressers, spinners, weavers,—and a production of cloth which an English manufacturer would study with interest. There are potters, painters, carpenters, and statuaries. There is a doctor attending a patient; and a herdsman physicking cattle. The hunters employ arrows, spears, and the lasso. The lasso is as evident as on the Pampas at this day. There is the bastinado for the men, and the flogging of a seated woman. Nothing is more extraordinary than the gymnastics and other games of the women. Their various games of ball are excellent. The great men are attended by dwarfs and buffoons, as in a much later age; and it is clear that bodily infirmity was treated with contempt, deformed and decrepit personages appearing in the discharge of the meanest offices. It was an age when this might be looked for; and when war would be the most prominent occupation, and wrestling the prevailing sport, and probably also the discipline of the soldiery; and when hunting, fishing, and fowling would be very important pursuits. But then, what a power of representation of these things is here! and what luxury coëxisting with these early pursuits! Here are harpers, with their harps of seven strings; and garments and boat-sails with elegant patterns and borders, where, by the way, angular and regular figures are pointedly preferred; and the ladies' hair, disordered and flying about in their sports, has tails and tassels, very like what may have been seen in London drawing-rooms in no very remote times. The incident which most reminds one of the antiquity of these paintings is, that the name of bird, beast, fish, or artificer is written up over the object delineated."—*Miss Martineau's Eastern Life*, p. 230.

This was the condition of Egypt and the state of the people when "the father of the faithful" visited the country. These were the prevailing customs and manners when the youthful Joseph was carried a slave to the banks of the Nile. Whatever difficulty may oppose the effort, it is necessary to arrive at some conclusion respecting the state of the Egyptian government at this period, and to make the most reasonable arrangement of the several dynasties thenceforward, until we arrive at the time when the annals of Egypt can be certainly synchronized with those of other nations.

In the consideration of this obscure subject, as on other occasions, the leading object of this work must be kept distinctly in view. Special reference must be had to the teaching of Holy Scripture; and special attention paid to the intercourse and connexion which from time to time took place between the Hebrews and this ancient people.

By a careful and extended investigation of all the monumental and written teaching which bears on this subject, it has been made sufficiently clear that the Shepherds were expelled from Egypt about the year 1845 B. C., (see *Appendix*, note 5,) by Amosis, who, having thus established the independence of his country, reigned twenty-five years, and became the founder of Manetho's eighteenth dynasty. The chronological table at the end of the chapter will place this and the following dynasties in juxtaposition with contemporary events in the history of the Hebrews and other neighbouring nations.

At this stage of Egyptian history we have the means of giving the titles and names to the sovereigns from the ancient monuments. (See *Appendix*, note 6.) The symbolical title assumed by Amosis is "Pharaoh," that is, "Sun," "avenging Lord of Upper and Lower Egypt:" his name, "Amosis," that is, "born of the Moon." There is peculiar propriety in the assumed appellation: having expelled the foreign intruders from his country, he calls himself, when entering on the undisputed government of Egypt, "the avenging Lord of the Upper and Lower Country." This was the Pharaoh whose dreams Joseph interpreted, and who received Jacob and his family, and appointed Goshen for the place of their residence. The immediate descendant of this prince was the first sovereign of the eighteenth dynasty.

AMENOPHIS 1.—The contents of his first or titular ring are, "Pharaoh, Director of Offerings." His name, given in the second ring, is, "Amenophis (I.,) Son of Amosis." He also appears to have been a very warlike and successful prince, although, as will be seen hereafter, it is possible that he obtained the public honour due at least to a portion of his father's exploits. In a grotto near Aboosimbel he is represented sitting in the middle of a small temple, attended by an officer of state, who holds over him a feather fan, and two other fly-flaps. In a collection of Egyptian antiquities now in the Louvre, are several small tablets, which not only commemorate the deeds of this king, but also show the affection with which his memory was cherished, and the manner in which this affection was evinced. These tablets appear to have been intended to be worn on the breast. On them this sovereign is represented grasping captives by the hair, carrying them with their heads downward, and preparing to destroy them with a curved battle-axe. Several of these captives are clad in leopards' skins, and are natives of the south; others, from their ample drapery, appear to belong to colder climates. Conventionally they represent the Ethiopian and Asiatic people; and we may conclude that Amenophis carried on wars successfully against both. It is curious at this distance of time to be able to trace out, not only the public events, but even some particulars in the family history of the Pharaoh who reigned in Egypt while the patriarch Jacob dwelt there. In a tablet in the British Museum this prince is represented with two women, one black, and the other of a fair complexion. The first bears the title of "Royal Dame;" and as her name is the same as that given to the queen of Amosis, it is fairly inferred that she was the widow of that prince; and that Amenophis is, in this instance, placed before us in company with his queen and the queen-dowager, whose name was *Ahmos Nofre Ari.*

From several monumental sculptures it is evident, that this sovereign was regarded with a degree of respect bordering on religious reverence. •In one of the little chapels excavated among the quarries of Silsilis in the reign of Manepthah, Amenophis I., along with Atmoo, and another Egyptian deity, receives an offering of incense from the king: and in the tombs of private individuals at Thebes similar honours are paid to him on the part of the deceased. One of these tombs is of the age of Manephthah I.; and it appears from the inscriptions that a special priesthood was instituted to pay these honours to Amenophis.

He was succeeded by his son, THOTHMOSIS I., whose title was, " Pharaoh great in the World through his Offerings;" his hieroglyphical name, " Thothmosis (I.,) like the Sun in his Rising." His wife was Ahmos. The flourishing state of the kingdom during his reign is fully attested by the splendid structures which he raised, and which still bear his name. Although some small and fragmentary remains have been found at Thebes which bear the name of Osortasen, it seems now placed beyond doubt that Thothmosis began the erection of the great palace of Karnak. The unequalled boldness and grandeur of the architectural designs for this erection will always be the wonder of the world. There appears to be unquestionable evidence that the plan laid down at the outset not only comprehended the noble structures and obelisks raised by this prince, but also, in great measure at least, those built by his successors on this site throughout the following centuries.

The advanced state of the arts at this period is abundantly displayed by existing remains. There is a memorial of Thothmosis I. found on the western side of the Nile, at El-Assasef. A gate of red sandstone of beautiful execution is still standing amid ruins bearing his name, with those of his successors. He here appears accompanied by the queen-dowager, wife of Amenoph I., as that prince had been represented accompanied by the widow of his father Amosis. She is described as wife and sister of a king, and as ruler of Upper and Lower Egypt. One of the monuments, recording the services of a military officer, mentions the wars of Thothmosis I. in Ethiopia, and also in the land of *Naharaina*, which is known to mean Mesopotamia. The kingdom of Egypt during this reign extended as far up the Nile as the Island of Argo in Upper Nubia, latitude 19° 12' N., a little above the Third Cataract, where a hieroglyphical tablet has been found bearing the names of Thothmosis I. and Amenoph III.

The reason which induced these sovereigns to rear the noble builings of Thebes is easily explained. This place had afforded a refuge for the native princes of Egypt during the long period that the Shepherds held dominion over the lower country. When, therefore, the intruders had been expelled, and all the resources of the kingdom restored to its legitimate rulers, they were disposed to employ their riches and efforts to ornament and enlarge their southern capital.

During the time that Thothmosis I. reigned in Egypt, the patriarch Jacob died in Goshen. How striking is the contrast between the most wonderful productions of man and the glorious revelations of God! Here, while all that human wisdom and wealth, science and skill, genius and perseverance, could possibly effect, were laid under contribution to rear the gorgeous and imperishable structures of Thebes, while immense political power and unbounded resources stood out in glorious array, and invested Egypt with undying fame,—an event occurred, in the tents of the humble Hebrews, which, in intrinsic importance and glorious results, far outvied all the lustre of Egyptian history. The patriarch who had talked with Jehovah, and wrestled with the Angel of the Covenant,—the dying Jacob, inspired by the prescient Spirit of God, was heard addressing his twelve sons in language which, even at that time, gave them wonderful intimations of the divine purpose and will in the election of the house of Israel; and which continues to be, in all succeeding ages, an illustrious evidence of the heavenly character of human redemption,—a splendid proof of the truth, faithfulness, and goodness of God.

THOTHMOSIS II. was the next sovereign. His assumed title was, "Pharaoh great in the World:" his royal name "Thothmosis (II.,) beneficent King of the World." His sway appears to have been as extensive as that of his predecessor; for his name has been found at Gebel-el-Birkel, (Wilkinson's Ancient Egyptians, vol. i, p. 52, note,) the *Napata* of the Romans. In his reign we first find mention of "the royal son," or prince, "of Ethiopia," from which circumstance it has been inferred that during this period Ethiopia formed a vice-regal government dependent on Egypt. Wilkinson seems inclined to conjecture that this addition was made to the dominions of Egypt by the marriage of Amenophis I. with an Ethiopian princess.

Our means of sketching the history of this country during the reign of Thothmosis II. are exceedingly limited: in fact, scarcely any records of his time have been preserved.

AMENSE, sister of Thothmosis II., succeeded him. Her assumed title was, "Pharaoh devoted to Justice:" her hieroglyphical name, "Amounsit." Her reign, says Wilkinson, has given rise to more doubts than that of any other sovereign of this dynasty. Whether she was regent during the minority of Thothmosis I. or Thothmosis II., or reigned supreme between them, or after the latter, are questions which have been fully canvassed by learned authors. Champollion-Figeac, and Mr. Osburn, have adopted the last-named conclusion, which seems supported by the greatest weight of evidence. That she was daughter of Thothmosis I. is proved by the obelisk before the granite sanctuary at Karnak. (Kenrick's Egypt, vol. ii, p. 212.)

The state of the arts during her reign is shown by a most remarkable specimen, still extant in the great obelisks at Karnak. They were erected by this queen in the same central court of that pile of buildings in which the smaller obelisks of Thothmosis I. stood, but are far superior to them in magnitude and beauty. Of their execution Rosellini thus speaks: "All the figures are delineated with such purity and freedom, cut with such art, and relieved within the excavated part with such perfection and precision of outline, that we are lost in astonishment in contemplating them, and wonder how it has been possible to work this hardest of materials, so that every figure seems rather to have been impressed with a seal than engraven with a chisel. The fragments of the companion obelisk, which are lying on the ground, may be handled: those parts which represent animals, in particular, are treated with such accuracy of design and finish of execution, as not to be surpassed by the finest cameos of the Greeks. The *pyramidion* represents Amunre seated, and placing his hand on the head of the king, whom he thus inaugurates. There is a peculiarity in the arrangement of the hieroglyphical inscriptions. The central column is occupied by the customary form of dedication; but the two lateral columns—which in some obelisks, as in that of Heliopolis, are left vacant, in others are filled by inscriptions of subsequent sovereigns—are here occupied more than half-way down with repetitions of the figure of Amunre on one side; on the other, of the dedicating sovereign, who offers to the god wine, ointment, milk, perfumes, and sacred *insignia*. The dedication and offering are usually in the name of Ment-Amen, (Amense,) but in some of the compartments the youthful Thothmosis III. appears, bringing an offering to the god."—*Kenrick*, vol. ii, p. 214.

It was in the early part of this reign, if our chronology is correct, that Joseph died; his wonderful interpretation of Pharaoh's dreams, and consequent advancement to honour, having occurred during the latter part of the reign of Amosis. It is probable that for a long time before his death, although treated with honourable distinction, he ceased to have any connexion with the affairs of government. Yet, although unconnected with the administration of public affairs, his death was a most important event both for Egypt and for Israel. It severed the bond which had long held the rising house of Jacob in friendly relation to the imperial power of the Pharaohs. Alien from each other in blood, language, habits, and religion, as were the two people; the Hebrew ex-minister, whose inspired wisdom had saved Egypt from being desolated by famine, soon after it had been delivered from foreign domination, would stand an admitted memorial of the obligation under which Egypt was laid to Israel, as long as he lived; but his death removed all this evidence, and left the authorities of Egypt to act as state-policy might suggest.

There seems, indeed, reason to believe that, even before the death of Joseph, the Hebrews had ceased to be regarded by the Egyptians as friendly visitors, who were at liberty to retire from the country whenever they pleased. This appears from the words used by Joseph just before his death: "God will surely visit you, and bring you out of this land." Gen. l, 24. It can, therefore, elicit no surprise, that, when this impediment was removed, jealousy was soon engendered, nor that this should soon issue in persecution.

Amense had two husbands, but was herself queen-regnant. We have undoubted proof that glass was known and used in Egypt during her reign, at least for ornamental purposes; a large glass bead having been discovered which bears her name. It is also certain, from sculptured representations, that the mode of irrigating land was similar to that of the present day, by the *shadoof*, or pole and bucket. It is worthy of observation, that the modern Egyptians have a tradition, that this mode of watering the land was derived from their Pharaonic predecessors. The manufacture of linen cloth, the arch, and other important inventions supposed to be of more recent date, are found delineated in sculptures executed during this reign.

THOTHMOSIS III. succeeded Amense. Kenrick supposes him to have been her brother; (Kenrick, vol. ii, p. 212;) but this notion appears to be satisfactorily refuted by the fact, that in the sculptures on the great obelisk at Karnak, Amense appears with this Thothmosis as a youth, (ibid., p. 214,) presenting offerings. Now, seeing that Amense reigned nearly twenty-two years, and that her brother Thothmosis II. reigned twenty years before her, this could not be, if her successor was also her brother. There can, therefore, be scarcely a doubt that he was her son. His title was, "Pharaoh, Builder of the World;" his name, "Thothmosis (III.,) Benefactor of the World." This prince is generally believed to have been the

Mœris of Herodotus and Manetho. His reign is one of the most glorious in the annals of the eighteenth dynasty. Monumental remains in great variety, bearing his name, prove that the limits of Egyptian rule had not been diminished in any direction.

The most magnificent erections of this prince are those with which Thebes was adorned; many of them still remain. There is a mutilated obelisk at Constantinople which is of this reign, and probably at first stood in the central court at Karnak. Another, of the same date, is at Rome, and was placed before the church of St. John Lateran by Sixtus V. This is the most lofty, and the most perfect in execution, of all that are extant; the central column of hieroglyphics, which bears only the titles of Thothmes III., was executed during his reign, while the lateral columns were added by his grandson Thothmes IV.

One of the most remarkable and "instructive memorials of this reign is a painting in a tomb at Quoorneh, copied by Mr. Hoskins in his 'Travels in Ethiopia.' It represents four principal nations of the earth bringing their tribute to the king, who is seated on his throne. Two obelisks of red granite, beside which the various objects are deposited by the bearers, and registered by the royal scribes, probably mark the great court of the palace at Karnak as the scene of the ceremony."—*Kenrick's Egypt*, vol. ii, p. 219. One part of this procession is composed of negroes, mixed with men of a red-brown colour, like the Egyptians. They bring only natural productions,—blocks of ebony, tusks of ivory, coloured stones, ostrich-eggs and feathers, a tree, gold and silver in rings, bags, and ingots, and a variety of animals. The name of the land has been read *Pount* or *Phunt;* but this gives no certain information of its geography. Another portion of the procession is specifically called "Nations of the South." From the products which they bring, they are evidently inhabitants of the African continent,—Libyans, Nubians, and Ethiopians. A third portion presents persons similar to the Egyptians and Libyans in colour, but differing greatly from them in costume. These bring vases of silver and gold, of beautiful form and workmanship. They probably represent the Phœnicians, and other nations of Palestine. Another company is composed of men of white complexion, with reddish hair and beards. They bring ring-money of gold and silver, coloured woods, precious stones, and vases. It is equally difficult to fix the geography of this portion of the procession, as it is to specify with certainty that of the preceding parts. Their dress and colour agree with those of the dwellers in Northern Media, on the south shores of the Caspian. A company of women with children, of this nation, and of people

of the south, closes the ceremony. As this representation can
scarcely be accounted for but on the supposition that it depicts an
historical fact, we may conclude that we have here a striking
exhibition of the wide range of Egyptian power and influence at
this period.

But if any doubt be entertained as to the strict historical character of this representation, there can be none as to the monument which is known as "The Statistical Table of Karnak." This document is of the reign of Thothmosis III.; and the inscription placed above it declares its object to be—to record the victories of this sovereign. It seems to be the identical tablet which the priests exhibited and explained to the Roman Germanicus, when he was at Thebes. (Tacitus, Annales, lib. ii, cap. 60.) It records a series of successful expeditions into different countries, with a particular enumeration of the tributes levied on them respectively. Although it is scarcely possible to do more than guess at the nations intended to be specified, several parts of the tablet having been mutilated, and the geographical terms which remain being exceedingly obscure and difficult of application; yet the enumeration of the tribute levied on those subject nations is most precisely given. As Tacitus observes, "The inscription further stated the tribute paid by the conquered nations; the specific weight of gold and silver; the quantity of arms, the number of horses, the offerings of ivory and of rich perfumes, presented to the temples of Egypt; the measure of grain, and the various supplies, administered by every nation; making altogether a prodigious revenue, no way inferior to the taxes of late years collected either by Parthian despotism, or the authority of Rome."—*Annals*, book ii, chap. 60.

Whether Thothmosis III. carried on these successful warlike operations in person or by his generals, cannot now be ascertained; but that at this period Egypt held many surrounding countries in tributary subjection, and was greatly distinguished among the nations for wisdom and power, must be received as an undoubted fact.

Another remarkable monument of this age is that which is known by the name of "The Tablet of Karnak." It is found in the interior of a chamber, evidently built for the purpose, in the palace of Karnak at Thebes; and represents Thothmosis III. offering gifts to a series of sixty-one kings, disposed in four lines around the walls.

But, after all, probably the most interesting remnant of sculpture relating to this reign which has been preserved to our time, is a tomb, at Thebes, of a person named *Pekshar̀e*, who is said to have been "a superintendent of great buildings" under Thothmosis III. On the walls of this tomb the singular representation is found which is spoken of in a preceding volume, (Hebrew People, p. 30,) and which describes the labours of the Hebrews under their taskmasters, while employed in making bricks. In that passage, the certainty of this application is fully proved; and we have here an undoubted evidence of that cruel bondage which Israel suffered in the land of Egypt. This fully accords with the date ascribed in this work to the Exodus, as may be seen by referring to the Appendix, notes 5 and 7.

It is worthy of observation, that although our arrangement gives but twelve years and nine months for the reign of this sovereign, some of the monuments speak of the thirtieth and thirty-first years of his reign; while at the same time the monumental allusions to Amense have been frequently defaced. Different theories have been propounded for the purpose of solving these difficulties. Bunsen and Lepsius suppose that Amense was daughter of Thothmosis I., and sister to the second and third sovereigns of this name; and that she exercised the powers of a regent during their minority. Champollion-Figeac and Osburn, on the other hand, maintain that she was sister of Thothmosis II. and mother of Thothmosis III., which seems the most reasonable hypothesis. In that case it becomes likely that the monuments were, after the accession of Thothmosis III., altered so as to make his reign begin with his birth, thus cancelling all that portion of the reign of Amense after the birth of her son, and appropriating all this period to him.

But whatever disputable points may stand connected with the chronology of this reign, we are fully entitled to regard it as identified with the hard and cruel bondage of the Israelites. This was the king that "knew not Joseph," the Hebrew ex-governor having died three years before his mother ascended the throne. Thothmosis III. either originated, or greatly increased, that violent persecution of the Hebrews which terminated in the Exodus.

AMENOPHIS II., the son of the preceding monarch, succeeded his father on the throne. His symbolical title was, "Pharaoh great in all Lands;" his regal name, "Amenophis (II.,) Ruler in the pure, just Land," that is Egypt. We know but little of the events of his reign, which lasted nearly twenty-six years. The obelisk at Alnwick Castle, brought from Egypt by Lord Prudhoe, is inscribed with his name; but it simply records the fact of his having erected two obelisks to the god Kneph. A sculptured representation of him is found in an excavated chapel at Ibrim, where he appears seated with two princes or great officers. One of them, Osorsate, presents to him the animal productions of the southern regions,— lions, jackals, and hares; an inscription above specifying their numbers. He also added to the erections at Thebes; but most of his works there have perished.

THOTHMOSIS IV., son of Amenophis II., succeeded his father. He assumed as his title, "Pharaoh, Edifier of all Lands;" and took for his name, "Thothmosis (IV.)" He reigned nine years and eight months. The hieroglyphical inscriptions of this reign, which are very beautifully executed, record the victories of this prince over the people of Ethiopia; and a *stele*, engraven on a rock of granite on the right bank of the Nile, opposite to Philæ, mentions a victory gained by him over the Libyans in the seventh year of his reign. He also appears in the tomb of an officer at Quorneh, seated on a throne; on the base of which are nine foreigners, apparently Asiatics, bound in the manner in which captive nations are represented on Egyptian monuments.

During the reign of this prince the persecution of the Hebrews was at its height. It is more than probable that he issued the sanguinary decree for the destruction of the male infants, as Moses was born in the seventh year of his reign.

AMENOPHIS III., son of Thothmosis IV. and his queen Manthemoa, next ascended the throne. His title was, "Pharaoh, Lord of Justice;" his regal name, "Amenophis (III.)" He reigned thirty years and five months, and was one of the most distinguished princes of the eighteenth dynasty. We have no evidence, prior to this reign, that Egypt had any permanent occupation of Nubia higher up the Nile than Semneh; but the temple of Soleb, which stands a degree farther south, contains proof that "under Amenoph III. the boundary of the empire extended thus far."—*Kenrick's Egypt*, vol. ii, p. 254. This sovereign appears to be the same as the Memnon of Manetho and Herodotus. If there be any truth in the tales which have come down to us respecting the exploits of Moses at the head of an Egyptian army against the Ethiopians, they must have been achieved in this reign. However this may be, it was under the government and patronage of Amenophis III., the brother of the princess who had adopted the persecuted infant, that the future leader and legislator of the Hebrews was brought up and taught "all the wisdom of the Egyptians," and became "mighty in words and deeds."

As this portion of Egyptian history was the period of Hebrew persecution, and the precursor of the Exodus, it may be important to show—as there is ample opportunity for doing—the extravagant, superhuman assumption which the sovereigns of Egypt at this time carried to such an extent as almost, if not fully, to amount to the claim of proper divinity. In the case of Amenophis III., there is reason to believe that this pretension was advanced in the most prominent and imposing manner. It was stated in the first volume of this work, (Patriarchal Age, p. 475,) that "a small edifice was erected by the side of every temple, the entrance of which was through the *adytum* or 'sanctuary;' so that it was, in the estimation of the people, the holy of holies, the perfection or crowning mystery of the entire worship." The reason for this is found in the prevalent doctrine that God created all things at first by the primary emanation from himself,—his First-born. And in perfect accordance with their principles of metempsychosis, this Divine Being was expected to become incarnate, and appear as an infant in this world. As such, he is always represented as the third person in the trinity of Egypt.

There can be no doubt that all this arose from a corrupted tradition of the primitive promise of a Redeemer, preserved among the early settlers in Egypt, and transmitted by them to their descendants. In the application of these doctrines, a practice at this time obtained of representing the Egyptian triad by the figures of the royal family. Thus the first person in this trinity is frequently exhibited by the sculptured representation of the Pharaoh who built the temple; the second person, or the Divine Mother, by that of his wife, the queen; and consequently their first son would assume the character of the Divine Word, the promised Seed. This was the case in a most remarkable manner in the instance of Amenophis III., the son and successor of Thothmosis IV. Prior to the birth of this prince, the queen is represented in the character of the goddess Athor, in the presence of the god Thoth, who, holding a roll of papyrus, is, as the Egyptian Hermes, supposed to be addressing her on her approaching maternity. In the next scene, the queen is conducted by the god Kneph into an apartment called *ma-en-misa*, or "the birth-place,"—the same appellation as is given to the most sacred part of the temple before described,—while the goddess Athor, who stretches toward her the key of life, leads her to the bed. Here attendant goddesses await her; and the scenes describe the mystical character of the place which is regarded as the birth-place of the infant god. In the next sculpture, Amunre is seen holding the youthful prince, whom a hawk-headed god has presented to him. He is addressing the child, and declares that he bestows upon him life, stability, purity, and happiness, magnanimity, and dominion on the throne of Horus. Afterward follow scenes describing the purification and inauguration of the young prince.

In this manner the birth of the Pharaoh is described who sat upon the throne when Moses was brought up at the Egyptian court.

By these significant ceremonies he is associated with divinity, and not very obscurely identified with the promised Seed, the incarnate Redeemer.

Horus, son of Amenophis III., succeeded his father. His hieroglyphic title was, "Pharaoh, Director of the Worlds, approved of the Sun;" his regal name, "the beloved of Amoun, Horus in the Assemblies." It is not likely that this prince made less pretensions to divinity than his father. A sufficient proof of this is found in the regal name which he assumed, *Horus;* this being the title of the infant deity who, in the mythology of Egypt, slew the great serpent by piercing his head; on which account he was identified with the Grecian Apollo, the Indian Chreeshna, and the Scandinavian Thor. This prince reigned thirty-eight years and five months. In a grotto near the Second Cataract, he is represented in the form of the youthful god Horus, suckled by the goddess Anouke. The principal monuments, however, of this reign are in the quarries of Silsilis. He here appears seated on a throne, carried on the shoulders of twelve military chiefs, while two others shade him with fans attached to long spears, and an attendant, keeping his face towards the king as he walks, scatters grains of incense on a censer which he holds out towards him. It is evidently the celebration of a military triumph, for a victory which he gained over the Africans.

It was in the seventh year of the reign of Horus that Moses interposed, in the hope of rescuing his kindred from their bondage, and was in consequence obliged to flee into Midian.

The successor of Horus was Ramses I. His title was, "Pharaoh, inexorable Avenger of Upper and Lower Egypt;" his name, "Ramses (I.)" It is a remarkable fact, and one which strikingly corroborates the arrangement which I have made of Egyptian history, that we are here, for the first time in this dynasty, puzzled with a discrepancy between the lists and the monuments. Little is known, too, of the reign of this prince. His tomb has indeed been found covered with rubbish, and utterly destitute of sculpture, but decorated with paintings, which show that it was erected, and that some of these were executed, during his lifetime. There is, indeed, no evidence that any monumental or other inscription to his memory was made after his death. His whole case is in perfect agreement with his being the Pharaoh who perished in the Red Sea. This prince sat on the throne when Moses returned from Midian. He was the subject of the plagues, and fell a victim to his insane resistance of almighty power. After this terrible calamity to the Egyptian state a new monarch ascended the throne,—

THE GENTILE NATIONS.

SETHOS I., whose royal title was, "Pharaoh, firm in Justice;" his name, "the Servant of Amoun, Sethos (I.)" Soon after his accession to the throne, he undertook a military expedition against the same nations whom the Thothmoses and Amenophis had previously reduced to subjection:—a fact which seems to indicate that some internal convulsion or weakness had emboldened these tributaries to throw off the Egyptian yoke. It is scarcely possible to conceive of any events more likely to produce this rebellion than the terrible humiliation of Egypt under the plagues, and the prostration of her power by the triumphant Exodus of Israel. The campaign thus commenced was eminently successful; and elaborate sculptures describe the prowess of the king, the rout of the enemy, and the reduction of their fortresses.

Similar sculptures exhibit other successful wars in which this prince engaged, and magnify his valour and triumphs. From these it has been inferred that Sethos carried his successful arms even into Asia Minor. These warlike operations took place during the wandering of the Hebrews in the wilderness; for Sethos reigned nearly thirty-three years. The tomb of this Pharaoh, discovered by Belzoni in the Bab-el-Melook, is the most splendid that has yet been unveiled to modern eyes. It contains a representation which is found repeated with some variations in the tombs of other kings, of this and the following dynasty, and which seems designed to assert the universality of Egyptian dominion. It would appear that, the successful wars of Sethos having restored to Egypt the political ascendency and splendour which had been so greatly obscured by the persecution of Israel and its consequences, the monarch assumed claims to an extent of dominion which had not been previously contemplated.

In this tomb, "the god Horus, the symbol of royalty, is preceded by four companies of men, of different colour, physiognomy, and costume. The first are plainly Egyptians: the third are blacks: the second, white, with bushy black hair, blue eyes, aquiline noses, and reddish beards; they wear short party-coloured tunics, with several tassels at the lower extremities: the fourth resemble the people called Rebo in the campaigns of Ramesis IV., wearing feathers in their heads and large cloaks, and having their bodies tattooed. Taken together, they appear to have conventionally represented the principal nations known to the Egyptians; and as these wars did not extend to Europe, we must seek the originals in Asia" (*Kenrick*, vol. ii, pp. 264, 265) and Africa.

A short time since, this was all that could be said respecting the wars of Sethos: but the labour and learning of Mr. W. Osburn have cast much light on this subject. He has shown that the hieroglyphic sculptures state that Sethos carried on wars with the land of *Canaan*. Not only is this national name identified, but others which refer to tribes and districts. In the pictures which celebrate the conquests of Sethos, he has found Tyre and Zidon, Arvad on the coast to the north of these cities, and the Hermonites in the hill-country adjoining. The Philistines are exhibited, and their personal appearance, dress, and warlike manners and armour defined. The Jebusites, Zuzim, and Hittites are also identified as having been vanquished by Sethos, as were also the Amorites and Moabites. There is no doubt that, from the peculiar nature of hieroglyphic inscription, a few errors will afterward be found in some of these solutions: yet it is an interesting circumstance, and one which serves to elucidate the history of Egypt, that its monumental annals generally recognise these Scriptural appellations, and refer to them in a manner so corroborative of the truth of Holy Writ.

Ramses II. succeeded his father. His assumed title was, "Pharaoh vigilant in Justice;" his name, "the beloved of Amoun, Ramses (II.)" He reigned five years and five months. To this sovereign belong the historical pictorial representations found in the temple at Brisoualli in Nubia; where the sculptures in the sacred sanctuary represent the youthful monarch suckled by Isis and Anouke; while in the vestibule he is delineated as mounted in his chariot, and accompanied by his two sons, also in chariots, routing the Ethiopians, who are shown flying and falling before the Egyptian heroes. In another part of the same vestibule, the king is seated under a rich canopy, while the fruits of his victory are displayed in a procession, in which the principal productions of Africa are presented to the king. In another part, the victories of this prince in Asia are celebrated in detail with great spirit.

The sculptures on the northern side of this cave describe the wars which Ramses II. carried on in Palestine. Following in the steps of his father, he successfully assailed the Jebusites, the Tyrians, and the Hittites. The sculptures are, unfortunately, much mutilated; but enough remains to identify these nations, and to prove that, just prior to the arrival of the Israelites under Moses on the banks of the Jordan, the power of the Canaanitish nations had been in a great measure broken by the successive invasions of Sethos and Ramses II. (See *Appendix*, note 8.)

Ramses III.—His title, as given in the hieroglyphic cartouche, is, "Pharaoh vigilant in Justice, *Sesostris*," that is, "approved of the Sun;" his name, "The beloved of Amoun, Ramses (III.)" This sovereign was the son of Sethos, and brother of the preceding Pharaoh. He was the great Sesostris, so celebrated in the history of ancient times.

It has always been a matter of difficulty to reconcile the warlike exploits of this Egyptian conqueror with the fact, that no notice whatever is found of him in the Hebrew history. Some learned writers have been led by this circumstance to arrange the Egyptian dynasties so as to make this reign take place before the Exodus. According to the chronological arrangement adopted in this work, no difficulty of this kind occurs, as the Hebrews crossed the Jordan in the third year of Sesostris; and his great campaign, commenced in his fifth year, would happen before the tribes of Israel had obtained any settled location in Canaan, or had made themselves objects of jealousy or enmity to the Egyptian warrior.

According to Herodotus, the first warlike measure of this monarch was a maritime one, directed against the coasts of the Red Sea and of the Persian Gulf. This, to a certain extent, failed for lack of nautical knowledge. On his return, he raised a great army; and, having made extensive arrangements for the government of the country in his absence, confiding the principal administration of affairs to his brother, he marched forth on a grand career of conflict and conquest. It is not possible to define with accuracy the route pursued, or the nations vanquished, by this Egyptian king; some of the ancients extending his conquests from India to the north of Europe, while some modern writers would limit his warlike operations almost entirely to Canaan. The entire scope of the history proves these extremes to be alike unworthy of confidence.

The first point of attack appears to have been the people to the south of Canaan. Here Punon, near Mount Hor, was besieged and subdued. While engaged in the reduction of this place, Sesostris received ambassadors from the *Shetin*, with proposals of peace; but the terms were such that he rejected them. Having subdued this fortified city, and thus established his power in the hilly region of Edom, Sesostris turned his arms northward. Here, however, we have no undoubted guide as to his course, and little can be offered beyond probable conjecture. (See *Appendix*, note 9.) But it would appear that Sesostris passed to the south-west angle of Canaan, where, accompanied off the coast by a fleet probably from Ascalon, he marched through the land of the Philistines to the south frontier of the Jebusites. From thence, fighting only with those who obtruded themselves on his way, by the same route and just in the same manner as Pharaoh-Necho did in after-ages, he reached the land of the Phenicians. This people had long before been in intercourse with Egypt. Here in all probability the king strengthened his friendly relations with those maritime tribes: nor is it unlikely that some coercion might have been used to enforce his wishes. That he came into this territory cannot be doubted; for, in the extreme north of Phenicia, there are yet extant monumental proofs of his prowess. These are sculptures in the solid rock found near Beirout, which distinctly bear the titular shield of Ramses III., with the characters, "the approved of Re."—*Trans. of the Royal Soc. of Lit.*, vol. iii, p. 105.

From Phenicia it is more than probable that Sesostris went to effect the great object of his campaign on the banks of the Euphrates. It has been already observed that, when in the south of Palestine, he received ambassadors from the Shetin, and that he refused their terms of peace. It is also apparent from the monuments, that this warlike people, finding their overtures rejected, took the initiative, and besieged the city which Mr. Osburn calls Hadanaz, and which was in alliance with Egypt. Having in a great battle defeated the enemy, and rescued his friends, he assails the capital of his foes, which, I think, stood somewhere on the banks of the Euphrates. That it could not lie in the hill-country of Judea is evident from the monumental delineation of the contest: for the attack is made by him "on a fortified city standing on a river, branches of which flow round its walls, and serve the purpose of a trench. The enemy, who wear long-sleeved tunics, have generally the head shaven, with the exception of a lock which falls over the back of the neck, and wear mustachios. Their shields are of different forms—some square, and apparently made of basket-work; others with wood, with incurved sides. The enemy are driven headlong to the fortress, and some of them have been precipitated with their horses and chariots into the river."—*Kenrick*, vol. ii.

The subject of these sculptures was regarded as so important, that another representation of it is given at Thebes on a gorgeous scale. A circumstance strongly corroborative of the correctness of the view here taken, with regard to the course of this conqueror, is found in the fact, that the Zidonians are described as assisting in this battle as allies of the Egyptians; (Osburn's Egypt: her Testimony, p. 86;) and, further, in the tribute imposed on the conquered people: for the treaty made between Sesostris and four chiefs of the Shetin is still extant. In this document "nothing can exceed the pompous arrogance of Pharaoh, and the abject crouching submission of the princes of Shetin. He grants them peace only on condition of entire submission, and an annual tribute of silver, precious stones, and spicery."—*Osburn's Egypt: her Testimony*, p. 91. These articles clearly indicate the eastern geography of the country. It may, therefore, be fairly presumed, that Sesostris marched his army from Phenicia through the vale of Lebanon, and thence to the banks of the Euphrates; and that by this means he not only virtually extended the frontier of Egypt to that river, but opened up a way to oriental commerce for Egypt, through the instrumentality of the Phenicians —a commerce afterward secured by Solomon on the same route.

It is not so easy to trace the subsequent progress of this conqueror. The priest who explained the Egyptian monuments of Thebes to Germanicus, declared that Rameses had possessed Libya, Ethiopia, Media, Persia, Bactriana, and Scythia, with the territories which the Syrians, Armenians, and their neighbours the Cappadocians, inhabit, extending his dominion from the Bithynian Sea on the one side to the Lycian on the other; (Tacitus, Annales, lib. ii, cap. 60;) upon which Mr. Kenrick remarks, "Now we know from the monuments that the claim of dominion over Libya, Ethiopia, and Syria was well-founded. In the time of Herodotus its memorials existed in Asia Minor, and may yet perhaps be found there. The valley of the Tigris was familiar ground to the military sovereigns of the eighteenth and nineteenth dynasties. Confirmed in so many points, why should not the accounts of the Egyptian priests be believed, when they tell us that Media, Persia, and Bactriana were also the scenes of the conquests of Rameses?"—*Kenrick*, vol. ii, p. 283.

The question which the learned writer here asks, may be answered by a reference to the undoubted exaggerations, not of the priests, (their expositions may on some points be sufficiently questionable,) but of the monumental inscriptions themselves. Without, therefore, making any claim on behalf of Sesostris to Media, Persia, and Bactria,—since, even if the armies of these empires had been subdued, Egypt could not hold military occupation of such an extensive territory,—we are fully justified in receiving the testimony of the monuments, when they are confirmed by competent historical authority. We may therefore safely conclude that, marching through Asia Minor, Sesostris probably reduced various states to subjection, and thus returned to Egypt.

Herodotus mentions a fact to which, as coming under his own observation, he attached great importance. He discerned an evident similarity between the Colchians and the Egyptians, in respect of their colour, hair, and general appearance; and on conversing with the former, he found them possessed of a distinct traditional remembrance of their Egyptian origin. It is well known that this country was famed for the production of gold—a circumstance very likely to tempt the cupidity of the Egyptian king. To this we may add the conjecture of Larcher, who, referring to the tradition handed down by Valerius Flaccus, considers it probable that Sesostris, attempting to pass into Europe, was defeated by the Thracians, and in consequence left a detachment of his army in Colchis to cover his retreat. One of the inscriptions on the rocks of Aboosembel is important, as corroborating our opinion as to the extent of this campaign. It declares that the king had employed the captives taken in his *Asiatic* wars on those works.

On returning to Egypt, Sesostris very narrowly escaped destruction through the treachery of his brother, who caused his tent to be fired in the night. From this danger the king escaped with the loss of two of his children; and having overcome every difficulty, he devoted the remainder of his long reign to the improvement of his country. In the chief city of every *nome* he erected a temple to the tutelary deity, and employed the captives whom he had taken in his wars to drag stones, and do the most laborious part of the work: so that all these buildings had inscriptions placed on them, purporting that they had been raised by the labour of captives, and not of Egyptians. The Exode of the Hebrews had removed a great number of men long devoted to this kind of slavery, and thus rendered the importation of these captives necessary to supply their place on these new public works. Diodorus (lib. i, cap. 4) relates that a company of these captives who had been brought from Babylon, unable to bear the severe labour assigned them, rebelled, and seized a fort near the river, where for a season they defended themselves, and wasted the neighbouring country; that they afterward obtained a pardon, and called the place by the name of their native land, Babylon.

After effecting great improvements in the country by his public works and legislative measures, Sesostris was afflicted with blindness, which, it is said, so affected his mind that he destroyed himself.

The successor of Sesostris was his son, MANEPHTHA, whose royal name was, "Pharaoh, strengthened by the Spirit of Amoun;" his title, "Manephtha, devoted to Justice." This reign, as might be expected from the length of the preceding one, was short, extending only to five years. With Rameses III. we lose the guidance of the Tablet of Abydos, and consequently have difficulty in giving accurately the names of the Pharaohs. No proper historical monuments of this reign exist. The *Rameseion* contains the portraits of the twenty-three sons of Rameses III., with their names and offices. The thirteenth, Manephtha, bears the addition of "King." He is represented at Silsilis in acts of adoration to various divinities No great building appears to have been raised by this sovereign.

When his name is found, it is in trifling additions made to the works of preceding monarchs. His tomb at Bab-el-Melook is one hundred and sixty-seven feet in length, and has been ornamented with great care in the portions near the entrance. Here one piece of sculpture still remains, of which the colours are as brilliant as when they were first laid on. Manephtha, crowned with a splendid head-dress, and clad in a long transparent robe, fringed at the bottom, stands before the hawk-headed god, Phre, who promises him length of days upon his throne. This is a sufficient proof of the practice of excavating the tomb during the lifetime of the king. (Kenrick, vol. ii, p. 294.)

After the death of Manephtha, his son, Sethos II., ascended the throne. His regal title was, "Pharaoh, vigilant in all Lands, the Friend of Amoun;" his name, "Sethos II., Servant of Phtha." He is represented at Silsilis as making an offering to Amunre, accompanied by an officer of his court, who puts up a prayer for the king. But Egypt had at this time rapidly declined from the glory to which it had been raised by the brilliant genius and prowess of Rameses III. We have no history of this reign; and the low and perilous condition of the monarchy is indicated at Silsilis by a curious and unique monumental inscription. This Pharaoh is represented as offering a prayer to Amunre, that his son may sit on the throne after him,—a prayer nowhere else found on the sculptures of Egypt. Taosir, or Taseser, the queen of Sethos II., is frequently represented as making offerings to the gods, sometimes alone, and at others in company with her husband. There is no date on any of the monuments of this sovereign; and everything indicates that either during his reign, or afterward, he was not fully recognised as a legitimate monarch of Egypt; though he bore the title, and held possession at least of Upper Egypt.

The son of the preceding Pharaoh succeeded him. His assumed title was, "Pharaoh, the Light of the Sun, Sesostris (II.;)" his name, "Si-Ptah Manephtha." Of this reign even less is known than of the preceding. He also appears to have been regarded as not justly entitled to sovereign dignity,—a fact which accounts for the appearance of his name on the monuments, where, as possessing supreme power, he could compel it to be placed, while it is omitted from the historical lists. With this reign the eighteenth dynasty terminated.

In closing this sketch of the period of Egyptian history which gave imperishable fame to this nation, and stands so prominently identified with the most interesting events of Hebrew history, it may possibly occur to the reader that there is here a serious discrepancy, if not a direct contradiction. It may be supposed that a people so wise, powerful, and refined,—so polished in art, and abundant in the enjoyment of all luxury and elegance,—could never be guilty of the atrocities which, according to the Scriptures, led to the divine interposition that produced the Exodus. It is remarkable, however, that this notion is abundantly refuted by secular history. The exquisite and imperishable monuments of Egypt bear undeniable and everlasting evidence to her tyrannical, cruel, and blood-thirsty character. Natural as the objection appears, it is perfectly annihilated by extant monumental inscriptions. We have before our eyes an abiding demonstration that, with all her wisdom and wealth, her prowess and art, her civilization and philosophy, Egypt was the power which, above all other ancient nations, might be expected to perpetrate the deeds of blood and darkness that the Bible charges on her in the case of Israel, and in consequence deserved to be made a special example of divine punishment. (See *Appendix*, note 10.)

In passing to the nineteenth and following dynasties, it will not be possible to be as minute as heretofore, inasmuch as great obscurity rests upon many reigns: even the names and titles can but seldom be identified on the monuments. I shall therefore give the lists of the dynasties, as far as can be ascertained, with such information as may be collected with reference to the several reigns.

NINETEENTH DYNASTY: FIVE DIOSPOLITAN KINGS.

	Years.
1. Sethos reigned	55
2. Rameses	66
3. Amenephthes	40
4. Rameses	—
5. Ammenemnes	26
Duration of the dynasty	187 years.

These are the kings of this dynasty, according to Eusebius. But no part of the Egyptian history—with the exception of one reign—is shrouded in deeper darkness than this. Neither the annals nor the monuments give any positive information. Mr. Osburn supposes the last king of the eighteenth dynasty to have been driven from his throne by a second invasion of the Canaanites or "Shepherds," and to have died in Ethiopia, leaving an infant son, Sethos Ramses, then only five years of age. I confess that the reasons assigned by him, from Manetho, for this decision, appear to me very unsatisfactory. Yet, knowing as we do the strength of numerous warlike tribes residing in the south of Canaan, or Edom, and wandering in powerful nomadic hordes in the Wilderness of

Sinai,* it cannot be unreasonable to believe that a confederation of these might take advantage of any weakness or disorder in the Egyptian state, and, for a while at least, successfully assail and ravage the lower and more exposed part of the kingdom.

Nor is it very improbable that this was done; and that, as Manetho intimates, after a while, the young king, supported by the power of Upper Egypt and Ethiopia, defeated and expelled these warlike intruders, and restored the integrity of the kingdom; the great and obvious error which writers, from Manetho to the present day, have fallen into, being the attempt to identify this eruption either with the descent or the Exodus of the Hebrews.

This Pharaoh, however, having possessed himself of the throne, took for his regal title, " Pharaoh, Guardian of Justice, the Friend of Amoun;" and for his name, " Rameses, Prince of On."

His reign was long and apparently prosperous. He restored not only the integrity of the kingdom, but its influence abroad. He appears to have gone over most of the lands which had been subdued by Sethos and Sesostris. We are distinctly told that he conquered the Shetin.

Having finished his foreign wars successfully, he pursued the course usually adopted by his predecessors, and devoted the spoils which he had acquired to the erection of a splendid temple. The magnificent palace-temple of Medinet-Abou, in Western Thebes, was raised by him; and its vast range of walls was covered with sculptured representations of his various wars. In one of these scenes, the king is represented sitting in his chariot, with an air of calm dignity on his countenance. Four great officers stand by him, presiding over the ceremony of counting each of the heaps of hands which have been cut from the enemies who had been slain. Each heap is said to contain three thousand. Close by are four rows of captives, bound in the usual manner. Immediately over the king is the address which he delivers to his army: it is in the form of a short poem or ode :—

> " The address of Rameses," &c., " to his royal sons,
> And to his servants who commanded his infantry and cavalry.
> Give yourselves up to joy;
> Let it resound to heaven.
> My falchion hath smitten the Hittite.
> I come, (and) terror fills their hearts.

---

* If the Amalekites possessed sufficient power to place in jeopardy a body of six hundred thousand fighting men, even admitting the latter to have been to a great extent undisciplined and unarmed, (although this is not mentioned,) they would be formidable foes on the frontier of any kingdom. Exod. xvii.

> I arise, conquering with the armies of Upper and Lower Egypt.
> I manifest you in the midst of them like springing lions,
> Or like hawks among the water-fowl.
> My heart is strong against them, like a bull against a ram.
> I have forded their rivers;
> I have laid waste their lands;
> I have burned their forts with fire.
> Amoun-Re hath put the whole world under my feet.
> I am a king upon my throne forever."—*Osburn's Egypt*, p. 101.

I add one further extract from Mr. Osburn's learned work, which has reference to the monumental records respecting this reign:—

"The mutilated state of these vast pictures prevents the possibility of anything like a connected account of the events of this war. Two actions of it are still remaining. The one is the surprise of a city or district of the Philistines, by the combined armies of the Egyptians and Zidonians. The other is an attack upon the fleets of the Philistines and Zidonians in harbour by the Egyptians. In both these pictures the defeat of the enemies of Egypt is as complete as in all other cases. In the land-fight, the army of the Philistines is vainly endeavouring to cover the flight of their wives, children, and possessions, in wagons of wicker work with solid wheels, and drawn by four oxen abreast. Their ranks are broken, and they are in inextricable confusion, while their wagons fall a prey to the Egyptian soldiers. The sea-fight is in every respect a remarkable picture, and deserves far more attention than it has hitherto received. As it occurs in the same series with the former, the event probably took place in the same war. Nothing, of course, can be known of the circumstances which induced the Zidonians, who in the former picture appeared as allies of Egypt, to join the ranks of its enemies on the present occasion. Such changes are of frequent occurrence in war. The occasion of the battle appears to have been a meditated descent on the coast of Egypt, by the combined fleets of the Zidonians and Philistines. The action took place either on the Egyptian coast or in its immediate vicinity. Rameses, at the head of his army, repulsed the enemy in their attempt to land, while the Egyptian fleet engaged with them by sea; both, on the authority of the picture, with incredible, yea, impossible, success. The entire fleet of the enemy was taken, and carried in triumph to Egypt; and the forces which had manned it graced the triumphal procession of the conqueror at Thebes."—*Osburn's Egypt*, p. 110.

The cruel character of this country and age is strikingly displayed in the picture of the king, who is represented armed with his bow, with each of his feet upon the necks of four of his enemies; while his four sons, all engaged in the same act, stand in line before him.

We have no precise information respecting other sovereigns of this dynasty, whose rule extended from the time of Othniel to that of Deborah and Barak. It is, however, a remarkable fact, that as the power of the Hebrew commonwealth became consolidated, and its political influence paramount in Canaan, so we lose all notice of the Canaanitish nations on the monuments of Egypt, where they are constantly recognised previously. After the reign of Sethos Rameses, the first king of the nineteenth dynasty, no allusion to the people of Canaan is found in the Egyptian sculptures, until the time of Rehoboam, when, as if to prove that the absence of these arose out of the altered condition of Canaan, and not from any change in the manners and usages of Egypt, we have gorgeous sculptured representations of the incursion of Shishak, and of his triumph over Rehoboam.

We proceed to the twentieth dynasty, respecting which we only learn that it consisted of twelve Diospolitan kings, who reigned one hundred and seventy-eight years, and that the greater number of them were called Rameses. Lepsius seems to have identified on the monuments Pharaohs of this name from Rameses IV. to Rameses XIV. We have no traces of foreign war or conquest during the reigns of these sovereigns. The principal memorials of Rameses V. are the lateral inscriptions of the obelisk which Thothmes I. erected at Karnak. They contain, however, no historical fact. His tomb in the Bab-el-Melook is small; the sarcophagus remains in it, and has been broken. Rameses VI. has in some instances effaced the name of his predecessor; but we have no memorials of his reign, and can only conjecture that it was long, from the unusual amount of labour employed in the preparation of his tomb. It is three hundred and forty-two feet in length, descending by a gradual slope to a depth of twenty-five feet below the ground, and is divided into a number of chambers. The whole surface of the walls and ceilings is covered with a profusion of coloured sculptures of minute size, chiefly astronomical and mythical. One of them represents the judgment-scene before Osiris, and the supposed return of a wicked soul to the world.

Of Rameses VII. there is absolutely no memorial, except his tomb, which is of much less finished execution than that of his predecessor. The sarcophagus is excavated in the rock of the floor to the depth of four feet, and covered with a slab of granite. Rameses VIII. is known only by the occurrence of his shield. The shields of the other sovereigns of this dynasty are much more crowded than those of the eighteenth dynasty. Rameses IX. was, according to Lepsius, the son of Rameses VII. He began a temple to Chons, on the right bank of the Nile, near Karnak; but left it imperfect, except the sanctuary. His tomb is small, and appears to have remained unfinished at his death, as the walls of some of the apartments have figures and inscriptions traced upon them, but not sculptured. The tombs of Rameses X., XI., XII., have also been ascertained. That of Rameses X. is executed with care, and adorned with astrological paintings. The seventeenth year of the reign of Rameses XI. has been found on a papyrus, and the second of Rameses XII. Of Rameses XIII. and XIV nothing beyond the names is known, which is the more indicative of the inactivity which characterized the last years of this dynasty, because Rameses XIV. reigned at least thirty-three years. Rosellini reckons a fifteenth, by whom a hypostyle-hall was added to the temple of Chons at Karnak, founded by Rameses IX. (Kenrick, vol. ii, page 338.)

According to the Arundelian Marbles, the fall of Troy took place in 1184 B. C.: and Pliny states that a Rameses then sat on the throne of Egypt. According to our arrangement this would happen during the reign of one of the latter Pharaohs of this name and dynasty. The rule of this line of kings ranged from the time of Deborah and Barak to that of Eli. The Hebrews were at that time expanding into a great people, and were gradually displacing all the old nations which had occupied Canaan. The Philistines alone appear to have remained unbroken in strength; and it is possible that there is in that fact more than at first meets the eye. This warlike people occupied the sea-coast in the southwest angle of the Promised Land. They stood, therefore, as a bulwark against Egyptian aggression. The wise providence of God seems strikingly displayed in the fact, that the last remnant of the martial power of Canaan which remained in the land, seemed alike designed to punish the Hebrews for their apostasy, when unfaithful, and to protect them from Egypt, while they remained devoted to Jehovah.

The rising power of the Hebrews, with that of Philistia, also shielded the Phenicians; and this maritime and commercial people rose rapidly into opulence and power, while the sway and trade of Egypt became more than ever circumscribed. Thus did Providence prepare the way for the political and commercial prosperity of the elect nation under David and Solomon.

THE TWENTY-FIRST DYNASTY: SEVEN TANITE KINGS.

	Years.
Smendes reigned	26
Psousennes	41
Nephercheres	4
Amenophthis	9
Osochor	6
Psinaches	9
Psousennes	35
The dynasty continued	130 years.

Tanis, or Zoan, now first appears in Egyptian history, as supplying a race of sovereigns to the imperial throne. This city stood on a branch of the Nile, the most easterly, and consequently the nearest to Palestine and Arabia, with the exception of the Pelusiac. Scripture plainly informs us that Zoan was built seven years after Hebron. We do not, indeed, know when the Jebusite town was founded; but it is mentioned in the time of Abraham. It is probable that Tanis rose into importance during the time when the shepherd-kings exercised supreme sway in Lower Egypt. In Psalm lxxviii, the miracles which accompanied the Exodus are said to have been wrought in "the field of Zoan;" (verse 43;) an expression which indicates that about the time of David this city was regarded as the residence of the Pharaoh who had "refused to let Israel go." In the age of Isaiah it was still considered as the capital of the Delta. "The princes of Zoan, and the princes of Noph," (Memphis,) are spoken of as equivalent to "the nobles of Egypt."

The ruins of this ancient city, although they have never been explored, are amply sufficient in extent to attest its magnificence. Its principal temple stood within an area of fifteen hundred feet by twelve hundred and fifty, and appears to have been built by Rameses-Sesostris, whose shield is seen in various parts of the ruins. It was adorned with an unusual number of obelisks. If its ruins had been explored with the same diligence as has been employed on those of Middle and Upper Egypt, some very important information would probably have been furnished for the history of this dynasty. This has hitherto been prevented by the rude character of the inhabitants, and the pestilential atmosphere of the district.

No sources of intelligence are at present accessible, which throw light on the manner in which the sceptre of Egypt passed from the Diospolitan dynasty to the Tanite. The temple which Rameses IX. erected to the god Chons (to which reference has already been made) exhibits a priest, "whose name has been read *Hraihor*, or *Pehor*, distinguishable by his shaven head and panther's skin, and denominated in his shield, 'High-Priest of Amun,' who at the same time appears to have performed the functions of royalty. In one compartment of the sculptures, Horus places on his head the white cap, and Nebthi the red cap,—acts symbolical of his investiture with the dominion of Upper and Lower Egypt. He even appears in a military capacity, with the title of 'Commander of the Archers.' Another priest, whose name has been read *Pischiam*, appears on the same building qualified with the titles of royalty. These names do not correspond with any of those in Manetho; and we are left to conjecture that, during the time that elapsed after the expiration of the Rameside dynasty, and before the establishment of the Tanite in full authority over Upper as well as Lower Egypt, the high-priests of Thebes assumed the royal style, and even military command. It would be agreeable to the practice of Manetho, not to include them in his dynastic lists, but to carry on his chronology by means of the Tanite kings, even though two or three generations elapsed before their authority was acknowledged in Thebes."—*Kenrick's Egypt*, vol. ii, p. 343.

During the rule of this dynasty the greatest political and commercial changes took place in Palestine,—changes which most seriously affected the sway and trade of Egypt. The military and political genius of David had not only consolidated the energy of the Hebrew people, and given to their hitherto isolated tribes a national character and power: it had also extended a commanding influence over the Phenicians, and, by dictating to them the terms on which they should carry on the traffic with the East, (a measure which Solomon secured by the erection of Baalbec in the Valley of Lebanon, and Palmyra in the Wilderness,) had completed their subserviency to the Hebrew government. The conquest of Edom by David fulfilled this scheme of policy. By these means the communication of Egypt with the East was completely cut off, and even the old-established caravan traffic through Petra, which had existed from the days of Joseph, was placed in the hands of the sovereign of Jerusalem. Solomon availed himself of all the advantages arising out of the geographical position of his country, and, by the aid of Phenician mariners, secured to Judea an important coasting-trade with the gold-coast of Arabia and India.

These measures of the Hebrew government had the effect of isolating the Pharaohs of Egypt from all their conquests in Asia, and shutting them out from all important commercial operations in the East. It is remarkable that, either awed by the daring valour of the Hebrews, or withheld by an overruling Providence, Egypt saw the progress of the Hebrew power and policy without striking a blow. A military junction with the Philistines, Edomites, Ammonites, or other warlike tribes, which were successively subdued by Israel, would have so obviously been for the interest of Egypt, that it is scarcely possible to account for the continued apathy of such a nation in those circumstances, without attributing it to providential interposition.

In the brief notices of Egypt which are found in the sacred Scriptures, there is enough to show that people not to have been indifferent spectators of these mighty changes in their political relations. When Joab, in the reign of David, slaughtered the males of Edom, Hadad, one of the royal family, having escaped to Egypt, was not only received and protected, but provided for as a royal prince, and was favoured with the queen of Egypt's sister for his wife: his son, too, was brought up in Pharaoh's house. It must be admitted that, in the early part of his reign, Solomon appeared to hold a very friendly relation to the reigning Pharaoh, and married his daughter. But even in the Scriptural notice of this event there is evidence, that Egypt had not ceased to regard Palestine as a theatre for warlike operations. We are told that when Solomon married the princess of Egypt, "Pharaoh King of Egypt had gone up and taken Gezer, and burned it with fire, and slain the Canaanites that dwelt in the city, and given it for a present unto his daughter, Solomon's wife." 1 Kings ix, 16. This city stood on the south frontier of the tribe of Ephraim, about fifteen miles N. W. by N. of Jerusalem: so that, even after all the martial triumphs of David, this Canaanitish town remained in the very heart of the country; and, in the early part of the reign of Solomon, a king of Egypt led an army along the western coast of Palestine, and sacked this city within a few hours' march of the capital of Judea. Such a fact casts important light on the international policy of ancient times.

When Solomon became enervated by luxury, and corrupted by sin, Hadad, Prince of Edom, went up from Egypt with the consent of Pharaoh; and, he having formed an alliance with Rezon, a daring freebooter, they succeeded in wresting from the Hebrew monarch Edom and a part of Syria. Hadad consequently became king of his native land, while Rezon reigned in Damascus. It is not stated that these persons received aid from Egypt in their efforts; but as it was obviously the interest of this nation that they should succeed, it can scarcely be doubted that they were favoured with indirect countenance and help, if not with open and avowed support.

During the reign of Solomon an active commerce in horses, chariots, and linen yarn was carried on between Judea and Egypt. Solomon not only furnished his own armies with horses and chariots from this country, but sold them again to the Hittites and the Syrians;

and, as if to indicate the thorough and monopolizing character of the Hebrew king's policy, it is distinctly stated that this was done by "*the king's merchants.*" 1 Kings x, 28, 29.

TWENTY-SECOND DYNASTY: NINE BUBASTILE KINGS.

	Years.
Sesonchis (Shishak) reigned	21
Osorchon	15
Three other kings omitted by Eusebius	25
Takellothis	13
Three others omitted by Eusebius	42
The dynasty continued	116 years.

The first of these kings is undoubtedly the Shishak of Holy Scripture; and as his invasion of Judah took place in B. C. 974, it must have occurred in the third year of his reign. It is a fact no less important than singular, that the monumental record of this event should exist at the present time in a perfect state, and exhibit an undoubted memorial of this historical event. Although much doubt in general attends the identification of names on Egyptian monuments, in consequence of its being necessary "to assume certain phonetic values for characters which do not occur elsewhere, or only in positions equally ambiguous; there appears to be no uncertainty respecting the most important figure of the whole," (in this monument,) "the third in the third line, which contains, in well-known characters, JOUDMALK, that is, *Joudah-Melek*, 'King of Judah;' which being followed by the usual character for 'land,' the whole will read, 'Land of the King of Judah;' these shields representing, not persons, but places, symbolized by a figure of their inhabitants."—*Kenrick*, vol. ii, p. 350. This monument is found on the external wall of the hypostyle-hall at Karnak.

There are other memorials of this sovereign at Karnak and Silsilis; but they are of a religious, and not of an historical character. If Sesonchis were the same as the Sasychis of Diodorus and Herodotus, (which, from an ingenious conjecture of Bunsen, is rendered very probable,) he was celebrated as a legislator, as well as a conqueror. To him is attributed the law which allowed a debtor to raise money by pledging the body of his father, on condition that, if he did not repay the money, neither he himself nor any of his family should be interred, either in the family sepulchre or elsewhere.

The state of the arts had now evidently declined. There are several statues of the lion-headed goddess *Pasht* which were executed about this time; one of them is in the British Museum. Mr. Birch pronounces it far inferior in design and execution to the statuary of Thothmes III.

A son of Sesonchis appears joined with him in an act of worship at Karnak. As was sometimes the case in Egypt, he united with the sacerdotal office the post of "captain of the archers." He did not succeed his father.

Osorchon is the next king in Manetho's dynasty, and his shield follows that of Sheshonk in the sculptures of the court at Karnak. The Books of Kings record no intercourse between Judah and Egypt, from the invasion of Shishak to the reign of Hoshea, who made an alliance with Seva or So, King of Egypt. The Second Book of Chronicles, however, says that in the reign of Asa, Zerach, an Ethiopian king, invaded Judah. Critics have supposed this Zerach to be the same as Osorchon, the successor of Sesonchis. All the circumstances of the case render this conclusion extremely probable. Zerach could not be one of the twenty-fifth or Ethiopian dynasty of Egyptian kings, since the earliest of these lived about two hundred years after Asa. The name "Zerach" is not very different from "Osorchon," when reduced to its consonants. We can scarcely believe that during Osorchon's reign any Ethiopian sovereign could have invaded Judah: for it is certain that at this time his sway extended over Upper as well as Lower Egypt; and, in order to accomplish this purpose, the Ethiopian army must have marched through the entire length of Egypt,—which is incredible. The sacred text, indeed, calls the invading sovereign an "Ethiopian:" but then this is found only in the Book of Chronicles, which was not written—at least, in its present form—till after the Captivity. And the use of this term may be accounted for, even supposing the war to have been conducted by one of the Pharaohs; for at this time the armies of Egypt were mainly composed of Libyan and Ethiopian troops. But, in addition to all this, the time exactly agrees. Rehoboam reigned twelve years after the invasion of Sesonchis; Abijah, his son, who succeeded him, three years; and the victory of Asa took place in the fifteenth year of his reign: so that thirty years elapsed from the invasion of Sesonchis to the defeat of Zerach. And as Sesonchis reigned twenty-two years,—nineteen of which were after his invasion,—and Osorchon fifteen years, his defeat by Asa (supposing him to be identified with Zerach) would have taken place in the eleventh year of his reign. When so many circumstances unite in the corroboration of an historical probability, in the absence of all opposing evidence, it may be safely regarded as an established fact.

There was also a reason for this war. Sesonchis had humbled Rehoboam, and spoiled Jerusalem: Judah would in consequence be regarded as a dependent, if not a tributary state. When, therefore,

Asa had made a league with the king of Syria who ruled in Damascus, and had built and fortified many places in Judah, Osorchon had just cause to apprehend, not merely the loss of all Egyptian influence in the East, but the probability that a powerful hostile alliance would be maintained against him. He accordingly assembled a great army, and invaded the south of Judah; but Asa, strong in the protection of Jehovah, went out against him, defeated his army in a great battle, and pursued him to Gerar on the southern boundary of Palestine. 1 Kings xv.

"The names of the three successors of Osorchon I. are not given by Manetho. Lepsius makes his immediate successor to have been Amunma PEHOR, who was probably his son. Another son, whose name was Sheshonk, filled the office of high-priest; and is mentioned in a funeral papyrus which appears to have accompanied the mummy of another high-priest of the name of Osorchon, the son of this Sheshonk, and consequently the grandson of Osorchon I. Neither of these appears to have ascended the throne. Pehor was succeeded by Osorchon II., and he by Sheshonk II. His shield is distinguished from that of the founder of the dynasty by the addition of the goddess of Bubastis, Pasht. The name of Takelothis was recovered by Champollion from a fragment of a piece of sycamore-wood, the remainder of which is in the Vatican; in which a priest, clad in the leopard's skin, is represented performing an act of adoration to *Phre*, in behalf of Takelothis's son. It has since been found on the wall at Karnak, with the date of the twenty-fifth year of his reign. The same inscription mentions the name of his queen, Keromana, and of his son and probably his successor, Osorchon, who is called 'High-Priest and Captain of the Archers.' Of Osorchon III., Sheshonk III., and Takelothis II., with whom the dynasty became extinct, no historical fact is recorded."—*Kenrick*, vol. ii, p. 356.

From a remark in the Canon of Eusebius it seems probable that under the twenty-third dynasty the Egyptians became a considerable maritime power, rivalling, if not excelling the Phenicians.

TWENTY-THIRD DYNASTY: FOUR TANITE KINGS.

	Years.
Petubatis reigned	40
Osorcho	8
Psammus	10
Zet	31
The dynasty continued	89 years

Of this entire dynasty no name had been found on the monuments, until very lately Lepsius has found a shield with the name of *Petse-*

pesht, the Egyptian word whence the *Petubastes* of Eusebius, and the *Petubates* of Manetho, were derived. A shield at Karnak, containing the name of *Psemaut*, has been ascribed by Lepsius to Psammus of this dynasty.

Neither Herodotus nor Diodorus affords any information respecting this dynasty. There are not even any private monuments which cast light upon the state of Egypt at this time. Everything seems to indicate that it was a season of decline and decay, which ranged from the sixteenth year of Joash King of Judah to the thirty-seventh year of Uzziah.

TWENTY-FOURTH DYNASTY.

	Years.
Bocchoris of Sais reigned	44

I have here adopted the numbers of Eusebius, in preference to the six years of Manetho, as rendered by Julius Africanus. Not that I have particular confidence in this reckoning; on the contrary, while I think the general line of chronology which I have laid down to be founded on unimpeachable historical *data*, yet, as regards the particular reigns, it would be mere affectation to pretend to undoubted accuracy. In the present instance the longer, instead of the shorter, term is selected, because the brief space of six years is far too short to work out a celebrity such as that which is unequivocally bestowed upon Bocchoris; and, further, because the former arrangement best agrees with the general course of events, and places Psammitichus and Nechao II. in more strict accordance with Hebrew history than would otherwise be the case.

The dynasty of Sais, as Kenrick truly observes, may be said to have been in fact prolonged to the time of the Persian conquest, the Ethiopian dynasty being intrusive, and the Dodecarchia only temporary. Sais, the city whence this dynasty obtained its name, stood near the Canopic branch of the Nile,—a district to which, as being the nearest and most accessible, the traffic of the Greeks was from the first attracted.

The name of this sovereign has been discovered on no monuments which can be referred with certainty to his reign. Diodorus calls his father Tnephachthus. According to the same writer this king was small in person, and contemptible in appearance, "but as to wisdom and prudence far excelling all the kings that were before him in Egypt." He is also supposed to have framed laws, defining the prerogatives and duties of the sovereign, and establishing equitable regulations respecting commercial contracts. Ælian, indeed, gives a very different account of Bocchoris, who, he says, obtained a very false reputation for the justice of his decisions. He alleges that, to grieve the Egyptians, Bocchoris set a wild bull to attack their sacred Mnevis; but that, as the assailant was rushing furiously on, he stumbled, and entangled his horn in the tree *persea*, when Mnevis gave him a mortal wound in the flank. To such accounts not much credit is due. Plutarch acknowledges the just decisions of Bocchoris, but calls him "a man of stern character." The probability is, that this Pharaoh reigned in a time of great declension and disorder, and that he made wise and energetic efforts to remedy existing evils,—efforts which, being partially successful, gave him great celebrity; but as these measures painfully affected those who were deriving private gain from public wrong, he was, to the extent of their influence, stigmatized by them as severe and cruel.

TWENTY-FIFTH DYNASTY: THREE ETHIOPIAN KINGS.

	Years.
Sabaco reigned...	8
(He took Bocchoris prisoner, and burnt him alive.)	
Sebichos, (Sevechus,) his son...	14
Tarkus..	18
Duration of the dynasty..	40 years.

The term "Ethiopian" is so indiscriminately applied to the Arab of Yemen, the Abyssinian, the native of Nubia, as well as to the inhabitants of other districts, that it becomes necessary, in introducing this Ethiopian dynasty, to ascertain the seat of its original power. On this point no uncertainty exists. The seat of the monarchy of Sabaco was the *Napata* of the Romans,—the same as Gebel-Berkel, standing about seven hundred miles above Syene on the banks of the Nile. Under the eighteenth dynasty Egypt ruled over the Valley of the Nile as far as this city. Its ruins even now bear the name of Thothmes III. But under the succeeding dynasties, the rising power of Ethiopia so far prevailed that the northern frontier of this kingdom included the Island of Argo; while, under the feeble twenty-third and twenty-fourth dynasties, it is not improbable that the Ethiopians occupied Thebes, and that Bocchoris held his crown as a tributary or subject prince. This supposition alone accounts for the statement, that, when taken prisoner by the Ethiopian monarch, he was burned to death. This is a conjecture of Mr. Kenrick, and one which seems particularly plausible, as Sabaco is celebrated as a just and humane sovereign, and therefore not likely to inflict such a terrible death on a captive prince, unless he had been guilty of some breach of faith or treachery.

We have no satisfactory information respecting this invasion. Herodotus calls the king who reigned in Egypt at this time Anysis;

and says that he was not put to death, but took refuge in the marshes of the Delta. But this account is utterly improbable. He also alleges that the monarch was blind, but that nevertheless he succeeded in escaping to the marshes, where he constructed an island of ashes and earth; that he maintained himself here fifty years; and that then, the Ethiopians having retired, he reässumed the reins of government.

But whatever might have been the manner in which the power of Ethiopia became paramount in Egypt, it is certain that it must not be regarded as the irruption of a barbarous people on a highly civilized country. On the contrary, Ethiopia at this period was as far advanced in cultivation as Egypt herself. The latter country had, in fact, proceeded far in declension; and it is probable that thus, by the ordinary operation of the human mind in such circumstances, the hardy, daring Ethiopian acquired an easy ascendency over the enervated Egyptian.

The name of the first sovereign of this dynasty, written *Shabek*, is found at Luxor, with the usual titles of Egyptian sovereignty. The sculptures on the internal wall of the *propylæa* raised by Rameses Sesostris having been injured or decayed by time, Sabaco renewed them, and substituted his own name for that of Rameses. These prove that Egyptian art still existed in considerable vigour. A statuette of the same king is preserved in the Villa Albani at Rome; and his shield has been found over a gate of the palace of Karnak.

Sebechus, or Sevechus, son of the preceding king, succeeded him. But it is impossible to distinguish this Pharaoh on the monuments from his father, as their phonetic names are written in the same characters. This explains the circumstance, that the name has been found on fragments with an indication of the twelfth year of the reign: these of course refer to Sebechus. It is stated in the Second Book of Kings that Hoshea, king of Israel, having made an alliance with So, or Seva, king of Egypt, (2 Kings xvii, 4,) refused to pay his customary tribute to Shalmaneser, king of Assyria. This event happened in the latter part of the reign of Hoshea, and in the beginning of that of Sevechus. This was the reasonable policy of the rulers of Egypt,—to maintain the power of Israel and Judah, the only barrier between their kingdom and Assyria. It is, however, very probable that in this instance the policy of Sevechus was defeated by the prompt energy of the king of Assyria, who had an efficient ally in the king of Judah; and, in consequence, the kingdom of Israel was subverted and destroyed.

Tarkus succeeded Sevechus. His name, written *Tarhak* or *Tar-*

haka, is found on the internal face of the *pylon* of a building erected at Medinet-Abou by Thothmes IV. Tarkus, or Tirhaka, was a very martial prince; and Strabo speaks of him as rivalling Sesostris. There may be much exaggeration in this; but it is not improbable that at this time, when the whole power of Egypt and Ethiopia were united under one warlike sovereign, the limitation of its martial glory might have been the result rather of the overwhelming power of Assyria, than of any real weakness. The account of Strabo in fact indicates as much, since he says that Tirhaka extended his conquests westward even to the Pillars of Hercules. At all events, it seems certain that Tarkus dreaded an encounter with this power. In the reign of Ahaz, Judah acknowledged the supremacy of Assyria; but when his son succeeded to the throne, strong in the holy confidence that Jehovah would protect his people, he threw off this allegiance, refused the customary tribute, and during many years maintained the independence of his country. In the sixth year of the reign of Hezekiah, Samaria was subdued, and the kingdom of Israel was soon afterward destroyed. Then there was no independent power intervening between the Assyrians and Egypt but Judah. Nor was this state left long unmolested. We are not informed of the relations which subsisted between Hezekiah and the reigning Pharaoh; but when, in the fourteenth year of the Hebrew monarch, Sennacherib invaded Judah, and Hezekiah had to purchase a brief respite by an enormous contribution, the officers of the haughty Assyrian, when delivering their insolent address in the name of their master, taunted the Hebrew king by saying, "Now on whom dost thou trust, that thou rebellest against me? Now, behold, thou trustest upon the staff of this bruised reed, even upon Egypt." 2 Kings xviii, 20, 21. This would of itself be sufficient to prove that some connexion between the two countries had been induced by their common danger. But all doubt is removed by the Scripture fact, that when these messengers returned to Lachish to their master, he heard that Tirhakah, the Ethiopian king, was marching against him. Chap. xix, 9. Upon receiving this intelligence, the Assyrian sovereign raised the siege of Lachish, and, fearing to encounter this formidable foe in an enemy's country, marched toward Egypt to meet Tirhakah. The king of Egypt in his turn began to fear; Hezekiah did not dare to pursue the Assyrians; and Pharaoh retired within the Egyptian frontier, while the whole country trembled in the prospect of a sanguinary invasion. But Egypt and Israel were both preserved by a miraculous interposition. The Assyrian army was all destroyed in one night by an angel of the Lord; and the boastful monarch was compelled to return to his own land in weakness and disgrace. This wonderful event is recorded in Egyptian history as distinctly and almost as fully as in the Hebrew Scriptures. (Hebrew People, p. 579.)

No satisfactory information can be obtained respecting the close of this dynasty. Herodotus says that the Ethiopian king was induced to retire from the country by a dream; and that he was succeeded by Sethos. This, however, cannot be true, inasmuch as we know that Tirhakah reigned when the Assyrian army was destroyed. It is not improbable that the conjecture of Kenrick is correct,—that Sethos, a priest, held a kind of subordinate sovereignty in Lower Egypt during the imperial sway of Tirhakah; and that martial monarch, having retired from before Sennacherib, perhaps into Upper Egypt, thus left the sacerdotal and unwarlike viceroy of Memphis to defend himself; a task to which he felt so unequal that he retired into the temple, and was told in a dream, that he should obtain deliverance from the Assyrian king. This promise was almost immediately fulfilled by the ruin of the army of Sennacherib.

TWENTY-SIXTH DYNASTY: NINE SAITE KINGS.

	Years.
1. Stephanates reigned	7
2. Nechepsos	6
3. Nechao	8
4. Psammitichus	54
5. Nechao II. (He took Jerusalem)	6
6. Psammuthis II	6
7. Uaphris	19
8. Amosis	14
9. Psammecherites	0 6 months.

We have no means of ascertaining whether this dynasty stood in any relation or connexion to Bocchoris of Sais: but, as Herodotus says that the blind king, who was driven into the marshes by the Ethiopian invasion, returned when they left the country, it is not improbable that Stephanates might have been of the same family. We have, however, no information respecting the first three sovereigns. Herodotus states that the Ethiopian king, before he left Egypt, slew Nechos, the father of Psammitichus; and that, on the death of Sethos, the Egyptians recovered their liberty; and as they could not live without kings, they chose twelve, among whom they divided the several districts of Egypt.

It appears therefore certain, that at this period Egypt was torn by civil discord, which terminated in a dodecarchy; the chroniclers selecting one line of kings as legitimate, in whom the succession is numbered. The account which Herodotus gives of this collateral sovereignty is as follows: "These princes connected themselves with each other by intermarriages, engaging solemnly to promote their common interest, and never to engage in any acts of separate policy. The principal motive of their union was to guard against the declaration of an oracle, which had said, that whoever among them should offer in the temple of Vulcan a libation in a brazen vessel, should be sole sovereign of Egypt; and it is to be remembered that they assembled indifferently in every temple.

"These twelve kings were eminent for the justice of their administration. On a certain occasion they were offering sacrifice in the temple of Vulcan, and on the last day of the festival were about to make the accustomed libation. For this purpose the chief priest handed to them the golden cups used on these solemnities; but he mistook the number, and, instead of twelve, gave only eleven. Psammitichus, who was the last of them, not having a cup, took off his helmet, which happened to be of brass, and from this poured his libation. The other princes wore helmets in common, and had them on the present occasion; so that the circumstance of this one king having and using his was accidental and innocent. Observing, however, this action of Psammitichus, they remembered the prediction of the oracle, 'that he among them who should pour a libation from a brazen vessel, should be sole monarch of Egypt.' They minutely investigated the matter; and being satisfied that this action of Psammitichus was entirely the effect of accident, they could not think him worthy of death. They nevertheless deprived him of a considerable part of his power, and confined him to the marshy parts of the country, forbidding him to leave this situation, or to communicate with the rest of Egypt.

"This Psammitichus had formerly fled to Syria, from Sabachus the Ethiopian, who had killed his father Nechos. When the Ethiopian, terrified by the vision, had abandoned his dominions, those Egyptians who lived near Sais had solicited Psammitichus to return. He was now a second time driven into exile among the fens by the eleven kings, from this circumstance of the brazen helmet. He felt the strongest resentment for the injury, and determined to avenge himself on his persecutors. He sent therefore to the oracle of Latona, at Butos, which has among the Egyptians the highest character for veracity. He was informed that the sea should avenge his cause by producing brazen figures of men. He was little inclined to believe that such a circumstance could ever occur; but, some time afterward, a body of Ionians and Carians, who had been engaged in a voyage of plunder, were compelled by distress to touch at Egypt: they landed in brazen armour. Some Egyptians hastened to inform Psammitichus in his marshes of this incident; and as the messenger had never before seen persons so armed, he said, that some brazen men had arisen from the sea, and were plundering the country. He instantly conceived this to be the accomplishment of the oracle's prediction, and entered into alliance with the strangers, engaging them by splendid promises to assist him. With them and his Egyptian adherents he vanquished the eleven kings."—*Euterpe*, cap. 147–152.

The battle which defeated the confederated kings, and gave Egypt to Psammitichus, was fought at Momemphis, near the Canopic branch of the Nile, and on the shore of the Lake Mareotis. Some of the opposing kings were slain; the rest escaped into Libya.

According to Herodotus, the dodecarchs, while they ruled together in amity, being determined to leave some permanent memorial of their joint sway, built the Labyrinth: but Diodorus ascribes this building to an earlier sovereign, although, from his account, it is not improbable that the primary erection had fallen into decay, and that the work of the twelve kings was reared on the same site.

Psammitichus, having established himself in power, rewarded his allies and native supporters by allotting them a district on the Pelusiac branch of the Nile, a little nearer to the sea than the city of Bubastis. The foreign troops had a settlement on one bank of the river, and the natives on the other, as, notwithstanding their association in the service of the same king, their national and religious prejudices were too strong to allow them to fraternize in one community. This place became afterward of the utmost importance to the destinies of Egypt.

Although no monument bearing the name of this sovereign remains in Egypt, there is ample proof that the whole country submitted to his sway. His shield is found in the palace at Karnak, and in a little island near Philæ. In the quarry of Tourah the design of a monolithal shrine, intended to be excavated, is traced on the rock in red paint, the cornice of which bears the shield of Psammitichus. Works of his reign are found in several European museums; but the most remarkable remnant of the art of this era is the obelisk which stands in the Monte Citorio at Rome. It was brought from Egypt by the Emperor Augustus, as a memorial of its conquest by the Romans. As a work of art, it is decidedly inferior to those of the age of Thothmes III.; but considering that seven hundred years had elapsed between these eras, the degeneracy is not so great as might be expected.

It seems to be an established fact, that the reliance of this monarch on foreign and party support alienated from him a large portion of his Egyptian subjects, although the precise occasion of the quarrel is not so clearly ascertainable. From the combined statements of Herodotus and Diodorus, it appears that the king of Egypt wished to subdue Ashdod, which had been taken and garrisoned by the king of Assyria; that for this purpose he invested it with an army, composed of native troops and his foreign auxiliaries; and that, he having given the latter the post of honour in the war, the former deserted him, and retired into Ethiopia. Herodotus ascribes this defection to the fact, that the garrisons in Upper Egypt had not been relieved for three years. But, whatever the cause might be, after this desertion had taken place, the king applied himself more diligently than ever to perfect the internal policy of his kingdom, and the cultivation of a friendly intercourse with Greece. Egypt, formerly the most inhospitable of all nations, now opened her harbours freely. To promote this intercourse, the king encouraged the study of Greek literature, and caused his own sons to be instructed in that language.

Toward the latter part of this reign Egypt was threatened with a foreign invasion. During the time that Cyaxares and his allies were besieging Nineveh an overwhelming army of Scythians entered Asia. Cyaxares attempted to arrest their progress, but was defeated. After ravaging the east, this terrible host marched toward the west. The prophet Zephaniah, who wrote a few years previously, is supposed to have predicted their character and progress with great spirit and fidelity. If, indeed, the passages referred to (Zeph. i, 4, 5, 6, and ii, 1) apply to this invasion, their appropriateness is undoubted: but notwithstanding the weighty support which Hitzig, Cramer, and Eichhorn have given to this opinion, it does not seem to be established. However this may be, after the Scythians had ravaged Media, they marched into Palestine, and menaced Egypt. They had advanced as far as Ascalon on the coast of Palestine, when Psammitichus met them, and by presents and entreaties prevailed on them to return. This took place about 618 B. C., and consequently in the thirty-seventh year of Psammitichus.

Necho, or Nechao, son of the preceding, succeeded his father 615 B. C. His first public work appears to have been an attempt to unite the Nile and the Red Sea by a canal: but this effort, after an enormous expenditure of wealth and life, was at length relinquished. Herodotus observes that "when Necho abandoned his plan of joining the Nile and the Red Sea by a canal, he engaged in military operations." It is more than probable that the peculiar aspect of political affairs in Asia induced him to forego his favourite project, and turned his attention to martial pursuits. On the expulsion of the Scythians, (612 B. C.,) Cyaxares resumed the siege of Nineveh;

and Pharaoh-Necho regarded this as a favourable opportunity for recovering the power which Egypt had formerly possessed on the banks of the Euphrates. He accordingly began the necessary preparations, and, 608 B. C., transported an army into Palestine, for the purpose of recovering military possession of Carchemish. But Josiah, the Hebrew king, drew together the whole strength of his kingdom, and marched out to oppose his progress. The Egyptian sovereign earnestly dissuaded him from his purpose, but in vain. The armies met at Megiddo. The result is well known. The good king of the Hebrews was completely defeated, and fatally wounded; so that he was taken to Jerusalem, where he died. This event appears to have totally deranged the plans of Necho. He was at Riblah in Hamath, when he heard that the people of Judea had made Jehoahaz, son of Josiah, king. Necho immediately sent for the newly-appointed sovereign to Hamath, when he was deposed and imprisoned, after a reign of three months. Necho then sent Jehoahaz to Egypt, where he ended his days, and made a younger son of Josiah, Eliakim, king, changing his name to Jehoiakim; imposing on him a tribute of a hundred talents of silver and a talent of gold. Whether Necho on this occasion did go on to Carchemish, is not certain. He might have thought it more important fully to establish his supremacy over Judea. We find him, however, four years afterward, proceeding to Carchemish with an army of Egyptians, Ethiopians, and Libyans. Jer. xlvi. He was then signally defeated. The sacred prophet tersely states, that Nebuchadnezzar " smote the army of Necho;" and the decisive effect of this stroke is indicated by the statement of another inspired writer: "The king of Egypt came not again any more out of his land: for the king of Babylon had taken from the River of Egypt unto the River Euphrates all that pertained to the king of Egypt." 2 Kings xxiv, 7. This decided the supremacy of Babylon. Egypt in future had to study the most effectual means of defence.

During this reign, according to Herodotus, Africa was circumnavigated by a Phenician fleet; of which the historian gives the following account: "For as to Libya, it shows itself to be circumnavigable, except where it borders on Asia. This was first proved, so far as I know, by Necho, King of Egypt. When he gave up excavating the canal that runs from the Nile to the Arabian Gulf, he sent out some Phenicians in ships, giving them orders on their way back to sail through the Pillars of Hercules into the Northern Sea, and thus return to Egypt. Setting out, then, from the Red Sea, they sailed into the Southern Sea. As often as autumn returned they landed in Libya, and planted some corn in the place where they happened to be. When this was ripe, and they had cut it down, they again departed. Having thus consumed two years, they, in the third, doubled the Columns of Hercules, and returned to Egypt. Their relation may obtain attention from others, but to me it seems incredible; for they affirmed that, having sailed round Libya, they had the sun on their right hand. Thus was Libya for the first time known."—*Melpomene*, cap. 42. In this relation of the father of history, it is observable that the difficulty which provoked his incredulity is the most satisfactory demonstration of the truth of the narrative. For, as Larcher observes, the phenomenon must have appeared as stated; "and this curious circumstance, which never could have been imagined in an age when astronomy was yet in its infancy, is an evidence of the truth of a voyage which, without this, might have been doubted."—*Larcher's Notes to Herodotus*, vol. ii, p. 34.

Necho was succeeded by his son Psammitichus II., whom Herodotus calls Psammus, and Manetho Psammuthis II. But as we do not meet with this latter name previously, there can be no doubt that Eusebius is correct, when he gives the name as above. This sovereign began to reign 599 B. C. No public building erected by him remains; but his name is found on several fragments of sculpture; as, for instance, in the citadel of Cairo, under the base of Pompey's Pillar at Alexandria. His titular shield is also found on the obelisk of the Piazza Minerva at Rome, which was executed under his son and successor Apries; and his name and titular shield also appear on a part of an intercolumnar plinth now in the British Museum. He is here delineated presenting an offering to the gods, who give him all power and victory, and put all lands under his sandals. Toward the end of his reign, Psammitichus II. made an expedition into Ethiopia: but as to the object or result of this war we are not informed. His shield is found at the Island of Snem, near the Cataracts of Syene. He died almost immediately after this expedition, and was succeeded by his son.

Uaphris, the Apries of the Greeks, and the Hophra of Scripture, ascended the throne 593 B. C. Until the beginning of his reign, Egypt had made no aggressions on Asia for the purpose of repairing the consequences of the defeat of Necho at Carchemish. But Apries, perceiving the gradual and steady progress of Babylonian ascendency in Western Asia, determined to make another effort to check this influence, and to extend the power of Egypt. He accordingly collected an armament, and invaded Phenicia. From the information supplied by Herodotus and Diodorus, it seems that he took Sidon, defeated the Cyprians, (who appear to have been allies, if not subjects, of the Phenicians,) and reduced the whole sea-coast of Phenicia. There can scarcely be a doubt that this was the overflowing flood predicted by Jeremiah. Chap. xlvii. Its coming from "the north" is explained by the fact that Phenicia Proper was the first scene of conflict. To this place the Egyptian army was conveyed in a fleet; and having gained several victories over the Phenicians, Apries marched his army toward the south, subduing all the strongholds on the sea-coast. He accomplished these objects, and produced on the king and court of Judea a deep impression of the great military power of Egypt. Zedekiah, having sent ambassadors to Apries, and obtained a promise of support, felt emboldened to violate his oath of fidelity to Nebuchadnezzar, relying on obtaining succour from Egypt. This led the king of Babylon to invest Jerusalem, when Apries proceeded with an army to relieve his ally. But Nebuchadnezzar was too good a general to remain before Jerusalem until the arrival of the Egyptians, and thus to place himself between two foes. He accordingly raised the siege, and proceeded to meet the host of Egypt. Apries did not venture, unaided, alone, and in the desert, to resist the Babylonish king: he retired, without hazarding a conflict, into his own land. Upon this Nebuchadnezzar returned, and took and destroyed the royal city of Judea; and thus were fulfilled the predictions of the prophets, that the apostate Hebrews would find no efficient aid in Egypt. (See Ezek. xii.)

After this storm had passed over, and Gedaliah, who had been left by Nebuchadnezzar as governor of Judea, had been slain, all the people that remained took Jeremiah the prophet, and fled into Egypt. Here they were kindly received by Apries; for we find them located with the prophet in the royal city.

After the ruin of the Hebrew monarchy, and the deportation of the survivors, who were carried into Chaldea, the king of Babylon prosecuted the war against the Phenicians and other inhabitants of the sea-coast. Whether Tyre, in consequence of the military measures of Apries, was avowedly subject to Egypt or not, it was hostile to the advancing power of Babylon: but it fell, after a long and desperate struggle, before the prowess of Nebuchadnezzar. Nor can there be a question that the conqueror swept the whole coast, and ravaged Egypt, in the same campaign. This was distinctly predicted by Ezekiel; and although Herodotus does not mention the fact, all probability is in favour of its having taken place. The language of the sacred seer is remarkable: "Nebuchadrezzar King of Babylon caused his army to serve a great service against Tyrus: every head was made bald, and every shoulder was peeled: yet had he no wages, nor his army, for Tyrus, for the service that he had served against it: therefore thus saith the Lord God; Behold, I will give the land of Egypt unto Nebuchadrezzar king of Babylon: and he shall take her multitude, and take her spoil, and take her prey; and it shall be the wages for his army. I have given him the land of Egypt for his labour," &c. Ezek. xxix, 18–20. Jeremiah, also, while in Egypt, asserts the same. After having hidden stones in the clay in the brick-kiln, near the palace of Pharaoh at Tahpanhes, he says, "Thus saith the Lord of hosts, the God of Israel; Behold, I will send and take Nebuchadrezzar the king of Babylon, my servant, and will set his throne upon these stones that I have hid; and he shall spread his royal pavilion over them." It was also declared that he would "break the images of Bethshemesh,"—Heliopolis. Jer. xliii, 8–13. That Nebuchadnezzar invaded Egypt, is, however, not only probable, and asserted by the voice of sacred prophecy; but it is also stated as a fact by Megasthenes, who says that he conquered a great part of Libya, which he could not do without passing through Egypt. The absence of any notice of this event by the Greek writers may be accounted for by supposing that, in accordance with the spirit of the times, the Babylonian monarch merely marched through and plundered Lower Egypt, without locating an army in the country, or extending his conquest to Upper Egypt.

It is necessary here to observe that, prior to this period, the colony of Cyrene had been founded, and had grown into considerable opulence and power. Battus, its founder, governed it forty years. Arcesilaus, his successor, ruled sixteen years. He was succeeded by Battus II., under whose government an invitation was sent to all Greeks to come and aid the Cyrenians in colonizing Libya. The Pythian oracle recommended compliance, and warned the people against delay. The result was that a multitude of persons from all parts of Greece soon congregated at Cyrene. As might have been expected, these could not be provided with allotments of land, without removing the native Libyans from their property, and treating them with great injustice. In those circumstances the king of Libya sent to solicit aid of Egypt. Apries, who saw it to be his interest to extend his influence over Libya, and at the same time to check the progress of a dangerous and increasing power in his neighbourhood, complied with the request, and sent an army into that country. But on this occasion he could not venture to employ his Greek mercenaries against their own countrymen: the troops were entirely native Egyptians. This was the first time that the free Greeks had to conflict with the troops of an old despotic monarchy. Here, as elsewhere, a contempt for the

limited numbers and unostentatious appearance of the Greeks
seems to have caused the ruin of their enemies. The Egyptians
marched negligently to the field, and were not only completely defeated, but almost entirely destroyed. Few of them returned to
their own country.

The news of this calamity produced a general insurrection in
Egypt. The few who returned, joined by the relatives and friends
of those who had fallen, immediately revolted. On hearing of this,
Apries sent Amasis, one of his favourite officers, to restore order
among the disaffected; but, while he was haranguing them for that
purpose, a soldier came behind him, and placed a crown on his head,
upon which the crowd saluted him as sovereign. Accepting the
proffered dignity and danger, Amasis placed himself at the head of
the revolt, and prepared to march against Apries. This monarch,
on being informed of his conduct, sent Paterbemis, an officer of high
rank, to bring Amasis alive into his presence. The rebel chief bade
him return, with a contemptuous refusal; and when with this message he appeared before the king, the infatuated sovereign ordered
his ears and nose to be cut off. This decided the fate of Apries.
The Egyptians who had hitherto supported him, disgusted at his
cruelty and injustice, went over to Amasis. Apries, was, in consequence, left alone with his Carian and Ionian auxiliaries. With
these, however, he marched to meet Amasis. The armies met on
the banks of the Lake Mareotis; and in the contest which ensued,
Apries was defeated and taken prisoner; and Amasis, although of
low origin, was then raised to the sovereignty of Egypt.

From the manner in which Herodotus records these events, the
conclusion is warranted, that Apries, by relying for the maintenance
of his power on his thirty thousand hired Greek troops, had grievously offended the native soldiery, and prepared the way for the
general defection that followed, when the defeat before Cyrene excited the public mind, and became a pretext for the rebellion, which
hurled him from the throne after a reign, according to Eusebius, of
twenty-five years.

Amasis, or Amosis, a native of a small town in the Saitic Nome,
and of plebeian birth, ascended the throne B. C. 568. He is the
first king of Egypt of whose personal character we have any knowledge. Of him we are told, that he appropriated the early part of
every day to the duties of his station; that he gave audience to all
that required it, and thus earned the reputation of a wise, just, and
good man. Yet after he had discharged these duties, he devoted
the rest of the day to pleasurable recreation. On being remonstrated with on this unkingly conduct, he is said to have replied,

"They who have a bow bend it only at the time they want it; when not in use, they suffer it to be relaxed; it would otherwise break, and not be of service when exigence required. It is precisely the same with a man: if, without some intervals of amusement, he applied himself constantly to serious pursuits, he would imperceptibly lose his vigour both of mind and body. It is the conviction of this truth which influences me in the division of my time." He thus silenced those who objected to his manner of life. He adopted another mode with those who despised him on account of his plebeian origin. Having "a gold vessel in which he and his guests were accustomed to spit, and wash their feet, of the materials of this he made the statue of some god, which he placed in the most conspicuous part of the city. The Egyptians, assembling before it, paid it divine honours; on hearing of which, the king called them together, and informed them that the image which they thus venerated was made of a vessel of gold which he and they had formerly used for the most unseemly purposes. He afterward explained to them the similar circumstances of his own fortunes, who, though formerly a plebeian, was now their sovereign, and entitled to their reverence. By these means he secured their attachment."

During this reign Egypt continued in great prosperity. The regular rise of the Nile diffused plenty throughout the land. A friendly treaty was established with Cyrene. The danger which threatened Babylon from the rising power of Media, took off all apprehension from that quarter. Amasis entered into an alliance with the king of Babylon, to support Croesus, King of Lydia, against Cyrus; but the rapid movements of the Persian warrior rendered their intended interference nugatory. In consequence of the ravages of Nebuchadnezzar, the Phenicians were so crippled in their resources that Amasis subdued Cyprus, and laid it under tribute. Although he was at first disposed to regard the Greeks with disfavour, as they had so strenuously supported his predecessor, yet he afterward manifested a friendly bearing toward that nation. He allowed them a free location in the city of Naucratis; and to those who came only for commercial purposes he gave sites, on which they might build altars to their gods.

Amasis was for a while on terms of intimate friendship with the Greek tyrant of Samos, Polycrates; but afterward renounced his friendship, on the plea that the Greek had enjoyed such uninterrupted good fortune as foreboded a melancholy termination of his career. Such is the poetic account of Herodotus. Diodorus, in all probability, comes nearer the truth. He states that Amasis renounced the friendship of Polycrates, because the latter paid no regard to an embassy which had been sent to him by the Egyptian king, exhorting him to abstain from outrages on his fellow-citizens, and on strangers who resorted to Samos. It was under the influence of this friendship that Pythagoras, who was of Phenician extraction and a native of Samos, visited Egypt. Whatever may be doubtful as to the wide range of travel and research attributed to this philosopher,—that he resided long in Egypt, and obtained a great acquaintance with its philosophy and religion, must be regarded as an established fact.

Architectural works of great splendour and magnitude were erected by Amasis; among which the *propylæa* of the temple of Minerva at Sais hold a distinguished rank. These, "for height and size, and the magnitude and quality of the stones employed, surpassed all others. These he brought from the quarries of Memphis, as well as the colossal figures and andro-sphinxes with which the *dromos* was adorned. A monolithal shrine of granite, from the quarries of Elephantine, excited the especial admiration of Herodotus. Two thousand men were employed to bring it down the Nile. From Elephantine to Sais was an ordinary navigation of only twenty days; but in this case three years were occupied, probably because the immense weight made it impossible to float it, except during the season of the high Nile. Its height was above thirty feet; its depth, from front to back, twelve feet; its breadth, twenty-one. After all the cost and labour bestowed on its extraction and conveyance, it was not erected in the temple of Minerva. As they were drawing it in, the superintendent of the works uttered a groan, through weariness of the labour, and the thought of the time that had been expended; and Amasis, either because he deemed this ominous, or because one of the workmen had been killed in the process of moving it on levers, would not allow it to be drawn any further. When Herodotus visited Egypt, it remained lying before the temple."—*Kenrick's Egypt*, vol. ii, p. 441. Amasis also erected a colossus, seventy-five feet high, at Memphis, before the temple of Pthah; and two of granite, twenty feet high, one on each side of the inner sanctuary. He also built a temple, of great size and magnificence, at Memphis: it was dedicated to Isis.

His reign, according to Herodotus and the lists, lasted forty-four years; according to Diodorus, fifty-five; but I have thought it safest here, as in the last reign, to adopt the numbers of Eusebius, who makes it forty-two years. Amasis died B. C. 526, and was succeeded by his son.

Psammenitus, on ascending the throne, was placed in circumstances of great difficulty and danger. Cyrus the Great had taken

Babylon during the reign of Amasis; but the nomadic tribes of the north having provoked him by their restless daring, he led an army against them, and perished in the enterprise. His son, Cambyses, on ascending the throne, immediately planned an expedition against Egypt. This was in course of preparation when Amasis died; and to his successor was consequently bequeathed the defence of the kingdom. This would under any circumstances have been a difficult task. The Medo-Persian empire was now paramount in Asia. The army of Cambyses was, therefore, composed of the best troops of the age.

It must have cast gloom on the prospects of Egypt, to remember that in every contest that had occurred between the armies of Egypt and those of the east, for several centuries, the former had invariably been worsted. The case of Sennacherib cannot be regarded as an exception, because in that instance there was no conflict, and the ruin of the Assyrians was confessedly miraculous. The great difficulty which the Persian monarch had to encounter was, to cross the desert from Palestine to Egypt. Here was a distance of about one hundred geographical miles in which no vegetation or water fit for drinking was to be found. If the land-marks had been removed from this desert, and no aid been afforded by neighbouring nations, it would have been a serious obstacle to the advance of an invading army. But all this advantage to Egypt was neutralized by the treachery of a Greek officer in the Egyptian service. Before the death of Amasis, that king had offended Phanes of Halicarnassus, one of the commanders of the mercenary troops. This person, knowing that Cambyses was preparing to invade Egypt, fled from his post, and, though hotly pursued and placed in great danger, he succeeded in reaching the Persian court, where, by the aid and information he afforded, Cambyses succeeded in placing his army in great strength before Pelusium.

It is said by an ancient author, that the Persians captured this key to Egypt by practising on the superstition of the Egyptians. Knowing in what veneration they held cats, dogs, sheep, and other animals, the Persian king collected a great number of these creatures, and drove them in the front of the army, as they proceeded to assault the city. The Egyptians, not daring to endanger the life of beings which they adored, allowed them to advance unopposed, so that Cambyses took the place without loss. Soon after this event the Egyptian king appeared at the head of his army; the Persians marched out to meet him; the fate of Egypt trembled in the balance. Before the battle began, the Greek mercenaries, to show their detestation of the treachery of Phanes, brought his children into the front of the army, cut their throats, drank their blood, and then proceeded to the conflict.

A singular omen is said to have portended ill to the cause of Egypt, just before this struggle took place. Rain fell at Thebes,—a prodigy never known to have happened but in that single instance. The battle was long and desperate: but Persia triumphed, and Cambyses pursued the wreck of the Egyptian army to Memphis. Desirous of avoiding further slaughter, he sent a Mitylenian vessel to Memphis to treat with the Egyptian authorities. But, enraged beyond measure at their defeat, the Egyptians no sooner saw the vessel approach, than they assailed it, and slaughtered all on board, being two hundred persons. Memphis was at once invested: it held out for a while, but was compelled to submit to the conqueror. Cambyses took a terrible revenge for the death of his crew, by causing ten times as many of the noble youths of Memphis, including the eldest son of the king, to be put to death. From Memphis Cambyses went to Sais, where he disgraced himself, and outraged the feelings of both Egyptians and Persians, by treating the mummy of Amasis with every indignity, and afterward burning it with fire. With the taking of Memphis the authority of Cambyses was established over Egypt, and the reign of Psammenitus terminated, having lasted but six months.

Libya and Cyrene bowed to the conqueror without a struggle, sent gifts, and submitted to tribute. The ambition of the proud Persian, however, extended beyond,—to Ethiopia in the south, and Carthage in the west. The first he endeavoured to reach; but the intervening desert defeated his purpose. After having decimated his army, in order to support the living on the flesh of their dead comrades, he was forced to retreat. Carthage was accessible only by sea; and as he could not induce the Phenicians to act against their own colony, and had no sufficient means of transporting his army independently of them, he was obliged to abandon his project.

TWENTY-SEVENTH DYNASTY: EIGHT PERSIAN KINGS.

	Years.	Months.
1. Cambyses (who in the fifth year of his reign in Persia became king of Egypt) reigned	6	
2. Darius (son of Hystaspes)	36	
3. Xerxes the Great	21	
4. Artabanus		7
5. Artaxerxes	41	0
6. Xerxes		2
7. Sogdianus		7
8. Darius (son of Xerxes)	19	
Duration of the dynasty	124	4

Much trifling conjecture has been employed to explain the cause of the Persian irruption into Egypt: but this is unnecessary. When all western Asia had been subdued, the invasion of an old and wealthy kingdom like Egypt followed as a matter of course.

It will be necessary here to regard the whole time of this dynasty as one reign. The succession of the several sovereigns, and their history, will be narrated in the chapter devoted to Persia.

As far as our information goes, Cambyses, on obtaining possession of Egypt, behaved toward the people with great moderation and forbearance The slaughter of the two thousand, in reprisal for the murder of the crew of the Mitylenian vessel, must ever be regarded as an act of monstrous cruelty and injustice. But this was not the deed of Cambyses: Herodotus is careful to inform us that it was the deliberate decision of "the king's counsellors." But, after the proud Persian had been compelled to abandon his attempt on Ethiopia, and had suffered the loss of fifty thousand men whom he had despatched to burn the temple of Ammonium, he returned to Memphis filled with grief and rage. On the pretence of his having stirred up the Egyptians to revolt, (which he might possibly have done in consequence of these disasters,) Psammenitus was put to death; and the magistrates of Memphis suffered in all probability in a similar way. On the return of Cambyses to that city, he found the people engaged in public rejoicings, upon which he immediately summoned the magistrates before him, and demanded the cause: they told him that their god Apis had appeared to them, as was his custom to do; and that when this happened, the Egyptians always held a festival. The king, however, persisted in regarding these manifestations as connected with the defeat of his attempt on Ethiopia, and accordingly condemned the magistrates to death. Unsatisfied with this vengeance, he sent for the priests; and as they gave him the same account, he insisted on seeing the god, and ordered Apis to be brought. When he saw the young steer with some strange marks on his body, he reviled their superstition; ordered the priests to be scourged, with every Egyptian who had participated in the festivities; and, drawing a short sword, he aimed a blow at the belly of Apis, but struck him on the thigh. Herodotus regards the conduct of the Persian king as proving his insanity: but it is more probable that he was afflicted with epilepsy, which rendered him irritable, and incapable, at certain times, of self-control.

Cambyses reigned over Egypt six years. No memorial is found of him in any temple; but his shield is seen on the road to Cosseir, near the Red Sea.

Under Darius, who bent the energies of his vigorous mind to consolidate and govern the great empire which his predecessors had by their military genius and energy won, Egypt was made one of the twenty satrapies into which the Medo-Persian dominions were divided. This satrapy included, besides Egypt Proper, Libya, as far as Cyrene, the Oases of the Libyan Desert, and the country between the Nile and the Red Sea. Aryandes, who had been left governor of Egypt by Cambyses, was made the first satrap; and, when Darius introduced the gold daric into this kingdom, he supplied a silver coinage to Egypt. His government was, however, so disagreeable to the Egyptians, that when Darius visited Egypt, he conciliated the people by offering a reward for the discovery of Apis, whose place was then vacant, and ordered Aryandes to be put to death. Darius is the only Persian king whose name is accompanied by a titular shield, and whose phonetic shield bears the Pharaonic crest of the vulpanser and disk, "Son of the Sun." Neither his, nor that of any other Persian king, is found on a public monument within the limits of Egypt.

Darius is supposed at this time to have obtained possession of the Great Oasis and of the Oasis of Sirvah, the temples in both bearing his inscriptions. He also resumed the excavation of the canal between the Nile and the Red Sea; and although he did not complete the underaking, he left a very small space unaccomplished. It is said that he was deterred from finishing the work by the discovery that the level of the Red Sea was higher than Lower Egypt.

We know little of the history of Egypt at this period: the projected invasion of Greece by the Persians seems to have fully occupied the mind of Greek historians; but it is certain that these events had a most important influence on Egypt. In 490 B. C. the Persian army was defeated at Marathon; and this decisive blow so encouraged the patriots in Egypt, that in 486 the whole country was in open revolt against the authority of Persia. We do not know who led this movement, nor what kind of government was established during the time that the dominion of Persia was in abeyance; but the interval of independence was short. In two years after this revolt Xerxes marched his army into Egypt, and, with scarcely a struggle, reduced it to entire submission, and left his brother Achæmenes satrap of the country. In consequence of this success, two hundred Egyptian vessels were engaged on the side of the Persian king in his attack on Greece. Nothing further is known of the internal history of Egypt, until the death of Xerxes, which took place 465 B. C.

Artaxerxes, having ascended the throne, found the empire in a state of great disorder and weakness, from the effects of the Greek campaigns. While he was engaged in repairing this disorder, and punishing revolted satraps, a gleam of hope was cast on the destiny of Egypt. At this time Inaros, a son of Psammitichus, probably a descendant of the Saitic princes, had obtained the sovereignty of that part of Libya which bordered on Egypt; and, encouraged by the difficulties which surrounded the king of Persia, he raised an army, crossed the frontier, and entered Egypt. He was immediately received as the deliverer of the country, and almost all the power of Egypt flocked to his standard. The Persian executive and tax-gatherers were immediately expelled, and the whole country submitted to Inaros. But this chief, well aware that he could not long maintain himself in this authority, unless able to resist all the power of Persia, lost no time in soliciting aid from Athens; and this power, hailing the opportunity with joy, sent him forty vessels with a force of about six thousand men.

In the mean time Artaxerxes had employed all the resources of his empire to collect a fleet and an army, for the purpose of establishing his authority in the west. He intended to commence his operations by the reduction of Egypt, and to command the army in person. His friends, however, advised him to give the command to Achæmenes, who had returned to Persia in consequence of the revolt. The king consented, and the satrap, at the head of his army, speedily entered Egypt.

Inaros, fully acquainted with the ground, and anxious to avail himself to the utmost of his resources, retired to the western frontier, where he had not only the Egyptian forces and Athenian auxiliaries, but also the strength of Libya, congregated to meet the enemy. Here a great battle was fought, in which the Persians were defeated mainly by the prowess of the Greek troops, and Achæmenes fell by the hand of Inaros. Immediately after this defeat the Persians retired to Memphis, whither they were followed and besieged by Inaros. He was, however, unable to reduce the citadel; and while he was thus occupied, another Persian army was equipped and sent into Egypt under the command of Megabyzus. This completely altered the aspect of affairs. The siege of Memphis was raised; the Greeks were compelled to burn their vessels and retire to Cyrene; Inaros and many others were taken prisoners, and carried to Susa, where the gallant chief was crucified five years afterward at the instigation of the mother of Achæmenes. By these means the greater part of Egypt was again brought under the dominion of Persia. The low and marshy lands about the mouths of the Nile, inhabited by a warlike population which had frequently been brought into contact with the Greeks, alone maintained their independence. Here Amyrtæus, who was descended from the Saitic dynasty, ruled in defiance of all foreign opposition.

Egypt was in this condition when Herodotus, the Greek historian, visited the country. It was then in a state of peace, and the Greek traveller passed in safety from the sea to the limits of Ethiopia. The frontier-towns and Memphis were occupied by Persian troops; but the worship in the temples went on as usual. Greeks were found in all the principal towns actively employed in commerce, and mingling freely with the Egyptians, notwithstanding the barrier which difference in manners and religion interposed between them. It is evident, however, that this subjection to Persia, although comparatively light, was very repugnant to public feeling in Egypt; so that, as soon as opportunity offered, it was ready to throw off the yoke. The situation of the country contributed to encourage such an effort. Far removed from the centre of government, and connected with the rest of the empire only at a single point, whatever disturbed the peace, or threatened the power of the dominant state, held out hopes to Egypt of recovering that political independence which she had maintained for many centuries. The death of Artaxerxes afforded such an opportunity. During the disputes and murders connected with the succession, there were some commotions in Egypt. These, however, led to no serious attempt to restore the national independence, until the second year of Darius, and even then it was either partially suppressed, or kept in check for eight years: for it was not until the tenth year of Darius Nothus, that the Persian rule was broken, and Egyptian independence secured.

TWENTY-EIGHTH DYNASTY.

	Years.
Amyrtæus the Saite reigned	6

It has been supposed that this sovereign is identical with the Amyrtæus who, when Inaros was defeated, and Egypt subdued by Megabyzus, established himself in the marshes of the Delta, and still maintained his independence. But the similarity of the name is insufficient to establish this identity, especially when it is considered that more than forty years elapsed between that event and the commencement of the Twenty-eighth dynasty. In all probability Kenrick's conjecture is just: that this Amyrtæus was grandson of the former, and son of Pausiris, who is said to have succeeded his father in his independent sovereignty.

We have scarcely any information from ancient authors respecting this reign, except that it is known that Amyrtæus maintained friendly relations with Athens, and entered into an alliance with the Arabians, in order to strengthen himself against any aggression on the part of Persia.

The monuments, however, bear testimony to the works of this sovereign. In the temple of Chons at Karnak is an inscription, stating that it had been repaired by him,—the first notice of the kind since Thebes was destroyed by Cambyses. There is a similar record in a temple dedicated to Sevek in Eilithyia: and Mr. Kenrick states that the sarcophagus in the British Museum, which Dr. Edward Daniel Clarke believed to have been that of Alexander the Great, was made for this monarch, and bears his shield.

TWENTY-NINTH DYNASTY: FOUR MENDESIAN KINGS.

	Years.	Months.
1. Nepherites reigned	6	
2. Achoris	13	
3. Psammuthis	1	
4. Nepherites		4
Duration of the dynasty	20	4

It seems at first sight strange that the Saite dynasty should close, and a new one be established on the throne of Egypt, without an effort on the part of Persia to reduce it again to subjection. The circumstances of the imperial government, however, explain the case. Just at this time the Medes revolted: soon afterward Darius Nothus died; and Cyrus, with the aid of the famous "Ten Thousand" Greeks, endeavoured to wrest the throne from his elder brother. Persia was, in consequence, in no condition to carry her arms into Egypt.

The name of the first sovereign of this dynasty is not found on any building in Egypt, but is inscribed on a statue in the Museum at Bologna. He sent substantial aid to the Lacedæmonians, when they were engaged in resisting the Persian arms in Asia Minor; but it happened to fall into the hands of the enemy.

After the death of Nepherites, Evagoras of Salamis solicited the aid of Achoris against Persia, and obtained supplies of corn, and fifty vessels. The name of this Pharaoh is found at Medinet-Abou, and among the ruins of Karnak. The quarries of Mokatlam also contain his shield; and there is a sphinx in the Museum of Paris, on the base of which his name is found hieroglyphically written, with the addition, "the beloved of Kneph."

Of the short reign of Psammuthis there are no records; but his shield has been found at Karnak.

THIRTIETH DYNASTY: THREE SEBENNYTIC KINGS.

	Years.
1. Nectanebus reigned	18
2. Teos	2
3. Nectanebus	18
The dynasty lasted	38 years.

There is considerable difficulty in fixing with precision the chronology of these reigns. It seems a settled point, that the Saite dynasty terminated B. C. 408. The lists give but twenty years and four months for the twenty-ninth dynasty; and yet there are many reasons for placing the accession of the thirtieth dynasty B. C. 380, instead of 388 or 387 B. C. One of the most important of these reasons is the circumstance, which has been strongly urged, that Nectanebus II. was only in the eleventh year of his reign when Ochus, B. C. 350, expelled him from the kingdom, and again subdued Egypt to the dominion of Persia. Yet it is not easy to reconcile this with the fact, that all the lists state the reign of the last of the Pharaohs to be eighteen years: and as, throughout, the authority of the ancient records has been admitted, so here I have adopted them as the safest guides.

The first event of consequence in the history of Egypt under this dynasty which meets our notice, is a Persian invasion of a most formidable character: the more so, because the oriental troops were strongly supported by an army of Greeks under Iphicrates. The Persian commander was Pharnabazus. With means quite sufficient to subdue the whole country, this expedition was rendered perfectly useless by the jealousy and suspicion which existed between the two generals.

The name of Nectanebus is found at Philæ on a temple dedicated to Athor; and also at Medinet-Abou in a small building of elegant workmanship, in which he appears presenting offerings to Amun Re and the other Theban deities. The thirteenth year of this king is mentioned on a stele preserved at Rome.

Teos, or, as he was named by the Greeks, Tachos, was the next sovereign. He had scarcely assumed the reins of government, when he was alarmed by the menacing attitude assumed by the court of Persia. He immediately applied to Sparta for assistance; and Agesilaus, willing to assist a nation friendly to the Lacedæmonians, went himself to Egypt with a strong force of Greek auxiliaries. It appears that the Egyptian king, having heard much of the fame of the Spartan warrior, was greatly surprised to see him a feeble and diminutive old man. He therefore refused to fulfil the intimation which had been given, by placing him in command of the army; but allowed him only the direction of the Greek force, while he put the fleet under the orders of Chabrias the Athenian. Nor was this the only instance in which the famed Spartan found himself grievously disappointed in the prosecution of this enterprise. Tachos, in raising funds for the war, as well as in the appointment of his officers, appears to have been guided by the advice of the sage Athenian. But this proved fatal to his cause. While his military policy rendered the Spartan his enemy, his financial measures were not only generally unpopular in Egypt, but peculiarly obnoxious to the priesthood. The Egyptian armament had, in consequence, scarcely commenced operations in Phenicia and Syria, before Nectanebus, nephew of the king, who commanded a section of the army,—advised by his father, who held an important post in Egypt,—revolted; and, being joined by Agesilaus and the Greek troops, compelled Tachos to fly to Sidon. The insurgents then defeated Mendasius, who had been named as heir to Tachos, and secured possession of the throne. Tachos, after having been thus driven into exile, repaired to the palace of the Persian monarch, where he was well received; and, having counselled a Persian invasion of Egypt, shortly after died.

Nectanebus II., having usurped the throne of his uncle, administered the affairs of the kingdom with considerable ability and success. Artaxerxes died in the ninth year of Nectanebus, and was succeeded by his son Darius Ochus. This prince was at once cruel and unwarlike. At first he gave way to indolence, and directed several attacks to be made on Egypt, which were always easily repelled; until, at last, roused by the ridicule which these failures excited, and especially by the defection of the rulers of Cyprus and Phenicia, who, in consequence of his sloth, had despised his power and revolted, he prepared himself for action, and marched, at the head of a formidable force, into Western Asia.

He commenced his operations by reducing Cyprus and Phenicia; after which, having added to his army ten thousand Thebans, Argives, and Asiatic Greeks, he proceeded toward Egypt. In passing the desert, he sustained a serious loss of troops in the quicksands; but he succeeded in reaching Pelusium with a powerful army. Nectanebus had made every possible provision for the defence of his kingdom, and the first operations of the war were conducted on both sides with great spirit. It appears, however, that the Greek auxiliaries in the service of Persia managed to out-general the Egyptian king, and establish themselves in force in the rear of his position. This forced Nectanebus to retire to Memphis,—a measure which compelled the garrison of Pelusium to surrender, and led to the subjugation of the whole country. For Ochus, having behaved with great moderation to the Egyptians who had fallen into his power, and having punished with death some Persian soldiers who had attempted to spoil the garrison of Pelusium, contrary to the articles of capitulation, produced an impression that those who submitted first would be treated best. The people, therefore, eagerly received him; and Nectanebus was compelled to fly into Ethiopia. Thus was Egypt again completely reduced, and made a province of the Persian empire, B. C. 350.

THIRTY-FIRST DYNASTY: PERSIAN KINGS.

	Years.
1. Darius Ochus reigned	12
2. Arses	2
3. Darius Codomannus	4

The fair promise of leniency and conciliation which the conduct of Ochus gave to Egypt during the war, completely vanished when his power was established over that kingdom. He not only imitated the outrages of Cambyses, but greatly excelled him in wanton cruelty. He caused Apis to be killed, dressed, and served up to a banquet, he and his friends feasting on his flesh. He commanded an ass to receive the honours due to the god. He spoiled the temples, taking away gold, silver, and sacred records. The latter were, indeed, restored, but only after extorting a large sum from the priests as the price of their redemption. The walls of the principal towns were razed, to prevent their being formidable in future. Wanton injustice, murders, profanations of sacred rites, and continual persecutions characterized his government; and thus Egypt groaned in affliction until he retired from the country. To show their abhorrence of his memory, the Egyptians substituted for his name, in their catalogue of kings, the figure of a sword, as the emblem of destruction.

Nothing is known of the internal government of Egypt from the departure of Ochus to the invasion of Alexander. The severe character of the administration may, however, be inferred from the fact, that the Macedonian conqueror was hailed with great joy by the people of that country.

THIRTY-SECOND DYNASTY: MACEDONIANS.

		Years.	B. C.
Alexander reigned		9	332
Philip Aridæus	} Ptolemy governor {	6	323
Alexander (son of the Great)		6	317
Duration of the dynasty		21 years.	

Alexander, having established his power in Egypt, had to leave it, for the purpose of prosecuting his gigantic schemes of foreign conquest. But, prior to doing this, he planned the building of a new city on the sea-coast, to be called after his own name, Alexandria. He made Cleomenes general overseer of this great work, and Dinocrates—who had become famous by rebuilding the temple of Diana at Ephesus, after it had been burned down by Eratostratus— architect of the buildings. He also settled the government on a plan as original as might be expected from his genius. Wishing that the land might be governed by its own established laws and customs, he appointed Doloaspes, an Egyptian, the civil governor of the whole country. But, not wishing to intrust him, or any other individual, with all the military power of such an important kingdom, he divided it into districts, and placed the military force of each in the hands of a separate lieutenant. These were all independent of each other; and their power was limited to the several sections over which they were called to preside. Egypt was governed in this manner during the life of Alexander. On his death his four principal generals agreed to place his natural brother Aridæus on the throne under the name of "Philip,"—at the same time appointing themselves to the government of four great divisions of the empire, which they were to rule in the name of the new king. Under this arrangement, Ptolemy obtained Egypt, Libya, Arabia, Palestine, and Cœle-Syria, and fixed the seat of his government in Egypt.

Throughout the remainder of this period incessant plots and counter-plots, wars, treasons, and murders, prevailed. In all of these, however, Ptolemy maintained his ground in Egypt. From the first, he aimed at ruling with justice and moderation, and adopted such measures as not only endeared him to the Egyptians, but induced many of the Greeks to go and reside in Egypt. But this anomalous state of things could not continue long. In 317 B. C., Olympias, the mother of Alexander, having returned to Macedonia, and got the principal power into her hands, caused Aridæus and his wife to be put to death. The youthful Alexander, the son of Roxana, was now called "king," and continued to bear that title until 311 B.C., when Cassander, who had for a long time shut him and his mother up in prison, had them both privately murdered. Thus was terminated even the nominal rule of the family of the great Macedonian.

THIRTY-THIRD DYNASTY: THE PTOLEMIES.

	Years.	Began B. C.
Lagus or Soter reigned	27	311
Philadelphus	38	284
Euergetes	25	246
Philopator	17	221
Epiphanes	24	204
Philometer	35	180
Euergetes II	29	145
Soter II	10	116
Alexander I. (Soter deposed)	18	106
Soter II. restored	7	88
Berenice	6 months.	81
Alexander II	15	80
Neus Dionysus	14	65
Ptolemy the Elder	4	51
Ptolemy the Younger	3	47
Cleopatra	14	44
Egypt a Roman province	30	30

As the reader has been already informed, Ptolemy ruled Egypt from the date of the death of Alexander the Great, although he did not assume the royal style and title until B. C. 305. For some years indeed after the death of the younger Alexander, there were incessant wars between those generals who had divided the empire among them. In the course of these conflicts Antigonus had wrested Phenicia, Judea, and Syria from Ptolemy; while Demetrius, the son of Antigonus, succeeded in subduing the Island of Cyprus, notwithstanding the utmost efforts of Ptolemy to retain it. But the restless ambition of Antigonus compelled the other generals to form a combination against him; in consequence of which a great battle was fought, near Issus, a city in Phrygia, B. C. 301, in which Antigonus was slain, and his son Demetrius compelled to fly at the head of only five thousand men. This confirmed Ptolemy in his government, and enabled him to consolidate his power, and devote his energies to the internal improvement of his kingdom.

In these efforts he displayed great moderation and practical wisdom. Notwithstanding his intense partiality for Greek manners, he did not attempt to Hellenize Egypt. On the contrary, he revived, as far as altered circumstances would allow, its ancient religion and form of government. He restored the priesthood to a large portion of their pristine power and privilege; renewed the division of the country into nomes; declared Memphis, although not the usual residence of the sovereign, the capital of the country; and its temple of Pthah the national sanctuary, where alone the kings could receive the crown.

These prudent measures were accompanied by a wise and liberal scheme of commercial policy. Under its fostering influence Alexandria rose into great power and prosperity. Merchants from all the neighbouring nations traded thither. Nor did Ptolemy, in his martial, civil, and commercial cares and plans, overlook the higher and more elevating pursuits of learning and philosophy. He planned or erected a splendid museum, or college of philosophy, and supported its professors and teachers from the public funds. These measures were too grand in their scope and character to produce much immediate benefit; but the basis was laid for future prosperity: a seed was sown which produced fruit through succeeding centuries. Another element which contributed in no insignificant degree to the welfare of Egypt was the large influx of Jews who were introduced into the kingdom. This importation was begun in the early part of his government. Enraged that the Jews, who had sworn allegiance to Laomedon, afterward refused to submit to himself, Ptolemy assaulted Jerusalem on the Sabbath-day, and carried away nearly one hundred thousand of the inhabitants into Egypt. (Hebrew People, p. 411.) But afterward, considering that the fidelity of this people ought to have entitled them to his respect, he treated them kindly, and trusted several important posts to their keeping, and allowed them the same privileges as they had enjoyed under Alexander. By these means many of this nation were induced to go voluntarily and settle in Alexandria and other parts of Egypt, where their industry and talents made them an important portion of the community. By this means the worship of the true God, and a large amount of revealed truth were placed prominently before the Egyptian people.

Another most valuable result of the establishment of a Greek sovereignty in Egypt, was the impulse which real learning and sound philosophy thereby received. With a sovereign, Greece gave Egypt her literature. The far-famed wisdom of Egypt had long before this become obsolete, and exhibited at best a kind of mummy-existence,— a lifeless resemblance of its former glory. But the patronage which Ptolemy gave to philosophy and art, opened up one of the greatest revivals of science and learning which the world has seen. By a remarkable coincidence, Egypt, although but the shadow of her former self, contributed most essentially to this important result. While Greece gave her learning, Egypt presented in return the *papyrus*,— a boon at that day only inferior, as a means of communicating knowledge, to the invention of printing. Before this time books had been written on linen, wax, or the bark of trees; and public records on stone, brass, or lead. But the *papyrus* afforded a medium so much more convenient and cheap, that it gave an immense impetus to learning, so that many persons then possessed books who had never previously seen them. Even in Greece and Rome this substance was almost exclusively used, as long as it could be procured.

Under these influences Egypt arose into new life and vigour, and again assumed a most important position among the independent nations of the world. Ptolemy had married Eurydice, the daughter of Antipater, and had by her his eldest son Ptolemy Ceraunus. But, having been greatly fascinated with Berenice, who came into Egypt as a companion to Eurydice, he married her also, and was ever after so much under her influence, that, in order effectually to exclude his eldest son from succeeding to the throne, he associated Ptolemy Philadelphus, the son of Berenice, with him in the government during his lifetime. During the year of their joint rule, the famous watchtower, or light-house, of Pharos was finished. It was a large square building of white marble, on the top of which fires were kept burning, as a guide to shipping entering the port of Alexandria.

Ptolemy Philadelphus succeeded to the undivided dominion of Egypt, B. C. 284, on the death of his father. Under his government Egypt attained the summit of power and fame. Here commerce was unrivalled; learning acquired an influence and honour unknown in any other nation of the day. The Museum of Philosophy and the Royal Library would have been the glory of any age or nation. Euclid, Conon, and Hipparchus had imparted to the schools all the weight of their great character. Manetho, the great Egyptian historian, wrote at this period; while Aristarchus, as a critic, and Apollonius Rhodius, as a poet, adorned and strengthened this galaxy of science.

But perhaps one of the greatest achievements of this age was the translation of the Hebrew Scriptures into Greek, at the instance of the sovereign. Thus the inspired books became patent to the world, and all the glorious truths of Old-Testament revelation were placed in the hands of the learned. No other language could at that time have obtained such currency for the sacred volume as the Greek.

It is a singular and significant fact, that just at the time when this Ptolemy was securing a translation of the Hebrew Scriptures, he was also engaged in the removal of the idol Serapis from Pontus to Egypt. For this image a most magnificent temple was erected in one of the suburbs of Alexandria. Here, too, was deposited that famous library which grew to be one of the most extensive collections of writings which the world ever witnessed.

Under Ptolemy Philadelphus, Egypt became the first maritime and commercial power of the age, and was scarcely second to any in military strength. By building a city on the western bank of the Red Sea, and another, named after his mother Berenice, almost on the frontiers of Ethiopia, he succeeded in engrossing all that trade which had successively enriched Judea and Phenicia. Like these nations, also, he added to this maritime traffic the overland caravan-trade with Arabia and the East.

This monarch, having heard that the Romans had succeeded, after a struggle of six years, in driving Pyrrhus, King of Epirus, out of Italy, sent ambassadors to Rome, congratulating the senate on their success. This being the first time that any Egyptians had appeared in Rome, and the Romans being flattered by the attention of a nation so celebrated as Egypt, they sent ambassadors in return, and thus established friendly relations between the two countries. It seems probable that this may have had considerable influence on the destiny of the rising republic. For when, twenty years afterward, the Carthaginians sent to request Ptolemy to lend them two thousand talents, to aid them in their war with Rome, the king of Egypt replied, "I will assist you against enemies or indifferent persons; but cannot, without a breach of fidelity, lend one friend any aid against another."

The tranquillity of the country was for a while disturbed during this reign by Magus, the king's half-brother, to whom he had intrusted the government of Libya and Cyrene. But Ptolemy repelled the aggression, and defeated all his efforts, and was ultimately reconciled to him. This prince died B. C. 246, having reigned thirty-eight years.

Ptolemy Euergetes succeeded his father. He was scarcely seated on the throne when he was drawn into a war with Seleucus Callinicus, King of Syria, in consequence of the murder of Berenice, sister of Ptolemy, who had been a wife to the father of Seleucus. Having collected a numerous army, Ptolemy crossed the desert; but instead of directing his march immediately to Syria, as might be expected from the peculiar cause of the war, he overran Palestine, Babylonia, Persia, and the rich provinces of Upper Asia, and came back laden with an enormous amount of spoils. On his return he attacked Seleucus, defeated him with great slaughter, and compelled him to take refuge in Antioch. The Egyptian army then returned home, having gained immense booty, but no real addition of territory, by the war. Not only was the wealth thus acquired prodigious, but we hear on this occasion, and, I think, for the first time, of works of art and *virtù* being carried off by the conqueror. Ptolemy, we are told, brought back with him two thousand five hundred pictures and statues, among which were many of the Egyptian idols which Cambyses had taken from Egypt. This greatly pleased the Egyptians, and they in consequence gave Ptolemy the name of *Euergetes*, "the Beneficent."

Having concluded this war, and made peace with the king of Syria, Euergetes devoted himself to the promotion of learning, and the completion of his father's object in the formation of a national library. With this design he sent learned men into distant countries, to purchase at any price such books as they thought desirable; and thus he greatly added to the literary treasures previously collected. Upon the death of Zenodotus, who had been librarian from the time of Ptolemy Soter, Euergetes invited from Athens Eratosthenes, a learned Cyrenian, to take this duty on him,—a trust which he discharged with honour to himself and great benefit to the institution.

Toward the close of his reign, Ptolemy Euergetes again directed his attention to martial pursuits; and having led an army southward, he made himself master of both sides of the Red Sea, as far as the straits which connect it with the ocean. Having perfectly succeeded in his object, he found on his return to Egypt, that Cleomenes, King of Sparta, was involved in a Grecian war. At first Ptolemy felt disposed to aid the Achæans; but taking offence at their application to Antigonus, King of Macedon, he sent considerable support to Cleomenes. Notwithstanding this aid, the Spartan king was completely defeated in the battle of Salasia, and compelled to take refuge in Egypt, where Ptolemy allowed him a yearly stipend of twenty-four talents, and promised, as soon as an opportunity offered, to assist him to recover his throne. But before any favourable occasion presented itself, Ptolemy died, and left the government to his son.

During this reign Egypt was restored to the zenith of prosperity. Her power secured the respect of every other nation; her civilization equalled, if not exceeded, that of all surrounding countries; while her commerce, far beyond that of all her contemporaries, filled the public treasury with wealth, and diffused plenty and contentment throughout the country. In looking back on the state of Egypt in those times, it seems as if, under the first three Ptolemies, it had arisen from the prostration of ages into an intelligence and power equal to that possessed by any nation of the day. But, alas! this exaltation was very short-lived. With Ptolemy Euergetes the sun of Egyptian prosperity sank from its meridian altitude, and began to verge toward decline. The authors of the "Universal History" say of him, "He was the last of his race in whom any virtue, humanity, or moderation appeared." Though we are hardly disposed to adopt this language, it may safely be said that in scarcely any other instance do we see such striking results flow to a country from the individual character of its sovereigns. Here is a nation rescued from a chaos of confusion,—political, commercial, general; for this was the condition of Egypt when conquered by Alexander. Yet under three successive rulers it rises into a proud preëminence in all respects over every neighbouring country. Again we look; and under the descendants of these kings the same land, without any external or other prominent cause, is seen reduced once more to weakness, confusion, and subjection. This circumstance will render the further account of its history more brief than might otherwise be expected.

Ptolemy, called *Philopator*, "a Lover of his Father," ascended the throne B. C. 221. He was a weak and wicked prince, and rendered his government odious and mischievous by resigning himself generally to the direction of unworthy favourites. By the instigation of his minister, Sosibius, he caused his brother Magus to be murdered, lest he might endeavour to secure the kingdom to himself. The death of Cleomenes, the exiled King of Sparta, who had been protected and provided for by the preceding king, soon followed. Antiochus the Great, who at this time ruled in Syria, perceiving the disorder and licentiousness which prevailed in the court of Egypt, thought it a favourable time to declare war against that country. Ptolemy, who seems not to have lacked courage, roused himself to the emergency, collected a great army, and proceeded to meet the enemy. In the beginning of the war, Antiochus obtained some advantages over the Egyptian troops: but shortly after, in a great battle fought at Raphia, near Gaza, he was completely defeated, with great loss; and Ptolemy obtained a large extension of influence in Palestine and Syria. Humbled by this defeat, and alarmed at the progress of Achæus in Asia Minor, Antiochus was anxious to make peace with Ptolemy; and the Egyptian king, although he had every inducement to prosecute the war, being equally anxious to return to his licentious pleasures, was ready to receive his overtures. A peace was in consequence concluded, by which Cœle-Syria and Palestine were confirmed as belonging to Egypt. This being done, Ptolemy went to Jerusalem, where he was well received, and treated the inhabitants kindly, until, having made a fruitless attempt to enter the inner sanctuary, (Hebrew People, p. 414,) he retired from the city threatening the whole nation of the Jews with extermination. It does not appear that he dared to assail the sacred city; but, on returning to Egypt, he published a decree, which he caused to be engraved on a pillar erected at the gate of his palace, excluding all who did not sacrifice to the gods whom he worshipped. By this means the Jews were virtually outlawed, being prevented from suing to him for justice, or from claiming his protection. But this was not the extent of his infliction. By another decree he reduced them from the first rank of citizens—to which they had been raised by the favour of Alexander—to the third rank. They were in consequence degraded so far as to be enrolled among the common people of Egypt. When commanded to appear for this enrolment, they were ordered to have an ivy-leaf, the badge of Bacchus, branded on their faces; those thus marked were consigned to slavery. Yet, notwithstanding the offering of sacrifice to the heathen gods presented a ready exemption from these dreadful penalties, but very few, out of many thousands of Jews, were induced thus to apostatize. The resolute firmness of the people in resisting the king's will being construed into factious obstinacy, he determined to destroy them altogether.

All the Jews in Egypt were in consequence collected and shut up together within the hippodrome, with a view to their execution. Five hundred elephants were drawn up to execute the king's wrath. Meantime the persecuted Hebrews betook themselves to earnest prayer; and we are told that when these animals were let loose, instead of slaughtering the Jews, they turned upon the soldiers and spectators, and destroyed great numbers of them. This circumstance induced the king to forego his purpose, and to restore the Hebrews to all the dignity and privilege which they before enjoyed.

During this reign the Romans, being again at war with Carthage, sent ambassadors to Egypt, to renew their ancient friendship, who brought magnificent presents to Ptolemy and his queen.

At the death of Philopator, B. C. 204, Ptolemy Epiphanes, being then a child of five years old, ascended the throne. In the early part of his reign another Roman embassy visited Egypt, when the king's counsellors took the opportunity of placing the young prince under the guardianship of the powerful republic. The senate of Rome accepted the charge, and sent Marcus Lepidus to act as guardian,—a trust which, after a short stay in Egypt, he conferred upon Aristomenes, an Acarnanian, who discharged the duties of this important office with integrity and ability for several years, until the king had attained the age of fourteen, when, according to the usage of the country, he was entitled to take the administration of the kingdom into his own hands. The folly of investing a person so young with absolute power was in this instance made fully apparent. The youth, who had been universally popular while under the direction of Aristomenes, was no sooner enthroned than he placed himself under the influence of worthless men, by whose advice he was led to the adoption of measures through which great disorders were introduced into every branch of the government; and at length his former able and honest minister was put to death.

Epiphanes married Cleopatra, daughter of Antiochus the Great. This marriage appears to have taken place when the young king was but about seventeen years old. It is generally supposed that he was taken off by poison, administered by his nobles, to prevent him from entering on a war with Syria, to which he had committed himself, when the national finances were so low that they feared they should have to contribute largely toward the expenses of the contest. He left two sons, Philometer and Physcon; and a daughter, Cleopatra, who was successively married to her two brothers.

Philometer, the elder of the two sons, then but six years old, was placed on the throne under the guardianship of his mother, Cleopatra, who for eight years conducted the affairs of the kingdom with great judgment and success. After her death, Lannæus, a nobleman of distinction, and Eulæus, a eunuch, were charged with the government of the country. One of their earliest measures was to insist on the restoration of Cœle-Syria and Palestine to Egypt,—these provinces having been wrested from the dominion of Egypt by Antiochus the Great. This demand led to a violent contest, which tended more than any preceding event to demonstrate the rapid decline of Egyptian power, and the rising sway of Rome.

The Syrian army, under the command of Antiochus Epiphanes, prosecuted the war with such vigour and success that it penetrated to the walls of Alexandria, and actually secured the person of the Egyptian king. Whether he was taken in war, or placed himself willingly in the hands of the Syrian king, does not clearly appear. But, however this may be, the Syrian monarch gained little by his acquisition. For, although he induced Philometer to enter into a treaty with him, this was instantly disallowed by the nation, who, regarding a sovereign in the power of an enemy as lost to his country, immediately raised Physcon, the king's brother, to the throne. This led to a second Syrian invasion, which resulted in the expulsion of Physcon; Antiochus restoring Philometer to the government, but retaining Pelusium, the key to the country, in the possession of Syrian troops. From this and other indications of the Syrian king's intentions, Philometer rightly judged that it was his design, by setting the two brothers in continued collision with each other, to retain Egypt virtually in his own power. Acting on this judgment, Philometer invited his brother to terms of reconciliation, which, by the aid of their sister Cleopatra, was happily effected.

The measures adopted by the two brothers to restore Egypt to an independent and prosperous condition induced Antiochus again to march an army into that country. He was on this occasion, however, compelled, by the prompt and energetic interference of the Romans, to abandon the enterprise. By agreement between the two brothers, they were to reign jointly; but they were no sooner freed from the danger of foreign aggression than they began to quarrel among themselves. This quickly produced an open rupture, in which Physcon succeeded in driving his brother out of the kingdom. He was, however, soon after restored by the power of Rome, which at the same time assigned Libya and Cyrene to Physcon. New disputes arose, and various contests took place between them, in all of which Rome regarded herself as entitled to act as the paramount ruler of Egypt, and to award its sovereignty according to her will.

Philometer was soon after provoked into a war with Alexander Bala, who had been raised to the throne of Syria mainly by his support. In the prosecution of this contest, the king of Egypt marched into Syria, where he completely routed the army of Alexander near Antioch, but died a few days after of wounds received in the battle. He left behind him a high reputation for wisdom and clemency. It was in his reign, and by his favour and that of his queen, Cleopatra, that the Jews under Onias were permitted to build the famous Jewish temple at Heliopolis.

On the death of her husband, Cleopatra endeavoured to secure the crown for their son: but some of the leading men inclined toward Physcon, and invited him from Cyrene, where he then reigned, into Egypt. The queen raised an army to oppose him, and a civil war was imminent, when an accommodation was arranged, through the mediation of Rome, by which Physcon married Cleopatra, who was his sister and his brother's widow, on the understanding that they were to reign with joint authority, and that Cleopatra's son by Philometer should be declared next heir to the crown. This agreement was no sooner completed than it was violated. On the day of his marriage Physcon murdered the son of Philometer in the arms of his mother, and commenced a career of iniquity and slaughter of which this was a fitting prelude. He indeed assumed the name of *Euergetes*, or "Benefactor," which the Alexandrians changed into *Kakergetes*, or "the Evil-doer,"—an epithet which he justly merited; for he was the most cruel and wicked, the most despicable and vile, of all the Ptolemies. To the Jews he evinced unmitigated enmity and cruelty, because they had espoused the cause of Cleopatra. To the Alexandrians he was no less cruel, because they had supported him,—and he feared lest those who had raised him to the throne should by the same power remove him.

During this reign three Roman ambassadors visited Egypt, while making a tour of the countries dependent on, or in alliance with, Rome. Their stay induced a cessation of Physcon's barbarous conduct, which, however, was renewed on their leaving. He then divorced Cleopatra his wife, and married her daughter, of the same name, who was his own niece; but not before he had subjected the young princess to the vilest indignity.

Such conduct excited the disgust of his subjects, and, accompanied as it was with excessive cruelty, produced a revolt which drove him from the kingdom. He, however, succeeded in recovering his position, and at length died in the sixty-seventh year of his age, having reigned twenty-nine years.

It is a fact as singular as unaccountable, that this most licentious and bloody prince, whose name is infamous, as associated with almost every crime, is notwithstanding celebrated by the most respectable ancient writers as a great restorer of learning, a patron of learned men, and withal an author of some celebrity himself. According to the testimony of Athenæus, it was his practice during the short intervals between his debaucheries, to apply himself zealously to the study of the polite arts and sciences; and he thus acquired so extensive a knowledge of all kinds of literature that he obtained the name of "Ptolemy the Philologist." The same author adds that he wrote a History in twenty-four books, and a learned Commentary on Homer. His History, Epiphanius informs us, was in great repute among the ancients: and Galen says that he enlarged and enriched the Alexandrian library by the purchase of valuable books at a great expense. Physcon left three sons,—Apion by a concubine, and Lathyrus and Alexander by his wife Cleopatra. By his will he left the kingdom of Cyrene to Apion, and the crown of Egypt to his widow in conjunction with either of her sons whom she should choose.

In the exercise of this discretionary power, the queen would have preferred Alexander, the younger son: but this was so distasteful to the people that she was compelled to admit Lathyrus to the joint sovereignty, and placed Alexander in the kingdom of Cyprus. Here we have a repetition of the mean and unnatural policy which at this period disgraced the government of this country. By repeated efforts the queen induced the people to withdraw their confidence from Lathyrus, and to consent to the return of Alexander. After reigning ten years, the former prince was obliged to leave Egypt, to which his brother immediately returned; Lathyrus repairing to Cyprus, and taking upon himself the government of that country. It was at this period that Lathyrus invaded Judea, then governed by Alexander Janneus, and obtained such advantages over him that the Jewish state was only saved from ruin by the aid sent to it by Cleopatra from Egypt. (Hebrew People, p. 443.)

In the mean time the younger brother, Alexander, having for nearly eighteen years, while bearing the name of "king," submitted as a slave to the violent and capricious will of his mother, became quite weary of her intolerable tyranny, and put her to death. This fact being made public, he was driven from the throne, and Lathyrus, or Soter II., restored, who reigned seven years longer. During this period the ruin of Thebes took place. Lathyrus, freed from the power of his rivals, undertook to restore the government of the kingdom to its former state. This led to an insurrection, of which Thebes was the centre. That ancient city not only refused to submit to the prescribed laws, but even struggled to regain its lost independence. The effort was vain. The king, having defeated the rebels in several battles, besieged Thebes, which, having held out for three years, was at length subdued, and was in consequence given up to the ravages of the soldiery, who committed such devastation that this noble capital was never afterward repaired, and consequently sank into ruin.

Lathyrus was succeeded by his only legitimate child, Cleopatra, whose proper name was Berenice. This princess, however, had scarcely assumed the sovereignty, when she was called to submit to the dictation of Roman power. Sylla, then perpetual dictator of the imperial city, no sooner heard of the death of Lathyrus, than he conferred the crown of Egypt on Alexander, a son of the king of that name who had been driven out of the country for having murdered his mother; he was consequently a nephew of the deceased king. On his arrival in Egypt, where Berenice had reigned six months, his presence occasioned great consternation. The Alexandrians were unwilling to create a rupture with Rome, and equally so to set aside a reigning sovereign on the nomination of another ruler by a foreign power. To avert the difficulty, they succeeded in persuading Alexander to marry Berenice, and reign jointly with her. This he did; but, in nineteen days afterward, caused her to be murdered. He, however, continued on the throne, and reigned fifteen years in a manner which might be expected from the atrocity of the commencement. At length the people, worn out by his exactions, and goaded to desperation by his cruelties, rose with common consent, and drove him from the throne. He made some fruitless efforts to induce Pompey to aid him to recover his crown, but died, a few months after his expulsion, in banishment at Tyre.

The Egyptians, having driven out this tyrant, selected a natural son of Ptolemy Lathyrus to fill the vacant throne. This prince, by a gift of six thousand talents (about £500,000) to Julius Cæsar and Pompey, was recognised as king of Egypt in alliance with Rome. He was named Ptolemy *Auletes*, or "the Flute-player;" but took on himself the title of *Dionysus Neos*, or "the New Bacchus." He was a fit representative of the fallen condition of the Egyptian state. More effeminate than any of his predecessors, priding himself on dancing in a female dress in religious processions, he was at the same time equal to his grandfather Physcon in the violence and viciousness of his conduct. After some time he was, like his predecessor, expelled from the throne. He succeeded, however, by immense gifts, in inducing Gabinius, the Roman governor of Syria, to attempt his restoration, which was at length accomplished; Archelaus, who had been invested with the government, having been defeated, and slain by the Romans. Auletes was thus restored to the throne, and died in peaceable possession of his dignity about four years after his restoration.

Auletes, on his restoration, had put to death his daughter Berenice; and at his demise left two daughters, Cleopatra and Arsinoë, and two sons. The first of these, Ptolemy the Elder, otherwise called Dionysius II., was, according to his father's will, married to his eldest sister, then about seventeen years old: and the juvenile couple were invested with the sovereignty of Egypt, under the protection of the Roman republic. It appears that this most celebrated Egyptian princess evinced considerable vigour and talent, even at that early age. So clever, indeed, was she, that the ministers who had been placed in charge of the national affairs were very anxious to get rid of her, and at length deprived her of her share in the sovereignty, and expelled her from the kingdom. Cleopatra, however, had a spirit equal to the occasion. She retired into Syria, raised an army, and in a short time marched upon Pelusium, prepared to dispute with her brother the sovereignty of the nation. It was while the hostile armies of the brother and sister lay within sight of each other, that Pompey, after the loss of the battle of Pharsalia, reached Egypt, expecting protection and support, but was put to death by the ministers of Ptolemy. Soon after this event, Julius Cæsar arrived in pursuit of his rival, and was presented with his head and his ring.

Cleopatra, whose licentiousness was quite equal to her talent and energy, caused herself to be secretly conveyed to the quarters of Cæsar, where she succeeded in captivating that mighty conqueror, and commencing an intimacy which resulted in the birth of a son, called, after his father, Neocæsar. The scandal of this conduct enabled Ptolemy and his ministers to rouse the public spirit of the Alexandrians, and of Lower Egypt generally, against the mighty Roman, to such an extent that he was placed in most imminent peril. Cæsar, however, disposed the handful of soldiers which he had with him in such a manner as to keep the Egyptians in check, until the arrival of Mithridates with large reinforcements, when he defeated the Egyptian forces with great slaughter. In the course of this conflict Ptolemy was drowned in the Nile.

Cæsar soon adjusted the affairs of Egypt to his own mind, placing Cleopatra on the throne. But as the Egyptians had a great antipathy to female sovereignty, he compelled Cleopatra to submit to the farce of marrying her younger brother, a lad eleven years old. She, however, held the power in her own hand, until he reached the age of fourteen, when by the laws of the country he was entitled to enter upon the joint administration of affairs. She then caused him to be poisoned. Arsinoë, who had been carried to Rome by Julius Cæsar, and compelled to walk, bound in chains of gold, before his triumphal chariot, was also assassinated at the instigation of Cleopatra.

The death of Cæsar convulsed the whole empire of Rome and all its dependencies, and swept away the last feeble figment of Egyptian monarchy and independence. On this occasion Cleopatra instantly decided to support the triumvirs against the murderers of Julius. On a charge of being unfaithful to this purpose, she was summoned to appear before Antony at Tarsus. Confident in the power of her charms, she obeyed, and effectually seduced that great captain. In fact, so besotted was he by this intercourse, that he neglected his affairs, and was at length so completely ruined, that, having inflicted on himself a mortal wound, he died in the arms of his wanton mistress. Cleopatra had two sons by Antony, and soon after his decease she shared the fate which she had brought on him. To avoid being made a spectacle at the triumph of Augustus, as he was proof against her seductive charms, she procured her own death by the bite of an asp. Egypt then became a province of the Roman empire, and continued in this state until the birth of Christ, and long afterward.

Thus Egypt flourished, and fell. Her history affords ample proof of the cultivation of the human mind in early times, and forms the great connecting link between European annals and the primitive nations. If our limits would allow, the subject would furnish rich materials for extended disquisition. We can, however, only observe that the chapter of history which has been thus sketched shows a most uncommon identity of character. In times so remote that the light of history scarcely renders objects visible, we just perceive colossal forms of civilization, learning, wealth, and power, standing out before us in wondrous array. As we descend the stream of time, when everything becomes well defined, Egypt appears equal in every respect to the proudest of her contemporaries. Yes, and strange to say, when her martial prowess had declined, and she fell beneath the sword of the invincible Macedonian, his genius, by the erection of Alexandria, laid new foundations for the stability and resources of Egypt, and made her, amid the waning of every other ancient kingdom, the mart of commerce and the seat of wealth. Notwithstanding the lengthened rule of the Ptolemies, who had been placed on the throne by Grecian power, and the overwhelming influence of Rome in the time of Cæsar, the adherence of the people to their old usages continued intact, and marked the last struggle which placed Egypt at the feet of imperial Rome. (See *Appendix*, note 11.)

A CHRONOLOGICAL TABLE OF THE KINGS OF EGYPT.

Year before Christ.	An arrangement of Dynasties and Reigns.	Length of Reign. Y. M.
1845	The Hyksos expelled from Egypt by Amosis, who reigned................................	25 —
	XVIII. DYNASTY.—SIXTEEN SOVEREIGNS.—348 YEARS.	
1820	(1) Amenophis I.................	30 7
1789	(2) Thothmosis I.................	13 —
1776	(3) Thothmosis II................	20 7
1755	(4) Amense (*sister of the last king*)................................	21 9
1734	(5) Thothmosis III. (*son of Amense*)..........................	12 9
1721	(6) Amenophis II.................	25 10
1695	(7) Thothmosis IV................	9 8
1685	(8) Amenophis III. (*Memnon*)	30 5
1655	(9) Horus.........................	38 5
1617	(10) Ramses I.....................	9 —
1608	(11) Sethos I.....................	32 8
1575	(12) Ramses II....................	5 5
1569	(13) Ramses III. (*Sesostris*)....	68 2
1501	(14) Manephtha...................	5 —
1496	(15) Sethos II....................	19 6
1477	(16) Sethos III...................	5 3
	XIX. DYNASTY.—FIVE KINGS.—187 YEARS.	
1472	(1) Sethos........................	55 —
1417	(2) Rampses......................	66 —
1351	(3) Amenepthes...................	40 —
1311	(4) Rameses......................	— —
1311	(5) Ammenemnes.................	26 —
	XX. DYNASTY.—TWELVE KINGS.—178 YEARS.	
1285	This was a Diospolitan Dynasty, most, if not all, of whom were called Rameses; but the length of the reigns is not given.	
	XXI. DYNASTY.—SEVEN THINITE KINGS.—130 YEARS.	
1107	(1) Smendes.......................	26 —
1081	(2) Psousennes....................	41 —
1040	(3) Nephercheres..................	4 —
1036	(4) Amenophthis..................	9 —
1027	(5) Osochor.......................	6 —
1021	(6) Psinaches (II.)................	9 —
1012	(7) Psousennes....................	35 —
	XXII. DYNASTY.—NINE BUBASTILE KINGS.—116 YEARS.	
977	(1) Sesonchis (*Shishak*)...	21 —
956	(2) Osorthon.....................	15 —
941	(3, 4, 5) Three other kings, names omitted........	25 —
916	(6) Tacelothis....................	13 —
903	(7, 8, 9) Three other kings, whose names are not given...................	42 —
	XXIII. DYNASTY.—FOUR TANITE KINGS.—89 YEARS.	
861	(1) Petubatis.....................	40 —
821	(2) Osorcho......................	8 —
813	(3) Psammus.....................	10 —
803	(4) Zet...........................	31 —
	XXIV. DYNASTY.—ONE SAITE KING.—44 YEARS.	
772	(1) Bocchoris....................	44 —
	XXV. DYNASTY.—THREE ETHIOPIC KINGS.—40 YEARS.	
728	(1) Sabaco.......................	8 —
720	(2) Sebichos (*Sevechus*)..........	12 —
708	(3) Tarkus.......................	18 —
	XXVI. DYNASTY.—NINE SAITE KINGS.—164 YEARS, 6 MONTHS.	
690	(1) Stephinates...................	7 —
683	(2) Nechepsos....................	6 —

THE GENTILE NATIONS.

Year before Christ.	An arrangement of Dynasties and Reigns.	Length of Reign. Y. M.
677	(3) Nechao I.	8 —
669	(4) Psammitichus	54 —
615	(5) Nechao II.	16 —
599	(6) Psammuthis	6 —
593	(7) Uaphris (*Apries, Hophra*)	25 —
568	(8) Amosis	42 —
526	(9) Psammecherites	— 6

XXVII. DYNASTY.—EIGHT PERSIAN KINGS.—111 YEARS, 4 MONTHS.

525	(1) Cambyses (in the fifth year of his Persian reign)	3 —
522	(2) Darius Hystaspis	36 —
486	(3) Xerxes (the Great)	21 —
465	(4) Artabanus	— 7
464	(5) Artaxerxes	41 —
423	(6) Xerxes II.	— 2
423	(7) Sogdianus	— 7
423	(8) Darius (*son of Xerxes*)	9 —

XXVIII. DYNASTY.—ONE SAITE KING.—6 YEARS.

414	(1) Amyrtæus	6 —

XXIX. DYNASTY.—FOUR MENDESIAN KINGS.—20 YEARS, 4 MONTHS.

408	(1) Nepherites I.	6 —
402	(2) Achoris	13 —
389	(3) Psammuthis	1 —
388	(4) Nepherites II.	— 4

XXX. DYNASTY.—THREE SEBENNYTIC KINGS.—38 YEARS.

388	(1) Nectanebus I.	18 —
370	(2) Teos	2 —
368	(3) Nectanebus II.	18 —

XXXI. DYNASTY.—THREE PERSIAN KINGS.—18 YEARS.

350	(1) Darius Ochus	12 —
338	(2) Arses	2 —
336	(3) Darius Codomannus	4 —

XXXII. DYNASTY.—THREE MACEDONIANS.—21 YEARS.

332	(1) Alexander (the Great)	9 —
323	(2) Philip Aridæus (Ptolemy, governor)	6 —
317	(3) Alexander (*son of the Great*: Ptolemy, governor)	6 —

XXXIII. DYNASTY.—THE PTOLEMIES.

311	(1) Lagus, Soter (who had previously governed Egypt 12 years, and, on the death of Alexander, is styled king)	27 —
284	(2) Philadelphus	38 —
246	(3) Euergetes I.	25 —
221	(4) Philopater	17 —
204	(5) Epiphanes	24 —
180	(6) Philometer	35 —
145	(7) Euergetes II.	29 —
116	(8) Soter II.	10 —
106	(9) Alexander I. (*Soter deposed*)	18 —
88	(8) Soter II. (*restored*)	7 —
81	(10) Berenice	— 6
80	(11) Alexander II.	15 —
65	(12) Neus Dionysus	14 —
51	(13) Ptolemy (the Elder)	4 —
47	(14) Ptolemy (the Younger)	3 —
44	(15) Cleopatra	14 —
30	EGYPT A ROMAN PROVINCE	30 —

CHAPTER II.

THE RELIGION OF THE EGYPTIANS.

REFERENCE to this Subject in "the Patriarchal Age"—The Importance of THEOLOGY to Religion—Egyptian Triads, their Relation to primitive Promise and Noah—The probable Identity of these Triads—Animal-Worship originated in the Cherubim, and carried out to an infamous Extent—General View of Egyptian Mythology—The MORALS of Egypt, recognised in Jurisprudence—Prominence given to Truth and Justice—Illustrations—The Doctrine of THE IMMORTALITY OF THE SOUL—Curious Corruptions associated with this Doctrine—Object of Embalming—The Doctrine of a future Judgment—The Opinions held by this People exhibited—Important Light imparted thereby on the Subject of Morals—The Hall of Judgment and forty-two Assessors—All resulting in everlasting Happiness or Punishment—Providence—General Accuracy of Doctrine, but neutralized by Polytheism—General Character and Influence of this Religion—Morals—Divine Sanction—Future Retribution—Spiritual Character—Remarkable Juxtaposition of Truth and Error.

SOME reference has been made to this subject in a preceding volume. (Patriarchal Age, p. 469, *et seq.*) To the brief sketch there given the reader is requested to turn, as an outline of the primitive Egyptian faith which it is not necessary here to repeat, but which it will now be our aim to expand into a succinct account of Egyptian idolatry, and its religious and moral influence upon the nation.

In the passages to which I refer, it was stated, on the authority of a learned and religious writer, that "the religion of Egypt underwent no alteration from the time of its establishment by Menes, to that of its abolition by Christianity." This sentiment is fully adopted in this work, in the sense in which, it is believed, the author intended it to be received; but in this sense it does not preclude progressive development and expansion, but specially refers to the principle and genius of the entire system. (See *Appendix*, note 12.)

In the prosecution of this purpose it is proposed to investigate in order the theology, morals, doctrines, and general influence of this religion.

The centre and soul of any religious system is its theology. Religion, as the term imports, unites—or, rather, *re-binds* (from the Latin verb *re-ligo*)—man to God. It is based on the presumption of man's alienation from his Maker, and therefore treats of the means and manner of his reunion with Deity. But then it inevitably follows, that the truth or falsehood, the purity or depravity, of the representation which is thus given of God, affects the entire character of the religion. Notwithstanding the numerous and minute delineations of deities, acts of worship, and religious rites, which we find on the monuments of Egypt, we have no native account of the religion of the country, much less of its primitive state. Not even a fragment of Manetho has come down to us on this subject: all we know from him has been given to us through Plutarch. Yet from the traditions which have been thus preserved, one fact stands out most unmistakably,—namely, that, "prior to the empire of Menes," the Egyptians "had their temple-service regularly organized;" (*Bunsen*, vol. i, p. 358;) and consequently the whole frame-work of their religious system was designed and brought into operation.

It has been already stated that anciently this people believed in the unity of the supreme God; and that human representations or incarnations of him were at first regarded as divine, rather by union with him, or emanation from him, than from their intrinsic nature; and hence had the name of the Supreme added to their own. Passing by all the speculation of Greek writers, and ascending to the primitive state of the Egyptian faith, there appears abundant reason for identifying its theology with the great departure from patriarchal religion which took place at Babel. Hence the triad,—Osiris, Isis, Horus. Again, we have Amout, Mout, Chons. In both these instances the triad consists of father, mother, and son. From what has been already stated, (Patriarchal Age, p. 475,) there can be no reasonable doubt that these deities arose out of a corrupted tradition of the first pair, in combination with the promised incarnate Seed, given under different names. (See *Appendix*, note 13.) It is, however, sufficiently evident that the circumstances of Noah, the second great father of the world, and his sons, had a great influence in the formation of the original idolatry of Egypt.

We have sufficient proofs of this in the obvious identity of Osiris and Noah,—a fact confirmed by the mutilation common to both, and the manner in which it was made prominent, and sacred in the case of the Egyptian deity. It is observable that Osiris and Isis are celebrated as the only deities worshipped in every part of Egypt; the birth of the son being sometimes regarded as prospective and approaching.

This allusion to the Arkite family is further corroborated. *Kneph*, according to Wilkinson, represented the idea of "the Spirit of God, as it moved upon the face of the waters." He was commonly exhibited with a ram's head, and regarded specially as the god of the Nile. But this deity was supposed to merge into three:—first, Kneph, the Spirit; then Pthah, proceeding from him, and thence regarded as his son; and lastly, Khem, (whose name is identical with the Scriptural *Ham*,) who was supposed to rule over the procreation of the human species.

Probably all these triads were at first identical, and intended to exhibit a personification of the supreme God under allusive representations of man's primitive history, and that of the Noachic family. But the moving agent in this process, although insidious, was not concealed. *The asp was sacred to Kneph.* The most poisonous winged serpent in the land was made the personification of the creator and ruling spirit! In fact, THE SERPENT WAS THE TYPE OF DOMINION! Its figure was in consequence affixed to the head-dress of Egyptian kings; and a prince, on his accession to the throne, was entitled to wear this distinctive badge of royalty. This Satanic assumption is embedded in the language to a considerable extent. "M. Champollion has satisfactorily accounted for the name *Uræus*, given to the snake, by suggesting that the word derives its origin and signification from *Ouro*, in Coptic, 'a king,' answering, as Horapollo tells us, to the Greek βασιλίσκος, 'royal;' and it is from this last word that the name 'basilisk' has been applied to the asp."— *Wilkinson's Ancient Egyptians*, vol. iv, p. 240. Of Pthah it may be necessary to observe, that he was regarded as the *Lord of truth*, and is said to have been produced in the shape of an egg from the mouth of Kneph, and represented the creative power of Deity. It cannot escape observation how closely this resembles the Divine Word. Wilkinson says, "The form of this deity is generally a mummy;" (*Ancient Egyptians*, vol. iv, p. 252;) but Cory shrewdly suspects that the bandaged figure rather represents "an infant swathed, as is the custom in the Mediterranean."—*Mythological Inquiry*, p. 42.

The principle of idolatrous substitution and representation having been once adopted, it was susceptible of infinite expansion and change. Hence, in the classic age, we find the great triad represented as composed of Osiris, Horus, Typhon; and Horus is set forth by Plutarch as the son of Osiris and Isis, begotten before they themselves were born, and born with them: a singular but remarkable allusion to the preëxistence of the promised Seed.

Typhon is the destroying principle; and, according to Plutarch, his proper name is Seth. Some have supposed this deity to be an introduction of later times after the great reformation in Persia. His name and character are, however, so involved in the legends of Osiris and Isis, that there seems reason for believing that, to some extent at least, even in early times the evil principle was recognised as divine,—an opinion confirmed by the appearance of his name, Seth, on the oldest monuments.

Our limits will not allow an enumeration of all the Egyptian deities; nor would any good purpose be served by it. Indeed, different opinions prevail, even among scholars, as to their number and character. Bunsen gives eight gods of the first order, twelve of the second order, and seven of the third order, with four genii of the dead.

It is essential, however, to pay special attention to that which forms the most extraordinary element of Egyptian idolatry, namely, animal-worship. On this subject a learned writer has expressed himself in language so strikingly corroborative of the views maintained in this work, that we quote him at length: "It is matter of very curious inquiry how mankind degenerated into the worship of animals, and the abominations of idolatry. It will have been observed in the preceding remarks that, among the heathens, the EAGLE was the token of the *ethereal power;* the LION, of the *light;* and the BULL, of *fire, heat, or the solar orb;* though these distinctions are not always very accurately maintained. These animals are, in fact, no other than the animals that composed the cherubim, which, in the antediluvian, patriarchal, and Jewish dispensations, were placed at the entrance of Paradise, and afterward upon the mercy-seat of the ark. They were deemed oracular; and above them rested the Shekinah, the cloud of glory, the visible symbol of the presence of the Lord, who is represented as sitting between them, or flying upon them.* The form of the cherubim was that of a bull, from which arose a human body, as a centaur, with four heads,—that of a bull, of an eagle, of a lion, and of a man, with wings and hands, and covered with eyes. In the heathen cherubim, among other remarkable variations, the head of the serpent is often substituted for the human head. The seraphim are considered to have been similar; and the teraphim were of the same form, but smaller figures, which were set up by individuals in their own house, and to which they resorted for answers. Zech. x, 2.

"The cherubim constituted the place of worship for all believers: they were termed the *pheni Elohim,* 'the faces,' (Zech. vii, 2, *passim,*) or 'presence of God;' and from between them issued oracles. Exod. xxv, 22. It would have been a singular omission, if the heathen, as they went off from the patriarchal worship, had not carried with them an institution so remarkable: accordingly we find the figures worked up into all their religious institutions, and the memory of them retained, even to the present day. The cherubim

---

* In this case our learned author is incorrect. The Lord is never represented as flying on the cherubim but in one mistranslated passage in the Old Testament. See my "Doctrine of the Cherubim," p. 37.

may be found in every part of the heathen world; and to the abuse of them, I believe, may be traced the worship of animals."—*Cory's Mythological Inquiry*, pp. 90–104.

It is observable that the curious compound figures which abound in Egypt and in the East, are almost always found at the entrance of sacred places. If anything is necessary, beyond what is given in the Preliminary Dissertation, to identify the animal-worship of Egypt with that of the cherubic figures, it is supplied by the fact—that the living Apis was required to have marks of this cherubic combination. The selected animal must have not only a white crescent on his side, and a particular lump under his tongue, but also the "resemblance of an eagle on his shoulders." And this, explained by antique bronze figures of Apis, gives not the addition of an eagle to the ox, but the form of eagle wings on his shoulders, similar to those of the Nimroud sculptures. These marks, as Wilkinson observes, were undoubtedly supplied by the priests: but this rather corroborates the opinion that the cherubic form was the model to which the living animal was, as far as possible, to be conformed.

These corruptions having been introduced, they were carried out to an amazing extent. "Among the Egyptians," says Clemens Alexandrinus, "the temples are surrounded with groves and consecrated pastures; they are furnished with *propylæa*, and their courts are encircled with an infinite number of columns; their walls glitter with foreign marbles and paintings of the highest art; the *naos* is resplendent with gold and silver, and *electrum*, and variegated stones from India and Ethiopia; the *adytum* is veiled by a curtain wrought with gold. But if you pass beyond into the remotest part of the enclosure, hastening to behold something yet more excellent, and seek for the image which dwells in the temple, a *pastophorus*, or some one else, who ministers in sacred things, with a pompous air, singing a pæan in the Egyptian tongue, draws aside a small portion of the curtain, as if about to show us the god, and makes us burst into a loud laugh. For no god is found within, but a cat, or a crocodile, or a serpent sprung from the soil, or some such brute animal: the Egyptian deity appears a beast rolling himself on a purple coverlet."—*Pædag.* iii, 2, p. 253. *Potter*.

Diodorus (lib. i, cap. 84) bears similar testimony: "The temples of Egypt are most beautiful; but if you seek within, you find an ape or ibis, a goat or a cat." These animals were treated with the utmost tenderness, and supplied with the most delicate and luxurious food. Nor was this attention and reverence confined to the priesthood. In the reign of Ptolemy Auletes, when it was his special interest to keep on good terms with the Roman people, a subject of the imperial republic, residing in Egypt, had unintentionally killed a cat,—an accident which excited the popular feeling to such an extent, that neither the awe of the Roman name, nor the utmost efforts of the king of Egypt, could save the unhappy man from death. The character and intensity of this insane devotion do not rest on the mere testimony of ancient historians. These animals, after being adored all their lives, were embalmed after death; and antiquarians have in recent times by their discoveries abundantly confirmed all that the ancients reported. "The embalmed bodies of bulls, cows, and sheep, dogs and cats, hawks and ibises, serpents and beetles, and, in short, nearly the whole zoology of Egypt, except the horse and the ass, have been found in excavations."—*Kenrick*, vol. ii, chap. 6.

Let us for a moment pause, and ponder on this exhibition of Egyptian theology. It may be said that this people retained some knowledge of the supreme God, and cherished the idea of his unity, power, and prescience. To some extent, in ancient times at least, this was undoubtedly the fact. Yet how all these views must have been defiled, corrupted, and debased by this idolatry! To exalt human nature, character, and passions to divinity, was to bring the Deity down to the level of manhood. To adore a brute, was to degrade the ideas of the worshipper respecting God to that contemptible measure. And this astounding degradation is a fearful fact. At a date prior to the monarchy of Menes, the founders of this nation made the fatal experiment. Although "they knew God, they glorified him not as God, but became vain in their imaginations." They made men representatives of Deity, and regarded eminent departed worth with idolatrous veneration. They perverted the pure rites of patriarchal worship, until every element of it was merged into a vile idolatry. The natural consequence of this—nay, I am not sure that the consequence is simply natural—the religious consequence of this was fully realized: "Professing themselves to be wise, they became fools. Wherefore God gave them up to" their vanity and folly, so that every luminary in the heavens, and almost every element on earth, were worshipped as divine. But, amid all this, one fact stands out conspicuous in the whole scheme:— the author-mind is fully exhibited. The unfailing badge of Egyptian idolatry is the sign seen in the centre of every temple, and paraded in every conceivable manner in the rites, ceremonies, sculptures, and pictures of Egypt. I allude to the winged globe and serpent. These are thus explained: "The globe denotes the Divine Nature; the serpent, his Word, which animates and impregnates the world; and the wing, the Spirit of God, which vivifies it with his motion."* Here, as in profane parody on such views of the Trinity as then obtained, we have a triad constructed, of which the Satanic form is the centre and ruling agent in respect of this world.

This theology, therefore, while it preserved many important truths respecting the nature of God, and his promises of mercy to the fallen race of man, completely overlaid them with a gross and elaborate idolatrous machinery, which, if it did not entirely conceal, must to a fearful extent have neutralized their influence. The great deceiver of man had pervaded this corrupt scheme with such multiplied exhibitions of the form in which he successfully urged the first temptation of mankind, that it appears as if, while the first object of the system was to isolate man from God by substituting anything, from the image of a man to a live cat or beetle, as an object of worship, its secondary design was to induce a recognition of the serpent-form as the highest exhibition of Deity. One important point is, therefore, evident: The theology of Egypt, instead of elevating the mind, and shedding on the spirit of the worshipper a clearer and purer light than human reason can afford,—which, in fact, is the proper province of this divine science,—darkened the intellect, and prostrated the man before dogs, cats, and beetles.

We direct attention, in the next place, to the morals inculcated by this system: and here it is cheering to observe, that, vile and contemptible as were many of the objects of worship, this system was free from the reproach resting on many so-called religious schemes; it did not repudiate all connexion with morals. On the contrary, moral character was deemed an integral element of religion. It was, indeed, the great merit of the religion of Egypt, that it taught the observance of moral law with reference to a future judgment. While making this statement, as an opinion which appears to be fully warranted by a general review of the system, it is but just to say that others have from the same premises reached an opposite conclusion. Probably, however, if we had more ample means of information, it would be found that, while the religion of Egypt taught the doctrine of future retribution as an article of faith, the multiplicity and various character of their several divinities almost entirely neutralized this doctrine as a popular element of religion, and left the public to a great extent unaffected by its salutary influence.

In respect of times so remote, and a country of which we have such imperfect knowledge, it is very likely that we can glean the best information on the subject of public morals by considering the character of their laws.

* This exposition is derived from a Syriac MS. attributed by Kircher to Sanchoniatho. (Cory's Mythological Inquiry, p. 99.)

Here it may be observed that special attention was paid to the jurisprudence of the country. Ten persons, the most upright and learned that could be found, were selected from each of the three principal cities,—Thebes, Memphis, and Heliopolis. "These thirty individuals constituted the bench of judges; and at their first meeting they elected the most distinguished among them to be president, with the title of 'arch-judge.' His salary was much greater than that of the other judges, as his office was more important; and the city to which he belonged enjoyed the privilege of returning another judge, to complete the number of the thirty from whom he had been chosen." They all received ample allowances from the state, in order that, possessing a competency, they might be inaccessible to bribes.

When engaged in his judicial duties, the arch-judge wore, suspended by a chain from his neck, a small figure ornamented with precious stones. This was a representation of the goddess worshipped under the two-fold character of TRUTH and JUSTICE, and was called *Thmei*. It has been supposed with good reason, that this was a corruption of the same patriarchal element, afterward developed in the Hebrew religion as the Thummim of the high priest.

The laws of the Egyptians were said to have been dictated by the gods, or more immediately by Thoth. This notion was common to many heathen nations; but it should not on this account be always treated as pretence and imposture. No doubt this was frequently the case. Legislators often gave out that they had received their laws from some deity, in order to secure for them acceptance and reverence. But it was not so in Egypt. No historical research can reach the origin of the Egyptian laws: "they were handed down from the earliest times." The plea of their divine origin was not, therefore, set up to procure their sanction, but was in all probability virtually true, inasmuch as they might have been founded on real revelations made to the early patriarchs by God.

It is remarkable that, throughout their code, truth was always identified with justice; and this combination was considered to be the cardinal virtue among the Egyptians. It was regarded as much more important than prudence, temperance, fortitude, and other virtues, which only affect the individual who possesses them, while truth and justice relate more particularly to others, and therefore act upon society at large. "Falsehood was not only considered disgraceful, but, when it entailed an injury on any other person, was punishable by law. A calumniator of the dead was condemned to a severe punishment; and a false accuser was doomed to the same sentence which would have been awarded to the accused, if the offence had been proved against him. But to maintain a falsehood by an oath was deemed the blackest crime, and one which, from its complicated nature, could be punished by nothing short of death."—*Wilkinson's Ancient Egyptians*, vol. ii, p. 32.

Murder, whether committed on a freeman or a slave, was punished with death. In this respect the Egyptians were in advance of Greece and Rome. In all instances in which a woman was capitally convicted, great care was taken to ascertain whether the condemned was in a state of pregnancy, in which case punishment was deferred until after the birth of the child.

Theft was sometimes punished with great severity. The nose of the criminal was cut off, and he was banished to a town built on the borders of the desert, and called, from the nature of the punishment, *Rhinocolura*. Yet, notwithstanding this, there was a recognised official, called "the chief of the robbers." Every one practising the profession of a thief gave in his name to this person; and every robbery, with all the detail of time, place, quantity, and value of stolen goods, was reported to him, as soon as the theft was effected. The party robbed, therefore, had always the option of applying to this chief, and receiving back his goods by paying one quarter part of their value.

Unlike the Greeks and Romans, the Egyptians did not allow to fathers absolute power over the life of their offspring; nor did they punish the murder of a child by its parent as a capital offence. But, as a medium course, they adopted a mode of punishment adapted to prevent the crime, and to lead the criminal to repentance. The person convicted of this offence was condemned to have the dead body of the child fastened to his neck, and was compelled, under the care of a public guard, to spend three days and nights in its embrace.

A woman convicted of adultery was punished with the loss of her nose; a man, to receive a bastinado of one thousand blows. If it was proved that the man used force, he was subjected to a terrible and inhuman punishment.

If we now examine the doctrines taught by this religious system, especially those respecting future retribution and providence, further light will be cast on the subject of the morality of ancient Egypt.

The doctrine of the soul's immortality appears to have been always known and believed in Egypt. But then, this tenet was held in connexion with that of transmigration. All our authorities concur in stating it to be the general belief among the Egyptians, that the souls of men survive their bodies, and return to life again in animals. "Herodotus fixes the period at three thousand years, when the soul returned to the human form: and Plato says, if any one's life has been virtuous, he shall obtain a better fate hereafter; if wicked, a worse. But no soul will return to its pristine condition till the expiration of ten thousand years, since it will not recover the use of its wings until that period; except it be the soul of one who has philosophized sincerely, or, together with philosophy, has loved beautiful forms. These, indeed, in the third period of one thousand years, if they have thrice chosen this mode of life in succession, shall in their three-thousandth year fly away to their pristine abode: but other souls, being arrived at the end of their first life, shall be judged. And of those who are judged, some, proceeding to a subterraneous place of judgment, shall there sustain the punishments they have deserved; but others, in consequence of a favourable judgment, being elevated into a certain celestial place, shall pass their time in a manner becoming the life they have lived in a human shape. And in the thousandth year, both the kinds of those who have been judged, returning to the lot and election of a second life, shall each of them receive a lot agreeable to his desire. Here, also, the human soul shall pass into the life of a beast; and, from that of a beast, again into a man, if it has first been the soul of a man. For the soul which has never perceived the truth, cannot pass into the human form."—*Wilkinson's Ancient Egyptians*, vol. v, p. 442. This curious notion of successive transmigrations of the soul has been so explained as to lead to the belief that the order observed was, "that the same soul enters the body of a man, an ox, a dog, a bird, and a fish, until, having passed through all of them, it returns to that from which it set out."

From this it has been inferred that the object of the Egyptians in the embalmment of deceased relations was, to preserve the body entire until the return of the soul. The fact that the lower animals were also sometimes embalmed, has been regarded, if not as confuting this notion, at least as throwing considerable doubt upon it. More has been made of this objection than it merits. Notwithstanding the circumstance of animal embalmment, which may not admit of satisfactory explanation, it seems probable that the notion of the return of the spirit to the same body might have had much influence in introducing the general practice of embalming human bodies.

Respecting the interesting subject of the future judgment, numerous exhibitions and illustrations are found on the monuments. But it is our misfortune to have to elicit the doctrine from these pictures. We are, therefore, in danger of resting an essential doctrine upon some merely poetic pictorial appendage. No sufficient literal description has reached us. It remains, therefore, for us to draw the soundest inferences from the *data* placed before us. " The judgment scenes, found in the tombs and on the papyri, sometimes represent the deceased conducted by Horus alone, or accompanied by his wife, to the region of Amenti. Cerberus is present as the guardian of the gates, near which the scales of justice are erected; and Anubis, 'the director of the weight,' having placed a vase, in the form of the human heart, and representing the good actions of the deceased, in one scale, and the figure or emblem of Truth in the other, proceeds to ascertain his claims for admission. If, on being 'weighed,' he is found 'wanting,' he is rejected; and Osiris, the judge of the dead, inclines his sceptre in token of condemnation, pronounces judgment upon him, and condemns his soul to return to earth, under the form of a pig, or some other unclean animal. Placed in a boat, it is moved, under the charge of two monkeys, from the precincts of Amenti, all communication with which is figuratively cut off by a man who hews away the earth with an axe after its passage; and the commencement of a new term of life is indicated by those monkeys, the emblems of Thoth. But if, when the sum of his deeds is recorded by Thoth, his virtues so far predominate as to entitle him to admission to the mansions of the blessed, Horus, taking in his hand the tablet of Thoth, introduces him to the presence of Osiris; who, in his palace, attended by Isis and Nepthys, sits on his throne in the midst of the waters, from which rises the lotus, bearing upon its expanded flower the four genii of Amenti.

"Other representations of this subject differ in some of the details. In the judgment of a royal scribe, whose funeral procession is described on the monuments, the deceased advances alone, in an attitude of prayer, to receive judgment. On one side of the scales stands Thoth, holding a tablet in his hand; on the other, the goddess of justice; and Horus, in lieu of Anubis, performs the office of director of the balance, on the top of which sits a cynocephalus, the emblem of Thoth. Osiris, seated as usual on his throne, holding his crook and *flagellum*, awaits the report from the hands of his son Horus. Before the door of his palace are the four genii of Amenti, and near them three deities, who either represent the assessors, or may be the three assistant judges, who gave rise to the Minos, Æacus, and Rhadamanthus of Greek fable."—*Wilkinson's Ancient Egyptians*, vol. v, p. 448.

In another MS., preserved at the Louvre, the deceased, Amenham, addresses a prayer to the god of light coming from heaven, whose eyes enlighten the material world, and dissipate the darkness of night. The picture which accompanies it represents many souls and men adoring a luminous disk. He next prays to Phre, the great god, manifested in the two firmaments under his two forms of Re, the rising sun, and Atmou, the setting sun; then again to Phre and Thoth, as gods of the sun and moon. Afterward he invokes Netphe, the mother of the gods; by whose bent body, covered with stars, all space was circumscribed: she was the impersonation of heaven. The bark of the sun is represented as sailing thereon, under the guidance of Moui, or light. His next petitions are presented to Osiris, the lord of Totou, the region of stability. The emblems of this divinity, and those of the ibis-headed Thoth, are enclosed in a serpent biting its own tail, the symbol of eternity. Afterward he prays to all the divinities presiding over the judgment of souls, and concludes with short ejaculations to Osiris, Nofre Tmoui, and the sacred cow of Hathor or Venus. (Antiquities of Egypt, p. 154.)

In order to a proper understanding of the Egyptian notions respecting the future judgment, it is necessary to state that they supposed the final judgment to be conducted by forty-two judges or assessors, each of these being imagined to take cognizance of a particular crime, so that the departed spirit, in passing before them in order, had to clear itself of the several sins in regular succession. Over these assessors Osiris presided, as the arch-judge did in the temporal courts.

The assessors appeared in a human form, with different heads. The first had the head of a hawk; the second, of a man; the third, of a hare; the fourth, of a hippopotamus; the fifth, of a man; the sixth, of a hawk; the seventh, of a fox; the eighth, of a man; the ninth, of a ram; the tenth, of a snake; the others, according to their peculiar character. It is proper to observe, that the appearance of these assessors differs in different rituals; but in all of them it appears that they were intended to represent the accusing spirits, each having a separate moral district under his particular care. (Wilkinson's Ancient Egyptians, vol. v, p. 76.)

In another ritual, a transcript of which is preserved in the British Museum, the deceased dedicates his heart to his mother and his ancestors, immediately after his adoration of the god Pthah. The second part of the ritual consists of eleven liturgical prayers to Thoth, the guide of souls, and, as we have already said, the impersonation of the divine wisdom. The soul implores this divinity to undertake for him, to cast down his enemies, to plead his cause with the gods of the various regions through which he has to travel, and finally to open for him the gates of the great hall of judgment, that he may pass through them in safety.

This formidable array of gods and monsters, however, was but introductory to a still more fearful ordeal that awaited the soul on its arrival at the terrible portal of the judgment-hall, where all the actions of its life while in the body were examined. This scene is by no means confined to the ritual which we are now considering. Its frequent occurrence on mummy-cases, votive tablets, boxes, and funeral remains of every description, sufficiently attests the very high importance that was attached to it by the Egyptians, and the conspicuous place that it occupied in their creed. Many of these pictures are much curtailed and abbreviated, according to the custom of the scribes on all occasions. In the most perfect of them the deceased is represented as standing immediately before the entrance of a vast hall in the attitude of supplication, and addressing a long prayer to the divinity who presides in it, Osiris, the supreme judge. He has for his assessors the two goddesses Thmei. The first of them, who was called "the Themis of the Left," because she occupied the left side of the hall, was president over the first twenty-one avengers: the other, "the Themis of the Right," had the charge of the other twenty-one assessors. The prayer to Osiris at the entrance of the hall reads thus: "O thou avenger, lord of justice, great god, lord of the two Themes, (Justice and Truth,) I worship thee, O my lord. I have spoken, speak thou to me thy name: tell me the names of the forty-two gods who are with thee in the great hall of justice and truth, living guardians of the wicked, fed with their bloods bring forward my righteousness, search out my sins." The deceased then proceeds to enumerate the moral offences of which he has not been guilty: "I have defrauded no man; I have not slaughtered the cattle of the gods; I have not prevaricated at the seat of justice; I have not made slaves of the Egyptians; I have not defiled my conscience for the sake of my superior; I have not used violence; I have not famished my household; I have not made to weep; I have not smitten privily; I have not changed the measures of Egypt; *I have not grieved the spirits of the gods;* I have not committed adultery; I have not forged signet-rings; I have not falsified the weights of the balance; I have not withheld milk from the mouths of my children." The offences that follow are peculiar to the climate and to the idolatry of Egypt: "I have not pierced the banks of the Nile in its annual increase; I have not separated to myself an arm of the Nile in its advance." These passages render it probable that, in ancient as in modern times, an important part of the revenue of Egypt was raised by imposing a tribute upon the lands overflowed by the annual inundation; so that to obtain any portion of these fertilizing waters secretly, was to defraud the state. This singular disavowal concludes thus: "I have not disturbed the gazelles of the gods in their pasturage; I have not netted the water-fowl of the gods; I have not caught the sacred fishes; I have not despised the gods in their offerings;" (in other words, "I have not given to the gods that which is imperfect;") "I have not bound the cattle of the gods; I have not pierced the god in his manifestation," as a sacred animal. The prayer concludes with petitions for purification and illumination.

The deceased then entered the great hall of judgment, and kneeling before the forty-two assessors, protested to each his innocence of the sin of which he was the minister of vengeance. The names of these terrible beings are descriptive of their appearance or qualities. The soul says to the first of them, "O thou that hast long legs," (art swift to pursue,) "I have not sinned." To the second, "O thou that dost try with fire, I have not been gluttonous." To the fourth, "O thou that devourest tranquillity," (that is, with whom there is no peace,) "I have not stolen." To the fifth, "O thou that smitest the heart, I have done no murder." To the sixth, "O thou with the two lions," (heads,) "I have not falsified measures." To the seventh, "O thou that hast piercing eyes, I have not acted the hypocrite." To the ninth, "O thou that dost make limbs to tremble, I have not lied." To the sixteenth, "O thou that dost delight in blood, I have not slain the cattle of the gods." To the twenty-second, "O thou that dost consume creation, I have not been drunken." The foregoing may suffice as specimens of what has generally been termed "the negative confession." Some parts of it remain still in much obscurity as to their import; others allude to offences of which it is a shame even to speak. (Osburn's Antiquities of Egypt, p. 157.)

We have stated that the forty-two assessors are ministers of vengeance, whose wrath is to be deprecated by the deceased. The names of all the forty-two, and the particular regions over which they preside, occur in the entire copies of this scene. In other copies they are represented sitting before their presidents. In the presence of the judge Osiris, these and other divinities, or genii, rigorously examined the conduct of the soul while incarnate on earth. The sentence which resulted from this judgment was full of joy to the good, and of woe to the wicked. They who by a faithful discharge of all their moral obligations, as children, as parents, as masters, as servants, as kings or subjects, and by the conscientious avoidance of vice under all its grosser forms, had been enabled to pass the ordeal, were permitted to go through the Hall of Themis; whence embarking on the infernal Nile, they are privileged to behold once more the disk of the sun,—a blessing for which the gods are very frequently supplicated on behalf of the deceased. With that luminary it would seem that they arose to heaven, and in his bark they navigated the celestial Nile, or primordial ether. At the fifth hour they were landed in the habitations of blessedness, where they rested from their labours. Here they reap the corn, and gather the fruits of Paradise, under the eye and smile of the "lord of joy in the heart," that is, the sun, who exhorts them thus: "Take your sickles, reap your grain, carry it into your dwellings, that ye may be glad therewith, and present it as a pure offering unto God." There also they bathe in the pure river of the water of life that flows past their habitation: from which it is evident that the Elysium of this religion was no more than a celestial Egypt. Over them is inscribed, "They have found favour in the eyes of the great God; they inhabit the mansions of glory, where they enjoy the life of heaven; the bodies which they have abandoned shall repose forever in their tombs, while they rejoice in the presence of the supreme God."

But a terrible fate impended over those who, being weighed in the balance of Amenti, were found wanting. In the first instance, as has been already observed, their souls were driven back to earth again by ministers of vengeance in the form of baboons, to transmigrate into that animal to which their besetting sin had assimilated them. The glutton, driven from the tribunal with heavy blows, became a hog; the cruel man a wolf; and so of others.

If, after their transmigrations, the soul remained polluted, its hope perished forever. It was then transported to the regions of darkness and eternal death, symbolized by the twelve hours of the night, and the lower hemisphere. God, under the symbol of the sun, is here also; but, as the avenger and tormentor, he makes the darkness his pavilion; his disk is black; no ray of light issues from him to illume their cheerless abodes. His object in visiting them is to superintend and preside over the punishments endured by the wicked in the seventy-five zones into which the lower hemisphere was divided. Each zone has an attendant spirit attached to it, who is also the executioner. In one of the zones the lost souls are bound to stakes, covered with wounds, which their executioners are still inflicting, brandishing their bloody swords, and at the same time reproaching them with the crimes they have committed while on earth. In another they are suspended with the head downward: elsewhere they walk in long and melancholy procession, with their hands bound across their breasts, and their heads nearly severed from their bodies; or with their hands tied tightly behind their backs, and their hearts torn from their bosoms, and dragging after them on the ground. In other zones, souls in the form which they bore when on earth, or in that of a hawk or crane, are plunged into boiling caldrons, along with the symbol of divine felicity, the fan, which they have forfeited forever. In the great representations of these fearful scenes, which are repeated in many of the tombs of the kings, the offences for which they endure these torments are specified over each zone, and it is declared concerning all the inhabitants of these abodes of misery, "These souls are at enmity with our God, and do not see the rays which issue from his disk; they are no longer permitted to live in the terrestrial world, neither do they hear the voice of God when he traverses their zone."—*Antiquities of Egypt*, p. 163.

The importance of the subject justifies this extended information respecting the doctrines of future retribution held in ancient Egypt; and to every intelligent believer in the truth of revelation it will suggest many important arguments corroborative of the teaching of Jude,—that even the early patriarchs were acquainted with the doctrine of a future judgment, and made it a prominent element of their religious teaching. Jude 14, 15.

The doctrines of the Egyptian religion on the subject of providence will next briefly engage our attention.

Here the paralyzing and destructive influence of polytheistic theology is plainly seen. As a general doctrine, providence was clearly and fully recognised by the ancient Egyptians. This was done to an extent which ought to confound not merely avowed infidels, but many who call themselves Christians.

Not only did this people consecrate each month, and even each day, to a particular divinity, but all nature was by them supposed to be pervaded with the essence of God. Almost every town and river, every tree and shrub, as well as every animal, was regarded as divine. The shining beams of the sun were looked on as divine influences: the mild radiance of the moon was invested with divine power. The sovereign was invariably regarded as the beloved of Deity: and divine interposition in human affairs was fully recognised and believed. We may adduce one proof of this, which is at once interesting and decisive. When Sennacherib the Assyrian, fearing the advance of the king of Egypt, while he was engaged in the conquest of Judea during the reign of Hezekiah, brought his army to the borders of Egypt, the Egyptian monarch repaired, as Hezekiah had done, to the temple of his god, and spreading his deplorable case before his deity, sought refuge in prayer. He was, the account informs us, assured in a dream that he should sustain no injury from the invading army. So it came to pass; for, as is well known from Hebrew history, the enemy was ruined without a conflict. The Egyptian account of this event has already been given; (see *Appendix*, note 11;) and it clearly shows the ruling idea of Egyptian sovereignty, that God not only interposed in the affairs of mankind, but that he did so specially in answer to prayer. This important fact demonstrates that, among the superior classes of Egypt, the priesthood at least, (for we are specially informed that this sovereign was a priest,) there remained a conviction of the divine unity, sufficiently clear and strong to induce them to repose confidence in the powerful interposition of the Supreme God, and in his gracious government of the human family. But then it is equally apparent that the masses of the people, ignorant of those important truths, and bewildered in the multitude of imaginary deities, would be strangers alike to confidence and consolation.

This assumption of the ignorance of the people is well founded. Wilkinson, their most assiduous apologist, is compelled to admit that, "though the priests were aware of the nature of their gods, and all those who understood the mysteries of the religion looked upon the Divinity as a sole and undivided being, the people, as I have already observed, not admitted to a participation of these important secrets, *were left in perfect ignorance respecting the objects they were taught to adore;* and every one was not only permitted but encouraged, to believe the real sanctity of the idol, and the actual existence of the god whose figure he beheld." (*Ancient Egyptians*, vol. iv, p. 175.) What, then, could be the confidence of the people in the providential interposition or protection of Deity? When the grand destinies of the people were confided to a deified lion, crocodile, cat, or dog, how could such their trust yield consolation? What could have been the real amount of reliance which those of a particular locality reposed in their gods, when they knew that the men of a different nome, but a short distance off, were killing and feeding on the same kind of animals as by them were considered to be divine?

To those, therefore, who, knowing the true character of the inverted theology, held fast to the patriarchal elements of revealed truth which had been preserved, to them divine providence might have been an important and efficient doctrine. But, with the people, who were left in ignorance, and who consequently regarded the bull Apis as being just as sacred as the Divinity of which it was the type,—with these there could be no rational confidence in providential government.

We hasten to make a few observations on the character and extent of the religious influence which this system imparted to the nation, as well as to individuals.

This is the most interesting and important aspect in which the religion of any people can be regarded. And here the religion of Egypt presented much to admire, and much to lament.

1. The morals of this system were, on the whole, sound. Vice was prohibited and condemned; truth and justice were sanctioned and enforced. In fact all the precepts already noticed (Patriarchal Age, p. 217) as pure patriarchal laws were found, with one exception only, in the statute-code of Egypt. It must be admitted, notwithstanding the apologies which learned writers have urged, that there is great reason to fear that Phallic worship produced even in Egypt impure and demoralizing results; but if such consequences arose, they occurred not with the sanction, but in violation, of Egyptian law.

2. This morality was enforced, not simply as conducive to human welfare, and, as such, necessary to individual and general happiness; it was enforced as of divine authority. The laws were regarded as of divine origin and obligation. The fact that this assumption has been falsely made in other countries, no more militates against the moral faith of Egypt, than it does against that of Christianity.

3. The propriety of moral conduct was not only urged as by divine authority, but by the explicit teaching of a future retribution; and a retribution, be it observed, which, after all the fanciful interposition of transmigration, finally issued in eternal misery to the wicked, and everlasting felicity to the righteous. Whatever doubts may exist as to the origin of any particular moral law, it is certain that these doctrines could only be adduced in sanction of morals by divine revelation: so that, in this instance, we have an unmistakable proof that important elements of Egyptian faith were derived from early divine revelation.

4. It is observable that this moral code was understood and taught in a truly spiritual sense. It was not merely mechanical action which was prohibited by the faith of Egypt. Neither conventional religious rites, ending in mere externalism, nor a compliance with the mere letter of a written law, met the demands made on the consciences of Egyptians. Let me quote in proof that remarkable expression found in "The Book of the Dead," used by a departed spirit even before it could have access to the assessors: "*I have not grieved the spirits of the gods.*" This phrase implies the deep and compassionate interest which, according to Egyptian theology, the deities took in the well-being of the people, and at the same time expresses the sincere and devout service which the people were required to render to their gods.

It appears, therefore, clear to my mind, that in Egypt an uncommon amount of pure patriarchal truth was preserved. Nor does it seem to admit of a doubt, that it was this which preëminently constituted the boasted wisdom of Egypt. However lightly esteemed by learned modern writers it may have been, this class of subjects attracted the attention of Pythagoras, Herodotus, and Diodorus, more than any other: and it was on these points that Egypt yielded to those sages the most important harvest of information. Here they read divinity which recognised the doctrine of the Trinity, and the hope of a future incarnation of God. Here they found a system of ethics based upon the tenet of the immortality of the soul of man,—upon his responsibility to his Maker for his deeds on earth,—and upon his appearance after death at the judgment-seat of God,—and also upon the infinitely important truth, that God himself is the exceeding great reward of the righteous, and will surely punish the wicked; that his favour is everlasting life, that his wrath is death eternal. (Antiquities of Egypt, p. 164.)

This country stands immortalized on this account. Amid all its follies and sins, the truth which Egypt preserved from age to age affords the brightest and the best *collateral* proof of the reality and power of patriarchal religion. But if this is conceded, it may be asked, "Why, then, so severely condemn this religion?" The answer is, On the ground of its vile, impure, and contemptible theology. While the native Egyptians held with wonderful tenacity great elements of patriarchal faith, they with equal devotedness clung to the master-error which had been promulged at Shinar. They consequently sank into an abyss of idolatrous infamy, such as was scarcely the fate of any other nation.

Ancient Egypt, therefore, stands before us as an intelligible and perpetual monument of the vital importance of the knowledge of God. Possessing an amount of revealed truth which in other respects might have made her the envy, and which did constitute her the teacher, of surrounding nations, she was, in one grand element of religion, the special victim of Satanic guile. God was shut out from the knowledge of the people. If the glorious doctrines of his unity, omnipotence, and omniscience, were preserved at all, they were held as corporate treasure by the priesthood and the initiated. The people were left to offer devotion to, and seek hope and consolation from, crocodiles, lions, asps, and beetles; while, over all this bestial array, the image of the serpent constituted the established sign of power and dominion.

In the case of this people, the saying of the apostle is preëminently true: They "knew the judgment of God, that they who committed such things were worthy of death;" and yet, unchecked by a just perception of the divine character, they did these very things.

Rom. i, 32. How grand, how truly sublime, is the subject here presented to our contemplation! God excluded, his honour given to vile reptiles, nay, even to the Satanic image,—the ETERNAL ONE thus scorned and rejected; while, nevertheless, his Spirit strives; every element of truth which the mind will consent to receive, is invested with special vigour and energy, and made—as far as divine oversight and providential arrangement (perhaps) could make it—permanent in its teaching and generally influential; the debasing consequences of their idolatry being, all the while, equally apparent. Well may the religious man exclaim, " O the depth of the riches both of the wisdom and knowledge of God! How unsearchable are his judgments, and his ways past finding out!" Rom. xi, 33.

148   THE GENTILE NATIONS.

CHAPTER III.

THE HISTORY OF THE ASSYRIANS.

HISTORY of Assyria resumed with the Reign of BELOCHUS—Absence of precise Information respecting this and succeeding Reigns—Probability that even in this Age the Power of Egypt was felt on the Banks of the Euphrates—Interference of Assyria in the Trojan War—Fragmentary Notices of ancient Reigns recovered from Inscriptions by Colonel Rawlinson—Connected Assyrian History begins about the Tenth Century, B. C.—ADRAMMELECH I.—SARDANAPALUS I.—His military Career and Successes—DIVANUBARA—The Annals of his Reign from the Black Obelisk and other Sculptures—SHEMAS ADAR—ADRAMMELECH II. or THONOS CONCOLEROS—The Termination of the Old Imperial Dynasty—ARBACES the Mede on the Throne of Assyria—The Mission of Jonah, and its Results—The Assyrians recover their Sovereignty—PUL obtains the sceptre—Menahem, King of Israel, destroys Tiphsah—Pul invades Israel, and extorts a thousand Talents of Silver from Menahem—TIGLATH-PILESER succeeds to the Throne—At the Solicitation of Ahaz, he invades Syria and Israel, and carries the trans-Jordanic Tribes and the Inhabitants of Galilee into Captivity—Colonel Rawlinson's Arrangement of the Information obtained from the Sculptures of Khorsabad and Kouyunjik—SARGINA usurps the Throne—His Annals and public Works—SENNACHERIB—His Campaigns from the Inscriptions—Remarkable Accordance between their Account of his War with Hezekiah, and that given in the Scriptures—The Destruction of his Army—His subsequent Reign—ESARHADDON—The Ruin of Samaria, and final Subversion of the Kingdom of Israel—The Captivity and Restoration of Manasseh—NABUCHODONOSOR—His Wars in the East—Defeat and Death of Phraortes—An Army under Holofernes sent into Western Asia—The General slain by Judith, and the Army surprised and routed—SARAC, or SARDANAPALUS II.—Alliance of Media and Babylon against Assyria—Nineveh besieged and taken—The Assyrian Empire subverted.

THE origin and early progress of this empire were stated in a preceding volume. (Patriarchal Age, pp. 434–441.) It will now be necessary to resume its history with the reign of Belochus, which began B. C. 1857. This sovereign continued to direct the affairs of his country at the time when Isaac died.

Unfortunately, however, no records of this and of several succeeding reigns have been preserved. A dry chronicle of the names of kings, with the period during which they respectively governed, copied from the national archives by Ctesias, the Greek physician, is all that has been transmitted to us in a verbal and authentic manner.

In a preceding chapter, when treating of Egyptian history, it was stated as a probable fact that, in the time of Thothmes III. of the eighteenth dynasty, the power of Egypt had been felt, and tributary gifts elicited, as far north and east as the banks of the Caspian, and the borders of Media. Further researches have rendered it all but certain that, even at that early period, Egypt and Assyria had been brought into close contact, and probably into hostile collision. A learned writer, (see Trans. Roy. Soc. Lit., New Series, vol. ii, p. 227,) from the same monumental materials, elicits the information, that this Egyptian warrior stopped at *Neniiev*, or Nineveh, and "set up his tablet in *Naharina*, (Mesopotamia,) on account of his having enlarged the frontiers of Egypt. Twenty-four ingots of glass were brought, as the tributes, by the chief of Saenkar or Singara, and as many from Bebel or Babylon. (See *Appendix*, note 14.) These wars could scarcely have been carried on, without bringing these two ancient empires into an adverse position toward each other. When it is remembered how strenuously Egypt, in later times, struggled for the possession of Carchemish on the Euphrates, the fact that this district was then visited by an Egyptian army will seem more probable than it might at first sight appear. But the facility with which nations then sought to avoid worse treatment by the presentation of gifts, and the readiness with which they threw off all sense of obligation as soon as the danger had passed away, will cause us to hesitate before we infer anything positive from such information respecting the proper extent of the territory of any empire.

Colonel Rawlinson has ascertained from the Assyrian sculptures, that a sovereign named after the goddess Derceto, or Semiramis, reigned in Assyria about 1250 B. C. His exact title has not been deciphered. But it seems likely that he built, rebuilt, or greatly enlarged the city of Nineveh on the Tigris, immediately opposite to the present town of Mosul.

We are further informed, that Teutames, the twenty-sixth king of this list, sent Memnon, who was the son of Tithonus, prefect of Persia, with an army, to assist Priam, King of Troy, when his city was besieged by the Greeks. This warrior, it appears, after having greatly distinguished himself, fell in that war. The statement of Herodotus, that the issue of this protracted conflict was regarded as sufficient to constitute the Greeks hereditary enemies of the paramount rulers of Asia, seems to countenance this tradition. (See *Appendix*, note 15.)

Great expectation has arisen, among the learned, from the recent wonderful discoveries which have been made in the ruins of the cities of this ancient country, and from the no less wonderful recovery of the art of reading the monumental inscriptions. Yet, although our knowledge of the power, manners, warfare, civilization, and arts of the Assyrians has been much increased, neither the great talent and perseverance which have been exerted abroad, nor the devoted inquiry which has been excited at home, has, as yet, given us such information respecting the history and chronology of this mighty empire as we should desire to possess. They have, indeed, enabled us to solve important problems respecting the history of the Assyrians, to verify many statements of Holy Scripture, and to form at least a tolerable idea of the national spirit, progress, and power of this empire during the last and most interesting period of its existence.

It is justly to be ranked among the most wonderful phenomena of divine providence, that here, as well as in Egypt, the extent to which the curse of Babel was carried, in the multiplication of dialects, should have so signally wrought its own cure. (See *Appendix*, note 16.) Yet, notwithstanding the rapid, extensive, and surprising success which has crowned the labours of learned and skilful men who have devoted themselves to the elucidation of the characters and language of the early Assyrian inscriptions, great, and, in many respects, unexpected difficulties have been found, which have much retarded a clear and positive identification of individual reigns. (See *Appendix*, note 17.) It has, however, been ascertained that, in the twelfth century before Christ, a sovereign reigned whose name has been rendered *Divanukha*. He built the city of Calah, upon the site which is now called "Nimrud." The identification of these two cities, Nineveh and Calah, is quite positive. Their names are found upon every brick, and almost on every slab, excavated from the ruins which cover their sites. It must not, however, be supposed, when we read of the building of a city of a certain name, that no city of that name or on that site existed before. Very frequently what is celebrated as the building of a city was only the rebuilding or enlarging of it, which is believed to have been the fact in respect both of Nineveh and Calah.

A royal cylinder has been recently discovered in a temple of Neptune near Nineveh, which appears to give the names of the two immediate successors of Divanukha. Colonel Rawlinson compares these names with Mardokempad and Messimordacus, preserved in the Canon of Ptolemy. The titles would certainly be thus read at Babylon; but the learned explorer is not quite satisfied that the planet Mars was called Merodach at Nineveh, as it certainly was at Babylon. (See *Appendix*, note 17.)

The next king of whom we have any account must have reigned in the eleventh century before Christ, following at no great distance of time the grandson of Divanukha. His name signifies, "the Servant of the Prince," or, "the Servant of the Son of the Noble House;" and, if expressed phonetically, may be read as ANAK-BAR-BETH-HIRA. The terms, however, "the Noble House," and "Son of the Noble House," occur so frequently in the inscriptions, both in proper names and in addresses to the gods, that they probably allude to some deified hero, or at any rate to some object of worship, of which the special title would in speaking replace the written periphrasis.

This king seems to be the first of whom we have any knowledge, as carrying the Assyrian arms into foreign countries. His exploits are recorded on a slab which was found at Nimrud, a relic of some ancient palace; and they are of value in defining the limits of the Assyrian empire at that early period. The king boasts that he had extended his sway from the Persian Gulf to the Mediterranean; but it is evident, from his lists of conquests, that neither Syria to the west, nor Asia Minor to the northwest, nor Media to the east, had yet been visited by the armies of Nineveh. At this time the empire comprised Mesopotamia, Assyria, and Babylonia; and incursions seem to have been then first made into Armenia, and the mountainous countries about the sources of the Tigris and Euphrates.

Connected Assyrian history may be said to commence in the tenth century before the Christian era, with the reign of ADRAM-MELECH I., as the appellation has been read by Colonel Rawlinson, —the first element being the name of the god Adar, and the second a royal title. This sovereign, in the judgment of the learned translator, must have ascended the throne shortly after the death of Solomon. Neither of this king, nor of his son, have any monuments been yet discovered. But the latter was certainly a warrior of note: for his conquests are often alluded to by his son, the great Sardanapalus. His name signifies, "the slave of Mars;" and Colonel Rawlinson suggests that it should be read *Anaku-Merodach*, (so in Hebrew ענק, " a collar,") and compared with the 'Ανακυνδαράξης of the Greeks.

SARDANAPALUS appears to have begun his reign about 930 B. C., in which case he would be the Ephecheres of Ctesias. He repaired the city of Calah, which had been founded by his ancestor Divanukha, building at that place the famous palace which has supplied our national Museum with the best specimens of Assyrian sculpture. He also erected at Calah temples both to Assur and to "Mars;" and he built a third to Uranus, or "the Heavens," at Nineveh; some relics of this latter building, which was repaired by Sennacherib, having lately been discovered. As a warrior, his achievements were well known to the Greeks; and these exploits he recorded in an inscription of about four hundred lines, engraved upon each face of an enormous monolith, which was placed in the vestibule of the temple of Mars at Calah. By a careful examination of all the fragments of this monolith, Colonel Rawlinson has obtained a complete and continuous copy of the whole inscription; and a translation of it is promised to the world at an early period. It describes, in most elaborate detail, the various expeditions of the king, and enables us to identify a multitude of cities and countries which are named in the historical and prophetical books of Scripture, but of which the positions have been hitherto unknown. Gozan, Hanan, and Rezeth, Eden and Thelaser, Calno and Carchemish, Hamath and Arpad, Tyre and Sidon, and Gebel and Arpad, are all distinctly named. So are the Arab tribes of Kedar and Hazor, Sheba, Teman, and Dedan. For the illustration of the general geography of Western Asia this inscription is not less important. The Tigris and Euphrates, the two Zabs, the Hermas and the Khaboor, are designated almost according to their modern names; and we have further the true native forms of Cilicia, Comagene, Sophene, and Gogarene, and of most of the other provinces, both north and south of the Taurus, which are named by the Greek geographers.

Other inscriptions, relating to this reign, have been discovered,— one in the northwest palace of Nimrud, which is repeated more than a hundred times. It contains a certain formula of royal commemoration, which, in regard to the titles employed and the general character of address, was adopted by all the succeeding kings of the dynasty in the dedication of their palaces. It thus begins: "This is the palace of Sardanapalus, the humble worshipper of Assarac and Beltis, of the shining Bar, of Ani, and of Dagon, who are the principal of the gods, the powerful and supreme ruler, the King of Assyria; son of the servant of Bar, (*Kati-bar,*) the great king, the powerful and supreme ruler, the King of Assyria; who was son of Hevenk the great king, the powerful and supreme ruler, King of Assyria." After this introduction, the inscription goes on apparently to notice the efforts made by the king to establish the worship of the Assyrian gods generally throughout the empire; and, in connexion with this subject, incidentally, as it were, occurs a list of the nations tributary to Nineveh, which is of considerable interest, as affording a means of comparing the extent of the kingdom, as it was constituted at that time, with the distribution given in later inscriptions, when the empire was enlarged by conquest.

A brief outline of this can alone be given. First are mentioned the people of Nahiri, (or Northern Mesopotamia,) of Lek, (perhaps the Lycians, before they moved westward,) of Sabiri, (the Sapires,) and of the plains sacred to the god Hem. There is then an allusion to the countries beyond the River Tigris, as far as Syria: and after several other names, Rabek is mentioned, which, from many points of evidence in other inscriptions, Colonel Rawlinson believes to be Heliopolis, the capital of Lower Egypt. The inscription adds: "I received homage from the plains of Larri to Ladsán; from the people beyond the River Zab as far as the city Tel-Biari; from the city of Tel-Abtan to the city of Tel-Zabdan; from the cities of Akrima and Karta, and the sea-coast dependent on Taha-Tanis, to the frontiers of my country. I brought abundance from the plains of Bibad as far as Tarmar; I bestowed (all) upon the people of my own kingdom."

Our learned author pertinently observes, "This list is no less remarkable for what it omits than for what it mentions. It would seem as if the sea-coast of Phenicia had not yet fallen under the power of Assyria, nor the upper provinces of Asia Minor, nor the high land of Media; and if Susiana and Babylonia were included,— as the mention of Taha-Tanis would seem to indicate,—they were not held of sufficient account to be noticed;" or rather were regarded as such essential elements of the empire as not to require mention. In a subsequent inscription, namely, that on the monolith already noticed, the period when Phenicia came under the Assyrian power is mentioned. It is there stated, that when Sardanapalus was in Syria, he received the tribute of the kings of Tyre and Sidon, of Acre, of Byblos, of Berytus, of Gaza, of Barza, (?) and of Aradus, —a complete list of the maritime cities of Phenicia.

It seems, therefore, that the wars of Sardanapalus issued in a considerable extension of the Assyrian empire in Western Asia. It was this, unquestionably, which made his name so celebrated in Greece. The inscription in the Nimrud palace, made in the early part of his reign, although evidently designed to set forth the extent of his dominions, omits all mention of the sea-coast of Phenicia; while the monolith which was reared to perpetuate his triumphs, parades all the cities of this country as rendering tribute to Assyria.

Sardanapalus was contemporary with Ahab, King of Israel; and received tribute from Ethbaal, King of Sidon, whose daughter Jezebel was married to the king of Israel.

The military career of this great warrior affords a most remarkable instance of the special providence which Jehovah exercised over the Hebrew people. While Sardanapalus was encompassing Palestine with his armies, and extending his power over every neighbouring people, God did not permit him to touch even apostate Israel, until every merciful means of restoring them had failed. The wicked Ahab, therefore, is left to the reproofs of Elijah, and not handed over to the proud and cruel Assyrian.

Sardanapalus was succeeded by his son DIVANUBARA; a name which signified, "the beloved of Divan" or "Hercules." Of the actions of this sovereign, who throughout a long reign appears to have displayed unfailing vigour and incessant activity, we have a remarkably extended and perspicuous account recorded on the Black Obelisk which Layard discovered at Nimrud, and which is now in the British Museum. Indeed, Colonel Rawlinson declares that "by comparing the obelisk inscription with the writing upon the votive bulls belonging to the centre palace, which were dedicated apparently at an earlier period of Divanubara's reign, and with the legend on the statue found at Kileh Shergat, which was designed especially to commemorate the king's southern expedition, we have as complete a register of the period as could well be desired. Of this register I will now accordingly undertake to give an explanation, merely premising that, although considerable difficulty still attaches to the pronunciation of proper names, and although the meaning of particular parts is still unknown to me, I hold the accurate ascertainment of the general purport of the legend to be no more subject to controversy than my decipherment of the Persian inscriptions of Behistun."—*Jour. of the Roy. Asiatic Soc.*, vol. xii, p. 431.

The inscription on the obelisk commences with an invocation to the gods to protect the empire. This occupies fourteen lines of writing. The whole cannot be read; but among other phrases are the following: "The god Assarac, the great lord, king of all the great gods; Ani, the king; Nit, the powerful, and Artenk, the supreme god of the provinces; Beltis, the protector, mother of the gods;—Shemir," (perhaps the Greek Semiramis,) "who presides over the heavens and the earth;—Bar, Artenk, Lama, and Horus;—Tal and Let, the attendants of Beltis, mother of the gods." The favour of all these deities, with Assarac, the supreme god of heaven, at their head, is invoked for the protection of Assyria. Divanubara then goes on to give his titles and genealogy. He calls himself "king of the nations who worship Husi," (another name for the god Shemir,) "and Assarac; king of Mesopotamia; son of Sardanapalus, the servant of Husi, the protector, who first introduced the worship of the gods among the many-peopled nations of Persepolis."

Divanubara then says, "At the commencement of my reign, after that I was established on the throne, I assembled the chiefs of my people, and came down into the plains of Esmes, where I took the city of Harida, the chief city belonging to Nakharni.

"In the first year of my reign, I crossed the Upper Euphrates, and ascended to the tribes who worshipped the god Husi. My servants erected altars" (or tablets) "in that land to my gods. Then I went on to the land of Khamána, where I founded palaces, cities, and temples. I went on to the land of Málac; and there I established the worship" (or laws) "of my kingdom.

"In the second year, I went to the city of Tel-Barasba, and occupied the cities of Ahuni, son of Hateni. I shut him up in his city. I then crossed the Euphrates, and occupied the cities of Dabagu and Abarta, belonging to the Sheta, together with the cities dependent on them.

"In the third year, Ahuni, son of Hateni, rebelled against me, and, having become independent, established his seat of government in the city of Tel-Barasba. The country beyond the Euphrates he placed under the protection of the god Assarac the Excellent, while he committed to the god Rimmon the country between the Euphrates and the Arteri, with its city of Bether, which was held by the Sheta. Then I descended into the plain of Elets. The countries of Shakni, Dayini, Enim, Arcaskán, the capital of Arama, King of Ararat, Laban and Hubiska, I committed to the charge of Detarasar. Then I went out from the city of Nineveh, and, crossing the Euphrates, I attacked and defeated Ahuni, the son of Hateni, in the city of Sitrat, which was situated upon the Euphrates, and which Ahuni had made one of his capitals. The rest of the country I brought under subjection; and Ahuni, the son of Hateni, with his gods and his chief priests, his horses, his sons and his daughters, and all his men of war, I brought away to my country of Assyria. Afterward I passed through the country of Shelár," (or Kelár,) "and came to the district of Zobah. I reached the cities belonging to Nikti, and took the city of Gedi, where Nikti dwelt." From the confusion evident on this part of the obelisk sculpture, and the parallel bull inscription, it seems probable that what is given above includes the third and fourth years.

We therefore pass on: "In the fifth year, I went up to the country of Abyari. I took eleven great cities; I besieged Akitta of Eni in his city, and received his tribute.

"In the sixth year, I went out from the city of Nineveh, and proceeded to the country situated on the River Belek. The ruler of the country having resisted my authority, I displaced him, and appointed Tsimba to be lord of the district; and I there established the Assyrian sway. I went out from the land on the River Belek, and came to the cities of Tel-Atak and Habaremya. Then I crossed the Upper Euphrates, and received tribute from the kings of Sheta. Afterward I went out from the land of Sheta, and came to the city of Umen. In the city of Umen I raised altars to the great gods.

From the city of Umen I went out, and came to the city of Barbara. Then Hem-ithra of the country of Atesh, and Arhulena of Hamath, and the kings of Sheta, and the tribes which were in alliance with them, arose; setting their forces in battle array, they came against me. By the grace of Assarac, the great and powerful god, I fought with them, and defeated them; twenty thousand five hundred of their men I slew in battle, or carried into slavery. Their leaders, their captains, and their men of war I put in chains.

"In the seventh year, I proceeded to the country belonging to Khabni of Tel-ati, which was his chief place; and the towns which were dependent on it I captured and gave up to pillage. I went out from the city of Tel-ati, and came to the land watered by the head-streams which form the Tigris. The priests of Assarac in that land raised altars to the immortal gods. I appointed priests to reside in the land, to pay adoration to Assarac the great and powerful god, and to preside over the national worship. The cities of this region which did not acknowledge the god Assarac, I brought under subjection; and I here received the tribute of the country of Nahiri.

"In the eighth year, against Sut-Baba, King of Taha-Dunis, appeared Sut-Belherat and his followers. The latter led his forces against Sut-Baba, and took from him the cities of the land of Beth-Takara.

"In the ninth year, a second time I went to Armenia, and took the city of Lunanta. By the assistance of Assarac and Sut, I obtained possession of the person of Sut-Belherat. In the city of Umen I put him in chains. Afterward Sut-Belherat, together with his chief followers, I condemned to slavery. Then I went down to Shinar; and in the cities of Shinar, of Borsippa, and of Ketika, I erected altars, and founded temples to the great gods. Then I went down to the land of the Chaldees, and I occupied their cities, and I marched on as far even as the tribes who dwelt upon the sea-coast. Afterward, in the city of Shinar, I received the tribute of the kings of the Chaldees, Hateni, the son of Dákri, and Baga-Sut, the son of Aukni,—gold, silver, gems, and pearls.

"In the tenth year, for the eighth time I crossed the Euphrates, and took the cities belonging to Ara-lura, of the town of Shalumas; and I proceeded to the country belonging to Arama" (who was king of Ararat.) "I took the city Arnia, which was the capital of the country; and I gave up to pillage one hundred of the dependent towns. I slew the wicked, and I carried off the treasures.

"At this time Hem-ithra, King of Atesh, Arhulena, King of Hamath, and the twelve kings of the tribes who were in alliance with them, came forth, arraying their forces against me. They met me, and we fought a battle, in which I defeated them, making prisoners of their leaders, and their captains, and their men of war, and putting them in chains.

"In the eleventh year, I went out from the city of Nineveh, and for the ninth time crossed the Euphrates. I took the eighty-seven cities belonging to Ara-lura, and one hundred cities belonging to Arama; and I gave them up to pillage. I settled the country of Khamána; and, passing by the country of Yeri, I went down to the cities of Hamath, and took the city of Esdimak, and eighty-nine of the dependent towns, slaying the wicked ones, and carrying off the treasures. Again, Hem-ithra, King of Atesh, Arhulena, King of Hamath, and the twelve kings of the tribes," (or "the twelve kings of Sheta,") "who were in alliance with them, came forth, levying war upon me. They arrayed their forces against me. I fought with them and defeated them, slaying ten thousand of their men, and carrying into slavery their captains, and leaders, and men of war. Afterward I went up to the city of Habbarie, one of the chief cities belonging to Arama" (of Ararat); "and there I received the tribute of Berbaranda, the king of Shetina,—gold, silver, horses, sheep, oxen, &c. I then went up to the country of Khamána, where I founded palaces and cities.

"In the twelfth year, I marched forth from Nineveh, and for the tenth time I crossed the Euphrates, and went up to the city of Sevenahuben. I slew the wicked, and carried off the treasures from thence to my own country.

"In the thirteenth year, I descended to the plains dependent on the city of Assar-Animet. I went to the district of Yáta. I took the forts of the country of Yáta, slaying the evil-disposed, and carrying off all the wealth of the country.

"In the fourteenth year, I raised the country, and assembled a great army: with one hundred and twenty thousand warriors I crossed the Euphrates. Then it came to pass that Hem-ithra, King of Atesh, and Arhulena, King of Hamath, and the twelve kings of the tribes of the Upper and Lower Country, collected their forces together, and came before me, offering battle. I engaged with them, and defeated them; their leaders, and captains, and men of war I cast into chains.

"In the fifteenth year, I went to the country of the Nahiri, and established my authority throughout the country about the headstreams which form the Tigris.

"Afterward I descended to the plain of Lanbuna, and devastated the cities of Arama, King of Ararat, and all the country about the head-water of the Euphrates; and I abode in the country about the rivers which form the Euphrates; and there I set up altars to the supreme gods, and left priests in the land to superintend the worship. Hasá, King of Dayini, then paid me his homage, and brought in his tribute of horses; and I established the authority of my empire throughout the land dependent on his city.

"In the sixteenth year, I crossed the Zab, and went against the country of the Arians. Sut-Mesisek, the king of the Arians, I put in chains, and I brought his wives, and his warriors, and his gods, captives to my country of Assyria; and I appointed Yanvu, the son of Khanab, to be king over the country in his place.

"In the seventeenth year, I crossed the Euphrates, and went up to the country of Khamána, where I founded palaces and cities.

"In the eighteenth year, for the sixteenth time I crossed the Euphrates. Khazakan of Atesh came forth to fight: one thousand one hundred and twenty-one of his captains, and four hundred and sixty of his superior chiefs, with the troops they commanded, I defeated in this war." This campaign is not only thus briefly noticed on the obelisk, but was also commemorated by the setting up of two colossal bulls, which were found in the centre of the mound at Nimrud. On these is an inscription, giving a more elaborate account of this war, and stating the numbers, as above, of the prisoners taken, together with thirteen thousand fighting men who were sent into slavery.

"In the nineteenth year, for the eighteenth time I crossed the Euphrates. I went up to Khamána, and founded more palaces and temples.

"In the twentieth year, for the nineteenth time I crossed the Euphrates; I went to the country of the Beráhui. I took the cities, and despoiled them of their treasures.

"In the twenty-first year, for the twentieth time I crossed the Euphrates, and again went up to the country of Khazakan of Atesh. I occupied his country; and, while there, received tribute from the countries of Tyre, of Sidon, and of Gubal." This latter name is the same with the Greek Βύβλος. The form occurs in the Hebrew Bible גבל. See Ezek. xxvii, 9; and 1 Kings v, 18.

"In the twenty-second year, for the twenty-first time I crossed the Euphrates, and marched to the country of Tubal. Then I received the submission of the twenty-four kings of Tubal; and I went on to the country of Atta, to the gold country, to Belni and to Ta-Esfereon.

"In the twenty-third year, I again crossed the Euphrates, and occupied the city of Huidra, the strong-hold of Ellal of Melada; and the kings of Tubal again came in to me, and I received their tribute

"In the twenty-fourth year, I crossed the river Zab; and, crossing away from the land of Kharkhar, went up to the country of the Arians. Yanvu, whom I had made king of the Arians, had thrown off his allegiance; so I put him in chains. I captured the city of Esaksha, and took Beth-Telabon, Beth-Everek, and Beth-Treida, his principal cities. I slew the evil-disposed, and plundered the treasures, and gave the cities over to pillage. I then went out from the land of the Arians, and received the tribute of twenty-seven kings of the Persians. Afterward, I removed from the land of the Persians, and entered the territory of the Medes, going to Ratsir and Kharkhar. I occupied the several cities of Kákhidra, of Taizánem, of Irleban, of Akhirablud, and the towns which depended on them. I punished the evil-disposed. I confiscated the treasures, and gave the cities over to pillage; and I established the authority of my empire in the city of Kharkhar. Yanvu, the son of Khaban, with his wives, and his gods, and his sons and daughters, his servants, and all his property, I carried away captive into my country of Assyria.

"In the twenty-fifth year, I crossed the Euphrates, and received the tribute of the kings of the Sheta. I passed by the country of Khamána, and came to the cities of Akti of Berhui. The city of Tarbura, his strong-hold, I took by assault. I slew those who resisted, and plundered the treasures; and all the cities of the country I gave over to pillage. Afterward in the city of Barhura, the capital city of Aram, son of Hagus, I dedicated a temple to the god Rimmon; and I also built a royal palace in the same place.

"In the twenty-sixth year, for the seventh time I passed through the country of Khamána. I went on to the cities of Akti of Berhui; and I inhabited the city of Tanaken, which was the strong-hold of Etlak. There I performed the rites which belong to the worship of Assarac, the supreme god; and I received as tribute from the country, gold and silver, corn and sheep and oxen. Then I went out from the city of Tanaken, and I came to the country of Leman. The people resisted me, but I subdued the country by force. I took the cities, and slew their defenders; and the wealth of the people, with their cattle and corn and movables, I sent as booty to my country of Assyria. I gave all their cities over to pillage. Then I went on to the country of Methets, where the people paid their homage; and I received gold and silver as their tribute. I appointed Akharriyadon, the son of Akti, to be king over them. Afterward I went up to Khamána, where I founded more palaces and temples, until at length I returned to my country of Assyria.

"In the twenty-seventh year, I assembled the captains of my army, and I sent Detarasar of Ittána, the general of the forces, in command of my warriors to Armenia; he proceeded to the land of

Khamána, and in the plains belonging to the city of Ambaret he crossed the river Artseni. Asiduri of Armenia, hearing of the invasion, collected his cohorts, and came forth against my troops, offering them battle. My forces engaged with him, and defeated him; and the country at once submitted to my authority.

"In the twenty-eighth year, while I was residing in the city of Calah, a revolt took place on the part of the tribes of the Shetina. They were led on by Sherila, who had succeeded to the throne on the death of Labarni, the former king. Then I ordered the general of my army, Detarasar of Ittána, to march with my cohorts and all my troops against the rebels. Detarasar accordingly crossed the Upper Euphrates, and, marching into the country, established himself in the capital city, Kanalá. Then Sherila, who was seated on the throne, by the help of the great god Assarac, I obtained possession of his person, and his officers, and the chiefs of the tribes of the Shetina, who had thrown off their allegiance, and revolted against me, together with the sons of Sherila, and the men who administered affairs; and imprisoned or punished all of them; and I appointed Ar-hasit, of Suzakisba, to be king over the entire land. I exacted a tribute also from the land, consisting of gold and silver, and precious stones, and ebony, &c.; and I established the national worship throughout the land, making a great sacrifice in the capital of Kanalá, in the temple which had been there raised to the gods.

"In the twenty-ninth year, I assembled my warriors and captains, and I ascended with them to the country of the Lek. I accepted the homage of the cities of the land, and I went on to Shenába.

"In the thirtieth year, while I was residing in the city of Calah, I summoned Detarasar, the general of my army; and I sent him forth to war in command of my cohorts and forces. He crossed the river Zab, and first came to the cities of Hubiska; he received the tribute of Daten of Hubiska; and he went out from thence, and came to the country belonging to Mekadal of Melakari. He then went on to the country of Haelka of Minni. Haelka of Minni had thrown off his allegiance, and declared himself independent, establishing his seat of government in the city of Tsiharta. My general, therefore, put him in chains, and carried off his flocks and herds and all his property, and gave his cities over to pillage. Passing out from the country of Minni, he next came to the territory of Selshan of Kharta. He took possession of the city of Maharsar, the capital of the country, and of all the towns which depended on it; and Selshan and his sons he made prisoners, and sent to his country, despatching to me their tribute of horses, male and female. He then went into the country Sardera, and received the tribute of Ataheri of Sardera. He afterward marched to Persia, and obtained the tribute of the kings of the Persians; and he captured many more cities between Persia and Assyria, and he brought all their riches and treasures with him to Assyria.

"In the thirty-first year, a second time, while I abode in the city of Calah, occupied in the worship of the gods Assarac, Hem, and Nebo, I summoned the general of my army, Detarasar of Ittána, and I sent him forth to war with my troops and cohorts. He went out accordingly, in the first place, to the territories of Daten of Hubiska, and received his tribute; then he proceeded to Anseri, the capital city of the country of Bazatsera; and he occupied the city of Anseri, and the thirty-six other towns of the country of Bazatsera. He continued his march to the land of Armenia; and he gave over to pillage fifty cities belonging to that territory. He afterward proceeded to Ladsán, and received the tribute of Hubu of Ladsán, and of the districts of Minni, of Bariana, of Kharran, of Sharrum, of Andi,—sheep, oxen, and horses, male and female. And he afterward penetrated as far as the land of the Persians, taking possession of the cities of Baiset, Shel-Khamána, and Akeri-Khamána, all of them places of strength, and of the twenty-three towns which depended on them. He slew those who resisted, and he carried off the wealth of the cities. And he afterward moved to the country of the Arians, where, by the help of the gods Assarac and Sut, he captured their cities, and continued his march to the country of the Kherets, taking and despoiling two hundred and fifty towns, until at length he descended into the plains of Esmes, above the country of Umen."

This monarch appears to have been succeeded by his son SHEMAS ADAR, who was followed by ADRAMMELECH II. As these were the last sovereigns of the old imperial dynasty, the only mode of reconciling the teaching of the inscriptions with the list of Ctesias is, to identify Sardanapalus with Ophratæus, Divanubara with Ephecheres, Shemas Adar with Æraganes, and Adrammelech II. with Thonos Concoleros. Nor does this arrangement involve any discrepancy. The second of these sovereigns, according to the list, reigned the unusual period of fifty-two years; while the inscriptions record a series of annual campaigns extending to his thirty-eighth year.

No doubt can be entertained as to the fact, that with Adrammelech II., or Thonos Concoleros, the old imperial dynasty terminated, and that ARBACES the Mede next succeeded to the throne. This is confirmed alike by the testimony of all ancient history, and is fully warranted by the inscriptions. The manner in which this was done is, however, one of the most disputed questions in ancient history. (See *Appendix*, notes 18, 19.) We have by careful inquiry into the subject been convinced, that Arbaces, being a Median officer, appointed in regular course with others to command the garrison of Nineveh, took advantage of his period of office to supplant his licentious and effeminate master, and seat himself on his throne.

No inscriptions have been found recording the actions of this king, although Colonel Rawlinson has discovered from damaged slabs evidence of the existence of a sovereign who reigned between Adrammelech II. and Pul. If our arrangement of these reigns is correct, this will be the sovereign who ruled Assyria, when Jonah went there on his mission from Jehovah. It is not improbable that future researches into the ancient mounds of that country may yet produce some native evidence of the preaching of the Hebrew prophet and its great results. It is, however, clear, that this period is as suitable to the circumstances detailed in the Scriptural account as any that can be found. If we had heard that one of the last rulers of the old imperial line had then reigned, we might have been struck with the improbability that a person so steeped in sensuality and sloth, as by universal consent these princes are said to have been, should promptly submit to the divine message, and unite with his people in self-denial, penitence, and prayer. But from a man who had dared to aspire to a throne to which he was not entitled, who had succeeded in reaching that dangerous elevation, and who was probably open to every sound of alarm in his own mind, and anxious to avail himself of any opportunity of blending his own with the general sympathies of his people,—from such a monarch the course pursued by the king of Nineveh, as recorded by the prophet, was just what might be expected.

Yet the subject of this narrative must always be regarded as a most extraordinary event. What could have induced a whole people to such instant and universal humiliation? The simple answer is afforded by the Scripture: "*The people of Nineveh believed God.*" Jonah iii, 5. It is, however, probable that the men of Nineveh were familiar with the wonderful interpositions of Jehovah on behalf of Israel. Having for centuries had intercourse with Egypt, this degree of religious knowledge would be inevitable; and hence we find that it was not until the Israelites had fallen into idolatry, and had assimilated their worship to that of the surrounding nations, that the Assyrians dared to assail them. Compare 2 Kings xviii, 22, with verses 33–35.

Pul succeeded Arbaces in the government of Assyria. The

name of this monarch has not yet been found on the inscriptions; but fragments have been identified as referring to his reign. Rawlinson believes Pul to have been connected with the old Assyrian line of kings; and Mr. Sharpe affirms, (Bonomi's Nineveh and its Palaces, p. 69,) that, "after the death of Arbaces the Mede, the Assyrians were able to make themselves again independent." It seems probable that after his decease the throne of Nineveh was secured by a native Assyrian, inasmuch as all the sculptures referring to this and the following reign indicate a return to the usages of the former dynasty.

Under this sovereign we meet with the first conflict between the Hebrews and the Assyrians, which, strangely enough, was begun by the former people. Menahem, having slain Shallum, King of Israel, and seated himself on his throne, was so fool-hardy as to lead an army to the banks of the Euphrates, where he stormed Tiphsah, a city belonging to Assyria, and destroyed its inhabitants with the most atrocious barbarity. 2 Kings xv, 16.

This assault was not long left unavenged. In the following year Pul marched an army into Samaria, of such magnitude and power that the affrighted king did not dare to meet it; but purchased a peace by the payment of ten thousand talents of silver. This circumstance is mentioned in an inscription found on a fragment of a slab in the south-west palace of Nineveh. Another fragment of Pul's annals, which is still lying in a passage of the same palace, seems to have contained a particular account of the expedition of this Assyrian king against Samaria; but the writing is so mutilated that little can be made out, except the name of the city.

TIGLATH-PILESER was the next king of Assyria. He also was brought into contact with the Hebrews by their own act. We have scarcely, in the whole history of that nation, a more striking instance of the evil consequences of their impiety and unbelief. Israel, under the reign of Pekah, entered into an alliance with Rezin, King of Syria, against Judah. The main object of this confederacy was the dethronement of the house of David, and the establishment of a son of Tabeal as sovereign of Judah. This produced a profound sensation at Jerusalem, when God sent Isaiah the prophet to King Ahaz, assuring him that this conspiracy should fail, and inviting him to ask any sign for the truth of this promise. The impious king declined to ask, on the plea that he would "not tempt God;" upon which the Lord gave, by the prophet, the glorious prophecy of the birth of Immanuel. Isa. vii.

But although Ahaz would not ask a sign of God, he was so alarmed at the union of these two powers against him, that "he took the silver and gold that was found in the house of the Lord, and in the treasures of the king's house, and sent it for a present to the king of Assyria," with this servile message to Tiglath-Pileser: "I am thy servant and thy son: come up and save me out of the hand of the king of Syria, and out of the hand of the king of Israel, which rise up against me." 2 Kings xvi. This course precisely falling in with the policy of the king of Assyria, he complied with the request, and proceeded to Syria, which he subdued, killing Rezin the king in the war, and taking Damascus. He then entered the kingdom of Israel, which he also subjected to his will; and, leaving the humbled king only the province of Samaria, he took all the cities on the east bank of the Jordan, and Galilee in the north, and carried the inhabitants away as captives to the extreme portion of his own kingdom on the banks of the river Kir. Ahaz went in person to Damascus, to thank the Assyrian for his aid. Thus began the long-threatened deportation of the idolatrous Hebrews into the land of their conquerors.

At the close of this reign we have again the light of recovered and translated inscriptions, to guide us in our way. In the next king we meet with the builder of Khorsabad, and have the aid of the inscriptions found in this city, and also in that of Koyunjik, to assist us in this and the following reigns.

These literary treasures, so strangely brought to light, have been arranged by Colonel Rawlinson in four classes:—

"1. First, the standard inscriptions, which contains the names and titles of the king, and a list of the principal tribes and nations subject to Assyria; with occasional notices of the building of the city of Khorsabad 'near to Nineveh, after the manner of Egypt,' together with a prayer to the gods for its protection.

"2. The second class consists of the long inscriptions on the votive bulls, which, without being strictly historical, go into much greater detail regarding the constitution of the empire, and name the various kings and chieftains subdued by the Assyrian monarch. There are also in those inscriptions very elaborate notices of the Assyrian Pantheon.

"3. The third or historical class consists of the slabs surrounding the sculptured halls, interposing between the bas-reliefs which represent the battles and sieges recorded in the inscriptions. Some of these records are in the form of regular yearly annals, while in others the entire history of the monarch's reign is given as a continuous narrative, without being interrupted by divisions of time. In some of these insciptions the geographical details are quite bewildering.

"4. The inscriptions of the fourth class are those on the back of the slabs, which were never intended to be seen. They are strictly religious, containing no geographical notices whatever, but merely noticing the building of Khorsabad by the king, and invoking the gods to extend protection to that city."—*Jour. of the Roy. Asiatic Soc.*, vol. xii, p. 458.

It will only be necessary here to present the reader with a tolerably copious abstract of the historical inscriptions relating to this period. The name of the founder of Khorsabad, as given in a phonetic form in the inscriptions, is ARKO-TSIN. He calls himself "King of Assyria and Babylonia," and of two provinces of which the titles are usually given as Saberi and Hekti, and which may be understood to denote that portion of Upper Asia immediately to the eastward of the valley of the Tigris. His three special divinities, who are named in every inscription immediately after the proclamation of his own titles, are Assarac, Nebu, and Sut. Then follows a catalogue of geographical names, which appears intended to mark out the limits of the Assyrian empire, and not to give a list of the merely tributary provinces.

It commences with the passage, "From Yetnan, a land sacred to the god Husi, as far as Misr and Misek," (or Lower and Upper Egypt,) "Martha or Acarri," (Acre,—which was the sea-coast of Phenicia,) "and the land of Sheta." The countries of Media, Vakana, (perhaps Hyrcania,) Ellubi, Rasi, and Susiana, are afterward mentioned in succession; and the list closes with a multitude of names of tribes and cities which belong to Susiana, Elymais, and Lower Chaldea, and the positions of which are illustrated by their contiguity to the great rivers Tigris, Eulæus, and Pasitigris. After these geographical notices, which are important as indicating the extent of the empire at the time, follow the annals, which extend from the commencement of the king's reign to his fifteenth year.

Before entering on the details of the next reign, it must be observed that we have here another change of dynasty,—a revolution. SARGINA, the Sargon of Isaiah, and the Shalmaneser of the Book of Kings, who succeeded Tiglath-Pileser, was not his son, nor in any way connected by relationship with the royal line, but a subordinate officer in the palace. "Polyhistor, in Agathius, calls him 'the head gardener;' and it is very possible that this may have been his real condition."—*Rawlinson's Outlines of Assyrian History*, p. 29. But, being a man of great daring, energy and capacity, he succeeded in grasping the reins of government, immediately after they had fallen from the hands of Tiglath-Pileser.

Having established himself on the throne, Sargina placed himself at the head of his army, and proceeded to consolidate the power of the empire by enforcing the entire subjection of those provinces which had evinced symptoms of insubordination, and to extend beyond its former limits the authority of Assyria.

The first campaign noticed on the sculptures was against Helubinerus, King of Susiana, who was defeated; and twenty-seven thousand eight hundred of his men, two hundred of his captains, and fifty of his superior officers, were carried into captivity.

The second campaign was against certain tributaries of the king of Egypt; and as in this passage (which is repeated several times in the halls) occurs the only mention of the Egyptian monarch's name, Colonel Rawlinson gives the clause as literally as possible: "Khanan, King of the city of Khazita, and Shelki, of the tribe of Khalban, belonging to the country of Misr," (or Egypt,) "prepared their forces for battle in the city of Rabek. They came against me; and I fought with them, and defeated them." This passage the learned translator applies to the frontier-towns of Egypt, (see *Appendix*, note 20,) and adds from the inscriptions, "I received the tribute of Biarku," or Biarhu, "King of Misr,—gold, asbatera," (perhaps tin,) "horses and camels," together with certain unknown articles, coming from Harida and Arbaka.

The next campaign presents some very interesting allusions. It was carried on against Kehek, the King of Shenakti, a city which is usually mentioned in connexion with Ashdod, and which must therefore be situated on the sea-coast of Palestine, being perhaps the same place as Askalon. Here occurs in the record a notice of peculiar interest. After the city of Shenakti was taken from Kehek, it was presented by the Assyrian king to Methati, King of Atheni. Colonel Rawlinson believes this to refer to Melanthus of Athens; and is supported in this judgment by the fact, that in the general inscriptions, which give a synopsis of the historical *data*, the city of Shenakti is said to be held by the *Yavana*. That this term refers to the Ionians seems certain. It is, therefore, likely that we have here an account of the presentation of a city by the king of Assyria to the Athenians, for naval assistance rendered by them during his wars. Colonel Rawlinson is disposed to think that many of the predictions and notices found in Isaiah (chap. xix and xx) were verified in this campaign.

The fourth campaign was against Amris, King of Tubal, who seems to have been supported by Arah, King of Ararat, and by Meta, King of Misek, and also by the tribe of the Amorites, here called Amári.

These campaigns are remarkable for their identity of character, and are almost all described in the same terms. The king of Assyria defeats the enemy in the field, subjugates the country, sacrifices to the gods, and then generally carries the people into captivity, supplying their places by colonists drawn from other parts of his empire, and appointing his own governors or prefects to rule these new communities. This uniformity is clearly attributable to the circumstance, that nothing was inscribed which could prove unacceptable to the royal warrior.

The following campaigns relate to wars successively carried on against Hamath and its dependencies,—Ararat and Minni,—Kharkhar and Media,—Syria,—and Susiana, Elymais, and Babylonia. In this list we find no notice of the capture of Samaria. Indeed, the year before this event is the last recorded in the annals which have been recovered. But it is unquestionable that the conquest was one of the triumphs of that reign. In a former campaign Sargina had subjected the king of Israel to tribute. 2 Kings xvii, 3. But finding afterward that Hoshea was forming an alliance with the king of Egypt, he sent an army to invest his capital, which fell into the hands of the Assyrians after a siege of three years, when the conquerer "took Samaria, and carried the people of Israel away into Assyria, and placed them in Halah and in Habor, by the river of Gozan, and in the cities of the Medes." 2 Kings xvii, 6. From this time Israel ceased to be a kingdom.

Although no inscriptions have as yet been discovered which furnish an account of these events, others very clearly prove that they actually took place in this reign. It seems that soon after the conquest of Syria and Israel, Sargina turned his arms against Carchemish, the city of the Hittites, on the Euphrates; and having spoiled this city, and brought from thence a great amount of wealth into the royal treasury, he set up a tablet in the palace of Sardanapalus at Calah, in celebration of the event. On this monument he for the first time assumes the title of "the Conqueror of the remote Judea;" so glorious in the estimation of the princes of the east was the subjugation even of a part of the Hebrew nation.

Not content with his success on the continent, it is asserted that Sargina sailed to the Island of Cyprus, and reduced it to subjection. There is still extant, in the Museum at Berlin, a statue of this king, with a suitable inscription, which was found in that island.

But Menander, quoted by Josephus, (Antiquities, book xi, chap. xiv, sect. 2,) says that Sargina failed in his efforts to subdue Tyre, although his army was employed against that city for five years.

Sargina makes no mention of his ancestors; but upon a clay tablet, of the date of Sennacherib, the name of Sargina's father is given as Nabosiphuni, and that of his grandfather as Kilapel. This sovereign was the builder of Khorsabad, from whence so rich a harvest of sculptured treasures has been procured, and which stands identified with the lower line of Assyrian kings. This city, named in the common idiom of the country after its founder, retained among the inhabitants the title of Sarghan, until the period of the Arab conquest.

It appears certain that SENNACHERIB succeeded his father Sargina, or Shalman, on the throne of Assyria. Respecting him the sacred Scriptures give us a considerable amount of information; but the monuments have as yet furnished no complete copy of the annals of his reign. Yet the patient and unwearied industry of those, to whose researches the world is so greatly indebted for important notices on this interesting subject, has brought together the materials for a tolerable account of the early part of Sennacherib's career.

It will serve to show the remarkable manner in which this knowledge has been obtained, if we notice the sources whence this account has been derived. The first is a clay cylinder, covered with inscriptions, which was found by Mr. Rich at Nineveh; and which, after lying for the last thirty years almost unnoticed in the British Museum, has been recently published in *fac-simile* by Grotefend at Hanover. This cylinder furnishes ample details of the first two years of Sennacherib's reign, and further contains a very interesting account of the king's early buildings at Nineveh. The second document is an inscription on a pair of bulls in Sennacherib's palace at Nineveh. Throughout all the historical portion of this inscription, which extends to the king's sixth regnal year, the writing is much mutilated; but, by the aid of the other texts, and a very careful examination of the slabs under every possible light, Colonel Rawlinson has succeeded in effecting an almost complete restoration. The third document—which is the most valuable of all, as it extends to the king's eighth year, and contains abundance of detail omitted on the bulls—is an inscription upon a clay cylinder, which was found at Nineveh many years ago, and was conveyed to England by Colonel Taylor in 1846. The original cylinder is said to be lost; but casts of it are extant,—one taken on paper by Colonel Rawlinson in 1835; and another taken in plaster by M. Lottin de Lavel, about ten years later: of these casts a great portion of the inscription can be recovered. From such materials, so wonderfully preserved, and so strangely brought into juxtaposition, the following account has been arranged according to Colonel Rawlinson's translations.

Sennacherib adopts the ordinary royal epithets assumed by his predecessors; but he also on many occasions takes the especial title of *Ebidu Malki*, " the Subduer of Kings;" and he further styles himself, " he who has reduced under his yoke all the kings of Asia, from the

Upper Forest which is under the setting sun," (Lebanon,) "to the Lower Ocean which is under the rising sun," (the Persian Gulf.)

His annals, as presented in those monumental remains, thus commence: "In the first year of my reign I fought a battle with Merodach-Baladan, King of Kar-duniyas, and the troops of Susiana, who formed his army; and I defeated them. He embarked on board his ships, and fled across the sea; concealing himself in the country, to Guzumman, the River Agammi, and the parts beyond it, he fled. His ships saved him. His standards, his chariots, his horses, his mares, his camels, and his mules, which he abandoned on the field of battle, fell into my hands. I then marched to his palace, which was near the city of Babylon; I opened the royal treasure-house, and rifled it of the gold and silver vessels, the hoards of gold and silver, altogether a vast booty; his idols, the women of his palace, all his chief men, &c., &c., each and all I seized and carried off into captivity. By the grace of Assur my lord, seventy-nine of the principal fortified cities of the Chaldæans, and eight hundred and twenty of the smaller towns which depended on them, I took and plundered. The nomade tribes of the Aramæans and Chaldæans, who inhabited the Mesopotamian country, I subdued and carried off into captivity.

"A man of the name of Bel-adon, the son of one of my confidential officers, who had been bred up in my palace, I appointed to be king of the country, attaching to his government the provinces of the north and east.

"At the same time I subjugated the Aramæan tribes, who lined the Tigris and Euphrates:—the Tehaman," (Teman of Scripture,) the Rikis, the Yetukh, the Hubad, the Kiheim, the Melik, the Gurum, the Hubal, the Damun, the Tebal, the Kindar," (Kedar of Scripture,) "the Ruhua, the Bakud, the Kamran, the Khagurin," (Hagarenes,) "the Nabaat," (the Nebaroth or Nabatæans,) "the Lihata, and the Aramæans Proper. I carried off to Nineveh two hundred and eight thousand men and women, eight thousand two hundred horses and mares, eleven thousand one hundred and eighty head of cattle, five thousand two hundred and thirty camels, one million and twenty thousand one hundred sheep, eight hundred thousand three hundred goats,—altogether an enormous booty."

It is worthy of observation that the king of Babylon, Merodach-Baladan, spoken of in this campaign, was the same who afterward sent an embassy to Hezekiah. This war is mentioned both by Polyhistor and Abydenus. It is further remarkable that the Assyrian annals speak of Kar-duniyas in the Lower Country, and not Babylon, as the capital of the nation.

The second year of Sennacherib's reign found him occupied among the mountains to the north and east. He seems to have crossed the Taurus into countries to which his ancestors had never penetrated; and his annals contain the usual amount of burning and plundering, sweeping off the old population, and planting fresh colonies in their place.

For the rest of the year, Sennacherib says, he was occupied in reducing Ellibi,—a name by which Northern Media is usually designated. The title of the king of the country, Aspabara, shows that he was of Arian extraction; and one of his cities, Marukarta, is well known in Armenian history. A large portion of Aspabara's territory was attached directly to Assyria; another of his principal cities was rebuilt, and, under the name of Beth-Sennacherib, was peopled by an Assyrian colony, and placed under the charge of the governor of Kharkhar (Van). From Ellibi, Sennacherib went on to Media, and received tribute from that nation, "which had never," he adds, "submitted to the kings my ancestors."

The annals of the third year are more important, and require to be given with more particular detail. "In my third year," says Sennacherib, "I went up to the country of the Khetta" (or Hittites). "Suliya, King of Sidon, had thrown off the yoke of allegiance. On my approach from Abiri, he fled to Yetnan, which was on the sea-coast." Mr. Rawlinson supposes Yetnan to be the same as the Rhinocolura of the Greeks, since it is always spoken of as a maritime city south of Phenicia, which formed the extreme limit of the Assyrian territory toward Egypt. He believes that we have here a remarkable fulfilment of the prophecy of Balaam against the Kenite, (Num. xxiv, 21, 22;) and proposes the following as a more correct reading for the former of these verses: "Thy dwelling-place is *Ethan*," (Yetnan,) "and thou puttest thy nest in *Sela*" (Petra). After which the learned translator asserts, "The transportation of the Kenites to Assyria, foretold in the next verse, is duly related in the inscriptions."

Sennacherib thus proceeds with a narrative of his annals: "I reduced the entire country; the places which submitted to me were Sidon the Greater and Sidon the Less, Beth Zitta, Sariput, Mahallat, Hussuva, Akzib, and Akka. I placed Tubaal on the throne in the place of Suliya" It seems probable that this person was related to the chief who in the preceding reign was intended, by Rezin, King of Syria, and Pekah, King of Israel, to supersede the house of David on the throne of Judah. Isaiah vii. The annals proceed: "The kings of the sea-coast all repaired to my presence in the neighbourhood of the city of Husuva," or Tyre, "and brought me the accustomed tribute. Sitka of Ascalon, who did not come to pay me homage, the gods of his house and his treasures, his sons and his daughters, and his brothers of the house of his father, I seized, and sent off to Nineveh. I placed another chief on the throne of Ascalon, and I imposed on him the regulated amount of tribute."

We are now brought to the point at which Sennacherib gives his own version of the campaign narrated in Holy Scripture, which terminated so disastrously for Assyria. We will give the account from the annals. The Assyrian monarch goes on to say: "In the autumn of the year, certain other cities, which had refused to submit to my authority, I took and plundered. The nobles and the people of Ekron, having expelled their King Haddiya, and the Assyrian troops who garrisoned the town attached themselves to Hezekiah of Judea, and paid their adorations to his God. The kings of Egypt also sent horsemen and footmen, belonging to the king of Mirukha," (Meroe or Ethiopia,) " of which the numbers could not be counted. In the neighbourhood of the city of Allakis" (Lachish) "I joined battle with them. The captains of the cohorts, and the young men of the kings of Egypt, and the captains of the cohorts of the king of Meroe, I put to the sword in the country of Lubanah" (Libnah). "Afterward I moved to the city of Ekron; and the chiefs of the people having humbled themselves, I admitted them into my service; but the young men I carried into captivity to inhabit the cities of Assyria. Their goods and wealth also I plundered to an untold amount. Their King Haddiya I then brought back from the city of Jerusalem, and again placed in authority over them, imposing on him the regulated tribute of the empire; and because Hezekiah, King of Judea, did not submit to my yoke, forty-six of his strong fenced cities, and innumerable smaller towns which depended on them, I took and plundered: but I left to him Jerusalem, his capital city, and some of the inferior towns around it. The cities which I had taken and plundered, I detained from the government of Hezekiah, and distributed between the kings of Ashdod, and Ascalon, and Ekron, and Gaza; and having thus invaded the territory of these chiefs, I imposed on them a corresponding increase of tribute over that to which they had formerly been subjected. And because Hezekiah still continued to refuse to pay me homage, I attacked and carried off the whole population, fixed and nomade, which dwelt around Jerusalem, with thirty talents of gold and eight hundred talents of silver, the accumulated wealth of the nobles of Hezekiah's court, and of their daughters, with the officers of his palace, men-slaves and women-slaves. I returned to Nineveh, and I accounted this spoil for the tribute which he refused to pay me."

How marvellous is this record! How strange that we should

just at this time recover the Assyrian king's account of his own wars! I will briefly note the points of agreement and of discrepancy found to exist in the Scriptural and monumental versions of this campaign.

It may be observed, in the first place, that the general scope of the inscriptions perfectly accords with the Scriptural account. We read in the Scriptures, (2 Kings xviii, 8,) that Hezekiah, in the early part of his reign, "smote the Philistines, even unto Gaza." Colonel Rawlinson, with great plausibility, supposes that this defeat of the maritime tribes of Philistia is spoken of in the inscriptions as a defection of the Ekronites; and the fact that the Assyrian governor of Ekron was, on the approach of Sennacherib, found at Jerusalem, seems to afford sufficient proof of this.

It was to this district that Sennacherib directed primary attention, when, in the fourteenth year of Hezekiah's reign, he marched into Palestine. He was there when he heard of the approach of the Egyptian army. Whether the statement of the inscriptions, that he engaged and defeated the Egyptian army before Lachish, is a grave fact or an Assyrian boast, cannot now be satisfactorily determined, although it seems probable that some collision between these forces took place.

There is a singular agreement between the Scriptures and the Assyrian records respecting the amount of gold which Sennacherib received from Hezekiah. Both state it to have been thirty talents of gold. 2 Kings xviii, 14. With respect to the sum contributed in silver there is a discrepancy; the sacred records mentioning three hundred, but the inscriptions eight hundred, talents. It seems, however, from the manner in which this is told in the inscriptions, that in the latter amount was included a portion of the plunder of the surrounding country.

It is true that the Scriptures do not assert that any considerable number of Hebrews were sent into captivity by this sovereign; while the sculptures say that not less than two hundred thousand were at this period sent into Assyria. But it is a remarkable fact, that Demetrius the Jew, who lived about two hundred and twenty years before Christ, and is quoted by Clemens of Alexandria, assigns to this reign the great Assyrian captivity of the Jews: so that it is probable some considerable deportation of the Jews then took place. The reduction of the greater portion of the towns of Judea, so ostentatiously claimed in the inscriptions, seems to be virtually admitted by the sacred writer, who briefly observes, "Now in the fourteenth year of King Hezekiah did Sennacherib King of Assyria come up against all the fenced cities of Judah, AND TOOK THEM." 2 Kings xviii, 13.

Still the fact, the great indisputable fact, is admitted:—Jerusalem was not subdued. "I left to him Jerusalem his capital city, and some of the inferior towns around it," says the boastful monarch. And why? Certainly not because of the military strength of the king of Judah;—for, had he been able, he would have defended the whole of his country;—but simply because the city of David was at that time protected by the power of God. How glorious is this proof of the truth and faithfulness of Jehovah!

Yet how singularly do the style and manner of the inspired writer and of the inscriptions contrast, when carefully collated with each other! We feel as if called to compare the cool and truthful statements of an authentic history of a war with the gasconading bulletins of the unscrupulous warrior who was the aggressor in the conflict.

The inscriptions do not, of course, say a word respecting the miraculous destruction of Sennacherib's army. It may be questioned whether the truth respecting that wonderful event was ever fully made known in Assyria. Besides the troops actually marching as the army of aggression, there must have been, to the west of the Tigris, an immense military force, spread over the several countries, and occupying various garrisons and important military and political posts. And a man of mind and energy, as Sennacherib undoubtedly was, would easily be able to collect from these a respectable body of troops, with which to return to his capital. It must not, therefore, be imagined that the Assyrian warrior fled as a fugitive to Nineveh, on the ruin of his grand army. It is much more probable that the inscriptions give the plan on which he acted; and that he exerted himself to the utmost to sustain the character of a conqueror, and to go back to his capital as one returning from a continued course of success. Yet the complete change of tone in the annals of the king, immediately after the termination of this campaign, is as perfect a corroboration of the Scriptural account of the miraculous destruction of his army, as could have been given without an explicit notice of the fact. As an instance, it may be stated that the events of his fourth year present a marked contrast to the detailed and magniloquent descriptions of the preceding periods. They are confined to a few meagre lines, and refer exclusively to an expedition against the Chaldees, undertaken, as Colonel Rawlinson conjectures, in order to punish Merodach-Baladan for having sent ambassadors to Hezekiah. Sennacherib does not appear to have conducted this war in person: he does indeed say that he went to the country of Beth-Yakina, (at the mouth of the Euphrates,) "where Suzubi the Chaldæan, who dwelt in the city of Bittuth, sustained a defeat. My troops pursued him; but he fled away, and his place was not found." The rest of the year was occupied in the reduction of Beth-Yakina. Sennacherib goes on to narrate, "Merodach-Baladan, whom I had defeated in the course of my first year, he fled before my chief officers, and concealed himself beyond the sea. His brothers, the offspring of his father's house, whom he had left on this side of the sea, together with the men of the country, I ordered to be conveyed from Beth-Yakina. The rest of the cities of Merodach-Baladan I destroyed and burned, and placed my son Assur Nadun over the government of the country in an independent position."

It has been generally assumed, that Sennacherib, immediately after the ruin of his great army, hastened to Nineveh, where he was almost immediately afterward slain by his two sons. But that this assassination took place immediately, or within fifty-five days, after his return to Nineveh, is only taught in a doubtful passage in the apocryphal Book of Tobit. Chap. i, 18-21. The account given by the sacred writer would rather lead to the opinion, that he survived the destruction of his army some considerable time: for it is said that, after this catastrophe, he "departed, and went and returned, and DWELT at Nineveh;" (2 Kings xix, 36;) an expression which would certainly indicate that he continued to reside there more than a few days.

This is, however, fully established by the inscriptions, which record the annals of five years after that memorable event.

In the fifth year of Sennacherib, there were two expeditions,—one against the tribes of Takhari; and the other against Manigama, King of the city of Vakku: but the geography of these places has not been clearly ascertained.

The inscriptions on the bulls at Nineveh close with an account of a maritime expedition, conducted by Sennacherib against the Chaldæans, who, to escape Assyrian tyranny, had embarked, with their gods and wealth, in vessels, and taken refuge beyond the sea in the city of Nagiat. Unable to reach them with his own people, Sennacherib brought artisans and mariners from Tyre and Sidon. These he assembled on the Upper Tigris, and thence, on rafts or vessels, floated them down to Beth-Yakina. Here they constructed and manned a sufficient number of ships, and, after sacrificing to the gods, crossed over to the city of Nagiat, which they destroyed, and returned laden with much booty. Nagiat was probably some important harbour in the Persian Gulf. The annals of the seventh and eighth years of Sennacherib's reign are also found on Colonel Taylor's cylinders: but, in consequence of the damaged state of the casts, Colonel Rawlinson is at present unable to furnish a translation of this part of the annals.

Besides these historical documents, the inscriptions referring to the reign and actions of Sennacherib are very numerous, and afford very important information respecting the disinterred buildings of Assyria. We are by these means instructed that it was before his Syrian campaign, that this sovereign began the embellishment of Nineveh. There were at that period four important buildings on the mound of Koyunjik:—the original royal palace; a temple to "the heavens," built by Sardanapalus; and two smaller edifices:— but these had all suffered from injury or decay, and Sennacherib undertook their repair. For this purpose he collected a host of prisoners from the Chaldæan and Aramæan tribes upon one side, and from Cilicia and Armenia on the other. The prisoners he distributed in four bodies, assigning three hundred and sixty thousand men for the repair of the great palace, and employing women almost to the same number in restoring the other buildings. The account given by Herodotus of the building of the tomb of Alyattes, the father of Crœsus, in Lydia, has excited surprise, on account of the prominent share which he ascribes to young women in the work. But the employment of females in such operations is very plainly recorded in the Assyrian inscriptions.

The palace excavated by Mr. Layard, whence he took the bass-reliefs of which such beautiful drawings have been recently published, was built in a later period of Sennacherib's reign. It was, in Colonel Rawlinson's opinion, executed for the most part after his return from his maritime expedition against the Chaldæans. Sennacherib also erected a palace on the mound, now called Nebi Yunus, in the centre of Nineveh; and another in the city of Tarbisi, three miles to the north of the capital.

The length of this reign is uncertain, and can at present be only approximately estimated. Further discoveries among the interred chronicles of Assyria may soon remove all doubt on the subject. The manner of Sennacherib's death is clearly stated in Scripture. While worshipping in the temple of his god Nisroch, he was assassinated by two of his sons, who afterward fled into Armenia.

ESARHADDON succeeded his father. His name and title are found in the inscriptions. On a Babylonian clay tablet in the British Museum the name is distinctly written as Assur-Akh-Adana.

This sovereign appears to have devoted himself, with great ability, energy, and success, to repair the losses sustained by his father. He had in the first place to resist the spread of revolt in the different provinces of his empire; and, with the exception of Media, he seems to have succeeded: but he does not appear to have thought the reduction of that nation practicable, with the forces which he could command.

At Babylon—which also took advantage of the weakness of the imperial state to assert its independence—he had better success. Having reduced that refractory province to obedience, Esarhaddon placed his son in command of it,—a situation in which he himself had been placed by his father Sennacherib,—and secured his government from further trouble in that quarter.

Having thus established his affairs in the east, the Assyrian sovereign proceeded to strengthen his interests in the west. His first step appears to have been to remove a considerable number of his subjects from Babylon, Cuthah, Ava, Hamath, and Sepharvaim, to Samaria and the other cities formerly occupied by the Ten Tribes of Israel.

This importation of people is spoken of in connexion with the capture of Samaria, as if it immediately followed that event. 2 Kings xvii, 24. But the authority of Ezra is decisive as to this being the act of Esarhaddon. Ezra iv, 2. It was most probably in connexion with this colonizing of the land of Israel, that the king of Assyria discovered reason to distrust the fidelity of Mannasseh, King of Judah: upon which he sent the captains of his host against him, and took him captive, "and bound him with fetters, and carried him to Babylon." 2 Chron. xxxiii, 11. The Hebrew king deeply humbled himself before God in his captivity, and the Lord heard his prayer, and turned the heart of the Assyrian monarch, so that he released Manasseh from his prison and his fetters, and restored him again to his throne, where he evidenced the genuineness of his repentance by a godly life and a righteous reign.

It was this sovereign who ruined the old palaces of Calah, which had been raised by a preceding dynasty, in order to obtain materials for the construction of a palace for himself. Of Esarhaddon's annals very important portions can be recovered from two cylinders placed in the British Museum by Mr. Layard, as well as from numerous clay tablets more recently found; but this has not yet been done. Nothing has hitherto been discovered that refers to that most important part of his reign which includes the captivity of Manasseh, and the transfer of tribes from the east to occupy the land of Israel, although records of these events may be expected yet to be brought to light.

Esarhaddon was succeeded by his son, whom Mr. Rawlinson calls Sardanapalus III., but who is known in history as NABUCHODONOSOR. A vast number of relics referring to his reign have been found. In fact, the *débris* of the temples built by him in Nineveh to Mars and to Diana are literally filled with clay tablets, broken cylinders, and other similar relics, covered with inscriptions. Besides the hoards already in the British Museum, thousands yet remain to be transmitted to this country.

That portion of these inscriptions which has been deciphered refers to the wars which this monarch waged in Susiana. It is extremely probable that, Babylon being held in doubtful subjection, and Media being avowedly independent, it required the utmost exertion of the imperial power to keep the neighbouring provinces in quiet submission. We consequently hear nothing of this monarch's power in Western Asia, until he had humbled the strength of Media. In this instance he was not the aggressor, but stood upon the defensive. Phraortes, King of the Medes, being confident in his martial prowess, marched against Assyria, with the avowed design of subduing that empire. The army of Nabuchodonosor met him in the plain of Ragau: for the Assyrian king had so fully prepared himself to meet the coming danger, that he actually entered the Median territories before his enemies had left them. In this great battle the king of Media was taken prisoner, and his army completely defeated. Intoxicated with his triumph, Nabuchodonosor slew his royal captive the same day. He then led his army against Ecbatana, the Median capital, which he subdued and spoiled; and having completely succeeded in this campaign, he returned to Nineveh, where he feasted his troops for one hundred and twenty days. Judith i, 16; ii, 1.

Having thus recovered his supremacy in the east, Nabuchodonosor in the following year sent a great army, under Holofernes as commander-in-chief, into Syria and Palestine, to establish his authority in those parts, and to chastise those provinces which had refused to furnish their stipulated contingent of forces for his Median war. The first object of attack by the Assyrian commander was the sea-coast of Phenicia, which he completely reduced, and compelled the people to send reinforcements to his army. After this, he was detained with his huge host a month in the plain of Esdraelon, for the provision of sufficient carriages and *matériel* for his army. He then proceeded to invest Bethulia, the key of all the hill-country of Judea. By enforcing a strict blockade, and cutting off the water, he had succeeded in reducing this little city to great straits, when Judah was saved, and the Assyrian army ruined, by the address and energy of a Hebrew heroine. Judith, having found admission to the tent of Holofernes, so fascinated him with her charms, that she obtained an opportunity of killing him; which having effected, she returned to the city with his head in her possession. Early on the following morning, the Hebrews, displaying to the Assyrians the head of their general, sallied out to attack them, when, panic-struck and without leadership, they fled in the utmost disorder; so that, instead of a battle, it was the rout and slaughter of the Assyrian host.

SARAC or SARDANAPALUS II. next ascended the imperial throne, and had to direct the affairs of government at a most disastrous crisis. By the death of Holofernes, and the rout of his army in the west, the martial power of the empire was, of course, reduced to the lowest state. But what greatly aggravated the danger of the new monarch was the fact, that Cyaxares, who had succeeded his father Phraortes on the throne of Media, proved to be a man of great capacity and an able warrior. Having recovered and restored Ecbatana, and re-organized the Median army, he took advantage of the loss of the Assyrian host at Bethulia, and the accession of a new sovereign, to renew hostilities with Assyria.

On this, as on the former occasion, the Assyrian king met his foes in the field. But the decay of imperial power was now manifest: the Medes triumphed; and the Assyrian, having succeeded in reaching Nineveh, was immediately shut up and besieged in his capital. The operations of this siege were, however, soon afterward completely deranged by an irruption of Scythians, who, pouring from the northwest into Asia, defeated the Median army, and completely overran all the neighbouring countries. For eight years these barbarians spread themselves through the east, and ravaged several nations in succession, until such excesses produced the inevitable results of disorder and disorganization. Availing himself of these indications, Cyaxares took advantage of a festival, and caused all the leaders of the Scythians to be invited to the houses of the Medes, and there to be simultaneously destroyed. Then, attacking the disordered and confounded troops, he drove them out of the country.

Delivered from this evil, the Median king turned again to the great object which filled his mind,—the conquest of Nineveh. But, previously to the renewal of his attack, he formed an alliance with Nabopolassar, King of Babylon, who had also declared his country independent of Assyria. This alliance was ratified by a marriage between Nebuchadnezzar, the son of Nabopolassar, and Amytis, the daughter of Cyaxares. Immediately afterward the confederate armies proceeded to renew the siege of Nineveh. According to Justin, the Assyrian king betrayed the utmost cowardice; and after a feeble resistance burnt himself and all his treasures, on a pile which had been prepared for the purpose in one of his palaces.

But Diodorus has given a much more probable account of this prince. He states that, relying upon an ancient prophecy that

Nineveh should never be taken until the river became its enemy, Sarac did everything which prudence and courage could suggest to resist the power of his foes. He sent off a great part of his treasures, with his children, to the care of his most intimate friend Cotta, Governor of Paphlagonia; stored up ammunition and provisions in abundance for the siege, and for the support of the inhabitants; and set his enemies at defiance. For nearly two years this state of things continued, the besiegers being unable to make any impression on the city, and the king of Assyria being too feeble to drive them from their post; until at length an unusual quantity of rain having fallen on the Mountains of Ararat, where the Tigris has its head, that river became so swollen that it rose above its banks, and the flood threw down about twenty furlongs of the city wall. The king, struck with dismay and despair at this unexpected fulfilment of the prophecy, had a pile prepared in his palace, and burnt himself, his concubines, and his treasures, to prevent them from falling into the hands of the enemy, who, having entered the city by the breach in the wall, sacked it, and razed it to the ground.

Thus perished Nineveh, after it had stood about nineteen hundred years from the time of Asshur, and had been the capital of one of the most extended empires that the world has ever seen.

It is impossible to turn away the mind from the contemplation of a political and military fabric, so venerable for its antiquity, so distinguished by its martial prowess, so wonderful in the literary and historic treasures of its ruined cities, without a thought respecting the great purposes of Divine Providence in the prolonged existence of this remarkable empire, and its connexion with the elect people of God, and the prophecies of Holy Scripture. (See *Appendix*, note 21.)

Having arisen out of the emigration of Asshur from his own appointed territory, in consequence of the usurpation of Nimrod, Assyria not only maintained her existence, but established her supremacy in Asia;—was the appointed agent of Providence in the subversion and captivity of the kingdom of Israel;—humbled in the dust an apostate king of Judah;—and, after recognising and bowing before the authority of one of Jehovah's prophets in sackcloth and penitence, became an illustrious subject of divine prophecy, and verified in her history some of the most sublime predictions which ever emanated from the prescience of Jehovah. Wonderful was Assyria in her rise,—her power,—her continued supremacy; still more wonderful in her fulfilment of sacred prophecy, and in sending forth from her ruined cities, after an entombment of twenty-four centuries, her records and annals for the instruction of the world.

CHRONOLOGICAL TABLE OF ASSYRIAN HISTORY.

B.C.	Kings' Names and Events.	Years Reigned.	B.C.	Kings' Names and Events.	Years Reigned.
	OLD ASSYRIAN LINE.			**OLD ASSYRIAN LINE CONTINUED.**	
1821	Balæus	52	934	Ephecheres	52
1769	Sethos Altadas	35	882	Acraganes	42
1734	Mamythus	30		(Whose deeds are recorded on the Obelisk.)	
1704	Ascalius	30			
1674	Sphærus	28	841	Thonos Concoleros	20
1646	Mamylus	30		**MEDIAN KING.**	
1616	Sparthæus	40	821	Arbaces	17
1574	Ascatades	42			
1534	Amyntas	50		**ASSYRIAN LINE RESTORED.**	
1484	Belochus II	25	804	Pul	51
1450	Baletores	34	753	Tiglath-Pileser	19
1425	Lamprides	37		(Who probably built the centre palace at Nimroud.)	
1388	Sosares	20			
1368	Lampares	30		**LOWER LINE OF KINGS.**	
1338	Panyas	45	734	Sargina (Sargon)	20
1293	Sosarmus	42		(The builder of Khorsabad.)	
1251	Mithræus	37	714	Sennacherib	9
1214	Teutames	32	705	Esarhaddon	38
	(Who sent an army, under Memnon, to assist Priam in the Trojan war.)			(Builder of the south-west palace at Nimrond.)	
			667	Nabuchodonosor	42
1182	Teutæus	44		(Who sent Holofernes into Judea, where he perished.)	
1138	Thineus	30			
1108	Dercylus	40	625	Sarac	19
1068	Eupacmes	38		(Who built the south-east palace at Nimrond.)	
1030	Laosthenes	45			
985	Pertiades	30	606	Nineveh destroyed by the Medes and Babylonians.	
955	Ophratæus	21			

CHAPTER IV.

THE HISTORY OF THE BABYLONIANS.

BABYLON the Seat of the first Postdiluvian Sovereignty—Conquered and subjected to Assyria—Policy of Assyria toward subject Countries—NABONASSAR—The Era bearing his Name—He was independent—NADIUS, CHINZIRUS, PORUS, and JUGÆUS, successively reign—MARDOCEMPADUS or MERODACH-BALADAN—His Embassage to Hezekiah—ARCHIANUS—HAGISA—MARADACH BALDANES—BELIBUS defeated by Assyria—ASORDANES—NABOPOLASSAR—Babylon asserts its Independence—Coalition of Babylon and Media against Nineveh—Scythian Invasion—Nineveh destroyed—The King of Egypt defeated at Carchemish—NEBUCHADNEZZAR—Takes Jerusalem—Carries away the principal Inhabitants into Captivity—Makes Zedekiah King—He rebels—Jerusalem again taken, and destroyed—Tyre taken, after a Siege of Thirteen Years—Egypt conquered—Nebuchadnezzar greatly improves Babylon by many Splendid Erections—Nebuchadnezzar's Dream of the Great Image—Explained by Daniel—Its wonderful Revelations—The Golden Image—Extraordinary Measures adopted for its Dedication—Heroism of the Three Hebrews—Glorious Revelation of the Son of God—Important Results of this Divine Interposition—The Dream of a Great Tree—Its Interpretation and Accomplishment—Noble Acknowledgment of the King—His Prophecy and Death—EVIL-MERODACH King—Liberates Jehoiachin from Prison—Neriglissar reigns—Forms a Combination against Media—He is slain in Battle—LABOROSARCHOD reigns—The BELSHAZZAR of the Book of Daniel—His Youth and Cruelty—He profanes the Sacred Vessels—Is slain—DARIUS takes the Kingdom, and appoints LABYNETUS Viceroy of Babylon—He rules subject to Media—Declares himself independent—Is defeated in Battle—Babylon taken by CYRUS—Labynetus taken at Borsippa, and sent into Carmania—Termination of the Babylonian Monarchy.

THE history of Babylon stands invested with special and peculiar interest, in consequence of its immediate connexion with the most terrible calamity inflicted on the Hebrew people, during the extended period to which this volume refers.

This country, as we have seen in a previous volume, (Patriarchal Age, pp. 431-434,) was the seat of the first kingly government established in the world after the flood. But, as there detailed, Babylon was conquered by Belus or Ninus, and added as a province to the Assyrian empire. It was in this state at the period when we are called to resume its history.

It must, however, be remembered, that in these ancient times the conquest and subjugation of a country did not prevent its retaining its separate national existence and government. No attempt appears to have been made to merge all the countries subdued by Assyria into one united and compact government. The kings of the several lands were allowed to reign, on their declaring their allegiance to the imperial throne, and furnishing to the sovereign the required tribute. When this promise was not kept, and the contumacy of the vassal king brought down upon him the irresistible power of the imperial army, no change was made in the ruling policy. The rebellious chief, with his family and friends, if not put to death, was removed in chains, and another person appointed king of the subject country in his stead.

This practice renders it extremely difficult to elicit with accuracy the precise times when important countries, such as Babylon, Media, and others, really obtained their independence, as it is possible that they may have claimed this privilege long before the imperial state would recognise it. This was the case in respect of Babylon; and many writers, overlooking this circumstance, have been led into serious errors.

The first of those kings who ruled in Babylon, after its subjection to Assyria, of whom we have any definite information, was NABONASSAR. He ascended the throne B. C. 747; and made the period of his accession to the regal dignity the commencement of the famous Nabonassarean Era; (see *Appendix*, note 22;) which, in conjunction with the Greek, Roman, and Christian, completes the four great cardinal eras of sacred and profane history. The principle of this era was an avoidance of intercalary days. The year consisted of twelve months of thirty days each, with five supernumerary days; and was in consequence very convenient for astronomical calculations, and for this reason was adopted by the early Greek astronomers.

As Babylon rose into prominence and power under the rule of this sovereign, Sir Isaac Newton was led to conjecture that Nabonassar was a younger son of Pul, King of Assyria, who, it is supposed, left the imperial crown to his eldest son, Tiglath-Pileser, and the throne of Babylon to Nabonassar. But this conjecture, which has been partially adopted by Hales and other learned men, has no solid foundation in history. It is unquestionably true, and is attested by Alexander Polyhistor and the Astronomical Canon, that Babylon had always kings of her own from the earliest times. And as Clinton truly observes, "These kings were sometimes subjected to the Assyrians, and sometimes independent; but they never acquired extensive dominion till the time of Nebuchadnezzar. Nabonassar was independent."—*Fasti Hellenici*, vol. i, p. 278. Respecting this reign no further information of importance can be obtained.

Nabonassar was succeeded by NADIUS, who is said to have reigned two years; and he was followed by CHINZIRUS and PORUS, each of whom ruled five years. JUGÆUS then ascended the throne, and reigned five years. Nothing whatever has been handed down to us respecting the public or personal history of these kings. Nor is it probable that their names, as here given, are those by which they were known in their own country, since these bear no affinity to the Chaldee or Assyrian names.

MARDOCEMPADUS succeeded Jugæus. He is certainly the Merodach-Baladan of Holy Scripture; and is the first king of Babylon who is noticed in the Old Testament as having had any intercourse with the Hebrew nation. It seems more than probable that, up to this time, Nabonassar and his successors had ruled in Babylon virtually independent of Assyria; although it is equally probable that this independence was never proclaimed at Babylon, nor acknowledged at Nineveh. This prince appears to be the first Babylonian ruler who directed his attention to the extension of his dominion in Western Asia. Having informed himself of the state of the countries bordering on the Mediterranean Sea, and having heard that Hezekiah King of Judah had recovered from a dangerous illness, he sent ambassadors to the Hebrew monarch, congratulating him on his restoration to health. The king of Babylon alleged that he was induced to send this embassy mainly by a desire to have some explanation of the sun's wonderful retrocession, as a sign of the Hebrew king's recovery. 2 Chron. xxxii, 31.

It is probable, however, that the motives which prompted the Chaldæan monarch to this step went far beyond mere kindly compliment or scientific curiosity. Babylon at this time was beginning to feel a rivalry with Nineveh; and undoubtedly, in this visit to Judea, it was intended to cultivate a good understanding with the most powerful king of Western Asia. The sculptures recently discovered among the Assyrian ruins cast important light upon this event. They inform us that after Sennacherib had lost his great army in his celebrated campaign in Palestine and Egypt, he prosecuted a series of wars against this Babylonish monarch, until he had driven him out of the country, and compelled him to seek refuge "beyond the sea." The juxtaposition of these events is remarkable. Sennacherib's army is destroyed, and he returns in disgrace and confusion. Hezekiah is taken sick, and recovers. Merodach-Baladan sends his messengers to the Hebrew court:—while, the Assyrian king having in some measure repaired his loss, and organized a military force, the first object to which he directs his attention is a war with this king of Babylon, whom he succeeds in driving out of the country.

The Assyrian inscriptions state that, having driven out Merodach-Baladan, Sennacherib appointed his son Esarhaddon to rule in Babylon,—a fact which still further confirms the jealousy which the intercourse between Babylon and Judah had excited in the imperial court. The name of ARCHIANUS, however, stands in the list as the next king; but no account whatever of his reign has been preserved. He was succeeded by HAGISA, who reigned thirty days: then followed MARADACH BALDANES. A fragment of Berosus, in the Chronicle of Eusebius, casts some light on this period. It says that Archianus was brother of Esarhaddon, and ruled in Babylon as his viceroy; but that Hagisa, or Acises, expelled him from the country, and seized the reins of government; and that this usurper, after a brief rule of thirty days, was slain by Maradach, who maintained himself in possession of power six months, when he was in turn cut off by BELIBUS.

After the expiration of three years, the king of Assyria, having resolved to reduce this refractory country to obedience, collected his forces, defeated Belibus, the usurper of Babylon, and carried him prisoner into Assyria. Babylon was thus again fully brought into subjection to the supreme state. It appears, from isolated notices of the fact, that Esarhaddon, in order to secure this noble city and wealthy province to his dominion, sent his son APRONADIUS, or ASORDANES, to govern Babylon. His rule is set down as having continued six years.

From this period to the accession of Nabopolassar, we have no further information beyond a mere list of the names of the kings and the length of their reigns. (See *Appendix*, note 23.) It seems highly probable that, during most of the intervening period, Babylon was subject to Nineveh. This was certainly the case B. C. 675, since about this time, when the king of Assyria subdued Manasseh, King of Judah, and led him into captivity, he took him, not to Nineveh, but to Babylon. 2 Chron. xxxiii, 11.

The accession of NABOPOLASSAR to the throne of Babylon was the beginning of a new era in the political progress and power of this state. This fact is so prominent in ancient annals, that Jackson calls him "the first king and founder of the state." It can scarcely be doubted that this progress was greatly favoured by external causes. At this period the rising power of the Medes had rendered them formidable enemies to the Assyrian sovereign. Babylon took advantage of this to assert its independence.

As described in a preceding chapter, the siege of Nineveh was interrupted by the sweeping incursion of the Scythians, which compelled the king of Babylon to turn his whole attention to the defence of his own country. After this storm had passed away, he again joined his forces with those of the Medes, and effected the entire destruction of Nineveh. This event occurred B. C. 606. Herodotus does not mention the presence of the Babylonians in this siege; but Tobit distinctly refers the capture of Nineveh to the joint forces of Media and Babylon. Tobit xiv, 15.

Pending these preparations against Nineveh by the united Medes and Babylonians, the king of Egypt thought this a favourable opportunity to make an effort to recover his ascendency in the east. He accordingly transported an army into Palestine, where he was reluctantly compelled to fight his passage through a Jewish army under Josiah, King of Judah. The result of this conflict has been already detailed. (Hebrew People, p. 342.) Having overcome this opposition, the king of Egypt marched against Carchemish on the Euphrates. The united army before Nineveh could not be diverted from their purpose by this invasion, and this very important city and military station was consequently suffered to fall into the hands of Pharaoh-Necho. 2 Kings xxiii, 29; 2 Chron. xxxv, 20. After this success, the Egyptian sovereign returned, securing Syria and Palestine in subjection to his authority by the way. In order to this, he appeared before Jerusalem within three months after Jehoahaz had ascended the throne, and, removing him from the government, he placed his brother Eliakim, whose name he changed to Jehoiakim, on the throne in his stead, and carried Jehoahaz in chains to Egypt.

Nineveh having fallen before the power of the combined forces, and the territories west of the Euphrates being assigned to the king of Babylon, as his portion of the empire, Nabopolassar sent his son with a great army to establish his power in these parts. The king of Egypt, being informed of this purpose, hastened to maintain the ascendency which he acquired in the east. But his efforts were vain. His army was smitten by Nebuchadnezzar, (Jer. xlvi, 2-10,) who pursued his enemy through Syria, Palestine, and even unto the borders of Egypt. The complete success of the youthful Babylonish chief in this campaign is described with equal brevity and force by the sacred writer: "The king of Egypt came not again any more out of his land: for the king of Babylon had taken from the river of Egypt unto the river Euphrates all that pertained to the king of Egypt." 2 Kings xxiv, 7. It was during this progress of the Babylonish army that the Rechabites took refuge within the walls of Jerusalem. Jer. xxxv.

We have not very ample particulars of this campaign. But it is fully apparent that Nebuchadnezzar on this occasion became master of Jerusalem, and put Jehoiakim in chains, with the purpose of taking him as a captive to Babylon; and that the king of Judah in this distress so humbled himself in the presence of his conqueror, that Nebuchadnezzar restored him to the government as his vassal, having first exacted an oath of fealty from him. Daniel and his companions, with many others of the noble families of Judea, were at this time carried away into Babylon.

Whilst NEBUCHADNEZZAR was thus employed in establishing the power of Babylon in Western Asia, he received intelligence of the death of his father: upon which, leaving the main body of his army under the command of his officers, and giving into their care the captives whom he had taken from the Syrians, Phenicians, and Jews, that they might conduct them to Babylonia, he hastened across the desert by the nearest course, with only a few attendants, to his capital. Here he found that order had been preserved; and he immediately entered upon the government of the kingdom. He now dispersed, into several parts of the kingdom, the captives whom he had taken, and adorned the temple of Belus with the spoils of the war. (Berosus apud Josephum, Contra Apion., lib. i, cap. 19.)

For three years Jehoiakim faithfully sent his promised tribute; but afterward, being encouraged to resistance by a new alliance with Psammuthis, King of Egypt, who had just then succeeded his father, he refused any further submission to the king of Babylon. It does not appear, from either sacred or profane history, that Nebuchadnezzar was able at the moment to chastise this insubordination of the Hebrew king. But it seems probable, that he ordered his lieutenants in those quarters to assail and harass the refractory sovereign. This seems clearly indicated by the sacred writer. 2 Kings xxiv, 2. While engaged in this warfare, Jehoiakim died; but in what manner the prophecy of Jeremiah respecting him was fulfilled does not appear. Jer. xxii, 18, 19; xxxvi, 30.

On the death of Jehoiakim, his son Jehoiachin succeeded him. This prince had, however, ruled but three months, when Nebuchadnezzar appeared in person at the head of a great army before Jerusalem. Hopeless of resisting such power, the Hebrew submitted, and "went out to the king of Babylon, he, and his mother, and his servants, and his princes, and his officers." 2 Kings xxiv, 12. By this ready submission he saved his life: for Nebuchadnezzar "carried away Jehoiachin to Babylon, and the king's mother, and the king's wives." Verse 15. On this occasion, also, "all the princes, and all the mighty men of valour, even ten thousand captives, and the craftsmen and smiths a thousand, and all that were strong and apt for war," were carried captive to Babylon. 2 Kings xxiv, *passim.* Hebrew People, p. 349.

Having thus prostrated the power of the Hebrew state, and carried away all the principal inhabitants, with all the treasures of the temple and the palace and the spoil of the city, leaving none behind but "the poorest sort of the people of the land," Nebuchadnezzar took Mattaniah, the uncle of the deposed king, and, changing his name to Zedekiah, made him swear by the name of the Lord not to rebel against him, nor to help the Egyptians. 2 Chron. xxxvi, 13; Ezek. xvii, 13–15; Esdras i, 48; 2 Kings xx, 17.

It does not clearly appear in what martial enterprises the king of Babylon was employed during several years after this event. It is probable that he was occupied in the conquest of some of those nations so signally set forth in the predictions of Jeremiah, Jer. xxv, 18–26; —most likely, those nearest to Babylon.

No portion of the wonderful incidents connected with this reign is more remarkable, than the precision with which the rising power of Babylon is made the subject of sacred prophecy. A collection of these predictions in order is well worthy of very serious attention; and shows how wonderfully the prescience of Jehovah was manifested in the providential government of the world at this period. Jeremiah, indeed, announced with the most wonderful exactness the exploits of this king; and that not only verbally, but on some occasions by the most significant types and figures. For instance: when the kings of the Moabites, Ammonites, Tyrians, and Zidonians were using all their influence to induce Zedekiah to join them in a coalition against Nebuchadnezzar, Jeremiah sent to each of the ambassadors of these nations, then at the court of Jerusalem for this purpose, yokes and bonds, as a present to their sovereigns, with this declaration: "Thus saith the Lord of hosts, the God of Israel; Thus shall ye say unto your masters; I have made the earth, the man and the beast that are upon the ground, by my great power and by my outstretched arm, and have given it unto whom it seemed meet unto me. And now have I given all these lands into the hand of Nebuchadnezzar the King of Babylon, my servant. And all nations shall serve him, and his son, and his son's son, until the very time of his land come. And it shall come to pass that the nation and kingdom which will not serve the same Nebuchadnezzar the King of Babylon, and that will not put their neck under the yoke of the King of Babylon, that nation will I punish, saith the Lord, with the sword, and with the famine, and with the pestilence, until I have consumed them by his hand." Jer. xxvii, 4–8.

Such interposition must not only have greatly affected the amount of resistance opposed to the progress of the Chaldæan conqueror, but also have given him great encouragement in the prosecution of his plans for the consolidation and extension of his dominions.

Yet all this was insufficient to induce even Zedekiah to render a willing subjection to Nebuchadnezzar. The diviners and sorcerers of these neighbouring countries, and the false prophets, who surrounded the person of Zedekiah, united, on the contrary, to assure the confederate princes of success in their effort. Jer. xxvii, 9, 14. Under this influence, after the lapse of several years, when the king of Egypt joined them, measures were taken by these princes for the promotion of their object. This was soon made known to Nebuchadnezzar, who immediately collected an army and marched into Syria. Here, when arrived at the place where the roads diverged to Rabbath, the capital of Ammon, and to Jerusalem, the king of Babylon halted, and proceeded to ascertain by divination which way he should take. Arrows, teraphim, and sacrificial victims, were all employed; (Ezek. xxi, 21, 22;) and the result of this process was a determination to advance upon Jerusalem. In his progress the Babylonian king took several of the fenced cities of Judah; after which he laid siege to Jerusalem, simultaneously investing Lachish and Azekah with other divisions of his army.

Pharaoh-Hophra, who now reigned in Egypt, was at the same time inordinately vain of his power, (Herodotus, Euterpe, cap. 169; Ezek. xxix,) and the most important member of the alliance of western states, which had united to resist the ambitious projects of the Chaldean king. On hearing of this invasion he immediately marched an army to the relief of Jerusalem. But in this instance, also, the repeated predictions of the prophets were verified: for no sooner had Nebuchanezzar raised the siege, and marched to meet the Egyptians, than Pharaoh at once retreated before him, without striking a blow, and returned into his own country.

Nebuchadnezzar hastened back to the Hebrew capital, which, after holding out for eighteen months, was taken. Zedekiah endeavoured to escape by night with his sons and chief officers; but he was pursued, overtaken in the plains of Jericho, and carried into the presence of the king of Babylon at Riblah, in Syria; where the conqueror caused his two sons to be slain before his eyes, and then punished him, in a way frequently employed toward rebellious vassals, by putting out his eyes, and sending him in chains to Babylon. (See *Appendix*, note 24.) Having completely destroyed the city and temple of Jerusalem, carried off all the wealth of the land as spoil, with the great body of the people as captives, Nebuchadnezzar directed the operations of his army against the surrounding countries. Rabbath, too, was destroyed, and its princes carried into captivity, while the Philistines, Moabites, Edomites, Arabs, and Syrians were also devastated and spoiled; according to the declarations which had been made by the sacred prophets respecting these nations. See

Nahum iii, 8-10; Jeremiah xliii, 8-13; xliv, 27-30; xlvi, 13-26; Ezekiel xxix, 30-32. Returning to Babylon, Nebuchadnezzar dedicated the spoil to his idol deities, distributed his captives in different parts of the kingdom, and recruited his army for the next campaign.

The following year Nebuchadnezzar began his military operations by the siege of Tyre. In this, as in other parts, the conqueror's progress, the difficulty of his undertaking, and his ultimate success, were distinctly foretold by the Prophet Ezekiel two years before he entered upon it. Ezek. xxvi; xxviii. This is one of the most memorable sieges on record, and exhibited equal determination and constancy in the attack and defence. Thirteen years of unavailing effort were expended on this wealthy commercial city; but in the fourteenth year it fell into the hands of its unwearied foe. The city, thus taken and totally destroyed, stood on the mainland: it was never rebuilt.

The attention of Nebuchadnezzar was now turned to Egypt, which he ravaged, as stated in a preceding chapter. (Page 97.) As this fact was so discreditable to their nation, the Egyptian annalists did not record it; and in consequence we have no mention of the event by Herodotus, Diodorus, or Strabo. A similar silence is maintained respecting the catastrophe of the Red Sea. Berosus, however, affirms that Nebuchadnezzar "subdued Egypt, Syria, Phenicia, Arabia, and excelled in warlike exploits all the Babylonian and Chaldæan kings who reigned before him." As already mentioned, (page 98,) Megasthenes asserted his conquest of Libya; (Josephus, Contra Apionem, lib. i, cap. 19;) and Syncellus says that the ancient Phenician historians related that Nebuchadnezzar conquered Syria, Egypt, and all Phenicia. (Syncellus, Chronog., p. 221.)

Having thus completely subdued all Western Asia, and freed himself from every apprehension of trouble on the side of Egypt, the king of Babylon returned with his army, laden with spoils, to his capital. He had now attained the summit of his ambition. Everywhere his power prevailed. In the east, if the Medes maintained a show of independence, it was merely nominal; and was allowed, because of the intimate family relationship subsisting between the two sovereigns, Nebuchadnezzar having married a sister of the king of Media. (See *Appendix*, note 25.) In every other direction, from Egypt and the Mediterranean to the extreme east, the Babylonish power prevailed. Nebuchadnezzar had commenced great alterations and improvements in his capital, even before he entered upon the siege of Tyre. He now completed these stupendous works, which have always been considered among the most remarkable erections of the world. Berosus thus speaks of them: " When he had thus admirably fortified the city, and had magnificently adorned the gates, he added also a new palace to those in which his forefathers had dwelt, adjoining them, but exceeding them in height and splendour. Any attempt to describe it would be tedious. In this palace he erected very high walks, supported by stone pillars; and by planting what was called a 'pensile paradise,' and replenishing it with all sorts of trees, he rendered the prospect an exact resemblance of a mountainous country. This he did to gratify his queen, because she had been brought up in Media, and was fond of a mountainous situation."—*Cory's Fragments*, p. 40. (See *Appendix*, note 26.)

Having thus fortified and beautified his capital, Nebuchadnezzar resolved to take the most effective measures for the consolidation of his power and the perpetuation of his empire. While occupied in this manner, lying on his bed, and revolving these matters in his mind, he fell asleep, and had a very remarkable dream, which, on his awaking, rested with unusual weight on his mind. Fully believing, in accordance with the national faith, that such visions were intended to convey important information respecting future events, the king immediately summoned to his presence the chief of his soothsayers, astrologers, and magicians, and required them to tell him his dream and its interpretation. The policy of the king in this instance is fully explained by his language. He distrusted the fidelity of these sages, and felt convinced that the same amount of supernatural wisdom which would enable them to give an authorized interpretation, would be sufficient to qualify them to declare the dream; while, in the latter case, his knowledge would enable him to test their fidelity; but, in the former, he would have no proof that their interpretation was anything more than mere pretence.

The wise men were confounded by this strange procedure, and promptly confessed their utter inability to comply with his demand. This so incensed the disappointed monarch, that he ordered all the wise men to be slain. Prior to this, Daniel and his three Hebrew companions, having greatly distinguished themselves in the attainment of knowledge, were enrolled among the number of the members of this sage body. When, therefore, the officer of the guard, in obedience to the king's command, was collecting all the wise men of Babylon preparatory to their execution, he had to include Daniel and his friends, informing them at the same time of their danger and of its cause. Daniel expostulated respecting the hastiness of the measure, and begged for time, that he might endeavour to furnish the required information. This respite was granted; and the prophet and his associates gave themselves to earnest prayer to God, that he would give to Daniel the knowledge necessary to save them from the impending doom. Their prayer was answered. The secret was revealed unto Daniel in a night-vision; and he accordingly presented himself before the king, and told him that he had seen in his dream a great and terrible image, the head of which was of fine gold, the breast and arms of silver, the belly and thighs of brass, and the legs of iron, while the feet were partly of iron and partly of clay. Astonished as the king was at hearing this exact description of his dream, he was still more so at its interpretation. Daniel—having assured him that it was not by his own wisdom that he had attained the knowledge of this secret; but by the special gift of God, who had given the dream and the interpretation thereof, that he might make known to the king what should come to pass hereafter—proceeded to unfold the divine teaching thus symbolically conveyed.

Addressing Nebuchadnezzar as a king of kings, possessing boundless power, dignity, and glory, by the direct and immediate gift of the God of heaven, Daniel told him that HE was *the head of gold;* that, after him, another kingdom should arise, inferior to him, as silver is to gold; and afterward a third kingdom, of brass, should bear rule over the earth; that at last a fourth kingdom, strong as iron, should put forth its power, and should be, at the same time, remarkable for invincible power and incurable intestine disunion; and that, during the period and rule of this fourth kingdom, the God of heaven should set up a kingdom, which, unlike all these successive transitory thrones, should embrace the whole earth, and continue to the end of the world.

It is scarcely possible, at this distance of time, to form any reasonable conception of the amount of information thus conveyed to the mind of this proud king. He must, at least, have been deeply impressed with the magnitude of the divine wisdom and power. He must have felt that a prescient and omnipotent Power ruled in this earth, before whom all human policy and martial prowess were as nothing; and that this Power had decreed but a temporary duration to his kingdom, extensive and elevated as it was; that there should be a succession of four prevailing monarchies, which should exercise paramount supremacy in the earth; and that, under the last of these, the kingdom of God should be established in the world.

No notion respecting antiquity is more unfounded than the supposition, that the king of Babylon and his courtiers would be at a loss to understand this announcement. From the earliest ages, the primitive promise lived in the memory and hope of mankind: and the form it assumed throughout successive generations was,—that a divine person, or "Son," should appear, who, subduing all evil powers, would establish one united and perpetual sovereignty in the earth. The interpretation of the king's dream, therefore, was calculated— and, very probably, was designed—to remove those vain-glorious thoughts which had occupied his mind, and to assure him that, so far from his own being the great and long-expected sovereignty, his kingdom was destined to be succeeded by three others, each wielding universal dominion, before the promised kingdom of God would come; and that, when at length it was set up, it should be so diverse, in its character and constitution, from all these, that it would break in pieces and destroy all these kingdoms, and stand forever. Dan. ii.

The revelations thus given by Daniel to the king were so satisfactory, that he raised the prophet to the highest honour, gave him great gifts, and appointed him RAB MAG, or chief of all the wise men, and ruler over the province of Babylon. Daniel immediately promoted his three friends to offices of trust and honour in the government of the province with which he had been intrusted.

Our next information respecting this reign announces the erection by Nebuchadnezzar of a golden image, of great height and splendour. This was set up in the plains of Dura in the province of Babylon. The simple addition of an image, even a large and golden one, to the objects already worshipped in a country so devoted to idolatry as Babylonia, would of itself excite no surprise, and scarcely call for observation. In this case, however, there are many extraordinary circumstances. In the first place, the king summoned, to meet him at the dedication of this image, "the princes, the governors, and captains, the judges, the treasurers, the counsellors, the sheriffs, and all the rulers of the provinces." Now, in an empire so extensive as that of Babylon, and so recently constituted, a measure of this kind must not only have involved great cost, inconvenience, and waste of time, but must, especially in recently-subdued countries, have been connected with some danger. This is so evident that it must be universally admitted, that nothing but a great and urgent reason would have led to such an abstraction of all the government staff, and the *élite* of all the officers of the empire from their post of duty, that they might meet together on this occasion.

The motive which operated in the mind of Nebuchadnezzar was, however, sufficient to induce him to adopt this course: and this is conclusive evidence that he aimed at something more than the addition of one more image to the Pantheon of Babylonia. Whether the exposition given in a preceding volume (Hebrew People, pp. 396, 586-589) be received or rejected, I think it must be

admitted that the king was moved to adopt this course by some
strong desire to bring the united religious faith and feeling of his
officers everywhere to bear upon their fealty to him, and to promote
the consolidation of his empire by this means.

Whatever might have been the king's motive in all this great
effort, it led to marvellous consequences. The pious determination
of the three Hebrew youths was formed; and they refused compliance with the royal mandate, to "fall down and worship the golden
image." They were in consequence cast into a fiery furnace.
Struck with such remarkable conduct, and enraged at this resistance to his authority, Nebuchadnezzar carefully watched the execution of the punishment. While thus occupied, he was amazed beyond
measure to find that the fire had no power on the bodies of the condemned men. Their bonds, indeed, were burned off, but their persons and their clothes remained unharmed by the destroying element;
and they walked up and down in the midst of the fire. Stranger
even than all was the appearance of a divine person, walking in
company with them through the fire, whom the terrified king, either
struck by the display of some well-known sign or appearance, or
taught by an immediate *afflatus* from heaven, at once recognised as
THE SON OF GOD.

Whatever personal, political, or religious design, then, was contemplated in the collection of this great assembly, it could have been
but partially secured, and was probably entirely frustrated. This
great, and at the same time select, concourse of the official and executive bodies of all the provinces of this immense empire are sent
back to their localities, not only under a deep impression of the
faithfulness and almighty power of the God of the Hebrews, but
with an assurance that, notwithstanding the hopes and expectation
of every people looked each to its own several country for his
appearance, the SON OF GOD was eminently the God of the Hebrews.

The religious effect of this miracle on this Hebrew multitude will
be noticed elsewhere: we simply observe here, that its political influence must have been great. What though Jerusalem lay in ruins,
and the Hebrews were scattered throughout Chaldæa in abject captivity? their fortunes could not be regarded as hopeless, their political interests could not be desperate, while an almighty God was thus
present to interpose in their behalf. When, therefore, "the princes,
governors, and captains, and the king's counsellors, being gathered
together, saw these men, upon whose bodies the fire had no power,
nor was a hair of their head singed," they saw before them living
proofs of the vitality of the Hebrew state,—a certain pledge that it

also should be delivered from the furnace of affliction in which it then was, and rise again to honour and power.

As no heathen monarch had ever before been the subject of such a large amount of prophecy and promise as Nebuchadnezzar, so no one was distinguished by such remarkable interpositions. Not only was he permitted to overthrow the Hebrew state, which had arisen under the special and immediate protection of Heaven, and had been miraculously sustained for many centuries; but universal sovereignty was in distinct terms promised to him, and he was actually put in possession of it. While he remained a proud and haughty heathen, although influenced by a mad ambition, he is called a "servant" of Jehovah, and direct punishment from God is denounced on all who refuse to submit to his authority. Jer. xxvii, 6–8. The result of this unparalleled success and elevation was intolerable pride, which subjected him to a most remarkable afflictive visitation.

Our information respecting this fact is brought before us in an extraordinary manner, being contained in a long and important proclamation or edict, issued by the king, which details all the circumstances of the case, with his solemn judgment thereon. It recites that the king saw in a dream a great and lofty tree, of unequalled strength, size, and beauty; that while he gazed on it a holy one came down from heaven, and cried aloud: "Hew down the tree, cut off his branches, shake off his leaves, and scatter his fruit: let the beasts get away from under it, and the fowls from his branches: nevertheless leave the stump of his roots in the earth, even with a band of iron and brass, in the tender grass of the field; and let it be wet with the dew of heaven, and let his portion be with the beasts in the grass of the earth: let his heart be changed from man's, and let a beast's heart be given unto him; and let seven times pass over him." The king said, that the dream made him afraid, and troubled him. He then called in his wise men; but they could not afford him any satisfactory solution of the dream. Daniel was then summoned: and, on hearing the strange recital, stood wrapt in mute astonishment for an hour; until the king said, "Belteshazzar, let not the dream trouble THEE." The prophet then, in a speech full of tenderness, power, and fidelity, told his master that the dream betokened the greatest personal calamity to the king. Identifying the sovereign with the tree, he thus explained its cutting down, &c.: "This is the interpretation, O king, and this is the decree of the Most High, which is come upon my lord the king: that they shall drive thee from men, and thy dwelling shall be with the beasts of the field, and they shall make thee to eat grass as oxen, and they shall wet thee with the dew of heaven, and seven times shall pass over thee, till thou know that the Most High ruleth in the kingdom of men, and giveth it to whomsoever he will." The prophet closed his address by earnestly exhorting the king to repentance, that, if possible, the infliction of this terrible evil might be delayed or averted.

No immediate prospect of the fulfilment of this prophetic doom appeared. Nebuchadnezzar still proceeded in his usual course, until twelve months after he had had this dream, when, while standing in his palace, admiring the splendour of his dwelling, and the magnificence and extent of his capital, he said, "Is not this great Babylon, that I have built for the house of the kingdom by the might of my power, and for the honour of my majesty?" Instantly a voice from heaven arrested his ear, and announced that the predicted infliction would now take place. And so it was: the same hour the king's reason left him: insanity, in its most humiliating form, affected his mind; and from this time he herded with beasts, and was a stranger to the comforts of humanity, until seven years had passed over him. It is possible that during these years Nebuchadnezzar had intervals sufficiently lucid to enable him to appreciate the extent of his loss, and the misery and degradation to which he was reduced. At the end of seven years he recovered his reason, and was restored to his kingdom. He immediately published, as a proclamation, that which is now found in the fourth chapter of Daniel's prophecy, and which was perhaps drawn up, at his request, by the hand of the prophet. It contains a noble acknowledgment of the truth, wisdom, goodness, and power of the true God.

Soon after this event, Nebuchadnezzar died, and left the kingdom to his son. We cannot, however, close the account of this extraordinary reign without observing, that it was in fact the Babylonian empire. The prophetic explanation given by Daniel of the first universal monarchy was as strictly accurate as it was bold and terse, when he said to Nebuchadnezzar, "THOU art this head of gold." Like Alexander of Greece, this king of Babylon, under God, gave power to his country. All before him was slow, almost imperceptible, growth:—all after him, rapid decay.

It may further be observed, that the numerous predictions respecting the future history of the world which this sovereign had received through the medium of Daniel, had given him a knowledge of succeeding events which have left traces on the page of profane history. In a fragment of Megasthenes,* preserved by Abydenus, it is stated,

* Megasthenes was a Greek author who wrote B. C. 300. He was sent by Seleucus to India, to renew a treaty with Sandrocottus.

"It is moreover related by the Chaldæans, that as Nebuchadnezzar went up into his palace, he was possessed by some god; and he cried out and said, 'O Babylonians, I Nebuchadnezzar foretell unto you a calamity which must shortly come to pass, which neither Belus my ancestor nor his queen Beltis have power to persuade the Fates to turn away. A Persian mule shall come, and by the assistance of your gods shall impose upon you the yoke of slavery; the author of which shall be a Mede, the vain-glory of Assyria. Before he should thus betray my subjects, O that some sea or whirlpool might receive him, and his memory be blotted out forever; or that he might be cast out, to wander through some desert, where there are neither cities nor the trace of men, a solitary exile among rocks and caverns, where beasts and birds alone abide! But for me, before he shall have conceived these mischiefs in his mind, a happier end will be provided.' When he had thus prophesied, he expired."— *Cory's Fragments*, p. 45.

It will be freely admitted, that if Daniel had fully communicated his several visions to Nebuchadnezzar, he would have been in possession of all the information given in the above extract: and nothing seems more probable than that, although from motives of policy he might keep the import of these to himself during his life, he might, just before his death, unburden his mind in such language as Megasthenes has given us,—language which will be found in perfect keeping with the thoughts, feelings, and character of the speaker. (Prideaux's Connexion, vol. i, p. 117.)

On the death of Nebuchadnezzar, EVIL-MERODACH ascended the throne. We have but slender information respecting this sovereign. The first act of his which is mentioned in Holy Scripture is the liberation of Jehoiachin, the captive king of Judah, from the prison in which he had been confined for thirty-seven years. 2 Kings xxv, 27. A Jewish tradition, already noticed, supposes the Babylonian prince to have been imprisoned by his father, and thus to have formed an acquaintance with the captive Hebrew. A cause is suggested for this imprisonment of the Babylonish prince by a statement of Xenophon to this effect, that during a hunting excursion he entered the Median territory, but was encountered and repulsed by a party of Medes under the command of Cyrus, who was then a youth.

Whether either of these traditions has any foundation in fact cannot now be ascertained: but it is sufficiently evident that his kindness to the captive king of Judah is the most prominent action of this sovereign's government which has come to our knowledge. He was slain, after a brief reign of three years, by a conspiracy, at the head of which was his brother-in-law, Neriglissar, who had married a daughter of Nebuchadnezzar.

NERIGLISSAR succeeded to the throne on the death of Evil-Merodach, and was greatly esteemed by his subjects for his justice and bravery.

He saw in the rising power of the Medes, and their close connexion with Persia, danger to the independence of his country: and it is highly probable that this apprehension was greatly strengthened by the predictions which Nebuchadnezzar had received from Daniel, and which would be preserved in the court of Babylon, as important guides to direct the policy of the state. He accordingly exerted himself to promote a powerful confederacy against Media. This was composed of the Lydians under Crœsus, the King of Cappadocia, the Phrygians, the Carians, the Paphlagonians, the Cilicians, and some Indians.

The Median monarch, in order effectually to resist this aggressive combination, first marched into Armenia, where the king, encouraged by these appearances of hostility, had thrown off his allegiance, and withheld his accustomed tribute. Having subdued and pardoned this prince, he proceeded to meet the confederated chiefs, who did not shrink from the conflict. A great battle was the result, in which the Medes were conquerors, and Neriglissar was slain. Crœsus of Lydia assumed the command of the defeated army, and retreated toward his own country; while the son of Neriglissar, LABOROSARCHOD, being a very young man, ascended the throne of Babylon.

This prince was the BELSHAZZAR of Daniel: he reigned but nine months; in consequence of which, his name does not appear in the Astronomical Canon of Ptolemy. Short as was his reign, he gave ample proof of his cruelty and dissipation. He wantonly slew the son of Gobrias, one of his principal nobles, because, while hunting, he successfully threw a dart at a wild beast which the king had hoped to kill. He also subjected another of his nobility to the most infamous and cruel treatment, because one of the royal concubines had praised his appearance. The crowning act of his short and inglorious reign was his profanation of the vessels of the house of the Lord at Jerusalem; which Nebuchadnezzar had taken away, and placed in the temple of his idol deity at Babylon.

This young and vain prince having assembled a thousand of his lords to a grand banquet,—while they were feasting with unbounded revelry, it occurred to him, that it would greatly add to the interest of the scene, and to his own honour, if he introduced these sacred vessels to his guests. The desire was immediately gratified. The sacred vessels were introduced. He drank wine out of them, and handed them to his guests, who, following his example, all united in extolling their own gods, by whose favour such trophies were placed in their hands.

While thus employed, the finger of a man's hand was seen writing on the wall opposite to the royal seat. To apprehend this fully, it must be stated that these royal halls were covered with sculpture and inscriptions. Every national triumph, and all the splendid actions of their several kings, were thus emblazoned before the eyes of all beholders. The finger of a man's hand thus miraculously adding to these records, of course, filled the assembly with consternation and alarm, and most of all dismayed the king, who in trembling haste summoned his wise men to his aid; but they could not read the writing. The queen, Nitocris, now appeared. She was the king's grandmother, and had been the wife of Nebuchadnezzar, and was therefore perfectly familiar with the history of that king's reign, and with the character and wisdom of Daniel. She accordingly suggested, that the sacred seer should be called; who, when he appeared, after a faithful reprehension of the king for his impiety, announced that the sentence so marvellously added to the inscriptions of the royal palace, was simply this: "THOU ART WEIGHED IN THE BALANCES, AND ART FOUND WANTING. THY KINGDOM IS NUMBERED AND FINISHED, AND GIVEN TO THE MEDES AND PERSIANS." (See also Hebrew People, pp. 354, 355.)

That same night Belshazzar was slain by conspirators; and, as the sacred record informs us, "DARIUS the Median took the kingdom, being about threescore and two years old." Dan. v, 31.

No portion of ancient history is more complicated or beset with greater difficulties, than this: and for further information respecting the chronology and order of this succession the reader must be referred to another place. (See *Appendix*, note 27.) It may, however, be stated here, that there is nothing in the conclusion to which we have come, or in the Scriptural account which we fully receive, contrary to the highest probability.

The sovereign of Media, with whom the Persians were in strict alliance, was brother of Nitocris, the wise and energetic queen-mother of Babylon. The race of Nebuchadnezzar was now extinct. Darius was the nearest of kin to the late royal line. The power of the Medes and Persians was in the ascendant. But a few months previously, the king of Babylon had fallen in battle against them, and all the confederate host had been routed by the Medo-Persian army. At this moment the young Cyrus was pursuing his career of conquest in the west of Asia. At the same time, it was known that the Median supremacy was just and clement. The king of Armenia had a short time before been pardoned, and allowed to retain the sovereignty of his country, even after he had been convicted of infidelity. Above all, the queen was well aware, that, with the deceased monarch, God's prophet had declared that the royal line of Babylon should cease, and the country become subject to the Medes and Persians. This was, indeed, not only known to the queen by previous predictions, but had also, on that eventful night of revelry, been heralded forth to all the assembled aristocracy by the venerable Daniel.

Can it, then, excite any surprise that this course was taken, now that there was no royal ambition to gratify? Need we wonder that the Babylonians did not decide upon appointing a king, and entering, under every disadvantage, upon a new Median war, rather than, by a ready submission to Darius, securing to themselves a mild and tolerant government?

The king of Media, on these terms, took possession of the kingdom, and treated it as the rest of his dominions. The sacred writer proceeds to say, that "it pleased Darius to set over the kingdom a hundred and twenty princes." The person he appointed as viceroy of Babylon was NABONNEDUS, or LABYNETUS, as he is sometimes named. It would seem, from the accounts of ancient authors, that he was the choice of the Babylonish people; it being extremely probable that, in those circumstances, the Median monarch would allow them a governor in whom they had the fullest confidence. Having made this appointment, and having heard, perhaps by public report, and possibly more fully from his sister, the fame and character of Daniel, Darius took him to his own capital of Ecbatana, and made him the first minister of his great empire.

Labynetus reigned seventeen years. We have no information respecting the early part of his government: but it seems that, having become accustomed to rule, he, after some years, turned his attention to the feasibility of obtaining the independence of Babylon. His first efforts were directed toward greatly improving the fortifications of his capital. At length, taking advantage of the conquest of Media, and the troubled state of the affairs of Cyrus, Labynetus assumed entire independence. How long he was permitted to enjoy this, does not appear. But at length the indefatigable Persian marched toward Babylon. Too confident in his strength, the king went forth, and met him in the field, but was completely defeated. Still the king of Babylon, relying on the strength of the city walls, refused to submit; and Cyrus was long detained by the siege, until at length, taking advantage of a public festival, he diverted the river from its bed, and caused his troops to enter, on each side of the city, in the night, which was thus taken by surprise, and completely reduced to subjection. Labynetus, on the capture of the city, retreated to Borsippa, the sacred palace and citadel, which were strongly fortified. (See *Appendix*, note 28.) Cyrus destroyed the principal part of the lofty walls of Babylon, before he left it.

Having subdued the capital, Cyrus proceeded to invest Borsippa; but Labynetus, seeing his circumstances desperate, submitted himself to the conqueror, and was sent into Carmania, where he ended his days. Thus terminated the glory and power of Babylon. We cannot, however, dismiss the history of this country without observing, that we have here the first of those four remarkable nations which were raised up by the special providence of God, made the subjects of wonderful prophetic revelations, and placed in singular proximity to the people of God. There is nothing in the history of the world comparable to the magnitude of this divine interposition. Its effect on the religious character and knowledge of the several countries will be elsewhere shown: but, as a grand element in God's government of the world, this divine vocation of nations to peculiar political power is truly wonderful. Babylon, after ages of subjection to Assyria, suddenly, and exactly when the Hebrew state was tottering to its fall, started up to the summit of martial power and political grandeur; and, having fulfilled her destiny in the ruin and captivity of the Hebrews, and verified the numerous predictions which had been delivered respecting her, she with equal rapidity, and almost without a struggle, descended first into her former subordinate position, and thence into absolute and perpetual desolation. (See *Appendix*, note 29.)

CHRONOLOGICAL TABLE OF BABYLONIAN HISTORY.

B.C.	Names and Events.	Years Reigned.
747	Nabonassar	14
	(Who made the date of his accession the beginning of the Nabonassarian Era.)	
733	Nadius	2
731	Chinzirus	5
726	Jugæus	5
721	Mardocempadus	12
	(The Merodach-Baladan who sent an embassy to Hezekiah.)	
709	Archianes, brother to Esarhaddon	5
704	Hagisa	30 days
	(Who killed the preceding Assyrian viceroy, and ruled independently.)	
	Maraduk	6 months
	Interregnum.	
702	Belibus	3
699	Apronadius	6
	(Babylon being again subdued to Assyria, this king, another brother of Esarhaddon, governs.)	
693	Regibulus	1
692	Mesesimordacus	4
688	Second *Interregnum*	8
680	Asaridin	13
667	Saosduchin	20
647	Chinladin	22
625	Nabopolassar	21
	(In conjunction with the Medes, destroys Nineveh, B. C. 606, and sends his son, Nebuchadnezzar, to subdue Western Asia.)	
604	Nebuchadnezzar	43
	(Destroys Jerusalem, B. C. 586.)	
561	Evil-Merodach	3
558	Neriglissar	5
	Laborosarchod	9 months
	(The Belshazzar of Daniel; his feast and death.)	
553	Labynetus	17
	(Rules at first as viceroy under Darius; but at length, assuming independence, is subdued by Cyrus.)	
536	Babylon taken by Cyrus.	

CHAPTER V.

THE RELIGION OF THE ASSYRIANS AND BABYLONIANS.

BABYLON the seat of the first post-diluvian Apostacy—Peculiar Religious Position of Babylon and Assyria—Epiphanius on the Early Declension of Religion—Information contained in his Statement—Fragment of Damascius—Its Important Teaching—The Chaldæan Oracles exhibit the same Fact—A Triad consisting of the Great Mother, Father, and Only-begotten Son—Further Development of Chaldæan Mythology—Chaldæan Deities—Their Origin and Peculiarities—Worship of the Heavenly Bodies, and of Fire—Chaldæan and Assyrian Idolatry began with Hero and Demon Worship in the Form of Triads—Mr. Faber on this Subject—Symbolical Representation of the Great Triad—Other Symbols—Assarac—Cherubic Figures—The Sacred Tree—A Garden called "Paradise" attached to each Royal Palace—The Palace itself a Sacred Temple—Doubts of Layard—Elaborate Proof of Fergusson—The King revered as a Divine Person—Proof of this—Manner in which the Kings evinced their Claim to this Character—This Idea shown to pervade the whole System—Remarkable Identity of Character which the Religion of Assyria and Babylon maintained through so many Ages—General Views—Gradual Declension in Theology—Worship of Fire—The Results of Hebrew Intercourse and Divine Interposition on the Religion of these Countries—Sabæanism not the Primitive Religion of Assyria—A large Amount of Patriarchal History and Religious Knowledge must have remained in the Primitive Nations long after the Dispersion—Patriarchal Longevity designed to prevent a Deterioration in Religion—Connexion with the Hebrews—Divine Interposition more likely on this Ground to be effective—Assyrian Intercourse with Egypt—Assyrian Knowledge of Hebrew History—The Mission of Jonah—Its Religious Results—The Destruction of the Assyrian Emigrants in Samaria by Lions—A Hebrew Priest sent to teach them the Law of the Lord—Babylon elated by the Ruin of Jerusalem—The King humbled, and all the People taught Divine Truth, on the Plains of Dura—Nebuchadnezzar's Insanity, Restoration, and Proclamation.

WHEN the antiquity and extensive dominion of these great empires, Assyria and Babylon, are considered, it is almost impossible to attach too much importance to an acquaintance with their religion.

Here, unquestionably, the first post-diluvian apostacy was carried into effect, and recognised as the established faith of a particular nation. Regarding Mr. Faber's induction—that the great principles of heathen idolatry were evolved, and generally adopted, before the Dispersion—as an established fact, we hold that these must have been incorporated into the national faith of Assyria and Babylon, before any other people would have obtained a settled location, and assumed a national form. Another circumstance serves to confirm this opinion: by the universal consent of all antiquity, the founder of the Babylonian state was one of the leaders, if not the prime mover, in the origination and development of this apostacy.

To Nimrod has been awarded, in all ages, the position of arch-apostate in this departure from the truth of God: and this being admitted, there cannot be a doubt that he enforced the adoption of this perverted faith as a part of the policy of his own government.

But while these circumstances clearly indicate the existence of some important facts, and the operation of certain principles, we must recollect that they prove the period to which our inquiry is directed to be exceedingly remote. We have here to discuss the nature of religious changes effected four thousand five hundred years ago, and to trace, as far as possible, their operation, influence, and development for the twenty centuries which ensued; and to attempt all this, under the great disadvantage arising from the circumstance that this people has perished from the earth, and been unknown among men during the last two thousand years. Much, therefore, cannot be expected in such an effort, beyond general heads of information. Accuracy in detail must in this instance be almost impossible. What can be gleaned, however, from authentic sources, it will be our aim to furnish; and from these *data* to supply general views of the character, morals, influence, and policy of this religious system.

In the absence of precise information respecting the early operation of idolatry in Assyria, it might be fairly presumed that those great errors which have been shown to have originated before the Dispersion, and to have wrought a total corruption in the theology of the world, had obtained in that country, and produced similar results to those which meet the eye of religious research in Egypt and other ancient nations.

We are not totally left to this barren induction, in respect of a subject of so much interest and importance. There are several facts connected with it, handed down to us by ancient Greek authors, who had opportunities of collecting, from the literature of Assyria and Babylon, important elements of information, which were current in their day, respecting the religion of those countries. These stores of instruction are largely supplemented by the extensive discoveries recently made in the sculptures and inscriptions of these ancient nations; which have shed a flood of light on the religious usages, rites, worship, sacred persons, and divinities of Assyria and Babylon. These sources of information, when studied under the direction of the general teaching of history, and with a due regard to the influence exercised by the numerous divine interpositions and communications of religious truth, through the instrumentality of the Hebrew people and of the Hebrew Scriptures, will, it is hoped, enable us to form a tolerably correct and full idea of the religion of these countries.

It may be desirable to call attention, in the first instance, to the following extract from Epiphanius: for although a part of it refers to a preceding period, altogether it shows the opinions which prevailed, at an early age, respecting the declension and deterioration of religion which took place at different times, and probably the account of the changes which it records is accurate :—

"The parents of all the heresies, and the prototypes from which they derive their names, and from which all other heresies originate, are these four primary ones.

"The first is Barbarism," (Patriarchism,) "which prevailed without a rival, from the days of Adam, through ten generations, to the time of Noah. It is called 'Barbarism,' because men have no rulers, nor submitted to any particular discipline of life; but as each thought proper to prescribe to himself, so he was at liberty to follow the dictates of his own inclination.

"The second is Scythism, which prevailed from the days of Noah, and thence downward to the building of the tower and Babylon, and for a few years subsequently to that time, that is, to the days of Phalec and Ragar. But the nations which incline upon the borders of Europe continued addicted to the Scythic heresy, and the customs of the Scythians, to the age of Tharra, and afterward. Of this sect also were the Thracians.

"The third is Hellenism, which originated in the days of Seruc with the introduction of idolatry: and as men had each hitherto followed some demonolatrous superstition of his own, they were now reduced to a more established form of polity, and to the rites and ceremonies of idols. And the followers of this began with the use of painting, making likenesses of those whom they had formerly honoured,—either kings or chiefs, or men who in their lives had performed actions which they deemed worthy of record, by strength or excellence of body.

"And from the times of Tharra, the father of Abraham, they introduced images and all the errors of idolatry; honouring their forefathers and their departed predecessors with effigies which they fashioned after their likenesses. They first made these effigies of earthenware, but afterward, according to their different arts, they sculptured them in stone, and cast them in silver and gold, and wrought them in wood, and all kinds of different materials.

"The Egyptians and Babylonians, the Phrygians and Phenicians, were the first propagators of this superstition, of making images, and of the mysteries; from whom it was transferred to the Greeks, from the time of Cecrops downward. But it was not until afterward, and at a considerable interval, that Cronus and Rhea, Zeus and Apollo, were esteemed and honoured as gods."—*Cory's Fragments*, pp. 53–55.

Although this statement is not regarded as detailing the potent causes which produced these changes, nor as specifying the exact times when these causes began to operate, we accept it as an important communication of the great stages of degeneracy, and of the order and time when these changes were so fully effected as to become open to public observation, and to stand patent to the world as accomplished facts.

Regarded in this aspect, it teaches that no great religious change, subsequent to the Deluge, was so fully effected as to be openly observable in the state of society, until the time of Peleg and Reu. The first of these was born about two years before the death of Nimrod. Further, we are informed that idolatry was reduced to an *established form of polity* in the time of Serug, who was born B.C. 2452, or two hundred and sixty years after the death of Nimrod. We are also told, that at this period idol-worship had become invested with special *rites and ceremonies*, and that it began with painting the objects of idolatrous regard; but that, in the days of Terah, it had become so developed that images were common. It is added, that it was not until some time afterward that Cronus, Rhea, Zeus, and Apollo, were esteemed and honoured as gods. And, lastly, we are informed that Babylon was one of the first of the nations which adopted and promulgated these errors. Indeed, we know from other evidence that the Babylonians were the first people that fully committed themselves to this national sin and folly.

Thus in Chaldæa was this master-evil introduced, and the true knowledge of God assailed by the rise, progress, and general prevalence of this fatal superstition. But it will be asked, "How did this scheme, in its systematic action, affect the knowledge of the one true God?" There can, indeed, be little doubt that the extract from Epiphanius is perfectly correct in stating that, before this time, individuals had been addicted to demonolatrous superstitions. It was, in fact, this which made practicable the impious attempt to introduce idolatry *as an established form of polity*, and which brought it into general operation.

It may be safely assumed, that at the beginning, as we have already stated, this error was not put forward as an avowed antagonist to the truth, but rather in the character of an addition, an auxiliary to it. The first notice we have of the operation of this system is in perfect accordance with this general rule. "The Babylonians," we are told, "like the rest of the barbarians, pass over in silence the one principle of the universe; and they constitute two,—Tauthe and Apason; making Apason the husband of Tauthe, and denominating her 'the Mother of the Gods.' And from these proceeds an only-begotten son, Moymis."—*Cory's Fragments*, p. 318.

In this brief but important passage there are some points which deserve especial notice. We are told that the Babylonians—and not they only, but the Gentile nations in general—preserved a strict silence with respect to the one true God,—" the one principle of the universe." They did not deny this: it would not have answered their purpose. This truth was, in that early age, too deeply imbedded in the faith, traditions, and judgment of all people. A denial of this cardinal doctrine would have raised resistance, and called forth startling proofs of its certain verity. No; but they were taciturn respecting the glorious unity of the true God; while other objects of veneration and worship were, with the utmost diligence and energy, spread before the mind, and by every sacred association urged on the acceptance of the people. Thus, while perfect silence was maintained respecting the divine unity, two persons are at first exhibited as divine; and then the triad is completed by the addition of their only-begotten son! Is it not truly astonishing that the two oldest primitive nations, Babylon and Egypt, should not only have adopted the first pair, with the promised incarnate Seed, as their divine triad, but that, after the lapse of so many ages, such unmistakable proofs of this should yet remain to attest the certainty of the fact?

That this was the case here, as in Egypt, cannot admit of a doubt; or if such existed, it would be dispelled by the significant terms "ONLY-BEGOTTEN SON." It is not merely a son,—a regal, a ruling son; but he is to be such a son as can have no equal, no parallel,—an only-begotten, divinely-promised son. It is further observable, that the woman is made the first of the triad, and called "the Mother of the Gods." (Ταύτην δὲ μητέρα θεῶν ὀνομάζοντες.) This arises out of the fact contained in the primitive promise, namely, that the incarnate Son was to be emphatically "the Seed of the woman:" and if this Chaldæan dogma had not come down to us through the language and medium of a nation of polytheists, we certainly should not have found the female parent of an *only*-begotten son called "the Mother of the *Gods;*" but rather, in strict accordance with the language employed by the Babylon of gospel times, "*the Mother of God.*"

The celebrated Chaldæan oracles are full of similar teaching. Mr. Cory says of them, "We meet everywhere with the doctrine of a triad." And although, with this learned and lamented author, I am disposed to make considerable allowance for the forgeries and corruptions which there is reason to believe the later Platonists introduced into these oracles, 1 quite agree with him in believing "that in them many of the remnants of the ancient system have been preserved;" and that "the fundamental tenet which they set forth is, that 'a triad shines through the whole world, over which a monad reigns.'"—*Cory's Fragments*, p. 318.

But while the fragment of Damascius gives us this important information respecting the origin of the Chaldaic triad, it proceeds further to develop the progress of Chaldæan idolatry. Although it had been stated so distinctly, that Moymis, the third person of the triad, was an *only-begotten son*, the account proceeds thus: "From them, also, another progeny is derived,—Dache and Dachus; and again, a third,—Kissare and Asorus; from which last three others proceed,—Anus, and Illinus, and Aus. And of Aus and Dauce is born a son called Belus, who, they say, is the fabricator of the world, the *Demiurgus*."—*Cory's Myth. Inq.*, p. 63; and *Cudworth's Intel. Sys.*, vol. i, pp. 488-492. Thus it appears that, having made the first pair and the promised Seed the triad which stands at the head of their theogony, the Babylonians had to exhibit a series of sacred persons, terminating with their hero-divinity Belus or Nimrod, who sustained the character of the great God, was their principal national deity in after-times, and is celebrated as the *Demiurgus*, or "Creator of the world." It seems extremely probable that this ancient fragment has preserved, and now presents to our view, an outline at least of the general plan upon which the idolatrous system of these countries was framed, and the order in which the more prominent errors were evolved and brought into operation.

But our task goes far beyond this. We have also to ascertain the extent to which this was carried, and the further progress of this fearful corruption, until it had reared up a system so full of impurity, and so opposed to divine truth, that it deserved to be called "Babylon the Great, the Mother of Harlots and Abominations of the Earth."

The first step in this inquiry should be directed to the theology of this religion. The names, number, and respective character of Assyrian and Chaldæan deities must be, as far as possible, ascertained. Hitherto little has been known on these subjects; and even now the means available for supplying this information are very limited, although from the resuscitated sculptures and inscriptions some valuable aid has been procured. The best arrangement and condensation of what has been thus obtained is given by Col. Rawlinson in his valuable "Outlines of Assyrian History," pages xviii–xxi, and is here subjoined entire in his own words:—

"The most important, and at the same time the most difficult, branch of study connected with the Cuneiform Inscriptions, is that which relates to the Pantheon;—important, because the names of the kings, and sometimes even the names of the countries which they rule over, are composed of the names of the gods;—difficult, because these names of the gods are usually expressed by arbitrary monograms, because several monograms often apply indifferently to the same god, and because many of the gods have, to all appearance, distinct and independent titles, in Syria, in Assyria, and in Babylonia. Colonel Rawlinson has bestowed much labour on this intricate branch of inquiry, but he has only in a partial degree overcome its difficulty: he has identified most of the deities worshipped by the Assyrians with the gods and goddesses of the Greek mythology, but in a few instances only has he satisfied himself of the vernacular pronounciation of the title.

"He presents, however, the following brief sketch of the Pantheon:—

"(1.) *Assur*, the patriarch 'Asshur' deified; Biblical 'Nisroch;' the tutelar divinity of Assyria, and the head of their Pantheon, but unknown to the Babylonians.

"(2.) *Anu*, the patriarch 'Noah' deified; 'Oannes' of Berosus: the name occurs frequently in composition: compare the nymph *Anobret* of Sanchoniathon, 'beloved of Anu;' *Telani*, 'hill of Anu,' native place of the Assyrian monarchs; and the name of *Shalman*, or 'Shalmaneser,' which in the Inscriptions is *Sallam Anu*, 'the likeness of *Anu*.'

"(3.) *Bel*, Belus or Jupiter, called on the obelisk 'husband of *Derceto*,' and 'father of the gods,' but not easily to be recognised in the later Inscriptions, as the title *Bel*, with a qualificative adjunct, was applicable to several other divinities.

"(4.) *Derceto*, or Semiramis, 'mother of the gods.' The native name was perhaps *Tarkat*, for which our copies of the Bible have *Tarkat*, as the deity of the Avites. 2 Kings xvii, 31. A famous temple of 'Atargatis' is thus described by Isidore, at 'Besechan,' or 'Ava,' on the Euphrates, near Hit; and all that part of Babylonia is distinguished in the Inscriptions by the name of the goddess. *Tarkat* was the special divinity of the first Assyrian dynasty, her name being usually attached to that of the king; and hence the family were named *Dercetades* by the Greeks. This fact also explains the pretended descent of the Assyrian kings from Semiramis.

"(5.) 'Saturn,' whose name is perhaps to be read '*Moloch*,' and who is sometimes placed at the head of the Pantheon, being styled the chief of the four thousand gods who inhabit the heavens and the earth.

"(6.) The planet 'Mars,' called *Merodach* by the Babylonians, (whence the Mirrikh of the Arabs,) but distinguished perhaps by another name at Nineveh. (The Greeks say *Thurras* or *Tur*.) He is called 'the god of battles,' and temples and memorial tablets to him abound both in Assyria and Babylonia. *Merodach* and *Nebo*, or 'Mars' and 'Mercury,' were the tutelary gods of Nebuchadnezzar, and the long Inscription at the East India House is almost entirely devoted to their glorification.

"(7.) 'The Sun,' one of whose names was *Shamas*, as in Hebrew and Arabic, but who seems to have been known by several other titles. He is called 'the guardian of the heavens and the earth,' and temples were erected in his honour in all the chief cities of Babylonia.

"(8.) The god *San*, whose title is found in the names of *Sennacherib*, *Sanballat*, &c., but whose character has not yet been identified.

"(9.) 'Diana,' associated with *Derceto*, of whom she seems to have been the daughter, and represented everywhere by a naked female figure. She was called *Tanath* or *Alath*, ('Alitta,') in Syria, as in the title of *Vabalathus* on the coins, for 'Artemidorus; and, according to Herodotus, her Assyrian name was *Mylitta*. But though her monograms can be everywhere recognised and her attributes partially explained, nothing has yet been found in the Inscriptions to show how the name was pronounced either at Nineveh or Babylon.

"(10.) *Hadad*, or *Adar*, 'the god of fire,' son of *Anu* or Noah, represented symbolically by *flames*, and called 'the vivifier of mankind,' 'the life of heaven and earth,' &c. That the Syrian designation of this deity was *Hadad* is shown by the Biblical title of 'Ben Hadad,' King of Damascus, of whose name, as it is found on the obelisk, the monogram of the 'fire-god' forms the principal element. Josephus, however, and the Greeks, frequently write 'Ader,' instead of 'Hadad;' and '*Adar*' is the true Babylonian word for 'fire,' as in the names of *Adrammelech*, *Adrameles*, *Atropates*, &c. The Sepharvites worshipped this god when they burned their children in the fire to *Adrammelech*. 'Hadad,' who is called by Sanchoniathon 'king of the gods,' was principally worshipped in Syria, and thus, according to Nicolaus, all the kings of the Damascus family assumed the name. His figure, as it is described by Macrobius, with rays darting downward to express beneficence, is frequently seen on the Assyrian monuments.

"(11.) *Ashteroth*, or 'Venus;' the name is written *Yastara* in the Inscriptions, and is frequently used as a generic appellation for all the goddesses of the Pantheon, like the *Baalim* and *Ashtaroth* of Scripture. In Babylonian she is called 'the queen of heaven and earth,' and seems to be confounded with *Nana*, the *Nannaia* of the Greeks, and *Nani* of the Syrians, which is the name still applied in Syriac to the planet 'Venus.' Where *Nana* is mentioned in the Nineveh Inscriptions, she is usually named 'queen of Babylon.' The name of *Nanabius*, King of Babylon, cited by Nicolaus, signifies 'beloved of Nana.'

"(12.) 'Rhea,' or 'Cybele,' whose name in Assyrian means 'queen of the gods;' she is usually associated with 'Saturn.'

"(13.) *Nebo*, or 'Mercury,' a deity held in great veneration both in Assyria and Babylonia; he is termed 'the king of heaven and earth,' or 'the ruler of heaven and earth,' and was the tutelar divinity of the family of Nebuchadnezzar.

"Among the other gods who have been identified with more or less of certainty, are (14.) the *Succoth Benoth* of Scripture; (15.) *Nit*, or 'Minerva,' adopted probably from Egypt; (16.) *Dagon*; (17.) *Murtu*, or 'Neptune,' the god of the sea, who was also, like *Hadad*, the god of fire, a son of *Anu*, or 'Noah,' and whose temple, erected by Sennacherib, is now being excavated in a mound near Nineveh; (18.) 'the Moon, of whose native name, however, no indication has been yet found.

"(19.) *Divan* or *Diman*, whom it is proposed to identify with the Greek Hercules, for Syncellus has preserved a tradition that this deity was called $\Delta\iota\delta\delta\tilde{\alpha}\nu$ by the Phœnicians, the Cappadocians, and the Ilians; and a further argument that *Divan* must represent a deified hero rather than a god is furnished by the fact that, although the name, expressed phonetically, and preceded by the determinative of divinity, enters into the composition of many Assyrian royal titles, it is yet never found in any invocation or list of gods, nor does there ever seem to have been a temple erected in his honour. We find also, (20.) 'the Heavens' personified and worshipped as a deity both at Babylon and Nineveh; and we further recognise a god, named *Dala*, (21,) whose title is to be found in the $\Delta\epsilon\lambda\alpha\iota\acute{\alpha}\sigma\tau\alpha\rho\tau\sigma\varsigma$ of Josephus, in Deleboras, 'beloved of *Dala*,' the name of an Assyrian king preserved by Macrobius, in $\Delta\epsilon\lambda\epsilon\phi\grave{\alpha}\tau$, explained by Hesychius as 'the star of Venus,' in Dalphon, the name of a son of Haman, &c.; and there are perhaps ten or twelve more of the Assyrian gods whose names and attributes are altogether obscure.

"The Assyrians have likewise preserved the titles of many stranger gods, whom they do not seem to have admitted into their own Pantheon. They were thus acquainted with the true God *Jehovah*, marking the term, wherever it occurred in proper names, with the sign of a divinity; and they distinguish in the same manner the gods of Susiana, *Khumba* and *Duniyas*, and the gods of Armenia, *Haldi* and *Bakbarta*."

Dr. Layard, in his new work (Nineveh and Babylon, p. 629) has given a list of thirteen deities; but it affords no additional information of importance, beyond what is above cited from Col. Rawlinson.

We find in the deification of ASSHUR in Assyria, and in the circumstance of his being unknown at Nineveh, a striking confirmation of the views advocated in this work respecting the building of Nineveh. (Patriarchal Age, pp. 344, 345.) If Nimrod, of the family of Ham, had been the founder of this city and empire, it is very improbable that Asshur, of the family of Shem, would have been the first and tutelar deity of the country. But if—as we have done—we take the words of the sacred writer in their plain and obvious sense: "Out of that land," Shinar, "went forth Asshur, and builded Nineveh, and the city Rehoboth, and Calah, and Resin;" then it might be expected that, as in almost every other idolatrous country, he would be the tutelar divinity of the nation: while, as Nimrod reigned at Babylon, Asshur would not be recognised there in that character: so that, in this instance, the position which Asshur occupies, as the first deity of the Assyrian Pantheon, may be fairly taken as a demonstration that our view of the origin of the empire is correct.

This deity is the Biblical Nisroch,—the Assarac of the sculptures. He was the great god of the nation; and, in fact, he represented in his person and worship the national faith of the Assyrian people. (Layard's Nineveh and Babylon, p. 637.)

The position of NOAH in this catalogue is in accordance with the usual course of idolatry in other ancient nations; and the prevalence of his divine appellation shows the early age at which his worship was introduced.

BEL, or BELUS, is a most important element in this list of idol deities. It is difficult to ascertain the precise manner in which this deity was added to the Pantheon. Two facts are unquestionable:—first, that this term has always been associated with the worship of the sun; and, secondly, that Bel, or Belus, was equally adored at Nineveh and Babylon. It is further to be observed, that the Assyrian Belus is said to have been the husband of Derceto, or Semiramis,—which would identify him with Ninus. From this it seems reasonable to infer, that in each country some distinguished warrior or hero was deified under this name; and that this apotheosis took place with reference to the worship of the solar orb. Further discoveries of inscriptions may possibly clear up this point. At all events it may be regarded as sufficiently evident, that Nimrod at Babylon and Belus, the father of Ninus, at Nineveh, (or probably Ninus himself,) were the persons thus raised to be objects of profane adoration.

Of DERCETO, or SEMIRAMIS, we have nothing to add to what has been found on the inscriptions, and already recorded of their history. (Patriarchal Age, pp. 439–441.)

The name of Saturn on the inscriptions is MOLOCH,—a circumstance which opens up a curious subject for inquiry, for which it is to be feared there are as yet no very available materials to work out a satisfactory solution. I allude to the fact, that this divinity is known to have been worshipped in connexion with the barbarous immolation of young children. Has this anything to do with the Greek fables of his destroying his own offspring? Or is there some common *substratum* of fact which will account for both?

Besides the personification of the SUN in the royal Belus, this orb was worshipped as a glorious luminary.

DIANA, or MYLITTA, appears to have sustained a very different character in Assyria from the virgin purity associated with her name in Europe. Herodotus has given an account of usages that obtained in the temple of this goddess at Babylon, when he visited that city, which it is necessary here to adduce:—

"The Babylonians have one custom in the highest degree abominable. Every woman who is a native of the country is obliged, once in her life, to attend at the temple of Venus. Such women as are of superior rank do not omit even this opportunity of separating themselves from their inferiors. These go to the temple in splendid chariots, accompanied by a numerous train of domestics, and place themselves near the entrance. This is the practice with many; while the greater part, crowned with garlands, seat themselves in the vestibule; and there are always numbers coming and going. The seats have all of them a rope or string annexed to them, by which each stranger may determine his choice. A woman, having once taken this situation, is not allowed to return home till some stranger throws her a piece of money, and leads her to a distance from the temple. It is usual for a man, when he gives the money, to say, 'May the goddess Mylitta be auspicious to thee!'—Mylitta being the Assyrian name for Venus. The money given is applied to sacred uses, and must not be refused, however small it may be. The woman is not suffered to make any distinction. She afterward makes some conciliatory oblation to the goddess, and returns to her house, never afterward to be subjected to similar forms. Such as are eminent for their elegance and beauty do not continue long; but those who are of less engaging appearance have sometimes been known to remain for three or four years, unable to accomplish the terms of the law. It is to be remarked that the inhabitants of Cyprus have a similar observance."—*Herodotus, Clio*, cap. 199. (See *Appendix*, note 30.)

The father of history, from the similarity of their rites, identified this goddess with Venus: but Colonel Rawlinson has found another Assyrian female divinity to whom he applies that term. This is ASHTAROTH, whom the Babylonians called "the queen of heaven," and who is the same that is spoken of by Jeremiah, and to whom the apostate Israelites burnt incense, and poured out drink-offerings. Jer. xliv, 17–25.

NEBO is supposed to embody the attributes afterward ascribed to Mercury. This divinity was revered in Assyria, as well as Babylonia; but in the latter country he was specially regarded as the tutelar deity of the family of Nebuchadnezzar, and the term is accordingly found incorporated in the names given to many of the princes of this line. The other deities do not call for particular observation.

Passing from the Pantheon of Assyria, we have to notice some of the idol deities of Babylon. The first of these is BELUS, or BAAL. Berosus, the Chaldæan priest of this deity, says, that when Chaos reigned,—who was described by the cosmogony of this people as a woman, presiding over the embryo elements of nature,—then "Belus came, and cut her asunder: and of one half of her he formed the earth, and of the other half the heavens." Afterward this deity is described as taking off his head; "upon which the other gods mixed the blood, as it gushed out, with the earth; and from thence were formed men, who on this account became rational, and partakers of divine knowledge. This Belus, then, divided the darkness, and separated the heavens from the earth, and reduced the universe to order." The account then proceeds to state that the animals which previously existed, "being unable to bear the light, died. Belus, upon this, commanded one of the gods to take off his head, and to mix the blood with the earth, and from thence to form other men and animals. Belus formed also the stars, and the sun and the moon, and the five planets."

The statue of this deity, as seen in his temple at Babylon, is described by Diodorus as in the attitude of walking. His words are: "Upon the top she placed three statues of beaten gold,—of Jupiter,

(whom the Babylonians call Belus,) Juno, and Rhea. That to
Jupiter stood upright, in the posture as if he were walking; he was
forty feet in height, and weighed a thousand Babylonish talents."
It is a singular fact, that we have now before us a representation of
this figure. In the Epistle attached to the Book of Baruch, and
which Jeremiah is supposed to have written to the captive Hebrews,
when they were being carried unto Babylon, he says, "Now shall ye
see in Babylon gods of silver and of gold and of wood borne upon
shoulders, which cause the nations to fear." Verse 3. A reference
to this Epistle in the Second Book of Maccabees (ii, 2, 3) proves
that the ancient Jews regarded it as genuine; (compare Isa. vi, 6,
7;) while, in strict accordance with the Sicilian historian and the
Hebrew prophet, on one of the slabs disinterred at Nineveh we have
a representation of several idols carried on men's shoulders, and one
of them erect in a walking attitude. But what seems decisive as to
the identity of the prophet's description with the sculpture is, the
very singular circumstance that the prophet, in describing the image
of this deity, says, "He hath also in his right hand *a dagger and
an axe.*" These will be allowed to be very unusual implements to
be carried by a divinity; yet in the recently recovered bass-relief he
is represented " with an axe."

In the same chapter Diodorus describes a goddess as seated in a
chair of state, made of gold, with two lions at her knees, and near
her two very large silver serpents. She has been supposed to be the
same with the Greek Rhea; but the Babylonish name has not yet
been obtained. Another female deity is also mentioned in this connexion. She has been believed to be identical with Here. She
appears standing, holding in her right hand a serpent by the head,
and in her left a sceptre ornamented with precious stones.

It will now be necessary to notice the worship of the heavenly
bodies, which extensively prevailed in those countries. It has been
generally believed that this was the primitive and universal religion
of the Assyrians and Babylonians. But although the opinion has
obtained such general acceptance, it does not appear, on examination, to be sustained by such weight of evidence as amounts to
rational proof. It may, indeed, be admitted as highly probable, that
an idolatrous regard for the heavenly bodies began even before the
Flood; (Patriarchal Age, pp. 235, 236;) and that many of the undivided community which journeyed to Shinar were greatly affected
by this heresy. But it seems to be an undoubted fact, that the
prime apostasy of Nimrod was of another kind, and, although
stealthily and insidiously introduced, issued in the establishment of
hero and demon worship, mainly in the form of triads of divinities.

It may, however, be regarded as certain, that the adoration of the heavenly bodies was afterward ingrafted upon this system of hero and demon idolatry.

Mr. Faber has thus stated this subject: "The hierophants of old appear to have been very early addicted to the study of astronomy; though, unfortunately, instead of pursuing their researches in a legitimate manner, they perverted them to the vain reveries of magic, and prostituted them to the purposes of idolatry. As they highly venerated the souls of their paradisiacal and arkite ancestors, considering them in the light of demon-gods, who still watched and presided over the affairs of men, it was an easy step in the way of apostate error, to imagine that they were translated to the heavenly bodies, and that from these lofty stations they ruled and observed all the passing events of this nether world. When such a mode of speculation was once adopted, whatever virtues might afterward be attributed to the planets, and in whatever manner the stars might be combined into mythological constellations, the first idea that must obviously have occurred to the astronomical hierophants, would undoubtedly be this:—Since they perceived the sun and the moon to be the two great lights of heaven, and since they worshipped with an especial veneration the Great Father and the Great Mother, they would naturally elevate those two personages to the two principal luminaries. Such accordingly was the plan which they adopted. Those ancient writers who have treated on the subject of Pagan mythology assure us, that, by what was called 'the *mystic theocrasia*,' all the gods of the Gentiles ultimately resolved themselves into the single character of the Great Father; and, in a similar manner, all their goddesses, into the single character of the Great Mother: and they further declare that, as all their gods melt insensibly into one, they are all equally the sun; and as all their goddesses no less melt into one, they are all equally the moon.

"Yet notwithstanding these avowed and recognised doctrines, the gods of the Gentiles are allowed to have been the souls of their ancestors, and are described as having once acted a conspicuous and sufficiently intelligible part upon earth. The only conclusion that can be drawn from these apparently opposite declarations is, that the demon-gods were worshipped in the heavenly bodies; and, agreeably to such a conclusion, we are unequivocally told, that the souls of certain deified mortals were believed to have been elevated after their death to the orbs of the sun, the moon, the planets, and the stars. Hence originated the notion, that all these celestial bodies, instead of being mere inert matter, were each animated by a divine spirit,—were each a wise and holy intelligence." *Origin of Pagan Idolatry*, vol. i, pp. 31, 32. (See *Appendix*, note 31.)

While these profound expositions apply generally to the whole range of idolatry, they do so with peculiar force and exactitude to the religion of Assyria and Babylon. But even in respect of these countries there is a perceptible difference in the development of those cardinal doctrines. In Babylon, for instance, the ramification of this system inclined to the *solar* form, while in Assyria it was decidedly in the *astral* direction.

There is, however, no more striking feature in the whole of this idolatrous system, than the multiplicity of compound human and animal forms which everywhere meet the eye. The first of these which deserves notice is the figure of a man, with the wings and tail of a bird, enclosed in a circle. Mr. Layard observes of this symbol, "We may conclude, from the prominent position always given to this figure in the Nimroud sculptures, and from its occurrence on Persian monuments as the representation of Ormuzd, that it was also the type of the supreme deity among the Assyrians. It will require a more thorough knowledge of the contents of the inscriptions than we at present possess, to determine the name by which this divinity was known. It may be conjectured, however, that it was BAAL, or some modification of a name which was that of the Great God among nearly all nations speaking the cognate dialects of a Semitic or Syro-Arabian language. According to M. Layard, this symbol is formed by a circle or crown—to denote time without bounds or eternity—encircling the image of Baal, with the wings and tail of the dove, to show the association of Mylitta, the Assyrian Venus,—thus presenting A COMPLETE TRIAD."—*Nineveh and its Remains*, vol. ii, p. 449, and note. Have we not here the key to this recondite symbol? All kinds of puerile conjectures have been put forth on this point: but this is one every way consistent and satisfactory. Nothing is more certain than that the Great Father was, from the introduction of idolatry, worshipped as Cronos or Saturn, or TIME, in all its wide and boundless range of duration. Then we have Mylitta, or perhaps rather Derceto,—"the Mother of the Gods" according to this system, and eminently the Great Mother, (Ibid., vol. ii, pp. 454, 455,) who was fabled in her youth to have been sustained by doves for a whole year, and after her death to have been changed into a dove; and under this symbol was universally worshipped in Assyria. Thirdly, Baal is presented as the Son, the Great God descending from the Great Father and Mother, and with them forming the Assyrian triad. (See *Appendix*, note 32.)

In fact, we have here Tauthe, Apason, and Moymis, symbolically combined as the great object of worship.

Dr. Layard's further discoveries, published since the above was written, greatly strengthen these conclusions. In the rubbish at the foot of one of the gigantic human-headed bulls, in the grand entrance to the palace of Khorsabad, were found four engraved cylinders. On one of these, made out of green felspar, "which," says the learned explorer, "I believe to have been the signet or amulet of Sennacherib himself, is engraved the king standing in an arched frame, as on the rock-tablets at Bavian, and at the Nahr-el-Kelb in Syria. He holds in one hand the sacrificial mace, and raises the other in the act of adoration before the winged figure in a circle, here represented as a triad with three heads. This mode of portraying this emblem is very rare on Assyrian relics, and is highly interesting, as confirming the conjecture that the mythic human figure, with the wings and tail of a bird, enclosed in a circle, was the symbol of the Triune God, the supreme deity of the Assyrians, and of the Persians, their successors in the empire of the east."—*Nineveh and Babylon*, p. 160.

The importance of this discovery can scarcely be over-estimated. The triadic figure, or symbol, in this instance, is precisely the same as those so frequently seen on the early Assyrian and Persian sculptures. Here is the human form, the circle, and the expanded wings; but from each of these wings another head is represented as rising, as if to mark out, in the most unmistakable manner, the great fact, that this symbolical representation was intended to exhibit the union of three personalities. Well may Layard say, that this confirms the opinion, that we have here "the symbol of the Triune God." The further prosecution of the subject, when we have specially to treat of the objects and manner of worship, will greatly enlarge and strengthen this view of the case.

But, passing beyond this symbolical representation of the primitive triad, we find the architecture and sculpture of these countries filled with figures compounding parts of the human body with those of birds and animals.

One of the most remarkable of these combinations occurs in the eagle-headed human figure. This, executed in colossal proportions, is not only found sculptured on the walls, and guarding the portals of the chambers, at Nimroud: it is also embroidered on the royal robes, and introduced in almost every possible variety of manner, connexion, and arrangement. It is supposed to represent Assarac,— the Nisroch of the Scriptures.

Besides this, numerous human-headed lions and bulls are met

with, many of them being of such gigantic dimensions and beautiful workmanship as to impress the mind with a strong conviction of the immense importance which the Assyrians and Babylonians attached to these curious and, to our view, unnatural compounds.

Directing our attention to these, in the hope of ascertaining their design and character, we are struck with the fact that, except when embroidered on raiment, they are always found in pairs, on each side of an entrance, as if guarding it. Another circumstance is very significant: with few and unimportant exceptions, these figures are combinations of the four cherubic creatures,—the man, the bull, the lion, and the eagle. These facts have led every careful student of Assyrian antiquities to regard these compound sculptured figures as standing in some connexion with the Mosaic cherubim, which were in a similar manner sculptured for the tabernacle and temple of the Hebrews, and embroidered on the curtains of both.

Layard says, "The resemblance between the symbolical figures I have described, and those seen by Ezekiel in his vision, can scarcely fail to strike the reader. As the prophet had beheld the Assyrian palaces, with their mysterious images and gorgeous decorations, it is highly probable that, when seeking to typify certain divine attributes, and to describe the divine glory, he chose forms that were familiar not only to him, but to the people he addressed,—captives, like himself, in the land of Assyria."

I have given the learned explorer's view, (much mistaken as I believe it to be in its reasoning, see *Appendix*, note 33,) for the sake of obtaining his countenance to the undoubted fact, that the compound Assyrian figures and the cherubic elements were identical.

Mr. Bonomi, who has most elaborately and successfully investigated these remains, observes, "These symbolical combinations we regard as derived from the traditional descriptions of the cherubim, which were handed down after the deluge by the descendants of Noah; to which origin, also, we are inclined to attribute their situation as guardians of the principal entrances of the palaces of the Assyrian kings. The cherubim guarded the gates of Paradise: the cherubic symbols were placed in the *adytum* of the tabernacle, and afterward in the corresponding sanctuary of the temple: and here in the Assyrian palaces they are never found except as guardians of portals."—*Nineveh and its Palaces*, p. 133.

To cite one more authority on this point, I give the following from the Rev. Mr. Blackburn: "We have glanced at the temples of the heathen, and seen these compound creatures, in various forms of debasement, placed in the avenues and the portals of their most celebrated fanes, as sentinels and guards; just as we see, in the sacred writings, the cherubim attending upon the throne of Jehovah, from the first cloudy pavilion that was pitched before the approaches to Eden, down to the celestial visions of Ezekiel in the plains of Assyria. These forms, I think, the Assyrians must have borrowed from the Jews, or rather from the earlier patriarchs: the doctrine, it may be, was lost in superstitious traditions; but the form and the symbol remained, as we see them in the present day."—*Nineveh: its Rise and Ruin*, pp. 176, 177.

This subject might be further elucidated, and those views sustained, if it were necessary; but the conclusion of Dr. Layard appears to be inevitable. "It will be observed," he says, "that the four forms (and those only) chosen by Ezekiel to illustrate his description,—the man, the lion, the bull, and the eagle,—are precisely those which are constantly found on Assyrian monuments as religious types. These coincidences are too marked not to deserve notice, and do certainly lead to the inference that the symbols chosen by the prophet were derived from, *or rather identical with, these Assyrian sculptures.*"—*Nineveh and its Remains*, vol. ii, p. 445.

Regarding this identity as an established fact, we might now proceed to the interesting inquiry, as to the object and design of the Assyrians in the adoption and general use of these curious figures. But this will be better accomplished after we have investigated some other elements of this religious system.

Another symbolical object which meets the eye in all the religious rites and services of this people is the *sacred tree*. This is the vine, the palm, or the fir; generally the last, which is highly ornamented with elegantly arranged groups of honeysuckle.

It may serve to convey some idea of the character of this symbolism, if we give a sketch of the sacred tree as it occurs in the large work of Dr. Layard,—"The Monuments of Nineveh."

Plate 7 exhibits two winged females standing one on each side of the sacred tree, with their left hands holding a garland, and their right hands raised as if engaged in some act of worship. Plate 7 (A) exhibits two winged human figures, kneeling one on each side of the sacred tree: they are evidently engaged in an act of devotion.

Plate 25 is an interesting and striking exhibition. In the centre stands the sacred tree, ornamented with honeysuckle: on each side is a king, holding a sceptre in his left hand, and raising the right, as if making some solemn covenant or engagement. Immediately above the tree, the celestial triad is represented by the circle, wings, and deity in human form: on this symbol of divinity the kings seem to be gazing with solemn interest; while behind each sovereign stands a winged human figure with the usual basket in the left hand, and raising a fir-cone over the shoulder of the king with the right hand. This is clearly intended to exhibit a most important religious ceremony.

But it is not only on the sculptures that the sacred tree is found: it entered into their architectural decorations; and to this we are undoubtedly indebted for that beautiful ornament, the Grecian honeysuckle. It equally pervaded all their designs for embroidery. One plate, (8,) showing the upper part of the king's robe, is nearly covered with figures of the sacred tree in almost every variety of form. Another, (plate 6,) giving the embroidery worn on the breast of the sovereign, contains the same sacred symbols in equal abundance and variety; the centre being the sacred tree, over which is the symbolic triad of divinities; and on each side a royal figure, the borders being filled with numerous devices of honeysuckle and other parts of these sacred emblems. This is not an unimportant circumstance. Dr. Layard, indeed, observes on this point, "From the constant introduction of the tree, ornamented with them, into groups representing the performance of religious ceremonies, *there cannot be a doubt* that they were symbolical, and were invested with a sacred character. The sacred tree, or tree of life, so universally recognised in eastern systems of theology, is called to mind; and we are naturally led to refer the traditions connected with it to a common origin."—*Nineveh and its Remains*, vol. ii, p. 472.

The allusive range of Assyrian sacred types to Edenic originals did not terminate here, but actually included the garden itself. This was placed in immediate proximity to the royal palace, and seems to have been arranged more after the fashion of an English park, containing numerous large trees, with a great number of animals of different kinds. Respecting this Dr. Layard speaks thus: "To the palace was attached a park, or PARADISE, as it was called, in which was preserved game of various sorts for the diversion of the king."—*Idem*, vol. ii, p. 246. It cannot, however, be admitted that the preservation of game was the principal object in the preparation of a place like this. The name given to it,—one consecrated to the highest realities of divine revelation,—the association of such a garden with the various Edenic symbols to which we have referred, (see *Appendix*, note 34,) and especially its immediate connexion with a consecrated temple and a sacred person,—all clearly show a higher and deeper design for such an appointment than that of a small enclosure for a royal hunt. The primitive intention, however passing ages might have obscured it, must have been in accordance with the genius of the whole system of Assyrian faith and practice.

We shall be induced the more readily to assent to this induction, when we perceive that the royal residence was a sacred temple, and the person of the king revered as a divinity.

On the first head, we may not be able to produce evidence so satisfactory as might be desired. Indeed, it has not satisfied Layard himself, as will be seen from the following words of that learned author: "Were these magnificent mansions palaces or temples? Or, while the king combined the character of a temporal ruler with that of a high-priest or type of the religion of the people, did his residence unite the palace, the temple, and a national monument raised to perpetuate the triumphs and conquests of the nation? These are questions which cannot yet be satisfactorily answered."—*Nineveh and its Remains*, vol. ii, p. 267.

No one will dispute the *dictum* of such a man, on such a point as this. But if these questions have not been satisfactorily answered, all that is possible seems to be done by Mr. Fergusson, who, writing two years after Layard, and availing himself of the important discoveries made in this interval, has given a careful and elaborate investigation of this difficult question:—

"Were these buildings palaces or temples?—a difficulty, however, not peculiar to this place, as the same uncertainty exists in Egypt: in Thebes, for instance, where, according to our usual nomenclature, it is impossible to say whether the great buildings there were, properly speaking, mere places of worship or residences of the sovereigns. That the king did generally, if not always, reside within these halls, seems nearly certain; and that all the great ceremonies and ministrations of government took place within these halls, are facts that can scarcely be doubted. Indeed, they seem at first sight to have been built almost wholly for these kingly purposes; whereas, on the other hand, the portion set apart for the image of the god, or exclusively devoted to religious ceremonies, is so small and insignificant as scarcely to deserve notice in comparison of the rest; yet these buildings were as certainly temples, and the only ones, of the most theocratic religion the world ever knew, though, at the same time, they were the palaces of the most absolute kings of whom we have any record. To name, therefore, these palace-temples or temple-palaces, as well as our Persepolitan buildings, we must redefine our words, and come to a clearer understanding of the terms we use, before we can explain what the buildings of which we are now treating really were.

"When we speak of a Greek or Roman temple we perfectly understand the term we use. It was a building simple in plan and outline, meant to contain the image of the god to whom it was dedicated, and wholly devoted to the religious ceremonies connected with the prescribed worship of that deity. A Christian church, in like manner, was in all ages a temple, wholly devoted to religious worship, without any secular use—a hall, in short, where people may congregate to worship the great God himself, or the saint to whom it is dedicated; but with the distinct idea that it is the house of God, sacred to the purposes of religion, and the fit and proper place in which to offer up prayer and sacrifice.

"In like manner, a palace in all the countries of Europe is, and always has been, merely a large house. It possesses the sleeping, eating, and state and festival apartments which are found in the dwellings of all men of the middle and even the lower classes,— larger, more numerous, and more splendid, of course, but dedicated to the same uses, and to them only. In modern times, a king is only a chief magistrate; in the middle ages, he was a leader; and neither Greece nor Rome ever had kings in the Asiatic sense of the word, at least, certainly not after Rome ceased to be Etruscan, or, in other words, Asiatic, in her form of government. In Persia, however, and indeed, *throughout the east*, the king is an essential and principal part of all forms of government, and virtually, also, the chief-priest of his people, and head of the religion of his country. We should have a far more distinct idea of the eastern kingly offices and functions in ancient days, if we called him 'caliph,' or 'POPE,' instead of 'king;' and were it not that with us the latter title is applied to only one potentate on earth, and we can scarcely understand the idea of there being, or having been, another, the term is just such a one as would directly define that union of temporal and spiritual power which we find united in the Persian monarch; and at the same time, as a necessary corollary, the term *bacilica*, in its original Roman sense, would as correctly describe the buildings we have been examining at Persepolis."—*Nineveh and Persepolis*, pp. 186-188.

Although this passage more directly refers to the ruins of Persepolis than to those of Assyria and Babylon, it so strictly applies to cognate usages in other eastern countries, and is, in the express terms of the author, so applicable to the royal residences in Asia, and the east generally, that I feel great pleasure in placing it before the reader. And here, it may be observed, we have no mere theorist,—no writer studying eastern antiquities for the purpose of deducing evidence in support of any peculiar religious dogmas; but a learned and intelligent man of science, investigating with intense diligence the remains of the ruined cities of ancient Asia for architectural purposes. In the prosecution of this labour, he educes the object and design for which the wonderful palace-edifices of the east were erected: and his conclusion is, that "the actual dwelling-places of the king they certainly were not;" (*Ibid.*, p. 188;) and further, that if "these buildings were not palaces, according to our usual acceptation of the term, still less were they temples;" (*Ibid.*, p. 189;) but that they were the seat and centre whence the king, in his compound character of political ruler and religious head of the people, administered the government, and prescribed for the faith and ecclesiastical polity of the country; where in fact a heathen pope sat in all the plenitude of his power.

It must not be supposed, when we hear temples mentioned as existing in Assyria or Babylonia, that such statements militate against what has been advanced. Although uniform in the great first principles of faith, the several nations and cities greatly differed in the details of their buildings. As an instance, Mr. Fergusson believes that he has discovered at Khorsabad, not only a building which he calls "the temple," but also the ruins of a range of houses, which he regards as the residence of priests. But then this temple is not only small in size, compared with the whole fabric, but was "situated in the very innermost recesses of the palace;" so that, in fact, it was part of the same pile of buildings. Of the celebrated temple of Bel at Babylon we really know but little, and cannot elicit any additional information from the meagre accounts which have come down to us: but it is highly probable that future explorations will bring to view proofs that in this respect Babylon, like Assyria and Persia, followed the same general rule.

It is important to keep in mind the fact, that these palace-temples were surrounded with Paradises, and that a stream, or streams, of water flowed through the latter,—rising, where that was possible, within the precincts of the temple. This was so universal in the east, that Larcher, in his Notes on Herodotus, (vol. i, p. 221,) observes, "We must bear in mind, that a temple of the ancients was very different from one of our churches. It comprised a considerable extent of ground, enclosed by walls, within which there were courts, a grove, pieces of water, sometimes habitations for the priests, and lastly the temple properly so called, and into which, most usually, the priest only was admitted."

It may, indeed, be safely gathered from all the information attainable in respect of these buildings, that they were the official residence of the sovereign; and that he stood so identified with divinity in the national belief, that they at the same time were regarded with all the reverence and sanctity of consecrated temples. (Layard, vol. ii, pp. 201, 267.)

We should here observe, that although the serpent-form does not appear so often and so prominently in the sculptures of Assyria as in those of Egypt, it is seen in such positions, and is repeated with such frequency, as to indicate very clearly its Satanic original.

It will be hereafter observed, that serpents are associated with the worship of fire on the sculptures of Koyunjik: and we have seen that the female divinities of Babylon, as described by Diodorus, are accompanied by images of this reptile. The statue supposed to be that of Rhea, the Mother of the Gods, had two colossal serpents standing before it; while that named "Juno" was exhibited holding a serpent in her right hand. A learned author, who has carefully studied this subject, inclines to the opinion that live serpents were kept to be worshipped at Babylon, as at Thebes in Egypt; and that this led to the fable of Bel and the Dragon. (Deane's Worship of the Serpent, pp. 41-47.) Further, it has been generally believed, that the serpent was the emblem borne aloft on the banners of Assyria, and the sign under which all their battles were fought; and that the emperors of Constantinople derived their dragon-standard from this people. When it is remembered with what devotion the soldiers of heathen countries regarded their chief ensign, the position of the serpent-form in the religious estimation of this people is easily ascertained.

Attention must now be directed more particularly to the character which the sovereigns of Assyria and Babylon sustained, or assumed, for the purpose of carrying out this politico-religious government.

On this subject Mr. Layard writes as follows : " A very superficial examination of the sculptures will prove the sacred character of the king. The priests, or presiding deities, (whichever the winged figures, so frequently found on the Assyrian monuments, may be,) are represented as waiting upon, or ministering to, him: above his head are the emblems of the divinity,—the winged figure within the circle, the sun, the moon, and the planets. As in Egypt, he may have been regarded as the representative, on earth, of the Deity; receiving his power directly from the gods, and the organ of communication between them and his subjects."—*Nineveh*, vol. ii. p. 267. And again the same author remarks, "The residence of the king, as I have observed, was probably at the same time the temple; and that he himself was either supposed to be invested with divine attributes, or was looked upon as a type of the supreme Deity, is shown by the sculptures. The winged figures, even that with the head of the eagle, minister unto him. All his acts, whether in war or peace, appear to have been connected with the national religion, and were believed to be under the special protection and superintendence of the Deity. When he is represented in battle, the winged figure in the circle hovers above his head, bends his bow against his enemies, or assumes his attitude of triumph. His contests with the lion and other formidable animals not only show his prowess and skill, but typify at the same time his superior strength and wisdom. Whether he has overcome his enemies, or the wild beasts, he pours out a libation from the sacred cup, attended by his courtiers and the winged figures."—*Ibid.*, p. 474.

It will thus be seen that the Assyrian sovereign was not only personally identified with the religion of his country, and occupied the position of sacred head of his people; but that he passed even beyond this dignity, and assumed an eminence as lofty as it was peculiar. The winged figure with an eagle's head has been identified by Rawlinson as Assarac, or the deified Asshur, the tutelar god of the Assyrian people; yet even he is seen on the sculptures ministering to the king. But, what is still more remarkable and significant, the winged figure in the circle has been shown to represent the primitive triad, and, of course, the centre figure in human form the divine son; yet this symbol, whenever it occurs, is placed over the head of the king, and—what is most striking—always *appears to be in the same attitude as the sovereign.*

I may notice two or three instances from Layard's "Monuments of Nineveh." One of the sculptures gives a vivid description of an attack on a fortified city. The ramparts are lined with bowmen, and the Assyrians are surrounding the walls, while the king in his chariot is bending his bow against the men on the walls, and is on the point of shooting. Above his head is the symbolic triad, with the centre figure directing the point of his arrow against the city, and exhibiting precisely the same action as the king. (Plate 13.) In another sculpture we see the great king returning in triumph from a campaign : he rides in his chariot, with his bow unbent in his left hand, and his right hand raised. Precisely such is the attitude of the human figure in the symbol of the divine triad above him. (Plate 21.) Again, we see two kings, one on either side of the tree of life, with their right hands raised: such is the attitude of the figure above.* (Plate 25.) What could be done to give a more clear and expressive declaration, that the king, throughout the whole of this system, was regarded as acting on earth in the character and power of the divine son above? For, be it observed, this figure is never seen over any one but the king.

It will now be necessary to glance at the manner in which these kings sustained and acted out this sacred character: and for this

---

* This has been supposed, with great probability, to represent two views of the great king, and not two several kings.

purpose the Babylonish kingdom will be regarded as succeeding to all the pretensions and powers of the Assyrian empire. Nebuchadnezzar and his successors will consequently be spoken of as if they had followed the last king of Nineveh on the Assyrian throne; the religion of the two countries being so similar as to render any distinction for our present purpose unnecessary.

Referring to the chapter on the History of Assyria, we call attention to the annals of Divanu-bara, son of the great Sardanapalus, which are recorded at length on the Black Obelisk. There, in the account of his first campaign, it is said, "I crossed the Euphrates, and ascended to the tribes who worshipped the god Husi. My servants erected altars in that land to my gods. Then I went on to the land of Khamána, where I founded palaces, cities, and temples. I went on to the land of Málar; and there I established the worship of my kingdom." Our limits forbid the mention of similar instances in detail. But here is one, and the first that meets us. It is a record of the first campaign of a young warrior-king. Yet, in scarcely more lines, there are three several declarations that he prosecuted his wars for the extension of his religion in other lands. This is described as the prime object in every case. Again, in the seventh year of his reign, having subdued Tel-ati, he says, "I appointed priests to reside in the land, to pay adoration to Assarac, the great and powerful god, and to preside over the national worship." In his fifteenth year, having subdued the country of the king of Ararat, he "set up altars, and left priests in the land, to superintend the worship." In the twenty-eighth year of his reign, having reduced the Shetina to obedience, he "established the national religion throughout the land."

These extracts are sufficient to show the religious authority assumed by the sovereigns of Nineveh in the early period of her history. We have the means of proving that in the later period of her annals the monarchs of Assyria had not abated one jot of their profane assumption. Let the latter part of the message which Sennacherib sent to the nobles of Jerusalem be read as ample evidence of this fact: "Hearken not unto Hezekiah, when he persuadeth you, saying, The LORD will deliver us. Hath any of the gods of the nations delivered at all his land out of the hand of the king of Assyria? Where are the gods of Hamath, and of Arpad? Where are the gods of Sepharvaim, Hena, and Ivah? Have they delivered Samaria out of MINE HAND? Who are they among all the gods of the countries, that have delivered their country out of mine hand, that the LORD should deliver Jerusalem out of mine hand?" 2 Kings xviii, 32–35.

Let this part of the address be carefully perused, and the reader will perceive that it does not discuss the relative military power of the parties. That matter was finished, when, with infinite contempt, Rabshakeh offered the Hebrews a truce, and a present of two thousand horses, if the king of Judah could set riders on them. Verse 23. The point in that part of the address which I have quoted has not respect to military strength, but to the relative power of deities. It was spoken in accommodation to the general polytheistic opinion, that certain gods presided over particular nations. But in this contest for divine power, who represents Assyria? We read of the gods of Hamath, Arpad, Sepharvaim, Hena, Ivah, and the Lord of Jerusalem; and others are mentioned in the version of the speech as given by Isaiah: but, strange to say, we hear nothing of the gods of Assyria. The pontiff-king of Nineveh arrogated this dignity to himself. If he had trusted in his god, the case had been altogether different: but the power poised against all the deities of the lands which he had conquered, and even against the Lord himself, was HIS OWN. "Who shall deliver out of MINE HAND?" is the profane boast with which he challenges to himself a power above all gods. It was this which called forth the word of the Lord: "Whom hast thou reproached and blasphemed, and against whom hast thou exalted thy voice, and lifted up thine eyes on high? Even against the Holy One of Israel." 2 Kings xix, 22. It was this profane daring to equal or excel the power of Jehovah which led to the fearful doom denounced against him: "Therefore will I put my hook in thy nose, and my bridle in thy lips, and I will turn thee back by the way by which thou camest." Verse 28.

It is certain, therefore, that the spirit of religious zeal, proud intolerance, and profane assumption, which characterized the sovereigns of Assyria in the early part of its history, was not merely continued, but rather increased, until the termination of the empire.

We have now to direct attention to Babylon, as exhibiting an embodiment of this religion. And here it may be observed that this was unquestionably the original seat of this system of faith, and the centre whence it emanated. Here, under the auspices of Nimrod, this fearful apostasy was established in connexion with kingly rule: here for a while both flourished; until, overwhelmed by the superior military power of Nineveh, Babylonia became a province of the Assyrian empire. After a very extended period of supremacy, this power in her turn fell before the combined army of Medes and Babylonians; and then that part of the old Assyrian empire and influence which lay to the west of the Euphrates naturally passed into the hand of the sovereign of Babylon.

Not only did this transition take place as the result of the ever-recurring changes in the martial power of nations: it was distinguished and consummated in a manner and by an agency of the most extraordinary character. Nebuchadnezzar, who succeeded to the throne of Babylon just two years after the destruction of Nineveh, was one of those men so distinguished for martial genius, daring ambition, and invincible energy, as to insure themselves the most prominent position in the age in which they flourish. In succeeding to the throne of Babylon, he succeeded to all the pretensions of the impious founder of that state, and to all those claims and powers which many centuries had sealed as the undoubted prerogative of the imperial sovereign of Assyria. A reference to a few points in his history will show whether he also assumed to be divine.

We have the advantage of pursuing this part of our inquiry under the guidance of sacred writ. We find this sovereign, immediately after he had established himself in the empire, and extended his sway from Nineveh to Egypt, gathering together all the chief officers, civil and military, from every part of his dominions, for a special and important purpose. But this was not, as might be at first surmised, either for a military or a civil object, but for one decidedly religious. The king had caused a great image of gold to be made, and set up; and the assembled multitudes were commanded at a given signal to bow down and worship this image. Reasons, which it is not necessary here to repeat, have been adduced, in a preceding volume, (Hebrew People, pp. 586–589,) for believing that this image represented Nebuchadnezzar himself in the character of the divine Son, the promised incarnate Seed; but, apart from this, there are important facts bearing on our subject in the inspired narrative of this event. Nebuchadnezzar, without preface or apology, prescribes an object of worship to his people. He does this as if it lay as much within his own legitimate authority, as to prescribe the boundary of a province, or the terms of military service. At the given signal all are required to fall down and worship the image. Dan. iii, 4, 5. Then this command is enforced by a threat, and by actual punishment. Verses 15, 21. It must be admitted that the stupendous miracle which saved the three young Hebrews, appears to have elicited from the king language which may, at first, be taken to imply a withdrawal of his assumed power, verse 28: but immediately after, he issues a decree, which, although in support of truth, and in vindication of the true God, is marked by the unchanged character of profane assumption: "Every people, nation, and language, which speak anything amiss against the God of Shadrach, Meshach, and Abed-nego, shall be cut in pieces, and their houses shall be made a dunghill." Verse 29. The whole conduct of Nebuchadnezzar, throughout the entire narrative, is, in fact, a positive assumption of the divine prerogative of prescribing an object of faith and worship for mankind.

But the existence of this assumption of divine attributes and powers is perhaps still more clearly seen in the following chapter. This gives an account of the king's vision of a great tree, with Daniel's interpretation of it, and the actual accomplishment of the predictions which it contained. It is to be feared that this well-known portion of Scripture has not received the attention which it merits. Let me ask, What was the precise object of all this wonderful interposition? It was simply this,—that Nebuchadnezzar might be brought fully to acknowledge the existence and supremacy of the most high God: "Till thou know that the Most High ruleth in the kingdom of men, and giveth it to whomsoever he will." Dan. iv, 25. And it is certain that the indisposition of Nebuchadnezzar to know and acknowledge this did not arise from a high reverence for any other god. As in the case of Sennacherib, the contest was between the claims of Jehovah and his own assumed dignity and power. This is rendered certain by the fact, that the culminating point of his crime was the inflated inquiry, "Is not this great Babylon, that I have built for the house of the kingdom by the might of MY power, and for the honour of MY majesty?" Verse 30. And we may well attach the strongest meaning possible to these terms, when it is known that they were immediately followed by a miraculous punishment, instant and terrible.

All this serves to show, that the principles and spirit which dictated the first great rebellion against God at Shinar, remained in active and powerful operation at the time of Nebuchadnezzar. But, after all, perhaps the strongest proof we have of this fact is the predictive declaration of the Prophet Isaiah respecting this king. In the fourteenth chapter of his prophecy, this sacred seer has given one of the most splendid prophetic odes to be found in the whole scope of holy Scripture. This prophecy is directed against a king of Babylon who was a great conqueror, who was succeeded by his son and grandson, after which the race was "cut off." This king of Babylon must therefore have been Nebuchadnezzar: the terms used by the prophet do not, and never have been supposed to, apply to any other person. In this prophecy we have not an account of this king's actions, but an exhibition of the thoughts and purposes of his heart, set forth under the guidance of that omniscient power which seeth what is in man: "Thou hast said in THINE heart, I will ascend into heaven, I will exalt my throne above the stars of God: I will sit also upon the mount of the congregation, in the sides of the north: I will ascend above the heights of the clouds; I will be like the Most High." Isaiah xiv, 13, 14. My view of the purport of this text, sustained by the authority of the Rev. G. S. Faber, has been given in the place already referred to: (Hebrew People, p. 588:) it will therefore be only necessary to add here, that these words fully teach that Nebuchadnezzar would aspire to divinity; that he would not be content with being regarded merely as one of the local hero-deities of heathen nations; that he would claim an equality with the Most High; that he would be supreme; further, that he would claim this as the incarnate Seed, who was to recover the seat in Paradise, which is here indicated by "the mount of the congregation in the sides of the north."—*Faber's Origin of Pagan Idolatry*, vol. i, p. 350.

It will be necessary now to place before the reader a brief recapitulation of the results to which we have been led in this portion of our inquiry.

It has been ascertained that the sacred places of this people were filled with figures combining the human with animal forms; that these combinations are always made by the union of two or more of the creatures spoken of as found in the Scriptural cherubim; and that this is done in such a manner as to leave no doubt on the mind that the human-headed and eagle-winged lions and bulls, which are now seen in the museums of London and Paris, and which still abound in the mounds of Assyria, were designed from traditional notions of the primitive cherubim.

We find a sacred tree associated with all the sacred rites of this people, and placed in such juxta-position with these cherubic sculptures as to lead to the conclusion, that it was incorporated into this religious system as a memorial of the tree of life in Eden.

It is certain that, attached to the royal palaces of Assyria, there were large enclosed gardens or parks; and the universal presence of trees and a river, and especially the peculiar adoption of the name and its application in holy Scripture, warrant the opinion, that these were memorial imitations of the garden of Eden, the scene of man's primitive happiness and fearful fall.

Further, it has been ascertained that the royal residence contiguous to this Paradise had a sacred character, and was as much a temple as a house, and thus appeared as a place consecrated to Deity.

Again, it has been shown that the sovereign was regarded as divine; that all the sculptures identify him in a remarkable manner with the divine Son in the sacred triad; that he assumed the care of the national religion, exerted himself to make it universal, and freely put forth the power of enforcing canons of faith on the people, and of dictating to them authoritatively on all points relating to religion.

Now, let it be remembered that all this took place in the neighbourhood where, and arose out of the people among whom, Nimrod, the great apostate leader, laboured to frustrate the purposes of the Most High by preventing the divinely appointed dispersion of the people, by his proud claim to be a universal sovereign, and his profane assumption of divine attributes. It is admitted on all hands that the promise of an incarnate Deity would form the most plausible basis for such a scheme of operation. For a moment let this be assumed, and it will be seen that all these elements of Assyrian religion are precisely those which under the circumstances might be expected. Here is the promised divine ruler and high-priest, surrounded with paradisiacal emblems, in a consecrated dwelling, adapted to his two-fold character, in close proxity to a Paradise, made as nearly as possible after popular traditions of the original, labouring to fulfil his mission by bringing all the world under his sway, and inducing them to receive terms of faith from his word.

The *substratum* of this system was historic truth and pure revelation. The thrilling events of man's primitive history were carefully brought out; every sacred place and sacred emblem were critically elaborated; ideas of primitive history and religion, hallowed by the lapse of ages, were brought into operation; the natural veneration due the man and woman whom God made, and placed in purity upon this earth, were all employed; and, more than all these, the language in which the antidote for man's misery in Heaven's mercy was first whispered into the ear of sinning mortals,—the promise of an incarnate Redeemer,—was added, to lay the foundations for the religion of Assyria and Babylon.

But all this truth was neutralized, perverted, and made the foundation on which was reared a superstructure full of evil. This was not done by rude opposition, but by insidious addition and vitiation. A proud, daring, ambitious man, urged on by the great author of all evil, having entrenched himself in those hallowed records of man's early history, daringly claimed divine honour, and thus prepared the way for unlimited idolatry.

Thus, as far as patient research can penetrate the obscurity of the subject, this system arose: and perhaps there is nothing in human history more remarkable than the identity of character which it maintained throughout two thousand years. In all the alterations of national prosperity or adversity, whether the seat of imperial power was at Nineveh or Babylon, the same system was maintained in respect of religion: so that, when, during the reign of Nebuchodonosor, Assyria was hastening to her fall, it is distinctly said of that king that "he had decreed to destroy all the gods of the land, that all nations should worship Nebuchodonosor only." Judith iii, 8. So intense, even then, was the claim to divinity made by the kings of Assyria. We have seen that this did not abate, when the seat of empire was restored to Babylon. Then Jehovah had to reduce Nebuchadnezzar to the condition of a beast, and to continue him in that abject state for seven years, before he would recognise the existence of any divine power beyond that which he claimed to centre in himself.

It has been found necessary to go more into detail with regard to this subject, than has been usual in this work, for two reasons. In the preceding volumes I was compelled to assume the existence of the facts and doctrines here developed; and it therefore became important that these assumptions should be fully justified. This course was also demanded by the circumstance, that this branch of the subject comes before us not only as an important element in the religion of those countries, but also as being equally identified with the religion of the world. The facts elicited in respect of Assyria and Babylon more or less illustrate and explain the religion of every other idolatrous country. At the same time they shed no unimportant light upon very interesting portions of the sacred record. (See *Appendix*, note 35.)

It will now be necessary to add such general observations about this system of religion and its influence on the people, as may arise out of the limited information which has been handed down to us by history, or gleaned from a study of the disinterred sculptures.

Here, as in other primitive heathen countries, there is found a gradual but marked deterioration in theology and objects of religious worship, In the earliest sculptures of Nimroud, the only object which the king is seen to worship is the winged figure in the circle, —the divine triad. He has, indeed, before him the sacred tree; but it does not appear that this is an object of adoration. It seems much more probable that this is employed only as a symbol of the tree of life. And this, the primitive form of worship among the Assyrians, as far as our means of information extend, strikingly confirms our view of the gradual and insidious manner in which the patriarchal faith was superseded by all the abominations of idolatry. Here was a symbolic representation of the true God, in his triune character, containing allusive representations of the great Father and Mother, with the promised Saviour as the incarnate Son, prominently exhibited as the centre and substance of Deity. The figure of the sacred tree would illustrate all this; and, by presenting to the mind an emblem of the happy seat from which man had been expelled, and to which it was believed he would be restored by the Saviour, the past history and future hopes of the world were concentrated to a focus, and that point was made the object of the earliest Assyrian adoration.

But truth alone is permanent and abiding; error is always subject to variation and change, and generally to a fearful progression from bad to worse. This is seen in the slender information supplied by the Assyrian sculptures on the subject of religion. Although no worship is represented on the ruins of Nimroud but that which is offered to the sacred triad, it is certain that idolatrous error had become widely extended and greatly diversified prior to the ruin of this ancient city. There has been found in the remains of that palace what has been called "the Hall of Nisroch." It is a chamber one hundred feet long and twenty-five broad: its entrance is by a doorway guarded on each side by one of those colossal-winged, human-headed bulls, now in the British Museum. With one exception, this room is covered with sculptured representations of Assarac, the deified patriarch, Asshur, the tutelar god of Assyria, called in Holy Scripture Nisroch. The exception to this rule is one slab, on which there is a representation of the king wearing a kind of necklace, consisting of emblems of the heavenly bodies, such as "the sun, the moon, a cross, a three-horned cap, and a symbol like two horns," (Bonomi's Nineveh and its Palaces, p. 261,) which Layard calls "a trident."

This Assarac—we know, from the annals of kings recorded on the sculptures generally, and especially from those on the Black Obelisk —was held forth as the great national deity. His worship was introduced wherever the Assyrian arms prevailed. Altars for his service were raised in every conquered country. It does not appear why he is thus represented. The wings and the eagle-head may, indeed, be regarded as cherubic emblems, although no reason has been assigned for their peculiar application in this instance. It is, however, probable that this selection was devised as a representation of the deified patriarch, under the influence of the maxims of mythic philosophy which obtained in the east at this time. This notion seems justified by the fact, that a fragment of the Oracles of Zoroaster, preserved by Eusebius, states that "God is he that has the head of a hawk. He is the first, indestructible, eternal, unbegotten, indivisible, dissimilar; the dispenser of all good; incorruptible; the best of the good, the wisest of the wise: he is the father of equity and justice, self-taught, physical, and perfect, and wise, and the only inventer of the sacred philosophy."—*Eusebii Præp. Evang.*, lib. i, cap. 10; *Cory's Fragments*, p. 239. Yet, although Assarac was the deified patriarch of the country, and uniformly recognised as the head of the Pantheon in all the royal annals, and withal dignified with such elevated attributes; and though his figure occurs so frequently on the sculptures; yet in no instance is the reigning king seen offering adoration to him; but, on the contrary, Assarac is seen ministering to the monarch. This is, perhaps, one of the most convincing proofs that can be furnished of the accuracy of the view which we have taken concerning the direct assumption of the highest divinity by the kings of Nineveh.

In the latter ages of the empire, however, we find considerable changes in the religious rites and objects of worship. At Khorsabad the primitive symbol of the trinity—the man with wings in a circle—has altogether disappeared. No visible type of this primeval doctrine remains. Here is found a colossal figure, which Mr. Bonomi shows good reason for believing to be Nimrod: but whether this conjecture is well founded, and -this mighty warrior was deified in Assyria, we have not as yet the means of deciding with satisfactory certainty. Here is also a human figure with four wings, which is conjectured to be Ilus or Cronos.

Whatever uncertainty may attach to the identification of the deities of this latter period of the empire, it is certain that the worship of fire had been introduced and become general. Although there are no traces of this in the earlier inscriptions, undoubted evidence of its existence is found on the sculptures of Khorsabad and Kouyunjik.

Among the ruins of the former city is a striking instance of this species of idolatry. Two eunuchs are seen standing before an altar, engaged in some religious service. They have the square basket, or utensil, seen on the older bass-reliefs. This sculpture casts important light on the singular ceremony so frequently seen on the Nimroud sculptures,—the presentation of the pine-apple, or fir-cone,—to which it has been found very difficult to attach any meaning. Here the fir-cone, painted red, as if to represent fire, is placed on the high stand or altar; a delineation which seems to justify the surmise that this cone was regarded as sacred, on account of its figure and inflammable qualities.

From the ruins of Kouyunjik there has been brought a still more curious representation of fire-worship. Two figures " appear standing before an altar, on which is the sacred fire. Two serpents appear to be attached to poles, and a bearded figure is leading a goat to the sacrifice."—*Layard*, vol. ii, p. 463. This seems to prove that this form of idolatry originated in Assyria, and was carried from thence into Persia. Mr. Layard also describes a singular altar found at Khorsabad, which is supported on three lions' feet; and which resembles so strikingly the Greek tripods, that the learned explorer conjectures that many of the forms and religious types, hitherto regarded as peculiar to Greece and Asia Minor, had their origin in Assyria.

Before I proceed to a general summary of the morals and religion of Assyria and Babylon, I will endeavour, as briefly as possible, to glance at the effects likely to be produced on the governments and people of these countries by their intercourse with the Hebrews, and the divine interpositions which arose out of this connexion.

Here the reader should be reminded at the outset, that whatever errors might have been concocted and disseminated by the rebellious conspiracy at Shinar, the masses of the population at that day must have been fully informed as to the great facts of the world's previous history. The Creation,—the Fall,—the promise of redemption,—the sin and violence of the old world,—the piety, the righteousness of Noah,—the doom of the antediluvians,—the preparation of the ark,—the Flood,—the accepted sacrifice of the arkite patriarch,—and the sin (whatever it was) which led to the malediction of Noah on Ham or Canaan,—all these facts, and a thousand more, unhappily lost to us, deep in significance, full of instruction, had been handed down from father to son, and had pervaded the public mind, and given a colour and a character to the opinions, the feelings, and even the prejudices of the people.

When, therefore, erudite authors describe the people of Assyria and Babylon as occupying a level country, and seeing the heavenly bodies through a clear atmosphere, and as thus being led to worship them as types of the power and attributes of the supreme Deity; and allege that this was their original theology; they must not expect their inferences to be believed by those who venerate the authority of Holy Scripture.

Do these writers really believe that the grandson of Noah survived the Dispersion? I do not hesitate to express my firm belief, that Divine Providence wisely ordained the longevity of mankind, at the beginning of the postdiluvian period, for the set purpose of making defection from the service of God as difficult as possible. My meaning will be fully apprehended by an inspection of the synchronistical chart in a preceding volume. (Patriarchal Age, p. 431.) From this it will be seen that, until after the Dispersion, the number of lineal descendants living contemporaneously was generally five: that is, a man's grandson was always born and arrived at manhood, before the man's own grandfather died.

In this state of society, and with such grand historical events—involving the mightiest operations of divine power, the most wonderful revelations of God's justice and mercy—living in the memory of the people, the notion that any great division of them could dispossess themselves of all this knowledge and its cognate ideas, and adopt Sabæanism as a general and original religious system, is utterly absurd, because it is impossible. The only way open to the tempter at that early age for the introduction of idolatry on a large scale, was in the way of insidious corruption of the truth.

So much of this same historical and religious knowledge as remained, would also serve to give effect to the salutary influence which an intercourse with the Hebrews was calculated to afford. It is a remarkable fact,—at least, it will be so esteemed by those who study the divine government of this world in relation to its bearing on the spiritual and immortal interests of mankind,—which Dr. Layard (Nineveh, vol. ii, p. 206) adduces, when he asserts that "a close intercourse" had existed between Egypt and Assyria, from the commencement of the eighteenth dynasty. This was the period, it will be remembered, when Joseph was carried to the banks of the Nile: so that this connexion was established just in time to render all the thrilling events of the Hebrew history in Egypt known in Assyria. And as this intercourse continued to increase during the succeeding dynasties, it cannot be doubted that such events as the miraculous Exodus of Israel, the fame of which, it is certain, was extended far and wide, (Josh. ii, 9–11,) must have been well known in Assyria. It is important to mark such facts as are thus brought to our knowledge by the Assyrian inscriptions, proving, as they do, that the position of the Hebrews, as the elect people of Jehovah, and as saved by him through the most miraculous interposition, was known among the principal nations of the ancient world.

The mission of Jonah next calls for attention. But of this we have no detailed information, beyond the simple statement of fact. A question, indeed, arises,—Would the message of Jonah itself have produced the results which followed, in the absence of all knowledge by the Assyrians of the Hebrew people? This does not seem probable. The facts are clearly these:—Jonah entered the city, and proclaimed, "Yet forty days, and Nineveh shall be overthrown." The people regarded this communication as the word of God: for it is said, "The people of Nineveh believed God, and proclaimed a fast," &c. This humiliation was universal, from the sovereign on the throne to the meanest subject: and God accepted this penitence, and turned away the evil which he had threatened to do, and did it not.

Taken in a religious aspect, it is impossible not to regard this as a most important event. It clearly implied the entire absence from the minds of the Ninevites of all real confidence in their own gods. This message did not come from them:—that must have been fully known. The result also implied, I think, some considerable acquaintance with Jehovah as the God of the Hebrews, and the mighty miracles of judgment and mercy which he had wrought. The brief antecedents of the history also serve to countenance this view of the matter. Without something of this kind it is scarcely possible to conceive of a great and powerful people, through all its ranks and ages, submitting to such a course.

Yet, if this supposition is correct, it must follow that, notwithstanding the continued practice of idolatrous corruptions, the Assyrian people retained a large portion of patriarchal truth; which, supplemented by the knowledge they had obtained of the God of Israel, was sufficient to point them out a way of escape from the threatened infliction. At any rate, they were then found possessed of such religious knowledge as enabled them on that occasion to engage in four of the most vitally important duties of practical religion.

First: They exercised faith in God: they believed the truth of the message delivered by the prophet, and admitted it, in all its fulness of meaning. Then they humbled themselves in sackcloth, and by fasting. This is most remarkable. In all that the Bible contains respecting patriarchal religion, fasting is not mentioned; nor does Moses enjoin any particular fast, except that on the great day of expiation. The sacred records, from Moses to Jonah, mention but two or three instances of fasting on account of some grievous calamity; and, I believe, but one of these included any considerable number of people: yet here we have a fast enjoined with the utmost rigour, throughout a great city like Nineveh! Again, the injunction to this people was, "Cry mightily unto God." How deeply expressive is this of earnest and continued prayer! Further, to this faith, penitence, and prayer, was added amendment of life: "Let them turn every one from his evil way." It is not possible to ascertain whether the communication of the prophet went beyond the proclamation of the threatening; but, taking the fact as it stands on the sacred record, this course of submission and obedience argues the possession, by the Assyrians of that day, of a large amount of sound religious knowledge, however extensively this might have been neutralized by idolatrous error. But even admitting the existence of all this knowledge, we cannot account for the ready and general submission of the Ninevites, without supposing them on that occasion to have been visited by a very gracious and prevalent influence of the Holy Spirit.

When the idolatrous kingdom of Israel was given into the hand of the king of Assyria, this divine interposition did not entirely cease. The Ten Tribes having been carried into Media, and none but the lowest, weakest, and poorest of the people being left in the land; and the men of Babylon, Cuthah, Hamath, and other places in the east, being brought to supply a population for Samaria and its neighbouring districts; these heathens introduced their own idolatry with themselves: in consequence of which, we are told, "the Lord sent lions among them, which slew some of them." Indeed, so terrible did this plague become, that a formal representation of the case was made to the imperial court; and one of the priests who had been carried into captivity was sent back again, to teach all the people the worship of Jehovah. Thus, even after Israel was ruined, and when the pride, cruelty, and idolatry of Assyria had brought that mighty empire to the verge of destruction, did Jehovah interpose to assert his proper sovereignty over the land which he had given to his people: and this was done in a manner which elicited from the haughty conqueror an acknowledgment of the fact, and a submission to the consequence, in the return of a captive Hebrew priest to teach the people the law of the Lord. In all this were attested an admission of the Deity of Jehovah, and a belief of his paramount power.

We pass on to the case of Babylon. The first instance of intimate intercourse between the Hebrews and this state was of an unfavourable character. It arose out of the subversion of the kingdom of Judah, and the destruction of the temple and city of Jerusalem by Nebuchadnezzar. Here was the centre and seat of Hebrew power and polity. Miracle and prophecy had been united for many centuries in the defence of this metropolis; and whatever knowledge respecting the God of the Hebrews, and his wonderful interpositions on behalf of his people, might have reached Babylon, they would all refer to the throne of the house of David, and to the sacred sanctuary at Jerusalem. When, therefore, these had been swept away by the martial power of Nebuchadnezzar, and the temple had been burned with fire, and Jerusalem was a heap of ruins, then would the king and people of Babylon regard their own gods as paramount in power, and the God and people of Jerusalem as alike subdued before them. This unquestionably accounts for the inordinate vanity of the king of Babylon. If the king of Assyria, after having subdued the Israelites of Samaria, gloried in the title of "Conqueror of the remote Judea," need we wonder that Nebuchadnezzar should be vain, after he had subverted the throne of David, and destroyed his city and the temple of his son?

There can be no doubt that, inflated with this success, and auguring therefrom the confirmation of his proudest purposes,—his own recognition as a divine religious and political head of his vast empire,—he made the golden image, and congregated the multitude of his officials on the plains of Dura. But, alas! what a defeat was that! How clearly, and publicly, and fully did Jehovah testify to this numerous host of the Babylonish aristocracy, that his arm was not shortened,—that, for those who were faithful in his service, he was still able and willing to exert his almighty power! It is scarcely possible to overrate the amount of knowledge, which the events of this day gave to the spectators, of the infinite wisdom, goodness, and power of the Hebrews' God. This would scatter to the winds all the profane assumptions of their king,—at least, so far as the people were concerned. Those who saw the affrighted monarch standing aghast at the sight of the Son of God walking in the midst of the flames, were not likely to recognise him again as a real divinity.

The wonderful vision of this king, and his predicted insanity, recovery, and consequent proclamation, must have largely contributed to open the eyes of the Babylonish people to the vanity of idols, and to an acknowledgment of the true deity and power of Jehovah. The decrees published by this sovereign, (Dan. iii, 29; iv, 1-37,) must have fallen as a glorious light on the darkness of Babylonish idolatry. Who can estimate the effects of such proclamations? Who can conceive of the besotted state of mind which would be necessary to impel men to neglect these, and trust in dumb idols? But, perhaps, nothing which occurred during this reign tended more fully to show the glorious perfections of Jehovah, than the prophecies of Daniel respecting the king's vision of the great image, which was explained as referring to the four great monarchies.

At first sight we perceive in the conduct of the king respecting his wonderful dreams nothing but a cool, calculating prudence. He would not be imposed on by the wise men, and therefore insisted on their telling him the particulars of the vision which had given him so much alarm. Terrified at the demand, they shrank from the effort,—when the enraged king doomed them all to instant execution. These measures, however, effected one thing of the utmost consequence, which they were never intended to do. They fixed public attention on this case. The dream, and the interpretation, that had placed the sacred college under sentence of death, from which all the members had been saved only by the revelations of the Hebrew prophet, could not be concealed: and, when made known, what did they declare? The infinite prescience and glorious sovereignty of the true God were asserted; the prevalent notion of local and national divinities was exploded; the great purpose of Jehovah to direct the entire government of the world, so that in his own appointed time the kingdom of God might be set up, was declared. Truly Jehovah left not himself without witness. Babylon, in all her apostasy and guilt, had glorious revelations of the wisdom, truth, mercy, and power of the true God.

Yet, notwithstanding this amount of divine interposition, and the consequent communication of much religious knowledge, Assyria and Babylon remained idolatrous and corrupt. We have not the means of tracing here, as distinctly as we could in regard of Egypt, the remains of pure patriarchal truth. But from the general analogy observable between the religion of these countries and that of ancient Persia, it may be safely assumed, that the doctrine of the soul's immortality, and of a final judgment, were firmly and generally believed. On the subject of morals but little can be said: but if we apply here a rule which generally holds good,—namely, that the laws and usages respecting women form the clearest indication of the moral condition of any people,—our estimate of the state of these nations will be low. The testimony of Herodotus, as to the prostitution of females of all ranks in the temple of Mylitta, is appalling; and yet it is the testimony of an intelligent and credible eye-witness. This practice was continued to the last period of the Babylonish history; and its prevalence is rather confirmed by another and independent statement of the same author. He says that no man was at liberty to make a matrimonial engagement for his daughter; but that all the marriageable females were periodically put up to public sale; and that, after the most beautiful had been first sold at high prices, and others less favoured at lower rates, the money so raised was distributed to portion such as were plain or deformed, so that all were thus disposed of. It is added that each man was bound to marry the woman whom he thus obtained. (Herodotus, Clio, cap. xcvi.) The Greek historian applauds this institution; but he will have no echo to his sentiments from any Christian mind.

On the whole, the religion of Assyria and Babylon does not present to our observation any wonderful range of invention, either in its theology, doctrines, or modes of worship. Less prominence is here given to these than in other heathen countries. In fact, the religion is marked by one great peculiarity, one grand distinguishing feature:—it was an enormous despotism. This was its character, its essential and distinguishing quality. A thorough investigation of this subject would require a dissertation. We can only glance at this primeval attempt to reduce the great body of mankind into a bondage of the most grievous kind,—a thraldom of soul,—a vassalage of spirit,—a subjection, perfect and entire, not only in civil and political affairs, but also in essentially religious matters, to the judgment and will of one man, misnamed "divine."

There is here presented to our attentive consideration a most important phase in the progressive development of human impurity. The antediluvian world perished through sins engendered in the absence of efficient political and religious government: "The earth was filled with violence." To prevent a recurrence of this evil, and its consequent suffering, the divine purpose appointed the dispersion of the postdiluvian population over the earth, under the heads of the several tribes. The sin of Nimrod was, at first, a vain attempt to counteract this purpose, by assuming to himself a divine character, and in this character claiming universal sovereignty over mankind. The miraculous intervention at Babel frustrated his impious purpose, and enforced the dispersion.

But, defeated in the extent of his great design, he clung to its principle and spirit with invincible tenacity. The results we see in the religion of Assyria and Babylon. Here we find every paradisiacal element exhibited with the most gorgeous profusion,—every primitive fact emblazoned with the greatest prominence,—all the essentials of a national faith brought out in pompous array. But when we come to investigate the operation of this system, and its influence upon the human mind, we find a dreary chasm. Viewed in this aspect, it loses its character as religion. On the one hand, we see a mortal man assuming divinity, and affecting to tyrannize over the faith and feeling, the judgment and conscience, of his fellows; we hear the voice of an earthworm outrage reason and heaven by the profane challenge, "I WILL BE LIKE THE MOST HIGH:" while, on the other hand, the countless numbers of men and women by whom he is surrounded are all regarded as called into being to do him homage, and live and think and feel in subjection to his will.

The withering curse of this profane subversion of all human right blasted the happiness, and paralyzed the intellectual development, of these nations. Men subjected to such domination might be fit tools for a military despotism; they might be better adapted, in consequence of the blind devotion to their king, to sustain him in his martial aggression on other nations: but for all the great and elevating purposes to which human nature is called, and for the accomplishment of which it is prepared by the possession of the noblest attributes, they were utterly disqualified. A military subordination was therefore reared up and maintained; an extensive empire was conquered, and by the same means long continued: but here was the end of its powers. Having accomplished this, it in turn sunk into subjection, and thence into perpetual desolation.

Such were the character, the doings, and the end of the first great antichristian aggression on the purposes of God and the liberties of man! Such were the spirit, the power, and the doom of the præ-Christian Popery!

CHAPTER VI.

THE HISTORY OF THE MEDES.

LINEAGE and Country of the Medes—Ecbatana, the Capital—Revolt of the Medes against Assyria—They recover their Independence—A Season of Anarchy—Public Spirit and judicial Efforts of DEJOCES—He is raised to the Sovereignty of Media—Establishes a regular Government and greatly improves the Country—PHRAORTES, a martial Prince, subdues Persia, and extends the Median Power over other neighbouring Nations—Invades Assyria, is defeated and slain—Ecbatana stormed and spoiled by the Assyrian King—CYAXARES invades Assyria—Defeats the Imperial Army, and besieges Nineveh—The Scythian Invasion—The Medes defeated—The Scythians overrun Asia—Their Massacre and Expulsion—The Lydian War—It is suspended, and Nineveh besieged a second Time, and taken—The Lydian War renewed—Terminated by the Eclipse of Thales—ASTYAGES reigns—Prosecutes various Wars—Belshazzar slain—The Kingdom of Babylon reverts to Astyages—Media conquered, and the Kingdom subverted by Cyrus.

THE Medes, who were descended from Madai, the third son of Japhet, occupied an important territory on the south coast of the Caspian Sea. It extended to Persia and Assyria on the south, and was bounded by Parthia and Hyrcania on the east, and Armenia on the west.

This country was generally mountainous, and a great part of it cold and barren. Its chief city was Ecbatana, which is said to have been erected by Dejoces. The walls of this capital are greatly celebrated by ancient writers, and are minutely described by Herodotus. They are seven in number, all of a circular form, and gradually rising above each other by the height of the battlements of each wall. The situation of the ground, sloping by an easy ascent, was very favourable to the design of building them, and perhaps first suggested it. The royal palace and treasury were within the innermost circle of the seven. The Book of Judith states that the walls of this metropolis were seventy cubits high and fifty cubits broad; that the towers on the gates were a hundred cubits in height, the breadth in the foundation sixty cubits, and that the walls were built of hewn and polished stone, each stone being six cubits in length and three in breadth. Of this noble city not a vestige now remains to mark the site on which it stood. (Ancient Universal History, vol. iv, p. 3.)

The Medes were, in the remotest antiquity, celebrated as a brave and hardy race, possessing all the requisites for making excellent soldiers. Their government was originally monarchical; and they seem to have had kings of their own in the earliest times. According to Lactantius, one Hydaspes reigned long before the Medes were conquered by the Assyrians: and Diodorus says, that Pharnus, King of the Medes, was, with his seven sons, defeated and taken prisoner by Ninus in the beginning of the Assyrian empire.

At the period when this volume resumes the history of these nations, the Medes were subject to the Assyrians, and their country formed a most important province of that vast empire. But in this state of subjection, there can be no doubt that they continued to be governed by their own kings; either hereditary descendants of their former rulers, or persons raised to this dignity by the imperial sovereigns of Nineveh.

It is impossible now to ascertain the line of succession of these sovereigns, or to mark out even their names, and the respective periods of their rule. It is known, however, that, during the time they were labouring under all the disadvantages of foreign domination, Media continued to hold a most important position, and to rank as one of the most martial and powerful provinces of the empire. In the Appendix of this volume (note 19, p. 547) reasons have been given for believing that the influence and power of this province were so great, that, at the termination of the reign of the feeble Assyrian monarch, Thonos Concoleros, a Median prince obtained possession of the imperial throne. The infusion of new life and vigour which was thus communicated to the government of Assyria, doubtless contributed to the successive conquests obtained during that and the following reigns. This was in fact the most glorious period of Assyrian history.

But it is apparent that the elevation of a Median prince to the throne of Nineveh did not satisfy the aspirations of the Median people, or sufficiently gratify the ambition of its chiefs. We accordingly find that, on the humiliation of Sennacherib, after the miraculous ruin of his great army between Palestine and Egypt, efforts were made to obtain the independence of Media. From the manner in which Herodotus states the case, it appears that the Medes were the first of all the nations of Upper Asia who asserted their national liberty, and revolted against the Assyrian power. This revolt, according to that historian, did not take place under the direction of the sovereign or satrap of the country, but by a general effort of the people; which proving successful, the Assyrian governor was expelled, and the paramount supremacy of that power was destroyed. For we are told, that, having secured their liberty, no national government was established; but the six several tribes of which the nation was composed lived apart, and according to their individual pleasure. The consequence of this was universal disorder. Injustice and rapine prevailed, while no effectual authority existed, sufficient to restore order, and conduct a government.

This great want was, however, soon supplied. DEJOCES, a Median, although living in a private station, was so distinguished for his wisdom and integrity, that, in this period of anarchy, many persons resorted to him for the settlement of their disputes, and the adjustment of their differences. He discharged this office with so much equity and intelligence, that at length his decisions were generally recognised, and his judgment appealed to, even by persons from the other Median tribes.

These public services were continued with so much zeal and talent, and received with such popular favour, that at length the whole people acknowledged him as their sovereign, built him a noble palace, and invested him with supreme authority. Dejoces appears to have fully justified the popular choice. He either founded, or greatly improved, Ecbatana, the capital of the country. His most earnest endeavours were devoted to elevate the manners and habits of his people; and having greatly improved their condition, he turned his thoughts toward the enlargement of his dominions, and succeeded by force of arms in extending his authority over some of the neighbouring tribes.

The length of the reign of Dejoces cannot be accurately ascertained. The open revolt of Media took place just after the ruin of the Assyrian army under Sennacherib, about 710 B. C.; but no information has come down to us showing how long the state of anarchy continued, nor what period of time elapsed while Dejoces was serving the cause of his country, before he was raised to the throne. (See *Appendix*, note 36.) It seems, however, to be admitted that this prince, after greatly benefiting his nation, by serving it in different ways for more than forty years, died B. C. 651, and was succeeded by his son

PHRAORTES, the son of Dejoces, was a very martial prince. He is called Aphraartes by Eusebius and Syncellus; and is certainly the Arphaxad of the Book of Judith. Some have hastily doubted this, because it is said in that apocryphal book that he built a very strong city, and called it Ecbatana,—a work universally ascribed to his father Dejoces. This error is fully corrected by the Vulgate Version, which says that "Arphaxad *added new buildings* to Ecbatana." This is unquestionably the recorded fact. A single reign is clearly too limited a period to build and perfectly to finish a noble capital: so the son completed what the father had begun.

This sovereign, being firmly seated on the throne, and having improved his capital, proceeded to extend his dominions. He overran, and brought into subjection to Media, several of the neighbouring countries. Herodotus says that "he singled out the Persians as the objects of his ambitious views, and reduced them first of all under the dominion of the Medes."—*Clio*, cap. cii. It has been objected, that Persia was subdued by his son and successor Cyaxares. (Ancient Universal History, vol. iv, p. 18.) This, however, is no valid objection. It has been repeatedly stated in the preceding pages, that the effect of conquest in those days was neither the annexation nor the military occupation of the conquered country, but rather the carrying away of valuable spoil, or of large gifts in lieu thereof, with a promise of annual tribute; and that, in consequence, if the subject power felt sufficient confidence, it would throw off the yoke, and, as the result, would probably be subdued a second or even a third time. This was perhaps the case with Persia.

Favoured with success in these enterprises, Phraortes dared to assail the imperial state, and turned his arms against Assyria. Nabuchodonosor prepared for the threatened attack with becoming spirit. He summoned all his vassal kings to meet him, with their promised contingent of warriors. Many of these, however, seeing his precarious condition, refused compliance. Undaunted by this defection, he collected as large an army as possible, and boldly marched to oppose the Median king. The conflict took place in the plain of Ragau, in which, notwithstanding his desperate valour, the Median chief was defeated and slain, and his army utterly routed.

Flushed with victory, the Assyrian sovereign marched into Media, stormed and took Ecbatana the capital, demolished its fortifications and most splendid buildings, and returned with all the spoil he could collect unto Nineveh, where "he rested, and feasted his own army a hundred and twenty days." Judith i, 14–16.

Although greatly weakened and distressed by these reverses, the spirit of the Medes was not broken; and while the imperial victor was revelling in luxury at Nineveh, they gathered the wreck of the army together, and placed CYAXARES, the son of the late sovereign, on the throne. The new king was in some measure relieved from apprehension by the march of the great Assyrian army under Holofernes into Western Asia; and being a brave and prudent prince, he devoted himself with great talent and energy to repair the losses which his country had received, and to prepare for taking advantage of any favourable change which might occur in the fluctuations of the imperial power. The death of Holofernes by the hand of Judith, and the surprise and rout of the Assyrian army before Bethuliah, soon after presented such an opportunity. Cyaxares accordingly hastened his preparations; and, anxious to revenge the death of his father, and to retaliate on the Assyrian capital for the recent spoiling of Ecbatana, he led his army toward Nineveh. Pending these events Nabuchodonosor died, and left the defence of his country to his son.

The new Assyrian monarch had to oppose this invasion with the wreck of the great army which had just returned broken and dispirited from Syria. Yet he boldly marched out, and gave battle to the Median forces. On this occasion he was doomed to defeat: his troops gave way, and, in despite of every effort, he, and those who escaped, were driven to take refuge within the walls of Nineveh, which was immediately afterward invested by the victorious Medes. Cyaxares vigorously pressed the siege, and would in all probability have speedily reduced that great city, formidable as were its fortifications; but his design was frustrated, and he was compelled to raise the siege, by an aggression as resistless as it was unexpected.

A formidable and countless host of Scythians, having driven the Cimmerians out of Europe, were in full pursuit of their flying enemies, whom they had followed to the borders of Media. Cyaxares, alarmed at this irruption, left Nineveh, and marched to meet this new enemy. In the battle which ensued the Medes were defeated; and the Scythians, finding no other power to oppose them, spread their ravages over all Upper Asia, and even marched to the confines of Egypt. The king of that country diverted them from their purposed invasion by costly presents. They then returned into Palestine, where some of them plundered the ancient temple of Venus at Ascalon, while others seized Bethshan, a city of the tribe of Manasseh on this side Jordan, which from them was afterward called Scythopolis.

For eight years the Scythians held possession of Asia, (see *Appendix*, note 37,) and revelled at pleasure, spreading desolation in every direction. At length the Medes devised the means of shaking off this destroying incubus, and putting an end to the evil. This was accomplished in the following manner: The Medes, perceiving that their enemies had in this lapse of time lost all military order, and had sunk into licentiousness and sloth, took advantage of a general feast, and by mutual concert invited as many Scythian leaders as possible to their several houses, where, freely indulging in drink, the guests were all cut off in their intoxication. The remaining Scythians were soon driven out of Media.

The destruction and expulsion of the Scythians from Media were immediately followed by a war between that country and Lydia.

Herodotus assigns a fanciful cause for this contest, which has not been generally received. It has been supposed that when, after the massacre, the remaining Scythians were driven from Media, they found refuge with Halyattes, King of Lydia, and were protected by him. Whatever occasioned the war, it was carried on with equal vigour and determination on both sides, and for some considerable time without any material advantage to either party.

Pending this war, Cyaxares having effected an alliance with Nabopolassar, King of Babylon, resumed the siege of Nineveh, which after a lengthened struggle fell before the power of its enemies, as stated in a preceding chapter. This event made the Medes the preponderating power in Asia, while the Babylonians occupied a position scarcely inferior to them in martial strength and political influence. These nations being in close alliance with each other, they were able, without difficulty, to subjugate the neighbouring states, and to extend their national and territorial aggrandizement.

The first step in this course, after the conquest of Nineveh, was the defeat of the Egyptian army at Carchemish. The king of Egypt had taken advantage of the conflict between Assyria and the united armies of Babylon and Media, to renew and extend the power of Egypt in the east. He accordingly marched a great army through Judea, and, having defeated and slain King Josiah, proceeded to the Euphrates, where he was totally routed by the combined forces, and compelled to relinquish all his possessions in Asia.

Having thus far effected his purpose, Cyaxares renewed the Lydian war. As before, this struggle was for some time indecisive. At length, both parties having prepared for a desperate conflict, it had commenced, and was being prosecuted with the utmost ardour, when the two armies became suddenly enveloped in the shades of darkness. (See *Appendix*, note 38.) Terrified by this uncommon circumstance, they retired as by mutual consent, regarding the prodigy as a sign of the anger of their gods. The truce thus unexpectedly occasioned was followed by a peace, arranged between the contending parties by the mediation of Nebuchadnezzar, King of Babylon, on the part of the Medes, and of Syennesis, King of Cilicia, on the part of the Lydians.

Media and Babylon continued to carry out their ambitious designs, sometimes acting in concert, and sometimes separately, subduing other countries formerly subject to Assyria. Cœlesyria, Samaria, Galilee, Jerusalem, Persia, and Susiana were thus reduced, and Media raised into a powerful empire. Cyaxares and Nebuchadnezzar were the principal agents in these successful wars. The king of

Media having thus realized the object of his ambition, died, after a reign of forty years, and was succeded by his son,—

ASTYAGES, whose first effort appears to have been directed toward effecting a more solid union with Persia, and to reconciling that numerous and powerful people to yield a willing obedience to his authority. They had suffered severely in the conquest of their country, and smarting under a deep sense of injury, were very unwilling subjects. To remove this feeling, Astyages is said to have given his daughter in marriage to Cambyses, a prince of the family of the Achæmenidæ, and of the royal tribe of Pasargadæ.

Of the reign of this sovereign, although it extended over thirty-five years, very few incidents have been recorded. He was brother of Nitocris, the celebrated queen of Nebuchadnezzar. In the early part of his reign, he had to subdue an insurrection which broke out in the province of Mazandran, bordering on the Caspian Sea. Having besieged the rebellious chief in his capital, he counterfeited a great want of provisions, and by his emissaries in the city purchased food of the keeper of the stores at an exorbitant price, until they were exhausted. He then summoned the citizens to surrender; which they were compelled to do by the discovery of this treachery. (Hales's Analysis of Ancient Chronology, vol. iv, p. 85.)

Astyages is said to have prosecuted other wars, with varicus success, against Syria, Asia Minor, Egypt, and Arabia.

While Cyrus was carrying on his Lydian war, the great nephew of Astyages, Belshazzar, King of Babylon, was slain by conspirators, who immediately proffered their submission to Astyages, as the nearest of kin to the royal house of Nebuchadnezzar, which had thus become extinct. Astyages accordingly assumed the sovereignty of this country, (see *Appendix*, note 39,) in the thirty-seventh year of his reign. He did not, however, on this account remove the seat of his government to Babylon; but, taking from thence Daniel the prophet, of whose fame he had heard, to be his prime minister, and such other persons as he required, he treated Babylon as a province of the great empire, the administration of which was carried on at Ecbatana, the Median capital; the local affairs of Babylon being placed under the direction of a viceroy, appointed for that purpose. (See *Appendix*, note 40.)

Here, in the Median capital, it was that the conspiracy was formed against Daniel which proved his fidelity to God, and led to his being cast into the den of lions, from which he was miraculously delivered.

Astyages in his old age, with a large unwieldy empire, was not equal to resist the rising genius of Cyrus of Persia. This prince, having subdued Lydia and other surrounding countries, turned his arms against the Median king. In this war, (as is more particularly detailed in the chapter on Persia,) Cyrus defeated and imprisoned Astyages, and established the Medo-Persian, or second great universal empire.

CHRONOLOGY OF THE MEDIAN KINGDOM.

B. C.
REVOLT, and War of Independence 710
The several Tribes under Self-government, 7 Years.
DEJOCES enters on Public Life 704
After serving his Country in a judicial Capacity, and in other Ways, he is raised to the Throne, his whole Period of public Service being 53 Years.
PHRAORTES or ARPHAXAD (22 Years) 651
He subdues Persia, and other neighbouring Countries; and, having invaded Assyria, is slain in a Battle with that Nation.
CYAXARES reigned 40 Years 629
Siege of Nineveh, and Scythian Invasion 620
Expulsion of the Scythians 612
Lydian War, and second Siege of Nineveh 608
Nineveh taken 606
Second Lydian War terminated by Thales' Eclipse 603
ASTYAGES reigned 38 Years 589
Babylon added to the Median Kingdom on the Death of Belshazzar 553
Media invaded, conquered, and its King deposed by CYRUS, who reigned 22 Years 551
Medo-Persian Empire.

CHAPTER VII.

THE PERSIANS AND THE MEDO-PERSIAN EMPIRE.

PERSIA a Province of the Assyrian Empire—Peculiar Interest attaching to this Part of Persian History—The Spirit and Prowess of the Blacksmith Kawah obtains the Independence of his Country—FERIDOON placed on the Throne—His long and just Reign—He divides his Kingdom between his Sons, SELM, TOOR, and ERIJ—Erij slain by his Brothers—The Assassins defeated and slain by MANUCHEHER, who reigns with great Celebrity—Sam, Prime Minister—Roostum, his Grandson, the great Persian Hero, born—NOUZER succeeds to the Throne—His cruel Reign—He is slain—Zoo expels the Enemy—His Son KERSHASP raised to the Throne, and afterward deposed—End of the Peshdadian Dynasty—The Kaianian Dynasty—The Median Ascendency concealed by imaginary Kings, KAI KOBAD representing Dejoces and Phraortes, and KAI KOOS Cyaxares and Astyages—Reference to the Eclipse of Thales—KAI KHOSRU, or CYRUS, succeeds to the Throne—The Account of Ctesias respecting his Parentage—The probable Career of this Warrior, until he defeats and deposes Astyages—Cyrus marries the Daughter of Astyages—The Death of the deposed King—Cyrus conquers Lydia—Takes Babylon, and establishes a universal Empire—His Conduct toward the Hebrews—The Restoration of Jerusalem begun—Extent of the Persian Empire—The Death of Cyrus—CAMBYSES—He prohibits the Progress of Building at Jerusalem—Invades and conquers Egypt—His impolitic Cruelty and Impiety—Usurpation of Smerdis the Magian—Death of Cambyses—Smerdis destroyed by a Conspiracy of Nobles—DARIUS raised to the Throne—His improved Mode of Government—The Case of Democedes, the Greek Physician—Makes an Edict in favour of the Hebrews—Reduces Samos—Babylon rebels—The Self-sacrifice of Zopyrus—Babylon is taken—Conquests in the East—A Body of Greek Troops wage War in Asia Minor, and burn Sardis—Darius contemplates the Invasion of Greece—Failure of the first Expedition under Mardonius—Battle of Marathon, and Ruin of the second Persian Invasion—Death of Darius—Persepolis—Behistun Sculptures—XERXES—Subdues Egypt—Makes vast Preparations for the Invasion of Greece—Crosses the Hellespont—Battle at Thermopylæ—The Persian Fleet defeated at Salamis, and their Army destroyed at Platæa—The Remnant of the Persian Fleet and Army destroyed at Mycale—Horrible Crime and Cruelty perpetrated in the royal Court—Xerxes assassinated—ARTAXERXES I. established on the Throne—Marries Esther—Ezra and Nehemiah sent to Judea—Revolt of Egypt—Peace with Athens—XERXES II.—SOGDIANUS—DARIUS NOTHUS subdues his Rivals—Demoralization of the Persian Court—ARTAXERXES II.—Revolt of Cyrus—He marches into the East—Is slain, and the Army dispersed, at Cunaxa—Retreat of the Ten Thousand Greeks—Continued Iniquity of the Court—Revolt and Death of the Heir-apparent—ARTAXERXES III. murders the royal Family—Restores Persian Authority in Egypt, Phenicia, and Cyprus—DARIUS III. undertakes the Government—Alexander invades the Empire—Triumph of the Macedonian.

ON resuming the history of Persia, we find it a province of the great Assyrian empire, having been subdued by Ninus or his immediate successor, and placed in entire subjection to the imperial government. (Patriarchal Age, pp. 453–455.) This period of subjection is shrouded from public view, and its disparaging influence on the national fame concealed, by the Persian historians describing it as the reign of a tyrant sovereign, Zohauk, who is fabled to have ruled for a thousand years.

The history of Persia, especially during the time which has now to pass under review, will always possess the deepest interest. This nation stood in intimate and peculiar relation to the elect people of Jehovah, in the most eventful period of their career,—placed in trembling jeopardy the fate of Greece, in the outset of her glorious course,—and by its fall immortalized the greatest military genius the world ever produced. This portion of Persian history, therefore, cannot fail to excite deep and serious attention. A knowledge of the real facts of this period is, however, a very difficult acquirement. Sir William Jones calls the season of Assyrian domination over Persia the " dark and fabulous " age; and that which we have now to review he designates the " heroic and poetical " age. And this is its true character, since we have to collect our information from the conflicting statements of ill-informed Greeks on the one hand, and from native writers, who disfigured all their annals with fable and poetry, on the other.

Amid this general darkness, however, we have clear and explicit information respecting the deliverance of Persia from her vassalage to Assyria, and her restoration to independence. As this foreign domination was described in the Persian annals as the tyranny of a monster king, named Zohauk, whose rapacity and cruelty were fast spoiling and depopulating the land; so the emancipation of Persia is spoken of as the defeat and death of this tyrant. This event was effected by the spirit and prowess of an humble blacksmith named Kawah. Zohauk having selected Kawah's two sons to be victims of his cruelty, Kawah rose in bold resistance. Having armed himself, and succeeded in rousing the spirit of his countrymen, he raised his blacksmith's apron on a pole as his banner; and, proceeding with the force thus collected, he defeated the royal troops. Kawah being afterward joined by great numbers of Persians, who now saw the dawn of hope for their country, the insurrection was continued, and extended, until Zohauk was defeated and slain, and Persia restored to liberty and independence.

FERIDOON—a young prince descended from the ancient royal family of the kingdom, who had hitherto lived in seclusion—joined the victorious blacksmith, and was, on the termination of the war, raised to the throne. The first act of the new sovereign was to appoint the old apron of Kawah as the royal standard of Persia; and as such it continued to be recognised during all the fluctuations of the national history, until the conquest of the kingdom by the Mohammedans, when it was taken, and studded with gems, with which it had been from time to time enriched.

This prince is said to have ruled with great justice and moderation. But, he having lived to a great age, his last days were imbittered by family feuds. When growing infirmities obliged him to relinquish the cares of royalty, he divided his dominions between his three sons, Selm, Toor, and Erij. But as the home-country of Persia was given to Erij the youngest son, the elder brothers demanded a new division, which the aged monarch refused; a course by which they were so greatly incensed, that they soon after put Erij to death: and, not satisfied with this act of cruelty, they embalmed his head, and sent it to his father. The aged sovereign was seized with frantic grief for the loss of his favourite son, and implored heaven to spare his life until a descendant of Erij should avenge his death. His wish was granted. MANUCHEHER, the son of a daughter of Erij, became the hope of the aged king. When grown to manhood, he commenced a war with the murderers of his father, who were both slain by his hand, and their forces defeated. Soon after this, Feridoon died, having previously placed the crown on the head of Manucheher, who reigned with great celebrity. In compliance with the advice of Feridoon, he took for his prime minister Sam, a Persian nobleman of great talents and integrity.

During this reign Roostum, the great martial hero of Persia, was born. He was the grandson of the prime minister Sam. Nothing can be more extravagant and romantic than the accounts given of the birth and prowess of this warrior by the poets of his country.

After a lengthened period of rule, Manucheher died, leaving his son NOUZER to succeed him in the government; whom he charged, on his death-bed, to be guided in all his conduct by the wise advice of Sam and of his sons. The youthful sovereign neglected this counsel, and pursued a course equally impolitic and unjust. In consequence of his cruel and oppressive conduct, his subjects were driven to the verge of rebellion. While in this state, the kingdom was invaded by a neighbouring potentate, Pushung, King of Turan; and the results of this contest were unfavourable to Persia. In one single combat, Kobad, a son of the famous Kawah, was killed by his adversary; and in another Nouzer himself fell by the hand of Afrasiab, the son of Pushung, who commanded the invading army.

Zal, a son of Sam, is said to have made a further effort to save his country from foreign rule. He raised a prince of the royal house, named ZOO, to the throne, who succeeded in expelling the enemy, and restoring the integrity of the kingdom. He was succeeded by his son KERSHASP, who was soon after set aside by Zal, as incompetent to govern. He was the last prince of the Peshdadian dynasty.

Having thus given the most probable account that can be extracted from the mass of fiction and fable handed down to us by the professed historians of this age, it will be necessary to observe that scarcely any part of it can be regarded as established historic fact, except that which exhibits the insurrection, prowess, and success of Kawah. These are fully attested by ample evidence. Sufficient indications of the extravagance of these annals generally will be found in the circumstance, that Feridoon is said to have reigned five hundred years, and Manucheher one hundred and twenty. It is, nevertheless, probable, that in all this romancing there is a *substratum* of fact, which it has been our object, as far as possible, to elicit, and to exhibit in the preceding account.

The reign of Kershasp was followed by the Kaianian dynasty, which continued to rule until the subversion of the kingdom and empire by Alexander.

It may be observed here, that, although the reign of Kai Khosru, or Cyrus, places us in the region of history, and we have, after that period, ample and authentic information; yet, down to the reign of the great Persian, the annals of this kingdom continue to be shrouded in darkness. The Persian lists give but two reigns between Kershasp and Kai Khosru,—those of KAI KOBAD and KAI KOOS. Sir John Malcolm conjectured, that the two reigns of Cyaxares and Astyages are represented by the Persian account of Kai Koos. This is probable. In fact, it seems almost beyond doubt, that, in order to conceal the subjection of their country to Media, the Persian annalists identified those Median sovereigns who had ruled over their land as their own kings; and, as such, had placed them in their lists, and given them an extravagant length of rule, sufficient to fill up the intervening space; following the same course in respect of Media as they had done in regard to Assyria. Hence the first king of the Kaianian dynasty is described as a descendant of Manucheher, of the Peshdadian dynasty. We are warranted in this hypothesis by the fact, that the same vanity actually induced the Persian scribes to invent a Persian lineage for Alexander of Macedon. (Malcolm's Persia, vol. i, p. 73.)

According to this supposition, Kai Kobad will fill up the space occupied by Dejoces and Phraortes. But the accounts left of his reign are so few, that they do not furnish any means of identification.

It is, however, not so with his successor, Kai Koos. He, while engaged in a great battle, is said to have been, with his whole army, struck with blindness,—a curious poetic version, after the eastern style, of the memorable effect of the eclipse of Thales on the army of Cyaxares.

KAI KHOSRU, the next sovereign, appears to be satisfactorily identified with CYRUS. Sir William Jones, a high authority on such a subject, has used the strongest terms to express his opinion on this point. He says, "I shall only doubt that the Kai Khosru of Firdausi was the Cyrus of the first Greek historian, and the hero of the oldest political and moral romance, when I doubt that *Louis Quatorze* and Lewis the Fourteenth were one and the same French king."—*Works*, vol. iii, p. 106.

In the case of this Persian hero, we are embarrassed by another of the great discrepancies which are found in the writings of Herodotus and Xenophon. And, as in other instances, so here I am compelled to take the Father of History as my guide. I do not come to this conclusion because I regard him as having furnished a clear, complete, and consistent account of the founder of the Medo-Persian empire; but because, with much that appears to be artificial and romantic, he seems to have supplied an outline of facts more consistent in themselves, in better accordance with the history of neighbouring nations, and more strongly supported by Persian tradition, than the narrative of Xenophon or any other writer. (See *Appendix*, note 41.)

Respecting the early years of this prince, it is probable that we have a key to his true history in the outline of the work of Ctesias which has been handed down to us. According to the account of the Greek physician,—who, having resided seventeen years at the Persian court in the reign of Darius Nothus, had important means of procuring information,—Cyrus was a Persian in no way related to the royal house of Media; but having succeeded in securing the sovereignty of Persia, and in vanquishing Astyages, King of Media, he gave out the story of his relationship to the deposed king, that he might by this means more easily secure the submission of the distant parts of the Median empire. To give effect to this report, and to secure his object, he soon after married Amyntas, the daughter of Astyages. This appears to be the most probable account; and the romantic tales of Herodotus and Xenophon must be regarded as the stories propagated by the Persian courtiers to feed the national vanity.

As it was the usual practice in the East at this period to select governors, or viceroys, from the royal families of the dependent countries, so it is probable that Cyrus was intrusted with the administration of affairs in Persia, and was thus enabled to train up a numerous body of brave and hardy soldiers. Nor is it improbable that the account of Xenophon is so far true, that he might be employed as a general in the imperial service, and have become a favourite with the soldiers by his prudence and daring; and that, as Herodotus states, Astyages had greatly alienated the hearts of his people from him by his excessive cruelty.

The information thus supplied by Ctesias may afford a key to many of the statements given by Herodotus and Xenophon, which are probably for the most part facts founded on a false theory. Cyrus is said to have ascended the throne of Persia B. C. 559. It does not follow that he then asserted his independence, or declared war against the imperial state. It might have been at this time that Cambyses his father died, the hereditary chief of the nation or province. In the following year, B. C. 558, the united army of Babylonians, Lydians, and their allies are said to have been defeated by the Medes and Persians under Astyages and Cyrus, and Neriglissar was slain. This may be true. Cyrus, as viceroy of Persia, might have been employed on such a service, and have greatly distinguished himself in it.

How the Persian warrior was occupied in the succeeding years is not known,—probably, in organizing his army in Persia. It could not be in the Lydian war, which Xenophon makes to follow the above battle, as the capture of Sardis did not take place until at least ten years afterward.

Having aspired to supreme dominion, Cyrus, B. C. 553, commenced his war of independence. From the hints thrown out by Xenophon in his Anabasis, this struggle continued some time. The empire was not *wrested* from the Medes without some difficulty. The Persian was, however, crowned with success. Astyages was defeated and taken prisoner, B. C. 551. The empire of the Medes was thus terminated, and the Medo-Persian empire established by the junction of both nations, with their dependencies. Herodotus says that Cyrus treated his captive kindly. The account of Ctesias, however, wears an aspect more like the political transactions of those times. He says, that Cyrus propagated the story of his relationship to the deposed monarch, and actually sent him to be ruler of the Barcanians; that, having married the daughter of Astyages, Cyrus after some time sent for him to see his daughter and himself; and that by the way the eunuch, who had the deposed king in charge, murdered him. Cyrus, to show his indignation of the crime, gave up the eunuch to the severest punishment. But as he was by the act freed from a dangerous rival, the innocence of Cyrus in the affair has been seriously impeached.

All the accounts of this era taken together show, that Cyrus had to act with the most consummate policy, in order to effect a fusion of the two nations, that they might be fully available for coöperation in the working out of the vast ambitious projects which he had formed. At first he gave the Persians no distinction in preference to the Medes, but earnestly cultivated the friendship and confidence of many nobles of the latter nation. Indeed, comparing all that has come down to us respecting the Persian conqueror, it would seem that he owed his great success to his profound sagacity and consummate statesmanship, quite as much as to his military genius and prowess.

Having sufficiently effected these objects, Cyrus marshalled his troops, and proceeded to extend his sway over the neighbouring countries. Aroused by his progress, Crœsus, King of Lydia, became exceedingly concerned; and having taken the utmost pains to procure information from the most celebrated oracles, and construing these responses favourably to himself, he crossed the River Halys, which separated Lydia from the provinces of the Median empire, and invaded Cappadocia. Cyrus, as soon as possible, marched to meet him; and it appears that a great battle was fought with no decisive effect. Yet Crœsus perceived his army to be inferior in numbers to that of the enemy; and finding that Cyrus did not renew the engagement on the following day, he returned immediately to Sardis, and instantly sent messengers in every direction, soliciting the aid of his allies,—a request which appears to have been promptly responded to: for soon afterward we find Crœsus at the head of a great army, consisting of Egyptians, Babylonians, &c., encamped on the banks of the River Pactolus in Lydia. Cyrus had been equally diligent in preparing for this encounter, and hastened his attack, in order that the battle might be fought before the arrival of the Lacedæmonians. He succeeded in this object, and obtained a great victory, principally, we are told, by opposing camels to the Lydian cavalry,—the horse, we are informed, having so great a dislike to the odour of the camel, that this manœuvre prevented the effective action of the most important section of the Lydian army.

Crœsus immediately retreated to Sardis, whither, next morning at day-break, Cyrus followed him. While directing his engines of war against the walls, as though he had determined on a regular siege, he at the same time employed some of the most expert climbers in his army, under the direction of a Persian who had formerly lived at Sardis, to endeavour to scale those parts of the fortifications which appeared to be almost inaccessible. These succeeded in their attempt; and the Persian troops thus obtained possession of the walls; upon seeing which the Lydians fled, and Sardis was taken.

We shall not detail what is said of the treatment of Crœsus by Cyrus in the conflicting statements of Herodotus and Xenophon. It will suffice that the Lydian king was saved, and afterward was generally found in personal attendance on the conqueror, who appears to have attached importance to his opinions and advice. In the war that followed, the troops of Cyrus subdued the remainder of Asia Minor and Ionia, including Halicarnassus, the native city of Herodotus, who might in consequence feel disposed to speak harshly of Cyrus, when occasion offered, as of one who had enslaved his country.

Having secured his conquest in the west, Cyrus reduced all Syria and Arabia, and at last invested Babylon. On the deposition of Astyages, Labynetus, his viceroy, assumed an independent power, and joined in the confederacy with Crœsus. He was now deprived of the assistance of his allies, and had to sustain alone a war with the overwhelming Medo-Persian host. Yet the king of Babylon did not shrink from the contest; but when Cyrus appeared before the city, he marched out and gave him battle. The effort was fruitless; the Babylonians were defeated and pursued into the city.

Cyrus immediately invested this proud metropolis; but its walls were of such height and strength, that the reduction of the place by the ordinary engines of war seemed a hopeless task. It is said that nearly two years were consumed in this siege. At length Cyrus adopted the extraordinary expedient of diverting the waters of the Euphrates from their channel. Having employed his soldiers in cutting a deep trench or canal in a place suitable for the purpose, he took advantage of a public festival, when general revelry prevailed in the city, and connecting his canal with the river, he let the waters run off, so as to leave the bed of the river fordable. A select body of troops were then marched into the city, through the arched opening in the walls by which the river entered it; and another through that by which it left. These forces, meeting, took Babylon by surprise: the gates were soon thrown open, and Cyrus was made master of this otherwise impregnable place.

There can scarcely be conceived a more circumstantial and complete fulfilment of sacred prophecy, than was furnished by this conduct and success of the Persian king.

Cyrus had now established a universal dominion. Media, and all its dependencies—Lydia, with all her surrounding and attached states, and Babylon, with every tributary country, together with his native Persia —were subject to his sway. And his mighty mind appeared equal to the burden of this vast empire. He consolidated its power, directed its general policy, and prosecuted his career of aggrandizement as though but a single nation depended on his will.

The most remarkable part of this extraordinary reign is the language and conduct of Cyrus toward the Hebrew people. We are tersely informed in Scripture that "Daniel prospered in the reign of Darius, and in the reign of Cyrus the Persian." Dan. vi, 28.

With the successive acquisitions of territory and power, Cyrus had a threefold accession to the honours of sovereignty. He was truly independent king of Persia B. C. 559. He conquered Astyages, and added the empire of Media to his dominions, B. C. 551: and, fifteen years afterward, B. C. 536, he subdued Babylon, and completed the establishment of his empire. This sovereign died B. C. 529. The period of his actual sovereignty was therefore thirty years. But as Media was previously the supreme state, the period of its conquest is that given in the Chronicles to the accession of Cyrus, who then succeeded, not merely to a sovereignty, but to the imperial government; while the Hebrew writers, who stood in so peculiar a relation to Babylon as the destroyer of their native land, (the king of that city still ruling over a great part of the Hebrew captives,) did not regard Cyrus as beginning to reign until he had reduced that country to subjection. Consequently, "the first year of Cyrus," spoken of in the Book of Ezra, is B. C. 536,—the first year of his universal rule.

When Cyrus deposed Astyages, and succeeded him in Media, he unquestionably found Daniel at Ecbatana, one of the most able and honoured ministers of state. The deliverance of the prophet from the den of lions, which had a short time previously taken place, must have occurred in Media, and not at Babylon, because the punishment was inflicted under the rigid application of Median law, which could not have been done at Babylon, since it was not usual to alter the internal economy and social laws of subject states, so as to make them precisely similar to those of the supreme kingdom. We are further informed, that "Daniel prospered in the days of Cyrus;" and the word is used so as to warrant the conclusion that he "prospered" in the same manner as he had done under Darius,—namely, by holding those elevated offices of trust and honour with which he had been invested by the Median monarch. It can scarcely be doubted, therefore, that in the confidential communications which took place between the king and his aged minister, Daniel would make known to Cyrus the wonderful revelations which had been given to him respecting the successive great monarchies which were appointed by Divine Providence to succeed each other in the earth.

It is a remarkable fact, that Nebuchadnezzar was fully informed of this succession, by special divine appointment, almost immediately after he had completed his conquests. It is equally certain, that Alexander of Greece, when setting out on his career of conquest, had these predictions read to him by the high-priest at Jerusalem. It would, then, be marvellous indeed if Cyrus, coming into daily and confidential communication with the prophet, should have remained in ignorance of these glorious revelations. Among numerous other proofs that he did receive such information, we refer to his edict in favour of the Jews.

Having put down all opposition, and extended his empire "from the River Oxus to the frontiers of Egypt, embracing Lydia and Asia Minor no doubt as far as the mountains of the Afghans which separate Chorassan from India, (Niebuhr's Lec. on Anc. Hist., vol. i, p. 110,) Cyrus turned his attention to the government of these vast dominions. One of the edicts published by him, in the first year of this universal reign, was the following: "Thus saith Cyrus, King of Persia, The Lord God of heaven hath given me all the kingdoms of the earth; and he hath charged me to build him a house at Jerusalem, which is in Judah. Who is there among you of all his people? his God be with him, and let him go up to Jerusalem, which is in Judah, and build the house of the Lord God of Israel, (he is the God,) which is in Jerusalem." Ezra i, 2, 3. (Hebrew People, pp. 362–364.)

At first sight this would appear a most extraordinary document. Cyrus had been, for the greater part of his life up to this year, engaged in war. He was bred in Persia, and of course a believer in the religion of that country. We have no definite information of his having had any intercourse with the Hebrew nation, with the single exception of his minister Daniel. It must be readily admitted, that under the ordinary impulses and calculations of worldly policy, the restoration of the Jews—of whom it may be fairly presumed that Cyrus had heard but little, and known still less—would not have been one of the first acts of his imperial sovereignty. But this is not only undertaken by him, but he explicitly states that he does it in obedience to a divine command. Nay, he does not scruple to ascribe all his extended power and dominion to the gift of the Lord God of Israel, whose injunction he thus obeys. Taking all the accompanying circumstances into account, this is a most remarkable edict, and, I am bold to say, can only be accounted for in any reasonable manner by supposing that Daniel had communicated to Cyrus the prophetic revelations of God respecting him, and his preördained interference on behalf of the Hebrew people. (See *Appendix*, note 42.)

This measure was effectual. A great number of the Jews, from different parts of the kingdom, gathered together their families and their substance; and, encouraged by the royal countenance, went in a body to Judea, where they proceeded to lay anew the foundations of a Hebrew state, and rebuild the holy city and temple, which had so long lain in ruins.

It is also remarkable, that this event affords one instance of the exact fulfilment of the prophecy of Jeremiah,—that the captivity should last seventy years; and one, too, peculiarly interesting to the prophet Daniel. As it was exactly seventy years from 586 B. C., when Jerusalem and the temple were destroyed, to 516 B. C., when the second temple was finished; so it was precisely seventy years from 604 B. C., when Daniel and his companions were carried into captivity, to 534 B. C., when the first body of Hebrews, by virtue of this edict, reached Judea, appointed Joshua high-priest, and laid the foundation of the second temple.

Thus did the continued exertions of the Persian hero, while aiming at the gratification of his own inordinate ambition, carry into effect the great purposes of Divine Providence respecting the government of the nations of this world. The kingdom symbolized by the head of gold had fulfilled its destiny, and passed away: that indicated by the breast and arms of silver had now extended her power over the nations. The "lion with eagles' wings"—which so strikingly represented the power of Babylon, where these identical figures guarded every approach to the palace-temples of her pontiff-kings— had perished; and now the Medo-Persian bear had arisen to devour.

How intensely fraught with teaching of the highest order is such history, regarded in the light of revealed truth! Here we look into the sacred page, and find the purpose of God clearly expressed in plain terms, and forcefully illustrated by the most energetic symbolical imagery. We look abroad in the nations of the earth: Babylon is triumphant in martial power, sitting as a queen among the nations; Media, possessing hereditary distinction for bravery and military prowess, is second only to the paramount state; while Persia, uncultivated and almost unknown, has scarcely yet made an impression on a page of history. Yet a series of contingent evolutions begins, involving the utmost energy of individual minds, and the most strange and unexpected collisions and associations of nations. Universal clamour, confusion, and war succeed: at length the storm is hushed,—peace reigns. We look; and out of this chaos of national strife has come, in all its predicted perfectness, the very event which the prophets of God had foretold. Cyrus, having organized Persia, and associated its rude hardihood with the military discipline and tactics of Media, by these united powers extends his dominion over Asia, and reigns supreme. And, to fulfil to the letter the utmost range of sacred prophecy, no sooner is he found in possession of this sway than he says "to Jerusalem, Thou shalt be inhabited, and to the cities of Judah, Ye shall be built." Thus the Hebrew people were placed in the way of working out their national and ecclesiastical polity, and of attaining a position in which all the purposes of redeeming grace, as predicted by their holy prophets, might be fully accomplished.

The empire thus established by Cyrus, and over which he reigned in peace for seven years, was immense in its extent. Bounded on the east by the Indus, and on the west by the Mediterranean Sea, on the north by the Caspian and Euxine, and on the south by Ethiopia and the Arabian Sea, the vast range of Central and Western Asia was subject to his sway.

The accounts which speak of the death of Cyrus are of the most conflicting description. Some affirm him to have been slain in war: Herodotus and Justin say the catastrophe took place while he was fighting against the Scythians; but Ctesias places this war at an earlier date, and says that he was killed by the javelin of an Indian. Xenophon, however, makes him die peacefully in his bed, while discoursing with his friends. On one point there seems to be a mutual agreement among ancient authors:—they all assert that Cyrus was buried in Pasargadæ, and that his tomb was found two centuries afterward by Alexander the Great. This fact seems decisive in favour of the statement of Xenophon. It is not likely that, if killed in Scythia or in India, he would have been interred in Persia.

Cyrus was succeeded by his son CAMBYSES, whom on his death-bed he appointed heir to the throne. The first incident of government that we meet with in this reign is the successful effort of the Ammonites, Moabites, and others, to prevent the further progress of the Hebrews in building the city and temple of Jerusalem. Ezra has recorded this fact; (Ezra iv, 6;) and Josephus (Antiquities, book xi, chap. ii, sect. 1, 2) has preserved the correspondence at length, and concludes his account with the statement, "Accordingly, these works were hindered from going on, till the second year of the reign of Darius." (See *Appendix*, note 43.)

The principal object which seems to have filled the mind of this king was the conquest of Egypt. Various tales have been circulated for the purpose of accounting for this strong desire. It is probable, however, that his motive was simply ambition. Cambyses saw, all around him, nations bowing to his sway, which had been conquered by his father and the preceding sovereign, and he longed to add to the empire a conquest of his own. Egypt, an old and wealthy kingdom, offered the greatest incentive to this passion. He accordingly began a series of preparations on a grand scale, which occupied him during the first four years of his reign.

At length the Persian king proceeded to carry out his long-cherished purpose. He had obtained, just before his setting out on this expedition, the greatest possible advantage, in the friendship of Phanes, a Greek officer of great capacity and courage, who had been previously employed by the king of Egypt as the commander of the Grecian auxiliaries in his service, but who, on receiving some affront from Amasis, had fled, and found succour in the court of Persia. This officer not only explained to the Persian king the resources of Egypt, and the nature of the country, but also put him in the way of obtaining water for his army while crossing the desert from Palestine to the Nile. Without a supply of this necessary, the transit of an army would have been impracticable: but this was secured, under the advice of Phanes, by an alliance into which Cambyses entered with the Arabian prince who ruled over the intervening country. Pending these arrangements, Amasis, King of Egypt, died, leaving to his son Psammenitus the kingdom, and the duty of defending it.

By the assistance which he had obtained, Cambyses appeared with his vast army before Pelusium,—the key to Egypt on the east. As noticed in the chapter on Egypt, it has been said that Cambyses obtained possession of this important post by collecting together a great number of cats, dogs, sheep, and other animals held sacred by the Egyptians, and by driving them before his army, when it advanced to attack the city. The Egyptian troops, not daring to raise a weapon against creatures which they revered as divine, allowed the Persians to come on without opposition, until it was too late: and thus the city was taken without loss.

The king of Egypt, on hearing of this movement, immediately led his troops to the Pelusiac mouth of the Nile, and encamped opposite the Persian army. Here a great battle was fought, which terminated in the defeat of the Egyptian king, and the ruin of his army. A very small proportion of his troops escaped, and took refuge in Memphis.

The further progress of Cambyses in Egypt, his conquest and cruelty, his fatal attempt on Ethiopia, and vain desire to wreak his vengeance on Carthage, have all been briefly detailed in the history of Egypt.

Cambyses was accompanied into Egypt by a brother named Smerdis. This prince appears to have possessed more muscular strength than any other man in the Persian army: for, when the Ethiopian king sent his bow as a derisive present to Cambyses, Smerdis was the only one in his army who could bend it. This greatly enraged Cambyses: a mind so limited and jealous as his could brook the presence of no superiority. He therefore devised an excuse for his brother's return to Persia. But, having soon afterward a dream, in which a messenger informed him that Smerdis had ascended the throne, and touched the heavens with his head, he became so alarmed and excited that he sent his favourite courtier Prexaspes into Persia, with orders to put his brother to death; which bloody command was fully carried into effect, although authors differ as to the manner in which this noble prince was assassinated.

From this period the life of the Persian king exhibited a continued series of acts of brutality and butchery. Cambyses had a sister named Meroë, whose name he gave to a celebrated island in the Nile. This princess he married; but, suspecting that she lamented the death of her brother Smerdis, he brutally kicked her when pregnant, so as to occasion her death. His character at this time evinced a degree of cruelty almost surpassing belief: he caused several of his nobles to be buried alive, and scarcely a day elapsed without some of his courtiers being sacrificed to his fury.

Prexaspes, who had murdered Smerdis at the command of the king, was now called to feel the violence of his temper. He was one day asked by Cambyses, what the Persians thought of him. The courtier replied, that they admired his wisdom, but regretted that he indulged to excess in wine. "They think, then," said the king, "that wine disturbs my understanding; but you shall judge." Then, after drinking more freely, he ordered the son of Prexaspes, who was his cup-bearer, to stand upright at the further end of the room. "Now," turning to the father, he said, "if I shoot this arrow through the heart of your son, the Persians have slandered me: but if I miss, I will allow that they have spoken the truth." He drew the bow; the youth fell: and, on the body being opened, it was found that the arrow had pierced his heart. Cambyses then asked Prexaspes whether he had ever seen any one shoot with a steadier hand: to which the servile courtier replied, that "Apollo himself could not have aimed more correctly." Such are the results of the contact of brutal tyranny with crouching slavery!

Cyrus had commended his captive, Crœsus of Lydia, to the kindness of his son; but about this time, being displeased with an answer which he had received from Crœsus, the king commanded him to be put to death. The courtiers delayed the execution, thinking that he would relent, which he soon did, and rejoiced to find that Crœsus was still alive; but he devoted to instant death those who had disobeyed his order.

Cambyses had entered on the eighth year of his reign, when he left Egypt to return to Persia. On his arrival in Syria, he met a herald sent from Susa to apprize the Persian army that Smerdis, the son of Cyrus, was proclaimed king, and to command their obedience. This revolution arose out of the following circumstances: When Cambyses left Persia for the invasion of Egypt, he committed the government of the country to Patizithes, one of the principal Magi, who had a brother very much resembling in person Smerdis, the brother of Cambyses, and called by the same name. Although the death of this prince had been kept from the public, the Magian had obtained intelligence of the event; and knowing that the tyranny and extravagance of Cambyses had become insupportable, and that the name of Smerdis was popular, he placed his brother on the throne, as the son of Cyrus, and sent heralds through the empire proclaiming his accession; trusting mainly, for the success of his attempt, to the odium attaching to the government of Cambyses.

The king, having assured himself by a careful interrogation of Prexaspes, that his brother Smerdis was really dead, and that the usurper was Smerdis the Magian, ordered the immediate march of his army to Persia. But when he was mounting his horse for this purpose, his sword slipped from the scabbard, and inflicted a serious wound in his thigh. The Egyptians, who recollected that it was by a wound in this part of the body that Cambyses had killed the sacred Apis of Egypt, regarded this as a judgment from heaven on his profane impiety; and, strange to say, our learned Prideaux entertained a similar opinion. During his stay in Egypt, the king had consulted the oracle of Butus respecting his destiny, and was told that he would die at Ecbatana. Knowing no place of this name but the capital of Media, he regarded himself safe in Western Asia. But while lying ill from the effects of his wound in a small town in Syria, he asked the name of the place, and learned to his dismay that it also was called Ecbatana: upon which he abandoned himself to despair, and died about twenty days after the accidental infliction of the wound.

Before his death, Cambyses had charged the nobles and officers of his army not to submit to the Magian Smerdis, who was undoubtedly a usurper. But after his death this statement was disbelieved: for Prexaspes faltered in his story, and admitted that he had not slain Smerdis with his own hand, being, it is supposed, bribed to do so by the Magi: so that the army and the nation for some time submitted to the new ruler.

The suspicions of the nobles were, however, soon excited by the scrupulous care which the Magi took to prevent the new sovereign from being seen. This induced one of them, named Otanes, to attempt to discover whether Smerdis was the son of Cyrus or an impostor. He possessed an advantage for prosecuting this inquiry peculiar to himself. His daughter had been the wife of Cambyses, and had after his death passed in the same capacity to his successor. Otanes, therefore, went to his daughter; but as she had not seen Smerdis the son of Cyrus, and was only admitted to the presence of the king at night, she could not resolve the doubt. It then occurred to Otanes, that Smerdis the Magian had, for some great crime committed during the reign of Cyrus, been deprived of his ears: he therefore charged his daughter to ascertain, when next called to the bed of the king, whether he had, or had not, been deprived of his ears. Delicate and dangerous as was the task, so anxious was she to meet her father's wishes, and to ascertain whether she was the wife of a king or of an impostor, that the next time she found her husband fast asleep, she made sure of the fact that his ears had been removed. The princess lost no time in communicating this fact to Otanes, who presently informed a friend. These two ultimately associated five other noblemen in the plot; and, having, by the dignity of their position, obtained access to the palace, they slew Smerdis and his brother Patizithes, and thus put an end to this impudent usurpation. It is said that the death of these impostors was followed by a general massacre of the Magi, and that nothing but the cover of night prevented their extermination.

Having effected their purpose, the conspirators deliberated as to the kind of government which should be established; (see *Appendix*, note 44;) and they having ultimately decided on continuing an hereditary monarchy, and having agreed on the means by which the next sovereign should be appointed, in the prosecution of their plan, DARIUS the son of Hystaspes, of the Achæmenean family of Persia, was raised to the throne.

Before his elevation to the sovereignty, Darius had married the daughter of Gobryas, one of the most daring of his associates in the destruction of the Magian impostor. To this wife he, after his accession, added the two daughters of Cyrus,—Atossa, who had been the wife of her brother Cambyses, and afterward of the Magian; and Artystona, who had not previously been married, and who became the most favoured of his wives. He also married Parmys, the daughter of Smerdis, the son of Cyrus; and Phædyma, the daughter of Otanes, who had been married to Smerdis the Magian, and was the means of his being detected.

Having strengthened his position by these marriages, Darius proceeded to improve the government of his vast empire. He effected this by dividing it into twenty separate governments or satrapies, over each of which he placed a governor or satrap. I am inclined to think that we have, in this measure of Darius, the first really practical movement toward the organization and establishment of an empire, in the strict and proper sense of the term. Every preceding conqueror had either left the several nations intact, under some new prince or king; or else transported the inhabitants from one country to another; a plan which appears to have been resorted to when the former arrangement was not likely to prevent them from struggling to recover their independence. The first mode was very defective, and allowed the continuance of every national partiality and prejudice, feeling and desire; while the latter destroyed the wealth, and all the productive agencies—social, commercial, political, and military—in order to prevent future insurrection. The course pursued by Darius secured a much larger amount of good, with none of this sacrifice and loss. By associating several distinct nations into one government, the manners and customs of each were assimilated; the caution of one people acted as a check on the daring of another; so that good government grew to be not only possible, but easy, and the chances of rebellion and intestine war became very slender indeed.

A circumstance occurred about this time which is worthy of notice, it having first directed the attention of the Persian court to the invasion of Greece. Darius, having hurt his foot while hunting, found that the Egyptian physicians, to whose care he intrusted himself, were making no progress with the cure of the wounded limb; and, apprehensive of being disabled for life, he inquired for other medical aid. As the result of this inquiry, he learned that there was in the city a Greek slave, named Democedes, who had been brought from Samos. Darius having sent for him, and induced him to undertake the cure of his foot, his skill was successful; and after a short time the foot was perfectly restored. The king loaded him with gifts, and introduced him to his wives as "the man who had restored the king to life." Democedes had now a sumptuous house, and in fact everything but that which he so ardently desired,—namely, his liberty. At length Atossa, the king's wife, was afflicted with a desperate disorder, and in her distress she applied to the Greek physician, who engaged to cure her, provided she would use her influence with the king in favour of an object on which his own heart was set. The queen promised, and Democedes cured her; and then he claimed her good offices to enable him to visit Greece.

She acted under his instruction; and, not daring to apply for his release, she urged the king to invade Greece, telling him that the Greek physician could procure every information for him, and that she greatly desired some women of Sparta, Athens, Argos, and Corinth in her service; and that it became Darius, in the prime of his manhood, to attempt some great enterprise.

Darius was roused by the queen's speech, and soon afterward sent fifteen trusty Persians with Democedes, to travel in Greece, and bring him a particular account of the coast and the military position of the country. A great part of this survey had been completed, when Democedes escaped from his companions, who had to return to the mortified and incensed king with the communication that he had been duped and deceived.

In the third year of his reign, Darius rendered very essential service to the Hebrews. After the death of Smerdis, the edict of that king had lost its force: but the Jews, disheartened by repeated interruptions, did not resume the reëdification of the city and temple; and in consequence of this apathy they were subjected to divine chastisement. Their vintage and harvest failed; and they were specially informed by a prophet, that their negligence in not rebuilding the house of God was the cause of this providential visitation. Hag. i, 6, 8–11. Roused to diligence by these inflictions, the Hebrews resumed their appointed work. This, as usual, called forth the opposition of the Samaritans, who on this occasion did not apply directly to the royal court, but to Tatnai, the governor whom Darius had appointed over the province of Syria. This officer appears to have behaved on the occasion with great judgment and discretion. He proceeded to Jerusalem, and demanded of the Jews by what authority they acted; and on their producing the decree of Cyrus in their favour, Tatnai wrote to Darius to inquire whether this document was genuine, and to learn the king's wishes in the matter.

Darius caused a search to be made; and on this occasion Ezra is careful to inform us, that this record was found at Ecbatana, or, as he writes it, "Achmetha, the palace that is in the province of the Medes." Ezra vi, 1–12. Darius renewed this decree; and ordered that the remaining vessels, which Nebuchadnezzar had taken from the house of God, should be restored; and that resources for carrying on the work should be supplied to the Jews out of the revenues of the province; at the same time threatening with instant death all who might hereafter obstruct this important work. Prideaux observes, on the authority of Lightfoot, that, in gratitude for this decree, which was dated from the palace at Shushan, the eastern gate

in the outer wall of the temple was called " the Gate of Shushan."
Josephus (Antiquities, book xi, chap. 3) has given a different version of the reasons which induced Darius to evince this favour to the Jews; but it appears rather too fanciful for sober history.

During this period the empire had been maintained in peace. The first war in which Darius was engaged was connected with the reduction of Samos. But while this was being carried on under the direction of Otanes, a more important rupture occurred nearer home, in the revolt of the Babylonians. It is probable that the lengthened absence of Cambyses and his army in Egypt, and the numerous difficulties which Darius had encountered after his accession, had given the inhabitants of this proud city hopes of retrieving their independence. On the first intelligence of this revolt, the king collected an army, which greatly terrified the rebellious Babylonians. They saw, from the power of the imperial force, that their only hope was to sustain a lengthened siege: and in order to do this, they adopted the horrible expedient of strangling the great body of their women and children, that their provisions might last for the longest possible period.

Darius soon appeared before the city, and closely invested it: but the Babylonians were so confident in the strength of their defences, that they danced upon the walls, and treated the king and his army with the greatest possible contempt. Nor did they miscalculate their resources. After a siege of nineteen months, Darius seemed as far from the attainment of his object as when he began. But what no amount of military daring or energy could effect, the self-sacrifice and duplicity of one of his nobles enabled him to secure.

The name of this officer was Zopyrus. He appeared before Darius with his nose and ears cut off, his back lacerated with scourging, and presenting a most pitiable, mangled, and bloody spectacle. He soon removed the astonishment of the king, by telling him that he had inflicted these injuries on himself, for the purpose of procuring the success of the royal enterprise; that in his mangled and bloody condition he was going to Babylon, and would say that he had been thus cruelly treated by Darius, and was therefore his bitterest enemy. He then concerted a series of measures which Darius was to carry out, and which would, as he expected, enable him to admit the Persian troops into the city.

This explanation being given, Zopyrus hastened as a deserter to Babylon. He being seen from the walls running and looking behind him, as with great anxiety, the guard descended and admitted him. Zopyrus told his concerted tale; upon which he was presented to the Babylonish assembly, when the wily Persian told them that he had advised Darius to raise the hopeless siege, and that for this fault the king had treated him so cruelly as to reduce him to the miserable condition in which he appeared before them. He concluded his tale of woe by imploring them to allow him to fight in the front rank against his former master. Deceived and deluded by these specious representations, the Babylonians took him into their confidence.

Zopyrus now told them, that on a particular day Darius would march a body of a thousand troops against a certain post; and that if they would place a corresponding force under his direction, he would destroy them. The Babylonians, taking every reasonable precaution, complied. As had been told them, they saw a body of one thousand men approach the gate of Semiramis. Acting under the direction of Zopyrus, the Babylonians sallied out, and completely destroyed them. He then said, that about a certain day he expected a larger body to assail the gate of Nineveh, when he would in like manner effect their destruction. This promise also he fully redeemed. Afterward he warned them that a troop of four thousand men would about such a time attempt the Chaldæan gate. Again Zopyrus led the assault, and again the whole body of the invading force was destroyed. The sacrifice of these seven thousand men had been fully arranged between Darius and Zopyrus. This success filled the Babylonians with unbounded joy. They saw in these victories the prospect of destroying the invading force in detail. Their confidence in Zopyrus was at its height, and he promised them a complete triumph. Soon afterward Darius ordered a general assault. Zopyrus promised to repeat his victories; but in the heat of the struggle, instead of destroying the Persians, he by a preconcerted signal admitted them into the city. The result of this treachery was fatal. Babylon fell prostrate beneath the power of the conqueror. Darius stained his triumph by crucifying three thousand of the most distinguished Babylonians. He also reduced the height of the walls, carried away the gates, and prohibited the use of arms by the inhabitants; these being precautions against any future attempt at insurrection.

Immediately after the complete reduction of Babylon, Darius commenced his invasion of Scythia,—an effort remarkable for nothing more than the madness of the enterprise, the number of troops employed,—nearly 700,000,—and the distance to be marched,—about one hundred and fifty days' or nearly five months' journey. If the project of Miltiades to destroy the bridge across the Danube had been carried into effect, but few, if any, of this vast host would have returned. The enterprise was begun in ignorant precipitancy, and finished under consummate disgrace.

Darius appears now to have turned his attention to the east, in the hope of retrieving his fame and extending his territory. In this he seems to have been successful, although we are not in possession of the details of the expedition. Herodotus says, "A very considerable part of Asia was discovered by Darius. That prince, wishing to ascertain whether the Indus flowed into the ocean, sent out ships with persons in whom he had confidence, especially Syclax of Calyandria. They embarked at Caspatyras, in the Parthian territories, following the eastern course of the river toward the ocean. Hence sailing westward, they arrived, after a voyage of thirty months, at the same point from whence the Phenicians sailed to circumnavigate Libya. In consequence of this voyage, Darius subdued the Indians, and became master of that ocean."—*Melpomene*, cap. xliv. In connexion with these discoveries, acquisitions were made in India which formed the twentieth satrapy of the empire, and produced a yearly revenue of six hundred talents in golden ingots. (Thalia, cap. xciv.)

From the period of the Scythian invasion, the Persian interest in the west had been in a state of continual oscillation. Thrace and Macedon had acknowledged the supremacy of Persia by giving the ambassadors of Darius "earth and water:" but no real subjection was shown to the imperial court. At length Aristagoras—a nephew and son-in-law of Histiæus, who had saved the royal army in the Scythian campaign by preserving the bridge across the Danube—commenced an insurrection of the Greeks against Persia. Sparta declined to take part in it, but Athens joined the confederacy. This united army crossed over to Ephesus, and succeeded in laying the city of Sardis in ashes. But their measures were hastily taken and ill supported; and, on encountering the Persian forces, they were completely defeated.

This led Darius seriously to contemplate the entire reduction of Greece. He was so enraged against the inhabitants of the capital of Attica, that he implored Jupiter that he might be allowed to be revenged on them, and employed an attendant to remind him three times a day of the Athenians.

The first armament sent on this service was commanded by Mardonius, the king's son-in-law. But this army was surprised by the Thracians, and suffered great loss, the Persian general himself being wounded in the conflict, while the Persian fleet encountered a storm in doubling Mount Athos, by which they lost three hundred ships and twenty thousand men. Mardonius returned into Asia with the wreck of this great army.

But Darius, with the resources of an immense empire at his disposal, could not brook the complete frustration of his purpose. While preparing another army, he sent heralds to the several states of Greece, demanding their submission. Ægina and many of the smaller cities signified their compliance; but Athens and Sparta felt so outraged at the demand, that, forgetting the sacred character of the messengers, they instantly put the heralds to death. This violent measure hastened the departure of the Persian army. Darius had on this occasion intrusted the command to Datis, a Median officer, and Artaphernes, his own nephew. On reaching the sea-coasts of Ionia, they collected an army of three hundred thousand men, and a fleet of six hundred ships. This immense force commenced the war by taking Naxos. Eretria was next subdued, and the inhabitants sent captives to Susa. The Persian army then passed over to Attica; when, at Marathon, ten miles from Athens, this mighty host of two hundred thousand men and ten thousand horse were entirely routed, and those who escaped with life were chased in confusion to their ships. Thus terminated the second Persian attempt to invade Greece.

The rage of Darius at this defeat was unbounded. He immediately commanded preparations to be made for an invasion on a larger scale: but while these were going on, Egypt revolted. The Persian monarch, whose mind rose with the emergency, determined to astonish the world by simultaneously conducting two wars,—one in Egypt and the other in Greece. Before his arrangements were completed, he had to settle a dispute in his family respecting his successor. The claimants were Artobazanes, who claimed the crown by virtue of his birthright; and Xerxes, the son of Atossa, the daughter of Cyrus, who asserted his right to the throne because he was the first son born after his father was a king, and should therefore have the precedence of a son born when his father was a private citizen. By the advice of Demaratus, the exiled king of Sparta, Darius decided in favour of Xerxes, and appointed him his successor. This was the last public act of Darius: he soon after died, leaving the prosecution of his vast projects, in the recovery of Egypt and the conquest of Greece, as a legacy to his successor. (See *Appendix*, note 45.) Darius had acquired the reputation of an able military commander; and he did much to foster the rising interests of the Hebrew people.

Before closing our account of this reign, some reference must be made to the great city Persepolis, the ruins of which cast important light on the history and the religion of Persia. Of the origin of this capital we know literally nothing. It is not mentioned either by

Herodotus, Ctesias, Xenophon, or Nehemiah, although they all frequently allude to Susa, Babylon, and Ecbatana. This silence may perhaps be accounted for, by the fact that this city does not appear at any time to have been the settled residence of the Persian kings, although there was at Persepolis a magnificent palace. This edifice, glorious even in its ruins, seems to have been one of the noblest structures that art ever reared. A question has, indeed, been raised as to whether Persepolis and Pasargadæ were not two names for the same city. Scholars generally, however, have decided that these were different places.

It is also necessary to refer to an account of the early part of this reign, of a very extraordinary character. On the western frontiers of Media, on the great road leading from Babylon to the east, stands the sacred rock of Behistun. Rising abruptly from the plain to a height of one thousand seven hundred feet, it was approached with reverence, and regarded as consecrated to the Supreme God. On the face of this rock, which was smoothed down for the purpose, about three hundred feet above the level of the ground, there stands an elaborate sculpture. It is so inaccessible, on account of its height and the perpendicular form of the rock, that it is difficult and dangerous to approach sufficiently near to read it.

The nature of this sculpture is peculiar. It contains pictorial representations of Darius as the great king, with two attendants standing behind him; and before him—one being prostrate under his right foot—are ten men, with a rope round their necks, thus confining them together in a line, and their hands bound behind their backs. Above, just before the king, is the symbol of the divine triad, as seen in the sculptures of Assyria. Above, around, and beneath, in separate columns, are numerous cuneiform inscriptions. After this ancient record had taxed the labour and learning of many scholars, all of whom made some progress toward its decipherment, we have now before us a complete translation of it, the fruit of the learning and industry of Colonel Rawlinson. The origin, manner, and contents of this record are all so peculiar, that it was not thought desirable to incorporate it in fragments with the history, but to place it entire and at once before the reader in a note. (See *Appendix*, note 46.)

On ascending the throne, XERXES entered heartily into the martial measures which had been begun by his father, and hastened the preparations for the reduction of Egypt. Before he proceeded with this undertaking, he confirmed the Jews in possession of all the privileges conferred on them by Darius. At length he marched his army toward Egypt, and effected, almost without a struggle, the entire subjugation of that country, leaving his elder brother Achæmenes, as satrap, to administer the government of that nation.

The three following years were fully employed in preparations for the invasion of Greece. This measure was opposed by Artabanus, the surviving brother of Darius, and other eminent officers: but a great number of Grecian refugees, who had found succour at the Persian court, by practising on the ambition of the king, urged him onward in this insane project; Mardonius, who longed to repair the injury done to his military fame in the first invasion, exerting himself to the utmost to promote the attempt.

At length, the preparations were complete; and Xerxes, with perhaps the largest army ever assembled on earth, proceeded toward the Hellespont.

It is difficult to give serious attention, not to say credence, to the tales which are reported of the intolerable arrogance of this king; such as his sending an epistle to Mount Athos, his flogging, and casting fetters into, the Hellespont, and other acts equally extravagant and improbable. At length, however, a bridge was erected across the straits, over which the many-nationed host passed for seven days and nights without intermission, their speed being frequently hastened by the lashes of whips;—as if men who needed such a stimulus to action would be of any worth when opposed to the best soldiers in the world.

Having made a grand review of his army, Xerxes proceeded through Thrace toward Greece, while the fleet followed the line of the coast. During this march, the most particular attention was paid to religious services, sacrifices being offered at every suitable place according to the rites of the Persian religion. In fact, throughout the whole of these preparations and arrangements, everything appears to have been done that human sagacity could devise. Even large sums of money had been sent to Carthage, to induce that nation to invade the Greek settlements in Sicily, that *Mogna Græcia* might derive no aid in this struggle from her colonies. Thus was the prophecy of Daniel fully verified: "There shall stand up yet three kings in Persia; and the fourth shall be far richer than they all: and by his strength through his riches he shall stir up all against the realm of Grecia." Dan. xi, 2. Indeed, every part of the dominions of Xerxes appears to have contributed to this multitudinous host. (See *Appendix*, note 47.)

The Persian army now approached the Pass of Thermopylæ, where Xerxes found, as had been before reported to him, a small body of Spartans in possession of the defile. After waiting four days in the expectation that they would fly from his presence, the king sent against them a detachment of Medes and Cissians, with orders to bring them prisoners. It was, however, repulsed, although continually reinforced with fresh men; until Xerxes exclaimed, that he had many *men*, but few *soldiers*, in his army. At length the Medes were superseded, and the Immortal Band of Persians, commanded by Hydarnes, were sent against the Greeks, but with no better success. Xerxes, who witnessed the encounter, thrice leaped from his horse, in apprehension of the ruin of his whole army from this handful of men. At length, by the treachery of a Greek, the Persians were conducted by a narrow path over the mountains, so that a body of the army was enabled to pass, and completely enclose the Spartan troops. Seeing his desperate condition, Leonidas sent away his auxiliary forces, and, with his three hundred Spartans and seven hundred Thespians, not only withstood the attack of these hundreds of thousands, but became the assailant, and actually penetrated to the royal pavilion of Xerxes, from which the monarch had hastily escaped. But numbers at length prevailed, and the gallant Greeks fell, rather wearied with their own exertions, than vanquished even by multitudes. According to Herodotus, the Persians lost in this contest two of the king's brothers, and twenty thousand men.

Having obtained this passage, the Persians laid waste Phocis, and marched on Athens. This city they found almost entirely abandoned; the citizens having, by the advice of Themistocles, taken refuge on board their fleet. The few who remained defended their homes until they were all slain; and then Xerxes obtained the gratification of destroying this capital.

Before this event, there had been a naval engagement between the Persian and Greek fleets near Artemisium, in which the Greeks had the advantage, although the victory was not decisive. After the ruin of Athens, the Greek fleet having retreated to the Straits of Salamis, the Persians followed them: and it was on the next course of proceeding that the issue of the war clearly depended. The plan which wisdom and prudence dictated to the Persians, was the one strongly urged in the council of the brave Queen Artemisia,—namely, for the Persian fleet to beleaguer that of the Greeks, while the great Persian army should proceed to the reduction of the Peloponnesus. If this course had been taken the results of the war might have been different. Instead of this, however, Xerxes adopted the unwise determination of attacking the Grecian fleet. Compelled to do so under every disadvantage, on account of the contracted space, the Persians were completely defeated; two hundred of their ships were destroyed, and the rest driven on the coast of Asia, never again daring to appear in the waters of Greece.

Xerxes witnessed this battle from an eminence, where he sat surrounded by scribes to record the deeds of the day: but these had nothing to write except the ruin of their master's hopes. On the completion of this disaster, Xerxes trembled lest the Greek fleet should sail to the Hellespont, break down his bridge, and cut off his retreat to Asia. Leaving, therefore, three hundred thousand men under Mardonius to continue the war, he hastened his return with the remainder of his surviving troops. These endured terrible hardships during their march; and the king at length, worn out with disappointment and apprehension, left his army, and with a small retinue hurried to the Hellespont. Here he found the bridge destroyed: and he who had passed over with such a host returned in a single skiff.

But the disasters of Persia did not terminate here. Their Carthaginian allies were totally defeated in Sicily, where one hundred and fifty thousand were slain, and nearly as many sold into slavery. Mardonius passed the winter in Thessaly: and, before opening the next campaign, made the most liberal offers to the Athenians, if they would accept the friendship of Persia. He engaged to make good all they had lost in the war, to extend their possessions, to guarantee them their own laws, and make them the most favoured of the tributaries of Persia. Athens was deaf to every overture, and both parties prepared for a renewal of hostilities. Pausanius, King of Sparta, and Aristides of Athens, led the Greek army to meet the Persians. The former had about one hundred and twenty thousand, the latter three hundred and fifty thousand, men. The opposing forces met at Platæa, where the Persians were not only defeated but destroyed. Mardonius fell in the battle. Artabazus, who appears to have anticipated the result, made good his retreat with a body of forty thousand men: besides these it is said that not four thousand of the Persian army survived that fatal day.

On the same day another terrible defeat was inflicted on Persia. The remains of the naval imperial force had assembled near Mycale on the coast of Asia. The Greeks, having ascertained their position, proceeded to attack them. On their approach the Persians drew their vessels ashore, where they had an army of one hundred thousand soldiers, and had formed a strong rampart for their defence. But such terror was inspired by the Greek name, and such were the daring confidence of the one party, and the trembling apprehension of the other, that the Greeks stormed the rampart, defeated the army, and utterly destroyed the fleet.

Xerxes, who had halted at Sardis to learn the success of his generals, was no sooner told of these accumulated calamities, than he fled from Sardis, with as much haste as he had from Athens after the battle of Salamis, giving orders for the destruction of all the Greek temples in Asia Minor.

The remainder of this reign was distinguished by nothing but what covered the monarch with infamy. After plundering the temples of Babylon, while passing through that city, in order to replenish his exhausted exchequer, and thereby verifying the prophecies of Isaiah and Jeremiah, (Isaiah xlvi, 1; Jer. l, 2,) he returned to his court at Susa.

Here he sought to seduce the wife of his brother Masistes. Finding her inflexible, he hoped to conciliate her by marrying her daughter to his son; but this had no influence on the virtuous matron. The licentious king then turned his desires toward the daughter, now the wife of his own son; and her he succeeded in debauching. In consequence of this wickedness Artaynta, the daughter, became possessed of a rich mantle, which Hamestris, the wife of Xerxes, had wrought for him. This she displayed in public, so that the fact became known to the queen.

Enraged at the circumstance, and attributing all the blame to the innocent mother, Hamestris waited until the king's birthday came, when the kings of Persia were accustomed to grant the most extravagant favours to their friends; and then the queen asked her husband that the wife of Masistes should be given into her power. Xerxes, suspecting the object, and knowing the innocence of the woman, for a while refused, until, conquered by her importunity, he complied. He then immediately sent for his brother, and asked him to divorce his wife, and offered him one of his own daughters instead. Masistes respectfully declined the honour, and urged that his wife was the mother of his children, and was in every way agreeable to him. Xerxes in a rage threatened, and his brother left him.

While this conference was proceeding, the queen was working out her horrible revenge. She had given the wife of Masistes to the royal guards, and made them cut off her breasts, her nose, her ears, her lips, and her tongue; and, thus horribly mutilated, she sent her to her house. Masistes on his return found her in this condition. He immediately collected his family, and fled toward Bactria, of which he was governor, intending to rouse that warlike people to revenge his wrongs. But Xerxes, penetrating his design, sent a body of troops after him, by whom the injured prince, every member of his family, and all his followers, were put to death.

This tragedy was soon followed by another, involving the fate of its guilty author. Xerxes was soon afterward assassinated by Artabanus, the captain of his guards; and his eldest son shared the same fate. A few inscriptions belonging to this reign have been preserved and translated. They have chiefly a religious bearing, and cast no new light on the history. (See *Appendix*, note 48.)

After the death of Xerxes and his eldest son, the regicide conferred the crown on ARTAXERXES, the third son of Xerxes, hoping to reign in the name of the young prince. But the new king seized the first opportunity of revenging the death of his father and brother, by the execution of the assassin with his confederates.

Artaxerxes, although raised to the throne, and delivered from the faction of Artabanus, was far from secure in the possession of power. His elder brother Hystaspes was governor of Bactria; and he not only possessed a valid title to the throne, but was supported in his claims by the martial province over which he ruled. Artaxerxes, therefore, raised an army, and led them to Bactria, where a battle was fought between the two claimants for the crown, without any decisive result. Both parties retired, to prepare for a second encounter. But Artaxerxes having the resources of the empire at his command, while Hystaspes was shut up in a single kingdom, the former in the ensuing campaign obtained a complete victory, and the undisputed possession of the throne.

Having thus obtained his object, and his whole dominions being in a peaceful condition, the king returned to Susa, where he appointed a series of feastings and rejoicings to extend over a period of one hundred and eighty days. It was during this season of revelry that the events recorded in the Book of Esther took place; the fair Jewess of that name being then raised to the dignity of queen of the empire, as the wife of Artaxerxes. As the Scriptural account is so well known, it will not be necessary here to give even an outline of that narrative. It will, however, be desirable to refer to some of the results of this marriage.

This queen has been justly spoken of as "one of the very few that resist the allurements of splendour, that cherish kindness for their poor relatives, and remember with gratitude the guardians of their youth." When, therefore, we read of the appointment of Ezra, and afterward of Nehemiah, to go to Jerusalem, invested with plenary powers under the royal authority to restore the city, and reconstruct the Hebrew commonwealth, we see clearly the results of the queen's influence. And when the difficulties which these devoted men had to encounter are taken into account, it may be fairly presumed that nothing short of the favour with which they were supported by the imperial court could have enabled them to succeed in their pious and patriotic objects. To the appointment of these officers, under God, we have to attribute the second series of Hebrew national history: and their being called to high stations appears with equal clearness to be attributable to the elevation of Esther. So wonderful are the evolutions of Divine Providence!

In the early part of this reign the Egyptians revolted under Inaros, as already related; but this effort totally failed. At length Artaxerxes, wearied of war, commanded his officers to make peace with Athens on the best terms that they could obtain: and although these were sufficiently humiliating to the pride of Persia, the treaty was completed. By this compact it was agreed, 1. That all the Greek cities of Asia should be made free, and allowed to live under their own laws. 2. That no Persian ships should enter the Ægean Sea. 3. That no Persian army should approach within three days' march of these waters. 4. That the Athenians should commit no hostilities within the territories of the king of Persia. These articles being sworn to, peace was proclaimed.

The cruel death of Inaros, after an imprisonment of five years,—the revolt of Megabyzus, and his restoration to favour,—and the efforts made by Lacedæmon to enlist the Persians on their side when the war broke out between Sparta and Athens,—occurred in the latter part of this reign; but do not require to be mentioned at length.

Artaxerxes died in the forty-first year of his reign. Besides the substantial aid he afforded to the Hebrews, the peace with Greece was the great political event of this period—a measure which, undoubtedly desirable as it was for Persia, clearly indicated the decline of that empire, and foreboded the rapid downfal which immediately succeeded.

XERXES II., the only legitimate son of Artaxerxes, succeeded his father. He had, however, to contend against the wild disorder of seventeen sons, whom his father had by his concubines,—a post of danger for which his dissolute habits rendered him peculiarly unsuited. After a reign of forty-five days, having retired to rest drunk, he was murdered in his sleep by SOGDIANUS, one of his illegitimate brothers, who at once succeeded to power.

Sogdianus was, however, scarcely seated on the throne, before he evinced a very cruel disposition, commencing with the death of Bagorazus, a most respectable eunuch, and one of the confidential servants of Artaxerxes. This conduct so disgusted the nobility, that when his brother Ochus returned with an army from Hyrcania, of which he was governor, Sogdianus found himself completely deserted. OCHUS was in consequence raised to the throne, and Sogdianus put to death.

On assuming the government of the empire, Ochus took the name of Darius, to which historians generally have attached the term *Nothus*, or "Bastard," on account of his illegitimate birth. Arsites, a brother of Darius, perceiving the facility with which Sogdianus had displaced Xerxes, and Darius had supplanted Sogdianus, thought that he might serve Darius in the same manner. Having, therefore, obtained the counsel and support of Artyphius, the son of Megabyzus, he broke into open rebellion. As the usurping prince and his prime supporter appeared in arms in different parts, Darius marched against his brother, while Artasyras, one of his generals, proceeded against Artyphius. By the aid of his Greek mercenaries, Artyphius twice defeated the imperial troops: but, these being at length bought over by large gifts to the royal cause, he was reduced to such a desperate condition as to be compelled to surrender himself, and rely on the mercy of Darius. The king was disposed to order his immediate execution; but he was restrained by his wife Parysatis, a daughter of Artaxerxes by another mother, and a very clever and crafty woman. By her advice the king generally suffered himself to be guided. Under this influence, Artyphius was treated with clemency, while Darius proceeded with great energy against Arsites. This prince, seeing himself deprived of the principal support on which he had relied, and that his general, although a stranger, had been kindly treated on his submission, resolved to lay down his arms, and surrender to his brother, not doubting but that he should in a higher degree partake the royal clemency. The king, indeed, felt disposed to save his brother; but the same influence which had dictated a clement policy toward the general, now insisted on the destruction of both. At the instance of the queen, therefore, Arsites and Artyphius were put to death.

Throughout the remainder of this reign, the court, and in fact the whole empire, were involved in plots and counter-plots, murders, insurrections, and intestine wars. The principal direction of public affairs had been left in the hands of three eunuchs, who were influenced more by selfish and factious motives than by a desire to promote the public good. Not a few of these troubles were owing to the restless disposition of Cyrus, the king's youngest son, who had been appointed governor of Syria, and had used the influence of his position to foment war in Greece: besides which, he had put to death two noble Persians, nephews of the king his father, for no other reason than because they did not offer him the salutation usually given to royalty. This conduct displeased Darius, who required his attendance at court, and was disposed to remove him from his government. On the other hand, the queen laboured to induce the king to make him his heir. This, however, Darius positively refused to do: so the interview which took place between them issued in the confirmation of Cyrus in the government of Syria.

Soon after this interview Darius died, and was succeeded by his son ARTAXERXES, commonly surnamed MNEMON. The new king, according to the custom of the Persian monarchs, proceeded to Pasargada to be inaugurated by the priests of Bellona. He was there informed by one of the priests, that his brother Cyrus had formed a conspiracy against him, with a design to murder him in the very temple. Having received this information, the king commanded Cyrus to be seized, and sentenced to death. But even then Parysatis, his mother, had sufficient influence with the king to have this sentence reversed, and to get Cyrus sent back to his government in Syria.

Having reached his seat of government, and being enraged at the defeat of all his plans, and especially that he had been sentenced to death, Cyrus resolved to attempt the ruin of the king his brother, and the attainment of his crown. Finding it impossible to make the necessary preparations for such a great enterprise while his province was in perfect peace, he seduced the cities which had been placed under the government of Tissaphernes, so that they revolted from him, and submitted to Cyrus. This led to a war between the two governors; which being rather agreeable to the king than otherwise, he allowed them to raise what forces they pleased. Cyrus fully availed himself of this advantage; and having made great sacrifices and exertions, he soon found himself at the head of an army of thirteen thousand Greeks, and one hundred thousand regular troops of other nations.

With this armament Cyrus left Sardis, giving out the report that he was directing his arms against the Pisidians. But Tissaphernes, rightly judging that the preparations were on too large a scale for such an object, set out with all possible speed to give the king a true account of the doings of Cyrus; which information enabled the king to collect a great army, and march out to meet his rebellious brother. The battle took place at Cunaxa in the province of Babylon, where Cyrus, after having furiously assailed and twice wounded the king, was slain, and his forces in consequence were totally repulsed and dispersed.

After this battle, efforts were made by the royal forces to cut off the Greeks who had fought on the side of Cyrus; and their principal officers were treacherously destroyed. But, electing others in their stead, they beat off their assailants, and then commenced, and successfully accomplished, that masterly retreat of which Xenophon has given an eloquent and inimitable account in his Anabasis.

At this period of the history, the mind sickens, and turns away in intense disgust, at the recital of the treacheries, murders, and horrible atrocities perpetrated by means of the royal females of the Persian court. These seem generally to be presented to the mind by the history of the age as the *Furies* of the country, waiting on every change of the royal family, or when any new aspect of political relations appeared, to interpose with vengeance and blood. During this reign, one officer after another was delivered to the implacable Parysatis, for having claimed the honour of killing Cyrus; and these, instead of being rewarded, were put to death with unheard-of torments.

Even Statira, the beautiful and beloved wife of the king, after having put Udiastes to a horrible death, was herself poisoned by Parysatis, who, pretending to be reconciled to her, had invited her to supper, and divided between them a delicate bird, with a knife which had been poisoned on one side only; so that, while she ate one half with impunity, her victim died in convulsions in a few hours. Such atrocities prepare the mind for the ruin of the country in which they take place. In fact, when such crimes become common, as they were in Persia at this period, they afford indubitable evidence that the country is already ruined.

While the court was thus the scene of malice and bloodshed, the provinces were convulsed with anarchy and misgovernment. Agesilaus, King of Sparta, having formed an alliance with the Asiatic Greeks, prosecuted a series of rapid conquests in Western Asia; and if he had not been recalled, in consequence of the lavish distribution of Persian gold in Greece, would in all probability have dismembered the Persian empire, if he had not altogether anticipated the work of Alexander.

The latter years of the reign of Artaxerxes Mnemon were peculiarly unfortunate. He had no sooner got rid of Agesilaus and the Spartan Greeks, than he was harassed with an insurrection in Egypt, which, notwithstanding the great efforts he made for the purpose, he could not put down, owing to a disagreement between the Persian general and his Athenian auxiliaries. Then Cyprus regained its independence. Worse than all, domestic troubles of the most afflicting character pressed on the mind of the king. Darius, who had been declared his heir, conspired against the life of his father, and drew *fifty* of his brothers into the treason: (the king had one hundred and fifteen children by his several concubines:) but the sovereign was apprized of his danger, the conspirators were seized, and all, including the fifty-one sons of the king, were put to death.

This melancholy event raised a new question as to the succession to the throne. For this dignity there were three candidates,—Ariaspes and Ochus, sons of the king and queen, and Arsames, the son of the king by a concubine, but greatly beloved by his father on account of his princely virtues. Ochus succeeded in terrifying his elder brother, who was of a weak and yielding temper, to such an extent that he poisoned himself: shortly after which, the prince procured the assassination of Arsames. These calamities were too much for the aged monarch, who died under the pressure of his domestic troubles.

Ochus succeeded his father; and on his accession assumed the name of Artaxerxes III. No sooner did the intelligence of the death of the king reach Western Asia, than there was a general revolt. This would have been fatal to the empire, had not the leaders of the insurrection soon quarrelled among themselves, and so neutralized all their efforts. The danger, however, was sufficient to alarm the new king, and to excite his cruel disposition. Determined that no revolted province should have any of the blood-royal to set up against him, and that none of his relatives should conspire against his authority, he adopted the horrid expedient of putting them all to death. The Princess Ocha, his own sister and mother-in-law,—for he had married her daughter,—he caused to be buried alive. He shut up one of his uncles, and one hundred of his sons and grandsons, in a court of the palace; and then caused them to be shot at by archers, until they were all slain.

But even these wholesale murders did not suffice to keep his subjects in awe: Artabazus, the satrap of Asia Minor, rebelled, and, having procured the assistance of an Athenian army, obtained several victories over the royal troops. The king, however, by large presents succeeded in inducing the Athenians to withdraw their forces from the contest. Artabazus then procured aid from the Thebans, and by their help was again successful; but again the influence of Persian gold induced these auxiliaries to return home. Thus left to his own resources, Artabazus was vanquished, and forced to take refuge at the court of Philip of Macedon. The king, flushed with this success, marched against the leaders of an insurrection which had been promoted by Phenicia, Egypt, and Cyprus. He first proceeded to Sidon, which city was treacherously thrown open to him, and instantly destroyed. This severity so terrified the other cities of Phenicia, that they submitted to the Persian king, who forthwith proceeded toward Egypt, which was completely subdued, and treated by the conqueror with the greatest tyranny and cruelty. Cyprus was also recovered, and made a Persian province; after which the king rewarded Mentor, his able military commander, according to his merits, and gave himself up to ease and dissipation.

This conduct afforded his confidential eunuch Bagoas opportunity to effect a purpose which he appears to have formed in consequence of the king's impious attacks on the religion of Egypt. Bagoas was a native of that country; and, when he saw the sacred Apis slain, dressed, and served up for a feast, might well burn with intense indignation. Whatever might be the cause, it is certain that Bagoas poisoned his master; and it is said that, burying another body instead, he actually gave the flesh of the king for food to animals. Having despatched the king, the guilty eunuch raised his youngest son ARSES to the throne, and put all the others to death, that he might thus retain the power of governing in his own hand. (See *Appendix*, note 49.)

Arses did not long retain even a nominal sovereignty: Bagoas, finding him less tractable than he expected, put him to death also; and, not yet daring to assume the sovereignty himself, placed DARIUS surnamed CODOMANNUS on the throne. This person, although of the blood-royal, was not the son of a king, but a junior member of the family, who escaped in an unaccountable manner when Artaxerxes III. destroyed the members of the royal house. In the war which that king waged with the Cadusians, one of those barbarians challenged the whole Persian army to find a man to fight him in single combat. When no one else offered, Codomannus accepted the challenge, and slew the Cadusian. For this noble act he was rewarded with the government of Armenia, from whence he was called by Bagoas to accept the imperial crown.

Darius Codomannus, on entering upon the government of the empire, evinced even less disposition than his predecessor to be the servile creature of Bagoas, and was consequently doomed by that unscrupulous murderer to the same fate. The king, however, penetrated his design; and when the deadly potion was presented to him, he compelled Bagoas to drink it himself,—thus disposing of the traitor by his own means. Having accomplished this, he acquired possession of imperial power without further danger. The throne of Persia, however, at this time was of little worth. Alexander of Macedon ascended the throne the same year with Darius, and found ready to his hand all the preparations which Philip had made for the invasion of Persia. By the time, therefore, that Darius had fairly entered upon the government of his great empire, the ambitious Greek was marshalling his host for its invasion.

Darius appears to have done all that the disorganized and effeminate state of his dominions rendered possible: but to resist, with the means at his command, the genius and energy of Alexander, and the armour, discipline, and overwhelming power of the Macedonian phalanx, was impossible. In the second year of the reign of these kings, the battle of the Granicus was fought, and won by Alexander; and from that day everything pertaining to Persia really belongs to the history of Greece, which actually passed under the government of Alexander, as soon as the immense range of territory permitted him to take possession of it.

Thus perished the Persian, or Medo-Persian empire, which arose into power by the military genius and indomitable energy of Cyrus, like a meteor among the nations of the East,—obtained an extent of territory and a consolidation of political and military power beyond any nation that had previously existed,—and, having fulfilled its destiny in the accomplishment of sacred prophecy, (see *Appendix*, note 50,) and especially in the restoration of the captive Hebrews to the land of their fathers, at length rapidly declined in all the elements of national strength, as it increased in disorganization, impiety, and crime.

As a chapter in the history of the world, the annals of this empire present to our view the introduction of that system of policy by which one nation aggregated others into social, political, and military union with itself. Assyria stalked through the earth as a martial giant, robbing and crushing all by its immense power. Persia first expanded the grand idea of making an empire consist of united nations, just as a nation consists of associated districts. In the accomplishment of this result, the talents and energy of Darius were scarcely second to the genius of Cyrus. But how short-lived is the power of any people, unless continuously sustained by the influence of intelligence, morals, and religion!

CHRONOLOGICAL TABLE OF PERSIAN HISTORY.

B.C.	Names and Events.	Years Reigned.
	Persia, a province of the Assyrian empire. Kawah restores its independence, and raises Feridoon to the throne.	
	FERIDOON.	
	MANUCHEHER.	
	NOUZER.	
	ZOO.	
	KERSHASP.	
	(The chronology of these reigns is unknown.)	
	Persia in subjection to Media.	
560	Cyrus reigns in Persia. Subdues Media, B. C. 551; and Babylon, B. C. 536. By these and other conquests Cyrus establishes the Medo-Persian empire.	
529	Cambyses	8
	Conquers Egypt.	
	Smerdis the Magian reigned 7 months.	
521	Darius Hystaspis	36
	Promotes building of Jerusalem.	
485	Xerxes	21
	Invades Greece.	
464	Artaxerxes	41
423	Darius Nothus	19
404	Artaxerxes Mnemon	46
	Cyrus, the king's brother, rebels, aided by the Ten Thousand Greeks.	
358	Ochus, or Artaxerxes III	21
337	Arses is placed on the throne by the eunuch Bagoas, and after two years is put to death.	
335	Darius Codomannus.	
	Persia invaded by the Macedonian, and, after a short struggle, is subdued by Alexander.	

CHAPTER VIII.

THE RELIGION OF THE PERSIANS.

IMPORTANCE and Difficulties of the Subject—Great Aid supplied by ancient Inscriptions—The Religion of Persia identical in its original Elements with that of Assyria and Babylon—Opinion of Jacob Bryant on the first Zoroaster—Its probable Import—The Magi—General Elements of the Persian Faith—Deity of the King—Palace-Temples—Paradises—Sacred Tree—Cherubic Figures—Divine Triad—Persian Peculiarities in this Symbol—The supreme Deity in Persia represented with the Head of a Bird—The Religious System of Zoroaster—The first Triad: Cronus, Ormuzd, Ahriman—This changed to Ormuzd, Mithras, Ahriman—Their respective Character and Position—The Antagonism and Creations of Ormuzd and Ahriman—The Worship of Fire, its probable Origin—The System of Zoroaster professed to rest on Divine Revelation—The Creation of Angels, the World, and Mankind—General Accordance with Holy Scripture—The Fall of Man—The Prevalence of Evil—The Flood—Continuance of Depravity—Mission of Zoroaster—The Spiritual Nature of Man—Future Judgment—Resurrection—Doctrine of universal Restoration—Wicked Men, and even Ahriman, raised to Heaven—The Priesthood—Their Three Orders: Herboods, Mobeds, and the Dustoor—Altars and Temples—Perpetual Fire—Public Worship—Sacred Rites—Holy Water—Morals—Sound Principles mingled with much that is puerile and superstitious—The Faith of Persia formed a perfect Type of Papal Superstition—Observations on the Manner in which this Inquiry has been conducted—Folly of forming an Opinion on this Subject under the Influence of Grecian Mythology—Necessity of recognising the Founders of the Nation as Members of the great patriarchal Family—General View of the System.

THE authors of the "Universal History," in the beginning of a very unsatisfactory chapter under a title similar to that which stands at the head of this, say, "There is hardly any subject which hath employed the pens of authors, ancient or modern, that deserves to be treated with greater accuracy, or to be read with more attention, than this which we are now about to discuss." In these sentiments we cordially concur; and may add, that there is hardly any subject which presents a wider or more formidable range of difficulties than those with which the religion of Persia is encompassed.

It may be freely acknowledged that this has not been a neglected topic. On the contrary, scarcely anything connected with the condition of the ancient world has excited more attention, or provoked more violent controversy. The collision of opinion thus educed constitutes, in fact, one of the greatest difficulties which embarrass a dispassionate inquiry into the religion of ancient Persia. The reader will scarcely require to be informed, that every investigation of this subject must begin with the person and doctrines of Zoroaster, (see *Appendix*, note 51,) and that the results of the inquiry will mainly depend on the conclusions arrived at respecting the character and teaching of this sage.

All that labour and learning can do has been done, to collect and explain the passages bearing on this subject, which are found scattered through the pages of ancient authors. But, unfortunately, all these come to us through the agency of aliens or enemies. No native Persian, of the most brilliant period of her history, has left us a page respecting the religion of his country. Strangers, inquiring after the manners and customs of an ancient people,—hostile scribes, employed by those who had conquered the kingdom,—or the *literati* of other lands, picking up, at second-hand at best, what they could collect on this subject,—are the chief sources whence European scholars have had to draw their information respecting the faith of ancient Persia. It will readily occur to the reader, that, when placed in such circumstances, foreign authors do not afford us the best *data* from which to elicit sound information respecting a system of religious doctrines. Too much reliance must not, therefore, be placed on deductions from such sources.

In one respect we approach this inquiry furnished with important aids to which the authors of preceding times were strangers. The historical information supplied by all the remaining literary fragments of antiquity can only lead to probable conjecture on many important points. We have, however, in our hands the recovered sculptures of the east; and, by the light they afford, can not only form sound opinions respecting the meaning of these fragments, but actually enlarge the information which they communicate, and even correct their statements, when partial or mistaken.

In the first place, then, it is an undoubted fact, that the religion of Persia was reared on precisely the same foundation as that of Assyria. That the palace-temples were built on the same general plan in both countries is unquestionable, and has been proved beyond the possibility of a doubt by Mr. Fergusson in his very valuable work. (See Palaces of Nineveh and Persepolis, *passim.*) And this is not a mere isolated circumstance, remotely connected with the subject, as might at first appear to us under the influence of our European habits and ideas: it stands in immediate relation to the ruling element of this great religious system. It involves the character of the whole structure of the religious fabric. As was shown in the case of Assyria,—the peculiar compound of divine and regal dignity sustained by the king was really the centre of the whole system of faith. He was emphatically, by divine right, the religious, as well as the political, head of the people. His person was sacred: his official residence united the characters of palace and temple. In fact, we have in this single circumstance a common principle which substantially identifies the great scheme of Persian religion with that of the more ancient kingdoms of Assyria and Babylon.

Lest, however, it should be supposed that I build too much on a single circumstance, I will satisfy the reader by quoting a passage from Dr. Layard, which will be found conclusive. "Although," observes that indefatigable explorer, "we may not at present possess sufficient materials to illustrate the most ancient Sabæanism of the Assyrians, we may, I think, pretty confidently judge of the nature of the worship of a later period. The symbols and religious ceremonies represented at Khorsabad and Kouyunjik, and on the cylinders, are identical with those of the ancient monuments of Persia: at the same time, the sculptures of Persepolis, in their mythic character, resemble in every respect those of the Assyrians. We have the same types and groups to embody ideas of the divinity, and to convey sacred subjects. When the close connexion, in early ages, between religion and art is borne in mind, it will be at once conceded, that a nation like the Persian would not borrow mere forms without attaching to them their original signification. The connexion, as exhibited by art, between Assyria and Persia, is sufficient, I think, to prove the origin of the symbols and myths of the Persians."— *Nineveh and its Remains*, vol. ii, p. 441, and note.

There appears, therefore, sufficient reason for believing that Persia adopted the religious system and symbols of the Assyrian empire, as the foundation of her faith and ceremonial rites. This will afford us better means for fully apprehending the general scope and particular elements of this economy, than we should otherwise possess.

It may also be fairly questioned whether this is not what we are to understand by "the first Zoroaster." The learned Jacob Bryant says: "Of men called Zoroaster, the first was a deified personage, reverenced by some of his posterity, whose worship was styled *Magia*, and the professors of it *Magi;* and the institutors of those rites which related to Zoroaster. From them this worship was imparted to the Persians, who likewise had their Magi. And when the Babylonians sunk into a more complicated idolatry, the Persians, who succeeded to the sovereignty of Asia, renewed under their princes, and particularly under Darius, the son of Hystaspes, these rites, which had been, in a great degree, effaced and forgotten. That king was devoted to the religion of the *Magia*, and looked upon it as one of his most honourable titles to be called a professor of those doctrines. By ZOROASTER was denoted both the deity, and also his priest. It was a name conferred upon many personages."—*Analysis of Ancient Mythology*, vol. ii, p. 389. See note.

It seems therefore to be very probable, that the antiquity and Chaldæan origin of what is called "the first Zoroaster," is nothing more than an oriental mode of covering the foreign origination of the religion of Persia; just as the period of Assyrian domination was represented under the figure of the reign of the tyrant Zohauk for a thousand years. Hence Layard says: "The identity of the Assyrian and Persian systems appears also to be pointed out by the uncertainty which exists as to the birthplace and epoch of Zoroaster. According to the best authorities he was a Chaldæan, who introduced his doctrines into Persia and Central Asia. The Persians themselves may be supposed to have recognised the Assyrian source of their religion, when they declared Perseus, the founder of their race, to have been an Assyrian."—*Nineveh and its Remains*, vol. ii, p. 443. While, therefore, all exact information respecting the person spoken of as "the first Zoroaster," and the origin of this faith, is lost in the obscurity of remote antiquity, there can still be little doubt that it emanated from Assyria, and from thence passed into Persia.

Another circumstance is worthy of notice, as casting some light on the nature and progress of this religion. The priests were called Magi; and, according to Herodotus, during the most flourishing period of the Medo-Persian empire they were regarded as the only ministers of the national religion. (Clio, cap. cxxxii.) But they constituted one of the six tribes of the nation of Medes. (Clio, cap. ci.) It seems that, even after they were regarded as sustaining this sacred character, they had not altogether lost their sense of national identity and partiality. For it is evident that Cambyses regarded the reign of the Magian Smerdis as equivalent to the restoration of the sovereignty of the empire from Persia to Media; and hence we find the son of Cyrus, in his last illness, entreating the Persian nobles in his army to resist the usurpation of the Magi, and not to "permit the empire to revert to the Medes." (Thalia, cap. lv.) The government of the Magi, then, was regarded as a Median government,—a fact which is further proved by the wholesale slaughter of these priests after the death of Smerdis; of which it is said, that if night had not interposed its darkness just at the time when it did, the Magi would have been all destroyed. (Thalia, cap. lxxix.) But we have no means of ascertaining the manner in which this Median tribe obtained their sacerdotal character and ascendency; nor have we any information as to the way in which, or the period when, the Chaldæan mystic faith was deposited with this race of priests.

It will now be necessary to notice some of the leading, original, and essential elements of this religion. We will then furnish a general view of it, after it had been reformed and remodelled by Zoroaster.

It has been already observed, that the palace-temples of Persia were precisely similar in their general character to those of Assyria and Babylon; and, as was intimated, this fact shows the general identity of the two systems. This view is confirmed by a reference to all the essential features of this religious scheme. The divine character assumed by the king, under the direction of the Magi, is shown by the decree of Darius, that for a certain time no prayer was to be offered to any god or man, save unto the king only. This was also attested by the rigid religious reverence with which approach to the person of the king was prohibited, so that neither man nor woman was permitted to enter "the inner court" of the palace, unless specially invited to do so, on pain of death. Esther iv, 11. Those who were privileged with admission, were not permitted to smile or spit in the royal presence. (Clio, cap. xcix.)

But we are assured that this respect and reverence issued in actual adoration; that, in fact, the king stood, in the estimation of his subjects, "on the same level with the gods." The real worship of the sovereign was therefore a public duty of universal obligation. "None durst appear before the king without prostrating themselves on the ground; nay, they were all obliged, at what distance soever the king appeared, to pay him that adoration. Nor did they exact it only from their own vassals, but also from foreign ministers and ambassadors; the captain of the guard being charged to inquire of those who asked admission to the king, whether *they were ready to adore him*. If they refused to comply with that ceremony, they were told that the king's ear was open to such only as were willing to pay him that homage; so they were forced to transact the business with which they were charged, by means of the kings servants or eunuchs. (Plutarch, in Vitâ Themistoclis.) Indeed, the Persians gloried in this. Hence we find Artabanus, in his conference with Themistocles, observing, 'Among those many excellent laws of ours, the most excellent is this, *that the king is to be honoured and worshipped religiously*, as the image of that God which conserveth all things.' " —*Ancient Universal History*, vol. iv, p. 77.

In all other respects, the similarity between the ancient religion of Persia and that of Assyria holds good. The palace-temple of this adored sovereign was attached to a paradise with a sacred stream and trees. The compound cherubic figures are found in the sculptures of Persepolis and other ruins of Persia, as they are at Nimbrod, Khorsabad, and Kouyunjik. The sacred tree occurs with all the prominence in Persia that it does in Assyria. The triadic figure of the man, wings, and circle, is found over the head of Darius Hystaspis on the sacred rock at Behistun, as over the head of Sennacherib in his capital. All this indubitably attests the identity of these systems beyond the possibility of mistake.

There are, indeed, peculiarities in some of these cases, which it may be necessary to mention.

The triadic figure, with the circle, wings, and human form, is found nowhere more frequently, or in greater perfection, than in Persia. And this is by Layard, and other respectable authors, frequently called Ormuzd, that being the name usually given to the supreme god by the ancient Persians. I rather incline, however, to the opinion that the human figure in this symbol represented, according to times and circumstances, both Ormuzd and Mithras. The *Zendavesta* recognises as a fundamental principle *Zerwan*,—a term which is understood to denote "time,"—time in its widest range, without beginning and without end. This will be perceived to be identical with the first personality in the Chaldæan triad, which was stated to be Cronos, or "Time." There can be no doubt that in both countries this was a title given to the great father, or the patriarch of the tribe or nation. How far the most ancient triad of Persia represented three hero-gods—Oromasdes, Arimanius, and Mithras—I shall not undertake to decide: but the learned Mosheim has supported this opinion with great skill and erudition. (See *Appendix*, note 52.)

The human figure with the head of a bird, which on the Assyrian sculptures was called Nisroch or Assarac, is here represented as setting forth the great God. The first of the triads of Zoroaster preserved by Eusebius is to this effect: "But god is he that has the head of a hawk. He is the first, indestructible, eternal, unbegotten, indivisible, dissimilar; the dispenser of all good; incorruptible; the best of the good, the wisest of the wise: he is the father of equity and justice, self-taught, physical, and perfect, and wise, and the only inventer of the sacred philosophy." This seems to render it certain that, whatever usage obtained in Assyria, this form was chosen to represent the supreme Deity in Persia.

The *Dabistán* (Shea and Troyer's Trans., vol. i, p. 36) confirms this view. It states: "The image of the regent *Hormuzd* (Jupiter) was of an earthly colour, in the shape of a man with a vulture's face: on his head a crown, on which were the faces of a cock and a dragon; in the right hand a turban, and in the left a crystal ewer." On this passage Mr. Fergusson remarks: "'Pitcher' would be a more correct word than 'ewer,' to judge from the form of the vessel he carries on the sculptures; but from the same authority, we should read 'fir-cone' for 'turban.' Can it be an error of description by some one mistaking one object for the other? The fir-cone is not unlike the Persian lamb-skin or Parsee cap."—*Nineveh and Persepolis,* p. 295.

We see, therefore, that as far as any light has been cast on the præ-Zoroasterian period of the Persian religion, although it bears evident marks of a local and national character, it nevertheless accords in all its essential elements with that which had previously obtained in Babylon and Assyria.

The more important part of our task is, however, to exhibit this religion after its reformation. Our first attempt will be directed to the attainment of some definite idea of its theology.

At first, as I have already intimated, Zoroaster assumed the existence of a primary principle or deity named *Zerwan*, or "Time." From this incomprehensible being, we are told, there arose the two great active powers of the universe—ORMUZD, the principle of all good; and AHRIMAN, the principle of all evil. "And," observes Mr. Fraser, in his judicious outline of this faith, "the question why light and darkness, good and evil, were mingled together by a beneficent and omnipotent Creator, has been as much controverted among the Magian priesthood as by modern metaphysicians."—*History of Persia,* p. 150. These three appear to have formed the primitive Persian triad, and to have been represented by the circular ring, denoting the boundless Eternal as Cronos or Time; Ormuzd, in a human form, in the centre; Ahriman being set forth by a serpent which, encompassing the figure in its folds, passes his head out on one side and his tail on the other.

As it is utterly impossible, at the present day, to separate the actual tenets of the Persian reformer from the elements of the ancient faith previously received, no positive assertion can be advanced on this point,—although I have little doubt that some close approximation to this triad was common, long before Zoroaster. If we may rely on the induction of Mosheim, it would seem that in the early and isolated position of ancient Persia, *Oromasdes, Arimanius,* and *Mithras* formed the national triad of hero-gods. Subsequently, an intercourse with other countries having made more prominent the great eternal God, and the author of all evil, these were introduced, one as the first, and the other as the third, of the triad, which accordingly was exhibited as the combination of a circle, a human figure, and a serpent, under the names of Zerwan, Ormuzd, and Ahriman. Whether the last-mentioned triad was the production of Zoroaster, or otherwise, it was not the last effort of his reforming genius in respect of theology. For we are informed, that when the malignity of Ahriman led him to put forth all his powers to frustrate the benevolent designs of Ormuzd toward mankind, Mithras was brought into being, as a mediator between the Deity and his creatures.

It is not perfectly clear to what extent this new creation affected the divine triad, but it seems very likely that the first cause of all things, or Zerwan, was in this respect lost sight of, and Mithras placed in the centre, as the mediator embodied in human form. This change seems to be indicated in the Zoroastrian Oracle: "The Father perfected all things, and delivered them over to the Second Mind, whom all nations of men call the First:"—a remarkable confession of the fact that, by the multiplication of deities, the great eternal God, although once recognised as the first cause of all things, was ultimately lost sight of, and superseded by other deities. According to Psellus, a Greek commentator on this oracle, it would seem that this was supposed to arise from the ignorance of people generally respecting the plurality of *hypostases* in the Deity. For his gloss upon the oracle just quoted is to this effect: "The first Father of the Trinity, having produced this whole creation, delivered it to Mind, or Intellect: which Mind the whole generation of mankind, being ignorant of the paternal transcendency, commonly call 'the First God.'"

Ormuzd, Mithras, and Ahriman became, therefore, the recognised divine triad of the Magi, the First Great Cause having dropped out of their code. This supposition is fully confirmed by Plutarch, the earliest and ablest writer who has given us any account of this religious system. He observes: "They say that Zoroaster made a threefold distribution of things; and that he assigned the first and highest rank of them to Oromasdes, who in the oracles is called 'the Father;' the lowest to Arimanes; and the middle to Mithras, who in the same oracles is likewise called 'the Second Mind.'"
—*De Iside et Osiride*, p. 370.

Thus did the genius of Zoroaster modify the ancient theology of Persia, and introduce corresponding changes into the national symbols of this triad of divinities. It now becomes necessary that we form some definite conception of these several personalities.

Ormuzd is spoken of as the supreme god, and invoked in this character on all occasions. The term *Ormuzd* signifies "great king;" and he is called "luminous, brilliant." His attributes are perfect purity, intelligence, justice, power, activity, and beneficence. He is, indeed, regarded as a perfect image of the Eternal, "the centre and author of the perfections of all nature, the first creative agent produced by the Self-existent."

Now it has been contended that the Persians believed in and worshipped only the one true God. The authors of the "Universal History" roundly assert this; and Dr. Prideaux joins with them, as a disciple of Hyde, to this extent also; but with this difference,— that while the former omit all mention of Ormuzd, the learned author of the "Connexion" alludes to Ormuzd and Ahriman as "two angels." Happily we can now correct the speculations of these eminent scholars by the words used by the Persians themselves. We have the language dictated by Darius, Xerxes, and Artaxerxes, in our hands. We know their thoughts and sentiments from their words, and of course have the means of ascertaining the objects of their worship. What, then, is the fact? Did the kings and people of ancient Persia worship the eternal God, whom they are supposed to have known, and treat Ormuzd as a created angel? On the contrary, Darius Hystaspis, the contemporary of Ezra and Nehemiah, in his inscription on the sacred rock at Behistun, invokes Ormuzd as the supreme god. "Says Darius the king:—Ormuzd has granted me the empire. Ormuzd has brought help to me, until I have gained this empire. By the grace of Ormuzd, I hold this empire."—*Column I, par.* 9. And on the tomb of Darius at Makhsh-i-Rustam is inscribed: "The great god Ormuzd, (he it was) who gave this earth, who gave that heaven, who gave mankind, who gave life to mankind, who made Darius king, as well the king of the people as the lawgiver of the people." This is decisive as to Ormuzd being regarded not merely as an angel, but as a real divinity.

The following sentence, taken from an inscription of Xerxes, not only confirms this opinion, but proves that while Ormuzd was regarded as a god, he was not worshipped as the only deity revered by the ancient Persians: "The great god Ormuzd, the chief of the gods, (he it is) who has given this world, who has given that heaven, who has given mankind, who has given life to mankind, who has made Xerxes king." Ormuzd was, therefore, regarded as a god, and as the chief of the gods. The pure theism of the Persians, then, under the Achæmenian dynasty, vanishes before the knowledge supplied by the ancient inscriptions.

Mithras, according to this system, was created or produced by Ormuzd, to act as mediator between him and his creatures, and thus to counteract the malevolent designs of Ahriman. The mediatorial character of this deity was so strongly marked, and so universally recognised, that Plutarch affirms that "the Persians, from their god Mithras, called any mediator, or middle betwixt two, *Mithras.*"

It has been conjectured that this introduction of Mithras into the

Persian theology was the great reforming work of Zoroaster in this direction; and that the old triad—whether composed of Time, Ormuzd, and Ahriman, as the great God, with two others proceeding from him; the first, the author of all good; the second, of all evil; or of Oromasdes, Arimanius, and Mithras, as national hero-deities—was by this reforming Magian made to accord with the new views which he promulgated respecting the promised Redeemer and the great spiritual adversary of mankind, and exhibited as Ormuzd, Mithras, and Ahriman. Hence Porphyry refers to this Mithras as the great object of Zoroaster's labour, and at the same time as the creator of the world: "Zoroaster first of all, as Eubulus testifieth, in the mountains adjoining to Persia, consecrated a native orbicular cave, adorned with flowers, and watered with fountains, to the honour of Mithras, the maker and father of all things; this cave being an image or symbol to him of the whole world, which was made by Mithras."—*Porphyrius, De Antro Nymph.*, p. 254.

We can scarcely doubt from this description that the cave of Zoroaster was so devised as to represent not only the creation of the world, but also the garden, the primitive residence of man. But, however this may be, it is certain that this last-described form of the theologic triad in Persia assumed precisely the same position as that of Assyria occupied in the national estimation. Indeed, the professed identity of person between the king and the second person of this triad is rather more strongly marked than was the case in the older country. For not only did the Persian monarchs make a more open and absolute claim to divinity than the Assyrian kings: they also made their identity with the second person, or human form, in the sacred triad, more fully apparent. It will be remembered that in Assyria the human figure in the triad was always represented in precisely the same attitude as the king. On the monuments of Persia this resemblance is carried much further. The human figure which arises from the winged circle is here "the very miniature of the monarch below;" (Landseer's Sabæan Researches, p. 268;) so that, in the language of sculpture, this fact seems to say, "He who now walks the earth and reigns below, is *identical with* the second divine personality which shines in the sacred triad above."

Ahriman, the third personality in this triad, and the personification of the evil one, must be next noticed. He is described as essentially wicked: but it seems doubtful whether he was originally so. In one place he is represented "as a power originally good, but who, like Lucifer, fell from that high estate through rebellion and disobedience. Ormuzd gives the following metaphorical picture of his rival:—He is alone,—wicked, impure, accursed. He has long knees, a long tongue, and is void of good. He is called a king, however, and said to be without end."—*Fraser's History of Persia*, p. 152.

"M. du Perron concludes, that Zoroaster meant to assign priority of existence to Ahriman; and that, full of his own perfections, and blinded as to the extent of his power, when he beheld in Ormuzd a being of equal might, jealousy rendered him furious, and he rushed into evil, seeking the destruction of everything calculated to exalt his rival's glory. The Great Ruler of events, displeased at his arrogance, condemned him to inhabit that portion of space unillumined by light. Ormuzd, as he sprang into existence, saw his malicious adversary, and made vain efforts to annihilate him. The Eternal bestowed on him the power of calling into being a pure world; while, as if the impulses of good and evil were simultaneous, Ahriman immediately opposed to it a world of impurity."—*Fraser's History of Persia*, p. 151.

It is, however, important to observe that this malignant being was worshipped in the best days of Persia as truly divine. Hesychius, following the usual practice of the Greeks in giving their own names to foreign deities of a similar character, says, "Arimanius among the Persians is Hades," or Pluto. And Plutarch observes that, on the arrival of Themistocles at the Persian court, Xerxes "prayed to *Arimanius*, that his enemies might ever be so infatuated as to drive from among them their ablest men; that he offered sacrifices to the gods,"—and undoubtedly to the god to whom he had prayed, as the most prominent of them.

Besides this triad of deities, the Persians are said to have adored the sun and fire, as real gods; while, on the other hand, it is contended that neither of these was regarded as truly divine, but both as the tabernacles of the Deity, or as the fairest and best exhibitions of his character. However this may have been, the ever-burning fire was kept flaming on the Persian altars. There were certain places consecrated to this purpose, which were called by the Greek writers *Pyrœtheia*. Each of these contained an altar enclosed with gratings, within which none but the Magi, who had the charge of these fires, were permitted to enter. Thither these went every day, with a bundle of rods in their hands, when they remained an hour in adoration, and in supplying the everlasting fire. This element of the Persian religion is one of great importance, and deserves attentive consideration. Its origin is described by Firdusi in a strain of romantic poetry: but little real light has been cast by ancient writers, or oriental authors generally, on this recondite subject.

It has for a long time been fashionable to describe the adoration of the heavenly bodies as the primitive worship of mankind, on account of their glorious appearance; and the worship of fire, as the next step in the progress of idolatry, fire being the most natural and active representative of the solar orb. But all this is unsupported by the slightest historical evidence. The account given by Maimonides, (Patriarchal Age, p. 235,) and by Sanchoniatho, (Cory's Fragments, p. 7,) referring as they do to antediluvian times, cannot be said to bear on this subject. Looking, then, to the fire-worship of Persia, it appears that nothing like ancient evidence of the manner or period of the introduction of this idolatry is attainable. We are therefore left to a reasonable induction from admitted facts.

It has been already intimated, that the general opinion of authors on this subject has been given in favour of the origin of this practice in the way of scientific or philosophical reasoning: as if in primitive times mankind were found without any idea of God, and were thus led to the most likely natural objects for exhibiting to their minds the divine character and attributes. I am compelled fully and frankly to declare that I altogether dissent from this opinion. I do not believe that mankind in the early ages of the world were ever found in this state, or ever formed their theological notions on such grounds. On the contrary, the whole scope of our researches into the history and religion of the eastern nations establishes the judgment, that the details of the ancient idolatry, beyond the grand system of apostasy devised at Shinar, did not arise from philosophical reasoning, but from a corruption of primitive tradition.

Nor does there appear to be any reasonable doubt that the worship of fire was introduced in this manner. It is a known fact, that the first manifestation of God to the fallen pair was connected with an *infolding fire;* and that this was continued in some manner throughout patriarchal times. It seems to follow as a natural result, that when the minds of men were perverted to idolatrous practices, fire, which had from the beginning stood so intimately connected with the manifestations of God and his worship, should itself be held sacred, and become an object of adoration. (See *Appendix*, note 53.)

This exposition accounts for the conflicting opinions which have been expressed respecting the nature of the reverence entertained for the sacred fire; some asserting, with the authors of the "Universal History," that the "fire before which the Persians worship,—taking that word in an extended sense,—they acknowledge nothing of divinity therein; but, esteeming it a symbol of the Deity, they prostrate themselves before it, and then, standing up, they pray to

God;" (Ancient Universal History, vol. iv, p. 86;) while others allege that "fire held a distinguished rank among the Persian gods. The fire was, therefore, in that country, the holiest of all things. It was always carried about with their kings, wherever they went; they addressed their prayers chiefly to it; and even when they attended the service of any other god, they first offered up a prayer to the fire."—*Christmas's Universal Mythology*, p. 136. Both these opinions may be perfectly correct, if taken to apply to different times and circumstances.

Among the primitive patriarchs there might have been a reverential remembrance of *the infolding fire* cherished for a long time; and the Persian faith, as reformed by Zoroaster, might in this particular, as it was unquestionably in many others, have been made to approach so nearly to that of the Hebrews, as to have a perpetual fire maintained on the altar, which was to be always used for sacred purposes, but not as in any measure in itself divine: while it is equally possible, and even probable, that, under the operation of this institution, the sacred fire might in process of time become an object of profane adoration.

Having said thus much on the theology of this system, it will be necessary to proceed to detail other elements of this religion.

It may, then, be observed, in the next place, that this system, as reformed by Zoroaster, professed to be sanctioned by divine revelation. The stated object of this sage was "to revive the original purity of the law, to perfect its doctrines, and to enforce its observances:"—a scheme as grand in its design, and as clearly defined in its means, as was ever propounded by mortal man. To crown the whole, the Persian reformer declared that he had not only diligently collected and arranged the fundamental parts of the pure primitive creed, separating these from all the errors which had been introduced, but that he had also received from Ormuzd new revelations, which greatly added to the sacred code, and improved the institutions of religious worship: so that the religion of Zoroaster professed to rest on the basis of the clear and explicit teaching of divine revelation.

As we have already intimated, this system distinctly taught, as a first principle, "that God existed from all eternity, and was like infinity of time and space;" but that, besides this supreme Deity, there were two great principles essentially opposed to each other, as light and darkness, good and evil, Ormuzd and Ahriman. Of these we have already spoken: but it is important to add that the agent employed by the Almighty in the production of these opposite principles is his Word,—a sacred and mysterious being frequently mentioned in the *Avesta*, under the appellations of *Honover* and *Iam*. This being is said to possess "ineffable light, perfect activity, and unerring prescience;" and is the agent by whom every creative act of the Eternal is performed.

The first act of antagonism between the principles of light and darkness which this system reveals, was the creation by Ormuzd of the universe and its celestial inhabitants. These were the *Ferohers*, or the spiritual prototypes,—the "unembodied angels,"—of every reasonable being destined to live upon earth.

Ahriman, alarmed and enraged at these productions of his rival, flew with malign intent toward the light; but a single intimation from the WORD, or IAM, sent him howling back into darkness, where he immediately called into being a host of deeves and evil spirits, which were designed to oppose the works of Ormuzd.

According to this scheme of faith, at that period a proposal was made to Ahriman of peace and amity, accompanied by an exhortation to return to the paths of virtue. This, however, he rejected with scorn and defiance. Ormuzd then created six superior guardian angels: Bahman, to whose charge was intrusted the animal creation; Ardibehesht, the genius of fire and light, the guardian of all fires; Shahriwar, the spirit of the metal and the mine; Espendermad, the female guardian of the earth; Kourdad, who presides over running streams; and Amerdad, who watches over the growth of plants and trees. (Dabistán, vol. i, pp. 241–243.) Immediately when these six angels arose into being to further the holy designs of Ormuzd, six deeves were produced from the darkness by the voice of Ahriman, to promote his malignant purposes. In those contests a fabulous period of time is said to have elapsed, at the end of which "Ormuzd called into being the heavens and their celestial systems, the earth with its complicated productions; and fire was given as the representative of that divine and original element which animates all nature. Serooch, the guardian of the earth, and Behram, armed with a mighty club and arrows, were formed to repel the attacks of Ahriman. Mythra, the mediator between Ormuzd and his creatures, and *Rash Rast*, the genius of justice, with multitudes of spirits, were called forth to assist in repelling the powers of darkness; and angels were appointed to protect every being. The stars and planets, the months of the year, the days and even watches of the day, had each their attendant spirit: all nature teems with them; all space is pervaded by them."—*Fraser's History of Persia*, p. 156.

Through the agency of these spiritual beings a long period of peace and tranquillity is supposed to have been maintained, until the purpose of Ormuzd to create man awakened afresh the malignant activity of Ahriman. The Feroher being delighted with the tranquillity which prevailed on earth, Ormuzd sent it thither, that it might assist in eradicating evil, promising that the souls of human beings should finally return to their divine mansions. The Feroher consequently descended, and was embodied in the form of the sacred bull, Aboudad, the man-bull, the excellent, the pure, the principle of all good.

Ahriman, in the depths of hell, trembled at these proceedings, and, mustering all his evil spirits, ascended to the earth in the form of a monstrous serpent, when he covered the surface of the world with noxious animals; and, in the shape of a huge fly, he polluted everything by insinuating the poison of evil into all nature. By means of a burning drought he parched the face of the whole earth, and caused his deeves to inflict a fatal wound on the sacred bull. But Ormuzd had taken care that his benign purposes should not be so defeated. "From the right limb of the dying beast issued Kayomurz, the first man; and from the rest of its members sprung a multitude of those vegetable productions destined to render the earth fruitful. Its seed, carried to the moon, and purified by Ormuzd, produced a bull and a cow, from whence all animals took their origin."

Kayomurz was beautiful, pure, and intended to be immortal. But neither his virtue nor the power of Ormuzd could save him from the malignant energy of Ahriman, who, after a severe conflict, succeeded in destroying him. Still Ormuzd was steady to his purpose. The principle of regeneration, being preserved, and confided to the tutelar genius of fire, was purified by the light of the sun, and after forty years produced a plant, or tree, representing two human bodies: these were Maschia and Maschiana, the parents of the human race.

In the whole of this narrative of creation we find a very interesting analogy to the history of Moses: and it is not improbable that some of the apparent extravagance and fable with which we now find it invested, were originally patriarchal traditions, not altogether devoid of truth and meaning. At all events, we have here an account of the existence and pursuits of holy and evil angels: a fanciful account, it is true, but yet one which strongly asserts the fact, and proves it to have been an undoubted element of popular belief. Here also is a statement of the elevated condition in which human nature was first formed,—man's name signifying immortality, and his condition being conformed to the mind of Ormuzd. Equally significant is the account of the fatal wound inflicted by the evil one. Nor should we regard as mere fable the reproduction of human nature in a vegetable form; especially as we are told, in explanation, that the names given to the pair of mortals, according to M. Du Perron, signify "death," and that they were regarded as the children of earth just in like manner as a tree which is nourished by the soil in which it grows, and the heavens by which it is bedewed.

But the effects of the Fall, and the progress of depravity, are carried by the *Avesta* still further. For although Maschia and Maschiana were supposed, notwithstanding their humble condition, to have been created pure, we are told that they were tempted to rebel, and even to worship Ahriman. In consequence of this crowning iniquity, they were cut off, and consigned to hell, there to remain until the resurrection, while the earth was overrun with incarnate evil spirits. These were destroyed by a general flood. Still the descendants of the first human pair increased in number; and the activity and power of the evil principle also increased; until at length, to defeat the malice of the evil one, and to shield human beings from the effects of his power, Ormuzd decreed to give a new and authorized promulgation of his law through Zoroaster.

It is observable here, that the genius of this entire system is the antagonism of two opposite and equally potent principles,—good and evil. The intimate union of these in everything rendered it impossible, according to this theory, to destroy the works of Ahriman, who was himself indestructible. Consequently the entire ground-work and argument of this faith were the incessant collisions and alternate preponderance of these rival influences on human and rational agents.

The nature of man, by this scheme, is exhibited in a peculiar aspect. Kayomurz is described in glowing terms, as of lofty aspect, pure and dazzling substance. His body was composed of the four elements,—fire, air, water, and earth; and was united to an immortal spirit, by which it was animated.

But the soul of man, instead of being considered as a simple essence and individual spirit, was regarded by Zoroaster as compounded of five separate parts, each having its distinct and peculiar office.

First, the *Feroher*, or principle of sensation. This was regarded as having existed previously. In fact, it seems that this system taught that Ferohers were created by Ormuzd for every individual destined to appear upon earth; and that they remained, until the birth of the body, in their spiritual abode.

Secondly, the *Boe*, or principle of intelligence.

Thirdly, the *Rouh*, or *Rouan*, the principle of practical judgment, imagination, volition.

Fourthly, the *Akho*, or principle of conscience.

Fifthly, the *Jan*, or principle of animal life.

The four principles named first in order cannot subsist in the body without the last. When, therefore, they leave their earthly abode, the Jan mingles with the winds, and is thus separated from the other principles and dispersed. At death the Akho, also, is separated from the other elements of the soul: for, as its office led it always to urge the mind to do good, and to avoid evil, it cannot be regarded as partaking in the guilt of the soul, or as punishable for its crimes: so that, when the body ceases to exist, the Akho returns to heaven, where it continues in a state of separate existence similar to that of the Feroher before the birth of the individual.

According to this system, the *Boe*, the *Rouan*, and the *Feroher*, united together, form the responsible soul, and, as such, are held accountable for the deeds of the man, and will accordingly be examined in respect of them at the last judgment. But, according to the tenets of Zoroaster, nothing is annihilated at death; the materials of the body rejoin their respective elements,—earth to earth, water to water, fire to fire, and the life to air. It is believed that, for three days after death, the soul hovers around the body, hoping to be again united to it. On the fourth the angel Seroch comes and conducts it to the bridge of Chinevad, where it is appointed to its destiny until the resurrection. On this bridge, which connects earth with heaven, sits the angel of justice, *Rash Rast*, to weigh the actions of mortals; and according to his decision the soul is permitted to pass along the bridge into heaven, or is cast over, and falls into the gulf of hell, which yawns beneath.

If the good deeds of the individual preponderate, the soul is met on the bridge by a dazzling figure, which thus addresses it: "I am thy good angel (Kherdar): I was pure originally, but thy good deeds have rendered me purer;" and, passing his hand over the neck of the blessed soul, the angel leads it to paradise. If, however, the sins of the deceased person proponderate, he is met on the bridge by a hideous spectre, which howls out, "I am thy evil Kherdar: impure myself, thy sins have rendered me more foul; through thee we shall be miserable until the resurrection;" on which it drags the condemned spirit to hell, where Ahriman, as a perfect Satan, taunts it with its folly and its crimes. In this system the body is not regarded as subject to future retribution, being considered as a mere instrument in the power of the Rouan, and therefore not responsible for its acts.

The doctrine of a future judgment is prominent among the tenets of Zoroaster. During the last ages of the world the power of Ahriman will prevail, and in consequence desolation and misery be extended over the earth. Then the three prophets will appear; the last of whom, Sosioch, will be the precursor of the general judgment and the renewal of nature. Strange as it may seem, the judgment shall be preceded by a general resurrection. Although the human body was not thought sufficiently identified with the moral conduct of the person to make it a partaker of its sorrow or joy in the intermediate period between death and judgment, yet the material frame was destined to be restored and reunited to the soul.

Accordingly the *Avesta* taught that the genii of the elements, who had received the various component parts of all human bodies in charge, will on this great day of account be called upon to render up their trust. " The soul will recognise its earthly companion, and reënter it. The juice of the herb *Hom*, and the milk of the bull *Heziosk*, will restore life to man, who then becomes immortal. Then begins the final separation of the good from the evil. Sinners who have not in the intermediate state expiated their faults, are again sent to hell, but not for eternal punishment. The tortures of three awful days and nights, equal to an agony of three thousand years, suffice for the punishment of the most wicked. The voice of the damned, ascending to heaven, will find mercy in the soul of Ormuzd, who will withdraw them from the place of torment. The world shall melt with fervent heat; and the liquid and glowing metals shall purify the universe, and fit all beings for everlasting felicity. To the just, this ordeal proves a pleasant bath of milk-warm water: the wicked, on the other hand, shall suffer excruciating agonies; but it shall be the last of their miseries. Hell itself and all its demons shall be cleansed. Ahriman, no longer irreclaimable, will be converted to goodness, and become a ministering spirit of the Most High."—*Fraser's History of Persia*, p. 161.

These kindred sentiments as to the final salvation of lost men and devils, are most unequivocally taught in the sacred books of this religious system. We read, " But above all he (Zardasht) has said, 'God has commanded me: Say thou to mankind, they are not to abide in hell forever; when their sins are expiated, they are delivered out of it.' "—*Dabistán*, vol. i, p. 263. The ultimate fate of Ahriman is stated in the Zend Avesta as follows: " That unjust, that impure being, who is a *Div* but in his thoughts; that dark king of the Darwands, who understands nothing but evil; he shall at the resurrection recite the *Avesta*, and not only himself practise the law of Ormuzd, but establish it even in the habitations of the Darwands. Moreover, it is said that Ahriman, that lying serpent, shall at the end of ages be purified by fire, as well as the earth be freed from the dark abode of hell. Ormuzd and Ahriman, accompanied by all the good and evil genii, shall sing the praises of the Author of all good."—*Dabistán*, vol. i, p. 358.

It will now be necessary to afford some information respecting the priesthood, and the ceremonies, rites, and worship of this system. The priesthood were the Magi, originally a tribe of the Median nation, (see p. 290,) but who, by means now inscrutable, had secured to themselves the influential and honourable position of religious teachers and priests, not only among their own people, but also throughout Persia. This office, even after it became so widely extended, did not merge into the general mass of the community, but continued to be hereditary in the same tribe.

Of this priesthood there were three gradations, or orders,—Herboods, or ordinary priests; Mobeds, or superior priests; and the Dustoor, or superintending priest.

The Herboods were the lowest class of the Magi; and, as far as we can now form any conception of their duties, it would seem that their office bore some analogy to that of the Hebrew Levites, excepting that the Herboods were competent to sacrifice. Unlike other ancient nations, the Persians did not allow a layman to sacrifice. The presence of one of the Magi was essential to the performance of this rite.

Above this lower grade of Magi were the *Mobeds;* which term seems to have comprehended the ideas of "prefect, judge, superior." They held a superior rank to the Herboods, and were subordinate to the Dustoor,—a kind of intermediate superintendents of the affairs of religion in their several localities.

There was never but one *Dustoor*, or high-priest, at the same time. He held a position somewhat similar to an "archbishop, or rather a metropolitan, who was acknowledged the successor of Zoroaster, and deemed the supreme head of the Church."—*Ancient Universal History*, vol iv., p. 93.

Some authors have expressed considerable gratification at the similarity which they have perceived between the regulations of this priesthood, and that which obtains in Episcopal Churches. In one particular, however, the parallel does not hold; for the Magian priesthood had no fixed salaries, being paid voluntarily for each service as it occurred. Some writers have given copious rules which were established for the regulation and direction of the Magi; but it seems more than probable that these were drawn from the practice of the modern Parsees, rather than from the institutes of Zoroaster. Yet, at the same time, since this religion has been continued from the era of Darius Hystaspis to the present day, as the settled religious belief and practice of the same people, even the usages of the present time may in some measure illustrate ancient observances.

Before the time of Zoroaster, their worship was conducted in the open air; but he directed them to enclose and cover their altars, so that they might with the greater certainty maintain the perpetual fire, which was before so often extinguished by accident, through the weather or other causes. It is expressly asserted, that these buildings were by no means intended as the residence of Deity, or in any way to limit his omnipresence, but simply as places for the shelter of their fire-altars.

The priesthood appear to have been subject to very minute rules of discipline, and to have been compelled to an exact observance of order in the conduct of public worship. The religious services, according to this system, were generally conducted in the *pyrea*, or "fire-temples." In each of these stood an altar, on which the sacred fire was kept perpetually burning by the officiating Magi. When the people assembled for public worship, the priest put on a white vestment and mitre, with a gauze or cloth passing before his mouth, that he might not breathe on the holy element. Thus he read certain prayers out of the liturgy, which he held in one hand, speaking very softly, and in a whispering sort of tone; holding in his left hand certain small twigs of a sacred tree, which, as soon as the service was over, he threw into the fire. At these times, all who were present put up their prayers to God, for such things as they stood in need of; and when prayers were finished, the priest and people silently withdrew, with every appearance of awful respect.

It is not improbable that we have a specimen, to say the least, of this Magian ritual in the *Zend Avesta*. For this celebrated work does not, as many have supposed, contain a treatise on the Magian faith, or even a synopsis of the articles of their belief; but it is rather a series of liturgical services for various occasions; and, as the Abbé Foucher well remarks, "bears the same relation to the doctrinal works of Zoroaster, that breviaries and missals do to the Bible."

The ancient Persians kept six religious festivals in the year, in memory of the six periods of time in which all things were created. But on one point connected with these there is considerable difference of opinion among authors, some saying that these festivals were each followed by five days of fasting, in memory of God's resting five days, as they believe, after each of those periods; while others contend that they had no fasts, and rejected everything of the nature of penance. "God, they say, delights in the happiness of his creatures; and they hold it meritorious to enjoy the best of everything they can obtain."

In their religious rites much use was made of a kind of holy water named *zor*, which was regarded as powerful in repelling evil spirits; and the consecrated juice of a particular shrub called the *hom*, prepared with many ceremonies, was regarded as possessing wonderful efficacy, and is often spoken of in the sacred books. (See the Dabistán, vol. i, p. 345.) A drop of this juice was given to infants, to cleanse them from the impurities of the womb; and also to persons at the point of death.

A variety of other customs of a religious character were observed. On naming a child, a sacred ceremony was performed; but still more importance was attached to putting on the sacred cord (*kusti*), and the equally sacred shirt (*sadra*). This was, indeed, a most solemn act, as these articles were supposed to form an armour against Ahriman. According to the *Dabistán* the sacred cord was a woollen cincture, girded round the waist, in which they made four knots:—the first, to signify the unity of God; the second, the certainty of the faith; the third, that Zardasht was the prophet of God; the fourth, to imply "that, to the utmost of my power, I will ever do what is good."—*Dabistán*, vol. i, p. 344. As often as they ate flesh, fish, or fowl, they carried a small part of it to the temple, as an offering to God, praying at the same time that he would forgive them for taking away the lives of his creatures for their subsistence.

It will now be necessary to direct attention to the moral influence of this religion. And in respect of this important point, we have here, as elsewhere, great scarcity of information. Almost every other matter was thought worthy of being recorded, except the moral character of the great body of the people. It must be fully admitted, that this faith inculcates general benevolence; to be honest in bargains, to be kind to one's cattle, and faithful to masters; to give the priests their due, physicians their fees. But with these sound precepts others, fanciful and superstitious, are regarded of equal importance; for instance,—physicians are enjoined to practise their sanitary experiments on infidels, before applying them to the followers of the faithful Zoroaster. Dogs and cats are held in great regard, as animals that watch the approach of evil spirits, against which the disciples of Zoroaster are constantly on their guard. On the other hand, it is meritorious to kill serpents, frogs, toads, and other reptiles, as being the creatures of Ahriman.

But, perhaps, we shall obtain the most accurate and forcible exposition of the morals of this system by noting at some length the virtues which secured to persons admission to the splendours and joys of paradise, and the sins for which others were shut up in hell.

From this review it will be clear, that while real virtues are extolled, and positive vice punished, the most childish puerilities are placed on a level with either. A catalogue of the blessed, for instance, would comprise the spirits of the munificent and noble-minded; those who observed *Naû Roz*, the great festival on the first six days of the year; just princes; priests and high-priests; women obedient to their husbands; attendants on fire-temples; champions who fought in the ways of God; slayers of noxious animals; husbandmen; heads of families who have improved the world by gardens and water-courses; and those who solicited money of the wealthy for the cause of religion, or to relieve pious poverty. On the other hand, the inhabitants of hell were held to be,—men of vile passions; a shedder of innocent blood; he who seduced the wives of other men; a man who had omitted to perform one peculiar mode of worship; an adulteress; those who had not adopted the sacred cincture; one who had betrayed his trust; a cruel and unjust king; a man who had slain four-footed animals; one who had neglected both the concerns of time and those of eternity; a slanderer and liar; a false witness; a man who had amassed wealth by unlawful means; hypocrites; a man who had killed dogs; a woman who, while combing her head, allowed some hairs to fall into the fire, &c. (See *Appendix*, note 54.)

This crude and unreasonable operation of law, when taken in connexion with the certain deliverance from suffering which the vilest sinner was assured of at the last day, must have operated most perniciously on the conduct of the whole people. Nor must it be quite forgotten, in the consideration of this subject, that the laws of nature were publicly outraged by the incestuous marriages which took place constantly in the Persian court; and that the most inhuman cruelty and savage barbarism coëxisted there with the height of oriental refinement, wealth, and luxury. The morals of Persia appear, therefore, at a disadvantage, when compared with those of other ancient heathen countries.

But there is one feature of this whole system which deserves special and peculiar notice. If Babylon had the unenviable distinction of introducing and establishing the great præ-Christian Antichrist, Persia appears to have carried out his development to the utmost limits; so that we can scarcely find an essential element of Popery that did not form a part of this system of Persian faith.

In the illustration of this point, the Scriptural Christian will not misapprehend my meaning, when I speak of any divinely-appointed rite as pertaining to Popery; since all must admit that while there is a true and proper application of these terms, there is a thoroughly Popish sense in which they are used; and it is in the latter sense, and often in regard of the *opus operatum* doctrines, that the reference is here made.

It must be borne in mind that the divine character of the sovereign was here put avowedly and prominently forward. So fully was this done that his being worshipped as divine was enacted by absolute law, and not only enforced on his subjects, but regarded as essential even on the admission of a foreign ambassador to the royal presence. Besides this, it must be noticed that the intrinsic merit of good works was clearly taught. *Kirfah*, the term used to designate the meritorious character of an action, is defined to mean "a good work,—a merit which ABSOLVES FROM SIN." How fully this accords with the great doctrine of the antichristian apostasy on this subject, I need not stay to demonstrate.

Again: the great principles of priestly authority and efficacy were fully taught and enforced. In reading the following remarkable proof of this point, let it be remembered that the term *Dustúr* stands for "high-priest," "archbishop," or, perhaps even more accurately, "supreme pontiff:"—"It is manifest, from the principles of religion, that we must concede due authority to the Dustúr, and must not deviate from his commands, as he is the ornament and splendour of the faith. Although thy good works may be countless as the leaves of the trees, the grains of sand, the drops of rain, or the stars in the heavens, thou canst gain nothing by them, unless they be acceptable in the sight of the Dustúr. If he be not content with thee, thou shalt have no praise in this world. Therefore, my son, thou shalt pay to the Dustúr who teaches thee, the tithe of all thou possessest, (wealth and property of every kind, gold and silver.) Therefore thou, who desirest to enjoy paradise to all eternity, pay tithes to the Dustúr: for if he be satisfied with thee, know that paradise is thine; but if he be not content with thee, thou canst derive no portion of benefit from thy good works; thy soul shall not find its way to paradise; thou shalt have no place along with angels; thy soul can never be delivered from the fiends of hell, which is to be thy eternal abode: but pay the tithes, and the Dustúrs will be pleased with thee, and thy soul shall get to paradise without delay. Truly the Dustúrs know the religion of all (faithful) men."—*Dabistán*, vol. i, p. 313, *Hyde's Trans.*

Can priestly claims be carried beyond this? And then, this priesthood was divided into regular gradations, until the series terminated in the *Dustúr*, or "supreme pontiff."

In addition to these elements, analogous rites were established. As soon as a child was born, it was purified by the sacred *hom*. The priest was present when the child received its name: immediately after which the infant was taken to the fire-temple, when the priest poured water into the rind of a holy tree, and from thence into the mouth of the child, at the same time offering up a prayer. At seven years of age the child was confirmed, after receiving instruction, passing through certain ablutions, and being dressed in a particular costume, one part of which it was necessary for the priest to make with his own hand. The *zor*, or "holy water," was also an important element in these rites. Finally, the sacred *hom* was administered by the priest, just in the manner of extreme unction, immediately before the death of a believer.

Truly there is little originality in the superstitious adulterations which have been used to paralyze and corrupt the gospel. There were precisely the same errors in doctrine; the same vain and absurd, but proud and profane, claims of the priesthood; and nearly identical unmeaning or pernicious rites were attached to the form of worship. In fact, the same round of means was employed, under the same influence, and with the same success, to corrupt the pure patriarchal faith of God's appointment, as we have seen operating to the perversion of the gospel: so that the apparent paradox is perfectly true,—that, whereas Popish superstition is, in respect of the gospel, a novelty, it is, at the same time, only a re-cast of errors and superstitions of a much more ancient period.

As our conclusions respecting the religion of Persia, and that of her more ancient neighbours, Assyria and Babylon, differ in many important particulars from those of preceding writers, whose investigations have been received with great attention and respect, I think it necessary to observe, that I altogether disclaim a wish to establish any theory of my own, or to introduce any novelty into this very important subject. But I candidly confess that I have felt it necessary to adopt a rather novel course in respect of this inquiry. On this point I will speak freely,—though fully open to correction.

Until the recent discovery of the inscriptions, our knowledge of the religion of the ancient eastern nations was mainly derived from Greek writers. They, as is perfectly well known, coloured all their accounts according to the principles of their own mythology. If, for instance, a Greek writer saw a statue of an Assyrian deity, or heard an account of a Persian religious ceremonial, he would naturally give the first the name of the Greek deity who came nearest to it in attributes and character, and would identify the second with the most similar rites to be found in his own religious system. The consequence has been, therefore, that we have been accustomed to see the religion of the primitive eastern nations through a Grecian medium. And it is only in this way that we read in Herodotus of Rhea, Juno, and Mars, as if they were Persian deities, and of Mylitta as the Babylonian Venus; that Diodorus speaks thus of Jupiter, Rhea, and Juno; and that Xenophon makes Cyrus always offer his prayers to Jove. These names were unknown in the east, and are not translations, but applications of the names of Greek deities to those of eastern countries, on account of some real, or supposed, resemblance between their respective attributes.

This has not only led to embarrassment and confusion: it has altogether misrepresented oriental religion, by putting it forth under a Grecian form, and associated with Grecian names. If Greece had been the parent of these nations,—if Assyria, Babylon, and Persia had received their civilization and religion from Greece,— this would be a correct course: but it was quite otherwise. These nations flourished in civilization, and had their religious systems matured, when Greece lay prostrate in barbarism. Grecian tenets, manners, and doctrines could by no possibility, therefore, have affected these oriental systems. All that is Grecian in the accounts which reach us of their religions must, in consequence, be misleading.

But while all the efforts to assimilate the religion of the primitive eastern nations to a Grecian model must have a pernicious tendency, it is evident that there was a more ancient faith, and an earlier sacred history, with which these eastern nations were acquainted; a history which brought down to them the great deeds of their ancestors, and which stood associated with the most wondrous operations of almighty power; and a faith which arose out of glorious and immediate revelations made by God to man, and had been impressed on all their traditions, opinions, habits, and history. Now I maintain that while the course which I impugn must be injurious, it is equally so to study these religions without any reference to man's primitive history, and while ignoring the faith and doctrines of the patriarchs; as though Assyria, Babylon, and Persia had not derived their existence, knowledge, and religion from the men who had been congregated together at Babel. Whatever defects, therefore, may be found in the sketch which has been given of the religion of these countries, I am satisfied that it is an approximation to sound views on this important subject.

What, then, was the character of the religion of Persia, as a system? and what were its results on the national mind?

Like its predecessor and prototype in Assyria, it was the soul of despotism. All that was said on this subject at the close of the fifth chapter might be repeated here. The profane assumption of the sovereign led to the intellectual and moral debasement of the people, as an inevitable result. Beyond this it may be observed, that the difference between the faith of Persia and that of Assyria and Babylon appears to have arisen from two opposite and conflicting causes,—the revival of primitive truth, and the introduction of monstrous and pernicious error.

Here was a clearer knowledge of man, in his true relation to God, than obtained in the more ancient nations. The primitive purity and fall of man,—Satanic power and malevolence, with their results,—the appointment of a mediator, and his position in the trinity,—the certainty of a future judgment,—the resurrection, and immortal life,—all these are prime articles of religious faith, of great importance in any religious code; and these, associated with an immense amount of primitive and paradisiacal tradition, were found as recognised articles of faith among the ancient Persians. But then they were fearfully neutralized by additional errors. Not only was the Persian theology corrupted, as in Assyria, by polytheistic adulteration; the profane assumption of the priesthood must also have been a frightful evil. It divested moral actions of their proper character and quality, by making them entirely contingent for acceptance on the will of the priest. The multiplied ritual services, in which priestly efficacy was the only virtue, would tend to the same result, and introduce many childish distinctions, calculated to confound the understanding and pervert the mind; while the doctrine of a universal restoration to heavenly happiness and glory, not only of wicked men, but even of devils, would neutralize the influence of a future judgment, and render that doctrine of little, if of any, effect.

The combined result was, that in Persia, even more than in Assyria and Babylon, religion was a royal and priestly monopoly. The people were not taught, and scarcely considered: every sacred rite required the presence of a Magian priest; and the public—save in their attendance on their fire-temples, where they heard something frequently of prayer—were left to the fearful and ruinous influence of moral putrefaction.

CHAPTER IX.

THE HISTORY OF THE GRECIAN STATES.

ALTHOUGH occupying a small Country, and not possessing early Civilization, the Greeks arose to superlative Distinction in History—The Geography of Greece—The Origin of the Greeks—Pelasgians and Hellenes kindred Races—Legendary History—The Argonautic Expedition—The Theban Legends—The Trojan War—The Return of the Heracleids—State of the Grecian States in the Time of Lycurgus—Division into numerous independent Communities—Their Unity of Blood, Manners, and Religion—The Political and Civil Institutions of Lycurgus—Sparta subdues the Messenians—The State of Athens—Prevalent and long-continued Disorder—Solon—He regains Possession of Salamis—Succeeds in the Sacred War against Cirrha—Fearful State of Society—Solon invested with Supreme Power—His Reforming Measures, and new Political Constitution, established—Pisistratus obtains the Chief Authority—The Tyrant expelled, and Democracy established, by the Aid of Sparta—The smaller Grecian States—The Islands and Colonies—Causes which led to the First Persian Invasion—It utterly fails—A Second prepared, and disembarked at the Bay of Marathon—Completely defeated by the Athenians under Miltiades—Further Persian Preparations for the Conquest of Greece—Suspended by the Death of Darius—Xerxes at length determines on another Invasion—His immense Preparations and Vast Army—Checked at Thermopylæ—His Fleet defeated at Artemisium—Athens destroyed—The Persian Fleet ruined at Salamis—Xerxes retreats—Returns to Asia—Mardonius makes the most flattering Overtures to the Athenians—Which they nobly reject—Apathy of Sparta—Attica ravaged a Second Time—A United Greek Army at length opposes the Foe—The Persian Force is annihilated at Platæa—On the same day the Persian Fleet is destroyed at Mycale—Successful Prosecution of the War, followed by Peace with Persia—The Period, Causes, and Progress of Grecian Civilization and Advancement—Thales—Pythagoras—Greece attains her Highest Intellectual Elevation—Great Wealth and Power of Athens—First Peloponnesian War—Mischievous Policy of Alcibiades—Second Peloponnesian War—Ruin of Athens—Sparta Tyrannizes over the other Grecian States—Restoration of Athens to Independence—Xenophon and the Ten Thousand—Thebes—Pelopidas and Epaminondas—Philip of Macedon—His Improved Military Tactics—Takes advantage of the Disunion and Rivalry of the Greek States to make himself Master of the Country—Alexander succeeds his Father—Prepares for the Invasion of Persia—Battle of the Granicus—His uninterrupted Success—In Three Years he extends his Sway from the Mediterranean to India—His Death—State of Greece during the Victorious Career of Alexander—Aggression of Sparta on Macedon—Repelled—Tumults on the Death of Alexander, repressed by Antipater—Cassander—His Government—Interference of Rome—Progress of her Power—Greece a Roman Province.

IN approaching the history of Greece we are brought into contact with a people of the most extraordinary character and destiny. It was not because of early greatness, or ancient splendour, that this people stood preëminent among the nations of the world: for, many centuries after Assyria, Egypt and Persia were possessed of wealth, power, luxury, and learning, Greece was occupied by semi-barbarous tribes, with very imperfect political institutions, who were strangers even to the knowledge of letters. Nor was it because of the extended territory: for Greece, properly so called, is scarcely larger than the kingdom of Naples. Yet with this limited geography, and with a celebrity of so recent a date that the national records do not afford materials for a history of the nation until the eighth century before Christ, it had then established a character in the world, and has exerted a more potent influence on mankind at large than any other people.

Rising into prominence and power at this late period of the ancient world, Greece, in the progress of five hundred years, accomplished all that seems possible of attainment by giant intellect and cultivated genius. In all the elegant arts—architecture, painting, statuary—the Greeks distanced all their predecessors, and created a school which it has been the glory of every subsequent age to imitate. Every branch of literature—poetry, history, and the drama—was carried to perfection. Science, philosophy, and logic were cultivated with equal success. And, what is yet more strange, having thus evinced a rare combination of intellectual power, cultivated taste, and brilliant genius, the sons of Greece successfully repelled an invasion of their country, although assailed by the united forces of the most mighty nations of the world; and, having triumphed in this effort, they went forth in irresistible martial power, and bowed the world to their will. Every nation that could be reached was subdued; and Grecian power ruled, and the Greek language and manners pervaded, the civilized world.

Nor is the waning glory of this wonderful people less remarkable than the rise and progress of their power. For, when Greece, in her turn, fell before the military might of imperial Rome, it was the proud boast of the conquered, that they imparted to their conquerors more advantage in the communication of arts and elegance, literature and learning, than the Romans had obtained in martial honours or territorial aggrandizement by the conquest of the country. Thus Greece, as she fell into ruin and obscurity, enlightened and elevated the most powerful nation on earth.

There has been some difference of opinion as to the extent of Greece in respect of its northern boundary; some writers including, and others excluding, Epirus and Macedonia. The inhabitants of these countries owned the same origin as the Greeks; were of similar manners, language, and religion; yet, in the progress of ages, they became so alienated from the great body of the Greek nation, that our best writers agree in describing Greece Proper as bounded on the north by Olympus, and the Cambunian Mountains, which divide it from Macedonia.

Greece, so limited, extends from north to south about two hundred and fifty miles; and its greatest breadth, from the western coast of Acarnania to Marathon in Attica, is one hundred and eighty miles. This country is about half the size of England,—a geographical compass by no means proportionate to the martial power of the people, or to the influence which they exerted on the world.

As it seems necessary to give a very brief sketch of this territory, it may be first observed that it was naturally divided into two parts by the Isthmus of Corinth. That part which lay below this neck of land was anciently called the Peloponnesus, and recently the Morea; and that beyond, on the continent, contained Attica, Bœotia, Phocis, Ætolia, and Acarnania.

The Peloponnesus—so called in honour of Pelops—forms the southern region of Greece. It is a peninsula, surrounded by the sea, excepting where it is joined to the main-land by the Isthmus of Corinth. It has in its centre the far-famed Arcadia of poetical tradition. This is an elevated and hilly district, its highest peak being Mount Cyllene. It is an excellent pasture-country, and in its general features greatly resembles Switzerland; while its inhabitants as strikingly exhibit the Swiss character,—being equally fond of liberty and money. The god Pan is said to have resided here, and to have invented the flute with seven reeds. Here he was worshipped, and delivered oracles. Around Arcadia were seven other districts, or territories, all of which were well watered by streams that descended from its highlands.

Of these, Corinth lay immediately in the Isthmus, having a harbour on each side. It was thus possessed of immense maritime advantages, and facilities for commerce perhaps equal to any port of the world. To the south of Corinth lay Argolis, so named from Argos, its chief town. Here stood Tiryns, whence Hercules departed to begin his labours; and Mycenæ, the city of Agamemnon; Nemea, celebrated for its games in honour of Neptune; and Nauplia, now the celebrated Napoli di Romania. To the southwest of Argolis lay Laconia,—a country rough and mountainous, watered by the Eurotas, on whose banks arose the celebrated Sparta; yet, although this was one of the principal cities in Greece, its site cannot now be identified.

To the north and west of Laconia was Messenia. Pylos, one of the cities claiming to have given birth to Nestor, was situated in this district. Elis, the Holy Land of Greece, lay immediately to the north of Messenia. There rolled the Alpheus, on whose banks the Olympic Games were celebrated: and here stood Olympia, with its glorious temple, and colossal statue of Jupiter, the masterpiece of Phidias. Temples to Jupiter and Lucina also adorned the neighbourhood. On this spot Pausanias counted two hundred and thirty statues; and in the days of Pliny they had increased to three thousand,—and all these the work of eminent artists. What are all our museums, and collections of statuary, compared to this? To the northeast of Elis we find Achaia, watered by the mountain-streams from Arcadia; and between this and Corinth lay the ancient city and small territory of Sicyon.

From this rapid glance at the Peloponnesus, we turn to notice that part of Greece which is situated beyond the Corinthian Isthmus. Immediately to the east of this lay Attica; its form was nearly triangular. This has generally been regarded as the most beautiful part of Greece, although the soil was by no means remarkably fruitful. Athens, the city of Pallas, the centre of Grecian civilization, learning, and refinement, was the capital of the district. On the top of a hill close to the city, stood the Acropolis, which in the days of her glory was covered with the most beautiful architecture.

To the northwest of Attica lay Bœotia and Phocis, separated from Thessaly by the mountain range of Œta, through which the famous Pass of Thermopylæ alone afforded easy communication. The renowned Parnassus divided Bœotia from Phocis. Delphi, noted for its oracle of Apollo, stood on the south side of Parnassus. Here excellent pieces of statuary were exhibited in countless number; and the contents of treasuries, received from neighbouring princes and kings, astonished the beholder. Here, also, in the Amphictyonic Council, the first maxims of law were taught, and the principles of policy laid down and matured. The Pythian Games, surpassed only by the Olympic, were celebrated in this neighbourhood; and here, above all, the Castalian Fountain poured forth her streams sacred to the Muses.

It would have been scarcely necessary to notice Thessaly in this sketch, but on account of some very ancient recollections. Iolcos, whence the Argonauts sailed, was in this province. This was also the country of Achilles. To the west of Thessaly we find Ætolia and Acarnania.

Having thus glanced at the geography of Greece, it will be necessary, before proceeding to trace its history, to notice its early inhabitants, and, if possible, discover its primitive settlers. Without presuming to speak positively on a subject so full of difficulty, we may venture to observe that there appears reason to believe that, in the general dispersion of the descendants of Noah, this portion of the world was occupied by Javan, the fourth son of the arkite patriarch, and afterward principally by the family of his son Elishah. As it is not intended to maintain this opinion at length, it will be sufficient to observe in support of it, that continental Greece was originally called Ionia, which term our best scholars have supposed to have been derived from the name Javan; with which, they contend, it nearly agreed, according to ancient Greek pronunciation. It is also a curious fact, corroborative of this opinion, that the Septuagint Version of Holy Scripture always renders the Hebrew term יון *Javan* by the word "Greece." This fact not only proves the origin generally attributed to the Greeks by the learned, in the third century before Christ: it does more: for, inasmuch as it is scarcely possible generally to substitute the name of any other country without doing violence to the consistency of the sacred writer, (as, for instance, in an important passage in Daniel viii, 21,) so we have the authority of the inspired Hebrew text itself in favour of this opinion.

This is also the case in respect of Elishah; for Ezekiel speaks of the "isles of Elishah" in such a connexion as almost certainly to fix the designation upon the Greek islands. In conformity with this evidence, the peninsula and isles of Greece have been regarded as peopled by the descendants of Elishah, while Tiras is supposed to have been the father of the Thracians.

But whatever truth there may be in these conjectures, it appears to be an undoubted fact, that considerably more than a thousand years elapsed from the first occupation of Greece to the time when we obtain materials for a history of its inhabitants. It cannot, then, be a matter of surprise, that it has been found utterly impossible to trace up, by any satisfactory historical induction, to any particular primitive root, the people who are the subject of Grecian history.

There is, however, one question, lying at the foundation of Grecian history, which must be noticed and disposed of, before we fairly enter on the subject. The earliest occupants of the country are always spoken of by ancient writers as Pelasgians; while the great body of the Greek nation in historical times are called *Hellenes*. The debatable points are,—Whether these were different tribes speaking different languages, or in their origin essentially the same people?—and, secondly, By what means, or in what manner, did the Hellenes ultimately acquire universal ascendency in Greece? On these subjects the learned have been long divided, nor can it yet be said that the question is settled. While such men as Professor Wachsmuth and Dr. Thirlwall advocate one view of the subject, and Mr. Grote the opposite, it becomes us to express ourselves with great diffidence. Yet, notwithstanding this conviction, we must be allowed to say that we fully agree with the first-mentioned authors, that the Pelasgians and Hellenes were originally the same people.

The general prevalence of the Pelasgic people, or rather the

Pelasgic name, seems a fact constantly admitted by ancient writers. "All are pretty well agreed," observes Strabo, "that the Pelasgians were an ancient race which prevailed throughout all Greece, and especially by the side of the Æolians in Thessaly."—*Thirlwall's History of Greece*, vol. ii, sect. 4. This statement must not, indeed, be so construed as to exclude the existence of other and distinct tribes in ancient Greece;—for Strabo, as well as Herodotus and Thucydides, speaks of several of these;—but it clearly shows that the Pelasgians were the most powerful and widely-diffused people of Greece, whose language and manners gave a character to the whole country. Traces of their residence have, indeed, been distinctly found in Thessaly, Epirus, Bœotia, Attica, and the Peloponnesus,—especially in Argolis, Achaia, and Arcadia.

With respect to the Hellenes, it has been supposed that they originated from Hellen, who is sometimes called "the son of Zeus," but is generally regarded as the immediate descendant of Deucalion and Pyrrha, although he is often mentioned as the *brother* of the Grecian hero of the Deluge. But whether such a person as Hellen ever existed, except in mythological fable, or not, it is a settled matter that no historical researches can carry up the Hellenic tribe or people to this individual. Historically we only know the Hellenes as deriving their name and character from a people, or tribe, which anciently resided in Epirus. There were, in fact, two tribes bearing this name, resident near Dodona, who were probably nearly related to each other and to the ancient Pelasgians. Mr. Grote, indeed, joins his weighty judgment with that of preceding writers, in deciding, upon the authority of a passage in Herodotus which refers to the language of the Pelasgians, that they were essentially a distinct people from the Hellenes. We think Dr. Thirlwall's statement remains in all its strength, notwithstanding this objection; (Thirlwall's Greece, vol. i, p. 60,) and, such being the case, the general current of evidence naturally leads to the belief that the Pelasgians and Hellenes were kindred races.

By what means, then, or in what manner, was that great change effected which spread the Hellenic name and influence so generally over Greece? One point is clear: it is undoubted, that "the peculiar stamp which distinguished the Greeks from every other nation on the earth, was impressed on them by the little tribe which first introduced among them the name of Hellenes."—*Thirlwall's Greece*, vol. i, p. 97. At the same time, it is the decided opinion of this learned writer, that this change "was not effected simply by the conquests or migrations of this new people."—*Thirlwall's Greece*, vol. i, p. 97. The alternative inference appears inevitable,—that the Hellenic ascendency was that which a highly martial caste, raised by their daring energy above the need of labour, impatient of repose, and eager for warlike adventures, obtained over a weaker, but perhaps an equally civilized, people.

The late era at which Greece appears before us as a subject of history, is in some measure compensated by the length and grandeur of what may be called "the traditional period." The greatest labour and learning have been expended on this topic; but they have failed alike to elicit with any certainty the exact chronology, and the precise historical character, of the important events which are supposed to have transpired during the thousand years which elapsed prior to 800 B. C. It will, however, be necessary to mention the principal of these occurrences.

The Argonautic Expedition may be referred to as the first, in order of time, of these notable events. If from the immense mass of poetry and legend, bearing on this subject, anything definite can be inferred, it may be supposed that about 1300 B. C. Jason, a prince of Thessaly, having collected together a number of the most chivalrous spirits of Greece, sailed on an expedition, partly commercial and partly martial, to the shores of the Euxine Sea; and, having fought, conquered, and plundered, on their return home they planted a colony at Colchis, carrying with them a princess of the country which they had invaded. (See *Appendix*, note 55.)

The Theban legends may also be adduced, as of a similar character. As far as can be ascertained, the subject of these arose out of the introduction of the Phenician or Asiatic worship into Thebes by Cadmus. But it involved the singular and melancholy fate of Œdipus, a protracted war, ending in the capture of Thebes, and the consequent isolation of this district, in sympathy and interest, from the general concerns of Greece. (See *Appendix*, note 56.)

The Trojan war may be noted next in order. It may be doubted whether there was ever such an extended account, given to the world with such exquisite and unsuspecting simplicity, and so generally regarded as actual history, without any independent evidence of its historical existence, as that which we find in the Homeric epic. Perhaps, as Mr. Grote conjectures, such an effort as that of Homer would never have come into existence in an age in which historical records existed. However this may be, it is an unquestionable fact, that the narrative of Homer was currently received and reverentially cherished throughout Greece; and it is equally clear that all which can be said respecting even the basis of the story, (omitting all the dramatic machinery of gods, goddesses, and heroes,) is that it is possible. But then, as an eminent writer on the subject observes,

"As the possibility cannot be denied, neither can the reality of it be affirmed." (See *Appendix*, note 57.)

A further reference to Grecian legend is necessary, because it both relates to an important revolution in the government of the country, and in a great degree accounts for the numerous and powerful Greek colonies which, at the commencement of the historical period, we find established in different parts of Asia Minor. This legend, or series of legends, relates to the descendants of Hercules. After the death of this hero, his children were driven from Peloponnesus, and found refuge at Athens; and their descendants, after many ineffectual efforts, succeeded, in connexion with a powerful army of Dorians, in subduing the peninsula. In consequence of this irruption, numerous bodies, led by those who had previously possessed power and distinction, emigrated, and formed Greek colonies in various islands, and in different parts of Asia Minor. (See *Appendix*, note 58.)

Passing over the legendary period of Grecian annals without further notice, we enter upon the times when this wonderful people stand before our view in the light of history; and select, for the commencement of our research, the era when Lycurgus introduced his scheme of legislation into Sparta. This occurred, according to Thucydides, B. C. 817. At this time Amaziah reigned in Judah and Jeroboam II. in Israel, it being just one year before the death of Elisha the prophet.

In endeavouring to convey some idea of the peculiar position of Greece at this time within the narrow limits of a chapter, our attention must be directed to two or three particulars. We find Greece, unlike every other ancient nation, not only without any political unity and national sovereignty, but actually divided into just as many free states as it had cities. It is, indeed, true that in some districts the most powerful city held a kind of supremacy over the smaller ones, which was called by the Greeks "hegemony:" but this extended only so far as to merge the foreign political relations of the minor places in those of the capital; so that the whole district, in all peaceful treaties and warlike measures, would act together. It did not allow the principal city, however powerful, to interfere in the internal administration of the several minor civil communities.

Another peculiarity of the Greek people was the character of the union which subsisted throughout the entire nation. This was maintained, first, by the common bond of nationality. The whole Hellenic race regarded themselves, however subdivided, as one people. A family feeling pervaded the entire extent of the population, and induced a mutual fraternal recognition among all its members. This union was greatly promoted by the Olympian, Pythian, Nemean, and Isthmian Games. All these—which maintained a powerful influence on the public mind, not only throughout Greece, but in all neighbouring countries, for many centuries—were greatly conservative of Grecian unity. At these games, although strangers might be spectators, none but Hellenes could enter the lists, as candidates for the prize. As this privilege was highly valued, the limitation was greatly conducive to the unity of national feeling and regard.

But, after all, the great secret of the identity subsisting between the numerous cities and clans of Greece lay in her religious institutions. Apart from their common object, as mere festivals, the games above mentioned, to some extent, partook of a religious character, and in this respect exerted a powerful influence on the public mind. This was, however, but a single and comparatively unimportant element. The Hellenes everywhere worshipped the same gods, held their sacrificial services in common, and regarded themselves, through their heroes, as descended from these deities. The intensity of the unity of feeling thus produced cannot be exhibited more forcibly than was done by the Athenians. When their city lay in ruins, and they, and their wives and children, found refuge only on board their ships, or in the Isle of Salamis; at the time they were deserted by the Spartans, and received the most tempting overtures from Persia, the principal reason set forth by them for their noble conduct is thus stated by their envoys to Lacedæmon: "We, however, though deserted and betrayed by the Greeks, have steadily refused all his offers, [those of the king of Persia,] *through reverence for the Grecian Jupiter.*"—*Herodotus,* lib. ix, cap. 7.

The success of the Heracleids, by means of their Dorian auxiliaries, established that people as a ruling caste, and reduced the greater portion of the former inhabitants to slavery. But this victorious aggression, instead of introducing strength and consolidation into the country, caused disunion and weakness. The unequal distribution of property produced domestic quarrels, while the unsettled state of affairs at home embroiled the state in a tedious and harassing war with the Argives. This condition of things continued, subject to various fluctuations and changes, for more than two hundred years, when, at length, a man arose into influence and power, whose genius moulded the institutions of SPARTA into a permanent form, and rendered that state, small as it was in geographical extent, one of the most powerful of its day.

It had long been the custom in Sparta for two kings to reign at the same time, with conjoint power. This originated, according to Pausanias, in the accession of the two sons of Aristodemus, Eurysthenes and Proclus, and continued, notwithstanding the mutual jealousy and suspicion inseparable from a diarchy, through thirty princes of the former line and twenty-seven of the latter. In the early part of these dynasties, struggles were frequent between the kings and the people. In one of these a sovereign was killed: his son, succeeding to the throne, soon after died, and was followed by his brother Lycurgus. But this prince, discovering that his brother's widow was pregnant, held the supreme authority in trust, until the birth of the infant, which proving to be a son, he presented the child to the magistrates of the city as their king, and exercised dominion only in his name as regent. Notwithstanding this nobility of conduct, the mother of the infant prince, and her brother, having thrown out suspicions respecting the intentions of Lycurgus, he deemed it prudent to retire a while from Sparta, and travelled into Crete and other lands, observing their institutions, and forming his opinion as to the best political basis for the constitution of his own country.

The absence of Lycurgus was severely felt at Sparta. Those who were invested with authority evidently lacked the power to maintain it; difficulty and danger beset the state on every side. In this emergency, earnest and importunate entreaties were sent to Lycurgus to hasten his return. He complied, and, on arriving at home, was hailed with delight by all parties, since he was regarded as the only man able to heal the disorders which prevailed. He undertook the task: but, perceiving the magnitude of the engagement, he made use of every precaution. In the first place, he obtained the unambiguous approbation of the oracle at Delphi for his measures. He then secured the aid of a number of the principal citizens of Sparta, who engaged, if necessary, to support him with their arms.

These precautions taken, Lycurgus introduced his new system of government and polity. Our sketch of this system must be as brief as possible.

As a political code, it was, in the most strict sense of the term, a mixed government. The monarchical principle was maintained, but in a weak form; as the rule of two contemporaneous kings, reigning with joint power, was continued. The aristocracy was represented by a senate of twenty-eight persons; while every Spartan of thirty years of age, and of unblemished character, had a voice in the assembly of the people. In addition to this, the commons were represented by the *Ephori*. These corresponded to the tribunes among the Romans. At first they appear to have been appointed as minor officers connected with police and courts of law. In consequence, however, of the divided and enfeebled condition of the monarchy, these gradually assumed a censorial, inquisitorial, and judicial power, which enabled them frequently to overawe and control both the kings and the senate.

This alteration in the mode of government was, however, according to Plutarch, the least of the innovations of Lycurgus. The following are the more important measures which are ascribed to him. He ordered an equal partition of the land among all the citizens; so that those who had been rich had to divide their landed property with the poor. The entire territory of Sparta was partitioned into nine thousand lots, and the rest of Laconia into thirty thousand,— the number of their respective citizens. Having succeeded thus far, the lawgiver proceeded to enforce an equal division of all movable property. Finding this measure to be impracticable, he assailed distinctions of rank and the indulgence of luxury by more indirect means. Gold and silver currency was prohibited, and an iron coin substituted, of such small value that, to lay up ten *minæ*, (about £32 5s. sterling,) a whole room was required, and a yoke of oxen necessary to remove it. This alteration cut up avarice and luxury by the roots, and at the same time isolated Sparta from the rest of Greece, and in great measure interdicted commercial intercourse; for this money would not pass current out of Sparta. The consequence was, the greatest simplicity in all the houses, furniture, and manner of living.

These statements of Plutarch must, however, be taken as exhibiting the general character of Spartan policy and practice, rather than the measures which were introduced, and fully carried into effect, by the personal exertions of the lawgiver. It is certain that, in the days of Lycurgus, the whole of Laconia was not subject to Lacedæmonian rule; and it is open to serious doubt, whether an *equal* division of land was ever fully effected, even in Sparta itself. As early as B.C. 600, we hear complaints made respecting the influence of wealth, and the degradation of the poor, even in the capital.

A further arrangement of this legislator was the establishment of public tables, where all were required to eat in common. The rich offered great opposition to this regulation; but it was notwithstanding carried into effect. To it Lycurgus added a public arrangement for the education of youth. All children were, according to his institutions, regarded as the property of the state, and treated accordingly. Yet it is a singular fact, that while the men were trained to this practice, and dined on plain fare, their wives at home not unfrequently maintained a luxurious establishment.

The result of all these measures was to make the Spartan state thoroughly martial in its character. The city was like a great camp: every man was a soldier; bodily strength and mental vigour were chiefly prized, as they rendered the man a more efficient warrior. It will be seen that these laws could not be made operative on the whole population. Husbandry and tillage, handicraft arts and menial service, necessarily require a large proportion of every people. To provide for these without diverting the Spartan citizen from his martial exercises, a system of wholesale slavery was established. The victims of this oppression were called Helots. It seems they were originally captives taken in war, whose posterity were ever afterward doomed to this cruel bondage; while further conquests increased their number.

The laws and institutions of Lycurgus were not given in a written code, but reduced to short sentences like proverbs, called ῥῆτραι, *rhetrai*. All these were confirmed by the oracle of Delphi, and committed to memory by the people.

The first important war in which the Spartans were engaged was with their neighbours the Messenians. After a very protracted struggle, this contest terminated in the subjection of that territory to the Spartan dominion; but the sacrifices and efforts put forth to attain this end greatly weakened the power of the victors for a considerable period.

It will now be necessary to direct attention to ATHENS. The political history of this state may be carried back to the time of Theseus. Among his successors the most eminent were Mnestheus, who fell before Troy, and Codrus, whose generous devotion (as already stated) led to the abolition of monarchy. After the introduction of this change, thirteen archons of the royal family ruled in succession. From the year B. C. 752, the archons were chosen every ten years from the family of Codrus There were seven of these, reaching to the year B. C. 682. Nine annual archons were then elected by the nobility. All these changes, however, did but little to promote the well-being of the state. The people were reduced to a miserable condition. The equestrian order,—so called from their fighting on horseback,—having, in the infancy of martial tactics, infinite advantage over a rabble on foot, secured to themselves all authority, civil, religious, and military. The ancient laws, being few and simple, were insufficient to meet the demands of the age: consequently much was left to the discretion of the magistrates, who too frequently decided according to their class-interests or prejudices.

In these circumstances the very framework of society was shaken, and Athens seemed to tremble on the brink of ruin. To avert this calamity, Draco, the archon, was selected to prepare a system of laws for the reformation of the state. He undertook the task, but supplied a code of such unexampled severity that it was said to have been written in letters of blood. Death was the punishment for idleness, as well as for murder. At first these penalties were enforced, but they gradually sunk into disuse; and the legislator was obliged to withdraw to Ægina, where he died.

This unsuccessful effort was followed by a series of disorders and crimes, until at length a legislator arose, who by his brilliant genius and wisdom introduced an efficient measure of social and political reform. Solon was of purest heroic blood, and possessed a moderate fortune. In his earlier years, owing to the improvidence of his father, he found it necessary to engage in commercial pursuits, by which means he added to his substance and his knowledge. The energy of his mind, and his habit, in accordance with the prevalent custom of the times, of expressing his thoughts in simple verse, made him known throughout Greece; and he was classed with other six, as one of the Seven Wise Men. (See *Appendix*, note 59.)

The first political event of importance in which Solon engaged was the recovery of the Isle of Salamis. Megara had long successfully disputed with Athens the possession of this island; and her citizens had actually established themselves upon it; while the Athenians had suffered so much in the struggle, and felt so annoyed at the result, that they decreed the punishment of death to any one who should propose any further effort for its recovery.

Solon determined to remove this dishonour from his country. To effect this object, he composed an earnest poetic address; and, feigning a state of ecstatic excitement, he rushed into the *agora*, and, taking his stand on the stone usually occupied by the official herald, he recited his elegiac address to the surrounding crowd on the subject of Salamis. He so fully succeeded in this attempt that they rescinded the prohibitory law, determined to renew the war, and intrusted Solon with the conduct of the enterprise. He accepted the command, and conducted the invasion with so much prudence and valour, that he restored that important island to the government of Athens.

Another circumstance, which occurred soon after, greatly added to the reputation of Solon, and secured to him countenance and support the most important, in respect of his future career. Cirrha was a small seaport in the Gulf of Corinth, offering ready access to Delphi. The inhabitants of this place obtained enormous riches by levying exorbitant tolls on the passengers who landed there on their way to the temple. This was felt to be a national grievance; and Solon not only moved the Amphictyonic Council to insist on the removal of the evil, (see *Appendix*, note 60,) but, when the Cirrhæans refused to reform the abuse at his instance, a band of Athenians accompanied a joint force of Thessalians and Sicyonians, and, after a Sacred War of two years' duration, accomplished the desired object by completely subduing and destroying the town, except just what was necessary to make it a suitable landing place; and dedicated the whole plain, from the sea to the temple, to the Delphian god.

While, however, Solon saw his efforts crowned with success in these external measures, he found the internal condition of the country rapidly approaching a crisis which threatened to issue in a frightful disruption of all society. The people of Attica were divided into three factions: the *Pedieis*, or "men of the plain," comprising Athens, Eleusis, and the neighbouring territory; among whom were the richest and noblest families of the land; the *Diakrii*, the mountaineers in the north and east, who were very poor; and the *Paralii*, whose means and social position were intermediate. Among these there appears to have existed a long-continued class-struggle. But this was greatly aggravated by a still more fearful evil,—a general outburst of feeling of the poor against the rich, arising out of deep misery, acted upon by great oppression. The rich had hitherto dictated the laws: these were partial and unjust. The needy man borrowed money on the security, not merely of his substance, but also of his own body. Nay, more: not only might the insolvent debtor be sold to pay his debts, but even his minor sons, unmarried daughters, and sisters also, might be sold with him. In this manner great numbers had been reduced from freedom to slavery; some had been sold for exportation; and others had maintained their own liberty by the sale of their children.

It was when Solon had by his talents and integrity commended himself to all classes, as possessing every requisite for a great reformer, that this mutinous feeling had reached its height. This so alarmed the rich, that although it was known he had severely condemned their cruelty in his poems, they consented that he should be invested with supreme power, in the hope that he would thus conserve the state, and relieve them from the impending danger. He was therefore appointed archon, nominally as the colleague of Philombrotus, but with authority substantially dictatorial.

Solon began his reforms by a measure which satisfied neither the rich nor the poor. In his first effort he cancelled at once all those contracts in which the debtor had borrowed on the security either of

his person or of his land; forbade all future loans or contracts in
which the person of the debtor was pledged as security; and deprived the creditor of all further power to imprison, or enslave, or
extort work from his debtor, confining him to an effective judgment
at law, which would authorize the seizure of the property of the
latter. This regulation swept off the numerous mortgage-pillars
(see *Appendix*, note 61) from the landed properties in Attica, and
left the land free from all past claims. It liberated and restored to
their full rights all those debtors who were actually in slavery under
previous legal adjudications; and it even professed to provide means
for the restoration of those who had, for a similar reason, been sold
into foreign slavery. (Grote's History of Greece, vol. iii, p. 135.)

By this extensive measure poor debtors and small tenants,
together with many others in needy circumstances, were greatly
relieved. But this relief placed another important class in great
difficulty. These were they who, while they stood in the relation
of creditors to the poorest classes, were themselves debtors to the
richest. To meet the case of such, Solon had recourse to the desperate expedient of debasing the money-standard of the country to
the extent of more than twenty-five per cent. The middlemen consequently obtained relief to this amount, while their rich creditors
had to submit to an equivalent loss.

Again: Solon decreed that all those who had been condemned by the
archons to civil disfranchisement, excepting only those who had been
convicted by other legal courts for murder or treason, should be free.
The necessity for such measures—indeed, the possibility of introducing them—clearly shows the diseased and disorganized state of
the Athenian commonwealth. The policy of Solon, however, not
only warded off the imminent convulsion which had long threatened
the country; it virtually depressed the political power of the rich,
and restored the poorer classes to extensive influence in public
affairs.

Having succeeded thus far, Solon was requested to prepare a new
constitution for the country; which task he also accepted, and carried
into effect thus :—He divided the whole population into four classes,
without reference to their tribes and families, but regulated entirely
by their possession of property. The first of these, comprising the
richest portion of the people, whose annual income was equal to five
hundred *medimni* of corn or above, were alone eligible to be archons,
and to military and naval commands. A second class was composed
of persons whose income ranged from five hundred to three hundred
medimni. These were called "knights," or "horsemen of the state,"
they being supposed to possess sufficient substance to keep a horse,

and to perform military service in that capacity. The third class, possessing an annual income of from three hundred to two hundred *medimni* of corn, constituted the heavy-armed infantry of the Athenian army, and were bound to serve as such, each with his own equipment of complete armour. Five hundred *medimni* were equal to about seven hundred imperial bushels; and one *medimnus* was equal to a drachm, and of the same value as a sheep.

These three classes paid all the direct taxes that were levied. Of course duties on imports and other articles of consumption would be paid in common by all. These direct taxes were levied in the form of a graduated income-tax, so far as the several classes are regarded; but as an equal tax, when considered with reference to the several individuals composing each class. Thus the poorest member of the first class, with an income of five hundred drachms, would, on a levy of one per cent., pay fifty drachms. Every other member of that class, whatever his wealth, would pay a *pro ratâ* sum. The poorest member of the second class, with an income of three hundred, would on the same levy pay thirty drachms; while the poorest member of the third class would be required to contribute only ten.

The fourth class, composed of all persons whose annual income was less than two hundred drachms, or about forty dollars, (which would then purchase about two hundred sheep, or about two hundred and eighty imperial bushels of corn,) were exempt from all direct taxes, disqualified from holding any individual post of dignity, and only served in war as light-armed troops, in armour provided by the state. Although, by these institutions of Solon, the great body of the people, who were comprised under this fourth class, were deprived of the privilege of holding office, their collective importance was in other ways greatly increased. For, though ineligible to official dignities, they had to elect the archons and magistrates out of the first class; and, what is still more important, these, after having served their term of office, were responsible to the assembly of the people, and might be impeached and punished in case of misbehaviour.

Another of Solon's institutions still remains to be noticed. He created a senate separate and distinct from the Areopagus, and with different powers. In the institution of this body the object was to prepare subjects for discussion in the general assembly, to convoke and superintend its meetings, and to insure the execution of its decrees. This senate, as appointed by Solon, consisted of four hundred members, taken in equal proportions from the four tribes. Persons of the fourth or poorer class were not eligible to sit in this senate; they were, however, entitled to vote on the election of every member; and, being by far the most numerous section of Athenian citizens, they invariably held in their hands the virtual appointment of the senatorial body.

At the same time that these new institutions were called into being, the old-established Council of Areopagus (see *Appendix*, note 62) was recognised, and its powers enlarged; it being endowed with ample supervision over the execution of the laws generally, together with the duty of a censorial inspection of the lives and occupations of citizens, as well as the power to punish men of idle and dissolute habits.

These measures of Solon, although they did not establish a democracy, had a most decided and efficient democratic tendency. They, in fact, formed the foundation and framework of the vigorous democracy which afterward so long reigned supreme at Athens. When, however, we speak of Grecian democracy, we feel as if using a figure of speech; for while we read that all the people were invested with political rights, and allowed to take a part and exercise an influence in the affairs of the state, it must be remembered that the term "people" is limited to the Hellenic part of the population. The greater number of the inhabitants—perhaps as many as three-fourths of the whole—were slaves, and regarded as utterly destitute of all political functions, and without any interest in the state.

It seems scarcely credible that, after all these institutions of Solon had been introduced and established, the lawgiver should have lived to see the whole constitution placed in abeyance through the successful usurpation of supreme power by an individual. Yet so it was. The *tyrant* Pisistratus, as such sovereigns were always called in Greece, exercised the power which he had unjustly obtained with great wisdom and moderation. His accession to this dignity, however, led to various factions and intrigues, by which he was twice driven from Attica. Yet he again succeeded in establishing himself in supreme power, and continued to hold it until his death.

Hipparchus and Hippias succeeded their father in the government of Athens; but they did not inherit his prudence and ability. Yet, favoured by the *prestige* of his character, and the actual possession of power, they succeeded in maintaining their joint dominion fourteen years, when Hipparchus was slain by two young Athenians, whom he had provoked by an atrocious insult. The excessive cruelty with which Hippias punished all who took any part in the murder of his brother, and even those who were suspected of having any knowledge of the plot, produced such intense disgust in the public mind, that various efforts were made to expel the tyrant from the country. These, however, would in all probability have been unsuccessful, but for the peculiar influence which the Alcmæonids had just now obtained at Delphi.

This family, having been driven from Athens by Pisistratus, retired from Attica; and as the temple of Delphi was just then to be reërected after its destruction by fire, they undertook the contract, which they executed in a style of splendour far beyond the design. By this means, supplemented by costly donatives, the oracle was induced to denounce the tyranny of Hippias, and to insist on the return of the Alcmæonids. This was brought about mainly by the instrumentality of Sparta. Whenever any citizen of that country appeared before the oracle, either on public or on private business, the answer always included the injunction, "Athens must be delivered." The constant repetition of this mandate overcame at length the friendly feeling which the Spartans felt toward the house of Pisistratus. Pious reverence for the god prevailed; and an expedition was sent to Athens to coöperate with the Alcmæonids, which, although defeated in the first campaign, succeeded in the second, under the conduct of Cleomenes, the Spartan king.

Hippias being thus expelled, democracy was established at Athens. Calisthenes the Alcmæonid not only restored the Solonian constitution in all its integrity, but greatly enlarged it. For, whereas previously the free citizens of Athens were comprised in the four Ionic tribes, by which regulation a great number of free-born Hellenes were excluded from all influence in state-affairs, Calisthenes abolished these four tribes, and divided the country into several demes or cantons. These he afterward arranged into ten tribes, so that no entire tribe corresponded to any given district. By this means he destroyed local feuds, and introduced an organization by which the whole country was fairly represented. In each of these tribes he enrolled all the free native Athenians, the most respectable resident strangers who had immigrated into the country, and even some of the superior order of slaves. By such measures the whole body of the Ionic population were placed under the inspiring influence of institutions calculated to employ all their intelligence and to elicit all their energy: and their future history shows how they responded to the call.

Having thus depicted the condition of Sparta and Athens, the leading powers of Greece, it will be necessary to give a rapid review of the minor states.

THEBES.—The Bœotians, who had been expelled by the Thracians, after having found refuge in Thessaly, returned to the land of their fathers about the time of the Dorian migration, and became united with the Æolian tribes. Royalty was abolished here as early as 1126 B. C., and the Bœotians formed as many states as they had cities. The political constitutions of these diminutive dominions were vague and undefined, and frequently fluctuated between a loose democracy and a tyrant oligarchy. Thebes always stood at the head, and exercised a paramount influence over these associated tribes. Their general affairs were decided in councils, held in each of the four districts into which the province was divided; and these assemblies united to elect four chiefs, who were supreme magistrates in peace, and generals in war.

Of the civil constitution and political government of ACARNANIA, ÆTOLIA, and LOCRIS at this time, little is known. It is probable that their institutions were principally aristocratical. The states of THESSALY were generally ruled by individual chiefs with arbitrary power. EPIRUS was subject to a family of kings called Æacidæ, who claimed descent from one of the sons of Achilles.

In peninsular Greece, CORINTH was, next to Sparta, the principal state. Commanding by its position the Ionian and Ægean Seas, and holding the keys of the Peloponnesus, Corinth rose rapidly into opulence and power. From the time of the Dorian migration to the year B. C. 584, it was subject, with little intermission, to three successive dynasties of kings. At this period, Psammitichus, after a reign of three years, was driven out by his subjects with the aid of Sparta, when an aristocratical goverment was formed.

SICYON, and the other Achæan states, were subject to a series of revolutions very similar to those of Corinth. In ARCADIA, ARGOS, and ELIS, monarchical institutions had successively given way to republican govenments.

A similar change had taken place in the principal Grecian islands. Corcyra, which was occupied by a Corinthian colony about 753 B. C., had, prior to the Persian war, an aristocratical government. Ægina was peopled at a very early date by Myrmidons from Thessaly, and at first was ruled by kings; but subsequently adopted a republican government. Eubœa had received many colonies from the main-land of Greece, and, probably as a consequence, its several cities were not united by any political confederacy, each possessing a separate constitution. Its principal towns were governed by an aristocracy. Crete was greatly celebrated even in the heroic ages. After the death of Cleanthus, B. C. 800, republican institutions were established in the principal cities, which thenceforth became independent states.

The Grecian colonies demand a passing notice. They were greatly instrumental in the diffusion of knowledge, in accelerating the progress of civilization, and in facilitating commercial intercourse between different nations. In this notice it is not intended to refer to the early settlements of the Pelasgi in Italy, which properly belong to the history of Western Europe; nor to the martial colonies established by the successors of Alexander, which pertain to a subsequent period; but to those founded by the Hellenic race between the time of the Dorian migration and the Persian war.

Soon after the subjection of Peloponnesus to the Heraclidæ and their Dorian allies, a great number of Æolians quitted their native land in small companies, headed by different Pelopid princes; and, after staying some time in Attica and Thrace, they passed over into Asia, and occupied the coasts of Mysia and Caria. They also obtained possession of the islands of Lesbos, Tenedos, and the cluster called the *Hecatonnesi*, or "Hundred Islands." Twelve cities were erected by these colonies on the Asiatic continent, the principal being Cyme and Smyrna. These maintained their independence until the age of Cyrus, when they were subdued by the Persians.

The great emigration from Ionia took place some years after the Æolian, about B. C. 1044. It was the largest that ever left Greece, and was occasioned by the abolition of royalty at Athens on the death of Codrus. His sons, disdaining to live as private citizens in a country over which their father had reigned, and which they regarded themselves as justly entitled to govern, declared their resolve to emigrate into Asia. They were readily joined by a numerous train of followers; and, having procured a fleet and suitable munitions of war, they took their course to Asia Minor, and landed on the south coast of Æolis. After a series of sanguinary wars, they succeeded in expelling the barbarian natives, and obtaining possession of the country from Miletus to Mount Sipylus. The result of Ionian emigration was the establishment of twelve cities in this district,—Ephesus, Erythræ, Clazomenæ, Colophon, Myus, Miletus, Priene, Phocæa, Lebedos, Samos, Teos, and Chios.

Of these the last three were insular stations. Miletus was the chief of these colonies, and Ephesus the most renowned. Phocæa was one of the latest cities founded by the Ionians. It obtained its name from a later immigration of Phocæans, induced by the success of preceding adventurers. This city rapidly rose into commercial importance, and was particularly remarkable for its extensive trade with the remote parts of Western Europe, while Miletus engrossed the principal portion of the traffic to the Euxine and Black Seas. Having these separate sources of wealth, and maintaining a commercial intercommunication, these cities became, prior to 600 B. C., important rivals to Tyre and Carthage. Phocæa founded several colonies, the principal of which was Marseilles. Colophon attained special distinction for its formidable cavalry, whose resistless charge became proverbial. Samos was the most noted of the insular cities, and was distinguished by the extent of its trade and naval power. All these Ionian colonies were united by an Amphictyonic confederacy. Representatives of the several cities met at stated times in the temple of Neptune at Mycale: here they deliberated on all matters pertaining to the general interests of the union, but never interfered with the internal government of particular cities. This was by far the largest and most successful of the Greek colonies.

After the conquest of Peloponnesus, the Dorians still desired a more enlarged range of territory; and being checked by the Athenians at Megara, they departed in separate companies to the coast of Caria, and to the islands of Cos and Rhodes. This migration appears to have been made without any concerted plan or direct union between the parties. It resulted in the erection of six cities, which afterward formed the Doric confederation called Hexapolis. This comprised Halicarnassus, Cnidus, Cos, Ialysus, Camirus, and Lindus.

Besides the preceding, the Greeks established several flourishing colonies on the shores of the Euxine Sea, on the coasts of Thrace and Macedon, and in Africa and Sicily.

The citizens of Miletus were most prominent in the establishment of colonies on the shores of the Euxine Sea, the Propontis, and the Palus Mæotis. This enterprise was carried out from 800 B. C. to 600 B. C. Miletus, indeed, acquired and sustained the immense trade which filled the four harbours pertaining to that city, and provided and equipped a naval armament, amounting to nearly one hundred galleys of war, principally by means of these northern colonies and their trade. Having established these important towns, —Lampsacus, near the Hellespont; Cyzicus, an ancient city, of which they obtained possession about 751 B. C., on the coast of Asia; Perinthus, on the coast of Thrace, just opposite to it; Heraclea, on the Black Sea; Sinope, in Paphlagonia; Amisus, in Pontus; and Phasis, and other cities, on the eastern coast of the Euxine,—they not only extended their commerce into southern Russia, but even penetrated overland into the countries now known as Khiva and Bokhara.

The coasts of Thrace and Macedon were nearly covered with Greek colonies, principally founded by Corinthians and Athenians.

On the coast of Africa stood the celebrated city of Cyrene, founded, in obedience to the Delphic oracle, by a company of

Dorians from the Isle of Thera, B. C. 651. This city rose into great commercial power and importance, and was long a rival to Carthage. The government was at first monarchical; but, like all other Greek states, it afterward became a republic, and ultimately merged into the kingdom of Egypt, in the time of the Ptolemies.

In Sicily, Syracuse, founded by a body of Corinthians B. C. 735, took the lead, and ultimately became the metropolis of the island. Here also, as elsewhere, royalty was established at first, but soon gave way to republican institutions.

Even this very brief review of the early history of the Greek tribes, and of the practical development of their institutions and resources, will enable us to form some idea of this extraordinary people. Their progress in civilization, and successful cultivation of the useful arts of life, enabled them to provide for all their wants, and promoted a rapid increase of population; while their restless energy and daring spirit of enterprise led them to grasp at the commerce of the western world. Their colonies covered the coasts of Asia Minor and the Archipelago, studded the shores of the Euxine, and extended even to Africa and Sicily; pursuing everywhere a liberal policy, and carrying on extensive commercial operations. Perhaps no nation ever resembled our own so much as Greece, B. C. 650. Impelled by a dominant spirit of daring, and thirst for gain and authority, and sustained by equal wisdom and prowess, the Grecians outgrew the limited territory of their fathers, and, while they carried their language and institutions to distant lands, drew from every quarter means of progress and elements of power.

In one striking peculiarity, they were unlike every other people. With a perfect identity of national lineage and character, they were divided into nearly as many independent states as they had respectable towns. Their colonial and commercial progress was, therefore, the result of local or individual effort. This state of things, while it gave the utmost encouragement to private enterprise, prevented the possibility of any great national movement, in the way either of commerce or of war, beyond the limits of their own land.

At this period of her history Greece had to sustain an invasion, equal, perhaps, in violence and power to any which ever assailed an independent nation. This was the first Persian war. It seems to have arisen out of several circumstances as proximate causes. The first of these occurred before the abolition of monarchy at Athens by the expulsion of the family of Pisistratus. Democedes, while a captive in Persia, having cured Atossa, the wife of Darius, of a dangerous tumour, induced her to propose that he should be sent to survey Greece, ostensibly for the purpose of subjecting it to Persia, but really that he might find the means of returning to his own country. The king of Persia consenting, the wily Greek effected his escape, and sent back a most offensive message to his late master. This rankled in the mind of Darius, and led him to meditate the means of revenge. There seems every human probability that this warlike prince, under the influence of these feelings, would have attempted an invasion, and have effected his purpose, if his mind had not been previously filled with a determination to subdue Scythia. (Grote's History of Greece, vol. iv, p. 353.)

At this period the paramount influence of Persia appears to have been acknowledged throughout all eastern Europe and the neighbouring islands. For when Darius crossed the Hellespont, and marched through Thrace to the Danube, on his insane attempt on Scythia, we find a bridge constructed for him over this broad river by the Ionians. In fact we may always notice, that those operations which require particular intelligence or energy are performed for him by Greeks or Phenicians. The Ionians who had constructed this bridge were left to guard it during the absence of the Persian king on his expedition; during which time they were instigated by bands of Scythians to destroy it, and thus shut up the Persian invader to inevitable destruction. Miltiades, at that time sovereign of the Thracian Chersonese, strongly urged the adoption of this policy. But he was overruled by the influence of Histiæus; and the Persian army, having utterly failed in their attempt, returned in safety. In the mean time Hippias, the son of Pisistratus, having found refuge in the Persian court after being exiled from Athens, solicited the aid of that nation to secure his return to power.

While all these circumstances tended to bring about a rupture between Persia and the powerful states of Greece, that event was hastened by the violent conduct of Histiæus, who had saved Darius and his army by preserving the bridge across the Danube. He soon discovered, that an essential service rendered to an absolute monarch is often as dangerous as an offence. Finding himself exposed to great peril on this account, he concerted with his nephew Aristagoras, and excited the Grecian colonies in Asia to revolt against Persia. In this effort he was aided by twenty ships from Athens. At first the insurrection was successful. Sardis, the capital of Lydia, was taken, and great wealth fell into the hands of the captors. But Aristagoras did not possess the genius and prudence necessary to a great commander. Reverses soon followed; the Persians triumphed; Aristagoras fled into Thrace, where he was murdered; and Histiæus, after desperate attempts to resist Persian power, and establish himself in different cities, was taken and crucified at Sardis by the Persian satrap.

Darius, acting under the influence of the feelings of resentment called forth by this revolt, manifested his anger against those who had in any way promoted it. He accordingly sent ambassadors to the Grecian states, demanding from them severally their homage, but requiring from Athens in addition that she should receive back the exiled Hippias. All the states, except Athens and Sparta, complied with his request; but these republics returned a haughty defiance. This reply, as might be expected, induced the proud Persian to prepare for the invasion of Greece. As mentioned in a preceding chapter, Mardonius was accordingly sent with a large army to carry out his purpose. He was accompanied by a fleet; and succeeded in subduing the Island of Thasos and the kingdom of Macedon; and was advancing toward Thessaly, when the fleet, while proceeding, that it might coöperate with the army in the Thermaic Gulf, encountered a terrible storm as it was passing Mount Athos, by which 300 ships were destroyed, and at least 20,000 men drowned, or cast on the desolate shore, to die a still more terrible death from cold, hunger, or wild beasts. This catastrophe rendered the advance of Mardonius on Greece impossible. The remains of the fleet and army returned to the Hellespont, and passed over to Asia.

Darius, still intent on his purpose, while preparing a vast armament for another invasion, sent heralds to the several cities, to demand from each the formal tokens of submission,—earth and water. This demand was generally complied with; but at Athens and Sparta it was not only rejected with intense indignation, but even the heralds bearing the message, notwithstanding the sacredness of their character, were instantly put to death.

This threatened danger led to the public acknowledgment of Sparta as the leading state of Greece, and to her acceptance of this distinction. This is important, inasmuch as, according to the highest authority, "it is the first direct and positive historical manifestation of Hellas as an aggregate body, with Sparta as its chief, and obligations of a certain sort on the part of its members, the neglect or violation of which constitutes a species of treason."—*Grote's History of Greece*, vol. iv, p. 431. This result was occasioned by an appeal from Athens to Sparta, as the head of Greece, against the Æginetans, for having given earth and water to the Persians, which they regarded as treason to Hellas. The Spartans responded to this appeal. Their two kings went to Ægina, and not only insisted upon the inhabitants continuing faithful to Greece in the coming struggle, but actually selected ten of the most eminent citizens, and took them to Athens to be kept as hostages for the performance of the promise.

Meanwhile, as the result of two years' preparations, the Persians assembled a great army and fleet. This armament, having passed along the coast of Asia to Samos, struck across the Ægean Sea, ravaging several islands in their course. They landed in the Bay of Marathon, on the east coast of Attica. Hippias, the former tyrant of Athens, returned with the Persian army. He had landed at the same place forty-seven years before, then a very young man, with his father Pisistratus; and, although accompanied by a comparatively small force, soon obtained the government of Athens. No doubt, he expected on this occasion, by the aid of the immense Persian host, a still easier acquisition of power. These hopes would be greatly strengthened by the fact, that up to this time the tide of Persian success had been uninterrupted; for the campaign of Darius in Scythia did not present the aspect of defeat. (Grote, vol. ix, p. 481.)

But the character of the Athenians had greatly changed during the interval. More than eighteen years the political arrangements of Cleisthenes had been in operation. The ten tribes, each with its constituent demes, had become a part of the established institutions and habits of the people. The tendency to intrigue and cabals had been in great measure cut off. The people were now accustomed to exercise a genuine and self-determined decision in their assemblies. They regarded themselves as identified with the state; and consequently the Persian invasion was an aggression on the personal liberty and property of every individual.

Besides this great improvement in the public character of the Athenians, it happened that at this time this city boasted the presence and aid of three statesmen, each of whom would have immortalized any country in any age. MILTIADES, who had so earnestly urged the destruction of the bridge across the Danube, while Darius was engaged in his Scythian expedition, had been compelled to return to his native city, where his eminent bravery and well-known decision of character raised him to an important command. THEMISTOCLES and ARISTIDES were younger men. The former, in addition to other high qualities, possessed boundless sagacity and invention, and was what would now be called a consummate diplomatist. The latter, together with great talents, always evinced an inflexible and universally acknowledged integrity.

At this juncture, with the immense host of Persia but a short distance from Athens, and supported by a vast fleet on the coast, the Athenians first despatched a messenger to solicit the immediate aid of Sparta. A strange superstition, or a still more culpable motive, induced this most powerful state to decline marching against the enemy until after the full moon,—a delay of at least five days.

The peculiar manner in which the Athenian forces were commanded also offered serious obstacles to a successful prosecution of the war. The army, being collected from the ten tribes, was commanded by ten generals, one from each tribe, with equal powers; every one of them having the direction of the whole army a single day in regular rotation. When these generals met to consult on the best course of resisting the enemy, they were equally divided in opinion; five voting for marching at once to attack the enemy, the other five for delay. Fortunately, however, the polemarch Callimachus, who had the casting vote, influenced by the powerful arguments of Miltiades, supported the proposal for an immediate attack.

We have no means of ascertaining with precision the numbers engaged in this conflict. The Athenian army appears to have comprised about 10,000 men, and the Persian at least ten times that number. The reputation of Miltiades was such, that all the generals waived their right to command in his favour. He accordingly led his troops against the Persian army near Marathon, and, after a short but severe encounter, routed it, and pursued the invaders to their ships. Notwithstanding this terrible defeat, the power of the Persian host was so great that it was proposed at once to sail to the harbour of Athens, and attack the city in the absence of the army. Miltiades, however, perceived the object of the enemy's movement, and effected a rapid return to the city, before the arrival of the fleet. Being thus defeated on the field and in his strategy, the Persian commander returned to Asia, and the liberties of Greece were maintained.

Perhaps no successful warrior ever occupied a higher position in the estimation of his country than Miltiades, after the battle of Marathon; but it was of short duration. Intoxicated with success, he urged the preparation of a great armament, with which he attacked the Island of Paros, but was defeated and wounded; and, returning in disgrace, he was tried, fined, and cast into prison, where he died.

Themistocles and Aristides now conducted the affairs of Athens, and greatly extended the influence of the state by martial prowess abroad, and by the improvement of its jurisprudence at home. Their rivalry, however, issued in the banishment of Aristides by ostracism; (see *Appendix*, note 63;) after which, Themistocles largely added to the naval power of his country, and secured the complete ascendency of Athens in the Grecian seas.

Although Darius, on the return of his expedition from Greece, was gratified to behold the long line of captives which Datis his general had taken at Eretria, he was exceedingly mortified that his attempt on Athens had not only failed, but that the arms of Persia had been covered with defeat and disgrace. Under this strong feeling against Athens in particular and Greece generally, Darius resolved upon collecting the entire strength of his empire for the accomplishment of his purpose and the gratification of his revenge. For three whole years the various governors and satraps were employed in making the necessary preparation for this war. Nor did the revolt of Egypt intimidate this martial prince. He had collected such an immense array of force, that he felt able to undertake the reduction of Egypt and the conquest of Greece at the same time. Death, however, sudden and unexpected, compelled him to bequeath his plans and prospects to Xerxes, his son and successor.

This prince did not immediately enter into the designs of his father. It required the utmost efforts of Grecian exiles, (Grote, vol. v, p. 5,) and the Persian counsellors who were partial to the project, to induce him to undertake this long-threatened invasion. But he was at length persuaded to enter upon the enterprise, as it is said, as a religious duty. (Grote, vol. v, p. 13.)

It is doubtful whether, in the whole history of the world, an armament equal in magnitude to this one ever proceeded to make war on any kingdom. It comprised levies from forty-six different nations, constituting a total of about 1,700,000 foot soldiers, besides 80,000 horse, numerous war-chariots, from Libya, and camels from Arabia, with an estimated total of 20,000 additional men. (See *Appendix*, note 64.) Besides this land-army, eight other nations furnished a fleet of 1,207 triremes, or ships of war with three banks of oars, on board of which Persians, Medes, and Sacæ served as marines. The real leaders of this vast host were native Persians of noble blood, who were distributed throughout all the divisions of the army.

This estimate has been by many able writers thought extravagant; but as it is that given by Herodotus, who had the advantage of conversing with those who were eye-witnesses of the enumeration of this vast host, it may be taken as the best approximation to the correct number that can be now obtained.

The measures devised for the transit of this army were commensurate with its magnitude. A bridge of boats, fastened together and to either shore by strong cables, was thrown across the Hellespont. This, however, was destroyed by a storm before it was used; at which the Persian monarch was so incensed, that he is said to have descended to the childish absurdity of upbraiding, flogging, and casting fetters into the waters of the strait, as a punishment for their insubordination. Afterward two other bridges were prepared; and over these the vast military array of Persia marched, taking up seven whole days in their transit over this distance of about an English mile in length. Besides this great work, Xerxes had a ship-canal cut through the isthmus which connects Mount Athos with the mainland, so wide that two of his large war-vessels could pass through it abreast. By this means the fleet was saved from the danger of rounding that stormy promontory.

When Greece became fully acquainted with the magnitude of these preparations, universal alarm prevailed; and a congress of the representatives of all the Grecian states who were determined to maintain their freedom, was held at the Isthmus of Corinth. Although this meeting did not result in any settled plan of operations, it did much to heal the feuds existing between the several states, and to induce a general union of feeling and a nationality of purpose. Meanwhile the oracles gave most appalling intelligence, and the prevailing sentiments were apprehension and distrust.

The first active measure toward repelling the invasion was the defence of the Pass of Thermopylæ. This was undertaken by Sparta, as the leading state of Greece. The force appointed for this service was led by Leonidas, one of the kings of that state, at the head of a band of three hundred citizen-warriors of Lacedæmon, with five hundred *hoplitæ* of Tegea, five hundred from Mantinea, four hundred from Corinth, and about two thousand one hundred from other places; besides four hundred Thebans, whose fidelity to the cause of Greece was very questionable. This famous pass consisted of two narrow openings at each end, just broad enough to drive a single chariot through: between these two extremities there was an interval of about a mile of wide open road, on the sides of which were several hot springs. This combination of circumstances gave it the name of *Thermopylæ*, or "the Hot Gates."

Another consideration led the Greeks to adopt this position. The Persian fleet accompanied the army, coasting its way as it advanced. Here, however, the large island of Eubœa lay immediately off the mainland, forming in the intermediate space the Meliac and Opuntian Gulfs; so that the Persian fleet had to encounter the dangerous navigation outside the island, and to be separated to a great distance from the army, or to sail through the narrow channel, where the small but effective Greek fleet would fight at nearly as great an advantage as was possessed by the soldiers who defended the pass. This position was accordingly occupied by the united navy of

Greece. When, however, the Persian fleet arrived, their numbers and strength were so imposing that the Greeks were terrified into an immediate retreat into the narrowest part of the channel,—a movement which neutralized entirely the defence of Thermopylæ, since it afforded an opportunity for the fleet to advance, and land troops in the rear of the Greek army. But before the Persians had sufficient information or time to avail themselves of this advantage, a terrible storm or succession of storms made frightful havoc of their ships. According to the lowest estimate, four hundred large vessels of war, besides numerous transports and small craft, with a countless number of men and an immense amount of stores and treasure, were lost. The Greeks attributed this storm to the interposition of their deity Boreas. The hurricane certainly had so damaged the Persian fleet that the Greeks felt emboldened to resist its progress, and for that purpose returned to Artemisium.

Xerxes at first could scarcely credit the report that a small band of Spartans would dare to resist the march of his army through the pass : he, however, soon found it to be true. Not only did they resist, but for two successive days hurled back in confusion and disgrace all that survived of the best troops in the Persian army who were sent against them. The proud Persian, maddened by this defeat and loss, thrice leaped from his horse in frantic agony. All his efforts, however, would have been vain, had not a Greek deserter told him of a narrow path across the mountain, by which he was enabled to march a body of troops to the other side of the pass, and thus, taking Leonidas in the rear, completely hemmed him in. The Spartan king was aware of this path, and had intrusted the defence of it to the Phocians, who, being assailed by the Persians at midnight, sought safety in flight. On hearing of this misfortune, Leonidas sent away his auxiliary forces, and retained with him but one thousand chosen troops. He did not wait for the attack, but, sallying forth into the broad space, he assailed the Persian host, and inflicted a terrible slaughter on the invaders, until, wearied rather than vanquished, the Spartan king fell, and his brave companions were destroyed.

About this time the Greek fleet obtained a great victory over that of the enemy at Artemisium; but this was rendered of no effect by the fatal loss of Thermopylæ, since there was no other tenable position to the north of the Isthmus of Corinth. The career of Xerxes was now marked with fire and blood. The Greeks in general abandoned their towns, and all the property which they could not remove; while the Persian host, after pillaging all that they could take, burned and destroyed the remainder. This was even the case with Athens. That noble people, knowing that it would be impossible to defend their city, removed their women and children to places of refuge in the adjacent islands, while all able to bear arms passed over to Salamis, to resist the enemy to the utmost.

Xerxes was allowed to gratify his revenge in the entire destruction of the Attic capital. This was, indeed, his prime object in the invasion of Greece; and it was the limit of his success. Intoxicated with this gratification, he decided on attacking the Greek fleet in the harbour of Salamis, and had the intense mortification of seeing his great navy completely ruined. The fleet being mainly composed of Phenicians, Egyptians, Cilicians, Cyprians, &c., differing in language from each other, and having no plan for acting in concert, the battle had no sooner begun in the narrow straits, than the whole fleet was thrown into confusion, and, hemmed around by the skilfully managed Greek ships, was destroyed, to an immense extent, without the possibility of successful defence. Xerxes was an eye-witness of the combat; and, on perceiving the result, he resolved to secure his personal safety by an immediate return to Asia. Leaving Mardonius with three hundred thousand chosen troops, the Persian monarch, with the residue of the army, hastily retreated by the way by which he came: but on reaching the Hellespont, he found his bridge destroyed, and had to cross the strait in a common fishing-boat.

The progress and result of this invasion thus far yield very important information on the character and relations of the Grecian states. It is almost incredible, yet it is an undoubted fact, that, while this immense army was marching through Thessaly, Greece had not seriously begun to prepare measures for the defence of the country; that when Leonidas and his devoted band took their station at Thermopylæ, not only was there no general and well-organized plan of resistance, but the most insane and criminal neglect of national interests existed. It was just then the time of celebrating the Olympic Games on the banks of the Alpheus, and the Carneian festival at Sparta and in most of the other Dorian states; and thus, while not merely the freedom, but even the existence, of Greece was at stake, a mere handful of men are sent to withstand myriads, that the body of the nation may enjoy these solemnities. This course is the more extraordinary, inasmuch as the frontier of Thessaly was clearly the proper place for the defence of Greece. If, by a wise arrangement, the strength of the several states had marshalled there, the attack of the proud Persian must have proved an unmitigated failure. But when, in consequence of the defeat of Leonidas, the Persians poured their troops into Greece, there was then no tenable position for the Greek army but the Isthmus of Corinth; and consequently all Doris, Bœotia, and Attica were left to be ravaged by the enemy.

But while all the disgrace and loss connected with the conquest of these states and the burning of Athens were caused by the fault of the Greeks, the entire failure of the expedition arose out of an equally false movement of Xerxes. If, instead of the foolish attack on the Greek fleet in the harbour of Salamis, he had pushed on his troops against Corinth, it is more than probable that, according to the opinion of the sagacious and brave Queen Artemisia, the ships of the Peloponnesian states would have retired from the fleet to protect their own homes; and thus, instead of one united Greek naval armament, there would have been opposed to the Persian navy only a number of small and ineffective squadrons.

After the flight of Xerxes, Mardonius with his army retired to Thessaly, where he wintered. Before renewing the war the following spring, he sent to the Athenians, offering to rebuild their city, and to give them the friendship of Persia, if they would secede from the Greek alliance. This measure greatly alarmed Sparta, who immediately sent ambassadors to Athens, imploring that people to reject the proposal. The Athenians nobly declared that great as were their sufferings and difficulties, they would maintain the war with Persia, while a single Athenian remained alive. They at the same time urged the immediate presence of a Peloponnesian army in Bœotia, to resist the advancing foe. This, in defiance of all sound policy and just principle, was refused; and Attica was once more desolated with fire and sword, the Athenians again taking refuge in Salamis. At this juncture Mardonius renewed his offers of friendship to the Athenians, which they rejected with scorn and contempt.

At length the Spartans were roused to action, fearing the defection of the Athenians or the return of the Persian fleet, either of which events would create a danger which no fortifications at the Isthmus of Corinth could avert. The Spartan force was commanded by Pausanias. On the approach of the Greek army, Mardonius retired to Bœotia, where he could fight at considerable advantage. Thither he was followed by the Greeks; and, after numerous evolutions and skirmishes, a great and decisive battle was fought near Platæa. This was brought about in great measure by accident. Pausanias, finding his post on the Asopus very favourable for the Persian cavalry, retired in the night to a position on higher ground near Platæa. Mardonius, mistaking this movement for a retreat, ordered an immediate and general attack. The result was the total defeat of the Persians: Mardonius and two hundred thousand of his men lay dead on the field, and of the remainder of the army only forty thousand escaped under Artabazus to the Hellespont. The invading legions were thus annihilated, Greece delivered, and a countless booty of wealth realized from the Persian camp.

By a singular coincidence, on the same day that the battle of Plataea was fought, the Persian navy, although drawn ashore at Mycale, and protected by sixty thousand men, was stormed and destroyed by the Greek fleet. These victories decided the issue of the conflict. Pausanias, enabled to assume the aggressive, continued the war against all the Persian dependencies in the Ægean Sea, and consummated his triumph by the capture of Byzantium, which was even then an important city.

Although this celebrated general allowed himself to be so intoxicated by his success and consequent wealth that he miserably perished, and Themistocles by the artifice of the Spartans was involved in his crime and died in banishment, the war was continued against Persia, principally under the direction of Cimon, the son of Miltiades, until, in 449 B. C., after a conflict of more than fifty years' duration, a peace was negotiated, which confirmed the independence of Greece, and of the Greek cities in Lower Asia, shut out all Persian vessels from the Ægean waters, and prohibited any Persian army from coming within three days' march of the sea. To this successful issue did the valour of Greece bring a war with the most powerful empire of the world at that time.

As our limits prevent our going into detail of the events connected with the rebuilding and fortification of Athens on an extended scale, (see *Appendix*, note 65,) in defiance of the petty jealousy of Sparta; as well as of the various political measures by which the former state, through daring maritime and commercial enterprise, became the leading power of Hellas; it will be necessary to direct particular attention to the real condition of Greece in this the most glorious period of her career.

It is extremely difficult to ascertain whence the peculiar and distinguishing excellence of the Greek character arose, and to trace the combination of fostering influences under which it grew up to such maturity and power. But it is certain that this growth was as rapid in its progress as it was remarkable in its extent, and grand in its results. It was after B. C. 660 that the Greeks are known to have cultivated the art of writing. Even the poems of Homer were unwritten at this period; and it was some time later that prose composition began to be cultivated. Pherecydes of Scyros, B. C. 550, is by several authors regarded as the first Greek prose writer; nor did any one acquire eminence in this department of literature until fifty years afterward.

It is also remarkable that inventions necessary to the existence of works of art in any tolerable measure, were introduced at an equally late period. The art of welding iron was unknown in Greece until just before 600 B. C., when it was discovered by Glaucus of Chios: and about the same time the art of casting copper or brass in a mould was invented at Samos. Prior to this, all Grecian statuary consisted of rude and ill-formed representations. Even the "memorial erected in honour of a god did not pretend to be an image, but was often nothing more than a pillar, a board, a shapeless stone, a post," fixed so as to mark and consecrate a particular locality. Sometimes, indeed, there was a real image, but of the rudest character, formed of wood, and always made for each separate divinity after a particular type or figure. About 580 B. C., a disposition was evinced to alter the material, and to correct the rudeness of the figure. Marble was introduced, and some artists of Crete acquired renown by working with this material. Ivory and gold were also used, to cover and adorn images made of wood.

It is also observable that about this period we meet with the earliest architectural monuments of Greece. The greatest Grecian temples, known to Herodotus, were built about, or soon after 600 B. C.

In tracing the primitive development of the Greek mind, it must not be forgotten, that in the early times, when prose literature was unknown, poetry and music were extensively cultivated. Grote, indeed, supposes music to have first led to this poetic cultivation. However this may be, it is certain that poetry was a most important agent in the development of Grecian greatness. This was perhaps as much owing to the manner in which it was used, as to the peculiar power and influence which it is adapted to communicate. It was not confined to works of imagination, and wasted in rhapsody, but was made to adorn and inspirit the most important public and private duties. Not only were the minds of this people excited and elevated by the sublime conceptions of Homer, and instructed by the Theogonies of Hesiod; but the same agent, strange as it may sound in our ears, was used to propound political constitutions and systems of law. Solon announced his various reforms, and gave forth his canons of government in verse. A metrical work on astronomy was ascribed to Thales.

The immense development of Grecian art, from 600 B. C. to the days of Pericles, forms a wonderful phenomenon in human history. It could only result from an uncommon diffusion of genius; and genius is a providential gift. While, therefore, we refer to means which promoted intellectual progress, we regard it as impossible for any consistent believer in divine revelation to consider the varied talent and the noble intellectual achievements of Greece in any other aspect, than as divinely-appointed means for accomplishing the predetermined purposes of the great Governor of the world.

It may, however, be observed, that one cause of this rapid improvement was evidently the result of the eminently practical tendency of Grecian effort. If we refer, for an instance, to the Seven Wise Men, whose talents and genius have consecrated their names to the highest honour, as great agents in the world's civilization; we do not find them to have been remarkable for their researches into abstract science; for, as a celebrated contemporary of Aristotle declared, they were not "wise men," or "philosophers," in the sense which those words bore in his day, but persons *of practical discernment in reference to man and society.*

The peculiar political constitution of the Grecian states must have greatly fostered the art of public speaking; and it is probable that nothing more effectively contributed to the general intellectual cultivation of the people than this practice. After the close of the Persian war especially, the requirements of public speaking called forth a class of rhetorical teachers, whose united efforts greatly aided the enlargement and refinement of the Grecian mind.

It must not, however, be supposed that this great mental development which immortalized Greece, was the spontaneous result of mere native energy. On the contrary, perhaps no country ever gained so much from foreign teaching. Thales, the most celebrated of the Seven Wise Men, the father both of Grecian science and of the Ionic philosophy, is acknowledged to have obtained his information from abroad. He is known to have visited Egypt and Asia; and it is extremely probable that a mind so energetic and inquisitive would lose no opportunity of seeking knowledge at the fountainhead. He might, therefore, have seen the wonderful Babylon in its glory, with its temple-observatory of the Chaldæan priesthood, and all the treasures of knowledge and research which it contained. He might also have surveyed the still more wonderful Nineveh, before its destruction by the Medes; and, in these primitive seats of life and learning, might have acquired the principles of science, and the results of enlightened and long-continued observation.

This supposition reconciles what else appears contradictory in the accounts which have come down to us respecting this sage,—namely, that while all that is reported of his mathematical knowledge consists of some problems which are contained in the first book of Euclid, he is said by Herodotus to have predicted an eclipse which actually occurred. It is easily conceivable that he might have obtained the latter information from the learned Chaldæans, while his own scientific attainments were on a comparatively limited scale.

Pythagoras was another such instance. He is said to have spent thirty years in travels which extended from Gaul to India. The time and extent of these journeys may be over-estimated; but it can scarcely be doubted that he visited Egypt, Phenicia and Babylon. These countries at that period retained their primitive character and national independence. Amasis, the last of the native kings, reigned in Egypt; and Nebuchadnezzar, or his immediate successor, ruled in Babylon, where the remains of the Hebrew people were then held in captivity.

Pythagoras returned with much important scientific treasure. He was the first European who traced in outline the true theory of the universe, which, two thousand years later, was revived and more fully taught by Copernicus. His principal tenets will be shown in the chapter which treats of the religion of Greece: but it must not be forgotten that, besides carrying out his religious and political objects, he greatly enlarged the general knowledge and the mathematical and physical science of Greece.

Our limits forbid enlargement on this topic: reference to an epitome of this intellectual progress must therefore suffice, in the observation that, from the time of Pythagoras to the days of Pericles, cultivated genius and the elegant arts rapidly rose to the highest perfection ever attained in any age or nation of the world.

The era succeeding the Persian war, which was rendered so glorious to the Greeks by the noblest triumphs of intellect and art, was followed by one so full of calamity and disgrace to the national character, that the mind recoils from the recital of such events; and we therefore purposely give but a very brief outline of them.

Athens attained, under the government of Pericles, the summit of her greatness. Not only did she stand foremost in the various departments of science, literature, and art, but in other respects her acquisitions were equally wonderful. Unbounded wealth had been gained, an unrivalled extent of commerce secured, and a corresponding naval force and colonial empire organized. In the short period between the battle of Mycale and the first Peloponnesian war, Athens had established her authority over more than one thousand miles of the coast of Asia; had taken possession of forty islands, together with the important straits which joined the Euxine and the Ægean; had conquered and colonized Thrace and Macedon; and had extended her powerful influence over the countries and tribes still further northward.

This amount of success rendered Sparta and the other Grecian states extremely jealous and envious of Athens. To such a degree was this feeling carried, that nothing but a pretext was wanting to create a formidable confederacy against Attica. A dispute with Corinth respecting some colonial possessions induced that state to seek the aid of Sparta,—a request which was immediately granted, and produced a general war between the two great sections of the Greek nation. The parties to this contest were singularly balanced in their power to maintain it. Athens, with her commercial and colonial resources and maritime strength, seemed far more than a match for Sparta and all her allies: but while this power was overwhelming at sea, the large extent of coast and scattered countries from which it was drawn prevented Athens from bringing an army into the field sufficient to meet that of her associated enemies. Each of the belligerents prosecuted the war according to their means. Sparta invaded and ravaged Attica by land, and the Athenian fleet desolated the coasts of Sparta. This unnatural contest was continued for about nine years with varying success, when it terminated in a peace, or rather truce, for fifty years, made on the basis of a mutual restitution of the captures made by each party during the war. This took place B. C. 422.

One short year sufficed to terminate this hopeful return of the Greek people to a pacific policy. Corinth, regarding her interests as neglected in this treaty, privately incited the Argives against Sparta. This in itself might have been harmless, had not Alcibiades, a nephew of Pericles, induced the Athenians to afford secret support to this aggression. This man, although possessing talent, lacked principle, and was, moreover, the slave of an ungovernable ambition. His influence was sufficient to place the leading states of Greece again in an antagonistic position.

Having effected this object, he persuaded the Athenians to send a great armament against Sicily. Although the object was not distinctly avowed, it was intended by this means to establish the supremacy of Athens over that island. This was the culminating point of Athenian greatness and daring. The expedition entirely failed: the fleet of one hundred and thirty-four ships of war, besides transports and tenders, were either taken or destroyed. The army, after terrible defeats and privations, was compelled to surrender at discretion; after which the generals were put to death, and the common soldiers sold for slaves.

In the mean time Alcibiades, who had been at first one of the commanders of this expedition, but who had fled from his post and his country, to avoid trial on a charge of impiety, at first aided the

Spartans by his advice and counsel in their aggressions on Athens; but, having provoked their resentment by his vices, and being wishful to return to his native country, he negotiated with the Persian satrap of Western Asia, and thus effected an entire revolution in Athens, by which the democracy was destroyed, and the government confided to four hundred of the aristocracy. These, however, dreading the ambition and wiles of Alcibiades, refused to recall him; while their cruelty and rapacity soon disgusted their warmest partisans. Alcibiades, finding them unsuitable for his purpose, prosecuted his intrigues in another direction, and soon effected the restoration of democracy, and his own recall and return to power.

These events, followed by the efforts of Alcibiades after his return, delayed, but could not prevent, the fall of Athens. Some reverses in their naval warfare induced the Athenians to doom him to a second banishment. Then the Spartan fleet held the mastery of the sea; and, after a brief season spent in preparations, Athens was simultaneously assailed by land and sea; the Spartan King Agis commanding the army, and Lysander the fleet. The Athenians made an obstinate defence, but their cause was hopeless; they were compelled to surrender. The conditions were sufficiently humiliating. The democracy was abolished, and the government of Athens given to thirty persons named by the Spartans. All their ships but twelve were surrendered; all claim to their colonies and foreign possessions was given up; and the Athenians were bound to follow the Spartan standard in war. Harsh as these terms were, the Thebans and Corinthians clamoured for far more severe measures.

The Spartans, however, did not regard their triumph as complete without the death of Alcibiades. To the eternal infamy of Sparta, a party of assassins was despatched to a remote village in Phrygia, where the illustrious Athenian resided in solitude. Afraid to assail him openly, they set fire to his house; and although he nobly rushed through the flames, and slew the foremost of the assassins, he fell, overwhelmed by numbers: and with him perished the hope of Athens.

The triumph of Sparta in the ruin of Athens did not consolidate the power of the former state. If the result of this success had been the union of all Greece under one strong, wise, and liberal government, it might, notwithstanding the sacrifice and the suffering which it involved, have promoted the great cause of civilization and human improvement. But this was not the case: the different states of Greece still remained separate and independent; and, after the fall of Athens, they severally found—especially the minor ones—that they had fought and bled to rear up an enormous tyranny. This

conviction was greatly promoted by the conduct of Lysander, the
Lacedæmonian general, who proved to be the greatest oppressor
that Greece had ever raised to power. Independently of the feelings elicited by his conduct, it was found that no sooner had the
fury of martial feeling passed away, than those who had been the
most inveterate enemies of Athens reprobated the continued injustice
of the Thirty Tyrants, and the cold-blooded cruelty and unlimited
rapacity with which they conducted the government of that city.
Even the Thebans deeply commiserated the sufferings of the Athenians, and afforded a safe asylum to all who preferred exile to confis-
cation or death.

The result was soon seen in the assembling of a considerable band
of these refugees at Thebes, under the direction of Thrasybulus.
They first seized Phyle, and afterward the Piræus. Lysander
quickly sailed to the aid of the government, and blockaded the
insurgents. But, by this time, wiser and more liberal counsels
obtained even in Sparta; and Pausanias, the most popular of the
Lacedæmonian princes, marched with an armed force to counteract
the designs of Lysander. It is but seldom, even in the crafty manœuvres of Sparta, that we find one army so effectively employed
to circumvent the operations of another. The liberal views of the
Pausanias party were, however, most triumphantly sustained. The
Tyrants were expelled from Athens, the ancient constitution was
restored, and a general amnesty decreed. These important measures gave fresh existence to the fallen republic, and rendered possible a renewal of its glory and prosperity.

Soon after the restoration of democracy, the trial, condemnation,
and death of Socrates took place. His remarkable character will be
reviewed in another chapter; in which some observations will be
made on his course of action, and on the treatment which he
received.

Another event happened about the same time, of which it is difficult to say whether the military talent or the literary excellence
which it called forth, is most to be admired. On the death of
Darius Nothus, King of Persia, he left the crown to his eldest son,
Artaxerxes Mnemon, as has been already related. His brother
Cyrus, having been previously governor of the western provinces of
the empire, had greatly served the Spartans, by supplying them
with money to carry on the war with Athens. He now hoped to
obtain from them in return such aid as would enable him, with the
troops which he could collect in his province, to dispossess his
brother, and secure the throne. Thirteen thousand Greeks responded to his call, and among them Xenophon the Athenian.

After the defeat and death of Cyrus, and the treacherous massacre of the principal Greek officers, this noble band of soldiers elected other leaders; and, although in the centre of an enemy's country, and hundreds of miles from their own land, menaced as they were by the power of the whole Persian army, they determined to resist all aggression, and to retreat in martial order to Greece. Xenophon, who was one of the commanders, has given us an eloquent account of this successful and masterly Retreat of the Ten Thousand.

Nothing is more evident from the history of Greece at this period, than that the division of this beautiful country and its richly-endowed inhabitants into many independent states was the prolific cause of innumerable evils. It was this which prevented Greece from taking any important position among the nations of the world. This was in fact the plague-spot of Grecian history. If Athens or Sparta assumed an imposing attitude in respect of Persia, that empire, by the influence of gold, could instantly raise up a power in other Grecian states to thwart and defeat the effort; while the tyranny exercised by the principal of those states over the smaller ones was the cause of ever-changing combinations and wars, in which the national energies and wealth were squandered in suicidal contests.

Thus, when, after the triumph over Athens, Agesilaus, the Spartan king, had greatly increased the Lacedæmonian navy, and made himself formidable to Persia by some operations on the coast of Asia, the Persian king supplied Conon, an Athenian admiral, with funds to equip a fleet of even superior power, with which he defeated the Spartans, and utterly destroyed their naval power, and thus not only rendered Athens really independent, but gave her again complete supremacy in the Ægean Sea.

In the mean time, the proud and unjust conduct of Sparta toward Thebes called forth the energies and talents of two of the best statesmen and military commanders ever produced by Greece. Pelopidas and Epaminondas not only rescued their country from subjection, but broke the proud yoke of Sparta from the neck of Greece, and aspired to place Thebes at the head of the Greek people. At length, these great men having perished in battle, a general peace was established by the mediation of Artaxerxes, on the single condition that each state should retain its own possessions. Thus ended the third Peloponnesian war, B. C. 362.

For a short season after the decline of Theban power, Athens exercised a leading influence over the Grecian states: but the harsh injustice of her policy toward her colonies drove the most wealthy of them into rebellion, which crippled her resources, and destroyed her supremacy.

Long before this time, Philip, King of Macedon, who had been educated in the arts of war and state-policy by the great Epaminondas, had aspired to the supreme government of Greece. Having vanquished all opposition to his rule, and established tranquillity in his own country, he turned his attention to the improvement of the military tactics and discipline of his army. Having noticed the success with which Epaminondas had used a massive column against the long slender lines of his foes, Philip, improving on the genius of his teacher, introduced the celebrated Macedonian phalanx. These measures made him more than a match for any of his neighbours: and, though he carefully concealed his intentions respecting Greece generally, he took occasion of every pretext for assailing the several neighbouring states in succession.

He first subdued Pæonia, and made it a province of Macedon. He then vanquished the Illyrians, and brought them completely under his power. He next took advantage of the war between Athens and her colonies, and added Amphipolis, Potidæa, and Pydna to his conquests; and thus obtained the command of the coast from the mouth of the river Strymon to Mount Olympus. A large portion of Thrace was next added to his dominions; and, by turning his arms against the tyrants of Thessaly, and marrying a princess of Epirus, he secured an unbounded political ascendency in these countries.

The Argus of Greece, who with intense diligence watched every step of this progress, who detected the covert designs which influenced the conqueror, and who with matchless genius and power warned his countrymen against the fatal result, was Demosthenes, the most eloquent of the Greeks. He devoted life to this task: but the martial spirit of Athens had departed; and the eloquence of this master of speech, failing to rouse his countrymen to resist Macedon with effect, has become practically useful only as a model of public speaking for the world.

While Philip, having thus prepared himself, stood waiting for an opportunity to exert his power in southern Greece, a favourable one presented itself in the second Sacred War. This arose out of a collision of feeling between Phocis and Thebes. Unable alone to secure its object, the latter state solicited the aid of Philip, who joyfully responded to the call. It was just the opportunity which he had long desired. He soon overran Phocis, destroyed its cities, distributed its population into villages, and deprived it of its vote in the Amphictyonic Council, which was transferred to the king of Macedon. Philip thus obtained a *status* in the great assembly of the Greek nation, and that at a time when this council was at the zenith of its power. This was a most important gain to the ambitious Macedonian: the semi-barbarian origin of his people was thus covered, and he and they were identified as elements of the Hellenic nation.

Stimulated alike by these successes, and by some reverses and losses which he sustained at the same time, Philip steadily pursued his object. He destroyed Olynthus, subdued the Thracian Chersonese, and added the whole Chalcidian peninsula, with its valuable commercial marts and seaports, to his dominions. At length the third Sacred War gave him another occasion of appearing as the champion of the religion of Greece. He again entered Phocis, and totally destroyed the city of Amphissa.

Feeling himself now sufficiently strong to avow his purpose, he took possession of Elatea, the most important city of the Phocians after Delphi. As this measure could not be mistaken, so it did not allow procrastination: it was seen at once that Greece must either now submit to Philip, or at once resist him. Roused by the eloquence of Demosthenes, the latter alternative was chosen; and the Athenians and Thebans marched their united forces against the invader. They met at Chæronea, where, after a contest which brought no honour to the cause of liberty, Philip obtained a complete triumph. Demosthenes himself, valiant as he was in speech, threw away his shield, on which he had inscribed in golden letters, "To Good Fortune," and abandoned the contest even at the onset. Thebes suffered a terrible infliction as the result of this victory; but very lenient measures were dealt out to Athens.

The great object and result of this Macedonian success were soon apparent. The very next year, in a general convention of the Grecian states held at Corinth, it was resolved that all should unite in a war against the Persians, and that Philip should be appointed captain-general of the confederate forces.

It is a very remarkable circumstance, and one well worthy the attention of the Christian philosopher, that this triumph of Philip, which has been universally deprecated as the ruin of Greek liberty, and the establishment of an unprincipled tyranny, was the very event that placed the Hellenic nation before the world in precisely the position that had been predicted by inspired prophets, and which issued in the exact fulfilment of some of the most glorious prophecies that were ever delivered, under divine inspiration, to mankind.

Philip did not survive to begin the war upon which he had so long and so ardently desired to enter. He was assassinated, while engaged in making preparations for the contest, by Pausanias, a Macedonian nobleman, B. C. 336. Alexander succeeded his father: and although all the neighbouring states arose in simultaneous resistance to the power of Macedon, the youthful sovereign, with equal daring and prudence, soon reduced them to subjection. Thrace, Illyria, and Thebes were in an incredibly short time completely subdued, and the latter city entirely destroyed. The severity of this punishment spread terror throughout Greece : the other states immediately submitted ; and Alexander was soon prepared to enter on the war which had been bequeathed to him by his father, and which filled his whole soul.

Having marshalled his army, the king of Macedon proceeded to the Hellespont, which he crossed without opposition. His force, we are told, consisted of but five thousand horse, and thirty thousand foot,—a mere handful of men in comparison to the mighty armies which Persia frequently sent into the field. Yet with this well-trained and highly-disciplined band Alexander proceeded to assail the myriads of Asia, formidable as they were not only in numbers, but in union and the *prestige* of past success, and supported by boundless resources of wealth and population. The whole progress of this conflict, from the first action on the banks of the Granicus, where the Macedonian completely defeated a numerous Persian army, forms a very remarkable fulfilment of sacred prophecy.

Elated with this success, the Grecian conqueror marched to the Lydian capital, and occupied Sardis. He then returned, and secured Ephesus and Miletus; after which, pursuing his course unchecked, he reduced Cappadocia, Paphlagonia, and Cilicia, and at length opened his way to the heart of Asia, by defeating Darius in person, at the head of a numerous army, in the decisive battle of Issus. Alexander then in rapid succession subdued Tyre, Palestine, and Egypt. Having spent one year in accomplishing these preliminary measures, he proceeded in the spring of 331 B. C. to attempt securing the grand object of the war. In this campaign Alexander defeated Darius a second time at Arbela, occupied Babylon, conquered Media and Persia, and established his dominion over Parthia and Hyrcania. In the following year he added Bactria to his conquests, and consolidated his rule over his Asiatic possessions. The three years next ensuing sufficed to extend his sway to India, and to establish his government from Greece and Egypt in the west to the banks of the Indus.

This colossal power, however, was destined to be of short duration : and its decline was as striking a fulfilment of prophecy as its rise had been. Alexander died at Babylon, B. C. 323, of a disease generally supposed to have been induced by intemperance. For several years after his death, some member of his family was invested with the form of royalty, while his generals ruled in the several sections of the empire, professedly as lieutenants or satraps, but really exercising absolute power. Between these, on different pretexts, a war was continually waged for more than twenty years,— a season replete with treachery, assassinations, and every form of violence. At length, B. C. 306, four of the principal generals, having raised themselves to prominence and power, partitioned the empire between them. By this treaty Seleucus became sovereign of Upper Asia; Ptolemy governed Egypt, with Syria and Palestine; Lysimachus obtained the northern provinces of Asia Minor, in addition to the kingdom of Thrace; and to Cassander were assigned Macedon and Greece, with the addition of the rich province of Cilicia.

During the progress of Alexander's war in Asia, Greece remained in tolerable quiet, under the government of the several states, subject generally to his lieutenant, Antipater. Sparta was the only exception. Unable to arrest the progress of her rival's success, this state for a considerable time maintained her independence in sullen quietude. When, however, the Macedonian king had subdued Darius, and was preparing to march on India, the Lacedæmonians, urged on by their martial King Agis, declared war against Macedon. This contest was of short duration. One decisive battle sufficed to terminate the war and the life of the Spartan king, and to compel the Spartans to send an embassy, soliciting the clemency of the Macedonian monarch, which was generously given.

One of the most remarkable contests recorded in the pages of history took place about this time,—namely, that between the rival orators, Demosthenes and Æschines. Ctesiphon having proposed that a golden crown should be presented to Demosthenes, as a testimony of the rectitude of his political career, Æschines impeached Ctesiphon for the proposition, assailing the whole course of policy recommended by Demosthenes, and declaring that it had issued in the ruin of Grecian independence. Demosthenes defended himself so triumphantly that Æschines was sent into banishment,—a measure which Alexander allowed out of respect to the ancient states of Greece, although Æschines was the old and earnest friend of Macedon, and his rival quite the reverse.

Notwithstanding the awe inspired by the vast conquests of Alexander, and the immense resources which he consequently possessed, a very considerable commotion was produced by a decree which he issued,—that the exiles from the several states should be restored to their respective countries and possessions. While this uneasiness was spreading, and producing indications of approaching violence, intelligence arrived of the death of Alexander. The revolt which had just begun, soon became general. Demosthenes, who had been exiled, was recalled; and a powerful army of confederate Greeks, under the Athenian commander Leosthenes, marched against Antipater. The effort was vain. The Macedonian general, reinforced by a section of the victorious army of Alexander, soon put down all opposition, and established one ruling government over Greece. The democracy was again abolished in Athens; and the aristocratical government, as it had existed in the days of Solon, was restored, while a Macedonian garrison was placed in the port of Munychia. Similar changes were made in other states, which at first produced clamorous complaints; but the people soon found, that, under a strong and general government, they realized a larger share of real liberty than they had formerly possessed, and saluted Antipater as "the Father and Protector of Greece."

After the death of this able ruler, Greece shared in the dissensions, revolutions, and wars, which for many years afflicted almost every part of the empire of Alexander. In these struggles some of the Grecian states suffered severely. Polysperchon, who had been joined with Cassander in the regency of Macedonia, being engaged in a contest with his colleague, and anxious to secure the Greeks to his interests, ordered the removal of the governors appointed by Antipater, and the restoration of democracy. Athens exulted in the change, and, under the excitement of the occasion, put to death several citizens, on the plea that they were friends of Antipater. Among these perished the greatest ornament of his age and nation, —the great Phocion; a man who had served his country with consummate ability and incorruptible integrity until above eighty years of age.

Cassander, having obtained aid from Antigonus, soon recovered paramount authority in Greece; and, reversing all that Polysperchon had done at Athens, he appointed Demetrius Phalereus governor of that city. This officer discharged the duties of his station with so much wisdom and moderation, that the ten years of his government were exceedingly prosperous to the people over whom he ruled. The power of Cassander extended, with the exception of a very few cities, throughout Peloponnesus; so that Greece was again subjected to Macedonian rule.

During the convulsions which agitated the country on the death of Cassánder, Greece suffered from a desperate invasion of a host of Gauls, who were at length repulsed, the remainder proceeding to Asia. Soon after this calamity, it was invaded by Pyrrhus, King of Epirus, who, having subdued a great part of Macedonia, proceeded to invade Greece. He, however, perished in the attempt. Antigonus, having secured the Macedonian throne, next laboured to annex Greece to his dominions; but he also died during the war. His son Demetrius exercised a commanding influence in the affairs of Greece, without claiming sovereignty over it; while his successor avoided all interference beyond the limits of his own country.

Thus released from foreign aggression, the several cities of Greece sought to recover their long-lost independence. During the troubles and political convulsions which raged in Macedonia under Lysimachus and Ptolemy Ceraunus, the cities of Achaia gradually recovered their liberties. Sicyon, Corinth, and Megalopolis were by different means delivered from foreign domination, and attached to the Achæan confederacy. This fair promise for Grecian liberty was checked by the ambition of the Spartan King Cleomenes, who, having murdered the Ephori, and revolutionized his country, restored the code of Lycurgus, and turned his arms against the Achæans: aided by Antigonus Doson, King of Macedon, they so completely defeated him at the battle of Salasia, that he abandoned the contest, advised his people to submit to their conquerors, and took refuge in Egypt, where at length he destroyed himself. This was the expiring effort of Sparta. The successor of Cleomenes was the last ruler descended from the Heraclidæ.

Although this danger had again introduced the Macedonian power into Greece, the Achæan League was maintained entire and powerful; and, under the able conduct and prudent measures of its chief, Aratus, promised at length to accomplish its object in the restoration of Greece. Unhappily, however, the League being pressed by their old enemies the Ætolians, Aratus again sought aid of Macedon; which was granted by Philip, the son of Antigonus. This ambitious ally, conceiving a design to subject the states of Greece to his power, and regarding Aratus as an invincible obstacle to his purpose, had that noble chief removed by poison. This was not the greatest of the calamities which arose out of this alliance. Philip had just before become the active ally of Hannibal of Carthage; the Romans in revenge formed an alliance with the Ætolians; thus bringing the arms of this mighty republic to bear on Greece in its decline, weakness, and distraction.

Philopœmen, who succeeded Aratus as leader of the League, did his utmost; but, after the termination of the second Punic war, Titus Quinctius Flamininus, Roman consul, succeeded by his power, and especially by his policy, in detaching the Achæans from all connexion with Macedon, and then most pompously proclaimed liberty to Greece. This nominal independence, however, continued a very brief space. The country being soon after invaded by Antigonus of Syria, a Roman army interposed. A series of tedious operations took place, during which Philip of Macedon died, and Perseus his son succeeded to the throne. This prince was equally obnoxious to the Romans and to his own subjects. A collision with Rome followed, terminated by the decisive battle of Pydna, in which twenty thousand Macedonians were slain, and Perseus was taken prisoner, and led in chains to Rome.

Still the Romans pretended to recognise the independence of Greece, although at one time they summoned one thousand of the most eminent Achæans to Rome, where they were kept in prison seventeen years, without being admitted to an audience or brought to trial. Some of these on their return induced their countrymen to insult the Roman ambassadors, who had been sent to Corinth to arrange some disputes between the Achæans and Spartans. This of course produced a war, which in all its stages was disastrous to Greece. Corinth was taken and destroyed; and thenceforth Greece, under the name of *Achaia*, became a province of the Roman empire.

Thus perished the political existence of that people, who had by force of arms effected the grandest conquests which the world had ever seen, established the widest empire that had existed up to that time, and realized the highest literary, poetic, and artistic elevation ever attained by any people. Nor is there, perhaps, anything more remarkable in the history of this wonderful country, than that, when conquered and subjected to foreign rule, she should still have maintained the majesty of her intellectual superiority and cultivated power, and have become the recognised preceptress of her conquerors in all literature and science, civilization and art, the elegancies and refinements of manners and life; so that, while prostrate at the feet of her mighty rival, Greece was the director of the world's intellect,—Athens was the university of Rome.

Thus the third universal empire passed away, (see *Appendix*, note 66,) and introduced the fourth great dominion. The reader will acknowledge, without hesitation, that the rise, the progress, and the ruin of Greece present one of the most remarkable chapters in this world's history.

CHRONOLOGICAL TABLE OF GRECIAN HISTORY.

B. C.	Names and Events.
817	Lycurgus legislates for Sparta.
779	Commencement of the Olympiads.
662	Sparta conquers Messenia, seizes the country, and reduces the people to slavery.
594	Solon reforms the law at Athens.
560	Pisistratus usurps the government of Athens, and places in abeyance the laws of Solon.
527	Hipparchus and Hippias reign at Athens.
510	The Pisistratidæ expelled from Athens.
497	Death of Pythagoras.
490	The Persians defeated at Marathon.
480	Invasion of Xerxes—his defeat at Salamis.
479	The Greeks victors at Platæa and Mycale.
478	Athens rebuilt and fortified by Themistocles in defiance of Sparta.
444	Pericles rules at Athens.
431	First Peloponnesian War.
404	Athens taken by the Spartans, and governed by Thirty Tyrants.
400	Return of the Ten Thousand Greeks from Persia.
399	Death of Socrates.
397	Plato and Aristotle.
387	Sparta the paramount power.
371	Battle of Leuctra.—Thebes becomes the chief power of Greece.
362	Battle of Mantinea.—Death of Epaminondas.—Decline of Thebes.
357	First Sacred War.
350	General corruption of manners, and decline of Grecian power.
344	Macedonia, by the genius of Philip, obtains the ascendency.
333	Alexander conquers Persia, and reigns supreme.
323	Death of Alexander.—Athens continues the chief maritime power.
322	Athens makes a vigorous effort to throw off Macedonian supremacy.
301	Democracy again established at Athens.
244	Agis III. attempts the reformation of Sparta.—He at first succeeds, but is eventually cut off.
243	The formation and efforts of the Achæan League.
227	Cleomenes effects a revolution in Sparta.
146	The power of the Grecian states gradually declines, until the power of Rome prevails, and they form the province of ACHAIA.

CHAPTER X.

THE RELIGION OF GREECE.

The earliest Religion of this People appears to have been a strange Compound of the Adoration of the material Elements and Powers of Nature; united with a sacred Regard for Mythic Legends, which had been traditionally preserved—Expansion of this Scheme after the Return of the Heracleids, and the Establishment of the Dorian Power—Outline of Grecian Theology and Cosmogony—The Grecian Deities—Zeus—Hera—Apollon—Artemis—Hermes—Hephaistos—Aphrodite—Ares—Eros, and other minor Divinities—The Greek Triad—Evident Connexion of the whole Scheme with Scriptural Tradition—The Temples—Priests—Worship—Divination—Oracles and Mysteries—The Influence of Philosophy examined—Thales—His Doctrines, and the Ionic School—Pythagoras—His System—Failure in Greece, and wonderful Success in Sicily—The Character of his Teaching—Socrates—His Mode of Instruction—Doctrines—He claims a Divine Mission—The important Character and Influence of his Teaching—Plato—General View of his Object—His Doctrines—Grand Intellectual Development evinced in his Philosophy—But his Efforts unfavourable to Morals and Religion—Aristotle—His brilliant Intellectual Efforts—Inefficient in respect of Religion—Zeno and the Stoics—Physical and Moral Doctrines—Unsatisfactory Result—Epicurus—His System—Its pernicious Effects—General View of Grecian Faith—Importance of Divine Influence, and a recognition of its Power—The Effect of these four Schools of Philosophy fatal to the Religion of Greece—Utter Failure of every Influence to correct the Effects of a vitiated Theology.

The inquiring mind can scarcely have presented to it a more interesting or important subject for investigation than the religion of Greece. Limited as was the national territory occupied by this people, their numbers, energy, cultivation, wonderful attainments in all the polite and elegant arts, as well as their amazing prowess in war, and range of conquest, bring them before the mind as the aristocracy of the world's intellect and art. When we add to these considerations the important fact, that the elevation and empire of this people were the subjects of some of the grandest predictions ever uttered by the sacred prophets in holy writ,—and that their language was the medium through which the truths of the Old Testament revelation were first conveyed to the world, and the tongue in which the New Testament was originally given to mankind,—it cannot but be a matter of interest and importance to obtain answers to these questions: What were the theological doctrines and worship of this remarkable people? What was the religious condition of the Grecian communities?

In entering on this subject, it will be necessary first to glance at it in an historical aspect, in order to point out the prominent changes which were made in the religion of the country during the progress of its history.

As far as any information has come down to us respecting the religion of the first occupants of Greece in the traditions of the ancient Pelasgi, it appears that their system of faith, if such it can be called, was very similar to that ascribed to the earliest era of the world by the Phenician Sanchoniathon. It being generally believed that the intercourse between these countries, so early as 1300 B. C., was such as to introduce the Phenician alphabet into Greece, we cannot feel surprised at an apparent uniformity of religion. The foundation-principle of this system seems to have been, a superstitious reverence of the productive and destroying powers of nature, as being replete with a spiritual life and energy, which was supposed to pervade the universe. Thus the earth (Gaia) was worshipped as a goddess, from whose womb sprung the fruits engendered by the creative power of the atmosphere (Zeus); and in volcanic regions people, on the same account, paid divine honours to the fire which desolated their fields.

The idea generally entertained by the ancients,—and evidently arising out of the traditions respecting creation, and the action of the Holy Spirit on the chaotic mass,—that the whole material world was pervaded by a divine spirit, imparted a religious character to all the fanciful imaginations put forth with respect to these suppositious beings, and at the same time gave a personal identity to all the phenomena of nature and the vicissitudes of human life. With these elements of early error at the foundation of their faith, it appears to be now an admitted fact that the ancient Pelasgi held the doctrines, and celebrated among them the mysteries, of the Cabiri; which, as Mr. Faber has conclusively shown, mainly consisted in superstitious reverence for the eight persons preserved in the ark.

This mixture of natural powers and mythic legends was, however, found too narrow a basis for a system of religion adapted to the taste of an energetic community, rising, by means of civilization, agriculture, and commerce, into prominence and power. An expansion and adaptation of the elements of this early faith are therefore perceived to be in gradual operation. For instance: Demeter was originally Gaia, the divine mother Earth; but was afterward regarded as the patroness of settled habitations, marriage, and jurisprudence. This change was gradual in its progress, and was not completed until the ascendency of the Dorians had been fully established in Peloponnesus. Prior to this, Greece can hardly be said to have been devoted to idolatry; for actual idolatry, as denoting the worship of visible objects, was unknown. Prayers were addressed as to invisible deities; and sacrifices—the only decidedly religious duty which was recognised—were offered upon altars in the open air. A few heinous crimes were sometimes denounced, as exposing the guilty party to the vengeance of the gods; but morality during this period derived very slender support from religion. Soothsayers, who pretended to foretell future events, were numerous; but local oracles had not attained any great celebrity. It is important to add, that the doctrines of the immortality of the soul, and a future state of rewards and punishments, were taught in those days; but the ridiculous absurdities with which these were accompanied, tended, when men had learned to despise the fables, to throw discredit also upon the momentous truths which they had veiled.

After the close of the Heracleid war, under the ascendency of Dorian power, the new and enlarged system of Grecian idolatry was established throughout Greece: and it is a curious fact, that the principal agents in its introduction have been also the means of perpetuating a knowledge of the system to the present day. For, at the time that the old and new systems were struggling for the mastery over the public mind, Homer arose, and by his unrivalled invention and brilliant genius so used, exhibited, and adorned the new scheme, that it thenceforth triumphed over all opposition. (B. C. 1000.) Hesiod followed, about one hundred years later, and still further illustrated its principles, and strengthened its hold on the Grecian mind. Herodotus, the highest possible authority on the subject, assures us that the Greeks were indebted for their gods to Homer and Hesiod. We, may, therefore, look to the productions of these poets for an exhibition of the theology of Greece during the principal period of her history; and, indeed, until the teaching of philosophers shed an influence over the religious opinions of the people.

When we bear in mind that the subject under discussion is, the theological doctrines of the most intellectual, energetic, and enlightened of the ancient nations, it becomes a matter of painful interest to perceive one startling fact at the very threshold of our inquiry,— namely, that the Greeks had no idea whatever of the eternity of the deities they worshipped. On the contrary, they believed that the supreme power was held by other divine beings, long before these whom they now worshipped were called into existence. Although it does not come within the plan of this work to give any extended list of divinities, with their mythological extraction and history, it seems necessary to furnish a brief account of the origin of the gods, the world, and mankind, according to the principles of this religious system.

According to Hesiod, in the beginning was Chaos, then Gaia, (the Earth,) Tartarus, (the subterranean Abyss,) and Eros (Love). Gaia brings forth Uranus, (the Heavens,) the Mountains, and Pontus, (the Sea). Gaia and Uranus are the parents of the Titans, Oceanus, Cœus, Crius, Hyperion, Iapetus, Theia, Rheia, (or Rhea,) Themis, Mnemosyne, Phœbe, Tethys, and Cronos; also the Cyclopes, and the Hecatoncheires, ("hundred-handed" giants,) Cottus, Briareus, and Gyes. Ouranos, or Uranus, however, hated his offspring, and prevented them from coming forth into the light of day. Indignant at this unnatural behaviour, Gaia persuaded his son Cronos to mutilate his father, and usurp his throne. Cronos and Rhea then became the parents of Hestia, Demeter, Hera, Hades, Poseidon and Zeus. To prevent any of his children deposing him, as he had deposed his father, Cronos swallowed them immediately after their birth. As soon as Zeus was born, Rhea presented to the father a stone, which he swallowed instead of his child. Zeus was concealed in Crete, where he remained until he was full-grown, when he sallied forth, deposed his father, and, aided by the arts of Gaia or Metis, compelled him to disgorge the children whom he had swallowed, and whose bodies, on account of their divine nature, were imperishable. The stone which he had swallowed last of all, was the first object discharged from his stomach. This was set up by Zeus in the glorious Pytho, (Delphi,) as a sign and a wonder for mortal men.

Zeus now, in conjunction with his brothers and sisters, makes war on Cronos and the Titans. By the advice of Gaia, he releases the Cyclopes, who had been imprisoned in the bowels of the earth, and receives from their hands the thunder and the deadly lightning. He also releases the Hecatoncheires, and brings them back to the upper world. The battle had already raged ten years between the Titans and the Olympic gods, when these giants appeared to aid the Olympians. Earth trembled to its centre, and even Tartarus shook, as these combatants fought, while huge rocks were hurled on either side, and Zeus with flaming thunderbolts mingled in the war. The Titans were at length defeated, loaded with chains, and thrown into the depths of Tartarus, where, being closely imprisoned, they were carefully guarded by the mighty Hecatoncheires. But even this victory did not establish the throne of Zeus. Gaia brings forth another monster, of immense size and power, who is at length struck down, by the thunderbolts of Zeus, into the lowest depths of Tartarus. By this last success Zeus and his brethren and sisters became rulers of the universe.*

* I am considerably indebted for this summary to ARNOLD's Translation of STOLL's "Handbook of the Religion and Mythology of the Greeks,"—an able and excellent work.

It is well known that this mythic Theogony has been subjected to several modes of interpretation,—the physical, the historical, the theological, &c. It is also generally admitted that neither of these supplies a complete key to them. In fact, the Theogony of Hesiod is, to use the words of a learned writer, "a farrago, composed of the most heterogeneous ingredients."

Without pretending to afford a solution to this crude poetic version of numerous myths, I may venture to express an opinion that the broad *substratum* upon which the whole rests, is a union of corrupted traditions of the scenes which took place at Babel, terminating in the proud supremacy of the house of Cush. (See *Appendix*, note 67.)

According to this system, after the defeat of the rival Titans, the universe was governed by the heads of the triumphant tribe. And scarcely anything is more worthy of observation in this whole case, than the family character subsisting among these deities. They comprised the brothers ZEUS, POSEIDON, and HADES; the sisters HERA, HESTIA, DEMETER, with her daughter CORA; and the children of Zeus,—ATHENE, APOLLON, ARTEMIS, HEPHAISTOS, ARES, APHRODITE, and HERMES. Of these individually a brief notice must be given.

I. THE GODS OF OLYMPUS.

ZEUS, or Jupiter, the son of Cronos and Rhea, was regarded as the great sovereign of the universe, the father of gods and men. He claims to exercise unlimited authority, not only over men, but even over every other god, and boasts a sway greater than the united power of all other divinities. (Homer's Iliad, viii, 18.)

Yet, notwithstanding the strong terms in which these claims to supremacy, if not to omnipotent power, are put forth, when the system is fully investigated it is found that the absolute government of the world is not entirely in the hands of Zeus. The fact is, that the Polytheism of Greece had invested so many deities with divine powers and freedom of action, that no one individual deity could possess absolute sway. Zeus, therefore, although the most perfect and most potent of the Grecian deities, was frequently thwarted in his purpose, and controlled in his actions, by Moira (Fate). And as the inventive faculties of man had already done their utmost in the personification of divine powers, this Moira was allowed to remain,—a dark, vague, and incomprehensible influence.

The whole order of nature is ordained by Zeus; he is the source and fountain of rule and government. Kings are his representatives, employed by him to administer justice to mortals, and deriving their authority from his commission. He is the guardian of popular assemblies and councils: he punishes those who pervert the right, and enforces the obligation of oaths. The rights of hospitality, and the case of the exile and suppliant, are under his special care; and he is the guardian of the family and house.

It is also worthy of notice, that this system not only recognised the birth of this, the principal of their deities; it even admitted that he died, and his grave was shown in Crete: so that one who had been dead yet lived to reign and rule over gods and men.

Zeus not only held this place in the national faith, but was also, in many instances, localized. Hence we meet with the Cretan Zeus, the Bœotian Zeus, the Arcadian Zeus, &c. The most ancient worship of Zeus in Greece was at Dodona in Epirus: the principal statue was that executed by Phidias, forty feet high, of ivory and gold, to look on which was regarded as an antidote to pain and sorrow.

A full knowledge of future events, and the power of making them known to mortals by signs, omens, and prophecies, were attributed to this deity. His moral character, however, was far beneath these ascriptions of dignity. By his wife he had three children, Ares, Hephaistos, and Hebe. Athene sprung from his head. His children by other goddesses were Apollon and Artemis by Leto, Hermes by Maia, Persephone by Demeter, Aphrodite by Dione, the Horæ by Themis, the Graces by Eurynome, the Muses by Mnemosyne. By mortal women he had many children: the principal were Hercules by Alcmene, Dionysus by Semele, Perseus by Danaë, Castor and Polydeucas by Leda.

HERA (Juno) was eldest daughter of Cronos and Rhea, and sister to Zeus. This god, having formed a clandestine engagement with his sister, kept their marriage secret three hundred years. Hera was then acknowledged as his wife, and proclaimed queen of heaven. In this character she receives the deference of all other divinities.

Her marriage with Zeus is the most prominent event in her history. As his wife, she shares the counsels of her husband beyond what is permitted to other deities. This union was not, however, the most happy: Zeus and Hera frequently quarrelled; and the extreme licentiousness of the husband, not to mention other causes, fully accounted for these dissensions.

As Hera was the only lawful wife among the female deities of Olympus, she was the special patroness of married women, whom she protected and assisted in all their perils.

ATHENE, or PALLAS ATHENE, (Minerva,) is the daughter of Zeus. Homer does not mention her mother; but Hesiod says that, Zeus having devoured Metis, (Wisdom,) Athene sprang full-armed from his head. As Hera seems to be a female impersonation of Zeus, so Athene stands before us as an embodiment of his wisdom. This goddess exercises considerable influence in the council of the gods. Although she is described in the Iliad as sometimes opposing the designs of Zeus, she generally acts in accordance with his will; and, even when her wishes go beyond his, the affection with which he regards his favourite child generally enables her to secure her object. She is always represented as a virgin deity, full of sagacity and prudence, skilled in all the arts cultivated by both sexes, and always ready to act as a leader and teacher in military manœuvres, and even to mingle in the fight. She gives the patriot strength for the protection of his country, and leads the warrior to victory.

PHŒBOS APOLLON (Apollo) is the son of Zeus and the female Titan Leto (Latona). This amour being known by Hera, she persecuted Leto from place to place, until she found an asylum in Delos, where she brought forth twins, Apollon and Artemis.

Apollon was the favourite son of Zeus, and always acted in accordance with his father's wishes, while many other of the Olympian divinities frequently opposed the will of their sovereign. He is especially the prophet of Zeus, and the god of soothsayers and oracles; and to him in this character the Greeks attributed some of the most important events in their history. These prophecies, or oracles, were delivered in a poetical form; the poet, like the seer, announcing the will of the gods to mankind. Apollon is also the god of song and music, protects flocks and cattle, and delights in the foundation of towns and the establishment of civil constitutions.

It is a remarkable fact, that a divinity of such a mild, beneficent, and elevating character should be termed *Apollon*,—the same as the Scripture *Apollyon*,—"the Destroyer." This is supposed to be accounted for by the legend that Themis had an oracle in Delphi, the way to which was guarded by the dragon Python. Here, too, we have very evident allusion to the "old serpent:"—*Python*, from פתה *pythe*, "to over-persuade, to deceive." This monster Apollon slew, and took possession of the oracle, which thenceforth became the most celebrated in Greece, or in the whole world.

It may serve to show the confusion produced by the application of conflicting traditions of primitive history and religion, to observe that although Apollon was regarded as personating the promised Seed in the original promise of redemption, and was celebrated as ὁ Σωτήρ, "the Saviour," in consequence of this his great victory over the serpent, yet the true character of this idolatrous imagery is shown by the sacred writer calling the evil spirit which Paul cast out of the damsel at Philippi "a spirit of Python,"—the very title which Apollon had earned by this victory, and used a thousand years.

ARTEMIS, (Diana,) the daughter of Zeus and Leto, and sister of Apollo, was originally an ideal being of precisely the same character as her brother; he being a masculine, and she a feminine impersonation of the same attributes. In process of time, however, other and extraneous ideas were introduced into the religion of Greece under this name. As an instance, it may be stated that the Ephesian Diana was originally an Asiatic deity, having nothing in common with the Greek Artemis, which, under the rising power and prevalent influence of Greece, at length merged into this character and title. At Sparta this goddess was worshipped under the name of ἡ 'Ορθία, "the Upright," and boys were whipped at her altar until it was sprinkled with their blood.

HERMES, or Mercury, was the son of Zeus and Maia, a daughter of Atlas. Homer describes him as the acute, witty, active messenger of Zeus,—one who brings everything to a happy conclusion. He is not to be regarded simply as a messenger, but as a god who, charged with executing the behests of the supreme Zeus, also exercised his own judgment and power, by which he rendered many very important services to gods and men. Yet, while acting in this independent character, he was, besides, the executor of the will of Zeus, just as Apollo was its interpreter and propounder to mankind.

Hermes may, therefore, be regarded as a divinity with rather multifarious attributes and offices. He is the guardian of flocks and herds, which he renders prosperous. He is god of inventions, and of heralds, being himself the herald of the gods. He imparts the gift of eloquence; and is the god of commerce. In this aspect his moral influence is not particularly sound, since he is always ready to patronize thieves and cheats, provided they effect their purposes with skill and dexterity. He is the patron of roads, and the protector of travellers: he conducts the souls of the dead to the lower world: and he is the god of gymnastics. In all this wide range of offices, Hermes is regarded by this system as equally clever and beneficent, always the giver of wealth and prosperity.

HEPHAISTOS, (Vulcan.)—Before the days of Homer, this deity was regarded as a mighty, creative being; but after the genius of the father of poetry had established the supremacy of Zeus, he occupied a more subordinate position. He is the son of Zeus and Hera, and was in consequence of his ugliness cast out of heaven as soon as he was born. He was kindly received and brought up by Thetis and Eurynome. He was afterward readmitted to Olympus; but, having taken part with his mother against Zeus, he was again hurled from heaven by the mighty thunderer, and, after whirling the whole day, fell on the island of Lemnos.

He was the great patron of artificers, especially in metals; and is sometimes associated with Athene, a deity of much higher rank, as the instructer and protector of artificers. His marvellous workshop was on Olympus, where he made two golden female figures, on which he is represented as leaning. He built brazen palaces for himself and other deities on Olympus. For Achilles he made a wonderful shield; for Diomedes, a suit of armour. His wife was Aphrodite, the goddess of beauty, who had, however, less attachment to her husband than to the strong and handsome Ares, which was the occasion of much scandal.

APHRODITE (Venus) was, according to Homer, the daughter of Zeus and Dione; but, according to another myth adopted by Hesiod, she was the offspring of the foam of the sea. She is the goddess of love and beauty. Paris awarded her the prize of beauty, in preference to Hera and Athene. By her favourite, Anchises, she became the mother of Æneas, and for his sake greatly aided the Trojans in their famous war.

Aphrodite was originally an Asiatic divinity, like the Syrian Astarte,—one of the gods of nature, who creates out of water all the productions of the earth, and is therefore herself said to have been born from the foam of the sea. The worship of this goddess was imported from the east into Greece, where she was soon adored as a Grecian divinity. By her power gods and men were enslaved. All living things feel her influence.

ARES, (Mars,) the son of Zeus and Hera, is represented as the fierce god of war: he was the paramour of Aphrodite. Their children were Deimos, Phobos, Eros, Anteros, and Harmonia. Ares appears to have been designed to set forth the violence, ferocity, and brute courage exhibited in war, as Athene represented its genius, strategy, and intellectual requisites. Ares was not extensively worshipped in Greece, and very few statues were raised to his honour.

EROS, (Cupid,) the son of Mars and Venus, in the early mythology of the Pelasgi, is spoken of as one of the most ancient of the gods. Hence Hesiod says: "First of all was Chaos, then the broad Earth, and Tartaros, and Eros, the fairest of the immortal gods." This ancient god was worshipped at Thespiæ in Bœotia, where the Erotidia were celebrated in his honour once in five years. The son of Aphrodite and Ares, however, absorbed attention and devotion during the best ages of Grecian history. And whatever may be said of the dubious and abstract character of some other minor divinities, it is an undoubted fact that this Eros "was the living, breathing embodiment of popular belief."

According to this universal faith, neither Zeus, the lord of the universe, nor even Eros's own mother, is safe from his attacks. In heaven and earth, in the sea and the lower world, he reigns supreme as the all-conquering god. Borne aloft on golden pinions, armed with a bow and arrows, which he carries in a golden quiver, he shoots according to his will; and whoever is pierced with his shafts, becomes instantly sensible of the pangs and raptures of love.

Besides these, it will be necessary to give the names of other divinities more or less connected with the sacred halls of Olympus, although many of them occupy there a subordinate position. Among these may be reckoned HESTIA, (Vesta,) the goddess of the hearth and its fire, the patroness of domestic harmony, the guardian of the house, and the protectress of strangers and suppliants. MOIRA, (Parca, Fate,) the goddess who spins the thread of man's destiny. The word is sometimes used in the plural; and Hesiod speaks of three Moiræ, who were the daughters of Night. Although this divinity generally appears in a subordinate character, as watching over and predicting individual destiny, at other times she seems to exercise unlimited power over all the gods, even binding Zeus himself to her will, however much against his inclination. TYCHE, (Fortuna,) the goddess of accident and luck.

NEMESIS, the goddess who apportions to men the measure of happiness or misery which their actions merit; although she more frequently assumes the aspect of an avenging than of a beneficent deity. ATE, a personification of the infatuation or perversion of the understanding which leads men to sin. DIKE, (Justice,) the protectress of the just, and the enemy of injustice and wrong. When a judge passes an unjust sentence, she carries her complaint to the throne of Zeus. THEMIS, the goddess of law and order. She is represented as a divine being, who in conjunction with Zeus protects the right, and convenes and dissolves the assemblies of men. Her peculiar office, however, is to restore peace to Olympus, and check all insubordination and disorder among the gods. She is the counsellor and auxiliary of Zeus, and, like Dike, is sometimes called his assessor.

The MUSES, the nine goddesses of song. Their names and offices were as follows:—Clio, ("the Recorder,") the goddess of history; Euterpe, ("the Delighter,") of lyric song; Thaleia, ("the blooming,") of comedy; Melpomene, (the muse "of song,") the goddess of tragedy; Terpsichore, ("she who delights in dance,") the goddess of dance; Erato, (the muse "of love,") presiding over amorous poetry; Polyhymnia, ("rich in hymns,") the goddess of hymn; Urania, ("the celestial,") the muse of astronomy; Calliope, ("the melodious,") the goddess of epic poetry.

CHARITES (the Graces) are goddesses who preside over the charms of social life, the union of individuals in civilized communities, and the unrestrained joviality of the banquet.

Besides these there were the HORÆ, the goddesses of the weather, whose duty it is to open and shut the gates of Olympus,—to send rain and sunshine, cold and heat, rendering the earth fruitful. The HYADES, or goddesses of rain. The PLEIADES, the daughters of Atlas, seven stars favourable to navigation. IRIS, the rainbow, and the female messenger of the gods to earth and the lower world. HELIOS, the sun,—the son of the Titan, Hyperion. SELENE, (*Luna*,) "the moon." Eos, the goddess of the dawn. The WINDS, too, are divine beings, four in number: Eurus, the blasting east wind; Notos, the moist south; Zephyros, the dark, rainy west; and Boreas, the blustering north.

On Olympus, whose lofty peak rises above the clouds, dwell the gods in palaces erected by Hephaistos. Around and above them is a cloudless sky. No rain or snow falls in those happy regions; no rude wind disturbs the everlasting calm. On the highest pinnacle of the mountain is the palace of Zeus, where the other gods assemble at the feast or in the council. Hebe, the ever-youthful, and Ganymedes, the Phrygian boy,—whom Zeus stole from earth, and endowed with immortality,—offer them nectar and ambrosia, while the Muses delight their ears with melodious strains, and the *Charites* display their celestial charms. Iris conveys the messages of the gods from heaven to earth; the Horæ, goddesses of the seasons, open and shut the gate of Olympus; and Helios, the all-seeing, brings to gods and mortals the cheerful light of day. In the morning he rises from the eastern Oceanos, heralded by the rosy-fingered Eos, (the Dawn,) and at night sinks to rest beneath its western wave; for Oceanos, the mighty stream of the universe, flows around the earth and the sea. But all these divinities of nature are subordinate to the gods of Olympus, and obey the command of the sovereign Zeus. (See Stoll's Religion and Mythology of the Greeks, p. 10.)

It was an essential element of this faith, that when Zeus had completed the overthrow of Cronos and the Titans, the government of the universe was divided between himself and his two brothers. Zeus, with the deities previously named, retained the sovereignty of heaven, Poseidon that of the sea, and Hades the lower regions. It will be necessary to notice briefly these two remaining governments.

Poseidon (Neptune) was the son of Cronos and Rhea, and younger brother of Zeus. He obtained the rule of the sea as his portion of universal empire. His palace was in the depths of the ocean near Ægæ. Although younger and less powerful than Zeus, he felt sometimes disposed to resist the supremacy of his elder brother. His temper, like the element subject to his authority, was boisterous and uncertain; and when any individual had excited his anger, the god was sure to pursue him with the most relentless hatred. On some account, which has never been satisfactorily explained, Poseidon was regarded as the divinity to whom mankind is indebted for the invaluable services of the horse. Over the seas he exercised unlimited power. As he glides along the surface of the water in his chariot, drawn by brazen-footed horses, the waves are stilled, and the monsters of the deep arise to do him homage, while all the divinities of the water acknowledge him as their sovereign lord. All the phenomena of the ocean are dependent on his will. At his fiat, the waves rise in all the fury of their power; before his anger, the earth trembles: he dashes ships in pieces, inundates whole countries, opens fountains on the dry land, and breaks the rocks in pieces. In ancient times his dominion extended over all fountains, rivers, and lakes; but when the system of mythology was fully developed, his sway was more particularly confined to the sea. The Isthmian Games were celebrated once in three years, near Corinth, in honour of this deity. The prize was a crown, made of branches of the fir-tree. Besides the horse, the dolphin was sacred to Poseidon.

Amphitrite, the daughter of Nereus, was the wife of Poseidon. Her name signifies that she surrounds the earth with water. She was therefore originally the sea; but Hesiod incorporated her into his Theogony as the wife of the principal marine deity.

Oceanos, the mighty stream which surrounds the earth and the sea, and from whence spring the gods, the rivers, and the fountains; Nereus, the old man of the sea, the father of the fifty beautiful nymphs named Nereids, among whom we find Thetis, the mother of Achilles; Leucothea, the companion of the Nereids, the protectress of the shipwrecked mariner; Proteus, the ancient soothsaying deity, who feeds the seals of Amphitrite; Phorcus, ("the gray,") another aged sea deity; Glaucos, a god of sailors and fishermen; Triton, a powerful deity, son of Poseidon and Amphitrite; the Rivers and Acheloios; were minor deities attending on Poseidon and Amphitrite.

The third grand division of this system of divinities was presided over by Hades, (or Pluto,) the son of Cronos and Rhea, brother of

Zeus, and husband of Persephone. He is the sovereign of the lower world, where his power is as supreme as that of his brother Zeus in heaven, although, as younger brother, he is in rank inferior to the Olympian deity. This dark and mysterious sovereign of the infernal kingdom has a helmet which renders him invisible: his terrible voice summons mortals to the realms of death: he is stern and inexorable, and more dreaded by mankind than any other deity. As the residence of this divinity was situate in the interior of the earth, he was commonly regarded as the dispenser of vegetable life, and the bestower of mineral wealth. His sovereignty extended over all mankind; if not fully during their life, yet certainly at their death he was sure to establish his dominion over all.

PERSEPHONE, the daughter of Zeus and Demeter, is the wife of Hades. While engaged with her companions in gathering flowers in the Nysæan meadows, the earth was cleft asunder, and Hades, rising out of the abyss in his chariot drawn by immortal horses, seized on the terrified maiden by the permission of Zeus, and carried her off with him to the infernal regions, where she became his wife. In the Grecian faith she is always exhibited as enthroned with her husband, and sharing with him the government of the infernal regions, just as Hera does with Zeus above. In fact, Persephone seems to possess more than a feminine part of this dark sovereignty; for she exercises an especial authority over the ghosts of the departed, while Hades seems more concerned with the affairs of the living. She was, indeed, a female counterpart of her dark and terrible consort.

The subordinate deities and divine attendants at this gloomy court were the following:—THANATOS and HYPNOS, Death and Sleep, the sons of Night; the KERES, a plural feminine personification of Fate,—dark, malignant, inexorable goddesses, objects of universal hatred; the ERINNYES, produced by Gaia (the Earth) from the blood of Ouranos, when he was mutilated by his son Cronos. These are immortal representations of the vexation and anger of those whose rights have been violated. On the fifth day of every month they sally forth from their infernal habitations, to punish those who have violated their oaths, and to inflict vengeance on flagrant sinners; which they administer, not only by direct penalty, but also at other times by perverting the judgment of men, so as to lead them to pursue a course which issues in their own ruin.

Hecate is sometimes mentioned in connexion with the Erinnyes, and on other occasions as a separate and independent divinity. She was the dark and terrible ruler of the world of phantoms and supernatural appearances, the patroness and teacher of witches.

Besides these three divisions of deities, there was another, composed entirely of subordinate divinities, which pertained to the earth as the common seat and centre of divine government and providence. The principal of these were: 1. GAIA, the Earth, who brings forth and nourishes everything that has life,—the all-producing, all-sustaining mother. 2. The NYMPHS, goddesses of inferior rank. They were the daughters of Zeus, and were divided into four classes,—Mountains, Meadows, Fountains and Woodlands. They are evidently personifications of the beneficent powers of nature. 3. RHEA, Cybele, the sister and wife of Cronos, and mother of Zeus and his brother deities. She, too, was often confounded with the Great Mother, and not unfrequently mistaken for Gaia. Her priests in Galatia and some other places exercised a kind of ecclesiastical dominion over the land. 4. DIONYSOS, (Bacchus,) the son of Zeus and Semele; the god of wine. He was the patron of song and festive poetry, of the drama, and of a peculiar species of lyric, called *dithyrambus*. But he was specially a god of nature; and his care extended not only to the culture and production of the vine, but to all the vegetable world. At first his worship corresponded to the character of a beneficent and friendly being; but afterward such riotous orgies were introduced, that the rites became disgusting and demoralizing.

5. The SATYRS, companions of Dionysos. They represent, in a lower degree, the life of nature, whose best and noblest productions are symbolized by Dionysos. Silenus, Marsyas, and Midas, are gross individual representations of this class. 6. PAN, the son of Hermes and of the daughter of Dryops, was a pastoral and sylvan deity, who, from his similarity to the Satyrs, was numbered among the attendants of Dionysos, where he figures as a dancer, and persecutes the Nymphs with his importunities. 7. PRIAPUS, son of Dionysos and Aphrodite, the god of fertility, generally worshipped by means of most disgusting symbols. 8. CENTAURS, being half men and half horses. Satyr-like in their appearance and character, they were also regarded as attendants upon Dionysos. 9. DEMETER (Ceres.) This goddess was in early times identical with the divine Mother Earth; but was afterward worshipped as an individual deity, presiding over herbs and flowers, with corn, and every other vegetable requisite for sustaining the life of man.

Having thus given, in tolerable detail, an outline of the theology of Greece, it will be evident that while there are clear and distinct *substrata* of Scriptural tradition, moulding and directing the active energies which brought this system into operation, these are not of the same kind, nor used in the same manner, as those which were found in the faith of the primitive nations whose history and religion

have been referred to in the preceding chapters. In the case of
Greece, there was a far greater chronological and geographical
removal from the season and seat of the events recorded by Moses
as the foundation of human history, and of the divine revelations
made to mankind in connexion with the Creation, the Fall, and the
Flood, than existed in the case of older and more eastern nations.
There is, consequently, in this theology a less distinct recognition
of the first promise of redemption,—of the Seed of the woman, and
of the Divine Son,—than we find in Assyria, Persia, and Egypt.
Nor is this to be wondered at, when it is considered that at least
twelve hundred years elapsed from the Dispersion to the earliest
time at which we can obtain any information respecting the religion
of the Hellenes; and that, during a great part of this period, their
progenitors had, by leading a wandering and unsettled life, and from
other causes, descended, to say the least, to the verge of extreme
barbarism.

Yet, even in these circumstances, so strongly was the idea of a
triune personality in the Deity inwrought into all the traditions of
the religion of antiquity,—and so fully was it countenanced by the
theology of those ancient countries which were preceptors to Greece
in this branch of knowledge,—that the triad became nearly as
prominent in Grecian theology as in that of more ancient nations.
But this triad is clearly the three sons of Noah, as has been shown
in a preceding volume. (Patriarchal Age, p. 271.) But the curious
manner in which this is described merits notice. First, we are
informed that Saturn destroys his offspring, and that Zeus is alone
preserved by a trick of his mother. Then it is said that this deity,
having grown up in concealment, afterward succeeds in defeating
the purposes of his father, and, by a desperate but triumphant conflict, secures paramount authority; while his two brothers, who had
been destroyed by their father, are marvellously restored, and have
each a separate but inferior portion of the universe placed under
their individual government.

However extravagant the terms in which this mythic account has
reached us, they are not sufficiently so as to conceal altogether the
basis of Scriptural and historical tradition on which it rests. The
arkite patriarch had announced the divine purpose, that the three
primitive tribes should separate, and their families spread over the
earth. The head of the house of Ham resists this, and in violent
conflict compels the Shemitic clan to retire from the seat which had
been assigned to them; and the Cuthite race thus acquired dominion,
and for a season effected their purpose of securing paramount rule.
Yet, although the traditions of this feud and consequent struggle

are clearly recognised as elements in Grecian mythology, true to the ruling idea of the primitive error, their chief deities form a triad, and that triad is composed of the three sons of Saturn or Noah.

We proceed to notice the temples, priests, worship, oracles, divination, and festivals of this religion. We shall then be prepared to form some opinion respecting the general character and influence of this system of faith and morals.

Temples appear to have existed in Greece from the earliest times: they were always regarded as consecrated enclosures. At first the ground thus set apart for sacred purposes was distinguished by being encompassed by a string or rope; afterward stone-walls were built around the whole space. The temple itself was called ναός, (Atticè, νεώς,) and at its entrance fonts (περιρραντήρια) were generally placed, that those who entered the sanctuary, to pray or offer sacrifices, might first purify themselves.

In early times the temples were of the simplest construction, and frequently made of wood: but afterward exceedingly elaborate and costly stone buildings were erected for this purpose. Temples were always consecrated. The original idea, evidently traceable in the progress of temple-building, is, that these sanctuaries were at first not designed for places of worship so much as for a residence of the Deity. The character of the early Greek temples was dark and mysterious, no light being admitted but through the doorway: afterward apertures in the roof partially remedied this defect. The larger temples were generally divided into three parts:—the (πρόναος, or πρόδομος) "vestibule;" the (ναός, σηκός, or *cella*) "nave," and the (ὀπισθόδομος) "storehouse." It does not appear that the inner part was regarded by the Greeks as a place of more peculiar sanctity, as was the case in Egypt and some other countries, since it was usually the place for depositing the treasures. The *cella*, or "nave," was the locality where the image of the god was fixed, and was properly "the temple." Vitruvius states that the entrance of Greek temples was always toward the west; but most of the ruins that remain in Attica, Ionia, and Sicily, have their entrance toward the east. The architecture employed in the erection of these edifices was the first emanation of Grecian art, and preceded painting and statuary, as it also secured an earlier and equally glorious triumph in the perfection to which it attained.

The priests of Greece were admitted to this office by different means. There were in some of the cities (as at Athens) sacred families, in whom the priesthood was hereditary. On some occasions the sovereign, or chief of the state, appointed the priest, while at other times he was elected by the suffrages of the people, or appointed by lot. All these modes are distinctly referred to by Eustathius, when giving a comment on that passage in Homer's Iliad (vi, 300): "By appointment public at that time priestess of Pallas." The archbishop observes that "she was neither appointed by lots, nor by right of inheritance, nor by the designation of any single person, but, as the ancients say, elected by the people."

It was a standing rule, that all who entered on the priestly office should be perfectly free from every bodily defect or superfluity. Nor was bodily soundness alone sufficient: uprightness of mind was equally necessary, as it was an admitted principle, that nothing ought to approach the gods but what is pure and uncorrupt. It was also thought that sexual intercourse militated against the efficiency of the priestly office; and hence the priests of the Mother of Gods at Samos dismembered themselves,—an example which was followed by some others in different parts of Greece. As a milder form of procuring the same result, the "*hierophantæ* at Athens, after their admission, enfeebled themselves by a draught of the juice of hemlock. In short, it was very customary for those that attended on the more sacred and mysterious rites, by using certain herbs and medicaments, to unman themselves, that they might worship the gods with greater chastity and purity."—*Potter's Antiq.*, vol. i, p. 242.

They also frequently retired from the world and all its business, that, being free from cares, they might wholly devote themselves to the service of the gods. But though most of them were obliged to strict chastity and temperance, others were allowed to marry; and Eustathius tells us that it was but an institution of the later ages that the priestesses should be virgins; to confirm which, Homer (Iliad i, 99) may be cited to prove that Chryseïs, the cause of the subject of the Iliad, was daughter of Chryses, Apollo's priest, and, again, that Dares, the priest of Vulcan, had two sons. Nor, indeed, was this adherence to chastity the uniform practice of later times: for in some cases a plurality of husbands or lovers was a necessary qualification for a priestess.

In small cities all the sacred offices were frequently performed by one person. But where worshippers were numerous, several priests were appointed, and inferior officers, such as sacrificers, keepers of the temple, treasurers of the sacred revenue, and others. Of the different orders of priests no definite information can be obtained: for not only the several deities, but even the same god, had different orders of priests, in different localities and under diverse circumstances. It may, however, be observed that in all places of note there was a high-priest, whose office it was to superintend the other sacred officers, and to execute the most holy rites and mysteries of religion. At Athens they had many high-priests; every deity almost having one, who presided over the rest. At other places they had two classes of priests,—one devoted to the celestial gods, and the other to inferior deities and demigods, with a high-priest over each class. At Delphi there were five high-priests, who with the prophets had the chief management of all parts of divine worship.

The religious worship of Greece mainly consisted of sacrifices, sacred gifts, prayers, and imprecations.

The sacrifices were of four kinds :—

1. Vows or free-will offerings: such as those promised to the gods before, and tendered after, a victory; or those offered by husbandmen after harvest.

2. Propitiatory offerings; intended to avert the anger of an offended deity. Of this kind were all the sacrifices used in expiations.

3. Petitionary sacrifices; oblations presented to the gods for the purpose of obtaining success in any enterprise. So devoted were the Greeks in general to their religious faith, that they seldom undertook anything of moment without first having asked the advice, and implored the assistance, of the gods by sacrifices and prayers.

4. Such sacrifices as were imposed or commanded by an oracle or a prophet.

The origin of these sacrifices was unknown to the Greeks, and lost in unexplainable myths,—at least, with one solitary exception; namely, that which asserts "propitiatory sacrifices to have been first begun by Chiron the centaur;" (Potter's Antiquities, vol. i, p. 248;) which, if we are correct in assigning all these fabulous compound beings to traditions of the primitive cherubim, affords an intelligible hint of the connexion between the origin of sacrifice and the presence of the cherubim in the primitive family.

Some have laboured to show, that in ancient times sacrifices were confined to vegetable products; and Ovid has been cited in proof. This theory is, however, very unsatisfactory; especially as, from the manner in which Pausanias mentions the vegetable sacrifices of Cecrops, (Pausanius, lib. viii, cap. 2,) it would seem that this practice was a departure from established rule rather than a primitive rite:—an idea which is confirmed by the fact, that the laws of Triptolemus prohibited the Athenians from offering bloody sacrifices. It appears, therefore, that the primitive custom obtained in the earliest ages in Greece; but, its nature not being understood, it was for a time laid aside, and afterward resumed.

Three things appear to have been regarded as essential to a

solemn and complete sacrifice:—σπένδειν, "libation," θυμίαμα, "incense;" ἱερεῖον, "the victim."

The term by which the first of these is set forth literally means no more than "to pour forth," and is therefore synonymous with "libation." It evidently refers to what in the language of Scripture would be called "drink-offerings." The liquid generally used for this purpose was pure wine, unmixed with water. When the terms, "mixed wine," occur, they refer to the use of more than one kind of wine, and not to wine mixed with water. But although wine was most usually employed, it was not the only thing employed in libations, which also comprehended water, honey, milk, and oil. Water, we are told, was always used on the Athenian altars to Jupiter the Supreme. Honey was poured out to the Sun; oil, to Pluto; and wine mixed with honey, to the infernal gods. One thing was regarded as essential in all these libations, namely, that they should be offered in cups full to the brim; it being regarded as irreverence to the gods to offer anything that was not whole and perfect.

The second thing necessary to a complete sacrifice was comprehended under the general term "incense." not that this odoriferous compound was always used, but something bearing some analogy or resemblance thereto. Branches of odoriferous trees, and sometimes the vine, the fig, and the myrrh, were employed for this purpose: barley and other grain, with salt, also frequently made a part of this portion of the sacrifice.

The third and principal part of the sacrifice was "the victim." The kind of animal to be sacrificed depended upon the circumstances and condition of the person offering, and the nature of the deity to be propitiated. In respect of the former,—a shepherd would sacrifice a sheep; a neat-herd, an ox; a goat-herd, a goat; and a fisher, after a plentiful draught, would offer a fish to Neptune; and so with others, according to their vocation and property. The nature and position of the god, also, in some measure regulated the kind of sacrifice to be presented. Thus, to infernal and evil gods they offered black victims; to the beneficent, white; to the deities presiding over fruitfulness, pregnant victims; and to the barren, barren ones. To the masculine gods they presented males, and to the feminine deities they gave females. Besides these distinctions, others obtained, since almost every deity was supposed to have a partiality for certain living creatures, from which sacrifices to each were generally selected, or certain creatures were thought to possess qualities that rendered them specially fitting. Hence to Hecate they sacrificed a dog, to Venus a dove or pigeon. To Mars they give a bull, and to Ceres a sow. But, notwithstanding all these influences, the animals most frequently offered in sacrifice, besides the two last-mentioned, were the goat, ox, cow, sheep, and lamb; and, of birds, the domestic cock and hen. Some of these were more acceptable if of a certain age; as, for instance, a heifer, a year old, that had never been put to the yoke, was most grateful to the gods; and thus Diomedes promises Athene,—

> "A youthful steer shall fall beneath the stroke,
> Untamed, unconscious of the galling yoke."

But not only were animals thus selected and sacrificed: human beings were sometimes immolated in a similar manner. Lycaon of Arcadia offered a human sacrifice to Jupiter; and at that time this act was regarded as so atrocious, that he was said to have been transformed to a wolf on the spot. Yet in later ages Aristomenes sacrificed three hundred men,—one of whom was Theopompus, King of Sparta,—to Jupiter Ithomæus. (?) Themistocles sacrificed three Persians to Bacchus, on the eve of the battle of Salamis; (Plutarch's Life of Themistocles;) not to mention other cases occurring in Grecian history.

Some particulars respecting the manner of conducting sacrifice deserve notice. Great care was taken that the priests and priestesses were pure. Sometimes an oath was administered to them, referring not only to defilement in general, but also specially to sexual connexion.

After this, all the parties were purified with water, which had been previously consecrated for this purpose. Particular care was taken not only in the selection of the animal, but also to avoid all appearance of force in bringing the victim to the altar, as any demonstration of resistance on the part of the animal was fatal to the acceptability of the sacrifice.

When the animal stood accepted by the altar, the priest, turning to the right hand, sprinkled it with meal and holy water: he also sprinkled those who were present. After this he prayed: he then took a cup of wine, which he tasted, and then allowed the company to do so, when he poured the remainder between the horns of the animal. Frankincense, or incense, was then placed on the altar, and also on the forehead of the victim. Then the animal was slain; and, if by any chance it leaped after it had received the stroke, or bellowed, or did not fall immediately to the ground, or, after the fall, kicked, stamped, was restless, did not bleed freely, or appeared to die with difficulty, it was thought unacceptable to the gods; these being evil omens, as the contraries were tokens of the divine favour and good-will

An impression prevailed in Greece, that anciently the whole of the animal was consumed on the altar. If this practice ever obtained, it was early laid aside; and a part only, the *thighs*, was burnt on the altar as the portion of the gods. While this portion of the victim was being consumed, the priest, and the person who provided the sacrifice, offered up prayer to the god. At this time, on some occasions, instrumental music would be used; at others, the people would dance round the altar, singing sacred hymns; the first of which, called the *strophe*, was sung in turning from east to west; the other, named the *antistrophe*, in turning from west to east. Then they stood before the altar, and sang the *epos*, which was the last part of the song. The sacrifice being ended, the portion of the priest was given to him; a tenth part was also due to the magistrates at Athens. A portion of the remainder was generally appropriated as a festal meal for the parties present; and the residue would be taken home by the party providing it, or sold, as he might choose.

Another important part of Grecian worship was prayer and supplication: and a review of the conduct of the Grecian people in respect of this particular, will perhaps produce a result more favourable to their religious character than any other branch of the inquiry. Plato bears very decided testimony to the devotional habits of his countrymen by saying, "This at any rate is true,—that those who have even the least share of wisdom, always invoke the deity on entering upon every undertaking, whether small or great."—*Timæus, Davis's Trans.*, p. 331. As we have already noticed, prayer always accompanied sacrifice, but was not confined to these solemn occasions: on the contrary, the whole history of Greece shows that in public and private, by kings and princes, as well as by common persons, in respect of matters of national moment, commercial enterprises, or individual concerns, prayer to the gods was the general, daily practice of the people. Sometimes the suppliant approached the temple, and prostrated himself on the threshold: at others the most humiliating position would be taken, like that described by Homer:—

> "Oft would she smite the earth, while, on her knees
> Seated, she fill'd her bosom with her tears,
> And call'd on Pluto and dread Proserpine
> To slay her son."—*Iliad*, i, 350.

It may appear strange to associate oaths and imprecations with worship, even in a secondary meaning and in a remote manner; but, according to the religious sense of the Greek mind, these frequently partook of all the force and character of solemn addresses to the deity. The use of oaths and imprecations was sanctified by the practice of the gods. Even Jupiter scarcely expected his solemn asseveration to be received as truth, unless confirmed with an oath by the river Styx. This deity was regarded as the divine being who presided over oaths, and, as such, had the whole range of swearing and imprecation placed under his own immediate government. This must not be understood as conveying the notion, that the Greeks only swore by Jupiter,—a supposition totally incorrect. Plato refers to Apollo, Minerva, and Jupiter, as being thus appealed to. Demosthenes, in his oration against Midas, swears by these three deities; but in another oration he takes an oath by Jupiter, Neptune, and Ceres. The Athenians very often swore by divers gods, sometimes by all the gods, at others by the twelve great gods. The Spartans usually swore by Castor and Pollux. Women generally referred in their oaths to Hera, Artemis, or Aphrodite; or else Demeter and Persephone. The most solemn manner of taking an oath was by laying the hand on the altar, or by lifting up the right hand. The utmost importance was attached to the faithful adherence to an oath, insomuch that εὐσεβής, or "one that keeps his oaths," was a phrase regarded as equivalent in meaning with "*a pious* person:" and, on the contrary, ἐπίορκος, "perjurious," was the most infamous appellation that could be given to a Greek.

We pass on to a consideration of Grecian divination and oracles. It was a current opinion among the Greeks, that the gods frequently and familiarly conversed with some men, whom they endowed with an extraordinary perception of their counsels, and a considerable acquaintance with future events. These were called μάντεις, and μαντική was the general term for expressing all sorts of divination.

The μάντεις were the prophets, seers, or soothsayers of Greece. They either gave forth their predictions spontaneously, or responded to the inquiries of the heads of the people on great emergencies. At Athens especially these were as a class tolerated, protected, and honoured; and, according to Cicero, were always present in the public assemblies of the people. As early as the days of Homer, the pretensions of these persons to announce the divine will were fully recognised; and we see in Calchas an instance of the force and authority with which their communications were made.

A striking peculiarity of a considerable portion of the Greek *manteis* was their hereditary character. For not only did individuals claim to communicate the divine will by the special gift of some god, but in some families this gift was held to be hereditary, probably on account of their supposed descent from some deity, as the Iamids traced their descent from Apollo. (Pausanias, lib. vi, cap. 2.) This family spread from Olympia over a great part of Greece, exercising everywhere the prophetic office. The Branchidæ near Miletus, the Eumolpids at Athens and Eleusis, the Clytiads, the Telliads, and the Acarnanian seers, with others, were of this class.

These prophets have been divided into three kinds or classes, according to the manner of the inspiration which they claimed to exercise. The first were called $\delta\alpha\iota\mu o\nu \acute{o}\lambda\eta\pi\tau o\iota$, or $\Pi\acute{v}\theta\omega\nu\epsilon\varsigma$. These were believed to be possessed with prophesying demons. Their communications were sometimes not even made by the ordinary use of the bodily organs, but the demon spoke from the breast or belly of the prophet: at other times the possessing demon dictated to the prophet the answer which he should give. The Septuagint translators of the Old Testament believed these men to be referred to by Isaiah; (vii, 19;) and they accordingly rendered the phrase which the authorized translation reads, "And when they shall say unto you, Seek unto them that have familiar spirits, and unto wizards that peep, and that mutter," &c., by language equivalent to, "And if they say unto you, Seek unto them whose speech is in their belly, and those that speak out of the earth, and those that utter vain words, that speak out of the belly," &c. It was to this class that the damsel at Philippi belonged, who was possessed with "a spirit of divination;" ($\pi\nu\epsilon\tilde{v}\mu\alpha$ $\Pi\acute{v}\theta\omega\nu o\varsigma$·) which spirit Paul cast out, and thus prevented the further continuance of her soothsaying. This case affords undoubted proof, that, however numerous false pretenders to this gift might be, demons did sometimes really occupy individuals of the soothsaying profession, and enable them by this means to exercise supernatural powers. The claim, therefore, was not universally a pretence: it was certainly in some instances a sterling reality.

A second kind of *theomanteis* were called "enthusiasts," $\grave{\epsilon}\nu\theta ov\sigma\iota\alpha\sigma\tau\alpha\acute{\iota}$. These did not profess to be so possessed that the deity himself spoke in them; but to be so influenced that, governed, actuated, and inspired by him, they gave forth, under his exerting power, the sentiments with which he had imbued their mind. Of this sort were Orpheus, Amphion, Musæus, and several of the sibyls. It seems more than probable that at a very early period superhuman communications were delivered by some of these *manteis* or sibyls.

A third kind of prophets were the $\grave{\epsilon}\kappa\sigma\tau\alpha\tau\iota\kappa o\acute{\iota}$, or those who were cast into trances or ecstasies, in which they lay like men dead or asleep, without sense or motion; but afterward revived, and gave forth revelations of what they had seen or heard during these seasons

We cannot dismiss this important subject of prophecy without a further investigation into the nature and extent of the powers which were thus, in reality or pretence, exercised.

Whence came it to pass that in all nations there was a rooted and general belief, that certain persons were gifted with the power of foretelling future events? And whence arose the equally general persuasion, that this gift ordinarily stood associated with an ability and authority, in other respects also, to communicate the divine will? Thus Calchas, the seer of the Grecian army before Troy, was high-priest to the expedition, and was specially consulted in every emergency, as familiar with the will of God. Hence, during the plagues sent by Apollo in answer to the prayer of his priest Chryses, Achilles counselled, "Let us consult some prophet or priest, who would tell us on what account Phœbus Apollo is so enraged with us." Upon this Calchas rose,—he "who knew the present, the past, and the future, and who guided the ships of the Greeks to Ilium by his prophetic art,"—and said, "O Achilles, dear to Jove, thou biddest me declare the wrath of Apollo, the far-darting king. And I will declare it. Neither is he enraged for a vow, (unperformed,) nor a hecatomb, (unoffered,) but on account of his priest, whom Agamemnon dishonoured; neither did he liberate his daughter, nor did he receive her ransom. Wherefore has the far-darter given woes, and still will he give them; nor will he withhold his heavy hand from the pestilence, before that Agamemnon restore to her dear father the bright-eyed maid, unpurchased, unransomed, and conduct a sacred hecatomb to Chrysa; then, perhaps, having appeased, we may persuade him."—*Iliad*, book i. *Buckley's Literal Translation*. Although this is an extract from an epic poem, and of no historical authority whatever as to fact, it is unquestionably a clear and perfect exhibition of the universal belief and practice of the early Greeks respecting this particular doctrine.

It seems reasonable, in these circumstances, to ask, Whence did this strong and prevalent faith arise? Did the true God vouchsafe any measure of the inspiration of his Spirit to select individuals in idolatrous Gentile nations? This question assumes a startling aspect; and the possibility of its receiving an answer in the affirmative may alarm some readers. But, on the other hand, does it not seem an equally serious matter for us to shut out from nations so situated the only remedial means which (as far as we are instructed respecting the divine purpose in the dispensations of grace) could be used for their instruction and elevation? It is, however, a remarkable fact, that in respect of Greece, which was peculiarly separated from other modes of procuring a knowledge of divine things, we find a general recognition of prophets, in the character of expounders of the divine will, beyond what is discovered in eastern and more favoured nations.

On this subject the learned Mosheim observes: "It is well known that no nation in times past was so barbarous, and so forsaken of God, that he did not, now and then, raise up in it good and wise men, especially before the promulgation of the law by Moses, who abominated the popular superstitions and the worship of idols, and both recommended to the people, and themselves followed, a better and more holy religion. Even the Jews by universal consent allow that, prior to the time of Moses, other nations, as well as themselves, had their prophets. Wherefore, if those who think with Dr. Cudworth simply mean that no nation was altogether destitute of divinely-inspired men, from whence all who were so disposed might learn the knowledge of the true God, and the way of eternal salvation, *there would be nothing in this opinion to be found fault with.* But these learned men wish us to concede something more, and require us to believe that the Supreme Being sometimes disclosed his will, and a knowledge of future events, even to those whose minds were utterly devoid of true religion, and contaminated with the most perverse sentiments concerning God. Are we, therefore, to assent to this opinion? For my part, I consider we ought to decide that generally God can do, and sometimes for most just and holy resons did do, the thing in question."—*Intellectual System*, vol. iii, p. 26. (See *Appendix*, note 68.)

If this general admission be applied to the early ages of Greece,—and it might be easily shown that the denial of it presents still more formidable difficulties to our view,—then at least one great peculiarity in the religion of this people is accounted for. I allude to the deep and general conviction which pervaded them in all ages of their history, that the divine will, and a knowledge of future events, were specially communicated to favoured individuals by direct revelation, and thus made known generally. Unhappily, even in that land of intellect and science, we have no means of gathering up any particles of these ancient communications. For amid all the sciences of Greece, divinity had no place. Fragments of truth were certainly orally communicated, and in some cases preserved, but generally in ill-understood and inoperative fragments. This fact, however, so clearly set forth God as the only source of divine knowledge, that the Greeks, whenever at a loss for information on the subject, applied to the deity to obtain it.

But, while by this means the prophetic institute was as fully established in Greece as it was even in Judea, it became fearfully polluted and debased. Not only did it frequently sink into the action of human craft, jugglery, and falsehood, but in some instances it was certainly imbued with Satanic guile, and sustained by demon power. (See *Appendix*, note 69.) Thus did the malign agency under which idolatry arose to curse the nations, in that country as in others, poison the very fountain of divine knowledge, and turn what was mercifully designed as a channel for the communication of divine truth, into a means of disseminating Satanic error.

Of other methods of obtaining a knowledge of future events,—such as divination by dreams, by sacrifices, birds, lots, ominous words and things,—our limits will not allow us to treat. We will therefore proceed to notice the very important subject of Grecian oracles.

The unbounded respect which the ancients entertained for these oracles, and the confidence with which they relied on them, can scarcely be exceeded. However modern philosophy may discard their authority, and denounce the superstition which led men to be guided by them, the fact remains patent to the whole world, and stands foremost in the most brilliant period of the history of this most enlightened of ancient nations,—that the declarations of the oracles were fully believed to be really and truly divine revelations. Not only did the most powerful kings, as Crœsus, and the wisest lawgivers, as Minos and Lycurgus, consult these oracles, and act under their guidance, as they believed; but in matters of the highest national importance the oracular authority was decisive, and in those of the most vital interest to individuals the arbitrament of the Pythoness was held to be conclusive. Thus much is undoubted; and it must have been something more than low craft, or priestly jugglery, which could rear up such a universal conviction,—embedded as it was in the common faith and religious principles of the most enlightened people of the ancient world,—and maintain it in full vigour, credit, and efficiency for a thousand years.

Our opinion of the moving influence which, while associated with much craft, intrigue, and policy, was the real cause of the great ascendency which the Grecian oracles maintained for so long a period over the human mind, has been already given. And these views have been greatly confirmed by subsequent research, and by numerous opinions expressed by men best qualified to decide on the subject, of which the following may be taken as a specimen:—" Notwithstanding the general obscurity and ambiguity of most of the oracles given at Delphi, there are many also which convey so clear and distinct a meaning, that they could not possibly have been misunderstood; *so that a wise agency at the bottom of the oracles can-*

not be denied. The early Christian writers, seeing that *some extraordinary power must in several cases have been at work,* represented it as an institution of the evil spirit."—*Dic. of Greek and Roman Antiq.*, p. 670. And who had better means of investigating the subject? Who were ever so advantageously situated for forming a sound judgment as to these premises? And who from such *data* can rationally draw any other conclusion?

It has been a subject of surprise that Zeus should have had so few oracles. This, however, does not lessen, but rather enhance, the religious character of the Greek oracles. For it was not because they were regarded as unworthy of the supreme god, that his name was so seldom associated with them: on the contrary, Zeus was accounted the great source of all oracular revelations; but he was considered to be too highly exalted to become the immediate channel of communication with mankind. Other deities, therefore, and especially Apollon, and even heroes, were supposed to act as mediators between Zeus,—who alone possessed the books of fate, and was the grand repository of a knowledge of the future,—and men, by communicating to them his will. We append a brief notice of the most noted oracles of Greece.

The oracle of Delphi.—The temple in which this oracle resided was built over a small natural chasm in the earth, from which, from time to time, an intoxicating smoke arose. Over this chasm there stood a high tripod, on which the Pythia, or priestess, when the oracle was to be consulted, took her seat. The smoke arising was supposed to affect her brain with a kind of delirious intoxication; and the sounds which she uttered while in this state were believed to contain the revelations of the god. They were carefully written down by the *prophetess*, and given as the oracular response to the party inquiring of the oracle. The Pythia was always a female native of Delphi, and generally selected from a poor country family. During the great popularity of the oracle, there were two of these, who took their seats alternately. At first the oracles were given only once a year, but afterward certain days in every month were set apart for this purpose; and the order in which the parties inquiring should be allowed access, was carefully regulated. The Pythia always spent three days in preparation before she ascended the tripod. During this time she bathed in the Castalian well. All persons inquiring of the god had first to offer in sacrifice a goat, an ox, or a sheep.

Most of the oracular answers which are extant are in hexameters, and in the Ionic dialect. Some of these verses had metrical defects which exposed them to the criticism of the learned. At length poetic responses were entirely laid aside, and the answers given in plain Doric prose.

This oracle during its best period was believed to give answers and advice to every one who came with a pure heart, and had no evil design. If he had committed a crime, the answer was refused till he had atoned for it; and he who consulted the god for bad purposes was sure thereby to hasten his own ruin. No religious institution in all antiquity obtained such a paramount influence, not only in Greece, but in all countries around the Mediterranean, in all matters of importance,—whether relating to religion or to politics, to private or to public life,—as the oracle at Delphi. On the establishment of colonies, in all disputes between these and the parent state, and in all questions bearing on religious institutions, as well as a thousand others, the decisions of the Delphic god were held to be final and conclusive.

The first manifest decline of this authority was on the occasion of the great struggle between Sparta and Athens, when the partiality of the oracle for the former state became so manifest, that all the influence of Athens was estranged from it; and it thenceforth dwindled away, until, having sunk into neglect, it was abolished by the Emperor Theodosius.

Besides the oracle at Delphi, there were several others in which Apollon was believed to utter predictions. The principal of these were at Abæ in Phocis, at Didyma, on the hill Ptoön, &c.

The oracles of Zeus must be mentioned next in order. In these, however, the god did not make his revelations by direct inspiration, as was the case with Apollon. He merely gave signs, which men had to interpret.

The first of these was at Olympia. Those who came to consult this oracle had to offer a victim in sacrifice; and the priest gave his answers from the appearance of the dead animal. This was much frequented in ancient times, but did not long retain its influence, except in respect of the Olympic Games.

The most important of the oracles of Zeus in Greece was at Dodona. Here the oracle was given from sounds produced by the wind. The sanctuary was built on an eminence, and in immediate proximity to a grove of oak and beech trees. The sound of the wind passing through this foliage was interpreted as a revelation of the mind of the deity. In later days alterations were introduced, and in historical times this oracle lost the importance which it had previously enjoyed.

Other gods, and even heroes, had oracles; but there was nothing in them to justify an account of them in these pages.

Before passing on to other topics, it will be necessary here to notice those peculiar and important rites which were associated with the religion of the Greeks under the title of "mysteries." The general character and design of this institution, as an element of heathen idolatry, have been already discussed. We have now to direct particular attention to those which were celebrated in connexion with the religion of Greece. Of these there were several,—those of Zeus in Crete, of Hera in Argolis, of Athene and Dionysos at Athens, of Artemis in Arcadia, and others; but the most important and remarkable were the mysteries of Samothrace and Eleusis.

The common character of these Grecian mysteries consisted in their being services connected with particular sacrifices periodically offered during the night-season, and to which none but the initiated were permitted to have access. In these select services not only were sacrifices offered and devotional rites performed, but explanations of ancient traditions were given; and, in some cases, most affecting exhibitions of the divine attributes and works were, by scenic representation and verbal exposition, communicated to the assembled company. No religious institution in Greece exercised a wider range of influence on the public mind than this; but unfortunately, as it was a capital crime to divulge anything seen or heard on those occasions to the multitude without, it is extremely difficult to collect any definite information respecting them. Our limits restrict us to a brief notice of the Eleusinian mysteries; and we submit to this the more readily, inasmuch as these were by far the most important of all the Grecian sacred rights, and, as such, have called forth continued investigation, which has at length elicited a tolerable amount of information respecting these occult and recondite services.

There were minor mysteries celebrated under the same name; but our attention will be exclusively confined to the greater mysteries. These are supposed to have originated about 1400 B. C., and were celebrated at Eleusis, a borough-town in Attica, situated between Megara and the Piræeus, at the head of the Bay of Salamis. This service was celebrated annually, but with special pomp and importance every fifth year. The rites began on the 15th of September, and continued during nine days. On the first day the company merely assembled, no one being eligible to take a part in this great service who had not been initiated in the lesser mysteries, although crowds of mere spectators who were not thus qualified visited Athens on these occasions. On the second day, the persons who were to take a part in the solemn service went in procession to the sea, where they purified themselves by ablutions in two small streams, which there fell into the Gulf of Salamis. On the third day, called "the day of sacrifices," a mullet, and barley grown in the field of Rharos, were solemnly consecrated to Demeter, to whose honour the mysteries were dedicated. This ceremony, by bringing the crowd into association with the deity, led them to assume a serious and reverential air, whereas previously joy and hilarity prevailed. On the fourth day, a procession was formed, in which a basket called καλάθιον, containing pomegranates and poppy-seeds, was carried on a wagon drawn by oxen. This was followed by females termed κισσοφόροι, with osier panniers: into these the Athenians poured their offerings of poppy, carded wool, grains of salt, sesamum, pomegranates, ivy, reeds, cakes called φθόεις, snakes, and branches broken from neighbouring bay-bushes. The fifth day was called "the day of torches," because in the evening the company roamed over the fields with lighted flambeaux; after which they repaired to the temple of Demeter at Eleusis. This ceremony was supposed to represent the search of the goddess for her daughter Proserpine. The sixth day was termed "the day of Bacchus," when a small statue of this divinity was borne in triumphant procession toward the great temple, over what was called "the Holy Way." In this procession the crowd were crowned with vine-leaves, and danced to the melody of music, until, arriving at the mystical entrance, they passed into the sacred enclosure, and spent the night in exercises and services, which were universally regarded as more holy and solemn than any other element of the religion of Greece. (See *Appendix*, note 70.) After this night, those who had taken part in its service were called ἐπόπται, or "the fully initiated."

On the seventh day, the athletic pastimes took place; and the strong distinguished themselves by feats of masculine prowess, and the agile by their dexterity and fleetness. The eighth day was, it is said, added when Æsculapius visited Attica. On this day the ceremonies of the lesser mysteries were repeated. The ninth day was called "the day of earthen vessels," because on it bowls of wine, sanctified by the consecration of the hierophant, were dashed upon the ground as libations to Demeter; and the festival closed amid the wild and exulting shouts of those who had witnessed the mysteries of Eleusinia.

Even this rapid sketch of the mysteries may serve to show that all the intellectual and artistic resources of Greece were called into requisition to sustain the national faith,—a fact that accounts for the strong hold which such theologic absurdities had on the mind of this cultivated and polished people.

It now becomes necessary to direct our inquiries to the religious character of the several philosophical sects, or "schools," of Greece: for even a partial acquaintance with this remarkable people is sufficient to show that, with them, religion was not so much studied under the mode of divinity, theology, and morals, as under the form and name of "philosophy." We shall not, therefore, greatly err if we direct attention to the most important of these philosophical schools, as holding nearly the same relation to the national religion of Greece as our several sectarian denominations hold to the general religious character of our own country.

The first of the philosophic teachers whom it may be necessary to mention in this category, is THALES, who has been already noticed as one of the Seven Wise Men. He is celebrated as the founder of the Ionic school of philosophy; and he was unquestionably the first, and the leader, of a band or succession of philosophers, of whom Pherecydes, Anaximander, Anaximenes, and Anaxagoras were the most eminent. But this was not properly a "school," since they held no class of doctrines in common. In one important instance, however, they introduced a great novelty into the popular religious belief. It had been a standing dogma from the days of Hesiod, that the world originated by divine generation: Uranus and Gaia produced Cronus, or Time, when the universe was complete. In opposition to this notion, Thales taught that water was the first principle or basis of all things. But to what extent he recognised God as the Supreme Artificer, does not clearly appear. This single step was, however, of vast importance. It stripped creation, and, through it, material existence in general, of that incubus of quasi-divinity which had been supposed to affect all its operations; and placed the material world before the mind as a subject for rational and scientific investigation. It must be confessed that when Thales had exploded the old scheme of cosmogony, as a series of personal history and divine intermarriages, he did not carry out his principle to all cognate subjects, or lay down any solid rule for eliciting the truth. In morals, as well as in respect of physics, this philosopher is celebrated as having made a great advance on his predecessors. He is said to have been the author of the golden rule, "Not to do to others what, if done to us, we should resent." We see here, therefore, the earliest influence of Grecian philosophy on religion, in assailing the absurdities of its theogony, and extending its moral influence.

We have now to direct attention to the teaching of PYTHAGORAS. This extraordinary man was eminent in almost every respect; but it is only concerning the influence of his doctrine and practice on morals and religion that we shall refer to him. It seems that he established a society, which was engaged partly in the study of political subjects, and partly in those which were scientific. But this brotherhood was mainly distinguished as being held together by a religious sentiment or influence. Whether this was framed on any model which the industrious Greek discovered during his extensive travels, or was an invention of his own, cannot now be ascertained. But it has been sufficiently shown that this brotherhood was distinguished by many observances which approached very nearly to a monastic character. But Pythagoras did not hesitate to put himself forward as "an inspired teacher, prophet, and worker of miracles,—employing all these gifts to found a new special order of brethren, bound together by religious rites and observances, peculiar to themselves. In his prominent vocation, analogous to that of Epimenides, Orpheus, or Melampus, he appears as the revealer of a mode of life calculated to raise his disciples above the level of mankind, and to recommend them to the favour of the gods; the Pythagorean life, like the Orphic life, being intended as the exclusive prerogative of the brotherhood,—approached only by probation and initiatory ceremonies, which were adapted to select enthusiasts rather than to an indiscriminate crowd, and exacting entire mental devotion to the master."—*Grote's History of Greece*, vol. iv, p. 534. When we read this account of an ancient sage, given not by a novice, or for any particular purpose, or by a religious enthusiast, but by the hand of a master, we feel intensely desirous of knowing more of his doctrine and character. But, alas! this laudable curiosity can be gratified only to a limited extent. Pythagoras left no writings; unless we receive "the Golden Verses," on which Hierocles wrote a learned Commentary, as possessing some traditionary authority, and embodying the moral principles which he inculcated. If we could be certain that they exhibit a summary of his ethical system, he would be entitled to occupy one of the highest places among Pagan philosophers. When want of success induced him to leave Greece, he located himself in Italy; where the inhabitants of Crotona among whom he resided called him "the Hyperborean Apollo," and the satirical Timon ridiculed him as one "engaged in fishing for men."

Grote well observes, that "there is no reason for regarding Pythagoras as an impostor, because experience seems to show, that while in certain ages it is not difficult for a man to persuade others that he is inspired, it is still less difficult for him to contract the same belief himself. Looking at the general type of Pythagoras, as conceived by witnesses in and near his own age, we find in him chiefly the religious missionary and schoolmaster, with little of the politician. The primitive Pythagoras is inspired by the gods to reveal a new mode of life,—the Pythagorean life."—*History of Greece*, vol. iv, p. 535.

It is scarcely possible to form any idea, at this time, of the effect produced by such a man, with his powers of mind and religious professions, on the character and opinions of his countrymen. The fact as to his doctrine seems clear:—he taught the doctrine of the metempsychosis or transmigration of souls. We might think this dogma would be a sufficient antidote to every other, and render the teaching of the philosopher repulsive. However it might have been in Greece, it was far otherwise in Italy; and it may be fairly questioned whether the annals of the world contain a similar account of the religious results following the efforts of any heathen philosopher. I quote again the words of Grote:—On the arrival of Pythagoras at Crotona in Italy, "his preaching and his conduct produced an effect almost electric upon the minds of the people, with an extensive reform, public as well as private. Political discontent was repressed, incontinence disappeared, luxury became discredited, and the women hastened to change their golden ornaments for the simplest attire. No less than two thousand persons were converted at his first preaching; and so effective were his discourses to the youth, that the supreme Council of One Thousand invited him into their assembly, solicited his advice, and even offered to constitute him their *prytanis*, or president, while his wife and daughter were placed at the head of the religious procession of females. Nor was his influence confined to Crotona: other towns in Italy and Sicily,—Sybaris, Metapontum, Rhegium, Catana, Himera, &c.,—all felt the benefit of his exhortations, which extricated some of them even from slavery." Our learned author adds: "To trace these tales to a true foundation is impossible; but we may entertain reasonable belief that the success of Pythagoras, as a person favoured by the gods, and a patentee of divine secrets, was very great; that he procured to himself both the reverence of the multitude, and the peculiar attachment and obedience of many devoted adherents, chiefly belonging to the wealthy and powerful classes."—*History of Greece*, vol. iv, p. 546.

We have preferred giving the above extracts from this learned author, although rather disposed to demur to some of his words, and believing, with him, that the accounts of the effects produced by the ministrations of Pythagoras are in many respects overcharged. Yet, with all this concession, we ask the intelligent Christian,—How is the admitted *residuum* of truth to be accounted for? Under what influence, and by what light, did the heathens of Crotona discern the error and evil of factious complaint, incontinence, and luxury? How did they, who had so long been the slaves of these vices, now

in such numbers acquire a power to resist their fascinations, and to
alter their conduct and habits? But it is alleged, "This is false:
partial and untruthful biographers have merely adorned the character
of their hero with these additions." We ask, then, with equal confidence,—What led those lying heathens to discern this elevated
morality? Is it in the nature of things that heathens, under the full
influence of vicious habits, should sketch even in idea such purely
moral reforms? We confess we think not; and without admitting
the claim of Pythagoras to "inspiration," in the proper sense of that
term, we feel disposed to regard him as a man who, with many and
serious errors, possessed a considerable amount of sound morality
and sterling truth, under the influence of Him who "enlighteneth
every man that cometh into the world;" and we believe that, faithful to this teaching, he was, under the same influence, made the instrument of a great moral reformation. Nor does anything in the
future history of this people militate against such an opinion. They
were lured into political action and influence, and severely suffered
the consequences of such indiscretion in the loss of many of their
principal members: but, taught by this error, they existed long afterward in their proper character as a moral and religious body.

Since it is our main object to exhibit the agencies afforded by
Grecian philosophy, and adapted to promote sound morality and
enlightened religion, we may pass over the teaching of the Sophists
and of the Eleatic school, and proceed to direct attention to the person that fills the largest space as an efficient teacher in these departments. We, of course, refer to SOCRATES.

This extraordinary man was the son of a sculptor, comparatively
a poor man, but of pure Hellenic blood. For some considerable time
he worked at his father's trade, until, at length, he fully devoted
himself to public instruction. In adopting this, he did not establish a school, or gather about him a number of young men who paid
for their instruction, and to whom he delivered set discourses. On
the contrary, Socrates went continually into places of public resort,
and, by entering into conversation with people of all ages and ranks,
imparted instruction unto all. The principal means by which he
effected this was by propounding a series of questions, which were
all studiously directed to some important end, and designed to impart a knowledge of some essential truth. More than this, indeed,
was intended in the adoption and continuance of this mode of teaching. Socrates had a very low estimate of the real acquirements of
his countrymen, and indulged in extravagant ideas of the effect of
knowledge: in fact, with him "wisdom" was synonymous with
"virtue." By the mode of questioning which he adopted, he was

able to convict of ignorance almost all with whom he conversed. Indeed, to a great extent, this was his object, in order that he might lead them to acquire knowledge.

One instance of this course of action may be related, since it is not only amusing, but casts considerable light upon the character and conduct of this philosopher. One of his intimate friends and ardent admirers, when at Delphi, had propounded this question: "Whether any other man was wiser than Socrates?" and received from the oracle the response that no other man was wiser. Socrates says that he was greatly perplexed on hearing this answer, as he wished to respect the truthfulness of the oracle, but found it difficult to do so, conscious as he felt of so much ignorance. He, however, resolved to apply a very simple test to this difficulty. Selecting a distinguished individual, of great reputation for wisdom, he entered into conversation with him, and propounded questions, the answers to which soon convinced Socrates that the wisdom of his interlocutor had been greatly overstated, though he himself fully shared the popular opinion as to his own acquirements, and could not by any means be brought to doubt the extent of his wisdom. This reconciled Socrates to the decision of the oracle; for, said he, "The result I have acquired is, that I was a wiser man than he: for neither he nor I knew anything of what was truly good and honourable; but the difference between us was, that he fancied he knew them, while I was fully conscious of my own ignorance: I was therefore wiser than he, inasmuch as I was exempt from that capital error."—*Grote's History of Greece*, vol. viii, p. 562.

Socrates, throughout his life, evinced an exact regard for all the religious duties imposed by the national faith. As respects the subject-matter of his teaching, he differed from all the philosophers who had preceded him, and especially from Thales. That sage made the first assault on the mythologic dogmas of Greece, by propounding a separate study of the physical system of the universe: and this course was followed by all succeeding philosophers, who confounded morals and physics in strange combination. Socrates repudiated this method. Declaring that "the proper study of mankind is man," he recognised the security and happiness of man both as the single end of study, and as the limiting principle by which it ought to be circumscribed. He objected to any study of astronomy more than might be gathered from pilots and watchmen; he even set limitations to the learning of arithmetic; and as to physical science, it was out of the question. It is curious to look back and trace such idiosyncrasies in the giant intellects of old. But Socrates evidently regarded these branches of knowledge as being in such a state as to promise no practical result; and this was his ruling idea. He consequently urged a close and careful study of human matters, in opposition to those which he regarded as shut out from our research by the divine will.

It is, however, as a moralist, and as a religious teacher, that we have specially to regard Socrates. He not only introduced the innovation mentioned above, of extending his teaching generally and gratuitously, and of shutting out speculative science, and limiting his discourses to simple ethics; he went further, and prosecuted this work not as a profession, or merely as an ordinary duty of life, but in the spirit of a religious missionary. In this respect he stood alone among the teachers of Greece; neither Parmenides and Anaxagoras before him, nor Plato and Aristotle after him, assumed this character, which Socrates most distinctly claimed, upheld by his life, and asserted in his death. Nor are we at liberty to construe this divine mission as meaning no more than an ordinary providential appointment, or such a conviction of the divine will as may rest upon and direct the mind of any good man. Socrates asserted the presence with his mind of a special visitation from God. He tells us that he had been accustomed constantly to hear, even from his childhood, a divine voice, interfering, at moments when he was about to act, in this way of restraint, but never in the way of instigation. Such prohibitory warning was wont to come upon him very frequently, not merely on great, but even on seemingly trivial, occasions, intercepting what he was about to do or to say. Of this spiritual monitor he was accustomed to speak familiarly to his friends, assuring them that he always most implicitly obeyed it. All those who were about him knew that this prevented him from entering upon public life, and hindered his preparing a defence when he was indicted for a capital crime. This has been spoken of by later writers as "the demon of Socrates;" and moderns have argued against it under that aspect with great eloquence and force. But all this is beside the mark. Socrates never spoke of it as a personality, but always as "a divine sign, a prophetic or supernatural voice."

But, besides this retarding and guiding influence with which Socrates regarded himself as inspired, he believed himself specially commissioned to pursue a particular course of teaching. In dreams, by oracular intimations, and by other means, he considered himself as set apart, by the special mandate of the gods, to detect and expose the superficial wisdom of the Greeks, and to lead them to sound practical knowledge. The weight with which this impression rested on his mind, and the spirit in which he aimed at discharging such a duty, may be seen in the following extracts from his address to his judges: "Whatever be the danger and obloquy which I may incur, it would be monstrous indeed, if, having maintained my place in the ranks as an hoplite under your generals at Delium and Potidæa, I were now, from fear of death or anything else, to desert the post which the God has assigned to me,—the duty of living for philosophy, and cross-questioning myself and others. And should you even now offer to acquit me on condition of my renouncing this duty, I should tell you, with all respect and affection, that I will obey the God rather than you; and I will persist until my dying day in cross-questioning you, exposing your want of wisdom and virtue, and reproaching you, until the defect be remedied. My mission as your monitor is a mark of the special favour of the God to you. Perhaps you will ask me, 'Why cannot you go away, Socrates, and live among us in peace and silence?' This is the hardest of all questions for me to answer to your satisfaction. If I tell you that silence on my part would be disobedience to the God, you will not believe me. Nevertheless, so stands the fact, incredible as it may be to you."

It is only necessary to add, that while this great man evidently placed his system of ethics on too narrow a base in comprising all virtue in wisdom, his practice was far more sound than his theses; for none could urge more diligently or forcibly than he did the necessity of maintaining control over the passions, the regulation of the affections, and the exercise of constant self-denial. But one of the most important principles of Socrates was, that although he affirmed virtue to be essentially wisdom and knowledge, he at the same time argued that it could not be taught, but that virtue was vouchsafed or withheld according to the special volition and grace of the gods; so that, while he made well-doing the noblest pursuit of man, he regarded the best man as most beloved by the gods; and thus human weakness and want were placed in dependence on divine goodness and strength.

A full analysis of the teaching of this age, and a complete investigation of its influence on Greece, would require a volume. Our limits will only allow us to add a few words on the latter topic. Here we have not only the assertion of divine influence on the human heart, as necessary to virtue,—and the condemnation of all vice as folly,—but a living embodiment of these doctrines in the person of the teacher, who professed to live under such a deep conviction of a divine impelling call to this duty, that he determined to die rather than swerve from the course to which he had been appointed. And this active obedience was continued in an incessant course of instruction for thirty or forty years, (for Socrates was seventy when put to death,) until the Greek mind was so imbued with these doctrines, that it was urged on his trial by Xenophon, that every good man believed in the necessity of living under immediate divine influence; and all were taught that the gods were deeply concerned in the happiness and virtue of man, and had therefore specially called Socrates to the mission which he thus fulfilled.

We have no hesitation in assuming this case to exhibit a very gracious divine interposition. We regard the conduct of Socrates as that of a man enlightened and guided by the Author of all good, to lead the hearts and minds of the most intellectual heathen nation of the earth back to himself. It may be objected that Socrates did not denounce Greek polytheism, nor live an immaculate life. This is admitted: but he did enunciate, and by every energy of argument enforce the adoption of, great spiritual truths, which, if practically received, would have superseded the absurd and wicked system of Greek theology, by bringing the people into an intelligent obedience to the Spirit of God. And he did evince his personal obedience, so far as his mind was enlightened, in choosing to die with a good conscience, rather than to live in neglect of known duty.

PLATO, the disciple and successor of Socrates, followed his master as the leading philosopher of Greece. Yet although this sage exercised a more extensive influence over the Greek mind than any other individual before or after him, our notice of his teaching will be brief. Unlike Socrates in his object, Plato did not direct his great energies to the promotion of individual wisdom and virtue. He evidently regarded it as his more immediate vocation to establish the science of politics on great moral principles. His principal efforts were accordingly directed to the dissemination of such views of God and man,—of the mutual relation, and common interest, and relative duties of the human family,—as should contribute toward the formation of a model political community. So far as this design is concerned, we altogether overlook it; but it will be necessary to give a brief sketch of his religious and moral tenets.

The teaching of Plato respecting the divine nature was far in advance of the theology of his age and country; but it is, nevertheless, not an easy task to state precisely what were his exact opinions on this important subject. For it seems that, with the fate of his master present to his mind, Plato steadily kept his personal safety in view, and expressed himself with caution, if, indeed, he did not withhold much that he fully believed. Hence he says, "It is a difficult thing to discover the nature of the Creator of the universe; and, being discovered, it is impossible, and would even be impious, to expose the discovery to vulgar understandings." Considering this reserve,—coupled as it was with Plato's adopting the theoretical part of the teaching of Socrates, in preference to the practical,—we can only hope to attain an approximate estimate of his theology. It seems that he maintained the existence of two kinds of being:—one, self-existent, the potent cause of the world's creation out of preëxistent matter, which he regarded as coëternal with God; and the other, man. The world was framed out of this matter, distributed into four principal elements, into which, after the creation, the divinity infused a rational soul. Man was formed, as to his body, out of this material substance, while human souls were made out of the residue of the soul of the world. The human mind was therefore supposed to exist previous to the body, as an emanation from Deity. Invisible gods and demons had, according to this system, been previously created by the same cause out of the same spiritual substance. Plato, therefore, carried out the teaching of Socrates into theory, by supposing the existence of one Great First Cause, the Creator of the polytheistic deities of Greece; while the world, thus endowed with a rational soul,—an emanation from God,—was spoken of as "the son of God."

This brief sketch is sufficient to justify the statement of Grote, that "Plato was a great speculative genius;" which is further proved by the consideration, that in none of his works does he make the remotest allusion to the existence of malignant spirits, but accounts for the origin and existence of evil by reference to the intractable nature of matter. In consequence of Plato's ruling idea of political theorizing, his most explicit declarations of moral virtue are given in a figurative form, the man being represented as a political body. But it is sufficiently apparent that he exhibits this perfect virtue as comprised under four distinct heads: 1. Prudence, or wisdom; 2. Courage, constancy, or fortitude; 3. Temperance, discretion, or self-control; and, 4. Justice, or righteousness. To all this the teacher of the Academy added the doctrine of *metempsychosis*, or the transmigration of souls, believing that the soul of a man sometimes passed into the body of a brute, until, by occupying successive bodies, its moral character was changed, or confirmed. (See *Appendix*, note 71.)

Before proceeding to form an opinion of the teaching of Plato generally, a few other particulars must be briefly added. He allowed men to drink to excess in the Bacchanalian festivals, but not at other times. (Diogenes Laertius, lib. iii, cap. 39.) He did not recommend the worship of the one true God, but that of the twelve gods of

Greece, to whom he proposed to solemnize twelve monthly festivals. (De Legibus, cap. 8.) He says, "He may lie who knows how to do it in a fitting or needful season." He advises governors to make use of lies toward both enemies and citizens, "when it is convenient." But, what perhaps will be regarded as still more strange, in his sketch of a model republic,—which is intended to exhibit a community formed in the most rational and perfect manner,—Plato recommends that women, as well as men, should appear perfectly naked at public exercises; that the wives of the rulers should be common to all; and that young men who have distinguished themselves as warriors should be rewarded by having a greater liberty of commerce with women.

Looking, then, at the whole matter, it is difficult to give, in a sentence or two, an opinion of the effect of Plato's teaching on Greece. His merits as a great man, a profound genius, are undisputed. He contributed, perhaps, more than any other man to place sound learning on a substantial basis, and to promote its general cultivation. But, regarded as a moral and religious teacher, his influence on the state of Greece must have been most injurious. Whatever the faults of Socrates might have been, his doctrines and practice had an evident tendency to lead men to a careful and conscientious obedience to the teaching and influence of the Divine Spirit. This we are inclined to regard as the only conceivable means by which Greece at that period could have been regenerated, and restored to religious truth and sound morals. The course of teaching and general conduct of Plato did more than anything else to prevent such a regeneration. The glitter of his science fascinated the Grecian intellect; his broad scheme of philosophy, and profound elements of logic, dazzled the mind even of the sedate and serious; and individual subjection of mind to divine influence is scarcely heard of after the death of Socrates. In our judgment, a great and gracious dispensation was thus repelled; and Greece, instead of rising, sunk in respect both of morals and of religion.

As we do not investigate the philosophy of Greece in order to trace its subtle transmutations, nor to detail its intellectual conflicts, but to ascertain its moral and religious results, our further reference to this subject may be concise. ARISTOTLE, who had long been a pupil of Plato, after having been preceptor to Alexander of Macedon, returned to Athens, and established a school of philosophy at the Lyceum, in opposition to the Academy which had been founded by Plato. Perhaps nothing in human history can exceed the intellectual grandeur of this seminary. But for one purpose it was fruitless. Aristotle cast no additional light on the divine character;

but, by teaching the eternity of the world, obscured what had been previously known. His opinions of providence were doubtful in the extreme: "*If*," says he, "the gods exercise any care at all about men, *as it seems*." He recommended the destruction of all weakly or deformed children, and counselled other measures respecting population of a revolting kind. He spoke of one supreme God, but asserted the stars to be true eternal divinities. The greatest efforts and highest success of such a philosophy could not be promotive of sound morality or enlightened religion; but, by drawing away the most energetic and cultivated minds into a kind of intellectual idolatry, exercised rather a deteriorating and withering influence.

We have next to notice the tenets and influence of the Stoics; and, in so doing, must keep to the doctrines of the sect as taught by ZENO. The dogmas of this philosophic sect with respect to creation were very confused. They taught that a chaos, containing the first principles of all future being, existed from eternity; that this chaos, being at length arranged, and emerging into variable forms, became the world as it now subsists. This change was effected by the agency of two principles; it being distinctly taught that everything which operates, as well as that which is operated upon, is corporeal. The acting principle is sometimes spoken of as fire; at others, it is called "reason," or "God:" so that this fire must have been regarded as identical with deity. And this deity was defined to be "that law of nature which ever accomplishes what is right, and prevents the opposite;" and Zeno identified it, or Zeus, with spirit and predestination, or unconditioned necessity. Zeno seems to have referred the several chief deities of the Greek Pantheon to the different modes in which the great primary divine power was manifested.

On the subject of divine providence, this sect taught that God governed the world by a general providence, which did not extend to individuals, cities, or people: it was therefore only another name for necessity or fate, to which God and matter, or the universe which consists of both, are according to this doctrine inevitably subjected.

In reference to morals, the disciples of Zeno have claimed, and have been usually allowed to occupy, an elevated position: and in respect of mere external action, and of some of the principles inculcated, this award is just. Zeno considered virtue as the result of the perfect dominion of reason. All actions were regarded as good or bad,—even impulses and desires,—because they rest upon free consent; and consequently passive conditions or affections, when not influenced by the dominion of reason, are immoral, and become the source of immoral action. Raising this lofty standard, they assumed a perfect equality in the morality of actions of each class: that is,

all virtuous actions were equally virtuous, and all vicious ones
equally vicious. They thus described a wise man as raised above
the instincts of nature, experiencing neither pleasure nor pain,—
feeling no fault, exercising no pity,—in fact, as divine. Hence one
of them says, "As to the body, thou art but a small part of the universe; but in respect of the mind, or reason, neither worse nor less
than the gods."

This morality lacked essential support. The immortality of the
soul was denied: or, if admitted, the resurrection with which it was
associated was marked by an oblivion of all preceding existence.
"This restoration," says Seneca, "many would reject, were it not
that their renovated life is accompanied with a total oblivion of past
events." The whole system tended to raise man to a state of independence. Hence, in opposition to the threat, "I will fetter thee,
Epictetus," the sage replies, "Thou wilt fetter my feet, but Jupiter
himself cannot fetter my choice." But these lofty lessons failed in
their object. Even Zeno himself allowed a community of women,
tolerated incest, was guilty of the most unnatural impurity, and
ultimately committed suicide.

The tenets and influence of this sect cannot be regarded as affording any additional religious light, or moral purity, to the people of
Greece. On the contrary, they tended to confuse the understanding, and, under the pretext of seeking elevated moral virtue, to
alienate man still further from God.

We have yet another religious sect to consider, in its teaching and
influence on the mind of Greece,—the followers of EPICURUS.

It will first be necessary to notice the ethical doctrines of this
sect. The foundation-principle of this scheme was, that pleasure
constitutes the highest happiness of man, and should therefore be
aimed at as the supreme good. There can be little doubt that this
system arose in opposition to the philosophical scheme of Zeno.
For, as that philosopher began with necessity and fate, and proceeded
to carry out his views by ascetic and repulsive severity; so Epicurus
commenced with the freedom of the human will, and chose, as the
object to be aimed at, supreme pleasure or unruffled happiness.
From the terms in which this thesis was propounded, many have
supposed that the system gave license to the gratification of unbridled desire. But there is no reason for believing that Epicurus
used the term in this sense. On the contrary, we are told that
"pleasure with him was not a mere momentary and transitory sensation; but he conceived it as something lasting and imperishable,
consisting in pure and noble enjoyments. It was accordingly exhibited by the union of two terms,—$\dot{a}\tau a\rho a\xi i a$, 'freedom from pas-

sion, coolness, calmness,' and ἀπονία, 'exemption from bodily pain;' thus showing a freedom from pain, and from all influences which disturb the peace of our mind, and thereby our happiness, which is the result of it. The *summum bonum*, or 'chief good' of man, according to this system, consisted in this peace of mind; and the great problem of his ethics was therefore to show how it might be attained." It is said that of all the ancient systems this has been most violently opposed, and most extensively misunderstood; and, probably, it might with equal truth be added, that no system has been explained with so much latitude, and has led to such different results in its professed followers.

But it will now be necessary to notice other parts of this scheme. Epicurus not only adopted the atomic theory of physics in respect of the formation of the world, but even supposed the gods to be in like manner composed of atoms. They were conceived to live in the enjoyment of perfect peace and happiness. They had nothing to do with creation, nor with the government of the world, or affording influence to man. The system was consequently objected to as atheistic; and, whatever may be the theory, it had undoubtedly this practical result. A further essential defect of the Epicurean philosophy is found in the utter absence of any authorized law. Piety toward God, submission to his authority, resignation to his will, or trust in him, could not exist. The essential principle of the whole scheme was selfishness. Every man was counselled to avoid everything that would occasion him trouble, pain, or disturbance. Hereby all efforts toward the public good, and all offices of friendship, were cut up by the roots. The result of the system was, therefore, the destruction of religious principles,—the removal of man from all divine teaching, influence, favour, or responsibility; and the effect of it on its author and his more eminent scholars was indulgence in gross sensuality.

The system of Epicurus, therefore, appears like the last effort of human reason to separate man from his God, and to remove from his mind all really religious influence, and all efficient moral principle.

Although these several systems of philosophy have been noticed in the order in which they arose, it must not be supposed that they thus succeeded and superseded each other. On the contrary, each school continued a separate and independent centre of instruction and influence, after the last had been fully established: so that the Greek mind had to make its election between these several developments of the national faith; while these sects coëxisted, as has been already intimated, as so many religious denominations. But, although this was the case, the course of time clearly shows the progressive degeneracy of Greece, in religion as in other respects. Prior to the Christian era, the scheme of Epicurus had obtained very extensive, if not indeed a highly paramount, influence over the Grecian people.

It will now be necessary to give a brief review of this religion. We perceive in Greece a want of that rich amount of patriarchal tradition found to pervade older countries. There is also the absence of the profane monarchical assumption so prominent in the religion of the Asiatic nations. Looking at the history and political condition of Greece, nothing is more anomalous and strange than the existence of such numerous petty independent states as obtained in Greece among a people of the same blood, language, and religion. But, observing what occurred in almost every ancient kingdom, we see in this multiplicity of states perhaps the only means of saving that country from the curse of the pre-Christian Antichrist.

It will further be noticed, that the early ages of Greece exhibit, in connexion with her religion, a deep and general recognition of divine influence. It may be agreeable to many minds to repudiate the importance of this fact; but it must have been something more than political finesse which led the Athenians, in the depth of their distress,—with the ashes of their homes, and the charred walls of their temples, under their eyes,—to refuse the most flattering overtures of Persia, from pure devotion to their god. And it is remarkable, that it was under this aspect of the national religion, (notwithstanding all their idolatry and the absurdity of their notions in many other respects,) that Greece attained her preëminent intellectual superiority. It was in the age in which Anaxagoras was banished for denying that the heavenly bodies were deities, and asserting that they were inanimate bodies, that Grecian genius shed her mightiest energy on the world. It was in the time of Pericles that Socrates perished, a martyr to the doctrine of divine influence on the human mind. And as if to teach, in the most impressive manner, the utter inefficiency of the highest intellectual efforts to promote the elevation of man without a recognition of the existence of divine teaching, and an experience of its power, it was when Plato and Aristotle brought their unparalleled genius and intellectual power to bear on their country, that Greece began to descend from her high elevation.

It is a remarkable fact, that, however differing or antagonistic in other respects, the four great religious sects—the Academy, the Peripatetics, the Porch, and the Epicureans—might be, they displayed a regular gradation of departure from a recognition of divine influence, grace, responsibility to future judgment, and true moral principle, as arising out of divine command.

Another fact unfavourable to the candour and justice of Athenian administration is seen in the difference of treatment evinced toward real and pretended cases of impiety. Anaxagoras was banished, Socrates slain, and Plato swerved from his course of duty, through the determination of the ruling body to punish the slightest infraction of the national faith. But then this severity was only shown toward those who propounded views and doctrines of purer theology and sounder morality. Aristophanes might hold up to ridicule all that the national faith regarded as divine: and, when this was really done in an impious manner, and for the purposes of levity, folly, and vice, it obtained perfect toleration.

To those who talk of progressive intellect and advancing civilization, as synonymous with an increasing acquaintance with religious truth, the declarations of learned authors in the following language should be admonitory: "In the more enlightened periods, in the times even of Plato and his disciples, the clearest principles—we do not say, of moral purity, but—even of moral integrity were not better understood, and still less better observed, than in the days of Homer. Philosophy relaxed the hold of superstition upon the conscience, without substituting any efficacious restraint in its place; and 'it is evident,' to use the words of Mitford, 'from the writings of Xenophon and Plato, that in their age the boundaries of right and wrong, justice and injustice, honesty and dishonesty, were little determined by any generally received principle.' The philosophy of Epicurus had completely gained the ascendency in the age preceding the Christian era; and the greatest characters and most learned scholars wavered between the tenets of the theistical and atheistical systems. Corruption of manners, and the subtilties of scepticism, had reached a height of extravagance which it seemed scarcely possible to exceed. Human reason had lost itself in the labyrinths of philosophical speculation, and human virtue had been abandoned to the wayward direction of the fancy or the passions."—*Edinburgh Encyc.*, vol. x, p. 479.

We have in these evolutions of the religion of Greece the solution of a difficulty otherwise inexplicable,—namely, the prevalence of unbounded licentiousness of manners in the midst of the greatest triumphs of wisdom, genius, and art. Who can read of the courtezans of Athens and Corinth without amazement? Who can hear of the visits of Pericles, and even of Socrates, to the dissolute Aspasia, without feeling all his notions of propriety and congruity outraged?

But the depths of this iniquity cannot be written. The religion of Greece could not and did not sustain the moral dignity of female virtue. It was cloistered and crushed by cold austerity and cruel neglect; while unbridled licentiousness reigned, and the most abandoned of women rolled in wealth, and rioted in the acme of honour. It will be sufficient to add, that before, as it is said, dissoluteness of manners was introduced into Athens, the great Themistocles was drawn in a chariot across the Ceramicus, in the sight of a multitude of persons there assembled, *by four naked courtezans.* (Plutarch, in Vitâ Themistoclis.) So nearly did the manners of Ashantee find a parallel in the wisest city of the world! So ineffectual is enlightened intellect to sustain moral virtue, in the absence of religious truth!

CHAPTER XI.

THE HISTORY OF ROME.

IMPORTANCE of Roman History—Unusual Extent of its Legendary Portion—Arrival of Æneas on the Banks of the Tiber—Lavinium—Alba—Romulus and Remus—Rome—Death of Remus—Rape of the Sabine Virgins—Sabine War—Political Constitution of the first Romans—Numa—Tullus Hostilius—Albans removed to Rome—Ancus Martius—The Reigns of the Tarquins and of Servius Tullius—Tragic Fate of Lucretia—Abolition of Royalty—Junius Brutus—War with Porsenna—Destruction of Veii—Invasion of the Gauls—Distress of the Romans—Oppressive Character of the Laws respecting the Poor—Legislative Reform—Renewed aggressive War—All Italy subdued by the Romans—War with Carthage—The First Punic War—Sicily added to Rome as a Province—Further Extension of Territory on the Continent procured by the Romans—Sardinia seized—Hannibal—His deadly Enmity to Rome—His Measures in Spain—The Second Punic War—Hannibal invades Italy—His wonderful Success—Repeated Defeat of the Roman Armies—Scipio leads a Roman Army into Africa—Obtains successive Victories—Hannibal recalled to Carthage, and defeated—Peace between Rome and Carthage, on Terms dictated by Rome—War with Macedon, in which Rome is triumphant, Philip reduced to Submission, and Liberty proclaimed to Greece—Antiochus of Syria makes War on Rome—Is entirely defeated—War between Rome and Perseus, King of Macedon—He is completely subdued—Rapid Increase and vast Extent of the Roman Dominions—The Third Punic War—Destruction of Carthage—Continued Progress of Roman Power—Results of these successive and immense military Operations on the Parent State—Isolation of the Ruling Class from the People—Great Distress of the latter—Tiberius Gracchus endeavours to effect legislative Reforms for correcting these Evils—Is circumvented, and murdered—Caius Gracchus succeeds his Brother in his Efforts to redress the Grievances of the People—Carries several Measures—Loses his election on being proposed a third Time for the Tribuneship—Determines on armed Resistance—Is defeated, and slain—Progress of Patrician Power, and the Demoralization of Roman Governments—Jugurthine War—Marius Consul—Termination of the War, and Captivity and cruel Death of Jugurtha—War with the Cimbri—The Romans sustain several Defeats, but the Enemy is ultimately routed and destroyed by Marius—Civil Wars in Sicily and Italy—Italians incorporated as Roman Citizens—Factious Rivalry between Marius and Sylla—The former in a Tumult expels his rival, and makes himself Master of Rome—Sylla at the Head of an Army marches to Rome, and takes Possession of the City—He removes his Enemies from Power, and proceeds to conduct the War against Mithridates—The King of Pontus completely defeated—Rome subjected to fearful Carnage and Disorder by Marius and Cinna—Sylla grants Mithridates Terms of Peace, and, uniting the Army of Fimbria to his own, returns to Rome—Sylla defeats the Troops of the Consuls, and makes himself absolute Master of Rome—Fearful Extent of his Proscriptions, and consequent Slaughter of Soldiers and Citizens—His Death—Pompey defeats a Marian Faction in Spain—Destroys the Cilician Pirates—Defeats Mithridates, and annexes his Dominions to Rome—Conspiracy of Catiline at Rome—Defeated by Cicero—The First Triumvirate—Pompey, Crassus, and Julius Cæsar—Crassus slain in the Parthian War—Cæsar, commanded by the Senate to disband his Army, marches on Rome—Pompey retires to Greece—Is followed by Cæsar, and defeated—Flies to Egypt, and is slain there—Julius Cæsar sole Ruler of the Roman Dominions—Cæsar slain by Conspirators—Strange Irresolution and want of Unity evinced by the Conspirators after the Death of Cæsar—The selfish Policy, Peculation, and Ambition of Antony—Prudent Conduct of the young Octavius—He is elected Consul—Flight of Brutus and Cassius—The Second Triumvirate—Antony, Lepidus, and Octavius—Defeat and Death of Brutus and Cassius—Autony's disgraceful Residence in Egypt—Lepidus banished—Defeat of Antony at Actium—He commits suicide in Egypt—Octavius, as Augustus, supreme Ruler at Rome.

We now approach the culminating point of ancient history.

Rome was the last and the most extraordinary empire of pre-Christian times. Commanding a larger geographical territory,—wielding a greater amount of martial power,—possessing a more complete political organization,—and rising with buoyancy and triumph over more terrible calamities, than those of any preceding central government,—this empire stands before the mind as the most glorious embodiment of political aggrandizement and prowess which the annals of the ancient world ever recorded.

In one other respect Rome exhibits a unique appearance. Rich as are the records of Greece in the incorporation of ancient legends into its primitive history, the Latin annals very far excel them,—not only in the extent of their range, their copiousness, and their minuteness of detail,—but also in respect of their close approximation to the period when the Roman power obtained a complete ascendency over every other nation.

What may be properly termed "the legendary portion" of this history, stretches over five centuries, from the age immediately succeeding the Trojan war, about eleven hundred years before the Christian era, down to 500 B. C. Yet it is necessary, in order to obtain an acquaintance with the history of Rome, to acquire an accurate knowledge of the accounts furnished by the Roman historians of this period. Indeed, this is no less imperative than if these records stood before us attested by the most ample historical evidence. The progressive light which, dawning on the foundation of the eternal city, continued to increase until, at the period mentioned above, the national history is fully authenticated, is always sufficient to indicate the occurrence of great and important events, that in some manner were identified with the national existence; although it is insufficient to define with precision all their causes and circumstances, or to afford valid attestation to the accuracy of their respective details. Yet, as the fabulous and doubtful are so interwoven with national manners and indubitable facts, there is no point at which we can begin our inquiries but at the very *incunabula regni*,—ranging our research over the whole period; distinguishing, as far as possible, the fact from the fable, the certain from the doubtful; and thus obtaining the best possible view of this important, but very obscure, portion of history.

It may, to a cursory reader, appear very strange that the story of so large a portion of time, embracing events of the most thrilling interest, with which from our childhood we have been familiarized as undoubted verities, should be set down as being, to a great extent, doubtful and uncertain. Yet a careful and dispassionate investigation of the claims to credibility possessed by the earliest historians of ancient Rome, (see *Appendix*, note 72,) inevitably conducts us to this judgment, and compels us to doubt the truth of their annals for the first six hundred years after the foundation of the city, and their narrative respecting many important events even subsequent to that period.

The earliest information we can obtain respecting ancient Italy tells us that it was inhabited by several distinct races or tribes, which occupied different districts, and were frequently found engaged in warlike contests with each other. Among these, the Pelasgians, Latins, and Tuscans held a prominent rank; but they have little to do with the accounts given of the origin and rise of Rome. The foundation of that city is ascribed to Æneas and a band of Trojans, who, having escaped from Troy, are supposed, after much voyaging and many disasters, to have reached the banks of the Tiber. (See *Appendix*, note 73.) Here the legends state that under supernatural guidance they built a city, called Lavinium; and that their rising power provoked an attack from the Rutulians and Etruscans, under Turnus and Mezentius. The former of these chiefs fell by the hand of Æneas; the latter, by that of the son of the Trojan chief, Ascanius, whose descendants became sovereigns of Latium.

Our authorities proceed to state that, thirty years after the Trojans had obtained peaceful possession of the country around Lavinium, they deserted their city for the more elevated and secure position of Alba, which henceforth became the centre, where the thirty confederate cities of Latium offered their united sacrifices to the gods. (See *Appendix*, note 74.)

The foundation of Rome—which, amid all the clouds of fiction and fable, we must regard in itself as a fact—next presents itself to our notice: but beyond the mere fact itself we can obtain little information that can be relied on. At some undefined time after the removal to Alba, Procas, the king of the city, died, leaving two sons, and bequeathing the kingdom to Numitor, the elder, and his treasure to Amulius. The latter, possessing more enterprise and energy than his elder brother, and having the means of employing a numerous band of adherents, deposed Numitor, slew his son, and made his daughter Ilia or Rhea Sylvia a vestal virgin. Having thus, as he believed, prevented his brother from having issue to succeed him, Amulius ascended the throne.

This purpose was, however, defeated. Sylvia became pregnant by the god Mars; and was, in consequence of her sacred character, put to death. Her twin sons were also exposed as if to certain destruction, but were miraculously preserved, and finally slew the usurper, and restored their grandfather to the throne. (See *Appendix*, note 75.)

Having been made acquainted with their previous imminent danger and wonderful deliverance, the two brothers applied to the king their grandfather for leave to build a city on the spot, near the Tiber, where they had been saved. Their request was granted. But disputes arose between the two brothers, which issued in the death of Remus by the hand of Romulus or of one of his partisans. This event is placed by the best chronologers on the 21st of April in the third year of the sixth Olympiad; four hundred and thirty-one years after the destruction of Troy, and seven hundred and fifty-three before the Christian era.

Finding it difficult to obtain inhabitants for his city, Romulus offered an asylum and protection to all persons whose misfortunes or crimes induced them to leave their native residence: and, having by this means collected a sufficient number of individuals, he became the king of the new state. But, according to the poetic traditions which are here our only guides, it was easier to procure restless and hardy men for this new city than to induce women to accompany them. To supply this evident necessity, he resorted to a desperate expedient. Romulus appointed splendid games in honour of Neptune: crowds of the inhabitants of the surrounding cities assembled as spectators. In the midst of the sport, a host of young Romans rushed on the multitude, and carried off a sufficient number of maidens, whom they afterward compelled by force to become their wives.

This outrage led to a desperate war. Some of the minor cities in the immediate vicinity having been successively defeated in their efforts to punish the authors of this violence, Titus Tatius, King of the Sabines, led his forces against Rome. Romulus, unable to meet this formidable foe in the field, retired within the walls of the city, leaving a strong force to guard an important post on the Capitoline Hill. Tarpeia, the daughter of the commander of this position, fascinated with the bracelets worn by the Sabine soldiers, offered to admit them if they would give her what they wore on their arms. This condition was accepted, and she opened the gate of the fortress: but the Sabines, either misapprehending her meaning, or determined to defeat her object, are said to have thrown their shields on her as they passed, until she fell, crushed to death beneath their weight.

(See *Appendix*, note 76.) This treason brought on a general engagement, which continued for a long time, victory appearing to alternate from one army to the other. This conflict was at length terminated by the interposition of the Sabine women. They had by this time become reconciled to their husbands, and felt equally unwilling that either these or their fathers and brothers should be destroyed. They therefore rushed to the scene of conflict, and implored the combatants to cease. This led to a treaty, by which the two nations agreed to live in amity under their own chiefs in the same locality. This purpose was carried out by the building of a new city on the Quirinal and Capitoline Hills, to which the Sabines removed; while a *comitium*, or "place of common assembly" for both nations, was erected in the space between the Palatine and Capitoline Hills. This state of affairs continued until the murder of Tatius the Sabine king, some time afterward at Lavinium, left Romulus sole monarch of the united nations.

The wars between the Romans and the Tuscans, with which the Latin historians have crowded more than thirty years of the life of Romulus, are equally romantic, and do not merit recital. If, indeed, any real historical information has reached us respecting this period, it seems to refer to the political constitution and form of government which were adopted and maintained even during the reign of the founder of Rome. It appears that, from the beginning, there was a classification of the inhabitants. The wealthiest and nobly born were styled "Patricians;" those of inferior rank, "Plebeians." The dignity of the Patricians was hereditary, and they alone were eligible to all offices in the state. From these a senate of one hundred was taken, to aid the king by their counsel, who were called *Patres*, "Fathers." In order to unite the two separate classes of Patricians and Plebeians together, every Plebeian was allowed to choose a Patrician as his "patron," to whom he became a "client." The effect of this relation was, to afford the client protection and friendly aid; the patron being his counsellor and advocate in all suits of law, and his adviser and assistant on all occasions; while, on the other hand, the clients held themselves bound to respect and defer to their patrons, and to show them every attention. It also seems that the power of the crown was considerably limited by the agency of the senate: so that, from the beginning, Rome exhibited a combination of monarchical and aristocratical government.

The fate of Romulus is as uncertain as every other portion of the history of this period. One heroic legend states, that after a long reign he disappeared from earth, and became a god, under the name of the deity Quirinus. Another tradition ascribes his death to a tumult in the senate-house, where he is said to have been destroyed by an aristocratic faction.

The latter of these rumours derives support from the fact that, on the death of the king, the senate endeavoured to retain in its own hands the entire administration of affairs. Each senator was to exercise supreme power one day in rotation. It is said that this form of government lasted one year, when its defects became so manifest that the people insisted that the senate should elect a king. But when this was resolved upon, a difficulty arose as to the nation from which he should be taken,—the Romans or the Sabines. It was at length decided that the new sovereign should be selected from the Sabines by the Roman senators. By this arrangement Numa Pompilius, the son-in-law of Tatius, the last king of the Sabines, was unanimously raised to the throne. As the history of this reign is entirely legendary, it will not be necessary to say more respecting it, than that this sovereign is reputed to have evinced great wisdom and prudence in his government. It is said that he framed the entire ritual law of the national religion, greatly improved the internal policy and jurisprudence of the country, and maintained, throughout a reign of forty years, peace and tranquillity between his country and the surrounding states.

After the death of Numa, another interregnum followed, after which Tullus Hostilius, the son of one of the most distinguished soldiers of Romulus, was raised to the throne. Although the chronology of this period remains exceedingly obscure, we now approach the dawning of historical light. Niebuhr speaks of this reign as the beginning of a "mythico-historical" age. In the early part of it we hear of a war between Rome and Alba, occasioned by mutual acts of violence and consequent recrimination.

The historians state that, war being declared, the rival forces met on the frontier of the Roman territory; but that, instead of deciding the quarrel by a general engagement, it was agreed to stake the supremacy of the two nations on the issue of a combat between six heroes, three to be furnished by each army. As a striking evidence of the poetry which pervades the national annals of this period, it may be sufficient to state, that it is alleged that there were then in the Roman army three brothers, born of the same mother at the same birth, named the Horatii; and in the Alban army, three other brothers, born in a similarly extraordinary way, called the Curiatii; and, to complete the catalogue of wonders, the Roman mother and the Alban one are said to have been sisters. These six men advanced in front of their respective armies: and, it having been solemnly agreed that the nation whose heroes were defeated should in future be subject to the other, the combat began. After a while one of the Horatii fell dead; and soon after another sunk lifeless on the body of his brother. The Albans on this raised loud shouts of joy, fully expecting the victory. It was, however, soon apparent that the three Curiatii were severely wounded, but that the surviving Horatius was unhurt. The latter aware of the disadvantage of contending singly against three, turned his back and fled, until, perceiving his pursuers separated from each other, he returned, slew the foremost, and afterward the other two, in succession. In consequence of this triumph, Alba became subject to Rome.

It seems, however, that the Alban chief was far from being reconciled to this result; and accordingly, when the Romans were engaged in a war with the Fidenates, and the Alban forces were summoned as auxiliaries of Rome, the Alban dictator drew off his army just as the battle commenced, and took no part in the conflict. The Roman sovereign at first concealed his indignation at this breach of faith; but, taking advantage of the timidity which the Albans afterward evinced, he put the dictator to death, dismantled the city, with the exception of the temples, and removed the whole of the inhabitants with their property to Rome, where he provided them with habitations on the Cælian Hill. The abandonment of Alba, and the removal of its inhabitants to Rome, may be regarded as well-established historical facts. But whether this was effected solely by the power of Rome, or by the troops of that city in conjunction with the Latins, as suggested by Niebuhr, is a matter of uncertainty. The fact, that while Rome removed the inhabitants, the Latins occupied the territory of Alba, seems to corroborate to a great extent the conclusion of the German historian.

The wars which Tullus is said to have waged with the Latins, and the peculiar manner of his death by lightning from the anger of the gods, are altogether full of improbabilities, as well as destitute of historical authority.

Ancus Martius, alleged to have been the grandson of Numa, is placed on the list, as the next king of Rome. Like his ancestor, he is most celebrated for his legislative improvements and ecclesiastical reforms; in respect of which, he displayed great wisdom and spirit. He could not, however, like his progenitor, by maintaining continual peace, devote his entire energies to the internal regulation of his kingdom. A war with the Latins called off the attention of Ancus from peaceful pursuits. In this he appears to have been successful; and pursued, in respect of those whom he subdued, the same policy which had been exercised toward Alba. He destroyed their towns, and removed the inhabitants to Rome, where he prepared dwellings for them on the Aventine Hill. He also obtained some successes in war over Veii, and built Ostia at the mouth of the Tiber,—the first seaport town possessed by Rome. He also threw the first bridge across the river. These conquered Latins have been supposed by some authors to have constituted the original Plebeians of ancient Rome. The death of this king is said to have been occasioned by violence.

The following reigns belong to a most interesting and important, but, at the same time, exceedingly obscure, period of Roman history. The first of these, that of Tarquinius Priscus, deserves especial notice. He was a descendant of Damaratus, who fled from Corinth when Cypselus, having obtained power, was wreaking his vengeance on the citizens, whom he had proscribed. Carrying his great wealth with him, Damaratus settled at Tarquinii; where he took an Etruscan wife, and brought up his children in the manner of the country, adding to their education all the elegance and refinement of Greece. The poetic authority, which is here our only guide, proceeds to state, that Lucumo, the younger son of this Greek, having, by the death of his elder brother, become sole heir to his father's wealth, was induced by his wife, who had studied augury, to remove to Rome, where he was admitted to the rights of citizenship, and adopted the name of Lucius Tarquinius, to which Livy adds *Priscus*. The state in which he lived, and the amiable character which he evinced, procured for him, at the same time, the friendship of the king, and extreme popularity with the people: so much so, that the king, prior to his death, appointed Tarquinius guardian of his children; and the people, when that event occurred, with common consent raised him to the throne. (See *Appendix*, note 77.)

The reign of this sovereign is given in great detail by Dionysius, and is narrated at considerable length by Livy: but their accounts are so confused and contradictory, that no reliance can be placed on their accuracy. It seems, on the whole, probable, that the object of the martial conflicts of this long reign, which is stated to have extended to thirty-eight years, was to place the Etruscans, Latins, and Sabines in subjection to Rome; and also that the first Tarquin greatly improved Rome, by public buildings, and works of much utility and importance.

Tarquin was assassinated by the emissaries of the sons of Ancus Martius, in the hope of preventing him from bequeathing the kingdom to his son-in-law, Servius Tullius, who was a great favourite of the Roman people. This wicked attempt entirely failed. Servius concealed the death of the king, until he had taken effective measures for insuring his own accession to the throne. He then declared the murder of his father-in-law, and called an assembly of the people to elect a new king, when he was unanimously chosen to succeed to the vacant office.

Notwithstanding the extravagant fables and romantic legends, which profess to detail the wonderful birth and divine paternity of this monarch, we have sufficient evidence that his talents and energy were such, that he may be said to have laid the foundations for the future power and prosperity of Rome. He is reported to have conducted several successful wars; but his fame mainly rests on his political institutions. He formed a federal union between the Latin cities, placing Rome at the head of the united body; and he consolidated and confirmed the union, by instituting common sacrifices for the whole body on Mount Aventine. He also instituted a *census*, or record of the citizens, and of the property possessed by them; and distributed the right of suffrage to centuries, according to the property possessed by the six classes into which the people were divided. All his legislation appears to have been designed and adapted to limit the prerogatives of the Patricians, or aristocratic class, and to extend general freedom under wise and prudent regulations. This generous policy, however, cost him his life. Tullia, the daughter of the king, had been married to Lucius Tarquinius, the son of the preceding sovereign. The Patricians, impatient of the restraint which the wise measures of Servius had imposed on their tyranny and injustice, entered into a conspiracy with Lucius against the aged sovereign,—the unnatural Tullia being also a party to the plot against her father. By this means, Servius Tullius was murdered in the senate-house; and his son-in-law, surnamed Tarquin the Proud, ascended the throne in his stead, by the force and favour of the patrician body alone, the concurrence of the people not being sought.

The romantic poetry so generally imbuing the best accounts which we have of these reigns, abounds here to an unusual extent, and spreads doubt and uncertainty over every fact which is reported. It will, therefore, be sufficient to say, that it is generally believed Tarquin confirmed the supremacy of Rome over the Latins, and extended the Roman influence and territory. But this success was able to afford very transient prosperity to his house. While he was engaged with a Roman army in besieging Ardea, his son Sextus violated Lucretia, a noble Roman lady. Finding resistance unavailing, she submitted to the outrage; but as soon as an opportunity offered, she summoned her relatives, told them her tale of woe, and immediately stabbed herself. Lucius Junius Brutus,—who had, up to this period, concealed the workings of a mighty and daring spirit under the appearance of eccentricity, bordering on madness,—roused beyond all measure by this atrocity and its tragic consequences, immediately convoked an assembly of the people, and, exposing the bleeding body of Lucretia to the multitude, obtained a decree for expelling the whole family of the Tarquins, and abolishing royalty in Rome.

This revolution may be regarded as a purely patrician movement. It made scarcely any change in the condition of the great mass of the people, but placed the executive government in the hands of the aristocracy, who now possessed, in addition to all their legitimate influence, the superadded powers of royalty. In order to make this acquisition secure to the order, the administration of affairs was intrusted to two supreme magistrates, who were at first called "prætors," but afterward "consuls." The first persons selected to fill this important office were, Junius Brutus, and Collatinus, the husband of Lucretia.

The deposed king and his family did not relinquish their elevated station without a determined struggle. The Tarquins took refuge in Etruria, and induced that state to send ambassadors to Rome, to plead on their behalf. These persons, although entirely failing in their object by the usual public and avowed efforts employed on such occasions, had well-nigh accomplished their design by indirect means. In consequence of their having access to the junior branches of many patrician families, a conspiracy was organized, which, but for a singular accident, might have issued in the restoration of the expelled sovereign. A slave, having overheard the deliberations of the conspirators, gave information to the consuls. Brutus immediately proceeded to convict and punish the traitors; and, finding his own sons implicated in the crime, he instantly sacrificed parental affection to public duty, and ordered their immediate execution. As a result of this discovery, recourse was had to the most stringent measures against the Tarquins. The property of the whole family was confiscated, and every individual condemned to perpetual banishment. Even Collatinus, the consul, being related to the family, and having evinced some vacillation with respect to the conspirators, was included among the proscribed. Publius Valerius was elected successor to Collatinus; and soon afterward, the Etruscans having in support of Tarquin made war on Rome, Junius Brutus, and Ancus, the eldest son of the late king, assailed each other with so much fury, that both fell dead on the field of battle. The victory, however, was won by the Romans, and served to secure the safety of the infant republic.

Valerius soon became one of the most popular rulers of Rome;

and, as such, was distinguished by the surname of *Poplicola*, "the Friend of the People." The first year after the banishment of the Tarquins was rendered remarkable by two important events,—one relating to foreign, and the other to domestic, policy. In this year the first treaty was made between Rome and Carthage, having respect to navigation and commerce. This treaty remained to the time of Polybius, engraved on the base of a column, in the old Roman language. The other measure was the *lex de provocatione*, or "law of appeal." The Patricians had, up to this time, always enjoyed the right of appeal from the judgment of the supreme magistrate to the general assembly of their own order: and it was by this law declared, that Plebeians ought to have a similar privilege.

Even in this obscure period, when Rome prospered, her annals seem tolerably authentic; but, on the contrary, when she suffered serious reverses, we are enveloped in all the darkness of the most improbable legendary tales. We now enter upon the annals of one of these seasons. Driven for refuge and support from one state to another, the Tarquin family wandered up and down, until at length they secured the aid of Porsenna, the most powerful of the Tuscan princes. It is vain to attempt a narration of the war which ensued, as we have but the most scanty elements of authentic information respecting it; yet it may be safely inferred, that although the Tuscan warrior failed to restore his client to the Roman throne, he had such manifest advantage in the war as to reduce the Romans to a tributary condition, and to take hostages from them for the performance of their engagements under the treaty.

A series of wars with surrounding states followed, which had various results, and were accompanied by incessant struggles between the Patricians and the Plebeians; the aristocracy invariably oppressing the people, when relieved from external aggression; and being compelled to make great concessions in answer to their demands, in seasons of public difficulty and peril. This succession of conflicts led to the banishment, and ultimately to the death, of Coriolanus. The retirement of the plebeian soldiers, in time of great danger, and the consequent appointment of tribunes,—the fatal defeat of the Fabii,—all these events are fully narrated; but they come to us more in the character of legendary tales than of authentic history, and therefore require only this passing allusion.

The siege and destruction of Veii require more distinct mention. This was the largest and richest city of Etruria, and had frequently been a formidable enemy to Rome. The sovereign of this city having put to death some Roman ambassadors, and refused to make any satisfaction for the outrage, the Romans determined on the entire destruction of his capital. After the siege had continued several years, Camillus was appointed dictator; (see *Appendix*, note 78;) and he succeeded in obtaining possession of the place. Its riches were transferred to the victorious soldiery, its citizens were enslaved, its idols were sent to Rome, and the city itself was destroyed. Notwithstanding the lustre of this success, Camillus, on the charge of having embezzled a part of the spoil, was sentenced to exile. (See *Appendix*, note 79.)

This successful warrior had but just left the city in disgrace, when the Romans became involved in the most terrible conflict which they had ever seen. An immense host of Gauls, under their king, Brennus, are said to have crossed the Alps, and, after spoiling the country, to have laid siege to Clusium, a city of Etruria. That people immediately apprized the Romans of the invasion; who, being much concerned at the event, sent three noble citizens to ascertain the nature and extent of this incursion. These persons joined the besieged in a desperate sally, and greatly distinguished themselves in the conflict. Brennus, on being made aware of the circumstance, immediately sent to Rome to demand satisfaction for this irregular aggression on the part of her citizens; and, not receiving satisfactory redress, he at once raised the siege of Clusium, and marched toward Rome. The imperial city was in no condition to oppose such a host. An army, hastily gathered and inefficiently provided, proceeded to meet the enemy, about ten miles from Rome; but it was totally defeated. The victorious Gauls now approached the capital of the republic with irresistible power. The Romans in this emergency did all that was possible. They selected the most able body of men that could be collected; and, providing them with as large a store of provisions as could be got together, they shut them up in the Capitol. The rest of the inhabitants, with all the wealth that they could carry, abandoned the city, and sought refuge in the neighbouring towns. It is stated that about eighty of the principal pontiffs and Patricians remained in passive dignity in the senate-house.

On the arrival of the Gauls, no defence was made: they marched into the deserted city, slew the senators who had remained, ravaged the public and private edifices, and invested the Capitol. After making vain attempts to reduce this stronghold, Brennus—finding that his army was rapidly becoming disorganized through irregular living, and the effect of the climate, to which they were unaccustomed—agreed to evacuate the city on receiving a great ransom. The Roman historians state, that before this sum was actually paid,

Camillus returned at the head of an army, defeated the Gauls, and compelled them to retire. But the account of Polybius is much more probable; namely, that, while engaged in this war with Rome, the Gauls heard that the Veneti had invaded their country; whereupon they concluded a treaty with the Romans, and proceeded to protect their own land. (See *Appendix*, note 80.)

After the departure of the Gauls, the condition of the Romans was truly desperate. A city, mean at first, and now destroyed by rapine and fire,—walls which had been rudely constructed, and now partly demolished,—all the movable property that violence could seize, having been carried off; and all that barbarian cruelty could destroy, having been consumed,—these fragments of ruin remained to this people as their only portion. It need not, therefore, be matter of surprise, that there was a great indisposition among the people to undertake the restoration of the city. Many urged that the city of Veii, which had been abandoned, could be more easily restored to a habitable condition; and it seems that it was only by an accident, or a mean preconcerted manœuvre, that the purpose of removal was checked, and the restoration of the city begun.

The great talents and energy of Camillus soon restored Rome to a respectable position with relation to the surrounding states, many of which had altogether thrown off all recognition of her supremacy, in consequence of the Gallic invasion. But no sooner was the city repaired, and the military power of the state in a tolerable degree reorganized, than the old dissensions between the Plebeians and Patricians became as rife as before, in consequence of the almost unlimited power which the existing laws gave the rich over the poor. (See *Appendix*, note 81.) These political and social evils were now absolutely unendurable; and the only question which seemed to arise respecting them was,—whether they would issue in the entire demoralization of the community, or lead to furious and bloody collision.

A careful review of the history of this period induces the conviction that scarcely any agency which ministered to Roman greatness, throughout the entire period of her advancement, contributed more essentially to rear the colossal fabric which afterward ruled over the world, than that of those energetic and discreet men who at this period introduced the most important legislative reforms. These were Caius Licinius Stolo, and Lucius Sextius Lateranus, aided by an influential Patrician, Marcus Fabius Ambustus, the father-in-law of Licinius. These men propounded a series of laws adapted to the exigencies of the times. The first enabled Plebeians to be elected to the consular dignity. The second prohibited any person from holding more than five hundred acres of public land for tillage and plantations, and from having more than a hundred large, or five hundred small, cattle feeding on the common pasture. This law also specified the rents of the public as not to exceed a tenth of the corn produced, and a fifth of the produce of fruit-trees. The third law enacted that, in all cases of outstanding debts, the interest which had been paid should be deducted from the principal, and the balance paid by equal annual instalments during three years.

The opposition offered by the Patricians to these laws was very general and intense, and was carried through the long period of five years. Yet, during this whole time, the advocates of reform never allowed themselves to sink into supineness or despair on the one hand, or to rush into sedition and violence on the other; but, steadily keeping to their object, and directing their energies within the limits of the constitution, they ultimately succeeded in their wise and benevolent design. The only alteration effected in the project was, that the consuls should not act as civil judges in future; but that magistrates, under the name of "prætors," should be appointed to perform this duty.

Relieved from intestine discord, the Roman people put forth their power in martial aggression on the neighbouring states. In a series of wars, during which they sustained some very severe reverses, they proceeded to subdue in succession the Samnites, Umbrians, Etrurians, Sabines, and Tarentines. The latter state was powerfully supported by Pyrrhus, King of Macedon, who vainly hoped to rival the great Alexander; but he was completely defeated by the Romans under Dentatus, their consul. Rome by these efforts became the mistress of all Italy, from the northern frontiers of Etruria to the Straits of Sicily, and from the Tuscan Sea to the Adriatic.

At this period we have to mark the progress of Rome in a contest with a rival republic of first-rate power and immense resources. Carthage, originally a Tyrian colony, had acquired extensive dominions in Africa, conquered a considerable portion of Spain, occupied Sardinia, Corsica, and all the islands on the coast of Italy, and, in addition to all these, had subdued a great part of Sicily. With possessions so numerous, this mighty republic was unequalled throughout the world for her commercial enterprise, and was in consequence mistress of the sea. With such a power it would seem impossible for the Italian state successfully to contend. But in one essential particular the advantage was wholly in favour of Rome. The Carthaginians were not soldiers; they depended on mercenaries for military strength; while the Italian republicans were a daring, hardy, and martial race.

These two republics had been united by successive treaties of amity from an early period of Roman history. Their first collision arose professedly out of a dispute respecting the city of Messana in Sicily, but really for the political ascendency in that important island. The Carthaginians having obtained possession of the citadel of Messana, a large section of the people solicited aid from Rome; and the Romans, although reluctant to engage in such a quarrel, yet, rather than see their rivals in possession of the whole of Sicily, embarked an army for that island. Here their arms were as successful as on the Italian peninsula. They defeated the Carthaginians in several battles; and, although meeting with some reverses, they soon secured the alliance of Hiero, King of Syracuse, and laid siege to the important city of Agrigentum. Carthage sent a large army to the relief of this place, but in vain; for, after a severe conflict, they were compelled to retreat, and the garrison abandoned the city, which fell into the hands of the Romans. This was the largest and most important place which had been taken by Rome. An immense amount of spoil was secured, and more than twenty-five thousand of the inhabitants were sold into slavery.

The capture of this city filled the Carthaginians with rage, and inspired the Romans with new motives for exertion. Conscious that they could not carry out this war with any hope of ultimate success, while their enemies remained masters of the sea, the Romans turned their attention to the immediate construction of a fleet. Nothing more strikingly displays the characteristic energy and tact of this people, than their success in this enterprise. Although they were, up to this time, so ignorant of the art of ship-building, and of maritime affairs in general, that they could not construct a vessel, until they had secured the hull of a Carthaginian galley which had been stranded on the coast; (Niebuhr's History of Rome, vol. iii, p. 575;) yet they proceeded to work on this model with such diligence and ability, that in a short time they sent to sea a fleet with which they ventured to encounter that of the Carthaginians. In this engagement, the Romans succeeded (mainly by means of a newly-invented mode of boarding enemies' ships) in capturing fifty Carthaginian vessels. After this victory the Romans prosecuted with advantage the war against the Carthaginian possessions in Sicily, although, from the resolution, resources, and naval experience of their enemies, they made but small progress, even during eight years of conflict, toward the reduction of the island.

In those circumstances the daring spirit of Rome could brook no further delay; and it was therefore determined to carry the war into Africa. For this purpose a fleet and an army were prepared, and embarked for the African coast. The Roman fleet consisted of three hundred and thirty vessels, manned with more than one hundred thousand fighting men,—a portion of them being specially selected, as the flower of the Roman army. The Carthaginian fleet, sent out to oppose this armament, carried not less than one hundred and fifty thousand men. The opposing forces met in the narrow straits between Sicily and Africa, where a long-continued and desperate battle was fought. This was probably the greatest naval conflict which had, up to this period, taken place in the world. For many hours the success alternated in nearly an equal degree; but at length victory declared for the Romans, who, although they had twenty-four of their galleys sunk, inflicted a much more severe loss on their enemies, destroying thirty of the Carthaginian vessels, and capturing sixty-three. Utterly unable to continue the conflict, after sustaining such a loss, the Carthaginian fleet fled, and left their foes in possession of their prizes.

Rather incited to fresh efforts than satisfied with this success, the Romans returned to their harbour in Sicily, repaired and equipped their fleet with all possible expedition, and, embarking a further body of troops on board the vessels which they had taken, sailed for Africa. Having effected a landing, and taken the city of Clupea, near Carthage, on its eastern side, the Roman commander sent home for further instructions. The senate recalled the consul Manlius, who was ordered to return to Rome with the fleet; and commanded the other, Regulus, with the army to conduct the war in Africa. This was done. Manlius took with him twenty-seven thousand prisoners to Rome; and Regulus carried on the war with such spirit, that he soon shut up the Carthaginians in their capital, and drove them to sue for peace in very humble terms. If the Roman commander had not prevented it by the most extravagant demands, a peace highly honourable and beneficial to Rome, and disastrous to Carthage, might then have been concluded. But the conditions of Regulus were equivalent to the utter ruin of the Punic state, and were therefore resisted. Meanwhile, it happened that Xanthippus the Spartan arrived at Carthage; and, observing the conduct of the opposing parties, he declared that the humiliation of Carthage and the success of Rome were not owing to the relative strength of the two armies, but to the conduct of the generals. He enforced this opinion with so much reason, that the Carthaginian people insisted that he should be appointed to take the command of their army. The result justified the choice. The Spartan chief, having organized his troops, and arranged the several bodies suitably, marched out, offered battle to the Romans, and won a splendid victory. The Roman army was annihilated; the consul Regulus and five thousand troops were taken prisoners, and thirty thousand men were left dead on the field. Indeed, but two thousand escaped, who effected their retreat to Clupea.

After this victory both parties made preparations for carrying on the war on a larger scale than before. The first renewal of the contest was in a sea-fight off the coast of Sicily, in which the Romans obtained a complete victory, destroying above one hundred Carthaginian galleys, capturing thirty, and destroying fifteen thousand men. After this success the Roman fleet proceeded to Clupea, where they had no sooner landed their troops than the Carthaginian army appeared before the place. The two Hannos commanded, Xanthippus having returned to Greece: but notwithstanding the improved tactics introduced by the noble Greek, nothing could compensate his loss; the Romans were victorious, and their enemies were routed with the loss of nine thousand men.

With such alternate successes and reverses, the war was continued. Obliged, notwithstanding their victory, to retire from Africa by scarcity of provisions, the Roman commanders, returning with a large fleet, wished to signalize their voyage by some exploit, and for that purpose coasted Sicily, where they were almost annihilated by a storm. Out of three hundred and seventy ships, only eighty escaped shipwreck. To repair this disaster, another fleet was prepared, and some important successes were obtained in Sicily: but of this armament one hundred and sixty galleys were destroyed by another tempest; on which the Romans abandoned their purpose of being a first-rate naval power, and limited their fleet to fifty galleys. But this resolve was soon laid aside, further fleets were prepared, and the war was prosecuted with such success, that the Carthaginians took their captive Regulus from his dungeon, and sent him to Rome to negotiate a peace. But, when there, the noble Roman strongly advised the continuance of the war,—advice which the senate adopted; on which Regulus was sent back to his prison, where he soon after died.

On the renewal of the war, the Romans suffered some severe losses. Another fleet was destroyed by a storm, and Hamilcar Barca conducted the war in Sicily with great success. But all this was counterbalanced by a naval victory obtained by the consul Lutatius, over Hanno, which forever destroyed the supremacy of Carthage at sea, and placed Hamilcar in a position which compelled him to solicit a termination of the conflict. These circumstances led to the establishment of peace between the two nations, on terms highly favourable to Rome.

At the close of the first Punic war, the Romans enjoyed a short season of tranquillity. The temple of Janus was shut for the second time, and there was quiet at home and abroad. But it is sufficiently apparent that this war seriously injured the best interests of the Roman state; and Niebuhr sagely observes, that it "was one of the first causes of the degeneracy of the Roman people." But, independently of its moral effects on the citizens of the Italian capital, it led to serious results both at Rome and at Carthage. At the latter place, the rapacity and tyranny of Rome produced such an effect on the mind of the great Hamilcar, that he took his son to the altar of his god, and there taught the young Hannibal to swear eternal enmity to the Romans,—an exercise of parental influence which, in its operation, brought Rome to the verge of ruin. On the return of the Carthaginian mercenary soldiers from Sicily, the state was unable to pay all the arrears which were due to them; and the negotiations hereby occasioned led to a desperate war, in which Carthage stood opposed to other old Tyrian colonies in Africa, combined with the barbarous tribes of Libyans in the neighbourhood. The rulers of the Punic capital, however, after seeing their city brought to the brink of destruction, were able to cut off their enemies, and establish their supremacy. But this measure fearfully weakened the martial resources of the state.

The results of the war were no less remarkable on Rome. At its close Sicily was declared to be a Roman province. It was the first country, out of Italy, thus associated with the central government, and exhibited the origination and first action of that principle which led to the aggregation of numerous nations under one head, as the great Roman empire.

While Rome was recovering from the financial and general exhaustion occasioned by this war, and Carthage was struggling through her conflict with her revolted mercenaries, a similar rebellion took place in the Punic towns on the seacoast of Sardinia. Having extinguished the rebellion in Africa, a Carthaginian force was sent to put down the insurrection in Sardinia: but here Rome interposed, and not only protected the rebels, but compelled Carthage to abandon the island, and to pay one thousand two hundred talents, as the price of continued peace,—conduct which has been truly characterized as "one of the most detestable acts of injustice in the history of Rome."—*Niebuhr's History of Rome*, vol. iv, p. 56.

The Romans took advantage of this season of tranquillity to extend their power in Northern Italy, where they subdued the Ligurians and some Gallic tribes. They also determined to punish the notorious piracies of the Illyrians. A fleet and an army were soon equipped; and, as the result of this successful invasion, the greater part of Illyricum was ceded to Rome.

In the mean time, Hannibal, the son of Hamilcar Barca, had grown up to manhood, and entered on public life with all the spirit and energy of his father. Filled with hatred to Rome, and shut out from the Mediterranean islands by the terms of his father's treaty with that nation, he cast an anxious eye around, to discover a country from which he might obtain a martial force, and the necessary means for assailing the obnoxious rival of his fatherland. What he sought for, he found in Spain. The southern parts of this country, yielding all the products of Sicily and Sardinia, and being besides rich in silver mines, formed a very natural object of attraction to Carthaginian rulers, after the loss of those important islands.

Accordingly, when Hamilcar was driven from Sardinia, he proceeded to Spain, where he encouraged the prosecution of the silver mines, and made himself very agreeable to the natives. On the death of this great man, his son-in-law, Hasdrubal, took the command of the troops and country, and either entirely built, or finished the building of, Carthagena, (or New Carthage,) which is supposed by some to have been begun by Hamilcar. By these measures the Carthaginians acquired a political ascendency over a population numbering millions, from which they could recruit and extend their army, without being compelled to hire faithless mercenaries on exorbitant terms. Rome unquestionably viewed all these operations with dislike and suspicion; but the intermediate Gauls prevented her from attempting any coercive measures. After Hasdrubal had conducted the affairs of Carthage in Spain for nine years, he was assassinated, and Hannibal succeeded to the government.

This general was not long possessed of power before he determined to adopt measures of aggression against Rome. He accordingly marshalled his troops, and laid siege to Saguntum, a Greek city and colony on the Iberus; which, after a siege of eight months, he captured. Having thus acquired an immense booty he sent rich presents to Carthage, and proceeded to place his army in a state of preparation for an effort on a much grander scale. The Romans, displeased at the success of Hannibal, sent ambassadors to remonstrate against his conquest of Saguntum. The wily general immediately referred them to Carthage, where he well knew that his success had placed his influence in the ascendant. When they appeared before the Punic rulers, the Romans blamed Hannibal for his aggression on Saguntum. The Carthaginians insisted that he was justified in the course he had taken; and that it did not become Rome, while extending her conquests on every side, to complain of their acquisitions in Spain. Offended at this discourse, the Romans bade them choose peace or war; to which they responded, that they would choose neither, but take whichever was offered them. Hereupon the Romans said, "Then take war,"—an announcement which was received by the Carthaginians with acclamations.

An ample field was now opened for the daring energy, wonderful genius, and indomitable spirit of Hannibal. He immediately subdued the remainder of Spain, and crossed the Pyrenees, to march on Italy. Scipio, who was then consul, was sent with an army into Spain, to find employment for Hannibal in that country. But when he arrived as far as Marseilles, he found that his enemy had already reached the banks of the Rhone. He accordingly disembarked his troops, and proceeded to dispute the passage of the river: but Hannibal was too quick in his motions to be arrested by this force. Before Scipio arrived Hannibal had passed the river, and, disregarding every other object, crossed the Alps, and descended on the plains of Italy. Here he immediately captured Turin, and was soon informed that Scipio had arrived to oppose him, and was encamped on the banks of the Po. It is beyond a doubt, that the Carthaginian general suffered a severe loss of troops, horses, and elephants, in crossing the mountains; but it is equally certain that the Alpine Gauls, who bore a deadly hatred to Rome, flocked to his standard, and greatly recruited his army. The Roman forces, being greatly augmented by the arrival of the consul Sempronius and his troops, were prepared for active operations. By various irritating measures, Hannibal provoked his enemies to pass the river, and attack him; when a desperate battle was fought, which issued in the total defeat of the Romans. Those who escaped took refuge in Placentia; while Hannibal went into winter-quarters, and established an alliance with the Gauls of Northern Italy.

The next campaign was opened by Flaminius and Servilius, who, having been appointed consuls, proceeded at the head of two Roman armies against the invaders. Servilius occupied Ariminum, to oppose the progress of the Carthaginians, in case they should choose to proceed along the eastern side of the peninsula; while Flaminius took his position at Arretium, to guard the approach to the capital through Etruria. Hannibal adopted the latter course, and consequently came in contact with the forces of Flaminius. Having offered him battle on the plains in the neighbourhood without effect, he proceeded toward Rome, leaving the consul and his army in his rear. This measure roused the ire of the Roman commander, and he immediately followed the Punic army. Hannibal, however, took advantage of a thick fog, and a narrow defile in the mountains, to turn on his pursuers, when a brief conflict sufficed to destroy the consul and his army together.

When the intelligence of this action was proclaimed in Rome by the prætor, in these words,—"We are vanquished in a great battle; the consul, with great part of his army, is slain,"—general dismay filled the heart of the people, and the voice of the officer was drowned in lamentation. In this calamity the Romans appointed Quintus Fabius Maximus dictator; and his prudence, sagacity, and talent amply justified the choice of his constituents. Immediately on his appointment he proceeded to organize a force sufficient to repel the invader. Meanwhile Hannibal, not deeming it safe to advance on Rome, recrossed the Apennines, and directed his course to Apulia on the eastern side of the peninsula, where he did his utmost to lay waste the Roman settlements, and to detach the natives from their allegiance to Rome. Fabius, having raised four new legions, and organized the troops that had served under the consul Servilius, proceeded to meet the enemy. While on his march he issued a proclamation, requiring the inhabitants of all unfortified places within the range of the enemy's operations, to retire with all their movable wealth, and to burn and destroy their granaries, houses, and everything that could not be removed. Fabius then proceeded to the neighbourhood of Hannibal's quarters. The Punic chief at once offered him battle; but the wary Roman knew that his strength was delay. He therefore took advantage of every opportunity to harass the enemy, to cut off stragglers, and to engage in any skirmish on advantageous terms But he steadily refrained from a general battle; and, much to the annoyance and distress of the Carthaginian general, he maintained this cautious and prudent policy throughout his term of office. By this time, however, the Roman spirit had recovered its tone; but the conduct of Fabius, although eminently successful, was stigmatized as mean and cowardly.

In this state of public feeling the time arrived for the election of consuls, when C. Terentius Varro and L. Æmilius Paulus were raised to that dignity. The first seems to have been appointed on account of his bold and daring spirit,—a qualification regarded as essential to the adoption of energetic measures for the expulsion of Hannibal from Italy. The latter officer had obtained a triumph for his victories in Illyricum, and was supposed to possess sufficient coolness and judgment to prevent the rashness of his colleague from being injurious. With an army of eighty thousand foot, and more than seven thousand horse, these officers proceeded against the Carthaginians.

By this time Hannibal had possessed himself of the fortress and small town of Cannæ, on the Aufidus, where the Romans had stored considerable quantities of warlike ammunition and food. This acquisition, together with the fact that the Roman troops had obtained the advantage over the Carthaginians in some recent skirmishes, induced a strong disposition at Rome to hazard a battle; and instructions to this effect were forwarded to the consuls. These officers proceeded to carry their orders into effect. Varro, being eager for the contest, availed himself of his day for commanding, to place the army directly before the position of Hannibal, who immediately crossed the river, and arranged his forces in order of battle. The Roman troops were the most numerous; but they had not sufficient room to act with effect; while the superior genius and inexhaustible military resources of Hannibal gave him overwhelming superiority. The result was a defeat more terrible, in its extent and results, than any which Rome had received, except in the conflict with the Gauls on the Allia. The consul Paulus was left dead on the field; the consuls of the preceding year were also slain; and, with the exception of ten thousand men who had been posted to guard the camp, and three thousand who fled from the carnage, the Roman army appears to have been destroyed. Out of six thousand horse only seventy escaped with the consul Varro. This officer in some measure compensated his haste in beginning, and lack of judgment in directing, the battle, by the indomitable spirit which he evinced under the full pressure of the calamity. Despairing neither of himself nor of his country, he carefully collected the wreck of his troops, and manfully took up his position at Venusia, between the victorious Carthaginians and Rome, to resist to the utmost their approach to the capital.

The intelligence of this disaster filled Rome with deep affliction. But the spirit of this remarkable people rose with the emergency: they again appointed Fabius dictator, and he at once resumed his old cautious policy, which had obtained for him the surname of *Cunctator*, "the Delayer." Meanwhile, Hannibal, crossing over to the western side of the peninsula, occupied the city of Capua. Here the relaxing influence of the southern climate, and the indulgences and licentious practices into which his soldiery plunged, rapidly deteriorated their military strength, and prepared the way for that change in the relative power of the belligerents which soon took place.

Nothing more fully shows the lofty and daring spirit of the Roman people, than the fact, that while Hannibal was ranging through Italy, ravaging their towns, and destroying their troops, they maintained an army in Spain,—which cut off the supply of further reinforcements to Hannibal from that country,—and another in Sicily; and, hearing that their great enemy had formed an alliance with Philip of Macedon, they actually sent a third army into Greece.

It was in Sicily that military success first dawned on the arms of Rome after her terrible defeats. There, the prætor Metellus took Syracuse, which had been defended not only by the bravery of its citizens, but also by the wonderful talents and mechanical resources of the great Archimedes, who was slain in the capture of the place. Soon afterward Agrigentum, the last Carthaginian fortress on that important island, also fell into the hands of the Romans, who thus became masters of the country, which was thenceforth, in its whole extent, a province of Rome.

As Hannibal received no reinforcements from Carthage, he summoned his brother, who had long resisted the Scipios in Spain, to join him in Italy. Hasdrubal obeyed, and crossed the Pyrenees and the Alps in safety; but, while proceeding to join Hannibal, he was misled by his guides, and compelled at great disadvantage to hazard a battle with the Romans under the consuls Livius and Nero, in which he perished with his whole army. The first tidings that Hannibal received of this great disaster, were by the bloody head of his brother being thrown into his camp. Harassed by these reverses, Hannibal made earnest application to Carthage for more troops; but the rival factions of that devoted republic were deaf to his applications. They neither aided him to continue the contest, nor took any means of obtaining peace. Yet, under all these disadvantages, the heroic Carthaginian prosecuted the war; and, without any external resources, while shut up in the heart of an enemy's country, he maintained the struggle for sixteen years.

At length Scipio, who, notwithstanding his youth, had earned a high military reputation in Spain, was raised to the consulship, and earnestly solicited leave to invade Africa. At first the senate regarded the proposal as extravagant: but, moved by the arguments and solicitations of the young and successful soldier, they assigned him the province of Sicily, leaving it to him, if he could obtain resources, to make a descent on the African coast, while they refused to provide him with any more troops than could be raised in Sicily. There can be no doubt that the senate was at this time greatly embarrassed by the straitened condition of Rome; but it seems equally certain that in this instance it manifested a mean and unworthy opposition to Scipio, who was the darling of the people.

After spending one year in Sicily, making preparations,—which he did mainly by receiving, on account of his great popularity, numerous volunteers and munitions of war from Italy,—he passed over to Africa. Here he found himself opposed by three armies,—one Carthaginian under Hasdrubal, and two Numidian under Masinissa and Syphax. Scipio had previously detached Masinissa, the legitimate king of Numidia, from his allegiance to Carthage; and the latter now showed his treachery by leading the Carthaginians into an ambuscade, where many of them were destroyed, after which he openly went over to the Romans. The consul then entered into a correspondence with Syphax; and, having gained sufficient time by amusing the Numidian usurper, he broke off the negotiation, suddenly surprised their camp in the night, set it on fire, and thus routed and destroyed a great part of the army. After this success, Scipio laid siege to Utica. To save a place of so much importance, the Carthaginians mustered all their available forces. But Scipio again assailed the combined army of Carthaginians and Numidians, before they were fully prepared for action, and obtained a second victory of such magnitude, that the Punic army was completely driven from the field, and Utica and Tunis were simultaneously invested.

The government of Carthage, alarmed and confounded by these defeats, sent off expresses to Mago and Hannibal, commanding their immediate return for the defence of their own country. The former general died on the voyage, of wounds received in battle: the latter, with his army, returned in safety. Prior to his arrival, the Carthaginians had entered into negotiations with Scipio for a treaty of peace: but they no sooner saw the veteran general and brave troops, who had so long set at defiance the armies of Rome even in the heart of Italy, than they broke off their correspondence with the Roman commander, and resolved once more to try the fortune of war. The Carthaginians arrived at this determination in opposition to the judgment of Hannibal. He would have made peace on reasonable terms; but his countrymen were so elated by his presence that they refused. With secret misgivings as to the result, this brave man made the best possible preparation for meeting the enemy in the field.

The battle took place on the plains of Zama, where—after a desperate and long-continued conflict, during which the Punic veteran did all that military genius and experience, directing the operations of determined bravery, could effect—the Romans were completely victorious. Hannibal escaped from the field of carnage with a small body of horse, and soon reached Carthage. When the rulers of the city saw their idolized chief without an army, and heard that intrepid warrior declare that "Carthage had no resource but peace," their spirit sunk into abject submission, and they accepted the terms of peace, or rather of subjection to Rome, which were dictated by Scipio. By these terms Carthage had to deliver up all Roman prisoners and deserters; to surrender all her ships of war, except ten, and all her elephants; to pay toward the expenses of the conflict about two millions sterling; to agree not to make war without the consent of Rome; and to give one hundred hostages for the due performance of the treaty. When the Roman general returned home, he was honoured with a most magnificent triumph, and dignified with the surname of *Africanus*.

The successful termination of this war placed the Roman state at the head of all the nations of Europe, as a military power. And it lost no time or opportunity of availing itself of this advantage for the extension of its dominions. The Athenians, having suffered greatly from the attacks of Philip, King of Macedon, sought, and readily obtained, the aid of Rome. The consul Sulpicius at first, and afterward Quinctius Flamininus, at the head of the Roman legions, carried the war to the shores of Epirus.

Yet although the Romans had now obtained a great extension of territory, having established their supremacy over all Italy, Sicily, and the Carthaginian dominions in Spain, they had at the same time been reduced to the lowest extremity of financial distress, by their efforts to maintain the war. Indeed, this appears to have been the distinguishing feature of the Roman character: for no ancient nation ever made such sacrifices to maintain a military struggle, as did Rome on this occasion. When every mode of taxation failed, the state called for the voluntary contributions of its members, and received gold and silver ornaments and plate, which, together with a great debasement of the currency, enabled them to carry on the war to a successful termination.

Although the Roman army under Sulpicius succeeded in protecting the Athenians, it effected nothing decisive against Macedon. During two years the war languished, and the Roman arms obtained but little respect in the east of Europe. At length T. Quinctius Flamininus was sent to take the command of the Roman army in Greece. He immediately altered the seat and the character of the war. Having completely defeated the design of the Macedonian king in guarding a strong pass between Epirus and Thessaly, the Roman general compelled him to retire, throwing open to Rome almost the whole of the Peloponnesus.

At the opening of the next campaign, the opposing armies encountered each other in Thessaly. Here the advanced guard of the two nations met by accident in a thick fog; when a struggle immediately took place, which extended to the whole of the troops, and became a general battle. Victory declared for the Romans; and Philip, defeated and humbled, sued for peace. This was granted with a great show of liberality: for, while the Romans compelled the king of Macedon to surrender his ships of war, to reduce his army to five hundred men, to discontinue the training and use of elephants, and to pay one thousand talents toward the expenses of the campaign, they professed to have no design of aggrandizing themselves, but most pompously proclaimed liberty to Greece. When this proclamation was made at the Isthmian Games, as Dr. Taylor well observes, "it filled the foolish spectators with so much delight, that they virtually became slaves to the Romans through gratitude for freedom."

The Romans hastened the conclusion of this treaty, having heard that Antiochus, King of Syria, was advancing at the head of a great army along the seacoast of Asia Minor toward the Hellespont; which induced the Roman deputies, who had been charged with the conduct of the arrangements consequent on the close of the war with Philip, to meet the Syrian monarch, and to protest against his proceeding to Europe. To this address the haughty warrior replied with scorn, that he knew his own rights, and did not require teaching from the Romans; and that they had better set some bounds to their own ambition, before they presumed to dictate moderation to other states. Yet, notwithstanding this angry meeting, no immediate hostilities took place.

It must not escape observation, that these wars in Greece bring Rome under notice as a subject of sacred prophecy, and of that peculiar providential interposition which the fulfilment of divinely-revealed and publicly-recorded predictions so clearly implies. Macedon was the hereditary kingdom of Alexander, and the seat of his first sovereignty. Antiochus was one of the successors of that great warrior, and ruled over a large part of the empire which he had reared up. A victory over these powers would consequently, in the then state of other countries, have placed the conqueror as the fourth monarchy which had been so clearly predicted by the prophet Daniel. This was soon afterward obtained.

The Romans, notwithstanding their military strength, still felt a latent dread of the rising power of Carthage, cultivated and directed by the indomitable Hannibal. They accordingly availed themselves of some little difference which arose between the king of Numidia and the Punic rulers, to send a commission to Carthage: the real object, however, was, if possible, to get the veteran general into their power. When we consider the violence of the rival factions in that city, it seems probable that they might have carried this plan into effect, had not the experienced warrior sought safety in flight. On the arrival of the Roman commissioners, he received them in his state costume, and conducted himself with his usual ease and self-possession; but that night he abandoned the city, and embarked for the east, where he was soon found at the court of Antiochus. Rightly judging that this sovereign was the only one who possessed military means and martial spirit sufficient to offer any chance of success in a struggle with Rome, the brave old Carthaginian, faithful to his youthful oath, determined to do his utmost to induce the Syrian king to attempt the arresting of the progress of Roman power.

Antiochus readily entered into the views of Hannibal; and a plan of operations was devised, by which the Romans were to be assailed simultaneously in Italy and Greece,—in the former, by an army under the Punic general; in the latter, by Antiochus. Messengers were actually despatched to Carthage, to bring that power into coöperation with the design; but, this fact being made known to the faction opposed to Hannibal, they betrayed the secret to the Romans. War thus became inevitable, and Antiochus passed over to Greece. The Romans made vast preparations for this contest, and sent their consul Glabrio, at the head of a great army, into Greece. Antiochus, who had brought with him but ten thousand men, felt unequal to meet the enemy in the open field, and took his position at the celebrated Pass of Thermopylæ. Here he was attacked and dislodged, and his army almost entirely destroyed. The king himself, with only five hundred men, escaped. At first he took refuge in Chalcis, from whence he passed over into Asia.

The Romans, elated with this success, prepared to prosecute the war with increased spirit; and, having elected L. C. Scipio (brother of the conqueror of Carthage) consul, sent him, with his able brother as second in command, to conduct the war in Asia. Antiochus possessed vast resources, and might have been a most formidable enemy of Rome. He, however, devoted himself far more to sensual pleasures than to the stern duties of military life. But when he was aware of the approach of the Roman forces, he placed himself at the head of an army of eighty thousand men, and waited the arrival of the enemy near Magnesia, at the foot of Mount Sipylus. Here he suffered a severe defeat: his army was destroyed, and he compelled to secure his personal safety by a precipitate flight. The result of this victory gave to Rome all the possessions which Antiochus had previously held in Europe, nearly the whole of Asia Minor, and a sum equal to about three millions sterling, in addition to the spoil taken in the battle, which was immense.

The tone of command now assumed by the Roman functionaries in Greece gave great umbrage to the native rulers; and they eagerly desired to throw off the yoke, which had been almost imperceptibly, but with ultimate rigour, imposed on them. None felt this foreign domination so keenly as Perseus, who had succeeded to the Macedonian throne; and he cautiously, but diligently, proceeded to husband his finances, augment his army, and make alliances with his neighbours, with the view, in due time, of asserting and maintaining his independence. In making these preparations for resisting Roman domination, he did not fail to correspond with the natural enemy of that power,—Carthage; and, as usual, from the factious character of the government of that republic, this step was soon known in the Italian capital. An army was consequently sent against Perseus, who entered Thessaly at the head of his forces, captured several important towns, and encountered the Roman troops on the banks of the River Peneus, where, in an engagement between the cavalry and light infantry of the two armies, the Macedonians had the decided advantage, and the Roman consul was compelled to retreat. Perseus, however, was not by this success led away from a just consideration of the dangers of his position. Taking advantage, therefore, of this success, he immediately made proposals for peace, which the Romans, according to their invariable custom, refused to entertain after a defeat. The war was accordingly recommenced, and continued for three years, without giving the Romans any advantage over their enemies. At length Æmilius Paulus, son of the commander that was slain at Cannæ, was appointed to the command of the army. This general, by his prudent conduct and wise strategy, soon altered the aspect of the war. Having found the Macedonian army intrenched on the banks of the Enipeus, he carefully examined the ground, and made a successful effort with a company of his troops, by which a pass was forced in the mountain, and a way opened to the rear of the Macedonian camp. This measure compelled Perseus to retreat, and take up a position on the Haliacmon, near Pydna. Here the Macedonian king was followed by the Roman army, and compelled, by the nature of the ground, either to hazard a battle, or to separate his forces. He chose the former alternative: a severe conflict ensued, in which the Romans obtained a complete victory. Perseus fled,—but was pursued, and ultimately compelled to surrender to the Roman consul. About the same time, a Roman army, under the prætor Anicius, invaded Illyricum, and completely subdued it in a campaign of thirty days. Thus Macedon, Epirus, and Illyricum were added to the Roman dominions.

The result of these wars places Rome before the mind of every believer in the truth of divine revelation, as the *fourth* kingdom, the *first* having been that of Nebuchadnezzar of Babylon. The head of gold had fallen; the Medo-Persian empire, symbolized by the breast and arms of silver, had perished; and now the sway of "the brazen-coated Greeks" was terminated by the subjection of Alexander's direct successor in the paternal kingdom, and of his most powerful successor in Asia, to the dominion of Rome. The further progress of this power should, therefore, be considered under an abiding recognition of this providential arrangement. It will be found that the future history of Rome rapidly placed it in the precise position in which it was spoken of by the prophet,—namely, as under the rule of "kings." Dan. ii.

Released from the Grecian war by the conquest of Macedon, the Romans looked around on every side with unquenchable ardour, seeking for territory to seize, and nations to subdue. After various intrigues, which greatly extended their influence in Spain, Transalpine Gaul, and Asia Minor, it was resolved, at the instigation of Cato, to destroy Carthage. The rulers of this republic, although possessing a considerable increase of wealth and power since the close of the last war with Rome, had nevertheless conducted their affairs with so much sagacity and prudence, that when the Roman senate had determined on its destruction, they were at a loss for any reasonable ground for renewing the war, and at last had recourse to the cruel and absurd decision, that the inhabitants of Carthage should remove with all their effects from that city to another residence, ten miles from the sea. The rulers, and, in fact, the whole population of Carthage, perceived that their ruin was determined on; and that the proposed measure, although it might produce that result more slowly than the operations of war, would with equal certainty effect it. They therefore resolved on a determined resistance; and never was a resolution more manfully carried into effect. Rich and poor vied with each other in their efforts to defend their city to the utmost. Even the ladies cut off the long hair of which they were so proud, to make strings for bows and slings.

This unexpected unanimity and energy rendered the destruction of Carthage a work of greater difficulty than was anticipated. For more than two years they made a successful resistance to every effort of their enemies. But at length the Romans appointed Scipio Æmilianus, the adopted son of Scipio Africanus, to the command of their army in Africa; and his energy and genius soon brought the war to a close. He at first devoted himself to restore the discipline of the army, which had been allowed by former commanders to degenerate into disorder and licentiousness. Having removed this evil, and, by the justice of his measures, and the blandness of his manner, secured the confidence and respect of the neighbouring African nations, he proceeded to assail Carthage with all his power. The defence was able and obstinate, but vain. The Roman general stormed the outer wall, cut his way to the principal square of the city, spent six days in preparing for the reduction of the strong fortresses which guarded it, and at length obliged the garrison to surrender at discretion; whereupon Carthage was consigned to the flames, and great numbers of the inhabitants perished in the ruins of the place, rather than submit to their cruel enemies.

During the progress of the Third Punic war, fresh disturbances broke out in Greece. These were principally raised by an impostor, who pretended to be the son of Philip. The Achæans entered into the strife; but resistance to the legions of Rome was fruitless. Corinth, Thebes, and Colchis were completely destroyed, and Greece was fully subjected to the Roman government. About the same time, the Roman arms were equally successful in Spain, which henceforth became a province of Rome.

The unscrupulous rapacity, and boundless grasping at power, which impelled the Roman senate to these continued sanguinary wars, were equally evinced in the government at home. The rapid succession and vast extent of these military operations, the numerous offices which they called into existence, and the means of highly lucrative employment for the nominees of the senate, raised that body to an inordinate measure of power and wealth; while the taxes and duties, for the maintenance of these extended struggles, falling on the people, reduced them to the direst poverty and wretchedness. The government, therefore, while it exulted in territorial aggrandizement and martial power, became, through the operation of these causes, a proud and violent aristocracy, isolated from the people by class feelings, privileges, and powers, and hated by them in proportion to this isolation.

This state of things was perceived and lamented by the best and greatest Romans of the day; but the first who boldly attempted to check the oppression, and redress the grievances, of the people, was Tiberius Gracchus. The son of a consul,—his mother the daughter of Scipio Africanus,—he had access to the highest offices of state, and might have shared in the power and plunder enjoyed by the great, had he chosen to ally himself with them. He nobly aspired to higher aims. His soul was moved with indignation at the unchecked progress of corruption; and he resolved to devote his best efforts to remedy the evils which prevailed. With this object, he offered himself, and was elected, as a tribune of the people. Invested with the authority of this office, he soon perceived that one prominent part of the prevailing corruption lay in the conduct of members of the aristocracy with respect to the public lands; as an individual would frequently undertake the management of an extensive and valuable tract of country, which he would sub-let in small portions to numerous needy dependants,—making thereby an enormous profit to himself at the expense of the public. Gracchus, therefore, after consulting with the wisest and most virtuous of the citizens, and obtaining their concurrence in his proceeding, determined to enforce the Licinian prohibition against any individual holding more than five hundred acres of the public land. This measure roused the ire of the sordid and oppressive aristocracy, who, although they did not dare openly to resist the operation of an admitted law, were resolved, if possible, to prevent it from being carried into effect. The patriotic tribune, however, not satisfied with this measure, and seeing the poverty and distress of the people, and that the resources of the state, after its recent successful wars, were quite equal to its wants, proposed that the treasures bequeathed to Rome by Attalus, King of Pergamus, should be distributed to relieve the wants of the poorest citizens.

While the enactment of these and other similar measures was being carried into effect, the year of office for which Gracchus was appointed tribune expired. He was, indeed, proposed for reëlection; and would doubtless have succeeded, had not a combination of patricians and place-holders determined to risk all the crimes and hazard of a bloody tumult, rather than allow this intrepid advocate of the people to proceed in his course of reform. Nasica, a large holder of public lands, with others equally interested, daringly assaulted the unarmed multitude who supported Gracchus. In this commotion the earnest reformer of public abuses was slain, with many of his friends.

The cause for which Tiberius Gracchus died, did not perish with him. At the time of his death he had a brother, a mere boy, named Caius; who, undaunted by the fate of his relation, determined to devote himself to a similar line of conduct. When he arrived at a proper age, he was elected quæstor, and discharged the duties of that office in Sardinia with great ability and integrity. On returning to Rome, he was raised to the dignity of tribune. In this office he proposed, and carried into effect, some measures which bore with peculiar force against the murderers of his brother. He then turned his attention to the enforcement of the agrarian law. When a second time elected tribune, he procured the enactment of a statute which raised the equestrian order to the dignity of judges, and proportionately diminished the power of senators.

To neutralize the operation of his influence, the patricians set up Drusus, another tribune, as a rival to Caius Gracchus in the popular esteem. For this purpose he was enabled, with the sanction of the senate, to remit taxes, and make large grants of public money, to the people. The mean design of this measure was, indeed, so successful, that, when proposed for tribune the third time, Caius lost his election. This, however, did not deter him from the prosecution of his great object. But, with the loss of his office, he had lost his legal power to stem the torrent; while, by the same influence which shut out Caius from office, Opimius, the most factious and violent of the patricians, was elected consul. In this state of things a furious collision was inevitable, and soon occurred. One of the lictors, engaged in some sacrificial service, having made a coarse remark to the crowd which surrounded Caius and Fulvius, some of the party rushed on him with such force that he was slain in the broil.

This impolitic violence afforded the aristocracy the opportunity which they had long desired: the senate was convened, and Opimius declared dictator. Caius Gracchus and his friends, determined to carry their resistance to the utmost, took possession of Mount Aventine. But they had miscalculated their power, under the influence of their own ardent feelings. The people were neither sufficiently organized, nor proof against the seductions of the powerful and wealthy party arrayed against them. Consequently, even before they were attacked, great numbers who had at first surrounded Gracchus, departed from his side; so that when the dictator assailed the popular party, it was completely routed. Above three thousand were slain. Caius himself fell, at his own request, by the sword of a faithful slave, rather than come into the hands of his enemies.

With the death of the Gracchi perished the last remnant of constitutional liberty at Rome. Henceforth the government was conducted by an oligarchy, until at length it became an absolute monarchy.

We now approach, in the progress of this mighty nation, the period in which, notwithstanding the utmost degeneracy into which their institutions had fallen, they succeeded, through the genius and energy of a series of most extraordinary men, in placing Rome on the pinnacle of power, and, in fact, reigning supreme in the world.

We have the first development of this extraordinary cycle in the

Jugurthine war. Micipsa, King of Numidia, and son of Masinissa, divided his dominions, on his death-bed, between his two sons, Hiempsal and Adherbal, and his illegitimate nephew, Jugurtha. The latter, possessing an unscrupulous and daring mind, determined to seize the whole kingdom. He accordingly procured the murder of Hiempsal; and when Adherbal prepared to assert his own right, and punish his brother's murderer, he was soon defeated, and compelled to fly to Rome to solicit aid. Jugurtha, who knew the character of the nation with which he had to deal, sent emissaries to the imperial city with such large sums of gold, to be employed in bribing the rulers, that he prevented any effective interference from that quarter. The senate, indeed, decreed, that the Numidian dominions should be equally divided between Jugurtha and Adherbal; but when the latter had taken possession of his portion, Jugurtha declared war against him, took him prisoner, and put him to death This atrocity induced the Romans to send a prætor to Africa, pledging the public faith for the personal safety of Jugurtha, but commanding him to repair to Rome to answer for his conduct. He obeyed the summons; but the power of gold prevailed: for, while one tribune questioned the African king, another, with equal authority, forbade him to reply; and thus the ostensible object of the Romans was defeated.

Jugurtha by these means not only obtained exemption from punishment, but actually dared, even in the capital, to perpetrate new crimes. Learning that another cousin of his was in the Roman capital, and regarding it as probable that he would obtain from the senate some portion of the Numidian dominions, he procured his assassination. When this murder became known, and had been fully traced to its author, it was regarded as such a flagrant insult to the Roman power, that although the pledge of personal safety was held sacred, and he was allowed to return to Africa, the consul Albinus was instructed to proceed with an army to make war upon him. Jugurtha, however, was as wary in war as he was daring in crime; and he managed to foil the operations of the Romans for the first year without coming to any decisive struggle. When the consul returned to Rome to hold his *comitia*, he left the army under the command of his brother Aulus, whose mind seems to have been filled with an intense desire to gratify his avarice by seizing the treasures of the Numidian king. Rashly adopting a series of measures for the accomplishment of this object, he enabled his antagonist to surprise, defeat, and capture his whole army The proud Numidian determined to avail himself to the utmost of this success; so he made his captives pass under the yoke,—a practice adopted by the Romans themselves for symbolizing the total national subjugation of a conquered country.

All Rome was roused by this infamy. The senate disavowed this dishonourable surrender; while the tribunes demanded the sending of a commission to Africa, to make inquiries, and to punish those who had received bribes from Jugurtha. But this virtuous effort was poisoned at the beginning of its operation. Scaurus, one who had been most flagrantly guilty, got himself appointed on the commission of inquiry; so that this notorious criminal presided over the trial and condemnation of four consulars and a pontiff. Among them was Opimius, who had been the cause of the death of Caius Gracchus.

At this time Rome suffered most severely from several defeats which she received from the barbarous tribes of the Cimbri on the northern frontier of their empire. This foe had destroyed one consular army on the borders of Illyricum, whence they marched westward, until they were found again in prodigious strength at Narbonne in Transalpine Gaul. Here, again, they were met by the greatest army that Rome could command, under the proconsul Cæpio and the consul Manlius: but the barbarians were again victorious, and it is said that eighty thousand of the Roman troops were left dead on the field.

In the mean time, the war was carried on against Jugurtha by Metellus with great success; and the usurper was compelled to solicit aid from Bocchus, King of Mauritania, and to take refuge in his dominions. The Roman general commanding in this war derived great assistance in these struggles from Caius Marius,—a young officer of mean birth, who had risen from the lowest grade of the service to be lieutenant of the army. As the war seemed drawing to a close, Metellus was surprised to hear Marius solicit leave of absence, that he might go to Rome, and offer himself for the consular office the ensuing year. The general at first refused, with some contemptuous expressions respecting the youth of the aspirant. Afterward, however, when there was scarcely time for him to reach Rome before the day of election, leave was given. Marius improved the opportunity: he fled, rather than travelled, to Rome, and made such good use of the brief interval that he was not only elected, but, notwithstanding Metellus had been confirmed by the senate in the command of the army of Africa, he had that country assigned him by the assembly of the people as his province. Utterly disregarding the appointment made by the senate, he collected fresh levies, and organized an army, to proceed to his appointed province.

In doing this, perhaps chiefly by the daring energy of his own example and character, Marius continued to work out a complete revolution in Rome. Prior to this time the Roman legions were supplied from the respectable classes of society: men who possessed some property, and consequently had a stake in the country, were alone deemed eligible to fill the ranks of the heavy-armed infantry. But neither Latins nor Italians had yet been enrolled as Roman citizens, while the free population had been diminished by successive wars. In these circumstances, Marius induced the senate to concur in his recruiting from the lowest of the people; and he soon found himself surrounded by a hardy and daring body of men, ready to follow his standard to meet any enemy. But then, as an able writer observes, they were led forth "without a prejudice or a principle, ready at his bidding to turn their arms upon either friends or enemies." Uninfluenced by the patriotic feelings and conservative restraints which were sure to affect men in the position of the old legionaries, these newly-formed soldiers became the creatures of their chief; and in consequence we henceforth find Rome ruled over by military power.

Marius hastened to Africa, where Metellus had carried on the campaign very successfully, but, hearing that he had been superseded, retired to Rome, where he was honoured with a triumph. Marius prosecuted the war with ability and spirit; and although Jugurtha defended himself with consummate genius, and seemed inexhaustible in resources, Marius at length defeated him in a great battle, and Jugurtha was afterward delivered up to the Romans by his faithless allies. It is undoubtedly true, that this man had been guilty of the most enormous crimes; but the barbarity of his victors seems equally detestable. After being led in chains through the land which he had governed, and exposed before the triumphal chariot of Marius, on the day when he was rewarded for the glorious termination of the war, the wretched captive was cast headlong into the subterranean prison on the Capitoline Rock, and left to perish of cold and hunger through a mortal agony of six days.

When Marius triumphed for his success in Africa, he had just been chosen consul for the second time, and was at once appointed to conduct the war against the Cimbri in Gaul. Thither he proceeded; but he found his raw levies unequal to subdue these hardy barbarians. Acting, therefore, on the defensive, inuring his troops to discipline and exertion, he patiently prepared for the work which had been assigned him. It was, however, not until he had been appointed consul the fourth time, that he felt sufficient confidence in his legions to risk a pitched battle. The prudent delay of Marius inspired the Cimbri with contempt for his troops; but, at length, in

two successive conflicts, he defeated this huge host with immense
slaughter. Yet, notwithstanding these successes, a great army of the
Cimbri still survived, crossed the Alps, and descended to the banks
of the Po. The forces sent out to meet them retired in confusion at
their approach. Fortunately Marius arrived just at this moment,
effected a junction of his victorious legions with the army of Catulus,
his colleague in the consulship, and in a great battle routed and
destroyed this terrible host. It is said that one hundred and fifty
thousand were slain, sixty thousand taken prisoners, and great numbers of both men and women destroyed themselves rather than fall
into the hands of the Romans. Thus ended the third perilous invasion of the Roman state. Marius was instantly counted with Romulus and Camillus, as the *third* founder of the city, and the preserver
of his country.

About this time a second servile war in Sicily was terminated
with a fearful loss of life. A much more dangerous one, of a very
similar kind, also broke out in Italy. It arose out of the gross injustice with which the Romans persisted in treating the Italian allies.
After a murderous contest of three years, it was ended by the
Romans granting the freedom of their city to all the Italians who
laid down their arms.

Amid all these conflicts, it became very evident that the most
imminent danger of the state arose from the rivalry of two great
generals. Marius, now nearly seventy years of age, still retained
ambition and energy of character. His rival was Sylla, a soldier
of noble extraction, about forty-five years old, who had served under
Marius as quæstor in Africa, and greatly distinguished himself in the
last victory over the Cimbri. Both these warriors had been engaged
in the war waged by Rome against the Italians, although Marius
retired before its close, while Sylla was actively and honourably
employed to the end.

Mithridates, King of Pontus, one of the most formidable enemies
that Rome ever had in the east, had taken advantage of these commotions in Italy and Sicily to extend his power throughout Asia
Minor, and, in fact, to make himself paramount in Western Asia.
Considering the position which Rome had assumed, a war with this
power was unavoidable. The command of the enterprise was looked
for by Sylla as an object of intense desire: and Marius, old as he
was, felt no less anxious to obtain the distinction. But the latter
was always regarded by the senate with dislike; and he had recently
made himself specially obnoxious by a covert connexion with a factious tribune, Saturnius, who had occasioned an insurrection, in
which he and many others had been slain. Under such circum-

stances the senate appointed Sylla to undertake the war against Mithridates.

Marius, enraged at being deprived of this command, obtained the active aid of Sulpicius Galba, one of the tribunes, and commenced an active agitation against the government. Availing himself of all the elements of discontent arising out of the recent arrangement between Rome and the Italians, and holding out hopes to his partisans of their sharing in the spoil of Mithridates, if successful, he by these means gathered a party, raised a tumult, and assailed the consuls: blood was shed, and Sylla had to seek safety in flight. Meanwhile, Sulpicius, having cleared the forum of his principal opponents, proposed to an assembly of the people the appointment of Marius to the command in Asia, which was carried. Marius was now, in fact, the master of Rome; and prætors were sent to inform Sylla, who had proceeded to his camp, that he was superseded in his command, and required to deliver up the army to Marius. But the factious leaders of this movement had mistaken the character of the man with whom they had to deal. Sylla immediately appealed to his troops, told them of the indignity to which he had been subjected, and persuaded them that they were no less insulted and injured than himself. The great number of his officers, men of family and property, refused to unite in any violent measure; but the soldiers, to the extent of six legions, declared their readiness to follow their general; and, placing himself at the head of these, he marched toward Rome.

The Marian faction, as well as the senate and the people of Rome, were alarmed and confounded at this measure: they had no troops to meet this army in the field. Officers were sent to Sylla, forbidding his approach to the city. These were slain, and the legions advanced: by an artful manœuvre Sylla obtained possession of one of the gates of the city, and entered at the head of his troops. The people assailed the advancing soldiers from the windows and house-tops; but a threat to set the city on fire soon put down this opposition, and Sylla in turn was paramount at Rome. He, however, preserved strict discipline among his troops, but insisted on the proscription of twelve of his enemies. Sulpicius was betrayed and slain. Marius narrowly escaped by flight.

Sylla then assembled the people, and caused them to abrogate those laws by which the tribunes had been able to excite such formidable seditions, leaving the people in full possession of their suffrages. He then allowed them to elect two consuls: Octavius, a firm supporter of the senate, was one; and Cinna, a decided partisan of Marius, was the other. It is remarkable that, possessing such power, Sylla should have permitted this last appointment; but he satisfied himself with requiring Cinna to take a religious vow to maintain and administer faithfully the new laws which had been made.

Having effected these objects Sylla returned to the camp, and proceeded to his appointed sphere of action against Mithridates. Here he had a difficult part to act; but he succeeded. After affording his soldiers ample opportunities for obtaining booty, in order to secure their adherence to himself, he stormed Athens, which had been in alliance with Mithridates, slaughtered the inhabitants without mercy, and defeated the armies of the king of Pontus in two decisive engagements.

While these events transpired in the east, a strange revolution had been wrought in Rome. Sylla had scarcely left Italy before Cinna avowed a determination to annul all the regulations which he had so religiously sworn to maintain. He accordingly insisted on the recall of the exiles, and the restoration of the laws of Sulpicius. These propositions, however, met with violent opposition from the senate, from his colleague in the consulship, and also from the tribunes; and when these found that Cinna was determined to attempt carrying his measures by force, they anticipated his movements, flew to arms, expelled him from the consulship and the city, and elected Merula, a flamen of Jupiter, consul in his stead.

But Cinna, when thus cast as a fugitive on the world, did not despair. He immediately proceeded to the newly-created citizens in Campania; and, exciting their compassion for him, and their fears that their newly-acquired dignity was likely to be wrested from them, he induced great numbers to rally round him, together with many exiles of the Marian party, and among them Sertorius, an officer of distinction. He then went, clothed in black, to the Roman camp, and appealed to the soldiers. The sight of a consul in such distress so moved these men, that they insisted on marching under his orders. At the head of a Roman army Cinna proceeded to Rome. In the mean time, Marius, who was well informed of all that was passing, suddenly landed on the coast of Etruria, where he was soon joined by many of his party, and a large body of discontented slaves; so that he, also, gathering strength as he went, approached Rome. Other sections of the army joined the insurrection; and Rome was completely beleaguered by her own rebellious subjects. After some considerable delay, during which a pestilence raged with fearful violence, both in the city and in the camp, the senate was compelled to submit. Marius and Cinna entered the city triumphant; and a fearful scene of carnage and plunder ensued. Marius glutted his rage against all who had opposed his party without any limitation; while the soldiers, who had crowded to his standard for the hope of plunder, eagerly grasped the opportunity now afforded them, and Rome was filled with blood and rapine.

Having gratified the revenge of his partisans, Marius appointed himself consul, without even the formality of an election; and, with Cinna, undertook the government of the state. It was arranged that the latter should direct the affairs of Italy, while the aged general should collect an army, proceed to the east, and supersede Sylla in the war with Pontus. Daring as he was, it is generally thought that Marius dreaded an encounter with his younger rival in arms; it is, however, certain that he died soon after his appointment,—as is supposed, by suicide. Valerius Flaccus was now appointed consul, as colleague of Cinna.

Order being somewhat restored in Italy, Flaccus collected an army, and marched to the east, to watch the motions of Sylla: but while manœuvring his army in Greece, in the hope of obtaining an advantage over his able opponent, he was assassinated in his camp, and Fimbria, a violent and factious tribune, who may be supposed to have had some participation in the murder, succeeded to the command of the army. This new general, not willing to measure his strength against Sylla at the head of Roman legions, passed over into Asia, in the hope that he should distinguish himself by the conquest of Mithridates. With this view, he attacked the troops of Pontus wherever he could find them, ravaging every wealthy city in his way; and he would actually have captured the great king himself, if Sylla, determined not to allow his rival such a glory, had not afforded Mithridates the means of escape. Mithridates was, by these reverses, led to be anxious for peace, which Sylla, in his peculiar position, was equally disposed to grant. A peace was therefore concluded, by which Mithridates delivered up a large portion of his fleets and treasures, and was limited in his government to the dominions which he possessed before the breaking out of the war. Having secured this settlement, Sylla turned his forces against the army of Fimbria, where the use of his gold was so effectual, that that tribune, abandoned by his army, committed suicide; and Sylla, at the head of the united forces, marched toward Rome.

After a severe struggle against the forces of the consuls, and the armies which had been raised in Italy to oppose him, Sylla made himself absolute master of Rome, and, to a fearful extent, surpassed the most sanguinary cruelty of Marius. Citizens of every rank were proscribed, and murdered, in the most reckless manner. These murders were extended to the provinces. Tyrant power reigned, and wild disorder ranged unchecked throughout the Roman states. Having gratified his lust for blood to the utmost, Sylla caused himself to be elected dictator for an unlimited time; but, three years after, he retired into private life,—a measure which surprised every one, until, after a brief period, it was explained by his dying of a loathsome disease, brought on by intemperance and debauchery.

On the abdication of Sylla, the consul Lepidus endeavoured to grasp the power which had fallen from his hands: but, unequal to the task, he was defeated and abandoned, and perished. Delivered from this danger, the senate was alarmed at the progress of a Marian insurrection in Spain, where Sertorius had collected an imposing force in the interest of that faction. Pompey was sent against him; and, although the veteran warrior, Sertorius, was at first more than a match for the daring young officer, the latter contrived to bring the war to a successful close. Sertorius was murdered; and his troops, deprived of his talent and energy, were soon reduced by Pompey.

Before this result had been secured, Italy was convulsed by a revolt, as dangerous as it was unexpected and daring. Spartacus, a gladiator, became the head of an army, which either defeated or kept at bay all the forces of Rome, and held all Italy in fearful excitement and apprehension, for more than three years. This insurrection arose out of the practice of coercing slaves, captives, and criminals to butcher each other in the arena, for the amusement of Roman spectators. A large troop of these swordsmen, maintained for this purpose, had plotted together, thinking that war in another form would be as pleasing, and as profitable, as that which they had been compelled to wage on each other. They accordingly meditated escaping, and seventy-eight of them succeeded; and, after taking a temporary refuge in an extinct crater of Vesuvius, they procured an accession of numbers, seized a neighbouring fortress, made Spartacus their chief, and prepared to defend themselves. They did this with such effect, and their numbers swelled so rapidly, that at one period it is said they formed a body of one hundred thousand men. But the veteran legions of Rome at length prevailed; Spartacus was slain, and his troops were dispersed or destroyed.

Crassus and Pompey were now chosen consuls. Both being anxious to seize supreme power, they paid extravagant court to the people,—the former, by large donations of corn; the latter, by restoring the power of the tribunes. Pompey, having obtained the command of the forces sent against the Cilician pirates and Mithridates, proceeded on his mission. By measures equally spirited and sagacious he contrived to induce these daring plunderers to collect their vessels, which were distributed over every part of the Mediterranean, into one body; and he then defeated them in a single battle. Afterward he proceeded against them so effectually on shore, that he broke their strength, and put an end to their depredations. He also conducted the war against Mithridates with equal effect. After traversing Asia beyond the range of any previous Roman army, the king of Pontus was completely subdued, and destroyed himself, rather than fall into the hands of his conqueror.

While Pompey was extending the Roman dominions and glory in the East, Rome herself was brought to the brink of ruin by the conspiracy of Catiline,—a daring and dissipated noble, who had several times been defeated in attempting to procure elevated offices in the state, and at length determined to secure the object of his ambition by violence. For this purpose he had drawn into his designs some of the influential nobles of Rome, and had prepared such an extended scheme of revolt as could scarcely fail to be successful. The vigilance and ability of Cicero, who was then consul, saved Rome. He with boundless sagacity penetrated all the schemes of the conspirators, and at length so forcibly charged Catiline with treason in the senate, that the guilty man, overwhelmed with confusion, left the city. The consul then took his measures so adroitly, that he apprehended the chief conspirators, and confronted them with written proofs of their guilt. They were promptly placed on their trial, condemned to death, and immediately executed. Catiline, perceiving that nothing more could be done by policy, now took up arms, and assembled a body of about twenty thousand men: but he was defeated and slain by a consular army near Pistoria. In gratitude for his conduct on this occasion Cicero was saluted by the people, on the motion of Cato, with the title of "FATHER OF HIS COUNTRY."

Rome had now reached a point of political and moral disorganization which rendered the effective operation of any popular government impossible. Pompey had returned from Asia, and enjoyed the most splendid triumph which had been seen in Rome. But he was on ill terms with Crassus, who was perhaps the most powerful man in the state. A collision between these great men would have been fatal to Rome. It was prevented by him who was afterward destined to rule supreme over the Roman dominions. Julius Cæsar now possessed considerable influence. He was forty years of age, and had never commanded an army, or filled any public office of especial responsibility, except that of supreme pontiff. He had, however, by the exercise of his great talents, in the ordinary public business of the state, acquired so much popular favour and general influence, that his position in the Roman councils was one of distinguished eminence. Cæsar availed himself of the present emergency to use this influence with effect. He reconciled Pompey and Crassus, and, uniting himself with them, formed what is called "the First Triumvirate." According to the terms of this partnership of power, Cæsar led an army into Gaul; Crassus was elected consul, and proceeded to Syria; and Pompey, also consul, went to Spain.

Cæsar continued his command in Gaul eight years, during which time he not only subdued the whole of that country, but also brought under the dominion of Rome all the territory between the Pyrenees and the German Ocean; crossed the Rhine, and defeated the Germani in their own country; and passed over into Britain, and a least brought a portion of this island into professed subjection to Rome. While Cæsar was prosecuting these conquests, Crassus perished, with a great part of his army, in a war against Parthia Pompey became envious of his colleague's fame; and the death of Julia, Cæsar's daughter, whom Pompey had married, dissolved the last link of union between these two great men. It then became evident that, with their ambition and power, a collision between them would soon be inevitable.

The crisis was hastened by Cæsar's asking permission to hold the office of consul during his absence. He had previously, by lavish gifts, secured the most influential adherents at Rome, and among them the powerful and popular Caius Curio. This able and energetic tribune, perceiving that the senate would soon be induced to recall Cæsar, took advantage of a proposition of the consul Marcellus to that effect, to submit a distinct motion,—that both Pompey and Cæsar should lay down their military command. This proposition was carried in the senate by a great majority, and applauded with enthusiasm by the people without; but was not carried into effect. The senate feared Cæsar, and trusted in Pompey, and would not consent to place their idol in a private position. After considerable time had been wasted in negotiation, the senate passed a decree, by which Cæsar was commanded to disband his army before a specified day, on pain of being declared a public enemy. Antony and Cassius, as tribunes, interposed their *veto* against this vote. At first their right to interpose was disputed; but at length the difficulty was obviated by a vote which suspended the constitution for this purpose, and the proposed measure was carried, the opposition of the tribunes being thus set aside. The principal adherents of Cæsar in Rome immediately left the city, and fled to his camp.

Cæsar, on receiving this intelligence, acted with a promptitude and energy which astonished his enemies. He immediately sent forth his troops toward the Rubicon,—the small river which divided his province from the Italian peninsula,—entertained his friends as usual through the day, and at night followed his men in their line of march. It is said that he hesitated for a moment on the bridge over the narrow river; and then, exclaiming, "The die is cast," he passed over. Pompey, who had previously boasted that he had only to stamp with his foot to raise legions in any part of Italy, found himself utterly unprepared to meet the daring spirit of his rival in the field, supported as he was by those legions at whose head he had passed on in an uninterrupted course of conquest during the preceding eight years. It is beyond comprehension how the *imperator*, with all the power and resources of the vast Roman dominions at his beck, and with all his experience and personal influence, should have allowed himself to be taken so completely by surprise, as not to be able for a moment to meet his rival. As soon as he heard that Cæsar had passed the Rubicon, he immediately declared that he had no force in Italy equal to cope with him; and he and the senate retired from the capital with such precipitation, that they even forgot to secure the public treasures lodged in the temple of Saturn. This neglect was not thought of until they arrived at Capua, when no one dared to return and fetch them. All Italy was subdued in sixty days. Pompey sailed from Brundisium for Greece, to collect an army from the legions of that country and of Asia; while Cæsar marched in triumph to Rome.

This revolution—for such it undoubtedly was—differed essentially from every preceding assumption of absolute power in Rome. Cæsar evinced no disposition to shed blood. Even captives who fell into his hands while in armed resistance to him, he spared. This clemency produced a general feeling in his favour: nobles and senators returned to Rome; and, after a brief interval, the chief who had accomplished these wonders found the capital in such an orderly condition, that he felt quite at liberty to prosecute the war against his enemies in the provinces. He first proceeded to Spain, which had been Pompey's province, and where he had many partisans among the officers. These collected their strength, but were soon compelled to surrender to Cæsar. Marseilles held out awhile against him; but it was reduced. Here, too, he spared the lives of all captives, taking only their munitions of war and treasures. Having thus reduced all the Roman dominions in the west to his sway, Cæsar returned to Rome, where he was created dictator,—an office which he held only eleven days. Causing himself and Servilius Isauricus to be elected consuls, and the other great offices to be filled with his devoted friends, confiding the government of the city to Lepidus, and placing the troops in Italy under the command of Marc Antony, Cæsar followed Pompey into Greece.

This general had not wasted the time which had been so opportunely given him. All his influence in the east was called into requisition; and a large army—indeed, one far exceeding in number that of his opponent—was gathered, and prepared to defend his cause. On the arrival of Cæsar, both generals seemed reluctant to stake the issue on a decisive battle. After much manœuvring, a combat was fought, in which Cæsar was forced to retire with some loss, and which inspired the troops of Pompey with unbounded delight, and gave them a very false confidence as to the future.

After this conflict, Cæsar, whose army greatly needed provisions, proceeded to Thessaly; upon which the advisers of Pompey urged him to cross the narrow sea, and seize Italy; but that veteran did not dare to make a movement of such consequence. He preferred effecting a junction with a body of troops under the command of Scipio, which placed the hostile armies again in immediate proximity to each other. At length Pompey, who had evidently feared to oppose his raw levies to the veteran troops of Cæsar, confiding in his vast numerical superiority, offered battle on a plain near Pharsalia. The battle was neither very long contested, nor very bloody, although it decided the empire of the world. The cavalry of Pompey fled before the German horsemen opposed to them; and the infantry, assailed in front and flank, numerous as they were, could not resist the veteran legionaries of Cæsar. It is, indeed, probable that the real cause of this victory is found in the fact, that while the soldiers of Cæsar loved their general, felt personally interested in his cause, and were prepared to die in his service, those of Pompey, being hastily collected, had no sympathy or confidence in each other, or in their chief.

This victory made Cæsar the sovereign of the Roman empire. Pompey fled to Egypt, where he was slain. Cæsar followed, too late either to destroy, or to save the life of, his great rival, but in time to subdue Egypt after a desperate struggle. Having consolidated his conquest, he proceeded to Tarsus, passed through Cilicia and Cappadocia, and completely defeated the unnatural son of the great Mithridates in Pontus, in a war so short and effective, that it occasioned the celebrated despatch, *Veni, vidi, vici*, "I CAME, I SAW, I CONQUERED." Having established the dominion of Rome in the east, he returned to Italy, when he was again named dictator.

Returning to Rome, Cæsar found the public business deranged, and the city full of confusion, through the violent quarrels of Antony and Dolabella. Having, after some difficulty, reconciled them, the dictator sailed to Africa, where Cato with an army still maintained the cause of the fallen Pompey. His arrival was soon after followed by that of Cneius Pompey, with the remains of the host which had fought at Pharsalia. The troops of Cato and Pompey were then combined under the command of Scipio, so that it seemed as if the contest had yet to be decided, especially as Cæsar had not more than half the number of soldiers that were marching under the banners of his opponents. Strangely enough, this most perilous conquest was begun without the general's command. The celebrated tenth legion, which had been but just before almost mutinous at Rome, and had been disbanded, but afterward restored to favour, on this occasion was so determined to distinguish itself, that, when both armies were drawn up in order of battle, this body of troops rushed headlong on the enemy; and the dictator, finding it impossible to restrain them, gave the word, "Good luck," and led on the other legions to the conflict. The struggle was very short. The African elephants, on receiving the first shower of arrows, gave way, and threw the infantry into confusion, so that Scipio's legions made little resistance. This decided the fate of the world. Cato soon after killed himself at Utica; Scipio was taken and slain; Juba and Petreius fought, until the former fell, and the latter slew himself.

Cæsar now returned to Rome, and was received with the most extravagant adulation. In his triumph, his chariot was drawn by four white horses, like those of Jupiter. He was also declared dictator for ten years, and had his statue placed in the capitol, with a globe under his feet, bearing the inscription, "TO CÆSAR THE DEMI-GOD." After staying awhile at Rome, the dictator found it necessary to lead his legions again to Spain, where the sons of Pompey were in arms; but the star of Cæsar was still in the ascendant, and the last elements of the Pompeian party were crushed.

While the means by which Cæsar acquired uncontrolled dominion at Rome proved him to be the first soldier of his age, the fact that he managed to wield this power without assuming a title, or introducing a usage, unknown to the republic, or at variance with the precedents of its history, exhibits him as a profound statesman. He was created dictator, tribune, supreme pontiff, inspector of morals, and prince of the senate; so that the possession of all these legitimate offices gave him the command of the army,—a *veto* on all legislation,—the distribution of national finances. Even the order of society and the regulation of manners were placed under his cognizance; as were augury and religion, the direction of debate in the senate, as well as all executive and judicial power.

Having thus raised himself to absolute rule over the largest aggregation of nations ever formed into one government, this wonderful man contemplated vast plans, worthy of his genius and power. He prepared to revenge the defeat of the Romans under Crassus in a war with Parthia, and to make great improvements in Italy by colossal public works. But, notwithstanding the extent to which successive revolutions had prepared the Roman people for an autocracy, and although absolute rule, either in the hands of one individual, or by a domineering oligarchy, had actually governed Rome from the times of the Gracchi, there were many able and honest Romans, who mourned over the elevation of Cæsar, as the ruin of their country, and the total loss of its civil liberty. Brutus and Cassius were at the head of this party. After much deliberation, it was agreed to put an end to this absolute rule, and to restore the country to freedom by the assassination of Cæsar, on the fifteenth of March. So many persons were parties to this conspiracy, that the plot was in imminent danger of exploding before the hour arrived; and even on the morning of the day appointed for the murder, it seemed scarcely possible to prevent the whole project from being communicated to the intended victim. The plot was, however, concealed. Cæsar went to the senate-house, was there surrounded by the assassins, and fell, pierced by numerous wounds, at the foot of Pompey's statue.

Perhaps no man fills a larger space, or occupies a more prominent position, in the general history of the world, than Julius Cæsar. Whatever may be said of his ambition, it is certain that he reduced the conflicting elements of Roman society to order and harmony. He incorporated the most worthy and distinguished foreigners with the citizens, and even with the senate at Rome. He magnanimously rose above the cruel and cowardly practice of putting political opponents to death: and, as if military operations and the ordinary detail of government were insufficient to employ his unfailing energy, he, as supreme pontiff, prepared and published a correction of the calendar, which, of itself, would have immortalized his name.

Nor were the projects of Cæsar less in advance of his age than his actual achievements. He contemplated a system of legislation, and a condensed and harmonious arrangement of statutes, as a code of law, which would have anticipated the work of Justinian by six hundred years. He designed an elaborate survey of the vast regions subject to Roman dominion; and actually appointed a commission of geographers and mathematicians to construct a map so large in scale, and so full of detail, that it required no less than thirty-two years to complete the work. In addition to these, he projected emptying the Lake Fucinus,—draining the Pontine Marshes,—making a canal from Rome to Terracina,—opening a new road across the Apennines,—and cutting through the Isthmus of Corinth. The man who could do what Cæsar did, and project what he planned, was a man far too great to be simply a tyrant. That he had great faults, is undoubted; that he pursued a selfish and ambitious policy, is unquestionable: but, notwithstanding this, he will ever stand before the world as the greatest man whom Rome produced throughout the whole of her history.

On the death of Cæsar, all Rome was filled with terror. No one knew to what danger the public peace was exposed; nor on what principles those who had slain the dictator were prepared to govern the state, nor whether they were disposed to involve in the ruin of Cæsar his partisans and friends. But as he had contrived to grasp absolute power without any violation of established law, all the elements of government remained intact, and tranquillity and order were maintained until the day of Cæsar's funeral. On that occasion Marc Antony, by a studied oration over the dead body, a recital of Cæsar's will, and the exhibition of an image of the hero with his twenty-three wounds, as in the agonies of death, managed to inflame the passions of the people to such an extent, that they tore up the benches of the senate house, to burn the body on the spot; after which they attacked the houses of the principal conspirators, who were obliged to secrete themselves, in order to secure their personal safety.

Antony was ambitious to step into the position occupied by his departed patron; and his being consul at the time gave him an immense advantage in carrying out his views. In the mean time the conspirators evinced the greatest timidity and indecision, and the utter absence of all unity of purpose. Instead of regarding the death of Cæsar as the beginning of a course of measures which were to issue in the renovation of the vast republic, they acted as though it was the only result at which they aimed, and consequently gave their opponents the opportunity of defeating the object which they meant to accomplish. Antony, as Cæsar's executor, possessed all his papers, and, in addition, gained over to his service the late dictator's secretary. He then induced the senate, on the plea of preventing universal disorder, to confirm all Cæsar's acts and appointments; and managed to include in this confirmation the projects which Cæsar contemplated. This measure invested Antony with almost unlimited power. He sold appointments, gave donations, conferred magistracies, did, in fact, anything,—bringing his authority for all out of the pretended papers of Cæsar. By these means he not only repaired his own shattered finances, but was able to give a *bonus* to the soldiers, and to secure to himself important military influence. He at the same time introduced a state of things which induced Cicero to say, "The tyrant is dead; but tyranny still lives."

While Antony was pursuing this course, a new hero appeared on the stage. Octavius, a young man, eighteen years of age, a nephew of Julius Cæsar, had been adopted as his son, and left his heir, by the last will of the dictator. His friends strongly advised him, on account of his youth, to forego the perilous distinction which had been bequeathed to him; but Octavius possessed spirit equal to the emergency. He accordingly came to Rome, and boldly claimed the position which his uncle had assigned him: and when he found that he could not obtain from Antony, as his uncle's executor, a sufficient sum to pay the legacy which had been bequeathed to the Roman citizens, he sold the residue of the late dictator's estate, together with his own, borrowed what more was necessary, and paid the amount. This conduct rendered the young man extremely popular.

At length, the long-impending crisis approached. Brutus and Cassius, perceiving that Antony was preparing to sustain the position which he had assumed by force of arms, departed to the east, in the hope of inducing the Roman legions in Greece, Macedonia, and the neighbouring provinces, to assert and defend the cause of liberty. Antony retired into Cisalpine Gaul, and levied an army of veterans to support him; while Octavius, jealous of the pride and power of Antony, professed to adhere to the senate; and that august body, inflamed by the furious harangues of Cicero, sent the two consuls with their forces, accompanied by Octavius, against Antony. Between these armies two battles were fought. In the first, the consular army had the advantage; in the latter, Antony was entirely defeated, but both of the consuls were slain. This event placed Octavius at the head of the united armies of the state; while Antony fled to Lepidus, who commanded a formidable force in Spain.

In this state of affairs a negotiation took place, which reflects infamy on all the parties concerned. Octavius, who had been elected consul before he was twenty, opened a correspondence with Antony and Lepidus, which issued in the formation of a second Triumvirate. These men partitioned the power of Rome between them, on the basis of sacrificing individual friends to the blood-thirsty animosity of each other. By this sanguinary agreement, seventeen of the most eminent men in Rome, including the venerable Cicero, and great numbers of inferior note, were basely murdered. This Triumvirate was boldly proclaimed, and its terms read and ratified, in the camps of the respective officers. By this covenant, Antony, Octavius, and Lepidus were, under the title of "triumvirs," to rule over the Roman dominions conjointly. They were to have the appointment of all magistrates; and their decrees were to have the force of law, without the sanction of the senate or the people. By this treaty, the two Gauls were assigned to Antony; the two Spains to Lepidus; and Africa and the Mediterranean Islands to Octavius; Italy being regarded as held in common between them. Greece and the east were to be divided when Brutus and Cassius, who held them at the time with a republican army, should be defeated. Lepidus was then left, with his soldiers, in charge of the government at home; while Antony and Octavius, each at the head of twenty legions, marched into Greece against the forces of Brutus and Cassius.

Here the cause of liberty, which had previously perished in Italy, was staked on the issue of the war. The armies met at Philippi; and, in two great battles, the cause of the conspirators was ruined. Brutus and Cassius fell by their own swords; Antony and Octavius were triumphant, and added to their previous atrocities by their barbarous and bloody treatment of the most illustrious of the captives who fell into their hands.

After these victories, Antony proceeded to Asia, to reward his soldiers with the spoils of that country, while Octavius returned to Italy. On entering Asia, the former plunged into a course of sensual dissipation, fatal to his military success. But, on his going to Egypt, the wanton Cleopatra met him; and he at once became an unresisting captive to her charms, and fully gave himself up to a life of voluptuous indolence and unbridled dissipation. In the mean time Octavius returned to Italy. Here he found Fulvia, the wife of Antony, a proud and daring woman, exercising a powerful ascendency over the consuls, and virtually directing the government. Disputes of a serious nature soon arose between the young triumvir and the wife and brother of his absent colleague. Octavius, with his usual policy, first bestowed large gifts upon the soldiery, and then proposed to submit to their arbitration the matters in dispute between himself and Antony. The veterans, of course, accepted the offer, and cited the triumvirs to meet before them at Gabii. Octavius appeared; Antony was absent, being in Egypt: the affair, however, mightily increased the influence of Octavius with the army. Lucius Antonius, as consul, adopted a bold course, and drove the indolent Lepidus before him; but he was soon defeated by the troops of Octavius, and, being compelled to surrender, was sent into a kind of honourable exile, being appointed to a command in Spain. By this means Octavius obtained the entire direction of the affairs of Italy, and the command of all the legions in the west.

These events at length roused Antony from his besotted crime and folly in Egypt. He returned to Italy, and the state of affairs betokened a bloody struggle. But the veteran legions again insisted on an accommodation between their quarrelling commanders; and accordingly a new partition of the empire was agreed upon. Antony received Egypt and the east, with the charge of the Parthian war; Octavius was placed in possession of Italy and all the west; and Lepidus obtained Africa; while to Sextus Pompey, the only surviving son of the great triumvir, who had made himself formidable at sea, were assigned Sicily, Sardinia, and Corsica.

This hollow peace was, like many other of the Roman alliances of this period, cemented by a marriage. On his return from Egypt, Antony had treated his wife Fulvia with such neglect, that this high-spirited woman died of grief and vexation. In order, therefore, to secure a family union between Octavius and Antony, as the leading members of this alliance, it was arranged that the latter should marry Octavia, half-sister of Octavius. This being done, Antony repaired to the east, to conduct the threatened war against Parthia.

The first inroad on this alliance was a quarrel between Sextus and Octavius. The former, seeing how dependent Rome was on the sea for supplies, availed himself of his maritime power to cut these off, by which means the price of provisions at Rome was doubled. With considerable difficulty Octavius, having obtained the aid of Lepidus, drove Sextus out of Sicily, and compelled him to take refuge in the east, where he was soon after put to death by one of Antony's officers. Meantime, Lepidus determined to attempt acquiring undivided sway in the west, and, at the head of twenty legions, took possession of Messana. Octavius marched against him, and, as he had frequently done before, secured more by policy than by war. Proceeding alone and unarmed into the camp of his rival, Octavius so wrought on the soldiers, that they came over to him in a body; upon which Lepidus, finding himself abandoned, threw himself at the feet of the victor, and in the most abject terms begged his life. Octavius could afford to be merciful; so he sent his former rival into banishment, where he lived in obscurity more than twenty years.

While the adopted son and successor of the great Julius was thus making himself supreme master of all the western part of the Roman dominions, Antony, after spending some time in Greece, sent back his new wife, Octavia, to Rome, determined to devote himself to the Parthian war. But no sooner was this done, than he summoned Cleopatra to meet him in Syria; where he commenced, in her company, a fresh career of dissipation and folly. He had, indeed, so fully committed himself to the invasion of Parthia, that he could not withdraw from it; so, leaving his licentious mistress behind him, he proceeded to the east. But this war, which had been so long projected, and for which ample preparations had been made, was rashly begun, unwisely conducted, and terminated with defeat and disaster to the Roman arms.

Antony proceeded with such haste to the Parthian territory, in order to commence operations before winter, that, when he reached the first fortified city of the country, he found that he had outstripped the transit of his siege apparatus; and that, while he could not reduce the place without it, he could neither advance, leaving this strong fortress of the enemy in his rear, nor hope to receive the requisite *matériel* before winter. The Roman veteran had, therefore, no alternative but to retreat; and this inglorious movement was not effected without great difficulty and immense loss. At length, however, the Roman frontier was gained, when, instead of distributing his forces, and preparing for a more successful campaign in the ensuing spring, Antony hastened again to the arms of Cleopatra, and abandoned alike his public duty and his honour for the gratification of his vices.

Octavia did all that a virtuous matron could effect. Hearing of the reverse her husband had sustained, and knowing how he was employed, she obtained her brother's consent to visit him with such presents as were deemed suitable to his circumstances. Antony, informed of the coming of his wife, sent a message to meet her at Athens, forbidding her to proceed further; while he and the partner of his guilt went on to Alexandria. Octavia felt she could do no more to save a worthless husband from the fate he merited; so she returned to Rome, and devoted her time to the care of her children, and of those of her husband by Fulvia, his former wife. This sealed the fate of Antony; for it filled the Roman mind with disgust for the man who could act in such a vicious and contemptible manner. But, not satisfied with this conduct, he sent his wife a bill of divorce, and appointed his children by Cleopatra to kingdoms in the east, sending the notifications of this to Rome, and demanding their formal enrolment there.

It did not require this excessive amount of insult and injury to induce Octavius to prepare for war: his interest and his inclination led him to this course; and both parties saw that the sword must soon decide the fate of these rivals for power. Immense preparations were made on each side, and, as in a previous instance, Greece was again selected as the theatre of war. For a considerable period the armies lay encamped on opposite sides of the little gulf of Ambrăcia. Antony, influenced by Cleopatra, who dreaded not being able to escape in case of defeat, determined to stake the issue on the result of a sea-fight, which took place in the straits leading to the gulf. Here, while the battle was still raging, Cleopatra hoisted her sails and fled: Antony, renouncing his fame, and abandoning the troops who were shedding their blood in his cause, followed the guilty woman, and both reached Egypt in safety. But this conduct, more than the result of the battle, placed the legions of Antony in the power of Octavius. The conqueror proceeded into Asia, and, after a short period, to Egypt, where, after scarcely a struggle, Antony fell by his own sword, and Cleopatra perished by the bite of an asp, which she procured for the purpose.

Henceforth Octavius was absolute sovereign of Rome. As he did not ascend to this dignity by grasping an aggregation of republican offices, like his uncle, but as the successor of a Triumvirate which had formally assumed a power to rule irrespectively of the senate and the people, the constitution of the government became in theory, as in fact, an autocracy. With the fate of his uncle before him, Octavius took special care of his personal safety.

The Roman people seemed divested alike of all desire to retain their former liberty, and of all apprehension of tyranny. They showered every honour on Octavius,—dignified him with the appellation of *Augustus*,—actually enrolled his name in the list of deities to whom public prayers were addressed,—and in other respects treated him as divine. This wonderful man obtained this full amount of sway, B. C. 30; and in the following year he had so consolidated his power that, amid universal peace, the temple of Janus was shut. Augustus still reigned, when, according to the divine purpose, the Son of God was incarnated among men, and the God of heaven set up his kingdom in the earth. (See *Appendix*, note 82.)

CHRONOLOGICAL TABLE OF ROMAN HISTORY.

B.C.	Names and Events.	Years.
753	Rome founded.	
—	ROMULUS king.............................	36
716	NUMA fully established the Etruscan religion.	
679	TULLUS HOSTILIUS.	
640	ANCUS MARTIUS.	
618	TARQUINIUS	
	Sibylline Books bought.	
578	SERVIUS TULLIUS.	
534	TARQUINIUS SUPERBUS.	
	Rome exercises supremacy over the Latins.	
	Death of Lucretia.	
509	Expulsion of Tarquin.	
	End of the monarchy.	
508	First commercial treaty with Carthage.	
498	First Dictator appointed.	
493	Tribunes of the people created.	
445	Military tribunes.	
405	Siege of Veii begun, which lasted ten years, and led to the establishment of a standing army.	
390	Rome sacked by the Gauls.	
366	Plebeian consuls appointed.	
353	First Plebeian dictator.	
293	Census, 272,300 Roman citizens.	
264	First Punic War lasted.................	23
	Rome becomes a naval power.	
218	Second Punic War.....................	17
	Hannibal, from Spain, invades Italy, and threatens Rome.	
216	The Scipios carry on war in Spain.	
202	Battle of Zama; Carthage compelled to submit to peace.	
200	War with Philip of Macedon.........	3
192	War with Antiochus of Syria.	
	The power of Rome supreme.	
171	Macedonian war with Perseus.	

B.C.	Names and Events.
168	The battle of Pydna, when the Macedonian kingdom is destroyed.
165	Rome so enriched by the spoils of conquered nations that the citizens no longer pay taxes.
149	Third Punic War.
146	Carthage, after a desperate struggle, destroyed.
133	Tiberius Gracchus, endeavouring to introduce reforms on behalf of the people, is slain in a tumult.
123	Caius Gracchus, attempting to carry out his brother's designs, is also slain.
107	Marius six times consul.
106	Cicero and Pompey born.
100	Julius Cæsar born.
88	Bloody civil wars between the factions of Marius and Sylla, in which 150,000 Romans perish.
62	Pompey triumphs as conqueror of fifteen nations and four hundred cities.
60	First Triumvirate,—Cæsar, Pompey, and Crassus.
49	Civil war between Cæsar and Pompey.
48	Pompey slain; Cæsar master of the Roman empire.
46	Reformation of the Roman Calendar.
44	Julius Cæsar slain.
43	Second Triumvirate,—Antony, Octavius, and Lepidus.
	Bloody proscriptions; death of Cicero.
	War between Octavius and Antony.
31	Octavius, under the title of Augustus, reigns supreme over Rome.
29	Temple of Janus shut.

CHAPTER XII.

THE RELIGION OF ROME.

MISTAKEN Notion which obtains of this Religion—Rome greatly indebted to Etruria—The Religious Institutions of the Etruscans—Importance of the Establishment of these Religious Institutions in Italy, before the Rise of Rome to Power—The Etruscan Religion exhibited much important Truth and Divine Influence—Considerable Reference to Primitive Traditions, and the Recognition of a Future State and Judgment—The Founders of Rome educated in these Doctrines—All the Primitive Arrangement and Organization of Rome formed on an Etruscan Basis—Sabine and Latin Deities introduced by the Union of these Tribes—Numa and his Institutions—Reign of Tarquin—Servius Tullius—Corruptions in Theology and Image-Worship introduced—The Gods of Rome—*Dii majorum*—*Dii selecti*—*Dii minorum*—Sacred Persons—Priests—Augurs—*Fetiales*—Flamens—The Sacred Places and Rites of this Religion—Temples—Prayers—Vows—Sacrifices—Festivals—*Lupercalia*—*Bacchanalia*—*Saturnalia*—General View of the Roman Religion—Remarkable Unity maintained, notwithstanding so much Extension and Addition—Completeness of the Ecclesiastical Economy—It answered its Design so far as to pervade the public Mind with its Influence—Originally identified with many important Religious Truths—Inquiry into the Effect of this System on the People—The Knowledge of God which it gave to the People—The Opinions of Deity entertained by Philosophers—Analysis of the Religious Works of Cicero—The Result—The Philosophy of Rome afforded nothing better than Epicurean or Stoical Views of Deity—Knowledge possessed by the Romans of the Immortality of the Soul, and of Future Rewards and Punishments—Effect of this Destitution of Truth upon Roman Morals—The Description given by St. Paul—State of Domestic Manners—Condition of Slaves, and their Cruel Treatment—Horrid Cruelty displayed toward the Children of Sejanus—Awful Prevalence of Licentiousness and unnatural Impurity.

THE religion of the ancient Romans has generally been regarded as merely a recast of the Grecian mythology, with the names of its deities rendered into Latin, and its sacred ceremonies and rites adapted to the genius and state of the people. A very limited search is sufficient to show the fallacy of this notion, and the real original of this system of faith.

In tracing the early history of Rome, it was observed, that this grand ruling power arose by the daring prowess and indomitable military energy and genius of a rude, but hardy, race, who did not locate themselves in a previously unoccupied country, but obtained a settlement among, and gradually acquired paramount authority over, a more ancient and civilized, but less martial, people.

It is to this people that we are to look for the fundamental elements of the religion of Rome. For, as certainly as Rome, toward the close of her grand career, obtained a rich amount of knowledge and refinement from the conquered Greeks; so, in the early part of her course, did she receive an equally important schooling in all the arts of civilization, and the principles of religion, from the ancient Etruscans.

Our limits will not allow us to go into the disputed question of the origin of the primitive inhabitants of Etruria. A highly accomplished lady of our own country has succeeded in casting very important light on this obscure subject; and argues with great force in favour of the opinion, that this part of the Italian peninsula was first colonized by a body of people who emigrated originally from Resen in Assyria, located for some time in Egypt, and ultimately crossed the sea, and took up their residence in the province afterward called Etruria. However this may be, it is an undoubted fact, and one which will be hereafter considerably illustrated, that from hence Rome obtained her theology, ecclesiastical polity, and religious ceremonial.

It becomes important, therefore, as far as our scanty means of information will enable us, to form some definite idea of the religion of the ancient Etruscans.

The founder and patriarchal chief of Etruria was Tarchun: his origin and country are very doubtful; but he is celebrated as the founder of this ancient and cultivated state. The highly poetic tradition preserved by Cicero says, that, "while Tarchun was ploughing at Tarchunia,—most probably, ploughing the sacred foundation of its walls,—a genius arose from the deep furrow, with a child's body and a man's head, who sang to him the divinely-inspired laws of his future government, and then sank down and expired."—*Mrs. Gray's History of Etruria*, vol. i, p. 141. Further information has been gleaned respecting this legend, from which it appears, that this was the means employed for asserting the inspiration and consequent divine authority of the primitive laws of the ancient Etruscans.

Cicero calls this genius Tages, and says, he was the son of Jupiter, or the supreme god. It has been supposed that he was identical with—or, at least, an embodiment of—the same ideal representation which we find in the Phenician Tapates, or Tanates, and the Egyptian *Thoth*,—"the Coptic word which expresses 'hand,' and the man who was the first and greatest scribe, the deified writer and lawgiver of the wisest of nations."—*Ibid*, p. 142. The representation that Tages appeared with the head of a man and the body of a child, seems of easy interpretation. It clearly indicates the maturity of the wisdom which dictated the law, and the infancy of the colony which received it. At the same time, it showed the local seat of the legislation. The body politic, to whom this code was addressed, was in a state of infancy; but the laws propounded were ancient, matured, and perfect. Yet these inspired commands were not Phenician, Egyptian, or Assyrian, but Etruscan. The mysterious legislator arose from the soil of Etruria. Yet was he not a juvenile in intellect and experience: his head was that of a sage, "showing forth that his laws, full of mature wisdom and sound judgment, were yet of infant date to the land of Tarchun. He was not 'Tages transplanted from Egypt,' but 'Tages born again in this new country.' He belonged to the Resena, notwithstanding his gray hairs; he rose from their soil, and, while he appeared as the ruler of all their chiefs, he was adopted by the nation as their own child. He embodied himself in their spirit, he adapted himself to their situation, and he bade them live henceforward as a new people, in the land which God had given them."

Cicero and Censorinus say that Tarchun, on hearing the voice of Tages, at first screamed in fear, but afterward received the genius in his arms, learned his laws, which were delivered in verse, and then wrote them down. Hence arose the Books of Tages, which were twelve in number.

Some authors have, indeed, doubted whether these laws were immediately written, and suppose them to have been committed to memory, and thus disseminated. But this hypothesis is at variance with such a broad range of facts, that it is quite inadmissible. Etruria was not simply one state, but twelve; yet, throughout all these, there was a perfect uniformity of religious doctrine, and an entire unity of ceremony and discipline,—a state of things which continued throughout successive ages. This could not have been the result of merely vocal traditions. Variations in different states would inevitably arise, and time would as certainly produce changes and corruptions. Nothing but the existence of a written code could have maintained this uniformity.

The laws of Tages were received with great reverence, diligently studied and guarded, and so implicitly obeyed, that they not only gave a character and spirit to the faith of ancient Rome, but maintained their ascendency in Italy, until supplanted by Christianity. In fact, to the Romans Tages was the same as Menu to the Hindus, and, so far as the apprehension of the people extended, what Moses was to the Hebrews. Müller, indeed, calls his institutions "the Leviticus of the Romans." Servius states, that a nymph received Tages before he disappeared; but this is understood to refer to a celebrated priestess, named Bygoë, who afterward wrote a commentary on some of these laws; and so greatly distinguished herself by piety, learning, and zeal, that she was in consequence said to have nourished Tages, and sung to him.

We feel a great desire to give an explicit statement of the theology taught by the institutions of Tages; but we fear that our information is less satisfactory respecting this particular than on any other part of this religious system. We are told that "the Etruscans acknowledged only one Supreme God; but they had images for his different attributes, and temples to those images. But it is most remarkable, that the national divinity was always a triad under one roof."—*Mrs. Gray's History of Etruria*, vol. i, p. 147. Here we have again a further proof of the spread of primitive tradition, and the power which its truth had upon the minds of men, although separated to the greatest distance from the common centre of the world's primitive population. The Etruscan names for the three elements of this sacred triad were *Tina*, "Strength," *Talna*, "Riches," and *Minerva*, "Wisdom;" God being regarded as a supreme union of these prevailing attributes.

Notwithstanding the explicit manner in which this triad is said to represent these divine attributes, it seems certain that an impression of distinct personality was equally recognised. Tina, and the other gods, were called to witness on the most solemn occasions. He was specially invoked in sacred ceremonies, as at the election of Numa: "Father Tina, if it be thy will." From the expressions used on this occasion, it is certain that the Tina of the Etruscans became the Jupiter of Rome. But that people had other deities. Janus was their god of war; and is supposed to have included, not only the attributes of Mars, but also those of Saturn and Hercules. Sethlans, the god of protection against fire and other evils, very nearly corresponded to Vulcan. Pales was the Etruscan god of shepherds; Nortia, the goddess of fortune; Fides, the god of good faith: beside which, we meet with the names of other deities, such as Viridianus, Valentia, Vertumnus, Volumnus, Volumna, Voltumna, Pilumnus, and others, whose attributes are not now ascertainable. (Ancient Universal History, vol. xviii, p. 205.)

Augury was an essential element of this religion. Cicero speaks of it, in connexion with divination, as the *ars Etrusca*, and *disciplina Etrusca*. Ovid affirms that Tages was the first who taught the Etruscans a knowledge of the future; and Müller says, "Augury was considered as a covenant between God and man, where each must act his part; and the augur, in those early days, firmly believed that his thoughts and words were inspired." The most ancient and remarkable manner of Etruscan augury was by lightning. For Tarchun clearly had the means of drawing lightning from the clouds:

and the wide range of information collected by Müller proves that a command over the electric element was essential to Etruscan augury. Another important feature of this divine science was, that no augur could consult the gods, or ascertain their will, except in a place previously consecrated; and any spot so consecrated was regarded as a fane or temple. But no place was considered as a temple without such consecration. The responses obtained by lightning were always either simply affirmative or negative; while the omens furnished by the flight of birds were supposed to give more general information.

The Vestal virgins were another part of the institutions of Tarchun. These were appointed to guard and maintain the sacred flame, which was originally kindled by celestial fire,—either an electric spark, or a solar ray. This, according to some authors, was renewed every year on the first of March, and was, in the popular notion, a symbol of pure divinity. Those, however, who have carefully considered the manner of divine revelation to the primitive patriarchs, will easily discern, in this part of these sacred usages, a reference to the infolding fire of the primitive cherubim. If this sacred fire should by any neglect or accident be extinguished, it must be again relit by being drawn from heaven. These virgins were endowed with special privileges. They had the highest seats assigned them in places of public resort, and enjoyed the power of pardoning criminals whom they might meet on their way to the temple. They had the *fasces* carried before them, and were subject to no authority but that of the *pontifex maximus*, or "sovereign pontiff." These females were devoted to virginity during their term of office, which extended over thirty years; ten of which were employed in learning the duties of the office,—ten, in a performance of its duties,—and ten more, in teaching the art to their successors. If, during this term of thirty years, they were known to violate their vow of chastity, they were on conviction buried alive.

Every city and town had a principal temple, consecrated to the national triad of deities. Every city might have as many more gods, temples, and gates, as the inhabitants might choose; but it was obligatory, wherever the laws of Tages were received, to have one temple consecrated to this threefold divinity, and three sacred gates to the city. The most sacred of all the Etruscan temples was that in his own capital of Tarchunia. This, although dedicated to the triad, was usually called "the temple of Tina," he being the first of the three. Müller has given us the manner of selecting the site, and appointing the limits of the sacred spot. Tarchun, having chosen the most elevated spot, as best adapted to his purpose, close to the fortress of the city,—that the one might bless, and the other defend, the capital,—then obtained his omen that this was in accordance with the divine will. The omen was most probably a flash of lightning, which, as chief augur and *pontifex maximus*, he had the power of procuring. "He then pronounced with a loud voice, in the presence of a multitude of his people, these solemn words, in the name of Tina of the Resena: 'My temple and my sacred land shall extend so far as I please to make it holy, and to dedicate it by the mouth that now speaks. That holy object' (tree, or some other limit named) 'which I name, shall bound my temple to the east. That holy object which I name, shall bound my temple to the west. Between them I limit this temple with the drawing of lines, having surveyed it with the sight of mine eyes, after reflecting thereupon, and establishing it according to my good will and pleasure.' The augur then drew his *lituus* upon the ground, and was silent.

"This is probably what Plutarch and Tacitus call 'the prayer of consecration;' and it took place whenever the augur was called upon to make ground holy. The Etruscan lines, both on the ground and in the air, were in the form of a +, and were named *cardo*, or 'meridian,' *decumanus*, or 'horizon.' The four regions marked out by these lines were called *cardines*; and hence our word 'cardinal,' and our denomination 'cardinal points.' Each region was again divided into four; so that the ground occupied by the building contained sixteen points, each giving its peculiar augury; of which the north-east was the most fortunate; and when the augur was consulted or officiated, he placed himself in the position of the gods, who were supposed to inhabit the north.

"After the dedication of the ground was completed, the foundations which were marked out for the temple were surrounded with fillets and crowns, and then the soldiers who had happy-sounding names went in, and threw into the enclosed space branches of olive and other sacred trees. Then came the Vestals, and the children whose parents were alive; and they bathed the place in fountain and river water. Tarchun then sacrificed a bull, a sheep, and a pig: and, laying the entrails on the grass, he prayed to Tina, Talna, and M. N. V. *fa*, to bless the place. Then he touched the garlands in which the sacred corner-stone was bound, and raised it by a cord, while all the people shouted, and helped him. They then threw in metals, both worked and raw, of gold, silver, and copper, which were not dedicated to other gods, or rather to other attributes; and the ceremony was ended."—*Mrs. Gray's History of Etruria*, vol. i, pp. 151–153.

It will now be necessary to direct more particular attention to the sacred persons employed in connexion with this system of religion.

The first and principal of these was the augur. He was, in fact, in a religious sense, the human head of the people,—the visible representative of deity on earth. It was his high vocation to declare with absolute and despotic power the divine will. It was blasphemy to contradict him,—rebellion to disobey him. The augur ascertained the divine will by means prescribed in the sacred books, and then authoritatively declared and expounded it to the people. Without him there could be no election to any sacred or civil office; no king, dictator, *pontifex*, Vestal, fetial, or priest, could be called into office, or enter on its duties, but through the instrumentality of the augur. The foundation principle of all Etruscan civil and religious policy appears to be best expressed in the Scriptural maxim, " There is no power but of God : the powers that be are ordained of God." Rom. xiii, 1. It is necessary to add that the character of the deity, as exhibited by the augur, was of a highly elevated nature; but he was especially represented as having a fatherly regard for all the people, without distinction of rank or degree,—always open to their prayers, watching over their interests, punishing their crimes, rewarding their virtues, rendering it equally obligatory upon all to walk by one law, to observe one rule.

The person of the augur was sacred, and his office endured for life. He was thus raised above fear in the discharge of his duty; while he was supported at the public expense, that he might have no temptation of yielding to bribery. He was always of a noble family, no person of mean condition or low extraction being eligible to the office. It was necessary, not only that the augur should possess high birth, but also that he should be a man of sound judgment, considerable knowledge, and varied acquirements: for no general could march his army over a frontier, or across a river, engage in battle, or make a division of spoil, without the augur's permission. There could be no marriage or adoption in noble families without his consent. He could dissolve any assembly, nullify any election, and exercise a *veto* on all public business, by a declaration that such was the divine will. The power of the augur was, indeed, so great, that the danger to the state was only obviated by multiplying the number of them, and thus interposing the power of one as a check on the action of his colleague. When an augur died, his place was filled by the remaining augurs, either with or without the approval of the nobility. There was at least one augur in every city, and generally three in the most important and populous places. From a consideration of the great deference paid by all classes of society to this office, and the length of time the institution was maintained in paramount influence in Italy, it cannot be doubted that a deep religious conviction pervaded the people that the augur was, in truth, the authorized exponent of the divine mind.

The institutions of Tages in one particular greatly resembled the Hebrew dispensation. All that pertained to the national policy and institutions,—indeed the whole range of political economy and regal power,—were as much elements of divinely-appointed and religiously-regulated matters, as the most sacred services of augury or sacrifice.

Tarchun was the sovereign of the Etruscan nation. But afterward, when large cities arose as the capitals of the different provinces, a king was appointed to each of them: so that, while a common bond of nationality was recognised, each state was virtually independent, and each king absolute ruler in his own dominions, except so far as he was limited by the national statute-code of Tages.

Tarchun, with each sovereign after him, was also *pontifex maximus*, or "chief-priest." The priesthood were not a separate caste, or, indeed, a separated body from the rest of the people. In fact, every Lucumo, or noble of Etruria, was a priest, and could take auspices, being at the same time equally eligible to conduct affairs of state or to command an army in war.

From these statements it will appear that the institutions of Tages, as brought into operation by Tarchun, and made the basis of the civil and religious statute-code of Etruria, exhibited a very remarkable variety of that great spiritual assumption which we have already found to pervade all the eastern nations. Here, as well as in Assyria, Babylon, and Persia, we have a divinely-appointed and absolute sovereign,—one, too, who, in addition to regal dignity, not only holds in his own person the national high-priesthood, but is specially consecrated the representative of Deity on earth,—an authorized revealer and expounder of the will of God. We hear nothing, indeed, of the grounds on which these claims to reverential regard and divine knowledge are made to rest,—nothing of the promised Son, or expected incarnation of Deity; but, in every other respect, we have, in the combination of those three offices, all the powers and claims so proudly put forth by the sovereigns of the primitive nations of the east.

Yet, while this identity is clearly seen, it is equally apparent that it is brought before us in Etruria in a manner which seemed likely to neutralize the pernicious effects of these claims, at least to a very considerable extent. For, although all these offices centered in Tarchun, and thus gave him a *status* nearly similar to that of an

Assyrian or Persian potentate, the most sacred office of the three, namely, that of augur, was afterward given to another individual, and thus separated from the head of the state. The division of the nation into small states, or royal dominions, operated in the same direction: so that, while we perceive, in the essential elements of the Etruscan faith, a great similarity to the profane assumption of the cast, we see it so modified by future arrangements as to be prevented from working out that intolerant spiritual despotism which we have had to contemplate in those countries.

It will only be necessary to notice one other class of the sacred persons of Etruria,—the *fetiales*. These were always Lucumones, or nobles, and consequently priests. Their special function was to preside over and direct national treaties, and to seek reparation for national injury prior to the declaration of any war. When one tribe of the Etruscan nation, or any foreign state, had offended or injured any Etrurian government, the practice was to send to the offending party a deputation of *fetiales*, who, attired in a state-dress, and crowned with vervain, applied for admission to the senate. Here they stated their grievance, and asked for redress within a limited time. At the end of this period, if their representations were not attended to, they took Tina and the other gods to witness that they had performed their duty, and it was for their country to decide upon the event. On their return home, they announced to their own senate that war was now lawful. If this were resolved on, the *fetiales* returned to the frontier of the offending country, and then, casting a spear into the territory, called the gods to witness against the want of justice in that people, and their obstinacy in refusing to make reparation.

The Etruscans were a highly-civilized and well-educated people. Their arts and sciences are even now attested by imperishable monuments in every part of western Europe. But, more than this, the Etruscans were a religious people. They possessed, perhaps, as pure a theology as any Gentile nation of that period. For, although recognising a plurality of deities, they appear to have still retained their knowledge and reverence of one supreme governing God, whose will they professed to seek, and by whose laws they sought to walk. To what extent their devotion and obedience were sincere and effectual, we cannot now pretend to determine; but thus much is evident,—that they regarded God as the Father and Governor of men. They recognised his watchful care, believed in his ever-pervading providence, and continually taught the necessity of doing everything, public and private,—things of the least concern, and of the greatest magnitude,—in direct accordance with the divine will.

It is a remarkable fact, and one that has been too much overlooked, in the providential dispensations of God toward mankind,—that, prior to the rise of Rome to fame and dominion, this people were brought to Italy, established in power, and permitted to extend the influence of their civilization, science, and religion throughout that peninsula. From the Tiber, the southern frontier of Etruria Proper, their authority extended to Cisalpine Gaul; and their influence, potent in every respect, had a far wider range.

It was not by accident or chance that the band of martial spirits who began to rear up the fourth great monarchy,—which was to extend its rule over all the nations of the world, and usher in the glorious kingdom of God,—laid the foundation-stone of their political power in immediate proximity to this civilized and religious people. It cannot be doubted that the influence of Etruscan civilization and religion formed the manners, and moulded the character, of Rome. This being the fact, it would be very desirable to form a correct estimate of the Etruscan system of faith: but we have not information sufficient for this purpose. It is certain that this people retained among them a large portion of patriarchal truth; that by it they were led to a general and effective recognition of the government and providence of God, and the vital importance of entire subjection to the divine will; that prayer was a well-ascertained and frequently-practised duty; and, indeed, that they acknowledged that man's whole course of life on earth should be shaped according to the will of Heaven. Now it is impossible to account for the knowledge of such doctrines, and the existence of such practices, without admitting the action of a considerable amount of divine truth, and the presence of a large measure of divine influence. It is true that the theology of the people was becoming corrupt, and a multiplicity of inferior deities had begun to be introduced; but, prior to the foundation of Rome, it does not appear that this defection had become either so extensive, or had so fatally infringed on the prerogatives of the Supreme Deity, as to have materially affected the faith of the people, or their confidence in the divine administration.

There is abundant evidence, in the pictures and sculptures of the early Etruscan tombs, to attest the prevalent belief of the people in the primitive traditions, and in the doctrines of the immortality of the human soul, and of a future judgment. No eye familiar with Layard's "Monuments of Nineveh" can look over the elegant coloured plates of Mrs. Gray's "Sepulchres of Etruria" without perceiving the constant recurrence of the symbolical tree of life. Between every pair of figures in the painting or sculpture, in every variety of form, in the frieze and other ornamental portions of the architecture, the tree, its fruit and foliage, are always to be discerned.

Then, as to the future existence of the soul, numerous most significant pictures convey the ideas entertained by this ancient people. One or two instances will be sufficient to prove this. In the Grotto del Cardinale there is a remarkable frieze, representing a procession of souls to judgment, attended by good and evil angels; the former being represented white, and the latter black. In one instance, a singular struggle is seen between a good and an evil angel for the possession of a person, whose character was of such doubtful quality, that while the evil angel endeavours to draw off the car on which the spirit sits, the other interposes his power; and the group is seen standing still during the progress of the contest. In the Grotto del Tifone there is another remarkable painting, exhibiting a procession of souls. This is led by a good angel with a flambeau, who is followed by several spirits. Then comes an evil angel, whose complexion is black, and whose features are an ugly distortion of a negro countenance. Other souls follow this figure; and the procession is closed by another black evil angel, similar to the former. All the angels, good and bad, have living serpents about their heads, or in their hands. These have been supposed to symbolize eternity; but we rather incline to think them an intelligible and living exhibition of that form under which the great tempter introduced death and all its fearful consequences into the world.

However this may be, the angelic contest for the possession of a spirit, and the joyous appearance of the souls near the good angel, and the agonized aspect of those in proximity to the bad ones, clearly evince a firm belief in the doctrine of future rewards and punishments. Surrounded with a civilized population imbued with these religious views and doctrines, Rome was founded, and rose up into power.

We will proceed to notice those stages in the progress of Roman history which had a special influence on the foundation of the national faith.

If we may rely on Plutarch, it seems that Numitor brought up Romulus and Remus at an Etruscan college, and gave them all the instruction usually imparted to princely Lucumones. They would, therefore, be taught everything necessary to the performance of the service of the priesthood, of which every Lucumo was a member. When the two brothers, with their band of followers, went forth from Alba to found a new settlement, they were attended by augurs; and the site of Rome was selected by the divination of augury, according to the Etruscan usage. It has been remarked as a singular fact, that the religious guides of the new settlers should not be Alban augurs, or Latin priests, but Etruscans. Plutarch, in Vitâ Romuli, adds, that Romulus sent to Etruria for special assistance, and had the whole city and its arrangements and policy directed according to the religious mysteries, ceremonies, and written laws, of that people. So exact, indeed, was this attention to sacred guidance, that Rome from the first was called " the Holy City."

After the singular junction of the Romans and Sabines, as had been distinctly stipulated in the treaty, the Romans were bound to adopt the Sabine theology, laws, and customs, wherever these differed from those previously in use: and as the religion of the Sabines was essentially the same as that of Etruria, it followed that in future the religion of Rome must be entirely Etruscan. Under this arrangement, twelve altars were built, on which sacrifices were offered to the following deities,—Vidius, Jupiter, Saturn, Sethlans, Summanus, Vesta, Terminus, and Vertumnus. These were all Etruscan gods. To these were added Quirinus, or Mars,—a deity peculiar to the Sabine people,—with Ops, Hora, Sol, Luna, Diana, and Lucina, which were divinities common to the Sabines and the Latins.

From this statement it will be seen that while Rome secured all the advantages derivable from the civilization, learning, and religious doctrines of Etruria, she also received, at the very outset of her national career, an increased tendency to polytheism, by the incorporation of Sabine and Latin gods with those of Etruria.

Romulus also appointed two Vestals,—one from the Roman, and the other from the Sabine nation,—who were installed priestesses of Vesta. He also established a college of the Salii, or dancing priests of Mars; and he dedicated the Campus Martius without the walls to Mars, who, as Quirinus Mavors, or Marte, was common to the three nations. Temples were also built to the Etruscan Sethlans and Janus, the latter of whom had henceforth two heads, to represent the union of the two nations.

The prevalence of Etruscan institutions at Rome during the early part of its history may be inferred from another important fact. Neither Plutarch nor any other author of credit ascribes one single invention to Romulus: yet it is certain that in his time there were kings, palaces, colleges, augurs, priests, temples, shrines, ceremonial services, and, in short, all the elements of a state-religion in the full development of a broad and efficient economy.

Numa, the Sabine, succeeded Romulus. He was an eminently pious prince, and would not adorn himself with the ensigns of royalty, even when fully elected by the senate and people, until the augurs declared his appointment to this supreme office to be in accordance with the divine will. He instituted a body of priests, called *pontifices*, who were to have special charge of a bridge which he caused to be built across the Tiber, and who were bound to keep a feast of union on this bridge. Numa established a college of *fetiales*, twelve in number. He also instituted several other colleges, and appointed flamens, or hereditary priests, of particular gods: such as the flamen of Quirinus and Romulus, the flamen of Jupiter, the flamen of Mars,—whose wives were priestesses. This sovereign also doubled the number of the Vestal virgins, and built a circular temple to the goddess Vesta, where the fire was ever kept burning. Numerous other additions were made by him to the institutions of the religion of Rome; and all these were done in the spirit of the original books of Tages, that is, by professed revelation. Numa alleged that he was divinely taught through the medium of the nymph Egeria; and, to render the laws which he founded on these revelations of the greatest benefit to his people, he had them written, and caused the priests of Rome to get them by heart. It is a singular fact, and one which, fairly considered, greatly confirms the view which has been taken in the foregoing pages,—that, although Rome was a martial state, and acquired her supremacy by successful wars, yet the most prosperous of her early reigns, and those which did most to consolidate the national power, were those of the most peaceful and religious of her kings: and of these the rule of Numa is a remarkable example.

Some readers may imagine that the manner in which we speak of this subject is in contradiction to the doubts which are expressed in the preceding pages with respect to the history of Rome at this period. We beg, however, to observe, that we think those doubts to be perfectly warranted, and in fact imperatively called for, by the nature of the evidence upon which the history of this period rests. But it is very evident, that the civilized and religious condition of Etruria prior to the foundation of Rome, and the influence of this civilization and religion on the condition of Rome, and the religious institutions brought into operation during the early period of Roman history, are much more clearly authenticated than the names of kings, or the marvellous and improbable exploits frequently ascribed to them. If, therefore, it should be proved that no such prince as Numa ruled in Rome, we should nevertheless be compelled to believe that, about the time ascribed to his reign, the religion of Rome, which had been previously raised on an Etruscan basis, was greatly developed, extended, and strengthened by the addition of many important rites and institutions.

Plutarch mentions a tradition of this king,—that, while engaged in a religious service, he was informed that the enemy was at the gates; to which he simply replied, "I am sacrificing,"—as if to intimate that, while engaged in the service of the gods, he felt perfectly secure of divine protection. The same authority states, that at this period there were no images of any deity in Rome; from which it has been inferred, that such images were common at that time in other parts of Italy. But this is altogether unwarranted by the language of this eminent biographer. His words are: "Numa forbade the Romans to represent the Deity in the form either of man or beast. Nor was there among them formerly any image or statue of the Divine Being. During the first hundred and seventy years, they built temples, indeed, and other sacred domes, but placed in them no figure of any kind; persuaded that it is impious to represent things divine by what is perishable, and that we can have conception of God but by the understanding. His sacrifices, too, resembled the Pythagorean worship; for they were without any effusion of blood, consisting chiefly of flour, libations of wine, and other very simple and unexpensive things."—*Plutarch, in Vitâ Numæ.*

From this it appears that the absence of image-worship at Rome arose from elevated views of the divine nature; that the several deities worshipped were regarded more as separate attributes than as truly divine personalities; and that there is every probability that these views extended as wide as the influence of the Etruscan faith. The degeneracy of image-worship was brought into Rome by Lucius Tarquin, who introduced figures in human form as objects of adoration.

The remark of Plutarch, as to there being no bloody sacrifices at Rome in the time of Numa, must be taken with some limitation: for the offerings of a bull, a sheep, and a pig were coeval with the foundation of Rome, and were used under the sway of all her Latin and Sabine kings. It was probably only meant to intimate that Numa did not introduce any new sacrifices of this kind, notwithstanding his extensive additions to the ritual code in other respects.

The first Tarquinian dynasty is only remarkable, in respect of religion, for the glimpse which it affords of the story of the Sibylline Books. The account of the circumstance is as follows:—An old woman presented herself before the king, and offered to sell him nine books for three hundred pieces of gold. Being repulsed, she went away, burnt three, and, returning, demanded the same price for the six which remained. Being again refused, she burnt three more, and demanded the same sum for the remaining three, threatening to destroy those, unless the money was paid. Struck with her manner, the king repented, and purchased the books; after which the prophetess vanished.

The reign of Servius Tullius exhibits the further progress of change in the primitive elements of the national faith. We find that at this period the simple Etruscan triad had sunk into oblivion, and the idea was only retained in giving the designation of "the triune Jupiter" to the great god whom the Tuscans and Albans united to worship, both at Alba and Laurentum. It is further observable, that in the space of a little more than a century, which elapsed from the death of Numa to that of Servius, the progress of image-making and of respect for images was such, that at the latter period there was an image of the reigning monarch, made of wood and richly gilt, standing in one of the temples of Fortune in the city of Rome.

It would be vain to attempt to trace in detail the further change and extension of the religion of Rome. That state having entered on a career of conquest, every new province increased the number of national divinities, and added to the common stock of mythologic fable and religious doctrines, until at length, when the Roman power became paramount throughout Egypt, the north of Africa, and a great part of Asia, the religion of the Romans was, in the widest sense, the religion of the world. In treating on this subject, we must of course limit our consideration to that aggregate of religious elements which had become recognised by the state, in the imperial city, as the national religion. Of this it will be our endeavour to convey some idea. But the subject is full of difficulty, —not only from the immensity of its range, and from the fact that the Romans themselves never reduced their religion to a system,— but also because the information actually procurable can only be collected in detached fragments, and is but seldom found connected with any recognition of real religious principle or truth.

In proceeding to sketch the principal elements of this religion, it will be necessary, as in other instances, to commence with its theology. But this at once presents to our consideration a range of polytheism beyond anything witnessed in any other nation of the world.

The Romans divided their deities, as they did their senators, into several sections or classes. The first or highest rank of divinities were called *dii majorum gentium*. These were the great celestial gods: they were twelve in number. Of these, 1. The first and chief was JUPITER; 2. His wife and sister, JUNO; 3. MINERVA or PALLAS; 4. VESTA; 5. CERES; 6. NEPTUNE; 7. VENUS; 8. VULCANUS; 9. MARS; 10. MERCURIUS; 11. APOLLO; 12. DIANA.

These are generally given with the genealogy according to the Greek system of mythology; but it is very certain that this hypothesis neither explains the origin of these deities, nor the opinions of the Romans on that subject. JUPITER is set down as the son of Saturn and Rhea, and is said to have been born and educated in Crete, where he dethroned his father, and divided his kingdom with his brothers. But nothing is more certain than that the Roman Jupiter had his origin in the Tina of the Etruscans, sometimes worshipped as the triune Jupiter, and evidently the patriarchal deity of Etruria. JUNO, according to the faith of ancient Rome, was merely a female impersonation of the attributes of Jupiter. It does not appear that those from whom the Romans received the elements of their religious system had any deity corresponding to MINERVA; so that this divinity was probably imported from Greece. VESTA was an Etruscan goddess, patroness of the sacred fire. CERES is identical with the Greek goddess Demeter. NEPTUNE seems to be equally an importation from Greece; and VENUS is another of the same class. There is not the slightest trace of any such licentious impersonation in the Etrurian Pantheon. The Roman original VULCANUS was Sethlans, the Etruscan god who gave protection against fire and other cognate evils. MARS, the martial deity, was worshipped by the Etruscans as Janus, and by the Sabines under the name Quirinus. These appear to have been united by the Romans, and adored under the name of Mars, to whom were ascribed the attributes and origin of the Greek Ares. MERCURIUS was the Greek Hermes. APOLLO was introduced from Greece. DIANA, as a goddess, was common to the Sabines and Latins; but, after the introduction of Greek manners, the worship of this divinity was associated with the mythological account of the Greek Artemis, as a female impersonation of the attributes of Apollo.

These twelve constituted the principal deities of Rome: they were in fact the great gods of the nation, during the later period of its history. They were also called *dii consentes*,—an epithet which seems to cast light on the origin of Etruscan polytheism. The term is supposed to be derived from the verb *conso*, that is, *consulo*, and to have been originally applied to the twelve Etruscan deities who formed the council of the supreme god. It seems, therefore, that the notion of a council subservient to the will of the great god having obtained currency, the supposed members of this body were, in process of time, worshipped as divine, and termed *dii consentes*,— a term which was afterward applied to the twelve superior deities of Rome. The first ruling power ascribed by the Etruscans to these deities, was the government of the world and of time; a fact which perhaps accounts for the attributes ascribed to the Roman deities in after-times.

The Roman gods of the second section were termed *dii selecti*, and were eight in number:—1. SATURNUS, the god of time; 2. JANUS, the god of the year, who presided over the gates of heaven; 3. RHEA, the wife of Saturn, who was also called Ops, Cybele, *Magna Mater*, &c.; 4. PLUTO, brother of Jupiter, and sovereign of the infernal regions; 5. BACCHUS, the god of wine; 6. SOL, the Sun, who was sometimes regarded as identical with Apollo, and at others as of totally different origin; 7. LUNA, a female impersonation of the moon, the daughter of Hyperion, and sister of Sol; 8. GENIUS, the tutelary god supposed to preside over and protect an individual, from his birth to the end of his life.

It will be necessary to remark further on this section of Roman theology. SATURN, although generally identified with the family of Olympus, was an Etruscan deity. JANUS, who is here set over the year and the gates of heaven, was originally the Etruscan god of war; and hence, although, after the Romans conformed to the Greek mythology, Janus is superseded by Mars as the deity of war, and retires to the more peaceful presidency of rolling time, he is still, in accordance with his primitive character, so far recognised as concerned in the peaceful or warlike condition of the nation, that his temple was open in time of war, and shut during the season of peace. RHEA was generally described as a pregnant matron; but, in the later portion of Roman history, she was worshipped under the name of Cybele, and was represented by the figure of a cubical block of stone, which was brought with great pomp from Pessinus in Phrygia to Rome during the second Punic war.

PLUTO was the brother of Jupiter, and husband of Proserpine, the daughter of Ceres, whom he carried off, as she was gathering flowers on the plains of Sicily. Associated with this infernal deity were other divinities of an inferior rank, such as the Fates or Destinies,— Clotho, Lachesis, and Atropos; the Furies,—Alecto, Tisiphone, and Megæra, represented with wings, and snakes twisted in their hair, holding in their hands a torch and a whip to torment the wicked; *Mors*, "Death," and *Somnus*, "Sleep;" and others of less note.

BACCHUS, the son of Jupiter and Semele, was attended by Silenus, his nurse and preceptor, and by Bacchanals and Satyrs. Priapus, the god of gardens, whose worship was celebrated by emblems of the most gross indecency, was the son of Bacchus and Venus. SOL, "the Sun," was painted in a juvenile form, attended by the *Horæ*, or four Seasons,—*Ver*, "the Spring;" *Æstas*, "the Summer;"

Auctumnus, "the Autumn;" and *Hiems,* "the Winter." LUNA, "the Moon," is represented as the sister of Sol.

GENIUS, the demon or protecting god, was at first regarded as a tutelary spirit, which was supposed to preside over and to direct the actions of each individual. Some, indeed, held that there were two such,—one good and the other bad,—attending each person throughout his whole life; so that under this term we have a multitude of spiritual existences. Although, in the early ages, these spirits were regarded only as subordinate ministers of the gods, they were at length elevated to be the objects of adoration, had altars and statues reared to them, and extensively received divine honour.

Of the same kind as the Genii were the Lares and Penates, household gods who presided over families. These have frequently been confounded, as if they were identical; but this is an error. The Lares were human spirits, who were at first treated with reverence, and afterward received adoration, either from members of their family,—and, as such, were called *Lares domestici,*—or, on the contrary, from the people, who awarded them national honour for their noble and patriotic conduct: these latter were consequently designated *Lares publici*. The name *Lar* is Etruscan, and signifies "lord," "king," or "hero." The Lares were, therefore, the honoured or deified spirits of men who, after their death, were, either from fraternal regard or patriotic gratitude, revered or worshipped.

The Penates, however, were divine, and must be regarded strictly as household gods. Although sometimes spoken of as sustaining the same character, the Lares and Penates differed in this important particular:—there was never but one Lar revered in one family,—the hero-deity of the family; while the Penates are almost always spoken of in the plural, there being several deities revered as the guiding and protecting gods of the house.

We have next in order to mention the third section of Roman deities,—the *dii minorum gentium,* or inferior gods. These were of various kinds, and ranged over so wide an expanse of imaginative creation, that only a few of the most prominent can have individual notice.

The first portion of these were the *dii indigetes,* or heroes who had been raised to the rank of deities.

Hercules may be named as one of the first of this class. His name, character, and labours are well known, and require no particular elucidation. Castor and Pollux, sons of Jupiter and Leda; Æneas, sometimes called *Jupiter Indiges;* and Romulus Quirinus, with a host besides, belong to this class. Indeed, during the later ages of Roman history, it was regarded as a usual and necessary compliment to an emperor, to declare him a god immediately on his death.

Another section of the *dii indigetes* were termed *Semones*, probably from *Semi-homines*. Among these were Pan, the god of shepherds, and inventor of the flute, represented with horns and goat's feet; Faunus and Sylvanus; Vertumnus, an old Etruscan deity, who presided over the change of seasons and merchandise; Pomona, the wife of Vertumnus, the goddess of gardens and fruits; Flora, goddess of flowers; Terminus, an Etruscan deity, the god of boundaries, whose temple was always open at the top; Pales, a deity who presided over flocks and herds; Hymen, the god of marriage; and Laverna, the patroness of thieves. It is, indeed, difficult and unnecessary to enumerate all these imaginative creations. Respite from business was adored as a deity; bad smells,—common sewers, —were each represented in this section of divinities. Here, also, the Nymphs, who presided over every part of the earth, are found. Every river had its presiding deity, and the head or source of each was particularly sacred. Mountains and woods were equally favoured.

The judges of hell also belong to the Semones. The Romans worshipped in the same category all the virtues and affections of the mind,—Piety, Faith, Hope, Fortune, Fame; and even bodily diseases, such as Fever, &c., were adored as divine. It is scarcely possible to conceive of a more widely spread polytheism than this; which reached to such an extent that, notwithstanding the immense population of the imperial capital in the season of its glory, it was said that the gods were in Rome more numerous than men.

We proceed to notice, in the next place, the several orders of sacred persons, or ministers of religion, who were appointed to conduct the services of this religion.

Here it may be observed, as a preliminary remark, that in Rome there was no holy caste. No man, however elevated the religious office or appointment which he held, was thereby precluded from pursuing the ordinary avocations of life. The chief of the augurs, or the first priest of the nation, might at the same time be a soldier, an advocate in courts of law, or fill any other public or private office. It should be further noticed that the priesthood of Rome was of two kinds,—the first being common to all deities, and the other being limited to the service of some particular divinity. The superior priests of Rome were called *pontifices;* those of a more ordinary character, *sacerdotes.*

The origin of the word *pontifex* is extremely doubtful. The most probable solution is that it is formed from *pons* and *facere*, (in the signification of the Greek ῥέζειν, "to perform a sacrifice,") and that it consequently signifies "the priests who performed sacrifices upon the bridge." The ancient sacrifice to which this alludes was that of thirty men, or in later ages images of men, which were cast from the sacred or Sublician bridge, just after the vernal equinox, on the Ides of May. (Dionysius Halicarnasseus, lib. i, cap. 38.)

These sacred officers were the most illustrious among the great colleges of the priests. There can be no doubt that the institution had an Etruscan origin. The first time we hear of it in Roman history is in the reign of Numa, who, having built the *Pons Sublicius* across the Tiber, appointed *pontifices* to take charge of it, and to offer annual sacrifices there. At first there were four *pontifices*, Numa being the first, or *pontifex maximus*, and Marcius, one of the noblest of the Sabines, being one of the other four. For a long time after the institution of this order, when one of the pontiffs died, (for the office was always conferred for life,) the remaining *pontifices* filled up the vacancy. In 300 B. C., the Ogulnian law raised the number of *pontifices* to eight besides the *pontifex maximus*, four of whom were plebeians. This number was continued until the dictator Sylla raised the number to fifteen, and Julius Cæsar afterward to sixteen. In both these changes the *pontifex maximus* is included in the number.

The vocation of the *pontifices* is explicitly stated by Dionysius and Livy. It was their duty to act as judges in all matters pertaining to religion, whether private men, magistrates, or ministers of the gods were concerned. The first *pontifices* received a code of written laws from Numa. What was not thus exacted for every religious ceremonial, the *pontifices* had to supply. They had to inquire into the conduct of all persons to whom the performance of any sacrifice or religious service was intrusted. The priesthood, of every order or kind, were subject to their authority. Besides which, they were the teachers of religious law, and the interpreters of everything connected with the ceremonial service of the gods. They had also to take cognizance of all disobedience of religious rule, and inflict such punishment as they might think fit. They were accordingly called "teachers," "ministers," "guardians," and "interpreters, of holy things."—*Dionysius Halicarnasseus*, lib. ii, cap. 73; *Livy*, lib. i, cap. 20. In the execution of this important range of duties, the pontiffs were entirely independent, and were not responsible either to the senate or to the people.

The original sacred laws of Numa, having received considerable additions, were in process of time published,—at least, such parts of them as related to ritual law. At first, the *pontifex maximus*, although, like the other members of the college, he might hold any civil or military employment, was not allowed to leave Italy: but P. Licinius Crassus violated this usage; and his example was frequently followed with impunity, as by Julius Cæsar when he went to his province of Gaul.

The great body of the Roman priesthood may be considered under two distinct heads,—the first including, besides the *pontifices*, the augurs and the *fetiales;* the second, the *flamines*. The augurs were in Etruria called *auspices*, or *haruspices*. This, as we have seen, was an Etruscan institution, and in Rome was coëval with the first reign. Romulus appointed three augurs; Servius Tullius added one more; the tribunes increased the number to nine, and Sylla to fifteen. The practice continued long after the introduction of Christianity, and was with difficulty set aside by the influence of the gospel.

The duty of the augurs was to ascertain and make known the will of the gods, mainly for the purposes of state, or the direction of national affairs. The several augurs formed together a separate sacred college, under the presidency of the chief augur, who was called *magister collegii*. The augur usually made his observations at midnight, or during twilight. Taking his station on an elevated place, he offered up sacrifice and prayer, and then sat down with his head covered, and his face turned toward the east. Then he fixed his mind on the space, before he decided on the limits within which he would look for the expected signification of the divine will. This was gathered, according to their belief and practice, from five several sources:—1. Thunder, lightning, meteors, comets, &c.; 2. The chirping or flying of birds; 3. The manner in which the sacred chickens took or refused their food; 4. The peculiar appearance of certain animals; 5. Sundry other particulars, termed *dira*. They were directed in the performance of their duties by a threefold body of law and instruction: 1. The formularies and traditions of the college, which in ancient times met on the Nones of every month; 2. The *Augurales Libri*, which were regarded as divinely-authorized directions for this sacred service; 3. The *Commentarii Augurum*, such as those of Messala and of Appius Claudius Pulcher. These were studied as the best directions which the researches of wise men could afford for the proper discharge of these duties.

The power of the augurs with regard to these supposed manifestations of the divine will went far beyond that of the highest civil magistrates. The first had the power to interdict any public procedure by declaring the auspices to be unfavourable; the latter could only do so by giving previous notice of their intention. The influence of the augurs was greatest in the early ages of Roman history. In later times, the power of the tribunes frequently interfered with their authority; and in many other respects the augurs were coerced by the civil power.

The *fetiales* composed another sacred college, which was established on an Etruscan basis, and acted as protectors of the public faith. In Rome, as before in Etruria, this section of the priesthood was charged with the duty of conducting a kind of religious negotiation prior to any declaration of war. This was done just in the same manner as that previously described as obtaining among the Tuscans. The presence of the *fetiales* was so indispensable in the ratification of a treaty of peace, that, on the termination of the second Punic war, *fetiales* were sent over to Africa, who carried with them their own *verbenæ*, and their own flint-stones, for smiting the victim to be sacrificed.

These several kinds of priests were not devoted to any particular deity, but were common to all the gods, and consequently stood connected with the whole range of the national faith, and identified with all its wide scope of worship and ceremonial service.

On the contrary, the flamens were priests individually devoted to the service of some particular divinity. The name was given them from a cap, or fillet, which they wore on their head. The principal of these were the following:—

1. *Flamen Dialis*, "priest of Jupiter." This order was first appointed by Numa; but the priests were afterward elected to office by the people; after which they were solemnly inaugurated, and admitted to the performance of sacred functions, by the *pontifex maximus*. The flamen of Jupiter held an office of great dignity, but one associated with many inconvenient restrictions. He was not allowed to ride on horseback, nor to stay one night without the city, nor to take an oath, nor to wear a ring. He was forbidden to touch, or to name, a dog, a she-goat, ivy, beans, or raw flesh; with many other restrictions of an equally incomprehensible kind. The regulations respecting the *flaminica*, or flamen's wife, were no less stringent. He was required to wed a virgin according to the most sacred rites of religion; and he was not allowed to marry a second time: consequently, as the assistance of the *flaminica* was essential to the proper performance of some parts of the flamen's religious duties, on the death of his wife he was obliged to resign his office.

2. *Flamines Salii* were priests similar to the preceding, but devoted to the service and worship of Mars. They were twelve in number, and were instituted by Numa. They received this name because they were accustomed, in some of the sacred services, to go

through the streets of the city dancing, dressed in an embroidered tunic, bound with a brazen belt, having on their head a cap rising to a considerable height in the form of a cone, with sword, spear, and one of the *ancilia*, or shields of Mars. They used to go to the capitol, through the forum and other public parts of the city, singing sacred songs as they went. The most solemn procession of the Salii was on the first of March, in commemoration of the time when the sacred shield was said to have fallen from heaven in the reign of Numa. No one could be admitted into the order of the Salii, unless he were a native of the place, free-born, and one whose father and mother were alive. After the close of their solemn procession, the Salii had a splendid entertainment prepared for them. Tullus Hostilius doubled the number of these priests.

3 *Flamines Luperci* were the priests of Pan, and so called because they were supposed to protect the sheep from wolves. Hence the place where this deity was worshipped was called *Lupercal*, and his festival *Lupercalia*, celebrated in February; at which time the Luperci ran up and down the city with only a goat-skin about their waists, and thongs of the same in their hands, with which they struck those whom they met, especially married women, who were supposed thereby to be rendered prolific. There were three companies of Luperci, two of them of very ancient origin, named Fabiani and Quintiliana; and, in more recent times, the third was added in honour of Julius Cæsar. The first chief-priest of this section was Marc Antony; and it was while acting in that capacity at the Lupercalia, that he went almost naked into the Forum Julii, and, having delivered an address to the people, tendered to Cæsar a golden crown. The Luperci were one of the most ancient orders of priests, it being said that they were instituted by Evander.

The flamens of these three orders were also selected from Patricians. At first they were appointed by Numa; but afterward they were elected by the people. It is supposed that the *pontifex maximus*, when there was a vacancy, selected three persons, of whom the people chose one.

4. The fourth order of flamens were called *Politii* and *Pinarii*, and were priests of Hercules. These are also said to have been instituted by Evander. They jointly conducted the worship of Hercules for a long time, until the *Pinarii*, by either the advice or the authority of Appius Claudius, delegated their ministry to public slaves, soon after which the whole race became extinct.

5. *Flamines Galli* were the priests of Cybele, Mother of the Gods. They were so called because they were all mutilated. They used to carry the image of Cybele through the streets of the

city, imitating the actions and gestures of madmen, rolling their heads and beating their breasts to the music of the flute, and making a great noise with drums and cymbals. Sometimes they would gash their flesh, and utter dreadful predictions. The rites of Cybele were characterized by gross indecency.

The last sacred class which it will be necessary to mention, as devoted to the worship and service of a particular deity, is the Vestal virgins. Their original appointment and vocation have been already noticed: they were priestesses of Vesta. At first they were nominated by the king; but, after the subversion of royalty, on the occasion of a vacancy, the *pontifex maximus* selected twenty girls, between the age of six and sixteen; and from these one was chosen by lot to the vacant office of Vestal.

It was the duty of the Vestals to keep the sacred fire always burning, watching it alternately day and night. Whoever allowed it to go out was scourged; and the extinguishing of the fire was esteemed a great public calamity, and could only be expiated by extraordinary sacrifices. The fire, after being extinguished, was lit from the sun's rays, as it always was on the first of March in each year. The senior or principal of the virgins was called *Vestalis maxima;* and to her care it is supposed the Palladium was confided. The sacred rites of the goddess were wholly performed by the Vestals; and their prayers and invocations were always regarded as having efficient influence with the gods.

When a Vestal violated her vow of chastity, she was tried by the *pontifices*, and, being convicted, was buried alive with due funeral solemnities. Her paramour, if discovered, was scourged to death.

These were the ministers of the national faith who held a leading position in the metropolis, and were consequently regarded as possessing an important religious character. But, necessary as it is to understand their office and duty, it is even more important to have a clear idea of the means adopted to pervade the public mind throughout the land with religious sentiments, and to direct them in their worship. In this respect the religion of Rome, from the foundation of the city, presents an aspect of peculiar importance. Here, as in many other instances, Romulus, adopting an Etruscan institution,—by which, under the laws of Tages, the people and territory of Etruria were regularly divided into tribes and *curiæ*,—first parted his citizens into three tribes, and then each tribe into ten *curiæ*,—thus separating the people into thirty sections. Having done this, we are told that "he divided the land into thirty equal portions, and gave one of them to each *curia*, having first set apart as much of it as was sufficient for the sacrifices and temples, and also reserved some part of the land for the use of the public."—*Dionysius Halicarnasseus*, lib. ii, cap. 7.

This series of divisions of both the land and the people was not made merely for civil or political purposes, but also with a view to the establishment of efficient religious institutions. Indeed, Romulus is celebrated as being without an equal in his care for the religion of his people. "No man can name," says the author of the "Roman Antiquities," "any newly-built city in which so many priests and ministers of the gods were ordained from the beginning: for, without mentioning those who were invested with family priesthoods, threescore were appointed in his reign to perform divine service, both in the tribes and the *curiæ*. Whereas others generally make choice of such as are to preside over religious matters in a mean and inconsiderate manner; some thinking fit to make public sale of this honour, others disposing of it by lot; he would not suffer the priesthood to be either venal or distributed by lot; but made a law, that each *curia* should choose two persons, both above fifty years of age, of distinguished birth and virtue, competent fortune, and without any bodily defect. These were not to enjoy their honours during any limited time; but for life, freed from military employments by their age, and from the cares of civil government by this law."—*Dionysius Halicarnasseus*, lib. ii, cap. 21.

It is scarcely possible to overrate the importance of this statement. We have here, at the very outset of Roman history, a geographical division of that country, and two ministers of religion placed in special charge of the religious interests of the people of each district. It must be freely admitted that this usage was adopted from Etruria; but whencesoever it was derived, is it not the first time we ever meet with a territorial appointment of ministers of religion? Here we have unquestionably the origin of parishes and of a parochial clergy. Nowhere else, either among the Hebrews or the Gentiles, do we find anything approaching to this geographical division of the people into religious cures.

It does not appear that these priests, or, in fact, those of any other order, received any regular stipend for the performance of their religious functions. It rather seems that the honour and the *status* thus obtained, were regarded as a sufficient remuneration. Romulus is said to have set apart sufficient land to provide for the sacrifices and sacred rites which were enjoined; and Livy also states that Numa, who appointed the greatest number of priests and sacrifices, provided a fund for defraying these expenses. But this outlay, except in the case of the Vestal virgins, who had a regular salary, must not be taken to include anything more than the repairs of the temples, and the cost of sacrificial animals. In later times, indeed the priests claimed exemption from the payment of taxes, and the *pontifices* and augurs for a while enjoyed this privilege; but at length they were compelled to forego it. Augustus increased both the honour and the emoluments of the priests. It seems to be ascertained that everything necessary to the respectable maintenance of religious institutions was provided, but that the private fortune of the men elected to the priesthood rendered their having a salary unnecessary. There can be little doubt that the wages of the servants and assistants who waited on the temple, and the cost of sacrifices, were defrayed out of the public funds.

We have next to direct attention to the sacred places and rites of the Roman religion.

Even in the early portions of Roman history, we frequently hear of the worship of numerous deities; while, in much later times, we are informed of temples being erected to these same gods; and the information is given in a manner which leads to the impression that no temple had previously been erected to these divinities. The solution of this apparent difficulty is probably found in the fact that, adopting nearly the terms of Greece with her religious ideas, the Romans called any place set apart for the sacred service of religion a "temple," even although it contained nothing more than an enclosed space and a simple altar. This, in fact, seems to have been the primitive idea. For "temple," Latin, *templum*, comes from the Greek τέμενος, from τέμνω, "to cut off;" *templum*, according to Servius, being any place which was circumscribed and separated by the augurs from the rest of the land by a certain solemn formula. So that, in the sense of the early Romans, a temple was not an ecclesiastical building, but a consecrated place, whether containing a building or not. The act of consecration by the augurs was, in fact, the great essential necessary to constitute a place sacred. The Roman temples in later times were built in the Greek style; the entrance being, if possible, toward the west, while the statue of the deity was always placed in the interior opposite the entrance. It was also regarded as an important point, when practicable, to have the entrance to the temple by the side of a street or road; so that passers-by, without being diverted from their course, could offer their salutations to the god.

The worship of the Romans consisted chiefly in prayers, vows, and sacrifices.

Prayer was essential to every act of worship; and the order of words employed in the supplications to deity was regarded as of the utmost importance. These forms of prayer varied, of course, with the nature of the sacrifice. The great importance attached to precision in the forms of speech used in prayer, is supposed to have given rise to the notion, that some special virtue pervaded certain collocations of language; and hence sprung belief in the efficacy of charms and incantations. Those who prayed stood usually with their heads covered, looking toward the east. A priest pronounced the words before them : they often touched the altars, or the knees of the images of the gods, turning themselves round in a circle toward the right, sometimes putting their right hand to their mouth, and not unfrequently prostrating themselves on the ground.

Vows were presented to the gods by the ancient Romans with the same solemnity. In the hope of obtaining some desired good, they vowed temples, games, sacrifices, gifts, a certain part of the plunder of a city, and also what was called *ver sacrum*, that is, all the cattle which were produced from the first of March to the end of April. Among the Samnites, men were included in the things vowed. Sometimes they used to write their vows on paper or waxen tablets, to seal them up, and fasten them with wax to the images of the gods; that being supposed to be the seat of mercy.

Thanksgivings used always to be offered up to the gods for benefits received, and upon all fortunate events. It was believed that the gods, after remarkable success, used to send on men, through the agency of Nemesis, a reverse of fortune; to avoid which, it is said, Augustus, influenced by a dream, was in the habit of begging alms of the people once a year, in the hope that this feigned humiliation and adversity would satisfy the resentment of the malign goddess, and ward off real distress.

There was one peculiar manner in which the Romans testified their gratitude to the gods for any signal deliverance or special victory. When the senate decreed a *lectisternium*, as this service was called, tables were provided, which were covered with the choicest viands, as prepared for a sumptuous feast. Around these tables the images of the gods and goddesses, removed from their pedestals, and reclining on couches, were placed, as if enjoying a repast. The splendid triumph of Cicero over the conspiracy of Catiline was honoured with a public thanksgiving of this kind,—the only instance, as that great orator used to boast, of its having been conferred on a person without his having laid aside his robe of peace.

The most important part of worship consisted in sacrifice; and it was always necessary that those who offered it should be chaste and pure; that they should previously bathe, be dressed in white robes, and be crowned with the leaves of that tree which was thought most acceptable to the god whom they worshipped. It was essential that the animal should be without spot and blemish, one never yoked, but chosen from among a flock or herd approved by the priests, and marked with chalk. It was then adorned with fillets, ribbons, crowns, and gilded horns.

When these necessary preparations had been made, the victim was led to the altar by the assistants of the priests, called the *popæ*, with their clothes tucked up, and naked to the waist. The animal was conducted by a rope, which was not to be drawn tight, since it was necessary, as far as possible, for it to appear to come willingly, and not by force, which was always regarded as a bad omen. For the same reason it was allowed to stand loose before the altar; and if it ran away, it was regarded as a most calamitous circumstance.

These preparations having been made, and silence commanded, bran and meal, mixed with salt, were sprinkled on the head of the animal, and frankincense and wine were poured between its horns,— the priest first tasting the wine himself, and giving it to those nearest him to taste it also. This was called the "libation." The priest then plucked a few hairs from between the horns of the victim, and threw them into the fire. This being done, the animal was struck with an axe or mall, by the order of the priest; the assistant asking, *Agone?* "Shall I do it?" to which the priest replied, *Hoc age*, "So do." The victim was then stabbed with knives; and the blood, being caught in goblets, was poured on the altar. It was then flayed; and the carcass sometimes was wholly consumed with fire: the sacrifice was then called *holocaustum*. Usually, however, only a part was burnt, and the remainder divided between the priest and the person providing the animal. Upon this division of the sacrificed animal, the *haruspices* inspected the entrails, of which the liver was the most prominent element, and supposed to afford the most certain omens of future events. If the signs were favourable, then it was said that an acceptable sacrifice had been offered to God: if the contrary, then another animal was offered; and so sometimes several creatures were devoted before the desired appearances were realized. After this inspection, the part of the sacrifice which was devoted to the god was sprinkled with meal, wine, and frankincense, and burnt on the altar. When the sacrifice was finished, the priest, having again washed and prayed, formally dismissed the assembly.

At the close of the sacrifice followed a feast. If the rite was a public one, the feast was provided by the *epulones*, who were officers specially appointed to prepare banquets given in honour of the gods. In private sacrifices the person offering feasted with his friends on the parts assigned them. The victims offered to the celestial gods were generally white; their neck was bent upward, and the knife was applied from above, the blood being afterward sprinkled on the altar. On the contrary, the animals sacrificed to the infernal deities were black, their heads were bent downward, the knife was applied from beneath, and the blood was poured into a ditch. There was a corresponding difference in the dress and demeanour of the persons offering. Those who presented a sacrifice to the celestial gods came dressed in white, having bathed the whole body: they made libations by tossing the liquor out of the cup, and prayed with their hands raised to heaven. Those who sacrificed to the infernal gods were dressed in black, only sprinkled their bodies with water, made libations by turning the hand, threw the cup into the fire, and prayed with their palms turned downward, and striking the ground with their feet.

The ancient Romans sometimes offered human sacrifices. By a law enacted by Romulus, which has been called *lex perditionis*, persons guilty of certain crimes, such as treachery or sedition, were devoted to Pluto and the infernal gods, and, in consequence, any one might kill them with impunity. Afterward a dictator, consul, or prætor, might devote, not only himself, but any one of a particular legion which was composed entirely of Romans, and slay him as an expiatory victim. It seems that, in the early ages of Rome, human sacrifices were offered annually. Pliny mentions a law made A. U. C. 657, for prohibiting this horrid practice; but it is reasonably believed that this enactment referred only to private and magical rites; for fifty years after the enactment mentioned by Pliny, in the time of Julius Cæsar, two men were slain and sacrificed with the usual solemnities in the *Campus Martius*, by the *pontifices* and flamen of Mars. And, as a proof that this savage practice was not renounced in the most glorious period of Roman history, it may be stated, that Augustus, after having compelled L. Antonius to surrender to Perusia, ordered four hundred senators and *equites*, who had supported Antony, to be sacrificed as victims at the altar of Julius Cæsar, on the Ides of March, A. U. C. 713.

It will be necessary here to refer to some of the Roman festivals, as they were intimately connected with religion, and exerted a very considerable influence on the manners and morals of the people. Our notice, however, will only extend to three of the principal of these,—the *Lupercalia*, the *Bacchanalia*, and the *Saturnalia*.

The *Lupercalia* was a festival appointed to the honour of the Lycian Pan, and was celebrated in Rome on the fifteenth day of February. It was one of the most ancient Roman feasts, and was celebrated on the spot where Romulus and Remus were supposed to have been suckled by the she-wolf; and where a temple was erected, and a grove planted, in honour of this deity. The entire proceedings of this festival derived their character from the fact, that they were appointed in honour of Pan as the deity presiding over fertility. On this occasion goats and young dogs were sacrificed, and two noble youths selected, to whose foreheads the blood of these victims was applied, and afterward wiped off with soft wool dipped in milk; during which process the youths were required to laugh. After the sacrifice, the Luperci partook of a meal, and were plentifully supplied with wine. They then cut the skins of the sacrificed animals into pieces; some of which they tied around their bodies, and the others they used as thongs. They then ran naked through the streets of the city, touching or striking all whom they met in their way. Women rather sought than avoided these blows, as they were supposed to promote fertility, and to diminish the pains of child-bearing. The grossest impurity was practised in connexion with these rites in Egypt; and even in Rome they were promotive of vile indecency, and were sometimes connected with displays of shocking depravity.

The *Bacchanalia* was not, properly speaking, a Roman festival established by law, although it evidently sustained that character, and produced the same effects as if it had been so authorized. It was, in fact, an adaptation of the mysteries of Dionysus, or Bacchus, to Rome. It is said that they were introduced into Italy at an early period; although, from the assertion of Livy, it would seem that they were not known at Rome until a later date, and that even then their celebration was kept a profound secret. When, however, we state the nature and frequency of these orgies, this account will be received with great suspicion. The *Bacchanalia* were celebrated, at first, three days in every year, and that in the day-time, when women only were admitted, and matrons performed the necessary priestly offices; until, at length, Paculla Minia, a Campanian matron, being priestess, professed to have received a mission from the god, by which she was charged to alter the time of celebration from three days in the year to five days in the month, and also to allow men to be initiated and to celebrate these orgies at night-time. Thenceforward, according to Livy, these rites became scenes of the most abominable proceedings, of which the licentious intercourse between the sexes was the least evil. In fact, the account of the Roman author is filled with sickening details of the most revolting and abandoned villany. (Hist., lib. xxxix, cap. 9–17.) How seven thousand persons (for that is the number stated) could be initiated into a fraternity of this kind, and hold nocturnal meetings monthly, five nights in succession, without the knowledge of the public authorities, seems incredible.

When these orgies were denounced by the senate, B. C. 186, it is said that Rome was almost deserted,—so many persons, feeling themselves implicated in those proceedings, sought safety in flight. From this period these practices were forbidden by explicit law, except in case of special application to the senate. The *Liberalia* was devised as a pure and innocent festival in honour of Bacchus, instead of that which had been abolished: but there is reason to fear that the new institution soon sunk into all the abominations of the old one; for St. Augustine denounces the extreme licentiousness of this festival in his day. (De Civitate Dei, lib. vii, cap. 21.)

The *Saturnalia* was a festival to Saturnus, to whom was attributed the introduction of agriculture and the arts of civilized life into Italy. The whole of the month of December was regarded as consecrated to this deity: but the feast was at first celebrated during one day, was afterward extended to three, and again by Caligula to five. During the period assigned to this festival, universal feasting and merriment prevailed; no public business was transacted; the law-courts were closed; the schools kept holiday; to commence war was impious; to punish a criminal involved pollution. The scourge kept for the punishment of slaves was, during this time, locked up under the seal of the master. All distinction between master and slave was laid aside: even public gambling was allowed by the ædiles; and presents were generally interchanged between friends. In fact, many of the circumstances attendant on the Italian Carnival, and on the Popish mode of celebrating Christmas, are evidently borrowed from the Roman *Saturnalia*.

It now becomes necessary to take a general view of this great ecclesiastical establishment, in connexion with its theology, doctrines, and rites, for the purpose of forming some definite opinion of its moral and religious results upon the nation at large.

It is but just to admit, that we find in ancient Rome an ecclesiastical institution which, for breadth of range, combined influence, power, and completeness of detail, has no parallel in the ancient Gentile world. The political isolation of the several Grecian states, to a great extent, destroyed the unity of the national religious establishments, by introducing not only division, but diversity. In Rome, on the contrary, the very reverse was the case. Small in the beginning as were the Roman population and territory, the daring energy of that state went forward in a continued career of aggression and extension, until the world lay prostrate at the feet of the proud republic. Remarkable as this extensive range of conquest is, it is equally so that, while islands and continents submitted to the Roman power, the imperial government maintained, throughout the paramount influence of the seat of rule, and the identity and unity of its religious system. Aggregating to itself, with equal facility, territorial dominion and religious elements, grasping at the same moment the kingdoms and the gods of the conquered, the whole was still Rome, and all its adjuncts Roman. Whether in Greece or Judea, Egypt or Britain, the highest attainable civil privilege was, to be a citizen of Rome. So, when Greece, Egypt, and Phenicia had extended the Pantheon of Rome by the addition of their divinities, the religion of Rome was as united as before. The imperial state, exercising an irresistible power, moulded all these additions into the Roman character, and fully fused them into the great body of its ecclesiastical economy.

Looking at the external structure of this religious system, we can scarcely find anything of the kind more grand or complete:—the *pontifices*, headed by the *pontifex maximus*; the augurs, by the chief augur; the flamens of the superior triad of deities, and of the other gods and goddesses. When we contemplate these, composed of the aristocracy of the power, intellect, wealth, and genius of Rome,—supplemented by a weighty and influential parochial clergy, spread over the whole extent of Italy, and laying hold on the manners, judgment, and sympathy of the people in every locality,—we have brought under review a mighty ecclesiastical agency. And when it is further considered that all the elements and powers of this system were identified with the imperial government,—that the martial prowess of Rome looked to her religion for guidance, direction, and support,—that the national councils were always held in the presence, and subject to the interposition, of the highest ministers of the national faith,—that the sacred persons, rites, and usages, throughout the land, were recognised by the jurisprudence of the state, and incorporated into the entire policy of the empire:—when all this is considered, it will appear that the ecclesiastical institutions of Rome were designed and carried into effect on a scale of grandeur and completeness commensurate with the colossal power and extent of that mighty empire.

Nor can it be denied that these religious arrangements, and this system of ecclesiastical order, answered, to a great extent, the intended object. Under these influences, the Romans became a very religious people. No affair of state was prosecuted, no enterprise entered upon, without a diligent inquiry as to the divine will respecting it. No private individual of repute would build a house, take a journey, or enter upon any important business, without sacrifice and prayer. Religion, in fact, was continually recognised in all public and private affairs. The nation had its temples, deities, and state hierarchy. No office could be filled without the aid and action of a minister of religion. Nor was this practical piety confined to public affairs: on the contrary, it pervaded the community; every family had its gods, every house possessed its Lar and Penates. Marriage was contracted with religious services; every social and relative change and incident brought the parties into connexion with religious rites; and at death the funeral solemnities were equally associated with sacred ceremonies.

There is another important fact which deserves to be fully recognised and carefully considered in a review of the religion of Rome. That religion was, as we have seen, based on many pure and sound doctrines of patriarchal faith. It may be regarded as an undoubted fact, that the religion introduced into ancient Etruria taught the existence of one supreme God, insisted on the doctrine of his providential government of the world, recognised the influence and power of his Spirit on the mind and circumstances of man, admitted the immortality of the soul, and, to a considerable extent at least, indicated the doctrine of a future state of rewards and punishments. It was, therefore, the every-day doctrine of this people, that the divine will is the only proper rule of action; and that every one, both in his private and in his public capacity, is bound to act in obedience to the will of God.

Rome was founded, and its institutions established, under the pervading influence of these doctrines: and, as a proof that Romulus, Numa, and their successors adhered to the spirit of these truths, it must be remembered that, for about one hundred and fifty years after the foundation of the city, no image-worship was seen within its walls.

Still the question returns upon us,—What was the result of the operation of such circumstances and doctrines upon the mind of the Roman people, after their career of military conquest had filled them with affluence and the pride of power? In other words, What was the real religious condition of Rome when, sitting as a queen among the nations, she had appropriated to herself the wealth of many peoples, as well as the learning, refinement, and genius of Greece?

It is feared that a clear and candid solution of this question will communicate most humiliating information. First, in regard of theology, what did the Romans know and believe respecting the divine nature and government? It will be obvious, that we must here discriminate between the learned and the ignorant,—the philosophers and the educated classes of society, and those who had no information on these important subjects, beyond what was afforded by the traditions floating in public report and the tales of the poets. Of the latter we can say but little: they either believed the fictions of Ovid and Virgil, and the corresponding legends, which had been handed down from antiquity, or they did not. If they did, what notion could they have of God? or, rather, of the endless variety of gods? To believe in the universal pantheism of Roman legends and Latin poetry, would be to entertain such notions of the divine nature as must inevitably prevent the mind from realizing any sound opinion respecting the nature, government, providence, or attributes of Deity: while, on the other hand, to disbelieve these, was to sink into all the darkness and absurdity of atheism: for they had access to no further information, nor any means of obtaining additional enlightenment. This, it must be admitted, presents a deplorable picture of the great mass of the Roman people. If anything on earth deserves the name of superstition, it is a steady attention to religious requirement in utter ignorance of God. This was the condition of the Romans. With a host of deities, a regularly constituted hierarchy, countless temples, multifarious rites, and general devotion, the people had no accurate knowledge of God, or, rather, were utterly ignorant of his nature and attributes.

But it may be supposed that the learned and philosophical portion of the Roman people must at least have had some tolerably clear conceptions of the divine nature, and a reasonable faith in the goodness and power of God. It is an unquestionable fact, that such knowledge and affiance are very generally ascribed to them by the educated classes in our own country. It is of importance, therefore, that we obtain a solution of this difficulty, and ascertain what were the views entertained on this subject by the best-informed among the Romans in the later period of their history. Fortunately we have ample means for the prosecution of this inquiry. On no portion of the religion of the ancient world have we such full and satisfactory information as on this. Cicero, who held for a long time one of the most important offices in the ancient Romish hierarchy, as being the chief of the augurs, and who was evidently one of the best-informed men of his age, has written copiously on the subject under discussion, and thus placed in our hands the knowledge so much needed.

It will be necessary to sketch an outline of the works referred to, and then to give the substance of the information which they communicate.

Cicero treats of this subject in three works, which appear to have been designed as a series of treatises on theology. The first is entitled *De Naturâ Deorum*, "Of the Nature of the Gods;" the second, *De Divinatione,* " Concerning Divination ;" and the third, *De Fato,* " On Fate."

In the first of these Cicero introduces three eminent philosophers, who argue at great length the subject indicated by the title. The weighty matter is discussed in a brilliant series of addresses. Velleius opens the debate. He gives a brief but forcible review of the leading philosophers, beginning with Thales; proceeds to enumerate the schemes and creeds of twenty-seven of the most prominent teachers of different ages and countries; and then exhibits and lauds the system of Epicurus, because, as he contends, that philosopher placed the existence of the gods on its proper foundation,—the belief implanted by nature in the hearts of mankind; and, secondly, because he rightly pronounced their attributes to be happiness, immortality, apathy; representing them as "doing nothing, feeling nothing from without, rejoicing in their own wisdom and virtue, and being, although of mighty power, and infinite in their nature, as numerous as men." —*De Naturâ Deorum,* lib. i, cap. 19. Cotta, who was *pontifex maximus* at the time, is next introduced, as representing the New Academy. He forcibly assails every part of the system advocated by the preceding speaker; shows "that the reasons assigned by Epicurus for the existence of the gods are utterly inadequate; secondly, that, granting their existence, nothing can be less dignified than the forms and attributes ascribed to them; and, thirdly, granting these forms and qualities, nothing more absurd than that men should render homage or feel gratitude to those from whom they have not received, and do not hope to receive, any benefits."

The second book contains an investigation of the subject by Balbus. By him the matter is divided into four sections : 1. The existence of gods; 2. Their nature; 3. Their government of the world; 4. Their watchful care of mankind, or providence. The existence of gods he advocates from the universal belief of mankind,—the well-authenticated accounts of their appearances on earth,—from prophecies, presentiments, omens, and auguries,—from the evident proofs of design, and of the adaptation of means to a beneficial end, in the arrangements of the material world,—from the nature of man himself and his mental constitution,—from certain physical considerations, which tend clearly and unequivocally to the establishment of a system of pantheism,—and from the gradual upward progression in the works of creation, from plants to animals, and from the lower animals to man; which leads us to infer that the series ascends from man to beings absolutely perfect. In treating of the nature of the gods, the pantheistic principle is again broadly asserted :—God is the universe, and the universe is God; whence is derived the conclusion, that the deity must be spherical in form, because the sphere is the most perfect of figures. But while the universe is God as a whole, it contains among its parts many gods, among the number of whom are the heavenly bodies. Then follows a curious digression on the origin of the Greek and Roman Pantheon, and on the causes which led men to commit the folly of picturing to themselves gods differing in shape, in age, and in apparel, of assigning to them the relationships of domestic life, and of ascribing to them the desires and passions by which mortals are agitated. Lastly, the government and providence of the gods is deduced from three considerations:—1. From their existence; which being granted, it necessarily follows that they must rule the world. 2. From the admitted truth, that all things are subject to the laws of nature; but nature, when properly defined and understood, is another name for God. 3. From the beauty, harmony, wisdom, and benevolence manifested in the works of creation. This last section is handled with great skill and effect: the absurdity of the doctrine which taught that the world was produced by a fortuitous concourse of atoms, is forcibly exposed. The whole is wound up by demonstrating that all things serviceable to man were made for his use; and that the deity watches over the safety and welfare, not only of the whole human race collectively, but of every individual member of the family.

In the third book, Cotta resumes the discourse, for the purpose, not of absolutely demolishing what has been advanced by Balbus, but of setting forth, after the manner of the sceptics, that the reasonings employed by the last speaker were unsatisfactory, and not calculated to produce conviction.

The second work, *De Divinatione*, was intended as a continuation of the treatise on the nature of the gods, out of which the inquiry naturally arises. It exhibits the conflicting opinions of the Stoics and the Academy upon the reality of the science of divination, and the degree of confidence which ought to be reposed in its professors. In the first book Q. Cicero defends the doctrine of the Stoics. He divides divination into two branches,—the divination of nature, and the divination of art. To the first he ascribes dreams, inward presages and presentiments, and the ecstatic frenzy, during which the mind inspired by a god discerns the secrets of the future, and pours forth its conceptions in prophetic words. In the second are comprehended the indications yielded by the entrails of the slaughtered victim; by the flight, the cries, and the feeding of birds; by thunder and lightning, by lots, by astrology, and by all those strange sights and sounds which were regarded as the shadows cast before by coming events. Numerous examples are adduced to establish the certainty of the various methods, cases of failure being explained away by supposing an error in the interpretation of the sign, while the truth of the general principles is confirmed by an appeal to the concurring belief of philosophers, poets, and mankind at large. Hence it is maintained that we are justified in concluding that the future is revealed to us both from within and from without, and that the information proceeds from the gods, from fate, or from nature.

In the second book of this work, Cicero himself adduces the arguments of Carneades, who held that divination was altogether a delusion, and that the knowledge which it pretends to convey, if real, would be a curse, rather than a blessing, to men. He then proceeds to confute each of the propositions enunciated by the preceding speaker, and finishes by urging the necessity of upholding and extending the influence of true religion, and of waging a vigorous war in every quarter against superstition in every form.

In the third of the works referred to, *De Fato*, it seems to have been the object of the eloquent author to give a review of the opinions entertained by the chief philosophic sects upon fate, or destiny, and the compatibility of the doctrine of predestination with free-will; in which the most prominent place is assigned to the Stoics,—who maintained that fate, or destiny, was the great ruling power of the universe, the λόγος, or *anima mundi*; in other words, the divine essence, from which all impulses were derived;—and to the Academics, who conceived that the movements of the mind were voluntary, and independent of, or, at least, not necessarily subject to, external control.*

It is scarcely possible to overrate the importance of these works in assisting us to form a just estimate of the theology of heathen Rome. We have here brought under our inspection all that the most profound learning, exalted genius, and devoted research of imperial Rome could discover respecting the gods which it worshipped, and the sacred services in which it took a part, as the most essential elements of the national faith. And to what does all this amount? What is the substantial information thus obtained? We learn, indeed, that the philosophy of Greece had been imported into Rome, and that its results abundantly justify the estimate given of its influence in a preceding chapter. But, in respect of the theology of Rome, we find that the doctrines of Epicurus had obtained such an ascendency over the Roman mind, that an advocate of this system is put forth by Cicero as one of the most prominent representa-

---

* See a very able analysis of the works of Cicero in DR. WILLIAM SMITH's "Dictionary of Greek and Roman Biography and Mythology," to which we have been indebted.

tives of the national religion: and this advocate maintains, "that the gods must be acknowledged to be of human form; yet that form is not body, but something like body; nor does it contain blood, but something like blood."—*De Naturâ Deorum*, lib. i, cap. 18. He ridicules the idea of providence, as entailing too much labour on God, insisting on the dogma, that ease is essential to happiness; and he sneers at divine oversight and government, saying: "You have imposed on us an eternal Master, whom we must dread day and night. For who can be free from fear of a Deity who foresees, regards, and animadverts on everything; one who thinks all things his own; a curious, ever-busy God?"—*Idem*, cap. 20. He closes, exulting in a host of gods who take no thought of men: "Epicurus, having freed us from these terrors, and restored us to liberty, we have no dread of those beings, whom we have reason to think entirely free from all trouble themselves, and who do not impose any on others."—*Ibid*.

From this near approach to atheism, we turn to the doctrines of the Stoics, as advocated by Balbus: and what does he give us, instead of this inert Epicurean deity? He, indeed, insists upon divine providence and government; but when we come to look at the deity who governs, we are told that, "as the idea we have of the deity comprehends two things,—the one, that he is animated; the other, that nothing in nature exceeds him,—I do not see anything more consistent with this idea than to attribute mind and divinity to the world, the most excellent of all beings. Nor is it to be doubted that whatever has life, sense, reason, and understanding, must excel that which is destitute of them. It follows, then, that the world has life, sense, reason, and understanding, and is consequently a deity."—*De Naturâ Deorum*, lib. ii, cap. 17. But, although the world is a god, it is not the only one. The philosopher proceeds: "I cannot, therefore, conceive, that this constant course of the planets,—this just agreement in their various motions, through all eternity,—can be preserved without a mind, reason, and consideration; and since we perceive them in the stars, we cannot but place them in the rank of the gods." This applies to the planets; but of the fixed stars he adds: "The fixed stars have their own sphere, separate and free from any conjunction with the sky. Their perpetual courses, with that admirable and incredible constancy, so plainly declare a divine power and mind to be in them, that he who cannot perceive their divinity must be incapable of perception."—*Ibid.*, cap. 21.

Our limits forbid further quotations: these simple facts are sufficient for our purpose. They inform us, that a man of the most eminent station, learning, wisdom, and genius, while Julius Cæsar held the reins of empire, devoted himself of set purpose to present to the world a fair exhibition of the opinions entertained by his countrymen on the most important and difficult of all subjects,—the nature and attributes of God. And what are the great results of this inquiry? After the most profound and extensive research, it comes to this,—that Cicero could find nothing better than the abstract, inert divinity of Epicurus, or the wild pantheism of Zeno, to exhibit as the theology of Rome at the dawn of the Augustan era. It is true that Cotta, the *pontifex maximus*, is introduced as one of the interlocutors; but he advocates no system: he demolishes the arguments of the Epicurean, and doubts the conclusions of the Stoic, but he has nothing better to give.

Let the reader mark with care the inevitable conclusion to which these facts conduct us. They show, first, that the great system of religion—sustained as it was by gorgeous temples, and elevated hierarchy, a countless priesthood, continually recurring solemn rites and ceremonies—was virtually repudiated by the intelligent, the learned, and the cultivated classes throughout the land. They saw, they sanctioned, they sustained a gorgeous system of faith as an engine of government, and for political purposes; while they did not really believe in a single divinity whom they taught the people to worship, and whom they pretended themselves to worship.

But in what respect were these educated and elevated classes better informed than the ignorant and deluded masses upon whom they looked down? In no respect whatever. The deity of Epicurus, or the conception of Zeno, was no more an object of rational worship than the Capitoline Jupiter. It must be added, that the manner in which Cicero presents the subject to our view, suggests even a darker shade than has been yet expressed. I allude to the general prevalence of doubt as to all these doctrines. On every hand a wide-spreading scepticism prevailed; and Rome, when at the zenith of her glory, was rapidly gliding into the darkness of atheism. What a fearful commentary does this afford to the assertion of the apostle respecting this people! "Professing themselves to be wise, they became fools." Rom. i. 22. The primitive theology of Rome contained, with some admixture of error, much patriarchal truth. But, elevated to the highest point of wealth and power, and possessing every means of acquiring information, instead of humbly tracing out these simple truths, and adhering to them as grand waymarks in their theological researches, they fell into the snare which had ruined Greece:—they idolized human intellect. They adopted, with great zest, the various systems of Grecian philosophy. The result we have seen: theology became a subject of human speculation; and thus, with the highest professions of wisdom, they descended to the folly of worshipping the world, the stars, the universe, as divine.

Our reference to other religious doctrines shall be brief: for, with such theological doctrines, or to speak more correctly, with such entire absence of sound theological knowledge, it is very evident there can be no hope of finding clear views on any religious subject. But it becomes important that we ascertain what were the opinions entertained by the Roman people respecting the immortality of the soul, and future rewards and punishments.

On this, as on the former subject, it is easy to say what were the opinions of the ignorant and uneducated. It is admitted on all hands, that the fables and legends which were the staple of the poets floated on the public mind, and gave them the only ideas they entertained as to religion. If the Roman populace, therefore, believed these, they would look forward to Tartarus and the Elysian Fields as the future habitations of departed spirits; and a more gloomy and less influential result than that which would thus be obtained, can scarcely be imagined. For, while the punishments of Tartarus were everlasting, the pleasures of Elysium were terminated by the drinking of the waters of Lethe; after which the spirit, perfectly oblivious of all past events, returned to this world to inhabit another body. And as, in a continual recurrence of trials and temptations, it may be supposed that the spirit would in some one instance fail, there seemed no rational ground of expectation for any, but that they would ultimately terminate their career in Tartarean misery and darkness.

But the extent to which this view of future existence would influence the public mind, must be measured by the hold which it had on the judgment and feeling of the people. And this would be greatly affected by the opinions entertained by the upper and educated classes of society. It is not difficult to state their views on this subject. A passage in Cicero's Oration for Cluentius casts important light on them. Referring to the fables of the poets, he says. "If these are false, *as all men see they are*, what has death deprived him of, besides a sense of pain?"* It is clear from this statement, 1. That the fables of the poets constituted the only foundation accessible to the Romans for a belief in future rewards and punishments. For the entire scope of the writer's argument is this,—that if there is no

---

* The passage in the original is: *Nam nunc quidem, quid tandem illi mali mors attulit? Nisi forte ineptiis ac fabulis ducimur, ut existimemus illum apud inferos impiorum supplicia perferre, &c. Quæ si falsa sunt,* ID QUOD OMNES INTELLIGUNT, *quid ei tandem aliud mors eripuit præter sensum doloris?*

future punishment, then death can only deprive us of all sense of pain, and not inflict any. And to the fables of the poets he refers, as the only authority on the subject. If these are false, then he concludes, as of unavoidable necessity, that death is a prelude to no painful infliction. So that, according to this high authority, those who by education or intellect were raised above a belief in these fables, together with all those who by ignorance or scepticism were strangers to their influence, had no idea of future existence, and simply regarded death as a release from the ills of life. But, 2. Cicero in this passage intimates that this was the general condition of his countrymen: "If these are false,—*as all men see they are*,—then death can do nothing but afford relief from a sense of pain."

Lest the reader should feel a difficulty in concluding that the great body of the Roman people were thus ignorant of all the restraints and motives afforded by the doctrine of a future life, I adduce further and, I think, conclusive evidence. In the debate in the senate on the punishment to be inflicted on the criminals convicted of being concerned in the conspiracy of Catiline, Julius Cæsar argued against the infliction of capital punishment. In the course of his argument he boldly advanced the Epicurean dogma, "that death was no evil, as they who inflicted it for a punishment imagined;" and thence proceeded to insist on the doctrines of that sect respecting the mortality of the soul. Now, when Cato and Cicero, who were on the other side, came to reply to this speech, how did they meet this profane dogma? Here, in a challenge so publicly and prominently put forth, was a fine opportunity for these able and eloquent men to uphold their own immediate opinions on this subject, and the interests of morality at the same time. How did they answer this? They did not venture to vindicate a state of future rewards and punishments either by urging the doctrines of any philosophical sect, or by appealing to the judgment of their country. Their only resource was the replication, that "the doctrine of a future state of rewards and punishments was delivered to them from their ancestors." This most illogical reply, as Bishop Warburton observes, is a sufficient proof that there was not in the recognised philosophy of Rome any clear assertion of a future life; so that the licentious dogma of Cæsar could only be met by a reference to doctrines prevalent in ancient times. Nothing can more clearly illustrate the real state of the case can this. Rome had enjoyed clear views on this subject; the doctrine of a future state of rewards and punishments had made a prominent element in the national faith: but while this knowledge yet remained on record as an historical fact, to be appealed to by Cicero, it had passed away from the public mind. Wild speculation and Grecian philosophy had united their influence to obliterate the truth; and Romans in the time of Cæsar saw, feared, hoped for nothing beyond the grave.

What were the consequences of this fearful change on the morals and social life of this mighty and talented people, neither our limits nor our inclination allow us fully to detail. Without the knowledge of God and of a future life, man sunk to the level of a brute, or was only distinguished from mere animal nature by an intellectual power which enabled him to develop his impurity into an almost infinite range of vice and folly.

The inspired apostle, describing the moral condition of the Roman people, has placed on the sacred record a passage which so fully exhibits the depths of impurity into which they sunk after having renounced God, that it is seldom read, and it is to be lamented that its reading should be necessary. Yet such glitter and gaudy colouring has been thrown over the moral condition of Rome by its acknowledged patronage of elegance and art, and possession of wealth and power, that it becomes needful to state enough to justify the strong language of the apostle. This is also necessary, since it will show that the inevitable consequences of apostasy from God, combined with unlimited idolatry, are in fact a surrender of the human mind, individually and collectively, not only to the operation of the vilest human passions, but also to the uncontrolled dominion of Satanic power; and this notwithstanding the utmost influence of science, civilization, and martial prowess.

The first result of this general impiety that will be noticed, was the effect produced on the family economy of Rome. The education and cultivation of the female mind was almost universally neglected. And this can scarcely be regretted, as the Roman lady did not require cultivation for the part she had to act. The wife was placed completely in the power of her husband: he could divorce her at will, or, without that formality, lend her to a friend, receive her back for a while, and then hand her to another. Such, in fact, was the absence of interest and affection, in their proper sense, between husband and wife, that the copious language of Rome had no word to express jealousy. These facts are important: they lie at the foundation of all the bonds of society,—all the fabric of morals. This unnatural and irreligious character of matrimonial life was productive of an extensive system of adopting children,—a practice which showed the weakness of the parental affections, and led to other extensive evils.

Not the least of these ills was slavery, which, although not occasioned by these vicious domestic arrangements, was greatly aggravated by them. This political vice did in Rome most extensively what it must always do to a certain extent,—it demoralized society. The number of slaves in Rome was so great that, when debating the propriety of enacting a peculiar dress by which slaves might be known, the senate rejected the proposition, lest the badge, if adopted, should make the slaves aware of their number and their power. Slaves at Rome must, in fact, have made a large portion of the population. An individual sometimes held above four thousand; it was by no means uncommon for one person to have two hundred; and it seems to have been a conventional rule, that a person was regarded as having no claims to gentility, unless he had at least ten slaves. These persons could not marry, nor hold property, and were, in fact, notwithstanding much legislation on the subject, in the absolute power of their owners. And, perhaps, in no age or country was this power used with more barbarous cruelty. The whip which was generally employed for their punishment (*horribile flagellum*) is described as a terrible instrument. It had several thongs, firmly fastened to a strong handle: each of the thongs was weighted with pieces of bone or bronze throughout most of their length, and sometimes terminated with hooks, and were therefore significantly called "scorpions." The application of this to the naked back of the sufferer lacerated the flesh fearfully, and sometimes occasioned death. These inflictions were as frequent as they were severe; so much so, indeed, that it was common for a slave to be nicknamed according to the kind of flogging, or other punishment, to which he had been subjected.

The cruelty of Vedius Pollio in throwing slaves into his fishponds to be devoured is well known, and often cited in proof of the barbarities exercised by the Romans toward their slaves. But the motives which induced this abominable conduct are not so generally understood. It was not to feed his fishes,—nor merely to inflict the punishment of death upon culprits,—that this course was adopted; but rather to gratify an exquisite taste for a peculiar mode of inflicting torment. I will give the account in a literal translation of the words of Pliny: "He caused certain slaves, condemned to die, to be put into the stews where these lampreys or muraenes were kept, to be eaten and devoured by them: not that there were not wild beasts enough upon the land for this feat, *but because he took pleasure to behold a man torn and plucked to pieces all at once*, which pleasant sight he could not see by any other beast upon the land."—*Hist. Nat.*, lib. ix, cap. 23. Is it possible to conceive of a more diabolical passion than this? It might be supposed that to see a fellow-creature lashed to death, or torn limb from limb by wild beasts in the amphitheatre, would be a sufficient gratification for any savage; but this did not meet the *cultivated taste* for a sight of mortal agony, which animated the refined Roman in the days of Augustus: he must see every part of the victim simultaneously assailed, and the flesh rent from the whole body at the same moment. To gratify this horrid taste, a naked slave was occasionally thrown into his fish-ponds, when the ravenous lampreys would instantly fasten on every part of the body, and, by devouring the flesh of the devoted wretch, gratify the fiendish passion of his inhuman master.

Nor did female slaves fare better at the hands of their mistresses. Their being punished severely, and even flogged to death, became so frequent, that laws were at length enacted to prevent these atrocities. It will, however, sufficiently indicate the feelings which influenced Roman ladies, and the treatment which those unfortunate females received, who were entirely subject to their will, to state that the poets represent it as the common practice for the mistress to sit at her toilet to have her hair dressed, with instruments of punishment at her side; and for the female slave charged with performing this office, to be made to strip quite naked above the waist before commencing the operation, so that any fault, delay, or mistake in the process, might be instantly punished with stripes, inflicted by leather or twisted parchment scourges on the naked shoulders or bosom of the slave. (Ovid, Artis Aman., lib. iii, 239, 240; Martial, lib. ii, epig. 66; Juvenal, lib. vi, 498, &c.)

If it be necessary to add aught more to show the want of moral feeling and prevalent cruelty which imbued the Roman institutions under the first emperors, it may be supplied by the manner in which the children of Sejanus were treated after the death of their father. This man was the favourite minister of the Emperor Tiberius. After revelling in the pomp and power, scarcely less than imperial, with which his master endowed him, he was suspected, and, by a sudden and artful stroke of policy of the same sovereign, charged with high treason, and strangled in prison. His two children, a boy and a girl, although too young to partake of their father's crimes, were, on his account, also doomed to die. But what was called "the religion" of Rome forbade the execution of a virgin: so the child was first ravished in prison, and then brother and sister were put to death, and their bodies, after being dragged by hooks through the streets of the city, were cast into the Tiber. This took place during the life of our Saviour, and not long before his crucifixion.

But the culminating point of Roman iniquity and pollution is found in that abominable licentiousness so forcibly described by the apostle. The Roman laws of marriage afforded no guarantee of permanent union. The sacred tie might be dissolved at the whim or caprice of either party; which in practice gave a licence to libertinism in men, and also produced its effects on the female character. This was stimulated by their religion. Little attention was paid to the true character of deity; but the incest and amours of the objects of worship were gloated over with fatal avidity. Numerous services of religion also strengthened this vicious bias. Laws had, indeed, been made to check vice in females; but then a married woman might avert the effect of all these by appearing before the ædiles, and registering herself as a common prostitute. This was actually done; and it was not until a married lady of rank publicly appeared, tendered her name for registration, and claimed the legal privilege of living a life of debauchery, that the senate interposed to check this almost universal abomination. But then the new-made law was no protest against the immorality of prostitution, but simply a declaration that "no woman whose grandfather, father, or husband, was a Roman knight, should make her person venal."—*Tacitus, Annal.*, lib. ii, cap. 85. We shall sufficiently exhibit the awful extent of Roman licentiousness by giving the sentiments of two of their most eminent men. Cato, the stern moralist, encouraged young men to licentiousness, provided they abstained from adultery; and Cicero, chief of the augurs of Rome, thus pleads,—that "to find fault with meretricious amours, was an extraordinary severity, abhorrent not only from the licentiousness of that age, but from the customs and constitutions of their ancestors;" adding, "When was not this done? When was it found fault with? When was it not allowed? Can the time be named when the practice which is now lawful was not accounted so?"—*Cicero, Orat. pro M. Cœlio*, cap. 20.

But, according to the apostle and to fact, merely gross licentiousness did not constitute the reigning sin, the deadly plague-spot of Roman manners. A lower deep, in fact, the lowest depth of infamous and unnatural lust, fearfully prevailed; but on this most disagreeable subject a few words must suffice. It must, then, be stated that slave boys were reared for the express-purpose of unnatural impurity, and that handsome ones sold at most enormous prices. So prevalent, indeed, was this detestable vice, that Cotta, who was *pontifex maximus*, and is introduced by Cicero as one of the ablest debaters on the nature of the gods, voluntarily, and without any reason for doing so, in that very debate admits himself to be guilty of this iniquity, and speaks of other eminent men as doing the same, as though it called forth neither shame nor remorse. But the language which most fully proclaims the unbounded range of this turpitude throughout Roman society, comes from the lips of Epictetus. That philosopher, contemplating the character of Socrates, breaks forth into the following eulogy: " Go to Socrates:—consider what a victory he was conscious of obtaining! What an Olympic prize! so that, by Heaven, one might justly salute him, 'Hail! incredibly great, universal victor!' "—*Epictetus, Diss.*, lib. ii, cap. xviii, sect. 4. Now what had the Grecian sage done to call forth this extravagant laudation? Will the reader believe it?—he had remained in the same room with the young and beautiful Alcibiades without committing the vilest iniquity which could disgrace human nature. How common—how all but universal—must this vile conduct have been among the Roman people, to have made a single act of continence the theme of such extravagant praise!

Dark and terrible, therefore, as St. Paul's picture of Roman society confessedly is, it is not, and scarcely could be, beyond the reality. God and his truth had been renounced, and Satan reigned in all the plenitude of his power. Religion, in its wide range of operation, became an instrument of evil; religious rites and ceremonies sunk into agencies promotive of vice; men of notoriously abandoned character filled the highest places in the priesthood: and thus, in the midst of unbounded power and wealth,—while Livy and Plutarch wrote history, Cicero fascinated the world by his oratory, and Virgil and Horace charmed all by the sweetness of their numbers,—Satanic influence prevailed; vice triumphed, and preyed so destructively on the vitals of the state, that an eminent living writer observes, "Such a state of society already trembled on the verge of dissolution; and reflecting men must have shuddered at the frailness of the bands which still held it together."—*Merivale's Fall of the Roman Republic*, vol. i, p. 228. Truly, "the world by wisdom knew not God."

CHAPTER XIII.

A GENERAL REVIEW OF THE HISTORY AND RELIGION OF THE GENTILE NATIONS.

Mistaken Notions respecting the Accordance of ancient History with Holy Scripture—The elevation of Man in his primitive State—Remarkable Corroboration of Scripture by Facts in Ancient History—Gentile Religion an important Development of Mosaic Teaching—It contains wonderful Revelations of the Power and Providence of God—Ancient History, as a Fulfilment of Prophecy, a remarkable Attestation of revealed Truth—Relation of Revelation to the Teaching of Science—The Testimony of ancient History in Respect of Religion in remarkable Accordance with the Bible—Proofs of the Existence and Power of Satanic Influence—Infinite Absurdity of Idolatry—Yet it was universal—False Theories devised for the Purpose of accounting for the Existence of Idolatry, considered and refuted—Satanic Aggression on the Purposes of God and Happiness of Man—The Deluge one of its Results—Corruption of the patriarchal Faith—Attempt to frustrate the divinely-appointed Dispersion—Miraculously defeated—The Call of Abraham, and Election of the Hebrew People, still further show the Violence of Satanic Aggression on the Purpose of God—The Succession of great ruling Empires displays the Power of diabolical Influence—The World prepared for the Introduction of the Kingdom of God.

The history of the ancient heathen nations has been generally regarded as entirely separate from and unconnected with the Hebrew people and the Old Testament Scriptures; and, being investigated, especially in their most ancient periods, by the unaided light of their own imperfect records and legends, has not unfrequently been placed in an attitude hostile to the explicit declarations of revealed truth. This seems to have produced an opinion which, if not often avowed, has nevertheless obtained extensive currency and influence,—namely, that the whole experience, knowledge, and power of the Gentile world, prior to the birth of Christ, must be regarded as totally isolated from the Bible, if, indeed, it does not stand out in open protest against its teaching.

In some works of great talent and learning, efforts have been made to disseminate such views: but even where nothing of this kind is discernible, the history, chronology, learning, and prowess of Egypt, Assyria, Babylon, Persia, and other ancient nations, are spoken of as though they had nothing in common with the Hebrews, and consequently as if the truth of revelation had no bearing or relation whatever to them.

The collection of facts, both historical and religious, furnished in this work, will, it is hoped, form an effectual antidote to this prevalent error. The history of the great primitive and powerful nations has been carried up, in this and a preceding volume, to immediate proximity with the dispersion of the Noachic tribes, as described in the Book of Genesis; and it has been clearly and fully shown, that, instead of these peoples having subsisted throughout lengthened periods, which bid defiance to any reconcilement with Scripture chronology, they are all found to have arisen from patriarchs named by Moses as descendants of Noah, their lineage and posterity being thus fully identified with the sacred record. This result, it should be observed, has not been obtained by a forced application of the text of Scripture to these national histories, but has been mainly elicited from the ancient and incorruptible monuments of those nations. The pictorial literature extant on the monuments of Egypt, and the disinterred sculptures of Assyria, Babylon, and Persia, have been carefully studied; and found to teach lessons of history, religion, manners, and morals, in perfect harmony with, and in strong corroboration of, the Scriptural account. Nor must it be overlooked, in the consideration of this subject, that, brief as our sketches of national history confessedly and necessarily are, they are not merely one-sided selections of matter, but impartial condensations of national annals. No facts of an opposite tendency have been ignored; nor can any arrangement of authorized *data* set aside or neutralize the effect of the account which has been here given. What, then, is the general view which has been obtained of the history of these Gentile nations?

It has been found that, instead of the speculation being true, which obtained so much favour some time ago,—that man began his career in barbarism, and gradually worked his way, through successive ages of toilsome effort, to an acquaintance with the useful arts, moral comfort, and intellectual dignity,—the earliest ages of every primitive nation display a state of intelligence and civilization.

We have also found, in many points of conformity and agreement between the annals of these ancient nations and the Hebrew Scriptures, unmistakable proofs of the authenticity and integrity of the Bible. Who can read the Mosaic account of the descent of Abraham to the country of Ham, and that of the sojourn of Jacob and his descendants there,—and compare the institutions, usages, national laws, habits of thought, and conventional arrangements which they exhibit with the disclosures of the hieroglyphics, and the revelations afforded by the picture-sculptures of the Egyptian tombs,—without being compelled to believe that he is pondering over truthful collateral accounts of the same people? Let any candid person carefully look at the representation of brick-making by captives on the tomb of

Rek-sharè; and then, reading the Mosaic account of the Hebrews under their taskmasters, and observing the physiognomy of even a modern Jew, let him say if he has not before him a most striking pictorial illustration of the historical fact.

The record of the triumph of Shishak, still extant on the external wall of the hypostyle-hall at Karnak, where the "king of Judah" is read among the names of those subdued by the prowess of the conqueror, is another proof of the same fact. Nor are the omissions of reference to Palestine on Egyptian monuments less in point than those existing records. Although the several tribes which inhabited that country prior to its invasion by Joshua, are frequently found figuring on Egyptian monuments before that time; yet, from the period when the Hebrews possessed themselves of the land, nothing of the kind occurs, until we meet with the triumph of Shishak over the king of Judah in the days of Rehoboam. Facts like these, while they attest the verity of Hebrew history, equally show the truthful accordance of it with a sound interpretation of heathen annals, and the suppression of truth in the latter.

Sennacherib's account of his wars with Hezekiah, and the autobiography of the martial career of Darius on the Sacred Rock at Behistun, might be referred to, as similar striking examples of the concurrence and truth of these collateral histories; but we prefer here to dwell more particularly on those which identify the origin, institutions, and usages of the primitive nations, with the early history of the postdiluvian world according to the inspired record.

We may first refer to the similarity of names, which, to the extent it is known to have existed, cannot have been accidental. In Assyria, for instance, we not only find the Scriptural names of the patriarch Asshur on the sculptures, as giving a designation to the whole land, it being thence called "the country of Asshur;" but this father of the race stands before us, in these exhumed sculptures, as the deified hero of the people, and, as such, worshipped as "Asshur, the king of the circle of the great gods."—*Layard's Nineveh and Baylon*, pp. 629, 637. We have a similar case at Babylon. The name of Nimrod is as current in native history and legend, as in the pages of Scripture. Berosus, from the preserved records of that city at the time of Alexander, speaks of him as the first king of the country. His figure stands in majestic attitude on the walls of the royal palace at Khorsabad. The Birs-Nimroud evidently derives its appellation from the same source. In fact, the name of this great usurper and arch-apostate is alike imprinted on the soil of his country, and embedded in all the traditions and legends of its inhabitants to the present day.

But the most elaborate and decisive evidence that the Mosaic account of the origin of nations is the only true one, is found in the fact, that undoubted reference to the scenes of Paradise, to the incidents of man's primeval history, and to the circumstances connected with the Deluge, enter into, and form the more prominent elements of, the religion of the early era of these primitive nations. To cite these instances in detail, would be to re-write a great part of some of the preceding chapters. In respect of Paradise, we have not only the perpetuation of the thing, but even the name, in its application to the sacred park-like grounds which surrounded the palace-temples of the eastern kings; while the water flowing from the threshold, and meandering through the garden,—the trees which grew in it, and which, represented in gorgeous sculpture, adorned the interior of the sacred place,—the cherubic figures which stood at every doorway, and elaborately ornamented all its parts,—with the serpent-form, as the type of dominion and sovereign sway,—all attest the undoubted origin of the people, and the foundation of their civil and religious polity, to be a striking confirmation of the teaching of Moses, and of the general tenor of the word of God.

On this point I am bold to say, that the history and religion of the primitive nations, as detailed in this volume, taken in connexion with what was adduced in a preceding one of a cognate character, so fully accord with the statements of Scripture, and are of such a peculiar nature, entering into the vital elements of the constitution of nations, and affecting the most sacred verities of their faith, that the early Gentile nations thus stand before the mind as a grand development of Mosaic teaching, and present to us a wide range of important and undoubted facts, which are utterly irreconcilable with any other account of the origin and early history of mankind : so that, setting aside Hebrew history altogether, the Gentile nations alone, fairly considered, from an irrefragable confirmation of the verity of Holy Scripture.

But this is not all. The Bible not only extorts this evidence of its truth from the most remote and the darkest period of Gentile history : it brings us in contact with displays of divine power, in respect of several of those nations, of a kind equally remarkable. Who can estimate the effects which the plagues and the Exodus produced in Egypt? It is admitted that these events are not named in Egyptian monuments :—it is not likely that such a national humiliation would be thus recorded :—but they are clearly recognised as a part of Egyptian history by Manetho, as well as preserved in the traditions of other countries. The punishment of Nebuchadnezzar by the immediate power of Jehovah, is another instance, and one clearly referred to in Babylonish annals. The defeat of Sennacherib in his attempt to capture Jerusalem, must have been known by him to be of God. Perhaps sculptured monument was never charged with a heathen testimony to the interposition and power of Jehovah, more important as an attestation of revealed truth, than when the Assyrian workman received the dictation of his proud sovereign, and chiselled in the enduring slab the weighty words, "Hezekiah King of Judah did not submit to my yoke; but I left to him Jerusalem his capital, and some of the inferior towns around it." It can scarcely be doubted that the predictions respecting Cyrus brought him equally into contact with the divine word, and the infinite wisdom and power of God. Thus, to each of the old mighty nations of the world did Jehovah gloriously reveal himself, while they stood in all the pride of their power, and in possession of their wide range of dominion; showing himself to be the only true God, whose will no earthly potentate could successfully resist: and—for this is important to our argument—ample evidence of the certainty of such interposition remains to the present time.

More than this: not only do the early history and religion of these nations accord with Scriptural truth; not only does their meridian splendour stand associated with miraculous interposition; but God in his wisdom adopted a course of action and plan of government which brought Greece and Rome equally within the range of his influence, and completed the manifestation of his providence to the Gentile world. How glorious is the prospect! See the sacred seer of God standing before Nebuchadnezzar, or placing on record his wondrous revelations in the palace of Shushan. See him pointing out, with a ray of heavenly light, the fate of empires, the destiny of nations, from the day in which he speaks, through future ages. Recognising all the glory and power of Babylon, the revealed prescience passes on, and treats it as an extinct thing. Persia rises in her strength, symbolized by animal forms and the silver portion of the great image, until it also has accomplished its destiny, and the heraldic representation of the nation—the ram—is trodden down by the rough goat of Grecia, and the Macedonian conqueror rules the world. The prescience of God falters not after revealing the grand contingencies of two hundred and fifty years: onward the prophet leads: the great horn of this power, "the first king," is broken. His empire is divided into four less powerful states; but they exist only for a while: the prophet points out in the distance the rising power of Rome, shows its diversity from the other kingdoms by its republican form of government, exhibits its want of unity in consequence of consular rule and intestine division, even indicates the means resorted to in vain for removing this evil by intermarriages between the families of the chiefs and the heads of factions; and, above all, he predicts the iron power of this martial people, which breaks in pieces and bruises all other nations, and spreads its colossal rule throughout the world. And then, as if to place before mankind the grand object of this providential arrangement, this succession of empires, this overruling and governing of heavenly power, it is written, "In the days of these kings shall the God of heaven set up a kingdom, which shall never be destroyed: it shall stand forever."

The sacred record is, therefore, seen to lead us back to the dawning day of time,—to read to us an outline of man's primitive history, —to inform us respecting the wonderful influences to which he was subjected, and their great results in his character and history. We then turn from this teaching to the legends, records, and sculptures of these ancient nations, and find everywhere undoubted proofs exhibited by them in facts, doctrines, systems, and ceremonies, which must have been derived from the circumstances which the Bible records. The inspired volume conducts us to each of these ancient kingdoms, and asserts, that in them God wonderfully interposed, by revealing his omnipotent power and omniscient wisdom, in support of his own truth: and we find even these humiliating events recognised in their national histories, and proved by collateral facts. Again, we see divine truth taking its stand amid all the splendour and power of the first great monarchy, and predicting its fate, and the rise, character, progress, power, and destiny of every other great nation until the advent of the kingdom of God. We go to the histories of these empires, and we find these wonderful prophecies true to the letter in every instance, and so exactly exhibiting the wonderful changes, revolutions, and conquests which took place during this period, as to form an accurate outline of its general history.

We direct attention to this for the purpose of showing the remarkable accordance between the sacred record and profane history, and of proving that the origin, progress, and fate of ancient nations harmonize with the teaching, and both corroborate and illustrate the history, contained in the sacred pages of the Bible. But we do more than this. Finding in the Bible the germs of every heathen institution,—seeing here the truth, which is found perverted and distorted into frightful forms in their mythologies,—discovering history which is the parent of all theirs, and which accords with it in every essential element,—we are bold to claim for the Bible a power to afford men some information respecting the ancient Gentile nations. *We fearlessly assert that no man, whatever his learning, or intellectual power, or station may be, when speaking of ancient history, has any right to ignore the Bible.*

But it is confidently urged, that the information afforded by the Scriptures on subjects of science is incomplete; and that therefore we are not to go to their pages for instruction respecting astronomy, geology, or even chronology. To a certain extent this is freely admitted, and no man of information will go to the Bible hoping to find an authorized catalogue of the dynasties of Egypt, or a list of the kings of Assyria. But men of science must not presume on the ignorance of devout students of the sacred volume, so far as to hope to lead them, for this reason, to the wild inference, that what the Bible says on these subjects is false, or undeserving of attention. It is freely and fully admitted that the Bible does not afford a *complete* system of chronology; and it may be difficult to pronounce with certainty which of the three systems, founded on its different versions, is undoubtedly correct. Our opinion, and the reasons on which it is based, have been elsewhere given. But, however this may be, there is a range within which, if the Bible is true, the truth must be found. A shorter period than the Hebrew numbers, or a longer one than those of the Septuagint, cannot accord with Scripture teaching; and men cannot travel beyond these limits without impugning the integrity of revealed truth.

But we have sketched the history of these ancient nations to ascertain, not so much their political and civil, as their religious, condition. And what has been the result of our researches in this respect? Man is found everywhere in possession of important elements of truth. In fact, if one undoubted conclusion more than another is clearly deduced by our researches into the primitive history of man, it is that, instead of being a stranger to revelation, man derived his knowledge of civil, relative, and religious duty immediately from God. The circumstances respecting his food and clothing, and the means of providing them,—the sacred institution of marriage and its obligations,—the truth relating to Deity, and the manner of serving him,—must all have been subjects of revelation. Hence, we everywhere find man in possession of a *substratum* of divine truth, forming the basis or platform on which all his individual hopes and motives to action rest, and affording the great principle which holds him in civil society,—relationship to his fellows.

Another general axiom may be propounded. Men everywhere are found to be the subjects of divine influence. This is, indeed, one of the most remarkable features in the condition of mankind. The influence of God upon the mind, circumstances, and destiny of man was everywhere fully admitted,—at least, until in the latter ages, under the teaching of a false philosophy, atheism and scepticism began to obtain in Greece. Nothing is more manifest than this: we find it in Homer and Virgil,—in the autobiographies and bulletins of Divanubara, Sardanapalus, and Sennacherib,—in the sacred inscriptions of the Persian kings, as well as in the native records of those of Egypt. It was in this manner, more especially, that when God, " in times past, suffered all nations to walk in their own ways, nevertheless he left not himself without witness, in that he did good;" (Acts xiv, 16, 17;) from which it must not be supposed that unaided human nature was left to draw the inference of God and his goodness; but rather that his Spirit taught them by his internal operation on their mind. Hence it is said that they were " without excuse, because that which may be known of God is manifest in them; FOR GOD HATH SHOWED IT UNTO THEM." Rom. i, 19, 20. Destitute of outward teaching, they had more ample spiritual influence.

The nature of man, however, was so corrupt, that, whatever might be the case in individual instances, for the purpose of enlightening and renewing men in general the means were insufficient to the end. It is true that, under these circumstances, human nature flourished, and the natural powers of man were cultivated and adorned; so that military prowess, intellectual culture, works of genius, and every branch of science, elegance, and art, attained perfection. But then man's moral and spiritual condition was one of darkness, degradation, and ruin. And this, notwithstanding the ordinary influences of the Spirit were sometimes seconded by marvellous interpositions from heaven. Thus Egypt was favoured with the miracles of Moses; Nineveh, with the preaching of Jonah; Babylon, with the prophecies of Daniel, and the miracle of the three Hebrew youths; Media, with the deliverance of Daniel from the den of lions; Persia, with the revelations respecting Cyrus; and Greece and Italy, with the preaching of Pythagoras and other philosophers. Yet, amid so much divine influence, acting on this human greatness, man descended into moral ruin. Why was this?

It was because there was an agent at work more potent for evil than human infirmity, or even human depravity. If this had not been the case,—if man in moral degradation and spiritual ruin had, untouched by other influence, resisted the merciful impulses of Heaven, and resolved to the utmost to gratify his base and wicked propensities,—we might expect to find him wallowing in sensuality and licentiousness: he might riot in rapine and blood; deceit, lying, pride, passion, malignity, and violence, might be expected to pollute, disorder, and spread misery and guilt over mankind: but it is not easy to conceive that mere humanity would have devised such an aggression on the honour due only to God, and at the same time involving its own most extreme degradation, as is found to exist in the practice of idolatry. There is something so opposed to all reason, so very absurd, in the idea that any natural object, or product of human art or labour, can be divine, or that there can be a plurality of divinities, that the existence or prevalence of such opinions in the ancient world has been generally regarded as an inexplicable enigma. Hence writers have contented themselves with giving a history and description of this great moral aberration, and its results, rather than attempted to account for its origin.

One talented author, whose recent production is before us, speculates in this manner: " Man feels himself small and weak amid the forces of nature: he sees a power in operation which even the wisest cannot combat; and the more ignorant, the more brutalized he is, the more he feels his utter helplessness. But the wise man investigates causes, finds that the greater the force, the less it is visible and tangible; and therefore soon arrives at the conviction that the Great First Cause must be still more remote from the grasp of the senses. The philosopher of all ages, as far as we can trace back with any certainty, has been a pure theist. Such was Zoroaster among the Persians; such were the great founders of the Greek philosophy; and such were the patriarchs described in the Hebrew records. But the ignorant man, unable to follow the steps of the philosopher, but equally sensible of the presence of a superior power, looks only to the force in action, whatever it may be, and holds *that* to be divine; for, to the ignorant man, whatever or whoever is stronger or wiser than himself, is an object of veneration."

We should feel much disposed to question the last-mentioned premiss,—that "to the ignorant man, whatever or whoever is stronger or wiser than himself, is an object of veneration." It appears equally probable, and even more so, that it, or he, would be an object of envy. But not to dwell on this objection,—does not this theory of the origin of idolatry assume a startling aspect from the fact, that it would lead to the impression that all the wise and enlightened of mankind—those who, from their endowments and position, have always been the leaders of the public mind—are guided and led by the ignorant and the obscure?

Such a proposition seems utterly incredible. Here are the wise, the cultivated, the influential, with right and truth on their side; and here are the ignorant and vulgar, who have adopted a monstrous and ridiculous absurdity: yet it is supposed that the latter induced the former to adopt their views; or, at least, that, against the opinion and influence of the wise and great-minded, a grand system of doctrines, rites, and usages was brought into operation, in every part of the world, among every people. It may be regarded as bold to say that such an hypothesis involves a positive impossibility: but we do not shrink from asserting that such a mighty and universal revolution was never known to result from such influence.

This, however, is not the principal objection which we have to urge against this scheme. In common with all the theories of its class, it overlooks the most important body of facts relating to primeval history. Yet it is a great advance on the theories of the cognate schools of the last century; it does not place the first race of mankind among the brutes, but allows them to have been cultivated, civilized, and rational; yet it leaves them utterly without religion. Now we take leave to say, this was never the condition of any human community; and we challenge an investigation into all history for the decision of the question. A civilized community, composed, on the one hand, of cultivated intellectual philosophers, and, on the other, of sober, thoughtful, ignorant men, altogether without religious views, practices, or opinions, but setting itself, in its various individuals, according to their respective information and powers of mind, to excogitate some definite idea of Deity,—one class coming to the conclusion that God is one invisible and mighty being; the other, that the powers of nature, in all their wide variety, are to be reverenced as divine,—this, I say, has no countenance in actual fact; nothing approximating thereto has ever been seen in history; and it can only exist in the dreamy speculations of those who prefer to give prominence to the wildest vagaries, rather than submit to receive substantial information from the word of God.

No! the truth is, that man entered on his career of existence more fully identified and imbued with religious truth, and duty, and privilege, than with aught else. And after his terrible fall, instead of having the elements of religion diminished in number, or removed further from him, he became still more intimately associated with them. Then the promise and great purposes of redemption were brought under his notice, and urged on his attention and observance with redoubled force. He had before this time learned, by bitter experience, the existence, subtilty, and power of his adversary the devil; and had been taught to apprehend somewhat of the spiritual and endless ruin to which he stood exposed. He was informed of the new relation of the woman, as the predicted mother of the great Deliverer—of the promised Son, who was to endure suffering, and finally to bruise the head of the serpent. With the tree of life, **and** with whatever of a sacramental character was connected with it, he was well acquainted; and the tree of knowledge, with the dire consequences of eating its forbidden fruit, would be fully present to his mind. Then he would understand the promise of redemption, as it affected individual man in that day, on which Abel exercised faith, and secured salvation; and the newly-appointed means of access unto God,—the infolding fire, the cherubim, and the sacrifice, —all these religious elements were known to the first race of men; and no believer in the verity of Holy Scripture can doubt but that these had a hold on the human mind, far beyond any ordinary fact or communicated truth. These had all been ingrafted on human history, and embedded in the memory, judgment, and feelings of man, amid the pressure of the most fearful calamity that affected our nature, in connexion with the most wondrous revelations of God, and the mightiest efforts and triumphs of the powers of darkness.

It is equally clear that the immediate survivers of the Flood, in commencing their new course of life and action, as the fathers of a new world, and the progenitors of a new population, would have all these religious realities impressed anew on their minds in the most weighty and affecting manner. That this was so,—that they lived in the memories of their descendants, influenced their character and conduct, gave a tone to their views, were immortalized in their institutions, and referred to in their most solemn traditions, sacred persons, and sacred places, until long after the establishment of idolatry,—is proved most incontestably by the records, religions, and undoubted remains of the most ancient heathen nations. It is demonstrable, therefore, that idolatry did not arise out of such a state of society, and in such a manner, as is supposed by the author whom we have quoted; and it seems to be scarcely less than demonstrable, that it arose as a perversion of truth under the immediate agency and influence of Satanic power. The origin of idolatry, indeed, forms the most prominent result of that great and continued antagonism between truth and error, spiritual light and spiritual darkness, which is discerned in every part of the history of mankind in pre-Christian times. With our views of this conflict and its results,—ranging as the subject does over the times and persons whose history and religion have been treated of in the present and the preceding volumes of this work,—our labours may very suitably be brought to a conclusion.

That human history commenced as the battle-field of these antagonistic powers is an established fact, to which every believer in the Bible will yield a ready assent. Man and the partner of his life, in pristine purity, innocence, and peace, enjoying hallowed intercourse with God, lived in Paradise. Here they were assailed by a spiritual adversary, who is spoken of in the sacred record as the "old serpent,—the devil." By his subtilty they were seduced from their allegiance, and plunged into sin; by which act man's innocent and peaceful condition was terminated.

We here state most explictly, that this portion of the holy record is understood by us as a detail of certain matter of fact. It is no figurative, imaginative, or enigmatical account, but a plain narration of history. As it has to do with, and to speak of spiritual beings, whose attributes, appearances, and volitions must be expressed with some measure of accommodation, when described in the language of men, it may not, perhaps, be wise in us to scrutinize too critically the import of such phrases as, "The voice of the Lord walking in the garden," and, "The serpent was more subtle than any beast of the field which the Lord God had made. And he said unto the woman," in regard of the exact *appearances* which they represent: but that they truly speak of the presence of the Lord Jehovah, and of Satan, no doubt whatever is entertained; and the effect of their communication and influence on the human mind is, of course, regarded by us as unquestionably real.

No sooner had this fearful aggression on human happiness succeeded, than the predetermined and prepared scheme of redemption was propounded. The man and woman are punished, yet are cheered by a glorious promise: Satan is assured that his victory, although giving him a short-lived power to inflict suffering on human nature, shall certainly issue in his own preëminent abasement and misery.

The leading elements of the new economy, in so far as they referred to the instruction, faith, and practice of mankind, were then propounded. Man, removed from the tree of life, to which, in his new relative position as a sinner, he could no longer have access, is made acquainted with a new way of approach unto God,—by the cherubic emblems, the Shekinah, and animal sacrifice.

Under this teaching, and in this practice, the first pair proceeded, until their children attained maturity, and their two sons had, on their own account, and according to their own mind and judgment, to approach God in worship. Here again we see the aggressions of Satan, and the gracious influence of the Spirit of God. Abel, coming in the appointed way with his mind spiritually enlightened, offered his sacrifice *in faith*, and by that faith found salvation. Cain, led away by the wicked one, rejected the appointed oblation, and would do no more than present a thank-offering. His offering was rejected; and the result is well known. Enraged at his rejection, still further urged on by the influence which he had followed, he killed his pious brother. Although we have in this period but few historic incidents, we must take these as types of the history of the time. Other men grew up; and while some were obedient, many rejected the influence of Heaven, and followed that which was in more accordance with their own corrupt hearts. At length one appeared who was fully devoted to God. So entirely did he subject his heart to divine guidance, that he is said to have "walked with God." But the brief notice of this holy man does not seem to be recorded so much to make us acquainted with his character, as to show the results of this spiritual antagonism at that day. Men now became to a great extent ungodly: their ungodly deeds were manifest and general. They had gone beyond this: their conversation was not only wicked, but directed against God; they made "hard speeches against him." Jude 15. Enoch endeavoured to stem this torrent. He proclaimed the truth; he denounced the evil conduct and language which prevailed; and he predicted a future judgment, when the Lord should come to punish sinners. As if to give the highest sanction to such a character, and the fullest attestation to such a proclamation of truth, this saint of God was removed directly to glory.

Onward rolled the course of time, until another model of righteousness and faith was presented in the person of Noah. But, by this time, Satanic influence had so affected the world's population, that God announced his purpose to destroy mankind by a Flood. Noah was commanded to prepare an ark to save his house: he entered upon the arduous task, and, during the one hundred and twenty years this wonderful structure was being raised, he ceased not to preach the truth, and warn the surrounding multitude of their danger. But, unchecked in their career of sin, they went on, until the day that he entered his appointed refuge: no further respite was granted; the Flood came, and the population of the world was destroyed.

Who can contemplate this event without seeing in it a fearful result of this spiritual antagonism? Satan tempts; yet God reigns. Men sin; but God will punish. The continued success of the destroyer is cut short by this terrible judgment; while the signal fidelity of Noah is honoured by signal and miraculous preservation. Under the smile and benediction of Heaven, the redeemed family commence their new career. But here again Satanic guile and power are felt. Whatever may be the precise meaning of the language which describes that dark day in the life of the arkite patriarch, there can be no doubt of its recording a successful Satanic aggression. Nothing short of this could have called forth such a malediction as Noah pronounced on that occasion.

It seems, from a general review of the whole narrative, that the antediluvian population of the world lived in one general body, and, as far as can be ascertained, without the institution of any regular government, subject simply to the effect of communicated truth and spiritual influence. In those circumstances, "men loved darkness rather than light;" evil passions and desires engendered evil actions; and "the earth was filled with violence," until universal depravity ensued. It appears from several passages in Holy Scripture, and from the traditions of the ancient world, that it pleased God to command a totally different general economy for the new world. As soon as a sufficient population was provided, it was divinely appointed that the several tribes and families should separate, and travel to the geographical districts which had been assigned them, (Deut. xxxii, 8,) and which they were respectively called to occupy, under the direction of their hereditary chiefs. In accordance with this providential arrangement, the family of Noah dwelt in the neighbourhood of Ararat for some centuries, until, having sufficiently increased, they appear to have journeyed to Shinar, as a more eligible locality for the appointed separation.

Prior to this, there is every reason for believing that important innovations had been effected in the faith of this united body. Representations of paradisiacal scenes and figures had been made, and incorporated into the place and manner of patriarchal worship; while influential notions had been entertained respecting the promised Incarnate Seed, and his appearing in a priestly and regal character among men; and a religious veneration was cultivated for the first Great Father and his three sons, who were regarded as reappearing in the arkite patriarch and his three sons. These, with many other errors in doctrine and practice, seem to have been induced by the active agency of the evil one, prior to the arrival of the human host at Shinar.

There a grand aggression was made on the preördained purpose of God. Nimrod, the son of Cush, stirred up by the spiritual adversary, arose in proud rebellion against Heaven, and succeeded in persuading the multitude to set aside the idea of dispersion, and to locate in those plains, and to build a capital and a tower, which should perpetuate their unity, and be the centre of their location. There appears from Scripture and ancient tradition abundant reason for concluding that Nimrod induced the people to adopt this course, by putting himself forth as the Promised Seed, and, as such, entitled to rule over the whole race of mankind. In this assumption, as in other instances, the Satanic aggression only professed to aim at an alteration in respect of one part of the divine appointment: government was to be established, and professedly by divine authority; but the Dispersion was to be prevented.

It pleased Jehovah by a miraculous interposition to defeat this Satanic opposition: and the manner, brief as it is, in which this interposition was put forth, seems to indicate that it was done by some peculiar manifestation of the Holy Trinity,—perhaps similar to that which we find made to Abraham when Sodom was destroyed. "Let us go down," said the Lord, "and confound their language:" and thus the Dispersion was enforced, and the several tribes, miraculously prevented from acting in concert, went forth to occupy their respective territories. Still Nimrod and his adherents continued at Babel, and there established a kingdom, dispossessing Asshur; to whom, of right, that territory belonged, and who, in consequence, went forth and built Nineveh on the River Tigris, and there founded a sovereignty.

But the divine purpose was not only infringed by the disobedience of Nimrod in remaining at Babel,—it was in great measure neutralized by the corruptions in religion which had been previously disseminated, and which, carried into every quarter, produced one wide-spread range of wicked idolatry. By a subtilty and energy which Satan alone could infuse, all the religious promises, circumstances, and facts, connected with God's revelations to man and with man's early history, were so systematically perverted, that they dethroned and dishonoured God, filled man with vain imaginations and proud assumptions, and virtually handed over the several sections of the human family to the overwhelming power of Satanic error. It is a circumstance strikingly illustrative of the mighty influence which gave this profane conceit energy and power, that we find all the most ancient kingdoms of the earth fully adopting it, and, indeed, making it the basis of their political constitutions. Not only so, but the plan, as it appears to have been originally sketched, is enlarged and rendered practicable; so that, when the several primitive seats of human settlement were covered with national institutions, everywhere idolatry prevailed. Although, in every instance, one common family type is discernible in this false religion in all places, this was filled up and modified into an almost infinite variety of detail: and, as if to show forth the real author of this foul dishonour to God, and wickedness and folly in man, everywhere the serpent-form was made a special object of adoration, and worshipped as the symbol of power and dominion.

To rear up a standard of truth in opposition to this aggressive error, Jehovah selected a pious individual, and called him out of the very centre of this idolatrous population. Abraham obeyed, and went forth, receiving great promises and wonderful spiritual instruction from God. He journeyed far into the west, went down even into Egypt, and everywhere raised an altar to the true God, and worshipped him alone. To him the promise of an Incarnate Redeemer, from his own seed, was made; and a covenant of mercy was established with him, that he should be the progenitor of this great Saviour. Isaac and Jacob followed in the same footsteps: heirs of the same promise, they, too, maintained fidelity to God, and each received fuller assurance of the coming of the Promised Seed.

The descendants of the latter patriarch, after having suffered grievous persecution in Egypt, were delivered by the mighty power of God. Here commenced a great and prolonged struggle between the powers of darkness and the Spirit of God. Here, for the first time on record, did the energy of Satan dare avowedly to meet, and endeavour to match, the might of the Omnipotent. The issue covered the gods of Egypt with shame, inflicted grievous calamity on that unhappy country, and wrought out a wondrous deliverance for Israel. This people, now a mighty host, are taken under the special care of Jehovah. They are miraculously fed in the desert; water is brought for them from the granite rocks of Sinai. There also they receive a religious economy, an ecclesiastical system, and a political and moral code of laws, immediately from Heaven. Indeed, God not only made wonderful revelations of himself to the Hebrews in the communication of this system, but actually came down and dwelt among them in the form of a visible glory in the holy tabernacle. By these means he led them forty years through the wilderness, and at length brought them into the land which he had promised to their fathers.

In this career of mercy, the power of the evil one was frequently and fully apparent. Even while Moses was in the mount receiving the law from God, Aaron was led to make a golden image for the people to worship; and afterward, so rebellious had they become, that it seemed impossible to keep them from returning to Egypt,— a folly from which they were prevented only by special revelations of the Spirit of God given to seventy prophets, whose spiritual ministry seems to have met the case.

When the children of Israel were located in Canaan, this diabolical aggression was renewed with fearful effect. The Hebrews, who had been, by promise, prophecy, and miracle, wonderfully raised up to bear before all the world a testimony for God against idolatry, themselves plunged into the vile practice to a great extent.

Throughout the rule of the Judges, their history is one continued series of idolatrous apostasy, and repentance under the pressure of galling affliction. At length, by the instrumentality of Samuel and David, the evil seemed to be extirpated. Piety and prosperity reigned in Jerusalem; the Hebrew people rose to the highest pitch of national greatness. God gloriously manifested his presence among them; and the victory over Satanic influence seemed to be complete. Yet when the religion of God appeared to be most secure, it was successfully assailed in what might have been thought its strongest fortress. Solomon, the favoured of the Lord, sunk into sensuality and pride, thence into licentiousness, and at length into idolatry.

From this period, that foul sin was a plague-spot which destroyed the vitals of Hebrew weal. From the time when the kingdom of Israel was formed, its policy directly tended to the promotion of idolatry. This evil influence was not allowed to reign unchecked: the demon destroyer was frequently arrested in his fatal progress by divine interposition. This was in general most efficiently accomplished by the ministry of inspired prophets. On one occasion particularly these antagonistic powers seemed fairly brought into collision, and nothing human could present a more noble aspect than the intrepid Elijah confronting the four hundred prophets of Baal, and challenging the devotion of Israel for Jehovah as the only true God. The triumphant issue is well known; but it failed to destroy the evil. Onward rolled the fatal influence of the prince of darkness: Israel became incorrigibly idolatrous, and was destroyed.

Judah, still enlightened by a glorious succession of prophets, and held in check by the divinely-appointed services of the temple, fell by slower degrees;—but it did fall. Although Satanic influence was repelled by numerous interpositions, and checked by several reformations of religion, all these agencies offered a vain resistance to its action on the corruption and depravity of the human mind. The people, as a body, (for we do not at all in this review refer to individual faith or conduct,) gradually became pervaded by this delusion; their princes took the lead in the fearful apostasy; and even the priesthood became corrupt; until, at length, when the prescience of God revealed the secrets of the sanctuary to the prophet Ezekiel, every form of idolatry, with its foolish and filthy objects of adoration, in all their multitudinous detail, was found depicted on the walls of the chambers, even in the sanctuary of Jehovah! This appears to have been the culminating point of diabolical ascendency. The glorious Shekinah would no longer occupy a temple where Satan had his seat, and so abandoned the sanctuary to its fate. The terrible catastrophe came: Jerusalem, "the city of David," "the holy city," was polluted, destroyed, and trodden down by the heathen. The temple, which had been filled with the divine glory, and whose sacred sanctuary had for centuries been irradiated with the glorious Shekinah of God, was burned with fire. ICHABOD was engraven on every Hebrew institution, and the success of the destroyer seemed complete, in blotting from the earth such an illustrious witness for the truth and power of God as the Hebrew faith and temple-service had been.

It is difficult to conceive of a more completely successful aggression on a divinely-appointed economy than that which is here presented to the mind,—not only as it respected the Hebrew Church itself, but also in its bearing on the covenant-mercy of God, and the great scheme of redemption. All the promises and prophecies which had been given subsequent to the Deluge respecting the great Redeemer, his work, and kingdom, and glorious salvation, had identified these with the Abrahamic covenant, and the house of David, and Mount Zion. The Hebrew sacred service had been instituted with evident and marked typical allusion to the appointed Saviour. Indeed, the entire political arrangements, the origin and succession of the royal family of Judah, with the whole Mosaic ecclesiastical and religious appointments among the people, seemed designed to prepare the way for Messiah, and to unite their various agencies into one complete pledge and precursor of his coming. And yet in the destruction of Jerusalem, and the subversion of the throne of David, all these foreshadowings perished, and not a visible type remained; not an element was left of this elaborate and complete typical economy, to adumbrate the promise of redemption.

But although Satan seemed to have fully accomplished his purpose, it was soon manifest that the grand scheme of redemption rested not on the obedience of man, but on the unchangeable faithfulness of God. Never did the world witness more glorious revelations of Jehovah in support of his Church and his truth, than when his faithful remnant were captives, hanging their harps on the willows of Babylon: never were more wonderful attestations given to the promise of redemption, or more gracious displays of the divine prescience afforded, than there. So gloriously, indeed, did Jehovah work, that before a century had passed away the Hebrews were again located in their own land, worshipping again on the sacred mount, in a newly-erected temple, with the city of Jerusalem and their general polity in progress to entire restoration.

But while the goodness and power of God had thus wrought deliverance for his captive people, the power of the wicked one was being mightily exerted in the Gentile world. Idolatry became everywhere fully established. Babylon, intensely devoted to this Satanic superstition, passed away: Persia arose to rule the nations; but it was under the same malign influence. The king there, too, was worshipped as divine; and although the good Spirit had given a large communication of truth, it was so completely overlaid with the profane assumption of king and priests, that the people were left blindly to worship the sun, or the sacred fire.

Greece then arose to exercise supremacy over the world, and presented a marked display of the continued collision between these antagonistic powers. Highly endowed with intellectual might, richly favoured with divine influence, possessing every element of human greatness in most abundant measure, Greece was unfaithful to the light of truth and the influence of God. " Sin reigned unto death;" a low, corrupt, sensual, and debased idolatry prevailed; until the reasoning mind turned away in disgust, and disowned even the existence of God.

Rome was but an unworthy representation of Greece. Starting on her career of progress with much of truth and divine teaching, Rome became infinitely corrupt. Her idolatry was as vast in its range and as vile as was possible. Never rising so high in intellect, or genius, or art, as Greece, Rome plunged deeper, if it could be, in infamous impurity, until the inspired apostle declares, " God gave them up." Thus Satan reigned, during successive centuries grasping authority over the physical nature of man; (Acts xix;) directing and endowing the human mind, until, notwithstanding the possession of boundless power and immense learning, human nature in Rome sunk to the lowest level of infamous degradation, so that it may be questioned whether in any part of the world it can now be found so very vile. So vast, indeed, was the acquired influence and power of Satan, that he ostentatiously challenges universal sovereignty over the world, and, exhibiting " all the kingdoms of the world, and the glory of them," he proudly tells even the Son of God, " All this power and glory is delivered unto me." Luke iv, 5, 6.

But does the reader ask, " What has become of the restored Hebrews? those for whom Jehovah had done so much, and to whom he had given the most precious of his gifts,—the word of God?" Alas! they no longer bear an efficient testimony for God. They renounced the spirituality of his covenant; they made even " the law of God of none effect by their traditions;" they perverted the promises of redemption; they, while still professing to acknowledge and worship God, exhibited, with a few solitary exceptions, as fearful an instance of the triumph of Satanic guile over saving truth as any other people. Hence, over them also Satan exercises a fearful power, and reigns as "the god of this world."

Thus we see the human family, after so much revelation of truth and mercy, so large an amount of divine influence and divine interposition, proving the depth of human depravity by showing the inefficacy of all these means, not for individual salvation,—*that* these means could and did accomplish,—but to rear up and maintain in the world a living, conquering, enduring church, which should permanently exhibit the power, the purity, and the truth of God.

For the accomplishment of this grand result, the world was driven to the last great crowning promise of grace,—the establishment of the kingdom of God. For this it panted, as in agony, under the tyrant power of the destroyer. And the introduction of this glorious dispensation, by the manifestation of the Son of God, broke the power of Satan, brought in everlasting righteousness, and opened a fountain of mercy, which shall flow on until the whole earth is filled with his glory. Amen.

APPENDIX.

Note 1, page 18.—*Antediluvian Idolatry.*

The idolatry of the antediluvians is not only taught in the traditions preserved by Maimonides; "the Assumption of Enoch" also says, that this patriarch "prejudged both the worshippers and makers of idols and images, in his commination against them." The apocryphal character of this book is fully admitted; but it must be remembered that it was regarded by Tertullian with so much respect, that he thought it, with other authorities extant in his time, decisive on the subject of which this passage speaks. In addition to this, we must call attention to the interpretation, given in a preceding volume, of Gen. iv, 26. (Patriarchal Age, pp. 164–167.) In connexion with the observations referred to, it may be remarked that this text was not read by the Hebrew scribes, "Men profanely calling on the name of the Lord," as Kimchi and other Hebrew scribes render it,—with which reading the Jerusalem Targum agrees: הוא דרא " That was the age in the days of which they began to err, and made themselves idols," (טעירן *idola, errores,*) "and called their idols by the name of the word of the Lord." (See Paulus Fagius in loc. Owen On Images, p. 21.)

An argument to the same effect has been drawn from the language used by Moses, when writing on the subject of antediluvian wickedness. In Gen. vi, 12, we are told, "God looked upon the earth, and, behold, it was corrupt" (נשחתה). The same term is used in this and the following verse three times to specify the evil of this age. It is worthy of observation, that Moses in many other places uses this word as descriptive of idolatrous practices. When speaking of the defection of the people in the case of the golden calf, he says, using the same word, "They have *corrupted* themselves." Exod. xxxii, 7. It is again used in the same sense, Deut. iv, 25: "And shall *corrupt* yourselves, and make a graven image." Deut. xxxi, 29, and xxxii, 5, may be also cited as additional instances; thus affording strong presumptive evidence that the great corruption of the antediluvian age consisted of idolatry.

This conclusion is supported by Arabian traditions. The Koran makes the existence of antediluvian idolatry an article of faith. Chapter lxxi. It is taught that in the days of Noah five false deities—Wadd, Sowa, Yaghuth, Yauk, and Nesr—were generally adored, and that this wickedness occasioned the Deluge. (See also Sale's Preliminary Dissertation, sect. 1.)

Nor must it be forgotten that the earliest Gentile writer, Sanchoniatho, details various particulars which unite to sustain the authority of these traditions. He ascribes the introduction of the worship of the sun to the second generation, intimating that Cain himself indulged in this practice. Of the fifth generation from the first man this writer says, They "consecrated two pillars to fire and wind, and worshipped them, and poured out upon them the blood of the wild beasts taken in hunting: and when these men were dead, those that remained consecrated to them rods, and worshipped the pillars, and held anniversary feasts in honour of them." Again, in the eighth generation we are told that Chysor, who during his life had "exercised himself in words, and charms, and divinations," was after his death "worshipped as a god." Thus does every available source of information confirm the opinion that idolatry was introduced before the Flood.

NOTE 2, page 20.—*Was the Doctrine of the Trinity known to the early Patriarchs?*

There is scarely any question which can be propounded respecting the religion of mankind in remote antiquity of more deep and general interest and importance than this. Reference has already been made to this subject, (Patriarchal Age, pp. 266-272,) when reasons were assigned for believing that the assertion of this doctrine having been held by the disciples of Plato, is not to be relied upon, and that the notions which prevailed among the Platonists arose rather from the prevalence of idolatrous triads among heathen nations than from "any divinely revealed knowledge of the true nature of the divine *hypostasis*." Thus far a careful and extended subsequent examination of the subject has served to confirm the views previously advanced. If, however, this language is construed not merely to apply to the origination of the Platonic dogmas, but to deny the fact of any divinely revealed knowledge on this doctrine having been communicated to the early patriarchs, then I must be allowed to say that in this sense it does not express the opinions which a careful and more mature investigation of the evidence bearing on this subject has fully established in my mind. On the contrary, there does not at present occur to me any reasonable cause for doubt that the doctrine of the Trinity made one of the important religious revelations to the first men, and that it, in connexion with the doctrine of the incarnation, (respecting which also some knowledge was communicated,) led to the worship of human nature, and the adoration of the three sons of each great father as a sacred triad. This gave a distinctive colouring to the whole system of heathen idolatry. It must not, however, from thence be inferred that Plato possessed a knowledge of this doctrine. This philosopher, in fact, never taught the existence of "three subsistences in one divine essence." Consequently Cudworth is compelled to say, "We freely acknowledge, that as this Divine Cabala was but little understood by many of those who entertained it among the Pagans, so was it by divers of them much depraved and adulterated also. For, first, the Pagans universally called their trinity 'a trinity of gods,'—τὸν πρῶτον, τὸν δεύτερον, and τρίτον θεόν, 'the first, the second,' and the 'third god;' as the more philosophical among them called it also 'a trinity of causes,' and 'a trinity of principles,' and sometimes 'a trinity of opificers.' Thus is this cabala of the trinity styled in Proclus, ἡ τῶν τριῶν θεῶν παράδοσις, 'the tradition of the three gods.'"—*Intellectual System*, vol. ii, p. 314.

If, therefore, we apply the results of modern research into oriental countries and religious doctrines to the *data* collected by Cudworth, the result will be, that, instead of believing with that eminent man that "this mystery was gradually imparted to the world, and that first but sparingly to the Hebrews themselves, either in their written or oral cabala"—*Intellectual System*, vol. ii, p. 314—we shall find reason for concluding that some distinct intimation of the triune nature was given to man at the beginning,—a knowledge which was maintained in the Hebrew Church, increased by successive revelation, and finally

APPENDIX.

perfected by the discoveries of the gospel: while, on the other hand, the Gentiles, although receiving the tradition, prior to the general Dispersion, with sufficient distinctness to impress a character upon all their idolatrous systems, nevertheless in process of time lost sight of the true nature of the doctrine, and at the period of the birth of Christ were destitute of all sound knowledge on the subject.

It is too much to ask the reader to receive our *ipse dixit* on this important case; nor will space allow our citing the wide range of evidence which has led us to this conclusion. In these circumstances a very brief abstract must be supplied.

The learned Dr. Allix has elaborately argued, (Reflections, chap. xviii,) that Moses, in the Book of Genesis, mentioned nothing but what was then generally known. If this proposition had been satisfactorily established, the case would have been settled, as it is an undoubted fact that Moses in this book uses language which clearly teaches a plurality of persons in the Divine Nature; and, when the promise of the incarnation, and the mention of the "Word of the Lord" as a person, are considered, is such as could scarcely be used by those who were ignorant of the doctrine of the Trinity. But even if this proposition is not fully sustained, there yet remains sufficient evidence that some important measure of knowledge on this subject was communicated, either to the first man, (which is most probable,) or to the early patriarchs.

This will be seen if it be remembered that there exists ample reason for believing that Moses compiled the beginning of the Book of Genesis from pre-existent records; (Patriarchal Age, pp. 67–70;) and that these contain the allusions to a divine plurality to which reference has been made. The knowledge of this doctrine which these passages display cannot, therefore, be ascribed to revelations made to Moses, but to some age long prior to the date of his writing. But then it must be recollected that Moses, while writing for the purpose of rooting out of the minds of men all notion of polytheism, yet transcribes these singular solecisms in language, "*In the beginning*," ברא אלהים (*bara Elohim*) "the Gods created." He might have said, *Jehovah bara*, or *Eloah bara*, and thus have used a singular noun as the name of Deity. Instead of this, however, he transcribes this plural appellation of God thirty times in the history of the Creation. But then this plural noun is used in connexion with (*bara*) a singular verb, thus clearly indicating that this divine plurality is one God. Nor is it to be supposed that this was a peculiarity of manner or style of writing used by Moses; for in other places he uses the singular *Eloah*, (Deut. xxxii, 15, 17,) and frequently connects the plural *Elohim* with plural verbs and adjectives. Gen. xx, 13, &c.; xxxv, 10, &c. This conclusion is supported, and the knowledge of the triune personalities rendered still more probable, by the language used in other parts of the Book of Genesis. We are told (xv, 1) "that 'the Word of the Lord came unto Abram in a vision, saying, Fear not, Abram; I am thy shield and thy exceeding great reward.' Here the Word of the Lord is the speaker: 'The Word came, saying.' A mere word may be spoken or said; but a personal Word only can say, 'I am thy shield.' The pronoun 'I' refers to the whole phrase, 'The Word of Jehovah;' and if a personal Word be not understood, no person at all is mentioned by whom this message is conveyed, and whom Abram, in reply, invokes as 'Lord God.'"—*Watson's Institutes*, vol. i, p. 563. Again, Gen. xix, 24: "Then the Lord" (*Jehovah*) "rained upon Sodom and Gomorrah brimstone and fire from the Lord" (*Jehovah*) "out of heaven." We have here the visible Jehovah, who had talked with Abraham, raining the storm of vengeance from another Jehovah out of heaven, and who was therefore invisible. Thus two Jehovahs are expressly mentioned: "The LORD rained from the LORD." This language proves that a plurality of persons in the Deity was known to the writer of the Book of Genesis: and that one of them held the peculiar relation or title of "the Word of Jehovah :" and the manner in which this information is communicated demonstrates that the persons spoken of, who lived long before Moses, were familiar with this language.

As decisive evidence on this latter point we may refer to the words used by Abraham to the king of Gerar: "When God caused me to wander," &c. Gen. xx, 13. In the original it is, "When" אלהים (*Elohim*) "the *Gods* caused," &c. Jacob uses similar language, Gen. xxxv, 7: "Jacob built an altar, and called the place" אל בית־אל "*El-Beth-el*, because there God" in the original, אלהים *Elohim*, "*Gods*") "appeared unto him." These passages, regarded in their connexion and scope, will be sufficient to prove that a Trinity, or at least a plurality, of persons in the Deity was known to the early patriarchs, and probably even from the beginning. The opinions formed under the guidance of this evidence are greatly strengthened by the fact that important information was communicated to the first pair immediately after the Fall respecting the incarnation and redemption through a Mediator: and throughout all ancient idolatry we find this information blended with ideas of a Trinity, forming the leading elements of every system.

It is, indeed, "generally agreed among divines that Adam in the state of perfection knew God in Trinity and Unity."—*De Gol's Vindication*, page 105. Epiphanius is most positive on this point; and Jerome, Justin, Irenæus, Tertullian, and many others, entertained and defended the same opinion. It therefore seems reasonable to conclude, that some knowledge of a Trinity was communicated to the early patriarchs, and probably to Adam, either in his state of innocence, or immediately after the Fall.

NOTE 3, page 20.—*The Worship of Man.*

Few perversions of the truth by the corrupt imagination of fallen man are more strange, in their nature and results, than that of worshipping some of his own race. That an intelligent and rational creature should ascribe divine honour and power to one of the same species seems an unaccountable folly. Yet when it is examined, like every other wicked aberration of the human mind, it is found to arise from a perversion of truth. The revelations of Paradise, in their use or abuse, coloured and formed the religious doctrines of mankind in all after-ages. The primitive promise, that the Seed of the woman should bruise the head of the serpent, was evidently understood, not only so far as to form a solid foundation for human hope, but also to some extent as it respected the means by which the deliverance was to be effected. On one particular there can be no doubt, namely, that the promised Redeemer would be an incarnation of Deity.

It is difficult to conceive how such an idea as this could have obtained a place in the human mind, had it not been revealed. This topic has not received the attention which it merits. An incorporation of the divine with human nature! All analogy and all reason are against it. Yet we find this notion not simply propounded by any particular class of philosophers, but generally pervading the heathen world.

It is, however, the manner and connexion in which this singular sentiment is found among all heathen nations which so lucidly indicates its origin. In a preceding volume, the principal sacred persons of heathen mythology are clearly identified with traditions of Paradise. (Patriarchal Age, pp. 132, 133.) But if Apollo, Chrishna, Hercules, Orpheus, Thor, and others, derived their religious and mythological character from corrupted private tradition, how clearly this shows that we have here the leading idea of the adoration of human nature!

In all these instances it was believed that a union of the divine and the human natures existed; a union the most intimate and natural which the perverted reason of man could comprehend. On this basis was reared every kind of profane presumption, political and religious. Alexander, when greatly pressed for time, thought it expedient to traverse Egypt, and cross the desert, in order to have his divine paternity attested by the oracle,—believing this necessary to his success; while to this day the head of the Scythian Church claims the character of God incarnate. Numerous examples of a similar kind, in every age and country, might be adduced, (Patriarchal Age, pp. 331-333,) showing that the original and ruling idea in all this assumption was the promised Incarnation. It seemed, indeed, to have been an admitted fact, that a claim to the character of the *Incarnate One* was essential alike to universal sovereignty and human adoration. The sovereigns of Babylon united both these claims, and led the way in this career of insane folly and awful guilt. Hence the word of inspiration has said, "Babylon is a golden cup. The Gentiles have drunk thereof. Therefore are the Gentiles mad."

Nor is it wonderful that such notions should have pervaded the heathen world, when we find the expectation of the Incarnation so strongly asserted by our first parents, and remember that, under Satanic influence, almost every element of primitive truth was perverted in heathen idolatry.

It may be doubted whether we attach sufficient importance to the perfect humanity which was evinced in the earliest manifestations of the *Word of God.* The text, (Gen. iii, 8,) "And they heard the voice of the Lord God walking in the garden," is rendered by the Targumists, "*They heard the Word of the Lord God walking;*" and the Jerusalem Targum paraphrases the beginning of the next verse, "*The Word of the Lord called unto Adam.*" The Word therefore that called, was the Word or voice that walked. *Vox enim res est illa, de quâ dicitur, quòd ambulaverit in horto.* Maim., *Mor. Nevoch.*, par. 1, cap. 24. See also *Tzeror Hammor*, sect. *Beresh*, apud Owen, Exerc. x, in Heb. vi,1. The gloss of this last work is perfectly unequivocal: "*They heard his voice walking.*" Now this clearly shows that the Divine Word came to the first pair immediately after their sin, possessing the attributes of Godhead for judgment and punishment, and at the same time appearing as a man. So fully was this the case that the sound of his footsteps first terrified the culprits, and they fled. (Faber's Eight Dis., vol. i, p. 28.)

Eve made a singular confession of her expectation of this Incarnate One, when, on the birth of her first-born, she exclaimed, "I have gotten that man which is Jehovah the Lord." Gen. iv, 1. Here, as Dr. Lightfoot observes, "the mother shows her apprehension of the promise: 'For,' said she, 'I have obtained the Lord to become man.'"—*Works*, vol. ii, p. 12. "And it is very remarkable that Adam did not call his wife *Chava*, or *Eve*, 'the Mother of all living,' till after he had received the promise of the Messiah. Before, he called her *Ischa*, 'Woman;' but when God had assured him of a Saviour, a Deliverer, then he calls her *Eve*, or 'Life;' for so the LXX. rendered it: Καὶ ἐκάλεσεν Ἀδὰμ τὸ ὄνομα τῆς γυναικὸς αὐτοῦ, Ζωή. And why so? Why must she be called 'Life' who was the introducer of death?" Evidently in reference to the Seed of the woman who should give life to the world.

As the Word of the Lord appeared in Paradise as a man, so he came to Abraham as a man; so he wrestled with Jacob as a man. Upon which a learned author remarks: "In each case, we may observe the Angel of Jehovah, appearing indeed in the form of a MAN, but yet, though he is usually spoken of as *sent* by Jehovah, declared to be the God Jehovah *himself*. By way of cutting off all occasion of dispute, it may be proper to remark, that the human figure which was thus exhibited, was no mere aërial phantom, but a substantial body provided with the same organs that *our* bodies are. The MAN-JEHOVAH, who conversed with Abraham, suffered his feet to be washed by that patriarch, and literally ate of the butter, and the milk, and the calf, which was set before him,—the MAN-JEHOVAH, who wrestled with Jacob, was palpable to the touch."— *Faber's Eight Dis.*, vol. i, p. 34. It was under the influence of such facts that the ancients formed their ideas of the expected incarnation.

These impressions, which were perpetuated in the early ages of the world, at once predisposed men to acknowledge and adore deified humanity, and afforded opportunity for presumptuous and ambitious individuals to claim this divine character, and to demand this adoration. (De Gol's Vindication, p. 108.)

NOTE 4, page 54.—*The Geography and Population of Egypt*.

Of all the countries which have obtained political power and importance, Egypt seems the most peculiar in situation and geographical outline. Extending southward from the Mediterranean where the Nile falls into the sea, following the course of that river, Egypt reaches to Philæ, in the Cataracts of E'Sooan or Syene, a length of about five hundred miles. This was the extent of the country according to Strabo; and it has the advantage of having been oracularly decided by the high-priest at the temple of Ammon. (Herodotus, Euterpe, cap. 18.) The breadth is very unequal. At the coast what may be properly called Egypt is about one hundred and fifty miles wide; but this part, which includes the Delta, diminishes in breadth, until, reduced to the Valley of the Nile, it becomes very narrow. Wilkinson has computed Lower Egypt, including the irrigated land on each side of the Delta, as containing four thousand five hundred square miles, although the whole arable land of Egypt Proper does not much exceed two thousand two hundred and twenty-five square miles. The Valley of the Nile, formed by a narrow slip of land on each side of the river, and bounded either by rocky mountains or sandy deserts, is about eight or ten miles in average width, as nearly as such an irregular outline can be estimated. Besides this, there are many spots between the rocky hills suitable for cultivation, which would greatly add to the capability of the country to provide for a large population, especially in Upper Egypt. The Oases have also been sometimes included: but there is no evidence to show that they were occupied by the Egyptians in ancient time.

It is not easy to determine the complexion of the population. They were certainly not negroes, although, from the proximity of Nubia, there is no doubt that intermarriages frequently took place between the two nations. One of the early sovereigns of Egypt, Amenophis I., is accompanied on the sculptures with two wives, one of whom is always represented black. If the skin of the mummy retains its original colour, the question of complexion would be easily settled: but we do not know what effect embalming and the lapse of centuries have had in this respect. It is a singular fact that on the exterior cases, as in the ancient paintings, the men are represented of a red-brown and the women of a green-yellow. But this, as Kenrick observes, must be conventional. The real colour was probably brown with a tinge of red.

It is difficult to speak with accuracy as to the number of inhabitants who were found in Egypt, since it is not always possible to ascertain whether ancient writers refer to Egypt Proper, or to the entire territory which at the time was brought under subjection to the Egyptian government. Theocritus reckons the number of Egyptian towns as thirty-three thousand three hundred and thirty-nine; but then he includes in his calculation Ethiopia, Libya, Syria, Arabia, Pamphylia, Cilicia, Caira, and Lycia, which were at that period subject to Ptolemy Philadelphus. Herodotus gives no precise information on the subject. Diodorus states the population of ancient Egypt to have reached seven millions; but the text is obscure, as it is doubtful whether he intended to say that it continued so large to his own time, or was reduced to half the number. Josephus reckoned the Valley of the Nile to contain seven millions in the time of Vespasian, besides the population of Alexandria, which would make three hundred thousand more. Tacitus informs us that when Germanicus visited Egypt, he was told by a priest at Thebes, that this city formerly contained within its walls seven hundred thousand fighting men. But this probably applied to the whole country, and the passage is so understood by Kenrick. It is possible, however, that the population of Egypt may have been overrated on account of the number and magnitude of the public works which were executed in this country. The ability to construct these buildings would depend not upon the number of men in the country, but rather upon the proportion of time which each individual would require to provide for his own subsistence and that of his family: and it is very probable that the necessary provision for individual existence could be procured with more ease in Egypt than in any country of the ancient world. Diodorus says, "It costs not a parent, to bring up a child to man's estate, above twenty drachmas," which sum amounts to about twelve shillings and sixpence. Some writers have supposed that Diodorus meant the annual expense; but even then the necessaries of life must have been exceedingly cheap. Probably Egypt in her greatest glory might have contained about eight millions.

This estimate of population would justify the apprehension which was felt from the rapid increase of the Israelites. It has been shown, in a preceding volume, that the Hebrews at the Exodus were probably far above three millions. Such a number of persons, rendered enemies by oppression, at one extremity of a kingdom five hundred miles long, would give great reason for apprehension: hence the bloody measure adopted to check their increase. (Diodorus Siculus, lib. i, cap. 80; Tacitus Ann., lib. ii, cap. 60; Kenrick's Ancient Egypt, vol. i, chap. viii; Wilkinson, vol. i, p. 217; Hamilton's Ægyptiaca; D'Anville's Ancient Geography, &c.)

NOTE 5, page 57.—*The Chronology of Ancient Egypt.*

It is not intended here to go into any critical analysis of those pretensions to remote antiquity which appear to have been either designedly or ignorantly made by the Egyptian priesthood, and which have been urged in modern times, as placing Egyptian history in opposition to revealed truth. What was thought necessary on this subject was said in the first part of this work. (The Patriarchal Age.) And although, since the publication of that volume, a continental scholar has laboured to sustain the cause of Egyptian antiquity against the Bible, it is believed that a dispassionate consideration of a few simple facts will be sufficient to vindicate revealed truth. When it is considered that we have the works of no Egyptian author preserved to our day; that the fragments of Manetho were written B. C. 260; that the dynasties prior to the eighteenth are in some instances known to be contemporaneous; that even in respect to the eighteenth dynasty, the best Egyptian scholars are disputing as to its chronological position, differing in opinion to the extent of two or three centuries; and that the first event in Egyptian history which certainly synchronizes with that of any neighbouring nation, is the invasion of Judea by Shishak, B. C. 974: —I say, when all these admitted facts are considered, it may be safely asserted, that no reasonable claim can be raised, from such materials as exist, respecting early Egyptian history, of any weight against the explicit testimony of Moses, even if we receive him only in the character of an authentic uninspired historian. If Herodotus, or any other heathen author, had given the world as explicit an account of the origin of nations, and fixed as accurately the generation in which it took place, as Moses has done, the question would be regarded as settled: but the pride of man will not submit to the teaching of God. If, however, any further evidence of the truth of Mosaic teaching respecting this country is required, it may be found in the remarkable agreement which subsists between it and the history of Egypt, when the latter is adjusted on sound chronological principles.

With the eighteenth dynasty we enter upon the most flourishing era of Egyptian greatness; and at the invasion of Judea, B. C. 974, we have a sure test of Egyptian chronology, as that event unquestionably took place in the early part of the reign of Shishak. Besides these points, the expulsion of the Shepherd-kings, and the Exodus of the Israelites, must be recognised. It is no more possible to ignore these facts, than it is to ignore the Roman invasion or the Norman conquest of Britain; and, admitting them, they must more or less influence any arrangement of Egyptian dynasties. In fact, as Mr. Cory says, "the great problem of Egyptian chronology is, to find the position of the eighteenth dynasty. But in doing this, any attention to Holy Scripture is constantly open to censure as unscientific and unphilosophical; although it cannot be denied, that neither Egypt nor any other ancient nation has given us a chronology so consecutive, intelligible, and authentic as the Bible. It is thus that Eusebius is reflected on for attempting to reduce the chronology of other nations to the standard of the Jews." It will be necessary briefly to give an outline of the facts. Manetho was high-priest of the temple of Isis at Sebennytus in Lower Egypt about 284 B. C. He was well versed in Greek learning, and certainly had access to all the literary treasures of Egypt then extant. He wrote a History of Egypt in three volumes, in each of which he gave in detail the dynasties of the kings of whom the history treated. The work itself has perished, but the lists have been handed down to us in a tabular form. It is uncertain whether Manetho wrote them in this manner, or whether they were extracted by Christian writers from the body of the work, and arranged by them in their present form. This work, by the confession of the author, was not only derived partly from the sacred books, but also in part *from popular tradition.*

The first Christian author who treated of Manetho's History was Julius, a native of Africa, bishop of Nicopolis, commonly called Julius Africanus. He wrote early in the third century, and seems to have aimed at exhibiting the connexion which had subsisted between the histories of the Babylonians, the Egyptians, and the Jews. His works are also lost, except a few fragments. About one hundred years later Eusebius followed Africanus. His was a more comprehensive work, although similar in object to that of his predecessor. Five hundred years after the time of Eusebius, George the Scyncellus, a Byzantine monk, wrote a general Chronology, which has come down to us in almost a perfect state. This, together with an Armenian copy of Eusebius, is the only means we at present possess of examining the dynasties of Manetho. Eusebius, as has been already intimated, has been censured because he regarded Scriptural chronology as a standard, and endeavoured to bring that of Egypt into agreement with it: and it has been alleged that "this could be effected on no sound principles;—that he appears not to have scrupled at arbitrary and even unfair expedients to attain this end."—*Kenrick's Ancient Egypt*, vol. ii, p. 91. But when we inquire into the *gravamen* of this heavy charge, it is found to be this:—Eusebius regards some of the early dynasties as reigning contemporaneously in particular nomes. And this, we are told, is of "no authority," and countenanced by "no other ancient author." (*Ibid.*, pp. 96, 97.) But what is the fact ? In 1849 a European scholar, writing from Egypt, and verifying his statements by actual inspection of the monuments, before he transmitted them to Europe, avers, that he has found actual proof that two or more of these dynasties existed at the same time. (R. S. Pole's Horæ Ægyptiacæ. See Literary Gazette for 1829, p. 262.) The limits of this note do not admit the production of this proof in detail; but it is amply sufficient to justify the conduct of Eusebius.

For the purpose, then, of testing the accuracy of this author, I take his numbers entire. The eighteenth dynasty, as corrected by the old chronicle, lasted three hundred and forty-eight years; and in the chronicle of Eusebius, after the ninth sovereign there is a note to this effect: "Under him Moses led the Jews in their Exodus from Egypt." "If, then, this dynasty were arranged on this principle, and it were admitted that Amosis, after having expelled the Shepherd-kings, reigned twenty-five years before the commencement of the eighteenth dynasty, the early chronology of Egypt would stand as follows:—

	B. C.
Expulsion of Shepherd-kings by Amosis	1845
He reigned afterward twenty-five years.	
Commencement of eighteenth dynasty at his death	1820
Continued three hundred and forty-eight years.	
Commencement of nineteenth dynasty	1472
Lasted one hundred and eighty-seven years.	
Twentieth dynasty began	1285
Duration one hundred and seventy-eight years.	
Twenty-first dynasty began	1107
Continued one hundred and thirty years.	
Twenty-second dynasty began	977

The first sovereign of this dynasty was Sesonchis,—the Shishak of Scripture; and, according to this scheme, he invaded Judea in the third year of his reign, B. C. 974. Besides this, other important requirements are met by this adjustment. The Arundelian Marbles state the fall of Troy to have taken place B. C. 1184, and Pliny asserts that a Rameses then reigned in Egypt. Such was the fact at that period, according to the preceding reckoning. The Exodus took place, according to Russel and the chronology adopted in this work, B. C. 1608; and by the above plan Achenchases, the son of Horus, died in that year. Again: there is a monumental sculpture, representing the Israelites under their taskmasters making bricks, in the reign of Thothmosis III. According to the scheme I have adopted, this would take place about one hundred and fifteen years before the Exodus: and as the Israelites had been long oppressed before the birth of Moses,—so long, indeed, that it became evident that their numbers rapidly increased, notwithstanding their oppression, and the savage measure of destroying the male infants was adopted in consequence,—and the Exodus took place in the eightieth year of Moses, this is also a corroborating incident. Further: the date of Joseph's going down into Egypt falls in the early part of the reign of Amosis, after the expulsion of the Shepherds, and the descent of Jacob, three years before the death of this Pharaoh. In this instance, also, the Scriptural account which supposes the prince who made Joseph governor to be the same who received his patriarchal father, is justified. And, lastly, this arrangement places the accession of the eighteenth dynasty only two years later than the time fixed by Champollion Figeac from independent astronomical and historical *data*, which date is also supported by the authority of Mr. Osburn.

It would display a childish affectation to rest upon any exactitude of date to a year or two in a case of this kind; but confidence may certainly be challenged for this scheme, on the ground of its general accordance with historical and Scriptural fact, while it does not appear to be open to any serious objection. Nor is it unworthy of observation that other schemes of chronological arrangement either altogether overlook the date of the Exodus, or place it in circumstances altogether irreconcilable with the Scripture narrative and with the facts of the case. (Kenrick's Ancient Egypt; Cory's Chronological Inquiry; Wilkinson's Ancient Egyptians; Horæ Ægyptiacæ; Literary Gazette for 1829; Osburn's Ancient Egypt, and his Egypt: her Testimony to the Truth.)

NOTE 6, page 56.—*The Monumental Names of Kings.*

In the oldest monuments, as those of the Pyramids and tombs of Gizeh, the names of Egyptian kings are enclosed in oval shields or rings, and each king has only one. The characters included in the oval are phonetic, and express the name of the king as it was then pronounced. In later times, that is, in the eighteenth and succeeding dynasties, each king has usually two such shields or oval rings. Over the first there are generally delineated the figure of a bee, and a branch of a plant; over the second, a vulpanser, and the disk of the sun, which are read, "Son of the Sun." Where two shields are found, it is generally admitted that the second contains the proper name of the prince in phonetic characters. As to the contents of the first of these rings, there has been some little difference of opinion. Champollion considered these signs as symbolical titles; but perhaps Osburn has caught the correct idea, in regarding them as the inaugural and distinctive title assumed by each king on his accession to the throne. The name found in the second ring is that which corresponds to the lists of Manetho. (Kenrick's Ancient Egypt; Osburn's Egypt: her Testimony to the Truth.)

NOTE 7, page 65.—*Sir Gardiner Wilkinson on the Date of the Exodus.*

Nothing seems more extraordinary than the opinions expressed by this learned Egyptologist on this subject. He maintains that the Exodus took place during the reign of Thothmosis III., although he confesses that if it did, it must have been in the early part of his reign. Without raising any question as to the date of this event, which of itself would be sufficient to refute this notion, or referring to the general interpretation of Biblical critics, that the Pharaoh who ruled Egypt at the time of the Exodus was destroyed with his army in the Red Sea,—which will by most persons be regarded as a fatal objection to this learned writer's theory,—I rest simply on the undoubted fact, that the deliverance of Israel, and the consequent plagues of Egypt, arose out of a controversy which Jehovah had with the idolatry of Egypt; and that the result was a great punishment of that proud and wicked kingdom. This was notorious for ages,—was patent to the world. Hence the prophet asked so confidently, "Art thou not he which smote Rahab, and wounded the dragon?" Can it, then, be believed, as Sir J. G. Wilkinson teaches, that the Exodus occurred just as Egypt was rising to its greatest glory; that this event released Egypt from inconvenience, and increased her strength? Surely this is impossible! The Exodus, with its precursory plagues, must have been a fearful infliction on this land, and could not have occurred just prior to a series of unexampled triumphs and national successes.

NOTE 8, page 70.—*The Providential Preparation for the Israelitish Invasion of Canaan.*

When the host of Israel encamped at Kadesh-Barnea, and spies were sent to ascertain the condition of the people occupying the land of Canaan, their fenced cities and martial power overwhelmed the feeble faith of the Hebrews, and they said, "We were in our own sight as grasshoppers; and so we were in their sight." Thus the purpose of God, that they should at that time take possession of the land, was frustrated, and the conquest of Canaan delayed more than thirty-eight years.

To insure the accomplishment of this purpose at that period, two measures were devised, and carried into execution, both displaying marvellous condescension and mercy. In order to teach Israel to rely more fully on Jehovah, and to have confidence in the word of his power, they were led through the wilderness during this long period, and had, on many most critical occasions, to obtain deliverance from ruin by a sole and simple trust in the promise of God. On the other hand, the nations of Palestine, so proud in their martial glory, were at the same time assailed in successive campaigns by Sethos and his son Rameses II. with all the military force of Egypt; so that many of their strongest fortresses were destroyed, and their military power greatly diminished. By these means the Lord graciously paved the way for the accomplishment of his purposes,—the judicial destruction of the Canaanitish nations, and the establishment of Israel as a separate and independent nation.

NOTE 9, page 71.—*The Martial Career of Sesostris.*

Mr. Osburn—a scholar whose immense learning, especially in respect of Egyptology, coupled, as it is, with a deep religious reverence for Scripture truth, entitles him to great deference and respect—has here advanced a scheme which, after the most careful investigation, appears open to insuperable objections with regard to his view of the route of this monarch, and the scene of his conquests. Mr. Osburn, guided by his reading of the hieroglyphic sculptures, supposes the Egyptian army, after the reduction of Punon, to go northward by the Wady-el-Erabah, expelling the Arvadites and Jebusites; and that they then embarked on the Dead Sea, probably in the ships of the Arvadites. Having reached the southern end of the sea, it is said, "the hieroglyphics seem to indicate that the march of Sesostris lay through the countries of the Jebusites and Hittites." Having, in fact, sailed from the south of the Dead Sea to the north, he is considered to have made a double, and returned southward again to Hadessah, which is supposed to lie near Jerusalem. This city he captured; and the conquest is spoken of as the most glorious event of the war. Having effected this object, he is supposed to have gone north again, to embark on the Dead Sea, and thus to return to Egypt. The following appear to be serious and valid objections to this scheme:—1. It is a notorious fact, attested not only by all ancient history, but also by recent Assyrian discovery, that long before the days of Sesostris the kings of Egypt had extended their conquests to the borders of Assyria; and that Sesostris is both by Egyptian monuments and general history regarded as equal, if not superior, to any of his predecessors. 2. The *Shetin* with whom Sesostris fought the great battle of this campaign, and whose subjection was his greatest triumph, are always on the monuments associated with Naharina, or Mesopotamia, and are so mentioned on the Assyrian Obelisk. 3. The manner in which both the monuments and the Greek writers speak of the passage of Sesostris through Canaan, forbids the opinion that this was the great scene of the war. On the monuments the king is described as forcing his passage through the country; and Herodotus speaks of it as if he molested none but those who opposed him. Mr. Osburn, also, distinctly says, "It is sufficiently apparent that nothing of great importance took place during the progress of Sesostris to the land of the *Shetin;*" and certainly this was not in Palestine. 4. It seems altogether incredible that the Egyptian king should find a fleet able to transport his army on the Dead Sea. Who ever heard of ships on that sea? This fleet, too, belonged to his enemies, who are supposed in each instance to have made a peace with him, just exactly in time to place their fleet at his disposal. For these reasons I feel compelled to differ in opinion from such an accomplished scholar as Mr. Osburn, and to lay down in the text a different and, as I believe, a more probable route for this conqueror. (Osburn's Egypt: her Testimony to the Truth; Kenrick's Egypt under the Pharaohs, vol. ii, pp. 260, 278, 288; Papers by Mr. Birch on Egyptian Obelisks, in the Transactions of the Royal Society of Literature, New Series.)

NOTE 10, page 76.—*The Cruelty exhibited in Egyptian Sculptures.*

The importance of Egyptian sculptures to any extensive acquaintance with the early history of the country is universally acknowledged; but it is not so generally known as it should be upon what principles these representations, so far as relates to warlike triumphs, are constructed, nor the cruel and sanguinary spirit which pervades them.

The walls of the temples and palaces which are covered with these immense pictures are often sixty to eighty feet high, and from six hundred to eight hundred feet long. A general rule may be laid down in respect of those which refer to military affairs. The first scene usually depicted is the battle and the victory. The conqueror, who is always one of the Pharaohs, is represented of gigantic stature, accompanied by as many of his warriors as can be introduced. These are pictured as slaughtering multitudes of their enemies, trampling upon the fallen, driving over heaps of slain, taking and sacking their strong-holds, and leading off male and female captives. This exhibition, which represents slaughtering rather than fighting, is sufficiently coarse in its sanguinary character.

The next scene is the repose after victory. The conqueror sits in his chariot, and calls upon his troops to rejoice; while the prisoners are brought bound to his feet, and the number of the enemy which have been slain ere estimated by the number of their right hands which have been cut off, brought to the sovereign, and counted over in his presence.

The next scene is laid in Egypt, and in the temple where the picture is found. Here the conqueror offers to the gods the spoils which he has obtained, and drags to their feet long lines of captives. These are represented nearly naked, tied together by one cord, which passes round the necks of all of them. As if this did not inflict sufficient degradation and suffering, their arms are bound in a variety of ways, all calculated to produce intense agony. In fact, this is done in a manner which plainly denotes an intention to inflict torture;— as if, says a learned writer, "the cries of the wretched sufferers formed an important accessory to the diabolical ceremony."

Then we must not forget the common pictorial appendage to almost every one of these representations, and which may be regarded as the title-page or table of contents—or even as both combined—of the entire picture. In this part, one or more of each of the conquered nations or tribes is placed in a kneeling posture in a circular form, as if tied to a stake in the centre; while a gigantic figure of the king gathers a portion of the hair of each into his left hand, and destroys them with a scimitar or club, which he brandishes in his right hand.

The atrocious cruelty thus exhibited is magnified by other representations. When Sethos, who reigned next after the Exodus, is represented as returning to Egypt in triumph from his wars in Canaan, he is seen seated in his chariot, leading in four separate cords as many strings of captives from the vanquished tribes, whose arms are tied into forms which must have given exquisite torture. Two of them, chiefs, have had their hands cut off; while three heads, reeking in gore, are suspended about the chariot;—a representation by no means uncommon in the sculptures of Egypt. When the great Sesostris is depicted as returning in triumph to Egypt from his wars, not only is he accompanied by the usual strings of captives bound in the most unmerciful manner, but three of the chiefs of the vanquished tribes are represented suspended beneath the axle of his chariot, in a posture of the greatest pain and utmost degradation.

It is, therefore, certain that the art, science, philosophy, and religion of the Egyptians, in all their combined influence upon their great monarchs, failed to inspire even common humanity, or to save them from the most enormous and detestable acts of cold-blooded cruelty: and what gives the deepest stain to their national morals is, that they did not hesitate to record and emblazon this diabolical torture in connexion with their noblest triumphs.

NOTE 11, page 125.—*The Fulfilment of sacred Prophecy in the History of Egypt.*

PROPHECY I.—The first of these wonderful manifestations of the divine prescience respecting this nation, taking them in the order of their fulfilment, was

538   APPENDIX.

the interpretation given by Joseph to the dreams of Pharaoh; from which he foretold the seven years of plenty, and the subsequent seven years of famine. Gen. xli.

These predictions were literally verified: and all the extraordinary operations of these fourteen years must have made known to the people at large the power of Jehovah, and have challenged the recognition of all Egypt, as a standing proof of the infinite prescience of the God of the Hebrews.

PROPHECY II we have in the divine declaration given to Abraham: "Know of a surety that thy seed shall be a stranger in a land that is not theirs, and shall serve them; and they shall afflict them four hundred years; and also that nation, whom they shall serve, will I judge: and afterward shall they come out with great substance." Gen. xv, 13-16.

The long and painful bondage of Israel, and their triumphant Exodus, wonderfully fulfilled these prophecies.

PROPHECY III refers to the signal defeat of Pharaoh-necho at Carchemish. A more spirited and graphic picture can scarcely be found than that which is given by Jeremiah (chap. xxvi, 1-12) of the martial parade of Egypt in this campaign, and of its total failure. Our sketch of Egyptian history shows how exactly this prediction came to pass.

PROPHECY IV.—We have here an important class of predictions, which foretold the conquest of Egypt by Nebuchadnezzar. When Jeremiah was forcibly carried into Egypt after the rebellious Jews had slain Gedaliah, the word of the Lord came unto him; and having, in obedience to the divine command, hidden great stones in the approach to the royal residence at Tahpanhes in the sight of the men of Judah, he said, "Thus saith the Lord of hosts, the God of Israel; Behold, I will send and take Nebuchadrezzar the King of Babylon, my servant, and will set his throne upon these stones that I have hid; and he shall spread his royal pavilion over them." Jer. xliii, 10. Again: the prophet, having, as above, predicted the defeat of Pharaoh at Carchemish, adds: "The word that the Lord spake to Jeremiah the prophet, how Nebuchadrezzar King of Babylon should come and smite the land of Egypt." Chap. xlvi, 13-16. Ezekiel iterates the same predictions. Far away in the east, on the banks of the Chebar, he declared, "Thus saith the Lord God, I will also make the multitude of Egypt to cease by the hand of Nebuchadrezzar King of Babylon. He and his people with him, the terrible of the nations, shall be brought to destroy the land." Ezek. xxx, 10, 11. The same prophet, also, by divine command, announces in express terms the singular fact, that the spoil of the land should recompense the Babylonish army for their long and unproductive siege and ruin of Tyre. Chap. xxix, 18, 19.

Of the manner and extent in which these prophecies were fulfilled, we have but slender information; but the fact is unquestionable. Berosus declares that Nebuchadnezzar, as soon as he had received intelligence of his father's death, set in order the affairs of Egypt, and hastily crossed the desert to Babylon; (Cory's Fragments, p. 39;) clearly implying that Nebuchadnezzar had obtained the government of that country prior to this period. Megasthenes, also, expressly affirms that this Chaldean warrior conquered the greatest part of Africa; and it is evident that no conquests could at that time have been made in Africa, except through Egypt. On this point the testimony of Josephus is decisive. He says, "Nebuchadnezzar, having subdued Cœle-Syria, waged war against the Ammonites and Moabites: and, having conquered them, he invaded Egypt, slew the king who then reigned, and appointed another."—

Josephus's Antiquities, book x, chap. ix, sec. 7. Thus were these prophecies also fulfilled.

PROPHECY V exhibits several important particulars. Isaiah xix. First, it is foretold that great and ruinous discords and civil dissensions shall arise. Secondly, a complete conquest of the country is predicted, which is to be effected by a very fierce and cruel warrior, who should be peculiarly severe against the idols of Egypt. Thirdly, an extensive introduction and establishment of the worship of Jehovah in the land of Egypt are set forth. See, on the first point, verse 2: "And I will set the Egyptians against the Egyptians: and they shall fight every one against his brother, and every one against his neighbour; city against city, and kingdom against kingdom." This discord was uncommon in Egypt. Usually they were a united people: but here, not only was it predicted that they should come extensively into warlike collision with each other, but, even in Egypt, kingdom is to be arrayed against kingdom. Yet this description was verified to the letter, under the twenty-sixth dynasty, when the country was parcelled out between twelve different kings; and again, after a bloody war, united into one sovereignty. The chronological relation of these civil wars is no less remarkable than the fact of their existence. This dynasty, in precise agreement with the prophecy, is followed by the conquest of Egypt by Cambyses. Of this the prophet speaks thus: "And the Egyptians will I give over into the hand of a cruel lord; and a fierce king shall rule over them." Isa. xix, 4. This was abundantly fulfilled in the entire success and atrocious cruelties of Cambyses. But this conquest was predicted to stand associated with a terrible aggression on the idols of Egypt: "Thus saith the Lord God; I will also destroy the idols, and I will cause their images to cease out of Noph." Ezek. xxx, 13. Our history of the Persian invasion has shown how fiercely Cambyses carried into effect these threatenings. He slew Apis, burnt and demolished their temples, and to a great extent proscribed the religion of Egypt.

Lastly, these predictions speak of the introduction of the Hebrew religion into Egypt. It has been already shown that this actually took place. ("Hebrew People," p. 460.) It is a most remarkable fact, that all the old powerful monarchies were thus placed in immediate proximity with revealed truth and the pure worship of Jehovah:—Babylon, Persia, and Media were thus favoured, through the deportation of the Hebrews into these countries,—and Egypt, through the permission to erect a temple for the celebration of Hebrew worship, and through the authorized translation and circulation of the Old Testament in the Greek language.

PROPHECY VI is a general prediction, which, for breadth of meaning and extent of application, has but few parallels even in sacred prophecy. Ezekiel declared, "They shall be there a base kingdom. It shall be the basest of the kingdoms; neither shall it exalt itself any more above the nations: for I will diminish them, that they shall no more rule over the nations." Ezek. xxix, 14, 15. Again he says, "I will make her rivers dry, and sell the land into the hand of the wicked: and I will make the land waste, and all that is therein, by the hand of strangers: AND THERE SHALL BE NO MORE A PRINCE OF THE LAND OF EGYPT." Chap. xxx, 12, 13.

How wonderful is this prophetic revelation! Egypt, the proud, the martial, the wealthy nation! Egypt, renowned for her wisdom, her commerce, her legislation! *Egypt* is to become the basest of nations,—is to exercise no longer dominion over other nations: and, stranger still, there is no longer to be a prince of the land of Egypt! It is to be sold, with all it contains, into the hand of strangers.

But how do the facts, detailed by authentic history, and which even at this moment exist, agree with these strange prophecies? The only reply which can be given to this inquiry is, The accordance is perfect.

These revelations were uttered about 580 B. C. In 525 B. C. Cambyses conquered the whole country, and brought it into entire subjection to Persia. Thus it remained, with the exception of some brief intervals, in which an effort was made to recover its independence, until again fully subjugated by Darius Ochus. It was afterward seized by Alexander, and continued under his government until his death, when it passed to the Ptolemies,—a succession of Grecian rulers. The Romans followed, and made it a part of that great empire. Thus it remained, until about A. D. 641, when it was subdued by the Saracens. It afterward passed under the power of the Mamelukes, and is now governed by a Turkish viceroy. Here, then, is the fact, that a country possessing the finest geographical position in the world, has for the last 2,200 years been in uninterrupted subjection to foreign government, and that government frequently conducted by slaves, as in the case of the Mamelukes, and administered with the utmost tyranny and rapacity. Thus has Egypt been sold to strangers, and become the basest of nations; nor, during this lengthened period, has a really native prince filled the throne of Egypt.

Our limits only allow the citation of one more instance :—

PROPHECY VII.—This class refers to the total ruin and desolation of the land. Ezekiel, speaking in the name of the Lord, said, "I will also destroy the idols, and I will cause their images to cease out of Noph. And I will make Pathros desolate, and will set fire in Zoan, and will execute judgments in No. And I will pour my fury upon Sin, the strength of Egypt; and I will cut off the multitude of No. And I will set fire in Egypt. Sin shall have great pain, and No shall be rent asunder, and Noph shall have distresses daily. The young men of Aven" (Heliopolis) "and of Pi-beseth" (Pelusium) "shall fall by the sword: and these cities shall go into captivity. At Tehaphnehes also the day shall be darkened, when I shall break there the yokes of Egypt. And they shall know that I am the Lord." Ezek. xxx, 13–19. Again, we find it said, "The waters shall fail from the sea, and the rivers shall be wasted and dried up, and they shall turn the rivers far away; and the brooks of defence shall be emptied and dried up; the reeds and flags shall wither. The paper reed by the brooks, by the mouth of the brooks, and everything sown by the brooks, shall wither, be driven away, and shall not be." Isaiah xix, 5–7. "I will make the rivers dry; and I will make the land waste." Ezek. xxx, 12.

In this summary of universal ruin and desolation, we have three prominent particulars set forth :—

1. The total ruin of the great and ancient cities of Egypt. And here let it be observed that no other nation ever employed such a massive and durable style of architecture as the Egyptians did. Yet, in defiance of all that human art and energy could accomplish, the Scriptures are in this instance fully verified. I cannot do better than give the following passage in proof: "Though Herodotus numbered the cities of Egypt by thousands, yet all those which existed in the days of the prophets have long been in ruins. Egypt, of old exceedingly rich and populous, is now—except where still partially watered by the Nile, and cultivated—bare and depopulated. Its two great cities, Cairo and Alexandria, are bordered by the desert. And, with the exception of Rosetta and Damietta, and a few miserable villages, not a single town is to be met with, in traversing Lower Egypt from Alexandria to El-Arish, or from one extremity to the other.

Thebes, once famed for its hundred gates, may be called, from the magnificence of its remains, 'The Metropolis of Ruins.' The mummies so abundant at Memphis remain, though the city has perished. Heliopolis has now a single erect obelisk, to tell that the mounds around it were once the City of the Sun. At Bubastis, the Pi-beseth of Scripture, are lofty mounds and some remains of the ancient city of Pasht. A single street, with its central square, of the city of Alexandria, built after the era of the prophets, occupied a greater space than the modern city; while a small fishing-village, built of mud and brick, is the only representation of the royal Zoan!"—*Dr. Keith's Evidence of Prophecy*, p. 378.

2. These predictions announce a great alteration in the geographical conformation of the country. And this, too, is exactly verified. So greatly are the extent and course, even of branches of the Nile, altered, that an ancient bed now dry is shown at a distance of eighty miles from the nearest branches of that river. The Pelusiac branch of the Nile, once so famous, is now choked up. In fact, to a great extent, "the land is waste, and everything is withered, where the rivers have been turned far away, and the brooks are emptied and dried up."

3. It is predicted that these changes shall have a ruinous effect upon several articles of commerce, and especially on the paper reed. This is most precisely fulfilled. The *papyrus*, which for centuries afforded, not merely the best, but almost the only material suitable for writing, and which accordingly constituted a royal monopoly of great value, has become utterly useless. So minute and exact has been the fulfilment of the divine word in every particular respecting this ancient and wonderful country!

NOTE 12, page 128.—*The progressive Development of this Idolatry.*

That the religion of Egypt, while it remained in all its great principles essentially the same, was marked in its details by progressive development, is proved by a careful inquiry into any part of this remarkable system.

On this subject Mr. Kenrick says: "Herodotus observes that 'all the Egyptians do not worship the same gods in a similar manner, except ISIS and OSIRIS, the latter of whom is said to be Dionusos; these all worship in a similar manner.' His words do not imply that there was a diversity of belief, but of worship, manifesting itself in the sacrifice of certain animals in some of the nomes, which in others were held sacred to particular gods, and therefore never used for victims." The learned author proceeds to show that this difference did not arise, as has been supposed, from the fact that Osiris and Isis were *national* deities, and others merely local ones. This notion, he asserts, "is not warranted" by the words of the father of history; but that this difference of worship was rather to be attributed to "the later origin of the Osirian worship, which was diffused from some one point, with a rapid development and a uniform system."—*Egypt*, vol. i, p. 398.

Another evidence of this development is found in the introducion of the deity Serapis. The historical account of this event states that the first Ptolemy brought from Sinope in Pontus a statue of Jupiter Dis. On its arrival in Egypt, the famous Manetho, the high-priest of Sebennytus, not wishing to refuse compliance with the king's command, nor to admit a foreign deity into an Egyptian temple, pronounced the image to be the statue of Serapis. It seems evident from this, that Serapis was a deity previously known in Egypt. But as it is not found on any monument of the era of the Pharaohs, it could not have been one of the gods of primitive times.

It is further observable that this Osirian worship, which was introduced in the mediæval period of Egyptian history, stood intimately connected with the Syrian myth of Thammus and Adonis; and as both exhibit the same "fundamental idea of the suffering, dying, and resuscitated god," it becomes a question whether we are to regard this simply as a result of primitive tradition, or whether the light of subsequent revelation was used to embody a more perfect exhibition of suffering divinity.

However this may be, it serves to show the development of this idolatrous system. This is further seen in the following extract from a letter, which was some time since placed in my hands, by a learned, talented, and pious lady, long resident in Egypt. She says: "Among the tombs we entered belonging to the early pyramidal group, although curious and diligent in search, we could not find an instance of idolatrous worship; not even an image of Ptha or Vulcan, nor of Apis, nor of Lhem, nor any of the primitive gods of the Egyptians. Amun or the Ram, Thoth or the Ibis, were not to be found; neither Mnevis or the Calf, nor Athor or the Cow. No form or similitude occurred to indicate that they were deified. In fact nothing met our eye that could in the slightest way offend against the second commandment,—much less those compound bestial forms which so deform the temples and tombs of the later dynasties in Upper Egypt. The multiplied trinities of Egypt were not to be found in the sepulchres of the earliest race of the Pharaohs. Osiris, Isis, and Horus, with the rest of the vast hierarchy subsequently worshipped by this wisest of nations, were nowhere to be seen. We carefully sought for some clew to identify the worship of the eighteenth, nineteenth, and subsequent dynasties with the era of the pyramids, but found none."

It seems therefore certain that the pernicious errors which the apostasy at Shinar engendered, and shed forth to poison the nations, were not for a very considerable time so fully carried out to their final consequences as to parade a visible and tangible idolatry before the eyes of the Egyptian public.

NOTE 13, page 129.—*The Changes made in the Egyptian Triad.*

In no instance are identity of principle, and external titular change and expansion, more observable than in the multiplicity of the Egyptian triads. On this point I cannot do better than quote Mr. Osburn: "The primary form, or antitype, of the entire mythology, is a triad of divinities composed of AMOUN the father, MOUT the mother, and CHONS the infant son. This triad passes through an immense number of intermediate triads, until it reaches the earth, where, under the forms of Osiris, Isis, and Horus, it becomes incarnate. But a curious device exhibits the unity and identity of the whole of this circle of monadic triads. Horus, the lowest link, returns upward under a new emanation, Amoun Hor, and assumes the Amonian title, husband of his mother. Isis is blended with Mout, and their son Malouli is invested with the attributes of Chons, the infant son in the first triad.

"The triads intermediate to these two extremes presided over, and were worshipped in, the several nomes, or provinces, into which Egypt was anciently divided. *Sevek-ra-Hathor*, the Egyptian Venus, and Chons-Hor form the triple divinity of the Ombitic nome. That of the nome of Edfou, or Apollinopolis, was Har-hat, (the thrice great Hermes,) Hathor, and Harsout-tho (Horus the sustainer of the world.) The triad adored at Esne was Kneph, Neith, and the young god Hake, under the form of an infant; at Hermonthis, as Mouthou, Ritho, and Harphre; while at Thebes, the ecclesiastical capital of Egypt, the deity manifested himself under his primary and proper form of Amon-ra, Neith, and Chons. Thus each of the nomes into which Egypt was divided had its own religion," and exhibited a separate triad under different names, and, in some instances, with different attributes. And thus we have before us a proof, that the essential principle of the system was invariably maintained, while in names and details changes and adaptations to circumstances are constantly found. (Antiquities of Egypt, pp. 136, 137.)

NOTE 14, page 149.—*Glass sent as an Article of Tribute from Assyria and Babylon to Egypt.*

The fact mentioned in the text was regarded by the learned translator as so strange and improbable, that he marked the term "glass" with a note of interrogation between brackets [?] to indicate his doubt of its accuracy.

Subsequent discoveries have done much to remove this apparent improbability. At the recent meeting of the British Association for the Advancement of Science, Sir David Brewster said, "he had to bring before the section an object of so incredible a nature, that nothing short of the strongest evidence was necessary to render the statement at all probable:—it was no less than the finding in the treasure-house at Nineveh of *a rock crystal lens*, where it had for centuries lain entombed in the ruins of that once magnificent city." After giving the exact size of this curious article, and describing its state, Sir David concluded by expressing his opinion that this should "not be looked on as an ornament, but a true optical lens."

Sir David then proceeded to exhibit some specimens of decomposed GLASS found in the same ruins, and expressed himself as prepared to describe the process of decomposition; he having directed his attention to the subject some years ago, on the occasion of having found a piece of decomposed glass at St. Leonard's. Thus the fact of the manufacture and use of glass by the ancient Assyrians is clearly established.

NOTE 15, page 149.—*The Army sent from Assyria, under the Command of Memnon, to assist Priam during the Trojan War.*

This statement has afforded matter for much cavil and disputation, although it appears to be sustained by as ample an amount of evidence as can be expected to be adduced in respect of an era of such remote antiquity, and in connexion with events which, on the whole, rest on a very slender historical basis.

It may first be noted, that Herodotus states that the reason why the Trojan war was regarded as an aggression on the rulers of Asia was, because the whole of Asia was considered as one country, while Greece and every other part of Europe were regarded as entirely separate and unconnected with it. (Clio cap. 4.) This statement, coming from such an authority, renders the allegation, that Memnon was sent by the Assyrian Court with an army to aid Priam, much less improbable than it would otherwise appear to be.

But, on the other side of the argument, great stress has been laid on the silence of Homer, who, in his enumeration of the Trojan forces and their allies, makes no mention of Memnon, or his Assyrian contingent. It does not, however, seem reasonable to construe this omission, in a catalogue made at a certain period of the war, into an argument of sufficient weight to rebut a positive statement avowedly copied by Ctesias from the national records; especially as Homer in the Odyssey not only mentions the presence of Memnon in the war, but says that he killed Antilochus, the son of Nestor. (Odyssey, iv, 250.)

This, however, is not the only evidence to the truth of this statement. Polygnotus, who flourished as a first-rate painter in Greece, about 440 B. C., depicted, on the walls of the Hall of Strangers at Delphi, the capture of Troy. In this great work of art, with most of the heroes of the Trojan war, we find Memnon, who is painted with his hand resting on the shoulder of Sarpedon, another eminent ally of Priam. Near Memnon was delineated an Ethiopian boy, because all tradition represents Memnon as an Ethiopian. Pausanias reconciles the tradition with the statement of Ctesias, by saying that, although an Ethiopian by descent, Memnon did not go to Troy from Ethiopia, but from Susa in Persia. And, to complete the chain of evidence, Diodorus Siculus fully adopts the statement of Ctesias, and asserts that Memnon was sent on that service by Teutames, King of Assyria; and that he was the son of Tithon, Governor of Persia, and marched from Susiana, his father's province, with ten thousand Ethiopians, as many Persians, and two hundred chariots.

Perhaps the greatest obstacle to the reception of this account has arisen from the confounding of this Memnon with the eminent man of that name who erected several palaces, called *Memnonia*, at Thebes, Abydos, &c., and whose statue is at present in the British Museum. If, however, the plausible conjecture of Jackson be admitted, namely, that the great Memnon was ancestor of Tithonus,—prefect of Persia under Teutames,—who named his son after his eminent progenitor, the whole entangled mass of tradition is unravelled, and all cause for scepticism appears to be removed. (Russel's Connexion, vol. ii, p. 536; Jackson's Antiquities, vol. i, p. 252, note; Pausanias, Phocis, cap. xxxi.; Diodorus Siculus, lib. ii, cap. 2.)

NOTE **16**, page 150.—*The remarkable Means by which the Reading of ancient Monumental Inscriptions has been recovered.*

The statement in the text, that, to this extent at least, the magnitude of the curse of Babel has wrought its cure, is fully borne out. It may be necessary to inform some readers how this has been effected. The knowledge of the hieroglyphics of Egypt which we now possess is mainly attributable to the famous Rosetta Stone. This is a block of dark-coloured granite, which was found in Egypt by the *savans* who accompanied Napoleon in his great expedition to that country. Perceiving that it contained an hieroglyphic inscription, together with another in the Egyptian enchoral character, and a third in Greek, they attached great importance to the acquisition, and proposed to send it to France. Meantime, however, the victory of the Nile, and the surrender of Alexandria to the British army, placed this precious relic in the hands of Mr. Hamilton, author of the *Ægyptiaca*, by whom it was sent to England; and thus this curious block of granite was transferred to the British Museum.

It immediately attracted attention; and, on the obvious principle of proceeding from the known to the unknown, the Greek inscription was translated, when, to the astonishment of the translator, the last clause was found to run thus: "This decree shall be inscribed on a tablet of hard stone, *in the sacred, the vernacular, and in the Greek character.*" It was thus made known, that these three inscriptions contained the same subject-matter: and from this hint the

APPENDIX.   545

perseverance and talent of Dr. Young and others elicited a key to the hieroglyphical records of Egypt.

The same thing substantially took place with respect to the monuments of Assyria. They were found to be almost always trilingual and triliteral: that is, they were on the same monument engraved in three different languages, each language having its own peculiar alphabet. The object of this was, of course, to make the inscription intelligible to the individuals of different races, to whom these several alphabets and languages were familiar. Just as, in the present day, advertisements, and even the names of streets, in the city of Brussels, are posted or painted in French and Dutch; and just as now a governor of Bagdad would have to publish a proclamation in Persian, Turkish, and Arabic; so, in the days of Cyrus and Darius, the same course was pursued. And as the Greek translation on the Rosetta Stone, by giving a known exponent of every hieroglyphic which it contained, led to the decipherment of these obscure symbols; so the Persian text of these trilingual inscriptions has enabled genius and industry to obtain a tolerable acquaintance with the recondite matter veiled under the previously unknown arrow-headed, or cuneiform characters of ancient Assyria.

Thus the extensive multiplication of languages has afforded means of deciphering unknown inscriptions, which could not have been obtained, had this variety of language been less abundantly diffused.

NOTE 17, page 150.—*The peculiar Difficulty of identifying Assyrian proper Names.*

No portion of the vast range of inquiry opened up to us by the discovery of the ancient Assyrian sculptures is more interesting than the attempt to identify these exhumed revelations with persons and things previously known to us through the medium of sacred or profane history. The temptation is, indeed, almost irresistible to endeavour to fix on certain portions of personal or national history from the monuments, and to regard these as identical with the sovereigns spoken of in Scripture, or mentioned by ancient historians. But perhaps nothing is more detrimental to the cause of truth and sound learning than a hasty yielding to this impulse. It is sufficient to deter any from this course, to know that Mr. Rawlinson, after a most elaborate and successful investigation of the subject, confidently asserts, that " beyond, however, a mere string of titles difficult to understand, and possessing probably, if understood, but little interest, we know nothing of those kings forming the early Assyrian succession but the names." This is sufficiently discouraging, but is rendered much more so by what follows: " When I say, too, that we know the names, I merely mean that such names are recognisable wherever they occur: their definite phonetic rendering or pronunciation is a matter of exceeding difficulty, nay, as I think, of impossibility; for, strange as it may appear, I am convinced that the early Assyrians did not distinguish their proper names by the *sound*, but by the *sense;* and that it was thus allowable, in alluding to a king by name, to employ synonymes to any extent, whether those synonymes were terms indifferently employed to denote the same deity, or whether they were different words used to express the same idea."

In all probability, we have an instance of this in the alteration of the names of Daniel and his three companions. The new appellations stated to have been given to these four persons, seem to convey essentially the same sense as their proper names, having in every instance the title of a Babylonish deity, instead of the Hebrew word used to designate God, combined with some other terms which appear to express a similar sense to the parallel words in the original names.

35

In such circumstances, nothing but clear and invincible evidence will justify any identification of the names of the monuments with Scriptural or historical kings. (Rawlinson On the Inscriptions of Assyria and Babylonia, in the Journal of the Royal Asiatic Society, vol. xii.)

NOTE 18, page 150.—*The proper chronological Succession of the Reigns exhibited in the Assyrian Sculptures.*

In making the statement in the text, confirming the superior antiquity of the Nimrud sculptures, I am aware that I place myself in opposition to the opinions which Mr. Bonomi has advanced in a learned and very useful work on the same subject. I do so advisedly, believing that he has reasoned from false premises in the argument to which I refer. (Nineveh and its Palaces, pp. 302–304.) The most weighty of the arguments advanced in his work for the superior antiquity of Khorsabad, are based upon the general idea, that the arts of social life, delineation, sculpture, &c., were rough, and coarse, and rude, in the early portions of history; but that they gradually advanced here, as they did in Rome and Greece, until they attained perfection. I regard this notion as altogether fallacious. I am of opinion that the earliest ages of the really primitive nations (that is, those founded soon after the Dispersion, and whose founders had not sunk into barbarism by a long course of wandering and unsettled life) will be invariably found highly cultivated. It was so in Egypt and Assyria: and this fact is in striking accordance with Scripture.

In a question of this kind, however, I would not rely on any general induction—much less on a mere opinion of my own. I cite in proof of my views the following judgment of a competent authority, Dr. Layard: "It is impossible to examine the monuments of Assyria without being convinced, that the people who raised them had acquired a skill in sculpture and painting, and a knowledge of design and even composition, indicating an advanced state of civilization. *It is very remarkable, that the most ancient ruins show this knowledge in the greatest perfection attained by the Assyrians.* The bas-relief representing the lion-hunt, now in the British Museum, is a good illustration of the earliest school of Assyrian art yet known. It far exceeds the sculptures of Khorsabad and Kouyunjik, or the later palaces of Nimroud, in the vigour of the treatment, the elegance of the forms, and in what the French aptly term *mouvement*. At the same time it is eminently distinguished from them by the evident attempt at composition—by the artistical arrangement of the groups. The sculptors who worked at Khorsabad and Kouyunjik had perhaps acquired more skill in handling their tools. Their work is frequently superior to that of the earlier artists in delicacy of execution—in the details of the figures, for instance—and in the boldness of the relief; but the slightest acquaintance with Assyrian monuments will show, that they were greatly inferior to their ancestors in the higher branches of art, in the treatment of a subject, and in beauty and variety of form. This decline of art, after suddenly attaining its greatest perfection in its earliest stage, is a fact presented by almost every people, ancient and modern, with which we are acquainted. In Egypt the most ancient monuments display the purest forms, and the most elegant decorations. A rapid retrogression, after a certain period, is apparent; and the state of art serves to indicate approximately the epoch of most of her remains."—*Nineveh and its Remains*, vol. ii, pp. 280, 281.

NOTE 19, page 162.—*The chronological Position of the lower Line of Assyrian Kings, and their Relation to the Median Revolt.*

The only authority worthy of reliance who has furnished us with a list of Assyrian kings is Ctesias, who, whatever be his defects as an author, in this instance merely acted as a transcriber of public records which were fully open to his investigation. His list has been adopted in this work, and it terminates with Thonos Concoleros, who ceased to reign B. C. 821.

Besides this line of Assyrian kings, Ctesias gives a list of the kings of Media, nine in number, whose united sovereignty extended from the former epoch, B.C. 821, until after the capture of Nineveh, and the destruction of the Assyrian empire, B. C. 606.

As it is a well-known fact, that during this latter period the Medes revolted, and declared themselves independent of Assyria, many authors have hastily inferred that Thonos Concoleros was the Sardanapalus who reigned when Nineveh was taken by the united forces of Media and Babylon. The learned Rollin, following Diodorus, has fallen into this error, in common with many others. He makes Arbaces, the first Median king in the list of Ctesias, take and destroy Nineveh, and give liberty and independence to the Medes. (Ancient History, vol. i, p. 280. 8vo.)

But all this is in opposition to the fact, that Nineveh subsisted as an empire, in all its power and dignity, and with sway over Media, long after this date. In fact, all its aggression on Israel and Judah, its conquest of the former, and cruel deportation of the Ten Tribes to the mountains of Media, took place subsequently to the time of Arbaces. It is, indeed, certain that the Assyrian empire was not dissolved, nor the Median kingdom separated from it, until a considerable period after the reign of Thonos. To say nothing of the doubtful course to which this hypothesis in other respects leads, (such as two destructions of Nineveh, under two kings with similar names, by the same nations, at times far removed from each other,) it is altogether inadmissible.

Russel has, I think, solved this problem, by suggesting that Arbaces, a Mede by birth or office, succeeded to the throne of Nineveh, not by the subversion of the empire and the destruction of the city, but by securing to himself the reins of government, as they fell from the hands of Thonos Concoleros, and that he in fact was a Median sovereign on the imperial throne.

This supposition reconciles all the otherwise conflicting elements of the history of this portion of the Assyrian annals,—accounts for the rising power and martial glory which the kings of Assyria who are mentioned in Scripture displayed,— and unites the otherwise conflicting statements of Herodotus and Ctesias into one homogeneous narrative.

There was enough to justify this conjecture of Russel in the fragments of history which lay open to him; but these are strikingly corroborated in an important particular by the monumental inscriptions.

From these Layard concludes that he has ascertained the existence of "two distinct periods of Assyrian history;" that the people inhabiting the country at those periods were of different races, or that, by intermixture with foreigners, great change had taken place in their language, religion, and customs; and that this alteration took place between the building of the palaces of Nimroud and the erection of those of Khorsabad and Kouyunjik. (Layard's Nineveh, vol. ii, p. 232.)

Rawlinson, too, thus speaks on this interesting point: "Owing to domestic troubles, or to foreign invasion, there appears after this king (Adrammelech II.) to have been an interruption of the royal line; and in the interval which elapsed before the succession was restored, a very considerable change may be shown to have taken place in the manners and customs of the inhabitants of the country. So complete, indeed, does the social revolution appear to Mr. Layard, that he conjectures a new race to have peopled the country, or, at any rate, *a new dynasty*, with a new religion, to have acquired the kingdom. On this point, however, I am not altogether of Mr. Layard's opinion. I am willing to admit an *interregnum*; and I think it even probable, as the king who restored the empire is entirely silent as to his genealogy, that he was not a member of the Old Imperial family in the line of distinct descent: but at the same time I feel pretty certain, that no very long period of time could have elapsed between Evechius II. and the builder of Khorsabad."—*Journal of the Royal Asiatic Society*, vol. xii, p. 449.

Thus remarkably do the inscriptions confirm this induction from history. Thus do Rawlinson and Russel, each studying his own distinct source of information, pronounce in favour of these separate and succeeding dynasties. And what is equally remarkable, both of these scholars identify this second line of kings with the sovereigns of Assyria of whom we read in Holy Scripture.

The establishment of a Median ruler, in the person of Arbaces, on the imperial throne, may therefore be received as an undoubted fact. But further difficulties meet us in respect of the succeeding reigns. It seems equally certain from the concurring testimony of the numerous sculptures of Khorsabad and Kouyunjik that the founder of the former city had been an officer of the palace, in no way related to the imperial line of kings, but who succeeded in seating himself on the throne, and bequeathing the government of the empire to his son Sennacherib.

The difficulty of the case is, properly to adjust the intermediate reigns. We know, from the express teaching of Scripture, that certain kings ruled over Assyria at given times; and, even setting aside the authority of its inspiration, the sacred record has in so many instances been abundantly confirmed by the sculptures, that its testimony cannot be doubted. But while we know that these kings reigned, we neither know their lineage, nor even the names by which they were distinguished in their own country. While, therefore, the Scriptures record facts, they do not afford sufficient information to solve the difficulty. I am fully satisfied that we must wait further revelations from the historic treasure-houses of the Assyrian mounds.

But until this additional light shines upon the subject, the conjecture of Mr. Samuel Sharpe appears to meet the requirements of the case better than any other I have seen or can devise,—namely, that "after the death of Arbaces the Mede, the Assyrians were able to make themselves again independent."—*Bonomi's Nineveh and its Palaces*, p. 69.

On this principle our Chronological Table is founded, and the history of the several reigns written: and thus, while the upper and lower lines of Assyrian kings occupy their unquestionable position, the reigns of Pul and Tiglath-Pileser harmonize fully with the teaching of sacred and profane history.

It may indeed be objected to this scheme, that the list given by Ctesias of the successors of Arbaces is hereby repudiated. It is not so. It is probable that these really or professedly remained kings of Media. Indeed, this hypothesis seems to be confirmed by the fact, that Dejoces, who led what was, properly speaking, the Median revolt, and asserted the independence of that kingdom, with his successors, is placed in the list as succeeding Arbaces, although none of them, before Cyaxares, ruled over Assyria. It can scarcely be doubted that when the

Medes obtained the ascendency under the last-named king, they had the names of those who had ruled in Media from the time of Arbaces entered on the records as imperial monarchs.

NOTE 20, page 166.—*Evidence of Sargina's Wars with Egypt, and the Kind of Tribute sent thence to Assyria.*

There is nothing in the term *Rabek* which would lead an English reader to suppose it to be in any way connected with Egypt; and yet the explanation which Colonel Rawlinson gives in a very few words, renders this connexion scarcely open to question. That the Ra-bek of the inscriptions must represent On or Heliopolis, is rendered almost certain by the name of the Syrian Heliopolis, which was vernacularly termed Baal-bek, the Phenician *Baal* being exactly equivalent to the Egyptian *Rá* or "the Sun."

On the subject of the animals received from Egypt in tribute,—"horses and camels,"—the latter is evidently a doubtful translation, and may refer either to camels, elephants, or any other large animal. But it is strange to find the learned translator of the inscriptions doubt the exportation of horses from Egypt, when we know that one hundred and fifty years before this time Egypt was the great mart whence Solomon procured these animals in abundance. 1 Kings x, 28. (Rawlinson on the Inscriptions of Babylonia and Assyria, in the Journal of the Royal Asiatic Society, vol. xii, pp. 462, 463.)

NOTE 21, page 179.—*The Fulfilment of Sacred Prophecy in the History of Assyria.*

This kingdom was the subject of numerous predictions, peculiarly explicit in their language, and equally so in the manner of their accomplishment. We shall give a brief summary of the principal of these.

PROPHECY I. respects the Kenites and their captivity by the Assyrians: "And he looked on the Kenites, and took up his parable, and said, Strong is thy dwelling-place, and thou puttest thy nest in a rock. Nevertheless, the Kenite shall be wasted, until Asshur shall carry thee away captive." Num. xxiv, 21, 22. This prediction was uttered by Balaam just before the people of Israel crossed the Jordan. About 1568 B. C., eight hundred years afterward, this prediction was verified; and, stranger still, two thousand five hundred years after that, Assyrian sculptures are dug from ruined cities, which spread before our eyes the manner in which this prediction was accomplished, and the agency by which it was effected! The peculiar juxtaposition in which this prophecy stands, is worthy of notice. Balaam had just said, "Amalek was the first of the nations; but his latter end shall be that he perish forever;" while the Kenite was to be wasted, until carried into captivity by the Assyrian. Now, these tribes dwelt in immediate proximity to each other; and there seemed every human probability that they would share the same fate. Yet, on the contrary, when Saul went to destroy the Amalekites, he issued this proclamation to the Kenites: "Go, depart, get you down from among the Amalekites, lest I destroy you with them.—So the Kenites departed from among the Amalekites;" (1 Sam. xv, 6;) and Amalek was destroyed. The Kenites remained subject to the terms of the prophecy. They were wasted by several incursions and attacks, until at length, in the third year of the reign of Sennacherib, they were completely reduced, and carried captives to Assyria. Colonel Rawlinson declares, "The transportation of the Kenites to Assyria—is duly related in the inscriptions."—*Outlines of Assyrian History.*

PROPHECY II. The predictions respecting Sennacherib.—This remarkable manifestation of divine prescience and power was given through the prophet Isaiah. The Assyrians having completely subverted the kingdom of Israel, and carried the Ten Tribes into captivity, Sennacherib marched into Judea in all the pride of his power; and, having taken most of the strong cities of Judah and the principal fortified towns of the Philistines, regardless of the immense sum which Hezekiah had given him as the purchase of his favour and peace, he sent his officers to Jerusalem, demanding, in the most insulting and profane terms, the instant submission of the Hebrew king and his capital. Hezekiah immediately preferred his earnest prayer to Jehovah, and Isaiah was commissioned to give him an answer in the following terms: "Thus saith the Lord, Be not afraid of the words that thou hast heard, wherewith the servants of the king of Assyria have blasphemed me. Behold, I will send a blast upon him, and he shall hear a rumour, and return to his own land; and I will cause him to fall by the sword in his own land. Thus saith the Lord God of Israel, Whereas thou hast prayed to me against Sennacherib king of Assyria: this is the word which the Lord hath spoken concerning him; The virgin, the daughter of Zion, hath despised thee, and laughed thee to scorn; the daughter of Jerusalem hath shaken her head at thee. Whom hast thou reproached and blasphemed; and against whom hast thou exalted thy voice, and lifted up thine eyes on high? even against the Holy One of Israel. But I know thy abode, and thy going out, and thy coming in, and thy rage against me. Because thy rage against me, and thy tumult, is come up into mine ears, therefore will I put my hook in thy nose, and my bridle in thy lips, and I will turn thee back by the way by which thou camest. Therefore thus saith the Lord concerning the king of Assyria, He shall not come into this city, nor shoot an arrow there, nor come before it with shields, nor cast a bank against it. By the way that he came, by the same shall he return, and shall not come into this city, saith the Lord." Isa. xxxvii, 6, 7, 21-23, 28, 29, 33, 34.

Let the reader mark the tone of unqualified assurance which pervades this address, and remember that the person spoken to was virtually the master of the world. All the east had submitted to his power: Egypt trembled at his approach, as he ranged like a destroying lion over Syria and Palestine, while the Hebrew king and God's sacred seer were shut up in Jerusalem. Let this be noticed, and prophecy will stand before us in all the power and sublimity of divine truth.

It will not be necessary to go into any detailed proof of the fulfilment of this prophecy: that has been sufficiently done in the history itself. But it may be desirable to point out some of the most important particulars in this wonderful case.

1. The extended terms of the prediction clearly prove its divine origin. If the strongest possible confidence in the resources of Hezekiah, and in the impregnability of Jerusalem, had induced the prophet to indulge in the bitter irony which he penned, he would certainly have confined himself to the safety of the city. But he said, "He shall not shoot an arrow there, nor come before it with shields, nor cast a bank against it." Isa. xxxvii, 33. Now no confidence in the strength of the fortifications of Jerusalem would have justified, or could have called forth, this language. As nothing but the power of God could have prevented the fierce Assyrian from doing this, so nothing but the prescience of God could have dictated the declaration. Yet all was exactly fulfilled.

2. Attention is called to the manner in which Jehovah declares, that he will lead away the haughty warrior from the accomplishment of his purpose: "I will put my hook in thy nose, and my bridle in thy lips, and I will turn thee back." Verse 29. This must not be read as mere poetic imagery. It was the barbarous

usage of this age for a conqueror who had subdued a rebellious vassal king or chief, to insert a ring in the upper lip or nose of the wretched captive, and, fastening a cord to this ring, to lead him about according to his pleasure in this state of suffering and degradation. To this custom the terms of the text refer:— and how exactly were they fulfilled! Surely no captive thus brutally treated ever suffered more than this proud king, when, after the loss of his great army, he returned to his capital, and inscribed upon the imperishable record which we can now read, "*But I left to him* [Hezekiah] *Jerusalem, and some of the inferior towns around it.*"

3. The entire prophecy was fulfilled. He heard a *rumour* of the approach of the Egyptian army, and marched to meet it. The Egyptians retreated: he pursued, until in the desert the blast of God came over his huge host, and they became dead corpses. (Hebrew People, p. 579.) He returned to his own land, as had been foretold; and there, where it might least be expected, according to the exact terms of the prophecy, he *perished by the sword*. Who can trace such wonderful developments without feeling himself brought into contact with the arm of Him who reigns in heaven, and doth what he will among the nations of the earth?

PROPHECY III. The predictions respecting the destruction of Nineveh.—On this particular we might quote the whole book of the prophet Nahum, which, in a style as pure as its spirit is earnest and well sustained, breathes, from beginning to end, the doom of this great capital. We notice a few points:—

1. The cause of its ruin. This was twofold.

(1.) Its idolatry: "Out of the house of thy gods will I cut off the graven image and the molten image: I will make thy grave; for thou art vile." Nahum i, 14.

(2.) Its cruelty and injustice: "Woe to the bloody city! it is all full of lies and robbery; the prey departeth not." Nahum iii, 1.

A glance at the history of this country in any age, or under any reign, will prove this fact. Its idolatry was imprinted on all the usages of society, strongly impregnated the entire national policy, and so fully entered into individual affairs, that scarcely a man could be found whose name did not exhibit the appellation of one or more of the national idol deities. The cruelty and injustice of Assyria were as patent as its idolatry. Every nation and city and people were regarded as lawful objects of plunder and rapine. To assail a weaker power, rob them of their goods and wealth, and carry all who did not perish in war into captivity, was the ordinary course of Assyrian policy toward every surrounding country. The terms of the divine accusation against this people are, therefore, fully borne out by the facts given in their history.

2. The positive terms in which the ruin of this city was foretold.

"The burden of Nineveh.—God is jealous, the Lord revengeth, and is furious; the Lord will take vengeance on his adversaries. The Lord is slow to anger, and great in power." Nahum i, 1-3. "Behold, I am against thee, saith the Lord of hosts;—and it shall come to pass, that all they that look upon thee shall flee from thee, and say, Nineveh is laid waste: who will bemoan her; whence shall I seek comforters for thee? There is no healing of thy bruise; thy wound is grievous: all that hear the account of thee shall clap their hands over thee: for upon whom hath not thy wickedness passed continually?" Chap. iii, 5, 7, 19.

Thus spoke Nahum, and thus declared the purpose of Jehovah to destroy this proud and wicked people. Nothing can be more explicit than the assertion that these events were not to arise as ordinary operations of human policy, but by the immediate interposition of divine power. The terms, "The Lord is slow to anger, and great in power," may have a pointed reference to the readiness with which he turned aside the threatened punishment on account of the humiliation of the people on the preaching of Jonah. In all probability, it was afterward urged that Jonah's prediction would never have been fulfilled, if no repentance or humiliation had taken place. To rebut this, God admits his slowness to punish, and at the same time asserts his infinite power: and the whole issue of the prediction stands out, in all its details, an abiding proof of the verity and accomplishment of this divinely-declared purpose.

3. We call attention to the predictions which specify the agency by which all this ruin should be effected. Here we have several particulars to notice, inasmuch as there are several agents distinctly specified.

(1.) Water is spoken of as the first and prominent agent: "With an overrunning flood shall the Lord make an utter end of the place thereof." Nahum i, 8. "The gates of the river shall be opened, and the palace shall be dissolved." Chap. ii, 6. This was verified to the letter: for the history states that the combined armies of Media and Babylon had invested the place two years, and were still unable to take it, until the Tigris, swollen by unusual floods, washed down many furlongs of the wall, and threw the city open to its enemies. What makes this the more remarkable is the fact, that the king of Nineveh is asserted to have relied on a prediction that the city should not be taken until the river became its enemy. This suggests an interesting inquiry: Did the Hebrew prophets communicate the subject of their predictions to those heathen nations which were affected by their inspired revelations? And was the prophecy of Nahum the prediction referred to, as giving confidence to the king of Nineveh?

(2.) Secondly, a noble array of martial prowess is spoken of, as engaged in war against Nineveh and spoiling it: "He that dasheth in pieces is come up before thy face: the shield of his mighty men is made red, the valiant men are in scarlet: the chariots shall be with flaming torches in the day of his preparation. The chariots shall rage in the streets, they shall jostle one against another in the broad ways: they shall seem like torches, they shall run like the lightnings.—Take ye the spoil of silver, take the spoil of gold: for there is none end of the store and glory out of all the pleasant furniture. She is empty, and void, and waste: and the heart melteth, and the knees smite together, and the faces of them all gather blackness." Nahum ii. The history shows that the array of the besiegers, the attack, and ruin of the city by the Medes and Babylonians, perfectly accomplished these graphic predictions.

(3.) Fire is also spoken of as one of the agents employed in the consummation of this ruin: "The gates of thy land shall be set wide open unto thine enemies: the fire shall devour thy bars.—There shall the fire devour thee." Chap. iii, 13, 15. The history states that this was also accomplished; the king himself, with his concubines and treasures, being burnt in the centre of his palace. Besides, the fact of an extensive conflagration is proved by Mr. Layard's first discoveries among the ruins of this ancient city. He says: "We came almost immediately to a wall, bearing inscriptions in the same character as those already described; but the slabs had evidently been exposed to intense heat, were cracked in every part, and, reduced to lime, threatened to fall to pieces as soon as uncovered."—*Nineveh and its Remains*, vol. i, p. 27.

We see, therefore, that the manner of the ruin of Nineveh was thus exactly described by the prophet.

APPENDIX. 553

PROPHECY IV.—We here refer to those prophecies which speak of the total and irrecoverable ruin of the city and empire. Several passages in the Book of Nahum, many of which have been already referred to, are explicit on this point: "With an overrunning flood He will make an utter end of the place thereof.—Thus shall they be cut down.—The palace shall be dissolved.—She is empty, and void, and waste.—All they that look upon thee shall flee from thee, and say, Nineveh is laid waste.—There is no healing of thy bruise." Thus, under the plenary influence of the Divine Spirit, Nahum wrote, while Nineveh sat as a queen among cities, and Assyria was the most potent empire on earth. Some time afterward Zephaniah, with equal point and power, foretold the doom of this proud nation:—

> "The Lord will stretch forth his hand against the north,
> And will destroy Assyria, and will make Nineveh
> A desolation, a dry place like the desert:
> And the flocks shall lie down in the midst of her;
> And every kind of *wild beast*, the *pelican*,
> And the *porcupine*, shall lodge in her carved doors;
> Their cry shall resound in the windows;
> The raven shall be found in the porch.
> For he hath laid bare her cedar-work.
> Is this the joyous city? that sat in security;
> That said in her heart, *I am*, and, *There is none
> Beside me?* How is she become a desolation!
> A place for wild beasts to couch in!
> Every passenger shall hiss at her, and shake his hand!"
>
> Dr. Hales's Translation.

Can anything be more explicit, pointed, or full, than these predictions? A ruin, entire, universal, perpetual! And it should be observed that a doom like this is not the usual fate of cities and nations. One or two, specially marked out by God's providence, have met this fate; but their number is very small. Yet, against all probability, these express revelations of the Holy Spirit were completely verified. Zephaniah prophesied about 640 B. C., in 606 B. C. Nineveh was destroyed: and so perfect, so utter were its abandonment and ruin, that it never in any measure recovered from its fall; but continued to moulder in solemn silence, until in a short time its site became unknown, and for two thousand years it has lain in thorough desolation.

NOTE **22**, page 182.—*The Era of Nabonassar.*

The origin of this era is thus represented by Syncellus, from the accounts of Polyhistor and Berosus, the earliest writers extant on Chaldæan history and antiquities: "Nabonassar, (King of Babylon,) having collected the acts of his predecessors, destroyed them, in order that the reigns of the Chaldæan kings might be made as from himself."

If this statement may be relied on, it at the same time accounts for the absence of all definite information respecting the preceding reigns, and shows the lax manner in which the progress of events had hitherto been recorded.

NOTE **23**, page 184.—*Probable State of the Political Relation of Babylon to Assyria, prior to the Reign of Nabopolassar.*

All the accounts which have reached us concerning these countries, tend to perplex and confuse the mind in respect to this question.

554   APPENDIX.

The chronicles of the imperial state, as given from the sculptures in the last chapter, clearly prove that the paramount power of Assyria was maintained by periodical visitations of an overwhelming military force. No political organization had been introduced, by which the different nations were placed in social proximity with, and assimilated to, each other. Kings ruled by sufferance in all the conquered countries; and while they paid the required tribute, and evinced a suitable respect for the supreme governor, they appear to have been allowed to govern their respective countries in their own way.

Babylon must have stood in the first rank of all these conquered nations dependent on Assyria. Its revenues were calculated at one-third of those of the whole Persian empire: and the exceeding fertility of the soil, combined with the situation, wealth, and importance of the city, fully justifies this estimate. (Herodotus, Clio, cap. 192; Niebuhr's Lectures on Ancient History, vol. i, pp. 107, 108.) To retain the ascendency over this country, great efforts would be made; while at the same time a kingdom possessed of such resources must have had ample means of asserting its independence, except when coerced by the united power of the other parts of the empire. As this could only be done on particular occasions, and subject to frequent interruption, throughout the period of her nominal subjection to Assyria, Babylon would frequently, and sometimes for a long period together, be really independent.

NOTE 24, page 188.—*The Punishment of Zedekiah.*

The remarkable and apparently conflicting prophecies delivered to Zedekiah have seemed very enigmatical to general readers, and have afforded to ignorant critics some imaginary ground for cavil. Jeremiah had told the king that he should surely be taken prisoner; that his eyes should see the king of Babylon; and that he should be carried captive to Babylon, and should die there, not with the sword, but in peace, and with the burnings (or mode of interment) of his fathers, the kings of Judah: (Jer. xxxii, 4, 5; xxxiv, 3–5:) while Ezekiel had with equal explicitness declared, that he should be brought captive to Babylon, yet should not see it, though he should die there. Ezek. xii, 13.

So far from these predictions being contrary the one to the other, they were sufficient, if properly considered in relation to the usages of the Assyrians and Babylonians, to have indicated the fate to which the faithless king would be subjected in consequence of his apostasy and perjury.

Although there can be no doubt that Zedekiah was well informed on the subject, it is only lately that the punishment usually inflicted on rebellious vassal kings has been brought before our own observation. Among the recent discoveries in Assyria we have a sculptured slab, taken from the ruins of Khorsabad. In the centre of this there is represented the figure of the great king: and before him are three persons, the foremost of whom is on his knees imploring mercy, and the two others are standing in an humble posture. The king holds in his left hand three cords, which are fastened at the other end to three rings, which are severally inserted into the under-lips of these three captives. The cords attached to the standing figures are held loosely; but that fastened to the ring in the lip of the kneeling figure is drawn tight: by which means his face is brought nearly into a horizontal position; and while he is held in this posture, with his hand raised supplicating mercy, the king, with his right hand, is deliberately thrusting the point of a spear into the eye of the wretched sufferer. (Bonomi's Nineveh and its Palaces, p. 169.)

APPENDIX. 555

It was thus, there can be little doubt, that the last king of Judah was presented to the king of Babylon at Riblah; and thus that he received that punishment which, in so remarkable a manner, verified the apparently conflicting prophecies which had been delivered by Jeremiah and Ezekiel.

NOTE 25, page 189.—*The Median Princess whom Nebuchadnezzar married,—the Queen Nitocris.*

This wonderful female was daughter of Cyaxares, the King of Media, who, in conjunction with Nabopolassar, destroyed Nineveh. As she was alive at the death of Belshazzar her grandson, it is probable that she was betrothed to Nebuchadnezzar when a child. She is celebrated in all ancient history for the vigour of her intellect, and the number and magnitude of the works which she accomplished for the improvement and defence of Babylon. She perfected the works begun by her husband, and executed many others of a stupendous nature, especially the alteration of the course of the Euphrates, which she changed so as to make it offer great obstacles to any military operations against the city. Evil-Merodach was her son; and it is probable that the queen-mother directed many of the operations of the government during his reign.

But the stormy period which elapsed from the death of Nebuchadnezzar to that of Belshazzar, must have afforded ample scope for the talents of such a celebrated queen: and the position in which she appears at the awful moment when the hand-writing on the wall could not be read by the wise men, clearly shows that on every emergency, even when far advanced in age, Nitocris was always ready to interpose her counsel and advice. (Clinton's Fasti Hellenici, vol. i, p. 278; Ancient Universal History, vol. iii, p. 434; Herodotus, Clio, cap. 185-188.)

NOTE 26, page 190.—*The Magnitude and Splendour of Babylon.*

The accounts which have been given of the size and magnificence of this city will naturally be received with caution: yet enough appears to be undoubtedly true to excite astonishment and admiration. Babylon was laid out and built upon a perfect plan. Considering that this was the first seat of the posidiluvian population, and the site of their first monarchy, this fact argues the advanced civilization of mankind in that age, and clearly indicates that the barbarism and ignorance which afterward became so general, did not result from the original condition of human nature, but was produced by the divisions, the journeying, and the difficulties which many sections of mankind had to contend with, before they reached the destination which Providence assigned them.

The city of Babylon was a perfect square. Each of its sides was fifteen miles long: its compass was, therefore, sixty miles, and the extent of ground included within the exterior line of walls two hundred and twenty-five square miles. It stood on a level plain. The River Euphrates, passing through the middle of the city, divided it into two equal parts, parallelograms in figure. The walls were built of bricks, cemented with bitumen. Outside the outer wall was a deep broad ditch, lined with a brick wall on each side, and filled with water; over which were bridges, to afford access to the several gates. The walls were eighty-seven feet thick, and three hundred and fifty feet high. In these walls every side had twenty-five gates, which led to as many streets. These ran in a straight line quite through the city, at right angles to each other: so that Babylon contained fifty streets, each fifteen miles long, and about one hundred and fifty feet broad.

The intersection of these streets divided the city into a great number of squares, which were built on the four sides, leaving the inner parts of the squares for courts, yards, and gardens. On each side of the river were quays, enclosed from the city with high walls. In these, at the end of each street, were gates of brass, and from them steps descending to the river. Spanning this river, and forming a communication between the two parts of the city, was a bridge of very elegant construction, thirty feet wide. There were two palaces, one on each side of the river, of great size and splendour. These communicated with each other by a subterranean passage, tunnelled under the bed of the river. Of the wonderful pensile gardens mention has been already made. The gates of the city were of very massy and splendid manufacture, and were constructed of brass.

The temple of Belus was one of the most wonderful ornaments of this city. At its foundation, according to Herodotus, it stood on a square furlong. Bochart is of opinion, that it occupied the same site and foundation as the primitive tower, begun before the confusion of tongues. It had eight stories, approached by stairs, or an inclined plane, on the outside. In each of these stories were many large rooms with arched roofs, supported by pillars. Above the whole stood a tower, on the top of which was an observatory for astronomical purposes.

The accounts of the ancients respecting the great extent of this city were formerly discredited: they are, however, fully sustained by modern investigation and research. But there is one observation necessary, in explanation. It does not appear that the whole of this plan was filled up. Much of the ground laid out for building was unoccupied, even in the days of its greatest glory. Quintus Curtius tells us, that when Alexander took Babylon, a large portion of the space within the walls was ploughed and sown: and there is reason for believing that such was always the case. There was, indeed, even with some deduction, space enough left for streets and palaces to form one of the largest and most populous cities of the world. (Niebuhr's Lectures on Ancient History, vol. i, pp. 26, 27; Ancient Universal History, vol. iii, p. 424; Hales's Chronology, vol. i, p. 458; Herodotus, Clio.)

NOTE 27, page 198.—*The chronological Succession of Babylonian Kings after Nebuchadnezzar.*

As this is *the* question of Babylonian history, it is thought necessary to add to what has been already advanced on the subject in a preceding volume. (Hebrew People, p. 532.) The point at issue is just this,—Was Babylon taken by Cyrus at the death of Belshazzar, or seventeen years after that event? It might be safely said, that the learning and talent of modern times had decided upon giving a verdict in favour of the latter proposition, had not Fynes Clinton dissented, and placed the weight of his authority on the side of the former one. This renders it more necessary to investigate the subject at greater length, especially as this learned writer has failed to produce conviction in our mind in favour of his conclusions. Clinton observes, "The sum of the whole is this: If we adopt the system of Jackson and Hales, we suppose Herodotus and Xenophon to be both in error, in order to sustain the credit of Berosus and Megasthenes; and we obtain a result not very conformable to the tenor of Scripture. If we adopt the arrangement founded upon Josephus, we sacrifice the account of Berosus as erroneous, but we find the narratives of Herodotus and Xenophon perfectly consistent with each other and with Scripture. I have therefore no hesitation in adhering to this arrangement, as the least beset with difficulties, and in sacrificing Berosus rather than Herodotus and Xenophon."—*Fasti Hellenici*, vol. ii, p. 373. To this judgment I demur, and think an examination of the points so prominently set forth by the learned writer will place the reader in possession of satisfactory information on the subject. The limits of a note will not allow an extended discussion; but I will first inquire, whether "the narratives of Herodotus and Xenophon" are "perfectly consistent with each other and with Scripture." It is notorious that these historians are eminently diverse in their history of Cyrus. Herodotus describes this prince as exposed to death in his infancy, in consequence of the superstitious fears of his grandfather; and alleges that the person who preserved him was compelled to eat the flesh of his own murdered son, in punishment for having saved him. (Clio, cap. 119.) Xenophon, on the other hand, states that this same grandfather carefully and kindly brought up Cyrus. (Cyropædia, lib. i, cap. 4.) Herodotus relates that Cyrus invaded Media, defeated and deposed his grandfather, and kept him in prison until he died. (Clio, cap. 130.) Xenophon, on the contrary, says, that his grandfather always patronized him, and added a Median force to the Persian troops under the command of Cyrus, and employed him in a war against Armenia. (Cyrop., lib. ii, cap. 3, 4.) These, it will be seen, are not unimportant incidents, but facts of such magnitude as to affect the structure of the entire history.

But I attach even more importance to the allegation, that these writers perfectly agree with Scripture. Is this the case? Holy Scripture states, that, on the death of Belshazzar, the kingdom of Babylon was to pass to "the Medes and Persians." Dan. v, 28. How does this agree with Herodotus, who asserts that, long before the capture of Babylon, Media was subdued by Cyrus? Daniel affirms that, on the death of Belshazzar, Darius the MEDIAN took the kingdom; when, according to the Halicarnassean historian, at this time there was no king in Media, but a deposed captive in a prison. How, according to Herodotus, are the reign of Darius, and the affecting circumstances in which Daniel was placed, to be accounted for? Clinton supposes the two years of Darius to be included in the reign of Cyrus: (Fasti, vol. ii, p. 369:) but, according to Herodotus, there was no such king; Cyrus was himself the sovereign.

Nor do I think that Xenophon comes much nearer the Scripture account. Is there anything in the Cyropædia of this learned Greek to warrant the supposition, that, on the taking of Babylon by Cyrus, Cyaxares of Media assumed any power or authority over the conquered country? According to Daniel, this Median king *took the kingdom.* Let any one carefully peruse the last chapter of book vii, and chapters 1–4 of book viii, of Xenophon's "Institution of Cyrus," and judge whether his account is at all compatible with the supposition of a Median king administering the government of a great empire, and ruling over Babylon. According to Xenophon, Cyrus, on the conquest of Babylon, stayed there a considerable time; and there and then he assumed the state and conduct of a king; and in that city he remained, until he had made a settlement of his empire; nor was it until he thought that his affairs were well settled in Babylon that he ventured to leave it, and then it was not to visit Media, but Persia! It is, indeed, said, that when Cyrus entered the Median territory, "he turned off to visit Cyaxares." But does this language indicate that Cyaxares was regarded as the paramount sovereign, and Cyrus his commander-in-chief? On the contrary, Cyrus told him "that there were domestics and palaces set apart for him in Babylon, that, when he went thither, he might have *what was his own* to come to." Is this the language of a general to his sovereign? Nor does anything take place in this interview incompatible with the meeting of two independent sovereigns. How, then, it can be said that there is such an accordance between these authors and Scripture, I cannot understand.

But then we are told, that the result obtained by adopting Berosus and Megasthenes is "not very conformable to the tenor of Scripture." Far be it from me to disguise the difficulties of this very intricate portion of history. I think I have already shown, that just thus much may be predicated of the accounts of Herodotus and Xenophon. Then this becomes the question: "Which has the greatest measure of conformity to Scripture?" I will enable the reader to decide. The account of Berosus is as follows: "Nebuchadnezzar died after he had reigned forty-three years; whereupon his son, Evil-Merodachus, succeeded him in his kingdom. His government, however, was conducted in an illegal and improper manner, and he fell a victim to a conspiracy which was formed against his life by Neriglissooras, his sister's husband, after he had reigned about two years.

"Upon his death Neriglissooras, the chief of the conspirators, obtained possession of the kingdom, and reigned four years.

"He was succeeded by his son Laborosaarchodus, who was but a child and reigned nine months. For his misconduct he was seized by conspirators, and put to death by torture.

"After his death, the conspirators assembled, and by common consent placed the crown upon the head of Nabonnedus, a man of Babylon, and one of the leaders of the insurrection. It was in his reign that the walls of the city of Babylon, which defend the banks of the river, were curiously built with burnt brick and bitumen.

"In the seventeenth year of the reign of Nabonnedus, Cyrus came out of Persia with a great army; and, having conquered all the rest of Asia, advanced hastily into the country of Babylonia. As soon as Nabonnedus perceived that he was advancing to attack him, he assembled his forces, and opposed him; but was defeated, and fled with a few of his adherents, and was shut up in the city of Borsippus. Upon this Cyrus took Babylon, and gave orders that the outer walls should be demolished, because the city appeared of such strength as to render a siege almost impracticable. From thence he marched to Borsippus, to besiege Nabonnedus; but Nabonnedus delivered himself into his hands without holding out the place. He was therefore kindly treated by Cyrus, who provided him with an establishment in Carmania, but sent him out of Babylonia. Nabonnedus accordingly spent the remainder of his life in that country, where he died."—*Josephus Contra Apionem*, lib. i, cap. 20; *Eusebius, Præp. Evang.*, lib. ix.

The brief account supplied by Megasthenes, and preserved by Abydenus, is to the same effect. It states that Nebuchadnezzar "was succeeded by his son Evil-Maluruchus, who was slain by his kinsman Neriglisares: and Neriglisares left Lahassoarascus his son; and when he also had suffered death by violence, they crowned Nabonnidochus, who had no connexion with the royal family; and in his reign Cyrus took Babylon, and granted him principality in Carmania."— *Cory's Fragments*, p. 45.

We have in these accounts an outline of history, which I do not say *perfectly* accords with Scripture, since the Book of Daniel speaks of the third year of Belshazzar, while one of these annalists gives him a reign of less than one year: but they nevertheless exhibit a general agreement with the Bible. Here the Babylonian monarchy is, according to the explicit terms of Scripture, limited to Nebuchadnezzar, his son, and his grandson. Then Darius succeeds, with Nabonnedus as his vassal: and if we admit the statement of Herodotus as to the conquest of Media by Cyrus, (and if we do not we destroy the authority of the father of history in respect of this case,) then the conquest of Media by Cyrus would, by the subjection of his lord paramount, release Nabonnedus from his allegiance, and make him independent. Nor are the other objections, urged against this view, of more weight. The surmise, that the dynasty of Nebuchadnezzar should continue seventy years, is groundless. The difficulty of interposing a reign of seventeen years between Darius the Mede and Cyrus, is not insuperable. According to our scheme, Darius was acknowledged the supreme sovereign at the death of Belshazzar, and Nabonnedus his vassal. This relation was continued down to the conquest of Media. Daniel at Ecbatana would, therefore, see nothing interposed between the Median sovereignty and Cyrus.

If I were disposed to take any liberty with the tables, I should feel inclined to add two years to the reign of Belshazzar, thus bringing it up to the Scriptural number,—a course which the account of Berosus would seem to justify; since, as it is asserted that he was slain for misgovernment, it can scarcely be believed that he exposed himself to this violence in a reign of nine months. This emendation would conform the chronology to the sum of these reigns given in the Astronomical Canon and to Scripture. As, however, it would betray a silly affectation to attempt extreme accuracy in the dates of such a period of history, I have followed Hales and Jackson in the length of these reigns.

Undue stress has been laid on the authority of Josephus. It is, indeed, true that he calls Nabonnedus "Baltaser," and ascribes to him the events of the fearful night when the miraculous hand wrote on the wall. But then, in other respects, the Jewish historian is incorrect and contradictory. He makes the reign of Evil-Merodach eighteen years, and that of Neriglissar forty years. He says that the former was the son, the latter the grandson, of Nebuchadnezzar, and that Labosoardochus was the great-grandson of that king. He does not state whether Labynetus was of this line, or otherwise. But this is decidedly at variance with Scripture, which expressly limits the Babylonish sovereignty to Nebuchadnezzar, his son, and his grandson. Jer. xxvii, 7. Besides this, Josephus makes the capture of Babylon to follow Belshazzar's feast at some distance of time. His words are: "Now, *after a little while*, both himself and the city were *taken* by Cyrus."—*Antiquities*, book x, chap. ii, sec. 4. It is observable, he does not say that he was slain; while the Scriptures tell us that it was *in the same night* that the catastrophe happened. Again: having given, in his work against Apion, the account which I have quoted from Berosus, in which Nabonnedus is said to have been taken at Borsippus, and sent to spend the residue of his life in Carmania, Josephus adds: "*These accounts agree with the true history in our books.*"—*Contra Apion.*, lib. i, cap. 21. It is, therefore, scarcely fair to place Josephus in direct antagonism to the statement of Berosus.

But if Herodotus and Josephus are, to a great extent, reconciled with Berosus, Xenophon remains opposed to him. I would seriously ask, however, Is this a great objection? I am free to confess that I attach just the same amount of importance to it, as if it were urged that a statement in any of Sir Walter Scott's novels contravened Robertson and Hume. That I may not be accused of a hasty judgment, I will give the opinion of a competent judge respecting the historical credit due to this author. The Abbé Millot says on this subject: "Who, then, is to be believed? Xenophon's Cyropædia is plainly the work of a philosopher rather than a historian, a kind of moral and political romance. Is it not singular, that people will expect to find truth with certainty in a work which is interwoven with fables? After the learned Freret I must add, that Xenophon's conformity with the Scripture is imaginary."—*Gen. Hist.*, vol. i, p. 92. Indeed,

Xenophon, by a passage in his Anabasis, confirms the statement of Herodotus respecting the conquest of Media by Cyrus the Great, and therefore entirely destroys the authority of his Cyropædia.

Our limits forbid the production of further evidence. But it is necessary to observe the difference between the weight of the authorities who are adopted, and of those whom we repudiate. Berosus and Megasthenes wrote from the authentic annals found in the archives at Babylon; while Herodotus set down what he could collect as a traveller, and was, in consequence, often misled by popular reports: which was the case in respect of this portion of history; for he knew nothing of Evil-Merodach or Neriglissar, and made Labynetus the son of Nebuchadnezzar. (Clio, cap. 187, 188.) Now, it is perfectly true, as Clinton observes, that despots might tamper with and falsify the records of preceding reigns: and it is to this cause probably that we should attribute some of the chronological difficulties which beset these subjects. But, admitting all this, these annals must, after all, contain a broad *substratum* of fact, which commends them to our regard as the safest general guides.

Much might be added here as to the views taken by eminent critics and chronologers on these points; such as that Scaliger and Petavius both thought that Laborosarchod was Belshazzar. Ancient Christian writers generally seemed to regard Neriglissar as the Belshazzar of Daniel. This was the opinion of Eusebius, Cedrenus, Sulpicius Severus, Zonaras, and Syncellus. These are followed by Dr. Hales. But this scheme, although it obviates some difficulties, departs more from the accounts given by the ancient annalists; although, in common with that which I have adopted, it recognises the reign of Darius before the taking of Babylon, which I regard as the master-truth to be maintained throughout this very intricate part of history. It is not, however, by minute chronological criticisms, so much as by a comparison of the histories of Babylon, Media, and Persia during this period, that a sound judgment can be formed; and I hope a reference to the chapters on these several monarchies will exhibit so much harmony of historical statement as to induce a general reception of the views which I advocate.

NOTE 28, page 200.—*The Geography of Borsippa, where Labynetus took Refuge.*

Niebuhr, and several other authors, have spoken of this place, as if it had been a sacred city not far from Babylon,—perhaps misled into this notion by the phraseology of Berosus. Dr. Hales, however, conjectured that this Borsippa, where Labynetus took refuge after the capture of Babylon, was no other than the fortified citadel of that city.

This opinion appears to be amply confirmed by the researches of recent explorers and travellers. Those who have paid particular attention to the Assyrian and Chaldæan ruins, are, I believe, unanimous in the opinion, that the *Birs Nimroud* is the remains of this Borsippa. And this appears to be confirmed by all travellers. Buckingham says, while inspecting this identical ruin: "I inquired particularly after the ruined site called *Brousa*, or *Boursa*, by the natives, and supposed to mark the place of the ancient Borasippa of Strabo, the Barsita of Ptolemy, and the Byrsia of Justin,—the place to which Alexander retired when he was warned by the Chaldeans not to enter Babylon by the east. Near as this place was to us, however, and commonly as it was thought to be known among the people of the country, there was but one of all our party who did not absolutely deny its existence, contending that *Boursa*, or *Birs*, were but different ways of pronouncing the same word, which was no other than the name of the place on which we stood." From this statement I am inclined to conclude, that Dr. Hales is perfectly correct in his conjecture, that Labynetus took refuge in his fortified palace-temple, called Borsippa, at Babylon, which was regarded as the citadel of the place, being strongly fortified; and that modern authors have been led into an error, confounding this fortress with a small city in the neighbourhood. (Buckingham's Travels in Mesopotamia, p. 476; Hales's Analysis of Ancient Chronology, vol. i, p. 458, and vol. iv, p. 98.)

NOTE 29, page 200.—*The Fulfilment of Sacred Prophecy in the History of Babylon.*

The predictions respecting this kingdom and city are equally remarkable for their great number, peculiar point and perspicuity, and wide range of application. It will be necessary to notice them under several heads.

I. Predictions respecting the exaltation and power of Babylon, delivered when it was a state dependent on Assyria.

Isaiah speaks of the early weakness and obscurity of this people: "Behold the land of the Chaldæans: this people was not, till the Assyrian founded it for them that dwell in the wilderness: they set up the towers thereof, they raised up the palaces thereof." Isa. xxiii, 13. Yet, while it lay in this state of obscurity and vassalage, the divinely-illuminated seer realizes all the abundant wealth and military glory which it afterward acquired, and calls Babylon "the glory of kingdoms, the beauty of the Chaldees' excellency," (xiii, 19,) "the golden city," (xiv, 4,) " the lady of kingdoms." (xlvii, 5.) Even the vain confidence of Babylon, and her inordinate pride in vast military power, are at this early day graphically portrayed : "O virgin daughter of Babylon,—thou saidst, I shall be a lady forever. I am, and none else besides me; I shall not sit as a widow, neither shall I know the loss of children." Isa. xlvii, I, 7, 8. What can surpass the point and power of these prophecies?

II. Prophetic declarations that Nebuchadnezzar should possess unlimited power over the nations of Western Asia.

In the first year of the reign of Nebuchadnezzar, while he was yet struggling to consolidate his kingdom, and to coöperate with the Medes in the subversion and division of the Assyrian empire, Jeremiah thus wrote: "Therefore thus saith the Lord of hosts; Because ye have not heard my words, Behold, I will send and take all the families of the north, saith the Lord, and Nebuchadrezzar the king of Babylon, my servant, and will bring them against this land, and against the inhabitants thereof, and against all these nations round about, and will utterly destroy them, and make them an astonishment, and a hissing, and perpetual desolations. Moreover I will take from them the voice of mirth, and the voice of gladness, the voice of the bridegroom, and the voice of the bride, the sound of the millstones, and the light of the candle. And this whole land shall be a desolation, and an astonishment; and these nations shall serve the king of Babylon seventy years.—For thus saith the Lord God of Israel unto me; Take the wine-cup of this fury at my hand, and cause all the nations, to whom I send thee, to drink it. And they shall drink, and be moved, and be mad, because of the sword that I will send among them. Then took I the cup at the Lord's hand, and made all the nations to drink, unto whom the Lord had sent me: to wit, Jerusalem, and the cities of Judah, and the kings thereof, and the princes thereof, to make them a desolation, an astonishment, a hissing, and a curse; as it is this day; Pharaoh king of Egypt, and his servants, and his princes, and all his people; and all the mingled people, and all the kings of the land of Uz, and all the kings of the land of the Philistines, and Ashkelon, and Azzah, and Ekron, and the remnant of Ashdod, Edom, and Moab, and the children of Ammon, and all the kings of Tyrus, and all the kings of Zidon, and the kings of the isles which are beyond the sea, Dedan, and Tema, and Buz, and all that are in the utmost corners, and all the kings of Arabia, and all the kings of the mingled people that dwell in the desert, and all the kings of Zimri, and all the kings of Elam, and all the kings of the Medes, and all the kings of the north, far and near, one with another, and all the kingdoms of the world, which are upon the face of the earth: and the king of Sheshach shall drink after them. Therefore thou shalt say unto them, Thus saith the Lord of hosts, the God of Israel; Drink ye, and be drunken, and spew, and fall, and rise no more, because of the sword which I will send among you. And it shall be, if they refuse to take the cup at thy hand to drink, then shalt thou say unto them, Thus saith the Lord of hosts; Ye shall certainly drink." Jer. xxv, 8-11, 15-28.

Again: "In the beginning of the reign of Jehoiakim the son of Josiah king of Judah," or of Zedekiah, (for the text is doubtful,) this same prophet declared to the ambassadors of Edom, Moab, Ammon, and Tyre, "Thus saith the Lord of hosts, the God of Israel: Thus shall ye say unto your masters; I have made the earth, the man and the beast that are upon the ground, by my great power and by my outstretched arm, and have given it unto whom it seemed meet unto me. And now have I given all these lands into the hand of Nebuchadnezzar the king of Babylon, my servant; and the beasts of the field have I given him also to serve him. And all nations shall serve him, and his son, and his son's son, until the very time of his land come: and then many nations and great kings shall serve themselves of him. And it shall come to pass, that the nation and kingdom which will not serve the same Nebuchadnezzar the king of Babylon, and that will not put their neck under the yoke of the king of Babylon, that nation will I punish, saith the Lord, with the sword, and with the famine, and with the pestilence, until I have consumed them by his hand." Jer. xxvii, 4-8. False prophets, indeed, endeavoured to counteract the effect of these prophecies: "And Hananiah spake in the presence of all the people, saying, Thus saith the Lord; Even so will I break the yoke of Nebuchadnezzar king of Babylon from the neck of all nations within the space of two full years." Jer. xxviii, 11. But the falsehood was soon repelled with terrible effect: "For thus saith the Lord of hosts, the God of Israel; I have put a yoke of iron upon the neck of all these nations, that they may serve Nebuchadnezzar king of Babylon; and they shall serve him: and I have given him the beasts of the field also. Then said the prophet Jeremiah unto Hananiah the prophet, Hear now, Hananiah; the Lord hath not sent thee; but thou makest this people to trust in a lie. Therefore thus saith the Lord; Behold, I will cast thee from off the face of the earth: this year thou shalt die, because thou hast taught rebellion against the Lord. So Hananiah the prophet died the same year in the seventh month." Verses 14-17. The entire history shows how fully these predictions, in all their detail, were fulfilled.

III. We refer to that range of symbolical imagery by which the position and power of Babylon, as a universal monarchy, were set forth. It may, indeed, be objected, that in respect of this nation these were scarcely prophetic, as they were all enunciated after the rise of Babylon into power. But even then it must be admitted that they were all of them predictive of the decline of this power. They all stand as the first term of a series,—the first link of a chain: their juxtaposition with the prophetic announcement of a succeeding monarchy, therefore, clearly invests them here with a predictive character.

The first of these is "the head of gold" of the great image which Nebuchadnezzar saw in his dream. Each part of this predictive figure has received the most careful and critical attention; but I am not sure that the unity of the whole has been sufficiently noticed. Here, indeed, in the person and power of Nebuchadnezzar, we see this "head of gold." Yet is this but the first element in a grand series of providential evolutions, which are all ultimately to be crowned with the fulness of the glory of the kingdom of God. Dan. ii.

The next announcement of a similar kind is that in which the four great monarchies are represented as four great beasts, of which "the first was like a lion, and had eagles' wings." Until recently, this seemed to be altogether an arbitrary representation of Babylonia. We now know, from its being an exact description of the most remarkable colossal sculptured figures found in the ruined palaces of this country, that it sets forth a most notable national type or emblem. In fact, no one who has seen those gigantic sculptures in the museums of London or Paris, will doubt for a moment that these words set forth the kingdom and power of Nebuchadnezzar in that day, as clearly as the most careful account of the royal arms of England would at this time represent our own monarchy.

IV. We refer to the prophecies which relate to the termination of this kingdom, and the destruction of its power.

While the prophecies of Isaiah respecting the rise of this kingdom are so remarkable, Jeremiah with equal explicitness foretells her ruin: "I will punish the land of the Chaldeans, and will make it perpetual desolations. And I will bring upon that land all my words which I have pronounced against it, even all that is written in this book, which Jeremiah hath prophesied against all the nations. . For many nations and great kings shall serve themselves of them also: and I will recompense them according to their deeds, and according to the works of their own hands." Jer. xxv, 12-14. "For, lo, I will raise and cause to come up against Babylon an assembly of great nations from the north country: and they shall set themselves in array against her; from thence she shall be taken: their arrows shall be as of a mighty expert man; none shall return in vain. And Chaldea shall be a spoil: all that spoil her shall be satisfied, saith the Lord. Your mother shall be sore confounded; she that bare you shall be ashamed: behold, the hindermost of the nations shall be a wilderness, a dry land, and a desert. Because of the wrath of the Lord it shall not be inhabited, but it shall be wholly desolate: every one that goeth by Babylon shall be astonished, and hiss at all her plagues." Jer. l, 9, 10, 12, 13. "The word that the Lord spake against Babylon and against the land of the Chaldeans by Jeremiah the prophet. Declare ye among the nations, and publish, and set up a standard; publish, and conceal not: say, Babylon is taken, Bel is confounded, Merodach is broken in pieces; her idols are confounded, her images are broken in pieces. For out of the north there cometh up a nation against her, which shall make her land desolate, and none shall dwell therein: they shall remove, they shall depart, both man and beast." Jer. l, 1-3.

V. It will be desirable to notice some of the peculiarities of the ruin of Babylon which were prophetically set forth.

1. The manner of its first capture by Cyrus was exactly described by Isaiah, and even the name of the conqueror was given: "Thus saith the Lord to his anointed, to Cyrus, whose right hand I have holden, to subdue nations before

him; and I will loose the loins of kings, to open before him the two-leaved gates; and the gates shall not be shut; I will go before thee, and make the crooked places straight: I will break in pieces the gates of brass, and cut in sunder the bars of iron: and I will give thee the treasures of darkness, and hidden riches of secret places, that thou mayest know that I, the Lord, which call thee by thy name, am the God of Israel." Isa. xlv, 1–3. And, as if to point out precisely the diversion of the Euphrates from its bed, the expression is used, "That saith to the deep, Be dry, and I will dry up thy rivers." Isa. xliv, 27. Thus did Jehovah declare, nearly two hundred years before the event occurred, that he would neutralize all the efforts which the sovereigns of Babylon had made to render the river a defence to the city. It was also predicted that the city should be taken by surprise during a festival: "I have laid a snare for thee, and thou art also taken, O Babylon, and thou wast not aware: thou art found, and also caught." Jer. l, 24. "And I will make drunk her princes, and her wise men, her captains, and her rulers, and her mighty men: and they shall sleep a perpetual sleep, and not wake, saith the King, whose name is the LORD of hosts." Jer. li, 57. These scriptures were so exactly fulfilled, that Herodotus says: "They who lived in the extremities were made prisoners before any alarm was communicated to the centre of the place. It was a day of festivity among them; and while the citizens were engaged in dance and merriment, Babylon was for the first time thus taken."—*Clio*, cap. xci. Thus exactly does the prophecy accord with the history.

2. The remnant of the Hebrews were charged by Jehovah to leave Babylon, that they might not be involved in its ruin: "Go ye forth of Babylon, flee ye from the Chaldeans, with a voice of singing." Isa. xlviii, 20. "Remove out of the midst of Babylon, and go forth out of the land of the Chaldeans, and be as the he-goats before the flocks. For, lo, I will raise and cause to come up against Babylon an assembly of great nations from the north country: and they shall set themselves in array against her; from thence she shall be taken: their arrows shall be as of a mighty expert man; none shall return in vain. And Chaldea shall be a spoil: all that spoil her shall be satisfied, saith the Lord." Jer. l, 8–10.

3. The melancholy consequences to the city of its second siege under Darius. —Of the city that said, "I shall not sit as a widow, neither shall I know the loss of children," the prophet of God declared, "These two things shall come to thee in a moment, in one day, the loss of children, and widowhood: they shall come upon thee in their perfection." Isa. xlvii, 9. The manner in which this was fulfilled is marvellous. Herodotus says, that when Darius invested the place, determined to husband their provisions, "they took this measure,— excepting their mothers, every man chose from his family the female whom he liked best: the remainder were all of them assembled together and strangled. Their reserve of one woman was to bake their bread; the rest were destroyed, to prevent a famine."—*Thalia*, cap. cl. Thus did "the loss of children and widowhood" come on them in all their "perfection in one day."

VI. We notice some of the prophecies which declared the full and final ruin of Babylon.

"Come down, and sit in the dust, O virgin daughter of Babylon, sit on the ground." Isa. xlvii, 1. "Babylon, the glory of kingdoms, the beauty of the Chaldees' excellency, shall be as when God overthrew Sodom and Gomorrah. It shall never be inhabited, neither shall it be dwelt in from generation to generation: neither shall the Arabian pitch tent there; neither shall the shepherds make their fold there. But wild beasts of the desert shall lie there; and their houses shall be full of doleful creatures; and owls shall dwell there, and satyrs shall dance there. And the wild beasts of the islands shall cry in their desolate houses, and dragons in their pleasant palaces: and her time is near to come, and her days shall not be prolonged." Isa. xiii, 19–22. "I will rise up against them, saith the Lord of hosts, and cut off from Babylon the name, and remnant, and son, and nephew, saith the Lord. I will also make it a possession for the bittern, and pools of water: and I will sweep it with the besom of destruction, saith the Lord of hosts." Isa. xiv, 22, 23. "Because of the wrath of the Lord it shall not be inhabited, but it shall be wholly desolate: every one that goeth by Babylon shall be astonished, and hiss at all her plagues. How is the hammer of the whole earth cut asunder and broken! how is Babylon become a desolation among the nations! Call together the archers against Babylon: all ye that bend the bow, camp against it round about; let none thereof escape: recompense her according to her work: according to all that she hath done, do unto her: for she hath been proud against the Lord, against the Holy One of Israel. Therefore the wild beasts of the desert with the wild beasts of the islands shall dwell there, and the owls shall dwell therein: and it shall be no more inhabited forever; neither shall it be dwelt in from generation to generation. As God overthrew Sodom and Gomorrah and the neigbouring cities thereof, saith the Lord; so shall no man abide there, neither shall any son of man dwell therein." Jer. l, 13, 23, 29, 39, 40. "O thou that dwellest upon many waters, abundant in treasures, thine end is come, and the measure of thy covetousness. And they shall not take of thee a stone for a corner, nor a stone for foundations; but thou shalt be desolate forever, saith the Lord. And the land shall tremble and sorrow: for every purpose of the Lord shall be performed against Babylon, to make the land of Babylon a desolation without an inhabitant. And Babylon shall become heaps, a dwelling-place for dragons, an astonishment, and a hissing, without an inhabitant. The sea is come up upon Babylon: she is covered with the multitude of the waves thereof. Her cities are a desolation, a dry land, and a wilderness, a land wherein no man dwelleth, neither doth any son of man pass thereby." Jer. li, 13, 26, 29, 37, 42, 43.

The vast range of prophecy concerning this nation and city has compelled us to make a selection—and, considering their number, a very brief selection—from these predictions. But sufficient has been adduced to show to the most sceptical mind that Jehovah reigns in heaven, and rules among all the nations of the earth. We see here proofs of every kind, that the rise, progress, power, conquests, decline, fall, and final ruin of this proud nation, were all the results of divine appointment; that, arising out of ten thousand operations of the human mind, purely contingent in their character, the whole series of Babylonish history which resulted from these was, nevertheless, in strict accordance with the announced purposes of Heaven, and thus attested, at every stage of its progress, the infinite providence of the eternal Jehovah.

NOTE 30, page 213.—*The Testimony of Herodotus respecting the Temple of Mylitta at Babylon.*

Much cavil has been raised against this statement of the Father of History; some arguing on the general ground of its improbability: and even Dr. Layard throws doubts on it, because we find no indecent symbols on the Assyrian or Babylonish inscriptions. The judicious remarks of Larcher on the place afford an ample reply to all this scepticism: "If this custom be hostile to morals, it is no less at variance with modern usages. But that circumstance does not constitute a reason for reproaching Herodotus as a promulgator of falsehood. This author had been to Babylon, and had been an ocular witness of it. Jeremiah had, a century before, spoken of it. Strabo, who is as faithful an historian as he is an exact geographer, has subsequently mentioned it; and it would be rather presuming, were we, two thousand years afterward, to insinuate a doubt as to the fact. But to proceed to some details.

"I have observed, in the course of these Notes, that the temples of the ancients were not like ours. They comprised courts, groves, pieces of water, sometimes pieces of cultivated land for the support of the priests, and, lastly, the temple properly so called, into which no one but the priest could enter. The whole was enclosed by a wall, and was termed 'the sacred place.'

"This brings me to an objection raised by Voltaire, who remarks, 'It must certainly have been a rare festival, to see crowds flock together to have intercourse before the altar with the principal ladies of the city.'

"To this it may be answered, 1. It appears from Herodotus, that the women did not wait in the temple properly so called. 2. Our historian has himself anticipated the objection of Voltaire, by saying that the men took out of the consecrated precinct the women that pleased them. Strabo affirms the same thing: 'He has commerce with her, after having taken her out of the sacred enclosure.'

"'But,' continues Voltaire, 'can so infamous a practice have formed part of the civil policy of any people? Could the magistrates of one of the greatest cities in the world have maintained such a regulation? Could the husbands have consented to the prostitution of their wives? That cannot be true which is contrary to nature.'

"This shameful practice was, in all probability, established among the Babylonians before they became a civilized people. It became afterward a point of their religion. The magistrates, as superstitious as the rabble, would have esteemed it a crime to abolish it: and the less credulous among them were doubtless restrained from an expression of their opinion by the force of popular prejudice.

"Voltaire proceeds to insist on the jealousy of the oriental nations: but to this it may be answered in his own words, 'Superstition reconciles all sorts of contradictions.'

"Jeremiah clearly enough alludes to this custom in the letter which he writes to the Jews, who were about to be led captive to Babylon. Baruch vi, 42, 43. By these women encircled with cords, we may understand those who, as Herodotus relates, sat in the alleys of the sacred precinct, enclosed with cords; or perhaps the prophet meant to say, that their heads were bound with cords, as both Strabo and Herodotus assert.

"But, however this may be, I know of no historical fact that appears better established, or which we have less reason to doubt."—*Larcher's Notes on Herodotus*, vol. i, pp. 245, 246.

NOTE **31**, page 216.—*What was the true Principle and Meaning of Sabæan Worship?*

It is not an easy matter to arrive at a clear and distinct idea of the purpose and intention of those who introduced, and continued to practise, the worship of the heavenly bodies. If the opinion of Mr. Faber, quoted in the text, may be depended on, the case is sufficiently intelligible. The quotation from Maimonides, however, given in another volume, (Patriarchal Age, p. 235,) would lead to a different conclusion ; namely, that God had created the heavenly bodies, to act as his agents or ministers in the government of the world ; and that hence they were regarded with idolatrous devotion ;—the error of Sabæanism being, according to this theory, the attributing to the agent or minister the possession of intelligent and independent powers, which reside alone in the great Creator.

In deciding this question, however, we must not forget that the Chaldæans, who are ever celebrated for the worship of the heavenly bodies, are equally famous for their knowledge and practice of astrology; and that this was made by them the means of unravelling mysteries, and of foretelling future events. This science, therefore, in its profession, would be a fathoming of those powers with which the heavenly bodies were supposed to be invested ; and the power of so calculating the result of their combined influences as to be able to penetrate the secrets of their government, and thus to elicit a knowledge of future events. It is probable that both these solutions hold good in respect of different cases. In respect of Assyria and Babylon, we incline to the opinion that both of these were combined in the formation of their system of the worship of the heavenly bodies, and of astrology. But whether Mr. Faber has succeeded in detecting and explaining the causes which led to the origination of astrology, or otherwise, it is certain that his representation accords with the latest manifestation of it. In the last days of Paganism it was currently believed that the heavenly bodies were animated and directed by certain deified mortals. Even Philo ventured to adopt a philosophical notion almost amounting to this; and Origen was induced to assent to his opinion. (Faber's Origin of Pagan Idolatry, vol. i, p. 32, and note.)

NOTE 32, page 216.—*The Assyrian Triad.*

Much additional information may be expected on this recondite subject, when we come to investigate the religion of the Persians. They adopted and expanded the same symbol; and as they unquestionably received it from their more ancient neighbours, the Assyrians, and have left us much more ample accounts respecting their religious rites than that people, we may calculate on receiving through them further light on the subject. But it seems certain, that the earliest Gentile fragments which we possess contain allusions to the elements found in this symbol. We are told in the remains of Sanchoniatho which have been preserved by Eusebius, that "before these things the god Tauutus, having portrayed Ouranus, represented also the countenances of the gods Cronus and Dagon, and the sacred characters of the elements. He contrived also for Cronus the ensign of his royal power, having four eyes in the parts before, and in the parts behind, two of them closing as in sleep; and upon the shoulders four wings, two in the act of flying, and two reposing as at rest. And the symbol of Cronus, while he slept, was watching, and reposed while he was awake. And in like manner with respect to the wings,—that he was flying while he rested ; yet rested while he flew. But for the other gods, there were two wings only to each upon his shoulders, to intimate that they flew under the control of Cronus ; and there were also two wings upon the head—the one as a symbol of the intellectual part, the mind, and the other for the senses."—*P. æp. Evang.*, lib. i, cap. 10. This ancient extract renders it certain that it had become usual to depict emblematic representations of the deities; and that Cronus, or Time, was more particularly and prominently set forth in connexion with expanded wings.

NOTE 33, page 218.—*The Cherubim of Ezekiel, and their Relation to the compound Figures of the Assyrian Sculptures.*

The hypothesis of Dr. Layard—that Ezekiel, being well acquainted with the Assyrian figures, chose these forms for the purpose of presenting an imagery familiar to his fellow-captives in Assyria—is so very extravagant, that it calls for special notice.

In the first place, it is by no means certain that either Ezekiel, or the other Jewish captives, were well acquainted with the gorgeous sculptures found in the royal palaces of the great cities of Assyria. They were located, it is true, on the river Chebar, (now *Khaboor*,) which runs through the western part of Mesopotamia, and falls into the Euphrates at *Karkisia*, the Carchemish of Holy Scripture. Nineveh, then in ruins, was one hundred English miles distant, and Babylon above three hundred. It is true that, in the country towns, there might have been imitations of these figures on a smaller scale: but certainly the fact is not so clear as to allow of its being made the foundation of an argument.

But, however this may be, the hypothesis alluded to is utterly untenable; for neither Ezekiel nor the other prophets composed their sublime discourses in a spirit of cool, calculating accommodation to the circumstances and views of those to whom they were immediately addressed; but rather, borne along by the Holy Ghost, they spake as they were moved by that divine agent. (Hebrew People, p. 586.) And in this particular instance such was peculiarly the case. The prophet opens his book abruptly with the declaration: "Now it came to pass in the thirtieth year, in the fourth month, in the fifth day of the month, as I was among the captives by the river of Chebar, that the heavens were opened, and I saw visions of God." Surely one who has done so much toward the elucidation of sacred history as Dr. Layard, does not mean to say that this is mere poetic imagery, carefully contrived previously in the mind of the prophet, and specially adapted to the case of those by whom he was surrounded. And this is the manner,—or, if possible, with increased solemnity and the assertion of more special revelation—in which the prophet records the account of his vision: " The word of the Lord came expressly unto Ezekiel the priest: and the hand of the Lord was there upon him. And I looked, and, behold, a whirlwind came out of the north," &c. Ezek. i, 1–4. Then follows the account of the cherubic appearances. Afterward the prophet states that " he was carried in the visions of God to Jerusalem," and that there he saw the same glorious appearances which he had seen on the banks of the Chebar. In the process of the wonderful revelations that followed, Ezekiel, who, as a priest, must have been well acquainted with the interior of the Hebrew temple, and consequently with the form of the cherubic figures, says, "I knew that they were THE *cherubims*." Ezek. x, 20.

It is clear, then, from the whole scope of the subject, that the forms presented to the eye of the prophet were the results of pure revelation; that he knew they were cherubim, from their identity with the figures seen in the temple; and that their resemblance to the Assyrian sculptures could only arise out of the likeness of both to the primitive Edenic cherubim, the form of which had been preserved throughout the patriarchal age.

NOTE 34, page 220.—*Imitations of Paradise attached to the royal Palaces of the Assyrian Kings.*

It has been already shown that the different ancient Gentile nations, when scattered over the face of the earth, appointed and preserved, in connexion with their temples or sacred places, gardens, with two trees in the midst, and having a river frequently divided into four streams, in imitation, or as memorials, of the primitive Paradise. (Patriarchal Age, pp. 129–131.) And if (as we know to have been the case) this was done in Spain, Epirus, Campania, and other places far remote from the seat of the earliest postdiluvian population; what may be expected from those who, locating at Shinar, or settling on the banks of the Tigris, would have no temptation—scarcely, indeed, the opportunity—to throw off the recollections and associations arising out of the primitive history of mankind, which had been instilled into their minds by the patriarchs?

To say the least of these facts, they lead us to expect to find some paradisiacal enclosures in Chaldæa and Assyria, rather than the reverse. This expectation is justified by the statement in the text. But it is important that the certainty of the allusive or memorial character of these paradises should be fully established. I will attempt this as fully as the limits of a note will allow.

In the first instance, we may direct attention to the name given to these places, *Paradise*. This is not a native Greek term for "garden, shrubbery, or park." It is of oriental origin; and, as far as I can learn, was introduced into Grecian literature by Xenophon, who mentioned it as the name applied to the grounds attached to the residence of the Persian king. "Here Cyrus had a palace, and a large *paradise*, full of wild beasts, which he hunted on horseback, when he wished to exercise both himself and his horses. And the river Mæander flows through the midst of the paradise; the springs of it come out of the palace, and it flows through the city of Celænæ." Was this done without design? The palace built near the fountain which fed the river, and flowed from the residence of the king into the midst of the paradise, and from thence into the city:—is there not here a studied imitation of the Garden of Eden? Had Ezekiel any reference to these local paradises, when he said to the king of Tyre?—"Thou sealest up the sum, full of wisdom, and perfect in beauty. Thou hast been in Eden the garden of God." Ezek. xxviii, 12, 13. Or had the prophet reference to the primitive paradise, and to the imitations of it remaining in the land of his captivity, when he gave his beautiful description of the river of God, which flowed from the right side of the altar, and "issued out from under the threshold" of the temple; as the river flowed from the sacred residence of the oriental monarch to irrigate his paradise, and thence ran through the city? Ezek. xlvii, 1.

The Greek word Παράδεισος, "Paradise," comes from an oriental root, probably the Persic. But an equivalent Hebrew term is found in several texts in the Old Testament. Nehem. ii, 8; Eccles. ii, 5; Canticles iv, 13. In the first of these passages it is rendered, in our authorized version, "forests:" in the two following, "orchards."

Thus stood the case in a philological point of view, when the translation of the Seventy was begun. These men, fully versed in Hebrew literature and oriental learning, and possessing a perfect acquaintance with Greek, proceeded to render the sense of the Hebrew Scriptures into the Greek tongue, and came in due course to the text which states that "the Lord God planted a garden eastward in Eden. In what terms do they give this passage? They had the Greek word, κῆπος, "a garden or plantation,"—which had been in use by their best writers from the days of Homer,—and other cognate expressions. Not one of them, however, is employed to designate in the Greek language the primitive Paradise; but, on the contrary, the newly imported word from Persia, or that used so sparingly by the writers of the Hebrew Scriptures, rendered into Greek letters, is adopted and employed for this purpose. This in itself is a curious and important philological fact.

But the extraordinary aspect of the case does not terminate here. This is the word used by our Redeemer to denote the separate abode of happy redeemed spirits. Luke xxiii, 43. The inspired apostle employed this term to designate that state of glory in the third heaven, to which his rapt spirit was taken by the mighty power of God: and, what is still more remarkable, the same word is employed in the Apocalypse to set forth that glorious antitype of the earthly Eden, where the true and spiritual "tree of life" stands "in the midst of the paradise of God." Rev. ii, 7.

I do not wish to attach undue importance to any isolated fact, much less to any opinion of my own. But I submit it to the serious judgment of every one who holds the inspired character of Holy Scripture, whether the plain statement of facts given above does not clearly identify the royal garden-like enclosures of eastern monarchs as memorial imitations of the primitive Paradise? On what other principle can the Septuagint use of the term, and the New Testament adoption of it, be accounted for?—to say nothing of its obviously intentional similarity in every essential feature. In the absence of direct proof, I scarcely think it possible to obtain stronger inferential evidence.

NOTE 35, page 232.—*Babylon the Type of Papal Antichrist.*

In the Apocalypse we have the following scriptures: "And great Babylon came in remembrance before God, to give unto her the cup of the wine of the fierceness of his wrath." Rev. xvi, 19. "I saw a woman sit upon a scarlet coloured beast, full of names of blasphemy, having seven heads and ten horns. And the woman was arrayed in purple and scarlet colour, and decked with gold and precious stones and pearls, having a golden cup in her hand full of abominations and filthiness of her fornication: and upon her forehead was a name written, MYSTERY, BABYLON THE GREAT, THE MOTHER OF HARLOTS AND ABOMINATIONS OF THE EARTH. And I saw the woman drunken with the blood of the saints, and with the blood of the martyrs of Jesus: and when I saw her, I wondered with great admiration." Rev. xvii, 3-6. "I saw another angel come down from heaven, having great power, and the earth was lightened with his glory. And he cried mightily with a strong voice, saying, Babylon the great is fallen, is fallen, and is become the habitation of devils, and the hold of every foul spirit, and a cage of every unclean and hateful bird." Rev. xviii, 1, 2. "And a mighty angel took up a stone like a great millstone, and cast it into the sea, saying, Thus with violence shall that great city Babylon be thrown down, and shall be found no more at all." Verse 21.

These predictions, taken in connexion with the general scope of the book, clearly refer to the great antichristian heresy introduced and maintained by the Roman Popedom. Efforts have, indeed, been made to apply these passages to Pagan Rome, and to other heathen states: but these have signally failed. In addition to the arguments which have been generally used to rebut such allegations, it may be conclusively observed, that the charge against this Babylon is not idolatry, or cruel persecution, merely. This might have been alleged against other heathen nations, as against Pagan Rome. The great allegation here is *whoredom, fornication*: the state arraigned is *the Mother of Harlots*. Now, in the spiritual sense in which these terms are used in the prophetic Scriptures, they simply mean apostasy. Moab and Ammon, Tyre, Egypt, and Damascus, were threatened and doomed to ruin by the Old Testament prophets; but they were not charged with spiritual whoredom; and for this obvious reason,—they were not by peculiar religious privilege called into a special covenant relation to Jehovah. These did not, therefore, avow their devotedness, and pledge their fealty to him, as their spiritual Lord. But Judah and Israel, who were espoused unto the Lord, and afterward relapsed into idolatry, are charged in the Scriptures with spiritual adultery in the strongest terms. It is so here. The language quoted amounts clearly to a charge of the most vile and aggravated apostasy.

The question to be settled, then, does not so much respect the means and extent to which Papal Rome has exposed herself to the imputation of this character, and its consequent malediction; but is rather,—What was there so peculiar in ancient Babylon, that it, above every other heathen nation, was made a standing type of the great New Testament apostasy? I will endeavour to answer this inquiry, and thus afford a brief comparison of the Old and the New Testament Babylon.

1. The apostasy at Shinar began with a profession of advancing religion, and was carried out by a most careful attention to all the rites, sacred things, and consecrated practices of that dispensation.

The first clause of this statement has been sufficiently established in the Preliminary Dissertation: the second and third are manifest from the whole scope of this religion. Let the reader consider how exact and comprehensive the attention to primitive history and early religion must have been, when its results were so permanently impressed on the faith and practice of Assyria and Babylon for twenty centuries. Sacred places, persons, and things,—Paradise, with the tree of life, and all their accompanying emblems,—the cherubic figures, in endless variety,—were all carefully treasured up as the means of spreading before the public eye the elements of religion.

Was not this eminently the case with the Papal apostasy? Here is the same attention to external things, the same veneration for ancient emblems, the same visible and tangible religious *matériel*.

2. The apostasy at ancient Babylon was established by the union in one person of the religious and political government of the country, with a claim to extend its power throughout the world.

This was unquestionably the fact. It stands attested by every page of Assyrian and Chaldæan history. The palace-temples, or temple-palaces,—the ordinances of government,—and the cool and familiar manner in which projects for the invasion of peaceful and unoffending nations were put forth, and executed,—all show that this claim to politico-religious universal dominion was not an accident sometimes occurring, but a ruling characteristic of this government.

It is so at Rome. Earthly government and religious supremacy centre in one mind: although Christ said, "My kingdom is not of this world," the Papacy unites both. And if this political rule is not felt throughout the whole world, it is well known that the hinderance does not arise from the limitation of pontiff pretension, but from what is called "the heresy and disobedience of unfaithful states."

3. The grand element in the apostasy of Babylon was the claim to divinity which was set up by the king, as the promised incarnate Seed.

This fact is fully attested, so far as the claim to divinity is concerned. The manner in which the claim to identity with the Divine Son was put forth is not so fully explained. In the case of one king of Babylon, it was undoubtedly unqualified and absolute. Probably, in other instances, it was a claim to be the vicegerent, or earthly representative, of this divine person.

We have this, too, at Rome. According to Papal language, God upon earth sits enthroned at the Vatican. Divine powers are professedly exercised and divine acts are there ostensibly performed.

Our limits compel us to great brevity. But we may ask with confidence,—Do the extensive range of history, the world-wide geography of earth, afford another such parallel? Other nations have followed Babylon: other Churches have, in the most unaccountable manner, imitated Rome: but these two powers stand out as the bold and daring originators of parallel apostasies, which, in their respective times, have perverted truth, propagated error, and cursed the world with persecution and bloodshed, beyond any other evil known to mankind. Here they stand, type and antitype, as pencilled out by the revelation of God,—alike in sin,—to be alike in ruin.

NOTE **36**, page 245.—*The Time of Anarchy, and the Accession of Dejoces.*

The chronology of this nation, from the period of its revolt, is universally allowed to be one of the most obscure and perplexing to be found in history. It is clear that the revolt of Media could not have taken place before 711 B. C. On the other hand, it is an admitted fact that Xerxes ascended the throne B. C. 485; and that there were at least eight reigns from the accession of Dejoces to that of the son of Darius, and that these occupied at least two hundred and sixteen years: so that the accession of Dejoces cannot be brought lower than 701 B. C. The entire margin for discrepancy or discussion is thus reduced to ten years.

One important element in the adjustment of the chronology of these reigns appears to have been generally overlooked,—namely, the period which elapsed from the beginning of the revolt to the reign of Dejoces. Clinton very properly states, "Herodotus, indeed, implies an interval of some space between the revolt of the Medes, and the election of Dejoces to be king."—*Fasti Hellenici*, vol. i, p. 259. But this learned author is clearly unwarranted in the assertion, that "these *anni ἀβασίλευτοι* could not have been prior to the fifty-three years of Dejoces." The contrary is as cleary implied by the ancient historian, as is the interval itself. He says, "The Medes first of all revolted from their authority," (the Assyrians,) "and contended with such obstinate bravery against their masters that they were ultimately successful, and exchanged servitude for freedom. Other nations soon followed their example, who, after living for a time under the protection of their own laws, were again deprived of their freedom on the following occasion. There was a man among the Medes of the name of Dejoces, of great reputation for his wisdom," &c.—*Clio*, cap. 95, 96. It cannot, therefore, be reasonably supposed that the time of the struggle for liberty, and the period in which it was enjoyed, can be included in the reign of the man who is said by the writer to have again deprived them of their liberty. I have therefore placed the beginning of the revolt B. C. 710, allowing nine years to elapse from thence to the accession of Dejoces. This arrangement will place the subsequent reigns in perfect accordance with the well-ascertained dates which follow.

Note 37, page 247.—*The Period of Scythian Domination over Asia.*

This has generally been set down at twenty-eight years, on the authority of a passage in Herodotus. (Melpomene, cap. 41.) But that appears to be a very unreasonable length of time. After so many years, they would certainly have settled in some district. It is, therefore, much more probable that Trogus and Justin are correct, who limit the period to eight years, and who most likely obtained a knowledge of the true period from Ctesias.

This term also agrees much better with the incident recorded by Herodotus as the principal element in the story. He says that, during the absence of the Scythians in Syria, their wives had associated with their slaves; and that, on the return of the Scythian army, the fruit of this intercourse, now grown to manhood, appeared in arms to oppose its entry. Having sustained some skirmishes with spirit, they felt prepared to continue the contest; until one of the Scythians advised that *they* should lay aside their arms, and approach their opponents with horsewhips; saying, "While they see us with arms, they think themselves our equals in birth and importance: but as soon as they shall perceive the whips in our hands, they will be impressed with a sense of their servile condition, and resist no longer." They did so, and their opponents fled before them. Now this romantic account might be applicable to slaves cohabiting with their mistresses for a few years, but seems to be incredible when applied to men who had grown up to manhood in freedom. In fact, other passages in our author clearly point out the shorter number to be the correct one; which is also adopted and ably defended by Jackson. (Chron. Antiq., vol. i, p. 341, note.)

Note 38, page 248.—*Chronology of the Eclipse of Thales.*

There has been much mistake and confusion introduced into the accounts generally given of this Lydian war. It has been stated that this war arose out of the massacre and expulsion of the Scythians from Media; that it was terminated by the occurrence of the total eclipse, which had been predicted by Thales, exactly as the armies began to engage in a great and final struggle; and that, immediately afterward, the siege of Nineveh was renewed, and the city taken, B. C. 606.

The first of these statements, relating to the origin of the war, is undoubtedly founded in fact: but the order of events subsequently needs correction. Dr. Hales has fully proved that the eclipse predicted by Thales could not have occurred earlier than B. C. 603. (Analysis of Ancient Chronology, vol. i, p. 76.) The battle which was terminated by it must, in consequence, have taken place after the fall of the Assyrian capital.

It seems certain, therefore, that after the Lydian war had begun, Cyaxeres, having formed an alliance with Nabopolassar king of Babylon, suspended its operations, and resumed the siege of Nineveh; and, having succeeded in effecting the ruin of that city, afterward prosecuted his warlike enterprise against Lydia, which led to the remarkable circumstances mentioned in the text.

Note 39, page 249.—*Who was the "Darius the Mede" of the Book of Daniel?*

In the history of a nation which filled a very brief space in story, but which nevertheless abounds in historical and chronological difficulties, this is after all the great difficulty. On its solution hinges the entire arrangement of the reigns, and the judgment to be formed of some of the most important dates of the period. The question simply is, whether Astyages was the last king of Media, who was deposed by Cyrus; or whether he was succeeded on the Median throne by a son, Cyaxares II., who was "Darius the Mede," and ruled two years in Babylon after the death of Belshazzar. This, like many other difficulties of this history, arises out of the discrepancy which exists between the statements of Herodotus and Xenophon,—or rather from the interpretation which learned moderns have put on the words of these authors. Herodotus states that Cyrus invaded Media, defeated and deposed his grandfather, and kept him in prison until his death; and that this took place long before the capture of Babylon. (Clio, cap. 130.) According to the Father of History, therefore, Astyages was the last king of the Medes, and there is no room for any other Darius; while, according to Xenophon, when Cyrus took Babylon, his uncle Cyaxares II., son of Astyages, reigned in Media. It is therefore contended on the one hand by the authors of the "Universal History," Dr. Hales, Dr. Prideaux, and Rollin, that Astyages was succeeded by a son, Cyaxares II., who was the Darius of the Book of Daniel; while the Abbé Millot, Lempriere, Jackson, Malcolmn, and Dr. Russel hold that Astyages was the last Median sovereign, and in consequence the person spoken of as "Darius the Mede" by the Hebrew prophet.

I have been compelled to adopt the last-mentioned theory, both from its general accordance with the scope of history, and the evidence by which it is supported. On the first head, the reader will form the best opinion by a comparison of the several chapters bearing on the history of this age. In respect of the authority of the conflicting authors, it may be safely affirmed in the language of the Abbé Millot, that Xenophon's Cyropædia is plainly the work of a philosopher rather than of an historian,—a kind of moral and political romance: and even his Cyropædia is invalidated (in regard of this subject) by his history of the Expedition of Cyrus the Younger, where he says that the great Cyrus got possession of the empire of Media by gaining a victory over his grandfather Astyages,—a statement in accordance with the histories of Herodotus and Ctesias. (General History, vol i, p. 92.) Clinton coincides in this judgment, declaring, "In the narrative of Xenophon, where historical facts are mingled with romance, the true chronology of the reign of Astyages is not observed."—*Fasti Hellenici*, vol. i, p. 263, note i.

The indefatigable Jackson has, however, placed before us a condensation of the evidence on this subject, which must be conclusive: "No ancient historian or Greek writer, besides Xenophon, whose credit is questioned by Plato and Cicero, appears to have known anything of this Cyaxares: and all agree that Astyages was the last king of the Medes, who was dethroned by Cyrus, and succeeded by him in the Median kingdom: so that we may conclude that the second Cyaxares is a merely fictitious king, and that Darius the Mede was another person. Herodotus says that Astyages left no son; and Ctesias agreed with Herodotus, that Astyages was not succeeded in the Median kingdom by a son, but was conquered and deprived of his kingdom by Cyrus: nor does even Xenophon say that Cyaxares ever reigned at Babylon; so that, by even Xenophon's account, Cyaxares could not be Darius the Mede. The ancient Jewish History of Bel and the Dragon, says, that Cyrus succeeded Astyages, and Æschylus makes Cyrus the third king from that king of the Medes who took Susa, and conquered Persia; and he was Cyaxares the father of Astyages; and so Cyrus must succeed Astyages in the Persian and Median kingdoms. Dionysius of Halicarnassus says, that the Median kingdom was destroyed under the fourth king: the four kings were Dejoces, Phraortes, Cyaxares, and Astyages: so he knew nothing of the second Cyaxares. Dinon in his Persic History related, that Cyrus made war upon Astyages. Diodorus says, that Cyrus conquered and deposed Astyages. Plato and Aristotle agree in the same relation: and so do Strabo and others, and with them Africanus, Eusebius, and other Christian writers. Lastly, it was foretold by Jeremiah, (chap. xxv, 25,) that the Median kingdom should be destroyed before the fall of the Babylonian empire; but which was not true if Cyaxares, son of Astyages, was king of Media when Babylon was taken by Cyrus; and it is certain that the Medes were never conquered unless by Cyrus, when he dethroned Astyages; and all historians agree that this was several years before the taking of Babylon. It is, therefore, clear and undoubted, that the Cyaxares of Xenophon was not Darius the Mede, nor king of Media."—*Chron. Antiq.*, vol. i, pp. 411, 412.

It may be necessary to add, that the term "Darius" was not a Median proper name, but a title, *Darawesh*, "King." As used by the prophet Daniel, therefore, it simply means "the king of Media." It is a singular fact, that the oldest extant coins, *Darics*, which are supposed to have been made in the reign of the last king of Media, bear a name precisely similar to that of our principal gold coinage. They were from the royal title called *Darics*, which is exactly equivalent, in derivation and import, to our term "sovereigns."

NOTE 40, page 249.—*The Fulfilment of sacred Prophecy in the History of Media.*

As Media, in its individual nationality, had but little intercourse with the Hebrew people, it is not reasonable to expect a large amount of predictions in Holy Scripture relating to this nation. Accordingly, we find a few, and but a few, prophecies of this class. Yet even these are worthy of attention, as showing the perfection of the providential government of Jehovah, and the extent to which, in that age, his will was revealed to mankind through his holy prophets.

I. We have a prediction that, to some extent, Media would be brought into subjection or subserviency to Babylon.

This could not have been expected. Media took the lead in the subversion of the Assyrian empire. Babylon was, indeed, associated with Media; but the Chaldæans had never, like the Medes, dared alone to meet the full power of the imperial state. Yet when the Lord so fully proclaims the ascendency to which he has appointed Nebuchadnezzar, and directs the prophet to give the cup of his fury to all the surrounding nations, that they may drink, and serve the king of Babylon,—among those enumerated we find "the kings of the Medes." Jer. xxv, 25.

We have no precise information respecting the conquest of Media by Babylon under Nebuchadnezzar; but we know that he subdued Persia, which had been subject to Media. In fact, during the supremacy of the great Babylonian conqueror, we hear nothing of Media in history. It perhaps owed its exemption from a harsher fate to the fact, that Nebuchadnezzar's wife was sister of the king of Media. It is, however, certain, that this kingdom was by Nebuchadnezzar not only checked in its career of conquest, but stripped of its tributary states, and shut up within the limits of its own territory, in timid and servile inaction, during the period referred to by the prophecy,—which thus received an ample accomplishment.

II. It was predicted, nevertheless, that Media should assist in the ruin of Babylon. Isaiah said when denouncing, in the name of the Lord, the burden of Babylon, "Behold, I will stir up the Medes against them:" and again, "Go up, O Elam; besiege, O Media." Isa. xii, 17; xxi, 2. And Jeremiah, in the name of Jehovah, calls this nation to this duty: "Make bright the arrows; gather the shields: the Lord hath raised up the spirit of the kings of the Medes: for his device is against Babylon to destroy it; because it is the vengeance of the Lord, the vengeance of his temple."

These predictions also were exactly fulfilled. Cyrus, having conquered Media, before he took Babylon, associated Persia (or Elam) and Media in the enterprise of investing and subduing it. In fact, it was by the discipline and bravery of the Medes, united with the Persians, that both Cyrus and Darius took Babylon.

III. Again, Media is designated by the prophet as one of the elements constituting the second great universal empire. Hence the angel said to Daniel, "The ram which thou sawest having two horns are the kings of Media and Persia," Dan. viii, 20: so that, according to the laws of Divine Providence, Media and Persia stood associated as integral elements of this great empire, even to the time when it was assailed and subdued by "the king of Greece." Consequently all the prophecies referring to the rise, progress, and power of this second kingdom—such as that respecting "the breast and arms of silver" of the great image, and the second beast like a bear—had a distinct and explicit reference to Media in common with Persia—although it has been thought best to defer a special citation of them to the next chapter.

NOTE **41**, page 255.—*The personal History of Cyrus.*

The personal history of this conqueror is involved in much obscurity. Reasons have been already given for distrusting the statements of Xenophon; but it does not follow from thence, that we can fully rely upon Herodotus. As hinted in the text, there is much, in the account of Cyrus given even by this writer, which appears to be romantic, and, without good evidence to the contrary, would be set down as the result of his imagination.

It is, however, true, that we have the means of comparing the account of the Greek Father of History with a native author, who had access to the same records or traditions; and the similarity in their statements is such, as to leave no doubt whatever of their general accuracy, as respects the prominent events recorded.

Herodotus wrote about 456 B. C. He had not the advantage of a residence in Persia; and it can scarcely be believed that he understood any oriental language. He was, however, an intelligent, persevering, and learned traveller, who visited various countries for the purpose of collecting information for the composition of a general history. He had a great advantage in respect of the date of his inquiries. He was at Babylon about seventy-five years after Cyrus had ceased to reign over that country. It could not, therefore, be very difficult for such a man, in such a city, so soon after the death of a mighty conqueror, and the founder of an empire, to have collected some authentic information respecting the principal events in the life of Cyrus.

On the other hand, Firdusi was a native Persian, a poet of remarkable genius and learning, who wrote in A. D. 1009, about 1445 years after Herodotus. Having displayed uncommon powers, while residing in his native village of Shadab, he was summoned to the court of Ghazni, where, at the command of the great Sultan Mahmud, he composed in verse his famous work of *Shah Nameh*, which has been preserved, and is to this day read by all well-educated Persians with equal admiration for the recondite information which it communicates, and the brilliant poetry and purity of language in which its narrative is conveyed.

In this work we have a poetical history of the kings of Persia, from Kaiomars, the first sovereign, to the conquest of the nation by the Mohammedan powers. In such circumstances, and writing under such auspices, the writer would have access to all available sources of information. We know that records of every particular relating to the Persian sovereigns were carefully preserved. Esther x, 2. Whether these remained to the time of Firdusi may be doubted; but, at all events, being a native of the country and a perfect master of its language, he would have every advantage in acquiring a knowledge of the early history and antiquities of his nation; and it is strongly asserted by all Persian biographers, that Mahmud placed in the hands of the poet the ancient chronicles of the kings of Persia, and that from these he collected materials for his great work.

Whatever opinion may be formed as to the truth of these allegations, we have to compare the story of Herodotus with that which is collected from the poetry of Firdusi. There can be no doubt that the reader will agree with the learned author who has collected the prominent points common to both in the following judgment: "It is utterly incredible, that two different princes of Persia should each have been born in a foreign and hostile territory; should each have been doomed to death in his infancy by his maternal grandfather, in consequence of portentous dreams, real or invented; should each have been saved by the remorse of his destined murderers; and should each, after a similar education among herdsmen, as the son of a herdsman, have found means to revisit his paternal kingdom, and, having delivered it, after a long and triumphant war, from the tyrant who had invaded it, should have restored it to the summit of power and magnificence."—*Sir William Jones's Works*, vol. iii, p. 106.

In all these essential particulars the statements of Herodotus and Firdusi agree,—an agreement which, considering the different circumstances and eras of the authors, is sufficient to prove that here is a *substratum* of facts which may be relied on as the basis of an authentic history of Cyrus.

Respecting the other point of difference, namely, whether Cyrus conquered Media, and forcibly deposed Astyages, according to Herodotus,—or lived in harmony with him, and succeeded to his throne on his death, agreeably to Xenophon's Cyropædia,—there can scarcely be a question; for, first, the Father of History is in this instance not only supported by Plato, Aristotle, Isocrates, Anaximenes, Dinon, and Amyntas, but even Xenophon's own Anabasis may be quoted in contradiction of his Cyropædia. In the former work, speaking of the city Larissa, he observes, "This city, when besieged by the king of Persia, when the Persians were wresting the empire from the Medes," &c.: and, again, when speaking of the city of Mespila, and its extraordinary fortifications, he states that "here Media, the king's consort, is said to have taken refuge when the Medes were deprived of the empire by the Persians."—*Anabasis*, lib. iii, cap. 4. Now as it is certain that Cyrus was the person who raised the Persians to supremacy over Media, these statements are directly contrary to the romantic statement of the Cyropædia, where, without any struggle or contest, Cyrus is represented as living in perfect harmony with his grandfather Astyages, King of Media, and quietly succeeding to his kingdom on the death of his uncle, Cyaxares.

NOTE **42**, page 260.—*Was Cyrus made acquainted with the Prophecies of Daniel?*

We have given in the text *primâ facie* evidence that Daniel would make Cyrus acquainted with those wonderful revelations which God had given to the world through him respecting the succession of the four great empires that were appointed to exercise universal rule, before the introduction of the kingdom of God. Many collateral proofs might be found in the history of this monarch confirmatory of this view; but attention will here be confined to two; namely, the inscription on his tomb, and his edict in favour of the Jews.

"Pliny notices the tomb of Cyrus at Pasargadæ in Persia. Arrian and Strabo describe it; and they agree with Curtius that Alexander offered funeral honours to his shade there; that he opened the tomb, and found, not the treasures he expected, but a rotten shield, two Scythian bows, and a Persian scimitar. And Plutarch records the following inscription thereon, in his Life of Alexander: 'O man, whoever thou art, and whenever thou comest, (for come I know thou wilt,) I am CYRUS, the founder of the Persian empire. Envy me not the little earth that covers my bones.'"—*Hales's Ancient Chronology*, vol. iv, p. 102.

It may be observed here, that the fact of the tomb of Cyrus being found in this identical spot cannot be open to doubt. I presume, no statement supported by the unanimous testimony of Pliny, Arrian, Strabo, Curtius, and Plutarch, would be questioned by any person at all competent to give an opinion on such a subject as this. Then comes the inscription. What does it mean? Who is the person addressed, and addressed, too, as having the power of depriving the occupant of the tomb of earth to cover his bones; and whose coming is spoken of as such an established certainty? Plutarch says that "Alexander was much affected at these words, which placed before him in so strong a light the uncertainty and vicissitude of things." This might be the best solution which the heathen biographer could offer respecting the emotion of Alexander. But to the person who has carefully studied the predictions of Daniel, and to the great Macedonian who had these prophecies read to him by the high-priest at Jerusalem, would the words of the inscription appear to indicate not *uncertainty*, but rather *the certainty of the divine appointment*,—the obvious and undoubted operation of a supreme over-ruling Providence, before whose power all earthly potentates are as nothing.

In short, no pointed sense, no worthy meaning, can be given to this inscription, except we suppose Cyrus to have been informed of the succession of the four great empires, and the consequent subversion of Persia by Greece. Then, we see who is addressed by him as the man certainly coming: then the reference to his power is intelligible. In fact, on this principle of interpretation, the inscription is worthy of Cyrus; and the emotion of the conqueror, worthy of Alexander.

The edict issued in favour of the Hebrews is a similar proof of the acquaintance of Cyrus with these predictions. In the first instance, we cannot bring ourselves to believe that the language of this edict ran in the usual terms of the royal Persian proclamations, namely, "By the grace of Ormuzd." Ezra would never have rendered such a phrase by the terms "the JEHOVAH God of heaven." In fact, he never could have rendered such words into "JEHOVAH *God of Israel.*" It would be impossible for any Hebrew—not to say, a pious and inspired priest—thus to prostitute the most glorious and ineffable name of the Eternal. Besides, it has been shown that the Hebrew name of God was recognised as a divine appellation both at Nineveh and Babylon, and it would undoubtedly be so likewise in Persia.

We have, therefore, in this passage precisely the same recognition of the true God as we find extorted from Nebuchadnezzar. Dan. iii, 28; iv, 37. And it seems certain that this was done by the same means,—namely, a communication of those glorious revelations which God had made to Daniel respecting the providential appointment of a succession of great empires to rule over the world; accompanied, there can be no doubt, by those parts of Isaiah's prophecies in which Cyrus was pointed out by name, long before he was born, as a chosen instrument for the accomplishment of the divine purpose.

The mind loves to dwell on the intercourse between the martial Persian—with the world lying at his feet and waiting his commands—and the aged prophet, who had taught Nebuchadnezzar, and warned Belshazzar, and received from the all-prescient Jehovah an outline of the world's destiny, from the day of Jerusalem's ruin to the end of time. When will history be fairly and fully studied in the light of revealed truth?

NOTE 43, page 262.—*The successful Opposition of the Governors of Syria and others to the Building of Jerusalem, and the Evidence thereby afforded of the Integrity and Perfection of the national Records at the Court of Persia.*

The correspondence on this subject preserved by Josephus is important, not only as casting light on the position and difficulties of the pious Hebrews during the times of Ezra and Nehemiah, but also as evincing the completeness with which historic registers were kept at the court of Persia. The Jewish historian says: "But when Cambyses, the son of Cyrus, had taken the kingdom, the governors in Syria, and Phenicia, and in the countries of Ammon, and Moab, and Samaria, wrote an epistle to Cambyses, whose contents were as follows: 'To our lord, Cambyses: we thy servants, Rathumus the historiographer, and Semellius the scribe, and the rest that are thy judges in Syria and Phenicia, send greeting. It is fit, O king, that thou shouldst know, that those Jews which were carried to Babylon are come into our country, and are building that rebellious and wicked city and its market-places, and setting up its walls, and raising up the temple. Know, therefore, that when these things are finished, they will not be willing to pay tribute, nor will they submit to thy commands, but will resist kings, and will choose rather to rule over others, than be ruled over themselves. We, therefore, thought it proper to write to thee, O king, while the works about the temple are going on so fast, and not to overlook this matter, that thou mayest search into the books of thy fathers: for thou wilt find in them, that the Jews have been rebels, and enemies to kings, as hath their city been also, which, for that reason, hath been till now laid waste. We thought proper also to inform thee of this matter, because thou mayest perhaps be otherwise ignorant of it,—that if this city be once inhabited, and be entirely encompassed with walls, thou wilt be excluded from thy passage to Cœle-Syria and Phenicia.'

"2. When Cambyses had read the epistle, being naturally wicked, he was irritated at what they told him: and wrote back to them as follows: 'Cambyses, the king, to Rathumus the historiographer, to Beeltethmus, to Semellius the scribe, and the rest that are in commission, and dwelling in Samaria and Phenicia, after this manner: I have read the epistle that was sent from you; and I gave order that the books of my forefathers should be searched into; and it is there found that this city has always been an enemy to kings, and its inhabitants have raised seditions and wars. We also are sensible that their kings have been powerful and tyrannical, and have exacted tribute of Cœle-Syria and Phenicia. Wherefore I give order, that the Jews shall not be permitted to build that city, lest such mischief as they used to bring upon kings be greatly augmented.'

When this epistle was read, Rathumus, and Semellius the scribe, and their associates, got suddenly on horseback, and made haste to Jerusalem : they also brought a great company with them, and forbade the Jews to build the city and the temple. Accordingly these works were hindered from going on till the second year of the reign of Darius, for nine years more: for Cambyses reigned six years, and within that time overthrew Egypt; and when he was come back, he died at Damascus."—*Antiquities*, book xi, chap. ii, sec. 1, 2.

Josephus evidently attaches greater effect to this correspondence than it merits : for it is clear that this is the interference referred to by Ezra; (chap. iv, 6;) and there can be little doubt that it availed during the reign of Cambyses. But the same sacred writer distinctly refers to other efforts to stay the proceedings of the Hebrews, which were made in the following reign ; and a letter of the opponents is given by him at length, addressed not to "Ahasuerus," as Cambyses is called by Ezra, but to "Artaxerxes," who must have been Smerdis the Magian. Either, therefore, Josephus has misstated the case in referring the correspondence which took place with Smerdis to the preceding sovereign ; or, which scarcely seems probable, such communications took place in both reigns, one being cited by the historian, and the other by the sacred writer. It cannot be doubted that by "Ahasuerus" Ezra means Cambyses, as he immediately followed Cyrus ; and it seems equally certain that Artaxerxes was the Magian, he having preceded Darius,—all four being specifically spoken of by the sacred scribe.

But the correspondence, as given both in the Scriptures and by the historian, affords important information respecting the national records. The complainants appeal to these in proof of the independence, valour, and determined spirit of the Hebrews, in their previous history. Now, Jerusalem was destroyed before Persia had existence as a paramount state. Indeed, whatever records had been made of the resistance of the kingdom of Judah to the imperial power must at latest have been made at Babylon. But the seat of empire had been removed from this city to Ecbatana in Media, and again from Ecbatana to Susa in Persia : and yet so carefully had the imperial archives been transferred and preserved, that the sovereign, on an appeal from a distant province, could instantly ascertain its character previously to its being subdued by the imperial power. This fact speaks volumes as to the means which Berosus, Ctesias, Firdusi, and others, who in their respective ages had access to these records, would have of collecting authentic facts respecting the early times of the empire.

NOTE 44, page 266.—*The Deliberations of the Conspirators as to the future Government of Persia, and the Appointment of Darius Hystaspes to be King.*

It is curious to find, in the deliberations of these seven Persian nobles, every kind of government advocated which has obtained among men. According to Herodotus, Otanes argued in favour of democracy, as zealously as could any American of modern times, and testified the sincerity of his address by withdrawing altogether from any claim to govern, when he found that none of his companions shared his sentiments. Megabyzus advocated an oligarchy, and strongly urged the propriety of intrusting the ruling power to a select number of individuals eminent for their talents and virtues. Darius, on the other hand, argued in favour of monarchy ; and adduced various reasons for maintaining the same kind of government which had previously existed in the country.

It cannot escape observation, that although the advocates for these different kinds of government seem to have been fully conversant with all the arguments since urged in favour of these several schemes of national polity, not one of them appears to have had the remotest idea of that happy blending of each which is so directly adapted to neutralize their respective evil tendencies, and to elicit the good qualities of all; as is seen in the constitutional governments of modern times.

The result was, that of the seven, four were in favour of monarchy, two of oligarchy, and one of democracy. It was therefore decided that monarchy should be continued, and that one of the seven should be the first king. Having previously made sundry regulations, conferring special privilege on Otanes, as the first instigator of the measures taken against the impostor Smerdis, and on the members of their own body, "they agreed to meet on horseback at sunrise in the vicinity of the city, and to make *him* king whose horse should neigh first. Darius had a groom, whose name was Œbares, a man of considerable ingenuity, for whom on his return he immediately sent. 'Œbares,' said he, 'it is determined that we are to meet at sunrise on horseback, and that he among us shall be king whose horse shall first neigh. Whatever acuteness you have, exert it on this occasion, that no one but myself may attain this honour.' 'Sir,' replied Œbares, 'if your being king or not depend on what you say, be not afraid. I have a kind of charm, which will prevent any one's being preferred to yourself.' 'Whatever,' replied Darius, 'this charm may be, it must be applied without delay, as the morning will decide the matter.' Œbares, therefore, as soon as the evening came, conducted to the place before the city a mare, having previously ordered Darius's horse to be taken there.

"The next morning, as soon as it was light, the six Persians assembled, as had been agreed, on horseback. After riding up and down at the place appointed, they came at length to the spot where, on the preceding evening, the mare had been brought: here the horse of Darius instantly began to neigh, which, though the sky was remarkably clear, was immediately succeeded by thunder and lightning. The heavens thus seemed to favour, and, indeed, to act in concert with, Darius. Immediately the other noblemen dismounted, and, falling at his feet, hailed him king."

Such is the account given by Herodotus of the election of Darius to the sovereignty of Persia. (Thalia, cap. 80-84.) The truth of this statement is attested by an equestrian statue, on which was placed an inscription celebrating his elevation to the throne, and containing the name of the groom and also of the horse.

NOTE 45, page 272.—*The Succession of Xerxes to the Throne of Persia.*

The account given in the text is taken from Herodotus. Plutarch and Justin give a different version of the case, which, as being received by the emperor Julian as authentic, is worthy of notice. According to this statement, the case was not decided by Darius; but on his death both brothers claimed the sovereignty, and each was supported by numerous friends. Pending the settlement of this question, Ariamenes (called by Herodotus Artobazanes) went into Media, but not in a hostile manner. While he was there, Xerxes assumed the crown and robes of royalty. But on the return of his brother he put these off, and sent him presents, with a friendly message to this effect: "Thus your brother Xerxes honours you; and if the Persians should declare me king, I will place you next to myself." Ariamenes replied, "I accept your gifts, but presume that I am entitled to the throne of Persia. Yet for my brothers I shall have posts of distinction, and for Xerxes the first."

On the day fixed for the determination of the right to the crown, the Persians appointed Artabanus, the brother of Darius, to make the decision. Xerxes excepted to this, and preferred leaving it to the popular will: but his mother reproved him for the objection, and he withdrew it. Artabanus then, after reviewing the conflicting claims of the candidates, decided in favour of Xerxes; upon which Ariamenes rose up immediately, did homage to his brother, and placed him on the throne.

NOTE **46,** page 273.—*The Behistun Inscriptions, containing Darius's own Account of his Wars.*

The following Inscriptions possess great interest, as being to some extent an autobiography of Darius Hystaspis. Reference will be made to their contents mainly in the chapter treating of the Religion of Persia: but the reader will find, that besides the light which they throw on Persian theology, they present some historical notices of importance, such, for instance, as the claim of Darius to the crown of Persia on hereditary grounds, which will be recognised as a curious piece of state-policy.

"1. I am Darius the great king, the king of kings, the king of Persia, the king of (the dependent) provinces, the son of Hystaspes, the grandson of Arsames the Achæmenian.

"2. Says Darius the king:—My father was Hystaspes; of Hystaspes the father was Arsames; of Arsames the father was Ariyaramnes; of Ariyaramnes the father was Teispes; of Teispes the father was Achæmenes.

"3. Says Darius the king:—On that account we have been called Achæmenians; from antiquity we have been unsubdued; (or, we have descended;) from antiquity those of our race have been kings.

"4. Says Darius the king:—There are eight of my race who have been kings before me; I am the ninth: for a very long time we have been kings.

"5. Says Darius the king:—By the grace of Ormazd I am (I have become) king; Ormazd has granted me the empire.

"6. Says Darius the king:—These are the countries which have fallen into my hands:—by the grace of Ormazd I have become king of them:—Persia, Susiana, Babylonia, Assyria, Arabia, Egypt; those which are of the sea, Sparta and Ionia; Armenia, Cappadocia, Parthia, Zarangia, Aria, Chorasmia, Bactria, Sogdiana, the Sacæ, the Sattagydes, Arachosia, and the Mecians; the total amount being twenty-one (twenty-three?) countries.

"7. Says Darius the king:—These are the countries which have come to me; by the grace of Ormazd they have become subject to me; they have brought tribute to me. That which has been said unto them by me, both by night and by day, it has been performed by them.

"8. Says Darius the king:—Within these countries whoever was of the true faith, him have I cherished and protected; whoever was a heretic, him I have rooted out entirely. By the grace of Ormazd these countries, therefore, being given to me, have rejoiced. As to them it has been said by me, Thus has it been done by them.

"9. Says Darius the king:—Ormazd has granted me the empire. Ormazd has brought help to me until I have gained this empire. By the grace of Ormazd I hold this empire.

"10. Says Darius the king:—This (or the following) (is) what was done by me, before I became king. He who was named Cambyses, (Kabujiya,) the son of Cyrus, of our race, he was here king before me. There was of that Cambyses a brother named Bartius; he was of the same father and mother as Cambyses. Cambyses slew this Bartius. When Cambyses slew that Bartius, the troubles of the state ceased which Bartius had excited. (?) Then Cambyses proceeded to Egypt. When Cambyses had gone to Egypt, the state became heretical; then the lie became abounding in the land, both in Persia and in Media, and in the other provinces.

"11. Says Darius the king:—Afterward there was a certain man, a Magian, named Gomátes. He arose from Pissiachádá, the mountains named Arakadres; from thence, on the fourteenth day of the month Viyakhna, then it was, as he arose, to the state he thus falsely declared: 'I am Bartius, the son of Cyrus, the brother of Cambyses.' Then the whole state became rebellious; from Cambyses it went over to that (Bartius), both Persia and Media, and the other provinces. He seized the empire; on the ninth day of the month Garmapada, then it was he thus seized the empire. Afterward Cambyses, unable to endure his (misfortunes), died.

"12. Says Darius the king:—That crown, or empire, of which Gomátes, the Magian, dispossessed Cambyses, that crown had been in our family from the olden time. After Gomátes the Magian had dispossessed Cambyses of Persia and Media and the dependent provinces, he did according to his desire,—he became king.

"13. Says Darius the king:—There was not a man, neither Persian, nor Median, nor any one of our family, who would dispossess of the empire that Gomátes the Magian. The state feared to resist him. He would frequently address the state, which knew the old Bartius; for that reason he would adress the state, saying, 'Beware lest it regard me as if I were not Bartius the son of Cyrus.' There was not one bold enough to oppose him; every one was standing obediently around Gomátes the Magian, until I arrived. Then I abode in the worship of Ormazd; Ormazd brought help to me. On the tenth day of the month Bágayádish, then it was, with the men who were my well-wishers, I slew that Gomátes the Magian, and the chief men who were his followers. The fort named Siktakhotes, in the district of Media named Nisæa, there I slew him; I dispossessed him of the empire. By the grace of Ormazd I became king; Ormazd granted me the sceptre.

"14. Says Darius the king:—The crown that had been wrested from our race, that I recovered; I established it firmly, as in the days of old; this I did. The rites which Gomátes the Magian had introduced, I prohibited. I re-instituted for the state the sacred chants and (sacrificial) worship, and confided them to the families which Gomátes the Magian had deprived of those offices. I firmly established the kingdom, both Persia and Media, and the other provinces, as in the days of old; thus I restored that which had been taken away. By the grace of Ormazd I did this. I laboured until I had firmly established our family as in the days of old. I laboured, by the grace of Ormazd, (in order) that Gomátes the Magian might not supersede our family.

"15. Says Darius the king:—This is that which I did after that I became king.

"16. Says Darius the king:—When I had slain Gomátes the Magian, then a certain man, named Atrines, the son of Opadarmes, he arose; to the state of Susiana he thus said: 'I am king of Susiana.' Then the people of Susiana became rebellious; they went over to that Atrines; he became king of Susiana.

And a certain man, a Babylonian, named Natitabirus, the son of Æna..., he arose. The state of Babylonia he thus falsely addressed: 'I am Nabokhodrossor, the son of Nabonidus.' Then the entire Babylonian state went over to that Natitabirus. Babylon became rebellious. He (Natitabirus) seized the government of Babylonia.

"17. Says Darius the king:—Then I sent to Susiana; that Atrines was brought to me a prisoner. I slew him.

"18. Says Darius the king:—Then I proceeded to Babylon (marching) against that Natitabirus, who was called Nabokhodrossor. The forces of Natitabirus held the Tigris; there they had come, and they had boats. Then I placed a detachment on rafts; I brought the enemy into difficulty; I assaulted the enemy's position. Ormazd brought help to me; by the grace of Ormazd I succeeded in passing the Tigris. Then I entirely defeated the army of that Natitabirus. On the twenty-seventh day of the month of Atriyáta, then it was that we thus fought.

"19. Says Darius the king:—Then I marched against Babylon. When I arrived near Babylon, the city named Zázána upon the Euphrates, there that Natitabirus, who was called Nabokhodrossor, came with a force before me, offering battle. Then we fought a battle. Ormazd brought help to me: by the grace of Ormazd, I entirely defeated the force of Natitabirus. The enemy was driven into the water; the water destroyed them. On the second day of the month Anámaka, then it was that we thus fought the battle."

[End of column I, which extends to ninety-six lines, and the writing of which is generally in good preservation.]

"1. Says Darius the king:—Then Natitabirus, with the horsemen who were faithful to him, fled to Babylon. Then I proceeded to Babylon; I took Babylon, and seized that Natitabirus. Afterward I slew that Natitabirus at Babylon.

"2. Says Darius the king:—While I was at Babylon, these are the countries which revolted against me: Persia, Susiana, Media, Assyria, Armenia, Parthia, Margiana, Sattagydia, and Sacia.

"3. Says Darius the king:—A certain man, named Martius, the son of Sisicres; a city of Persia, named Cyganaea, there he dwelt; he rose up; to the state of Susiana he thus said: 'I am Omanes, the king of Susiana.'

"4. Says Darius the king:—Upon this (?) I was moving a little way in the direction of Susiana: then the Susians, fearing (?) from me, seized that Martius, who was their chief, and they slew him. (?)

"5. Says Darius the king:—A certain man named Phraortes, a Median, he rose up; to the state of Media he thus said: I am Xathrites, of the race of Cyaxares.' Then the Median forces, which were at home, (?) revolted against me. They went over to that Phraortes; he became king of Media.

"6. Says Darius the king:—The army of Persians and Medes that was with me (on service) that remained faithful to me. Then I sent forth these troops. Hydarnes by name, a Persian, one of my subjects, him I appointed their leader. I thus addressed them: 'Happiness attend ye; smite that Median state which does not acknowledge me.' Then that Hydarnes marched with his army. When he reached Media, a city of Media, named Ma..., there he engaged the Medes. He who was leader of the Medes could not at all resist him. (?) Ormazd brought help to me: by the grace of Ormazd, the troops of Hydarnes entirely defeated the rebel army. On the sixth day of the month Anámaka, then it was that the battle was thus fought by them. Afterward my forces remained at Kapada, a district of Media, according to my order, (?) until I myself arrived in Media.

"7. Says Darius the king:—Then Dadarses, by name an Armenian, one of my servants, him I sent to Armenia. I thus said to him : 'Greeting to thee: the rebel state that does not obey me, smite it.' Then Dadarses marched. When he reached Armenia, then the rebels, having collected, came before Dadarses, arraying their battle. —— by name, a village of Armenia, there they engaged. Ormazd brought help to me ; by the grace of Ormazd, my forces entirely defeated that rebel army. On the eighth day of the month Thurawáhara, then it was a battle was thus fought by them.

"8. Says Darius the king:—For the second time the rebels having collected, returned before Dadarses arraying battle. The fort of Armenia, named Tigra, there they engaged. Ormazd brought help to me ; by the grace of Ormazd, my troops entirely defeated that rebel army. On the eighteenth day of the month of Thurawáhara, then it was a battle was thus fought by them.

"9. Says Darius the king:—For the third time the rebels having assembled, returned before Dadarses arraying battle. A fort of Armenia named ——, there they engaged. Ormazd brought help to me ; by the grace of Ormazd, my forces entirely defeated the rebel troops. On the ninth day of the month Thaigarchish, then it was a battle was thus fought by them. Afterward Dadarses remained away from me . . . until I reached Media.

"10. Says Darius the king:—Then he who was named Vomises, a Persian, one of my servants, him I sent to Armenia. Thus I said to him : 'Hail to thee: the rebel state which does not acknowledge my authority, bring it under submission.' Then Vomises marched forth. When he had reached Armenia, then the rebels, having assembled, came again before Vomises in order of battle. A district of Assyria named ——, there they engaged. Ormazd brought help to me ; by the grace of Ormazd, my forces entirely defeated that rebel army. On the fifteenth day of the month Anámaka, then it was a battle was thus fought by them.

"11. Says Darius the king:—For the second time the rebels having assembled, came before Vomises in battle array. The district of Armenia named Otiára, there they engaged. Ormazd brought help to me : by the grace of Ormazd, my forces entirely defeated that rebel army. In the month Thurawáhara, upon the festival, (?) then was a battle fought by them. Afterward Vomises remained in Armenia apart from me, until I reached Media.

"12. Says Darius the king:—Then I departed: from Babylon I proceeded to Media. When I reached Media, a city of Media named Gudrusia, there that Phraortes, who was called 'king of Media,' came with an army before me in battle array. Then we joined battle. Ormazd brought help to me ; by the grace of Ormazd, I entirely defeated the forces of Phraortes. On the twenty-sixth day of the month of Askhama, (?) then it was we thus fought in battle.

"13. Says Darius the king:—Then that Phraortes, with the horsemen who were faithful to him, fled from thence to the district of Media named Rhages. Subsequently I despatched forces in pursuit, by whom Phraortes was taken and brought before me. I cut off both his nose and ears and his lips, (?) and I brought him to ——. He was held chained at my door ; all the kingdom beheld him. Afterward, at Ecbatana, there I had him crucified ; (?) and the men who were his chief followers at Ecbatana, in the citadel I imprisoned (?) them.

"14. Says Darius the king:—A certain man named Sitratachmes, a Sagartian, he rebelled against me. To the state he thus said : 'I am the king of Sagartia, I am of the race of Cyaxares.' Then I sent forth an army, composed of Persians and Medians. A man named Camaspates, a Median, one of my subjects, him I appointed their leader. Thus I addressed them: 'Hail to ye: the state which is in revolt, which does not acknowledge me, smite it.' Then Camaspates marched with his army. He fought a battle with Sitratachmes. Ormazd brought help to me; by the grace of Ormazd, my troops entirely defeated the rebel army, and took Sitratachmes, and brought him before me. Then I cut off his nose and his ears, and I brought him to ——. He was kept chained at my door. (?) All the kingdom beheld him. Afterward I had him crucified at Arbela.

"15. Says Darius the king;—This is that (which) was done by me in Media.

"16. Says Darius the king:—[The rest of this paragraph is illegible in the Persian inscription, except in a few detached words. A connected translation is given from the Median transcript, which is perfect.] Parthia and Hyrcania" (Warkán in the Persian, Vehkániya in the Median) "revolted against me! they declared for Phraortes. Hystaspes, who was my father, the Parthian forces rose in rebellion against him. Then Hystaspes, with the troops who remained faithful to him, marched forth. Hyspaostisa, a town of Parthia, there he engaged the rebels. Ormazd brought help . . . . by the grace of Ormazd, Hystaspes entirely defeated the rebel army on the twenty-second day of the month Viyakhna:" (Viyahnas in the Median:) "then it was the battle was fought by them."

[End of Column II, which extends, like the preceding, to ninety-six lines. The writing is a good deal injured by a fissure in the rock, which extends the whole length of the tablet.]

"Says Darius the king:—Then I sent from Rhages a Persian army to Hystaspes. When that army reached Hystaspes, he marched forth with those troops. The city of Parthia named Patigapana, there he fought with the rebels. Ormazd brought help to me; by the grace of Ormazd, Hystaspes entirely defeated that rebel army. On the first day of the month of Garmapada, then it was the battle was thus fought by them.

"2. Says Darius the king:—Then the province submitted to me. This is what was done by me in Parthia.

"3. Says Darius the king:—The province named Margiana, that revolted (?) against me. A certain man named Phraates, the Margians made him their leader. Then I sent to him one who was named Dadarses, a Persian, one of my subjects, and the satrap of Bactria. Thus I said to him: 'Hail to thee: attack that province which does not acknowledge me.' Then Dadarses marched with his forces; he joined battle with the Margians. Ormazd brought help to me; by the grace of Ormazd, my troops entirely defeated the rebel army. On the twenty-third day of the month Atriyátiya, then it was the battle was thus fought by them.

"4. Says Darius the king:—Then the province submitted to me. This is what was done by me in Bactria.

"5. Says Darius the king:—A certain man, named Veisdátes; a city named Tárba, in the district of Persia named Yutiya, there he dwelt. He rose up a second time; to the state of Persia he thus said: 'I am Bartius, the son of Cyrus.' Then the Persian forces which were at home being removed (?) from connexion with me, they revolted against me. They went over to that Veisdátes; he became king of Persia.

"6. Says Darius the king:—Then I sent forth the Persian and Median forces which were with me. Artabardes by name, one of my servants, him I appointed their chief. Another Persian force proceeded after me to Media. Then Artabardes, with his troops, marched to Persia. When he reached Persia, a city of

APPENDIX. 587

Persia named Racha, there that Veisdátes, who was called Bartius, came with a force before Artabardes in battle array. Then they joined battle. Ormazd brought help to me; by the grace of Ormazd, my troops entirely defeated the army of Veisdátes. On the twelfth day of the month Thurawáhara, then it was the battle was thus fought by them.

"7. Says Darius the king:—Then that Veisdátes, with the horsemen who remained staunch to him, fled from thence to Pissiachádá. From that place, with an army, he came back arraying battle before Artabardes. The mountains named Parga, there they fought. Ormazd brought help to me; by the grace of Ormazd my troops entirely defeated the army of Veisdátes. On the sixth day of the month of Garmapada, then it was that the battle was thus fought by them. Both that Veisdátes they took, and also they took the men who were his principal adherents.

"8. Says Darius the king:—Then that Veisdátes and the men who were his chief followers, the town of Persia named Chadidia, there I impaled (?) them.

"9. Says Darius the king:—That Veisdátes, who was called Bartius, he sent troops to Arachotia, against one named Vibánus, a Persian, one of my servants, and satrap of Arachotia; and he appointed a certain man to be their leader. He thus addressed them: 'Hail to ye: smite Vibánus, and that state which obeys the rule of King Darius.' Then those forces marched which Veisdátes had sent against Vibánus, preparing for battle. A fort named Capiscania, there they fought an action. Ormazd brought help to me; by the grace of Ormazd, my troops entirely defeated that rebel army. On the thirteenth day of the month Anámaka, then it was the battle was thus fought by them.

"10. Says Darius the king:—Another time, the rebels having assembled came before Vibánus, offering battle. The district named Gadytia, there they fought an action. Ormazd brought help to me; by the grace of Ormazd, my troops entirely defeated the rebel army. On the seventh day of the month Viyakhna, then it was the battle was thus fought by them.

"11. Says Darius the king:—Then that man who was the leader of those troops which Veisdátes had sent against Vibánus, that leader, with the horsemen who were faithful to him, fled away. A fort of Arachotia, named Arsháda, he went beyond that place. Then Vibánus with his troops marched in pursuit (or, to Nipatiya). There he took him, and slew the men who were his chief followers.

"12. Says Darius the king:—Then the province submitted to me. This is what was done by me in Arachotia.

"13. Says Darius the king:—While I was in Persia and Media, for the second time the Babylonians revolted against me. A certain man named Aracus, an Armenian, the son of Nañditus, he arose up; a district of Babylon named Dobáña, from thence he arose; he thus falsely proclaimed: 'I am Nabokhodrossor, the son of Nahonidus.' Then the Babylonian state revolted against me; it went over to that Aracus; he seized on Babylon; he became king of Babylonia.

"14. Says Darius the king:—Then I sent troops to Babylon. A Median of the name of Intaphres, one of my servants, him I appointed their leader. Thus I addressed them:—Hail to ye: smite that Babylonian state, which does not acknowledge me.' Then Intaphres with his forces marched to Babylon. Ormazd brought help to me; by the grace of Ormazd Intaphres took Babylon...On the second day of the month...then it was he thus"...[The three last lines are entirely lost in the Persian, with the exception of the concluding words, "Then he was killed;" and I have not the Median translation of this part of the inscription.]

"2. Says Darius the king:—[This column is throughout greatly defaced: in many parts the writing is wholly obliterated, and can only be conjecturally restored; the translation, therefore, is given with much less confidence than that of the preceding columns.] This is what I have done. By the grace of Ormazd have I done everything. As the provinces revolted against me, I fought nineteen battles. By the grace of Ormazd, I smote them, and I made nine kings captive. One was named Gomátes, the Magian: he was an impostor: he said, 'I am Bartius, the son of Cyrus:' he threw Persia into revolt. One, an impostor, was named Atries, the Susian: he thus said, 'I am the king of Susiana:' he caused Susiana to revolt against me. One was named Natitabirus, a native of Babylon: he was an impostor: he thus said, 'I am Nabokhodrossor, the son of Nabonidus:' he caused Babylonia to revolt. One was an impostor named Martius, the Persian: he thus said, 'I am Omanes, the King of Susiana:' he threw Susiana into rebellion. One was named Phraortes, the Median: he assumed a false character: he thus said, 'I am Xathrites, of the race of Cyaxares:' he persuaded Media to revolt. One was an impostor named Sitratchmes, a native of Sagartia: he thus said, 'I am the king of Sagartia, of the race of Cyaxares:' he headed a rebellion in Sagartia. One was an impostor named Phraates, a Margian: he threw Margiana into revolt. One was an impostor named Veisdátes, a Persian: he thus said, 'I am Bartius, the son of Cyrus:' he headed a rebellion in Persia. One was an impostor named Aracus, a native of Armenia: he said thus, 'I am Nabokhodrossor, the son of Nabonidus:' he threw Babylon into revolt.

"3. Says Darius the king:—These nine kings I have taken in these battles.

"4. Says Darius the king:—These are the provinces which became rebellious. The evil one (?) created lies, that they should deceive the state: afterward... caused...to be subdued by me. (?) As it was desired by me, thus...did (?)

"5. Says Darius the king:—Thou, whoever may be king hereafter, exert thyself to put down lying: the man who may be heretical, him entirely destroy. If it shall be thus kept up, (?) my country shall remain entire (or prosperous.)

"6. Says Darius the king:—This is what I have done. By the grace of Ormazd, have I achieved the performance of the whole. Thou, whoever hereafter mayest peruse this tablet, let it be known to thee, that which has been done by me, that it has not been falsely related. (?)

"7. Says Darius the king:—Ormazd is my witness, (?) that this record (?) I have faithfully made of the performance of the whole.

"8. Says Darius the king:—By the grace of Ormazd, there is much else that has been done by me that upon this tablet has not been inscribed. On that account it has not been inscribed, lest he who may hereafter peruse this tablet, to him the many deeds (?) that have been done by me elsewhere, it should seem that they are falsely recorded. (?)

"9. Says Darius the king:—Those who have been former kings in Persia in succession, (?) to them it is done, as by me; by the grace of Ormazd has been the performance of the whole; so it has been recorded. (?)

"10. Says Darius the king:—Be it known to thee, my successor, (?) that which has not been done by me, thus publicly, (?) on that account that thou conceal not. If thou publish this tablet to the world, (?) Ormazd shall be a friend to thee, and may thy offspring be numerous, and mayest thou be long-lived.

"11. Says Darius the king:—If thou conceal this record, thou shalt not be thyself recorded; (?) may Ormazd be thy enemy, and mayest thou be childless.

"12. Says Darius the king:—This is what I have done; the performance of the whole, by the grace of Ormazd, I have achieved it. Ormazd has brought help to me, and the other gods which are (brought help to me.)

"13. Says Darius the king:—On that account Ormazd brought help to me, and the other gods which are, (because) that I was not a heretic, nor was I a liar, nor was I a tyrant…My offspring above their place (?) above…by me with the tribes…was done. Whoever was an evil-doer, (?) him I entirely destroyed. [These lines are much defaced.]

"14. Says Darius the king:—Thou, whatsoever king who mayest be hereafter the man who may be a liar, or who may be an evil-doer, (?) do not cherish them; (?) cast them out into utter perdition.

"15. Says Darius the king:—Thou, whosoever hereafter mayest behold this tablet which I have inscribed, and these figures, beware lest thou dishonour them: as long as thou preservest them, so long shalt thou be preserved. (?)

"16. Says Darius the king:—As long as thou mayest behold this tablet and these figures, thou mayest not dishonour them; and if from injury thou shalt preserve them, (?) may Ormazd be a friend to thee, and may thy offspring be numerous, and mayest thou be long-lived; and that which thou mayest do may Ormazd bless for thee in after times.

"17. Says Darius the king:—If, seeing this tablet and these figures, thou shalt dishonour them, and if from injury thou mayest not preserve them, may Ormazd be thy enemy, and mayest thou be childless; and that which thou mayest do, may Ormazd spoil thee.

"18. Says Darius the king:—These are the men who alone (?) were there when I slew Gomátes, the Magian, who was called Bartius. These alone (?) are the men who were my assistants:—[The names are almost obliterated in the Persian, and several of them are imperfect in the Median. I have been able, however, to recover the following:] Intaphernes by name, the son of Hys…a Persian; Otanes by name, the son of…a Persian; Gobryás by name, the son of Mardonius, a Persian; Hydarnes by name, the son of…a Persian; Megabyzus by name, the son of Zopyrus, a Persian; Aspathines by name, the son of…a Persian."

[There is one more paragraph in Column IV, consisting of six lines, which is entirely obliterated in the Persian, and appears to be without any Median translation.]

Of the thirty-five lines which compose a supplementary half-column, it is impossible to give a complete translation, one side of the tablet being entirely destroyed. From such portions as are decipherable, it appears to contain an account of two other revolts; one in Susiana, conducted by a man named…imin; and the other by Saruk'ha, the chief of the Sacæ, who dwelt upon the Tigris.

Darius employed Gubar'uwa, (Gobryas,) the Persian, against the former rebel; and he marched in person against the latter, having previously returned from Media to Babylon. The details of the campaigns cannot be recovered, but they both terminated successfully.

The inscription then concludes with further thanksgivings to Ormazd, and injunctions to the posterity of Darius to preserve uninjured the memorial of his deeds.

The events described in the supplemental column must have taken place during the process of engraving the preceding record, and after the tablet containing the sculptured figures was finished. By a further smoothening of the face of the rock, Darius was enabled add the Sacan Saruk'ha, whom he had defeated in person, to his exhibition of captive figures; but there was no room in the tablet for the figure of the Susian rebel, who was discomfited by his lieutenant Gobryas.

TRANSLATION OF THE DETACHED INSCRIPTIONS WHICH ARE APPENDED TO EACH OF THE FIGURES EXHIBITED ON THE UPPER TRIUMPHAL TABLET.

Above the head of Darius is an inscription of eighteen lines, marked A in the engraving, containing an exact copy of the first four paragraphs of Column I, which have been already given. The writing is perfect; and the portions, therefore, of the lower tablet, which have been effaced, can be determinately restored. It is needless, I conceive, to repeat the translation. A Median translation, also quite perfect, adjoins the Persian original, but the Babylonian transcript is wanting.

B. Tablet attached to the prostrate figure on which the victor king tramples:—"This Gomátes, the Magian, was an impostor: he thus declared, 'I am Bartius. the son of Cyrus; I am the king.'"

C. Adjoining the first standing figure:—"This Atrines was an impostor; he thus declared, 'I am king of Susiana.'"

D. Adjoining the second standing figure:—"This Natitabirus was an impostor: he thus declared, 'I am Nabokhodrossor, the son of Nabonidus; I am king of Babylon.'"

E. Adjoining the third standing figure (the Persian legend is engraved on the body of the figure):—"This Phraortes was an impostor: he thus declared, 'I am Xathrites, of the race of Cyaxares; I am king of Media.'"

F. Above the fourth standing figure:—"This Martius was an impostor: he thus declared, 'I am Omanes, the king of Susiana.'"

G. Adjoining the fifth standing figure.—"This Sitratachmes was an impostor: he thus declared, 'I am king of Sagartia, of the race of Cyaxares.'"

H. Adjoining the sixth standing figure:—"This Veisdátes was an impostor: he thus declared, 'I am Bartius, the son of Cyrus. I am king.'"

I. Adjoining the seventh standing figure:—"This Aracus was an impostor: he thus declared, 'I am Nabokhodrossor, the son of Nabonidus. I am the king of Babylon.'"

J. Adjoining the eighth standing figure:—"This Phraates was an impostor: he thus declared, 'I am the king of Margiana.'"

K. Above the ninth, or supplemental figure with the high cap:—"This is Saruk'ha the Sacan."

[The name of Nebuchadrezzar is written indifferently Nabukhadrachar and Nabukhudrachar.]

NOTE **47**, page 274.—*Did the Jews fight in the Army of Xerxes?*

This question has been largely debated by the learned; but it seems scarcely open to reasonable doubt. It is perfectly probable that, in a general draft on the several provinces of the empire, the Jews, few in number as they were comparatively at this time, would be included. And this probability almost amounts to certainty, when it is considered that, from the geographical position of the seat of war, the principal levy of troops must have been from Western Asia.

Besides, Josephus explicitly declares that this was the case, and quotes in favour of his opinion the statement of Cheulus the poet, who, in the enumeration of this army, says, "At last there passed over a people, wonderful to be beheld; for they spake the Phenician tongue with their mouths; they dwelt in the Solymean Mountains, near a broad lake; their heads were sooty."—*Contra Apion*, lib. i, sec. 22. The learned Prideaux thus explains and defends the passage: "Jerusalem having also had the name of Solyma, (by abbreviation for Hiero-Solyma,) and all the country thereabouts being mountainous, and lying near the great Lake Asphaltitis, commonly called 'the Lake of Sodom;' this description seems plainly to suit the Jews, especially since it is also mentioned that they spake the Phenician language, the Syriac being then the vulgar language of the Jews."—*Connexion*, vol. i, p. 264. It is admitted that Scaliger and Bochartus attribute this to Solyme in Pisidia: but Eusebius and Salmasius being on the side of Josephus, the balance of authority, as well as evidence, is clearly in his favour.

NOTE 48, page 278.—*The Inscriptions relating to the Reign of Xerxes.*

These inscriptions relating to the reign of Xerxes, although tolerably numerous, possess no great variety or particular interest. They are found at Hamadan, at Persepolis, and Van. We here give them from the translation of Colonel Rawlinson:—

"The great god Ormazd, the chief of the gods, (he it is) who has given this world, who has given that heaven, who has given mankind, who has given life (?) to mankind, who has made Xerxes king, both the king of the people, and the lawgiver of the people. (2.) I am Xerxes the king, the great king, the king of kings, the king of the many-peopled countries, the supporter also of this great world, the son of King Darius the Achæmenian."

"Xerxes, the great king, the king of kings, the son of King Darius the Achæmenian."

"The great god Ormazd, the chief of the gods, (he it is) who has given this world, who has given that heaven, who has given mankind, who has given life (?) to mankind, who has made Xerxes king, both king of the people, and lawgiver of the people. (2.) I am Xerxes the king, the great king, the king of kings, the king of the many-peopled countries, the supporter also of this great world, the son of King Darius the Achæmenian. (3.) Says Xerxes the great king:—By the grace of Ormazd I have made this house. May Ormazd protect me, together with the (other) gods, and my empire, and that which has been done by me."

"The great god Ormazd, (he it is) who has given this world, who has given that heaven, who has given mankind, who has given life to mankind, who has made Xerxes king, both the king of the people, and the lawgiver of the people. (2.) I am Xerxes the king, the great king, the king of kings, the king of the many-peopled countries, the supporter also of this great world, the son of King Darius the Achæmenian. (3.) Says Xerxes the great king:—That which has been done by me here, and that which has been done by me elsewhere, all of it have I accomplished by the grace of Ormazd. May Ormazd protect me, together with the (other) gods, both my empire and my works" (literally, "that which has been done by me.")

"The great god Ormazd, (he it is) who has given this world, who has given that heaven, who has given mankind, who has given life to mankind, who has made Xerxes king, both king of the people, and lawgiver of the people. (2.) I am Xerxes the king, the great king, the king of kings, the king of the many-peopled countries, the supporter also of this great world, the son of King Darius the Achæmenian. (3.) Says Xerxes the king:—By the grace of Ormazd I have made this gate of entrance (or, this public portal.) There is many another noble work besides (or, in) this Persepolis which I have executed, and which my father has executed. Whatsoever noble works are to be seen, we have executed all of them by the grace of Ormazd. (4.) Says Xerxes the king:—May Ormazd protect me and my empire. Both that which has been executed by me, and that which has been executed by my father, may Ormazd protect it."

The great god Ormazd, the chief of the gods, (he it is) who has given this world, who has given that heaven, who has given mankind, who has given life (?) to mankind; who has made Xerxes king, both king of the people, and lawgiver of the people. (2.) I am Xerxes the king, the great king, the king of kings, the king of the many-peopled countries, the supporter also of this great world, the son of King Darius the Achæmenian. (3.) Says Xerxes the king:—King Darius, who was my father, he by the grace of God executed many a noble work; he also visited this place; in celebration (?) (of which) why did he not cause a tablet to be engraved? After that I arrived here, I caused this tablet to be written." . . .

NOTE 49, page 284.—*The Inscriptions relating to the Reign of Artaxerxes.*

"The great god Ormazd, (he it is) who has given this world, who has given that heaven, who has made mankind, who has given life to mankind, who has made me Artaxerxes king, both the king of the people, and the lawgiver of the people. (2.) Says Artaxerxes, the great king, the king of kings, the king of the nations, the king of this world:—I am the son of King Artaxerxes, Artaxerxes (being) the son of King Darius, Darius (being) the son of King Artaxerxes, Artaxerxes (being) the son of King Xerxes, Xerxes (being) the son of King Darius, Darius (being) the son of one named Hystaspes, (and) Hystaspes (being) the son of one named Arsames, an Achæmenian. (3.) Says King Artaxerxes:—I have made this well-sculptured piece of masonry for my own convenience. (4.) Says King Artaxerxes:—May Ormazd and the god Mithra protect me: (may they protect) both this province and that which I have done.

"ARTAXERXES THE GREAT KING."

It will be sufficient to observe of this inscription, that the orthography of the name of Artaxerxes, regardless altogether of etymological precision, and following to a certain extent the corrupted pronunciation by which the Medes and Babylonians sought to adopt the compound Persian articulations to their peculiar organs of speech, is decisive, I think, as to the foreign origin of the legend; and I would infer also from the same circumstance that the relic must be assigned even to a later date than that of the latest Achæmenian inscriptions at Persepolis.

NOTE 50, page 285.—*The Fulfilment of sacred Prophecy in the History of Persia.*

In a brief review of the predictions accomplished in the history of this nation, it may be best to notice,—

1. The predictive representation of the second universal empire given to the prophet Daniel under different symbols; and, first, as "the breast and arms of silver," in the great image which Nebuchadnezzar saw in his dream. This predictive symbolism was explained by the prophet, "*Thou* art this head of gold. And after thee shall arise another kingdom inferior to thee." This, therefore, could refer to no power but the Medo-Persian empire of Cyrus, which succeeded the Babylonian monarchy. Various conjectures have been put forth respecting

the *inferiority* of this kingdom to the preceding, which are generally of a most unsatisfactory kind. It was certainly not inferior in extent, nor—if the explanation of Daniel with respect to the first kingdom is received—in duration; and no argument can be drawn with propriety (although it has frequently been attempted) from the value of the metals; for the kingdoms represented by brass and iron are in some respects distinctly stated to be superior to those set forth by gold and silver.

I freely confess I feel doubts as to whether the term "inferior," used by our translators here, conveys the true sense of the original. It is the only instance in which the word is thus rendered, although it frequently occurs in Scripture. In eighteen other places in this Book, it is translated "the earth." If something of this kind, however, is the meaning of the term, I presume it must be understood as referring to the unequalled magnificence of the Babylonian kingdom during the reign of Nebuchadnezzar. The *fact* is, however, especially worthy of attention. There was Nebuchadnezzar in all the pride of his power; yet to him the prophet says, "After thee shall arise another kingdom." And so it was. Babylon sunk into ruin, and Persia rose into power in her place. Dan. ii, 39.

Secondly, the Persian empire is described as the second beast, "like to a bear." This appears to have been intended to signify the inordinate rapacity and cruelty of Persia. For "it had ribs between the teeth of it:—and they said thus unto it, Arise, devour much flesh." And surely no nation ever displayed more of these qualities than did this. From India to Egypt and Greece, it went forth to devour; and the punishments systematically inflicted by these kings were of unequal severity. Dan. vii, 5.

Thirdly, this empire is set forth under the symbol of a ram with two horns. "Then," says the prophet, "I lifted up mine eyes, and saw, and, behold, there stood before the river a ram which had two horns: and the two horns were high; but one was higher than the other, and the higher came up last. I saw the ram pushing westward, and northward, and southward; so that no beasts might stand before him, neither was there any that could deliver out of his hand: but he did according to his will, and became great." Dan. viii, 3, 4. This symbolism is thus explained to the prophet by the angel: "The ram which thou sawest having two horns are the kings of Media and Persia." Verse 20.

Remarkable as is this prophetic symbolism, it is so plain as to leave little room for comment. Of all the great monarchies, this alone was distinguished as a junction of *two* kingdoms. One of these, Media, was the most ancient and famous in history; the other, Persia, of recent rise to power, yet of surpassing potency. Hence the two horns of unequal heights—the last being the highest. Here, as in the case of Babylon, it seems very probable that the figure employed was a well-known symbol. The ram's head, with two horns made of gold, was, we are told, worn by the Medo-Persian kings instead of a crown. The national banner was a ram; and rams sculptured with two horns, one higher than the other, are found on the ruins of Persepolis. The rapid conquests of this power are vividly set forth by the ram "pushing westward, and southward, and northward," while there was no ability in any people to stand before him. It is not possible to conceive of a more exact prophetic symbolism than this.

II. We notice the special predictions relating to Cyrus, the founder and hero of this empire. The adaptation of this prophecy to Babylon has been already noticed. It will, therefore, here be only necessary to mention the dates, and to quote a few lines of this wonderful prediction. Cyrus ascended the throne of Persia B. C. 559; Isaiah ceased to prophesy B. C. 698; so that, at least one hundred and forty years before the accession of this warrior to the throne of his native country, the Hebrew seer published these remarkable lines:—

> "Thus saith the Lord, thy Redeemer, (O Jacob,)
> And he that formed thee from the womb, (O Israel :)
> I am the Lord who made all things;
> Who stretch out the heavens alone,
> And spread out the earth by myself:—
> Who saith to CYRUS, He is my shepherd,
> And shall perform all my pleasure :
> Who saith to Jerusalem, Thou shalt be built;
> And to the temple, Thou shalt be founded." Isa. xliv, 24, 28.
>
> "Thus saith the LORD to his anointed,
> To CYRUS, whom I hold by the right hand,
> To subdue before him nations,
> And ungird the loins of kings;
> To open before him (palace) folding-doors;
> Even (river) gates shall not be shut." Isa. xlv, 1.
>
> Dr. Hales's Translation.

When it is considered that this was not only written before Cyrus was born, but while Jerusalem stood in all her glory, and the temple in all its beauty, we see the full force of the prophecy. The sacred seer—realizing, under the teaching of the Holy Spirit, coming events—places himself in the midst of the desolations of the captivity, and calls Cyrus to the work which Divine Providence had assigned him.

III. We refer to the predicted invasion of Greece by Persia.

Daniel gives this prophecy in the following language: "Behold, there shall stand up yet three kings in Persia; and the fourth shall be far richer than they all: and by his strength through his riches he shall stir up all against the realm of Grecia." Dan. xi, 2. The prophet is careful to tell us that this was spoken in "the first year of Darius the Mede;" and consequently when Cyrus was reigning in Persia, it being the year before he subdued Media. Those *three* kings must therefore be Cambyses, Smerdis, and Darius; and the fourth, Xerxes. The history shows the boundless extent of his resources, and the intensity with which "he stirred up all against the realm of Grecia." There are few predictions on the sacred record more full and exact in terms, or which have been fulfilled in a more complete and elaborate development of historical events.

IV. We glance at predictions which set forth the defeat and captivity of Persia.

Here we might cite the invincible prowess of the Grecian goat, and his unqualified success. Dan. viii, 5-7. But this belongs rather to the history of Greece. It will here be only necessary to refer to a prophecy of Jeremiah: "Thus saith the Lord of hosts; Behold, I will break the bow of Elam, the chief of their might. And upon Elam will I bring the four winds from the four quarters of the heaven, and will scatter them toward all those winds; and there shall be no nation whither the outcasts of Elam shall not come. For I will cause Elam to be dismayed before their enemies, and before them that seek their life: and I will bring evil upon them, even my fierce anger, saith the Lord; and I will send the sword after them, till I have consumed them: and I will set my throne in Elam, and will destroy from thence the king and the princes, saith the Lord." Jer. xlix, 35-38.

APPENDIX. 595

Elam generally signifies Persia; and that it does so here, is evident by the reference to the *bow* of Elam,—the favourite and most formidable weapon of Persian warfare. Here, then, even before Persia is raised to power, does Jehovah predict her ruin. So it was with Babylon. Thus did the Lord guard the purity of his government, and show that, however nations or individuals might be raised by providential appointment to elevated power, this formed no sanction for their sin, which was sure to bring upon them divine judgment.

The exactitude with which these prophecies were fulfilled by the conquests of Alexander is so obvious, that they do not call for special remark.

NOTE 51, page 287.—*The conflicting Opinions and Controversy respecting Zoroaster and his Doctrines.*

For the reasons stated in the text, it becomes necessary to present, in as condensed a form as possible, an outline of the opinions promulgated by the learned respecting the character and teaching of this person.

To begin with a statement sufficiently startling:—it may be observed that M. Huet, a celebrated French bishop, put forth the opinion that Moses was Zoroaster; or that the latter was a fictitious personage, invented by the Persian Magi, for the purpose of introducing into their country the theological system which they had borrowed from the Jewish lawgiver.

The controversy respecting this sage, however, arises out of the statements advanced by the learned Dr. Thomas Hyde in his elaborate work on this subject. (Veterum Persarum et Parthorum et Medorum Religionis Historia.) In this work it is maintained, that the religion of the ancient Persians arose out of the doctrines taught by Zoroaster, a Magian sage who lived in the reign of Darius Hystaspis; and that this was the only person of that name.

Dean Prideaux, who has given in his valuable "Connexion" a lengthened epitome of Zoroaster's life and doctrines, adopts and defends the sentiments of Hyde, and is quoted as the great authority on that side of the question to the present day. This is done, however, with singular impropriety, and exhibits a remarkable instance of neglect in the continued publication of a standard work without correction. It is true that Prideaux in his "Connexion" maintained that there had been but one Zoroaster; but it is equally true that, being pressed by the arguments of his erudite cousin, Walter Moyle, Esq., of Bake, in Cornwall, he was led to alter his opinion, and admit the existence of two Zoroasters. "But your other answer," says the learned dean, "is far better, and *I think you are extremely in the right to suppose two Zoroastres. I think it impossible to reconcile the Grecian and Persian accounts upon any other hypothesis.*"—*Moyle's Works*, vol. ii, p. 75. Surely, after this, some notice of this change of sentiment should have been inserted in the subsequent editions of Prideaux's great work. But this has not been done; and the learned dean stands before the world, to this day, in direct contradiction to himself, and with this disadvantage,—that his error is in a popular work, but its correction is one very little known.

It is, however, argued in opposition to this opinion, that the Greek and Latin writers speak of several Zoroasters. Some of these are placed in such remote antiquity as to be altogether fabulous. Pliny says that Eudoxus placed Zoroastres six thousand years before the death of Plato, alleging that Aristotle concurred in that opinion. Hermippus and others say, that this sage was taught magic five thousand years before the siege of Troy; while Pliny himself expresses an opinion that Zoroastres lived many thousand years before Moses. Xanthus of Lydia reckons six hundred years from Zoroastres to the time of Xerxes; and Justin says that he flourished eight hundred and fifty years before the Trojan war.

There is no less diversity of opinion as to the number of persons of this name than there is as to the times when they lived. Sir Walter Raleigh observes, "Of Zoroastres there is much dispute. Arnobius remembereth four to whom the name of Zoroaster or Zoroastres was given: the first, Arnobius calleth the Bactrian, which may be the same that Ninus overthrew; the second, a Chaldæan, and the astronomer of Ninus; the third was Zoroaster Pamphylius, who lived in the time of Cyrus, and his familiar; the fourth, Zoroaster Armenius, the nephew of Hostianes, which followed Xerxes into Greece."—*History of the World*, book i, chap. xi, sec. 1.

Again: "Some eastern writers," says Mr. Richardson, "place Zerdusht thirteen hundred years after the Flood. Some make him the disciple of Elijah, or Elisha; others Ozair, Ezra, or Ezdras. Some consider him as Abraham; others, as the usurper Zohah; and some have conceived him to be Smerdis Magus."—*Diss.*, p. 231.

And, lastly, Dr. Thomas Burnet says, "Zoroaster was the prince and chief of the Magi, as many authors testify; but they differ much in the history of this Zoroaster, or of the Zoroasters. Some reckon one, some two, and some several. It seems to be certain, first, that there were at least two Zoroasters, both eminent for wisdom and Magism; one a Chaldæan or Bactrian, mentioned by many authors; the other a Persian, or Medo-Persian, concerning whom there is no doubt. Secondly, I clearly perceive that the affairs, ages, opinions, countries, writings, of these two are often confounded and blended together, both by the ancients and moderns."

Thus much respecting the personality of this sage, and the period when he lived. We append a few words concerning his doctrines. Here, too, we find equal difference of opinion. The authors of the "Universal History," following in the steps of Dr. Hyde, earnestly contend that after the reformation of Zoroaster the Persians were pure theists,—"zealous adorers of the one all-wise and omnipotent God, whom they held to be infinite and omnipresent; so that they could not bear that he should be represented by either graven or molten images; or that the Creator and Lord of the universe should be circumscribed within the narrow bounds of temples."—*Ancient Universal History*, vol. iv, p. 84. Dr. Hyde, indeed, goes further than this, contending that, taught by Zoroaster, the Persians not only maintained "the worship of the true God," but also "a rightly constituted Church, with a well-regulated hierarchy, with its triple order of priests and prelates, and also arch-prelates." This piece of *naiveté* strongly reminds me of the reply of a gentleman of Girgenti, (the ancient Agrigentum,) in Sicily, to a friend of mine. When asked if Girgenti was not an ancient bishopric, he answered, "Yes, sir; it was a bishopric some centuries *before Christ!*"

On the other hand, many erudite authors contend that Zoroaster introduced or continued the worship of fire,—the adoration of two conflicting independent principles, the one perfectly good, the other equally evil. Thus antagonistic are the sentiments of authors respecting the Persian sage and his doctrines.

NOTE 52, page 292.—*Probable Theology of Persia before Zoroaster.*

The learned Mosheim is of opinion that at first the Persian triad was formed of three hero-gods; and that afterward Zoroaster, in order to carry out his religious reformation, applied the names of these hero-divinities to other objects;

namely, Oromasdes to the divine principle of purity and goodness, Ahrimanius to the evil principle, and Mithras to the mediator deity. We insert his views at length:—

"In the first place, then, I lay it down that the gods of the most ancient Persians were three: *Oromasdes, Arimanius,* and *Mithras:* secondly, that these three were heroes, kings, and leaders, illustrious for good deeds and for the greatness of their achievements, and exalted to the rank of gods by the favour and reverence of the people. For, as all nations paid divine honours to the first founders and ancestors of their race after death, I see no reason why we should not suppose the same of the Persians. That Arimanius and Oromasdes [on the etymology of whose names see Beausobre, Hist. de Manich., p. 169] were mighty men and most renowned leaders in war, is shown by G. Wil. Leibnitz among others, Essais de Théodicée, par. i, sec. 138, p. 285. Add the recent German edition of Casp. Abel's Teutonic and Saxon Antiquities, cap. i, sec. 6, p. 22. I shall therefore confine my inquiry to Mithras. In my opinion, he was a strong and mighty man or king, who delighted chiefly in horses, dogs, and hunting, and who gave peace and security to his countrymen by ridding the Persian province of wild beasts, robbers, and other pests. His soul they imagined to have been transferred after death to the sun, and, from a grateful recollection of past benefits, paid to it divine honours, so as to seem to worship the sun itself. That this is not a rash assumption, but an opinion resting upon no slight foundation, will, I think, be shown by the arguments I am now about to adduce. I pass over what I have already more than once intimated, that the ancestral gods of every country were no other than the authors and founders of the race; nor shall I dwell upon the well-known fact, that *Mithras* belongs to those names which in Persia and the neighbouring countries were appropriated to men, [Mithra, the son of Labdacus,—Disp. of Archelaus with Manes, in Zacagnius's Monum., p. 67 ; Hagenbuch's Epistol. Epigraph., pp. 241, 242, 246,] because many, I know, suppose it to be probable, that those who bore this name received it from their parents from motives of religion toward the god. But, in order to establish my point, I shall appeal to the evidence of the images, mysteries, and sacrifices of Mithras. In the first place, the ancient Persians represented Mithras as a strong and powerful man, guarded with a sword and wearing the Persian turban, who, seated on the back of a bull, restrains, overpowers, and despatches the fierce beast, which is at the same time attacked by dogs. (See some representations of the kind in Anton. Van Dale's Diss. Novem in Antiq. et Marmora, diss. i, p. 18, &c.) In some images there are also a tame lion, a serpent, and a scorpion. [The ancients say that Mithras was a stealer of oxen, and a robber. See Hist. de l'Acad. des Inscript., tom. vi, p. 365, &c., where Maffeius also attempts an explanation of the words *Nama Sebesion,* found on some stones dedicated to Mithras.] Now, I ask of any one possessing even a slight acquaintance with such matters, whether anything could better represent a hunter and tamer of wild beasts. If there was nothing else, this image alone would in my mind sufficiently show the origin and exploits of Mithras. Very learned men, I am aware, following the example of the ancient scholiast of Statius, contend that these are symbols of natural things; namely, that the man signifies the sun, the bull the moon, and that the whole group represents the superiority of the sun to the moon. *Sol,* says this scholiast, *lunam minorem potentiâ suâ et humiliorem docens, taurum insidens cornibus torquet.* 'The sun riding on a bull turns it by the horns, showing thereby that the power of the moon is inferior to his own.' (See Vossius, De Idololatriâ, lib. ix, p. 776 ; Martini, Religion des Gaulois, lib. ii, cap. 34, p. 456.) But let those who are unwilling to employ their reason assent to interpretations like these. For my part, I conceive we ought to aim at simplicity in expounding the religions of antiquity, nor do I consider that ancient nations possessed so refined and subtle an intellect as to conceal things which are obvious to every one, under I know not what symbols and images. The superiority of the sun to the moon is evident to the sight, and known even to the most ignorant and uninformed. What man in his senses, then, would believe that the Persians, to impart a knowledge of this truth, with which all but the blind must be familiar, had recourse to so far-fetched a symbol? And what relation does a bull bear to the moon? What is meant by the dogs that are at the same time attacking the bull? What by the rest? If the bull be a symbol of the moon, because, like the moon, it has horns, others, I fear, by the same rule, may take it to be represented by a ram or a goat. And what shall we say of the notion itself imagined to be conveyed in this symbol? I ask whether it be possible for any reasonable man to suppose that a man slaying a bull is an apt image to show the sun to be superior in dignity to the moon. The same may be said of the other explications of this image. It is a custom among the later philosophers and grammarians to make their own conception the standard in judging of the notions of antiquity; hence, they insist that their monuments are symbols of other things, lest, forsooth, the ancients should appear to have entertained absurd and foolish notions respecting the gods, or at least cherished different opinions from their own. And yet learned men set the highest value upon these interpretations: whence it very often comes to pass, that they altogether misrepresent the ancient solemnities, and exhibit those barbarous nations as much wiser than they really were. Whereas, if they had duly sifted and examined the whole matter, they would no doubt have perceived that there are few of the explications afforded by Plotinus, Proclus, Jamblichus, and so many others, which do not themselves betray their own weakness and insufficiency. The victims recorded to have been sacrificed by the Persians to Mithras furnish me with another argument. Horses were sacred to this god, and publicly offered to him, as is manifest from innumerable testimonies of the ancient authors, Xenophon, Philostratus, Herodotus, and others. (See Vossius, De Idololatriâ, lib. xi, cap. 9, p. 132; Sam. Bochart. Hierozoic., lib. ii, cap. 10, p. 132.) This I interpret as follows; Mithras in his lifetime was passionately fond of horses, as their aid cannot well be dispensed with either in subduing savage animals or encountering with enemies. Hence the Persians, after his death, decreed that horses should be held sacred to his memory. Moreover, it was the popular belief in antiquity, that the shades of the dead retain in another world a fondness for the objects which they prized in this life. Among the Germans and other nations, as is well known, horses were slaughtered at the funeral piles of chieftains and warriors, to be employed by them for pomp or pleasure in the eternal abodes. In like manner, the Persians, knowing their king Mithras to have delighted in horses, judged it right to sacrifice to him, from time to time, fresh troops of horses, to enable him still to enjoy his ancient gratification in the empire of the sun. This view, indeed, is very far from being in accordance with those either of the ancients or moderns. Herodotus, Ovid, and others, suppose horses to have been consecrated to the sun on account of their swiftness.

> Placat equo Persis radiis *Hyperiona* cinctum,
> Ne detur celeri victima tarda deo.—OVID. Fast., lib. i, 385.

But this reason I hold to be altogether out of the question, and never once thought of till all memory of by-gone times had become obliterated. For if the Persians had regarded only the swiftness of the victim, it would have been much more appropriate to sacrifice to their god Mithras an eagle or some other bird, as in that respect far superior to horses. Or why should they not have selected the hare or the stag, proverbial for their swiftness, or some other more worthless animal, in preference to the generous, valuable, and most useful horse? The longer, indeed, I ponder over this matter, the more rooted is my conviction, that no more probable cause can be assigned for this worship of Mithras, than the one I have hazarded. I can easily fancy, however, that the Persians themselves by degrees naturally lost sight of the true reason why their ancestors offered this sacrifice; and, in the confusion in which, from various causes, ancient religions became involved, came to substitute a spurious one in its stead.

"Such was the religion of the ancient Persians before the time of Zoroaster. Arimanius, Oromasdes, and Mithras, men illustrious for their achievements, and supposed to have been translated after death to the stars, were the popular gods, and received public homage and worship. Among these, Mithras held the highest place, whose soul, owing to his pre-eminent virtues, was believed to have migrated to the sun."—*Cudworth's Intellectual System, Mosheim's Notes*, vol. i, pp. 475–477, 479.

NOTE 53, page 298.—*The Origin of Fire-Worship.*

Few particulars connected with the abstruse subject of ancient idolatry seem more strange than the entire absence of all reference to patriarchal tradition or Scriptural truth in the efforts to account for the origin and object of fire-worship. Herodotus, Plutarch, and Strabo, with their entire ignorance of primitive history, would, when considering the elements of oriental religion, naturally reason out to their own satisfaction the probable motives that led to certain observances. But that these speculations should have been adopted and followed by those who hold the Bible in their hands, and who possess a far more broad and accurate knowledge of the early history of Asia than those sages could obtain, appears very remarkable.

Let us for a moment refer to the appointment of the cherubim and the infolding fire before Paradise, as intimately associated with the worship of mankind immediately after the Fall. (Patriarchal Age, p. 147.) Observe that the prominent elements connected with this fire,—the ark, the cherubim, the sacred tree, the Paradise, &c.,—were all preserved in traditional remembrance, and incorporated into the religion of the primitive nations, after their fall into idolatry. Let it be further remarked, that this luminous appearance, identical with the Shekinah of Hebrew history, was so prevalent in the patriarchal age that Jehovah was in consequence called "the God of GLORY." Acts vii, 2. Let all these unquestionable facts be considered, and it will surely appear more probable that this cause led to the adoration of this element, than that it resulted from abstruse philosophical induction.

The account of the origin of fire-worship, as given by Firdusi, is as follows: "One day the king (Houshang) retired to the mountains, accompanied by some of his attendants: something appeared at a distance, of enormous magnitude, black, tremendous, and glossy. Its two eyes seemed fountains of blood: the smoke which issued from its mouth obscured the air. The prudent Houshang contemplated it circumspectly; he seized a stone, and prepared to assail it. He threw it with the force of a hero, and the serpent no longer annoyed the world. The stone struck upon a rock, and both fell to pieces by the percussion. A brilliant flame sprang from the contact; and thus fire became the production of stone. The king prostrated himself before God, and offered devout supplication for having thus obtained the sacred fire; for which he erected a sanctuary in that spot. He said, 'This fire is a divinity: let it be worshipped by all.' Night came; the mountain was covered with fire; it was surrounded by the king and his attendants. The event was celebrated by a feast, the name of which became that of the auspicious hero,"—*Malcolm's Persia*, vol. i, p. 185. It may not be possible to elicit much truth from a statement so romantic in its texture; yet we have here many of the usual elements of paradisiacal tradition. The royal hero,—the gigantic serpent, the attack of the latter by the former,—the destruction of the serpent,—and the sacred fire,—all these would lead us to suppose an allusion to man's primitive history in this case, however adorned with fiction and fable. It must be added, that while this exhibits the account furnished by the Persian historian of the origin of the worship of fire in that nation, the *Zendavesta* declares that Zoroaster received the sacred fire in heaven, when he received that divine volume from Ormuzd, and that he brought both at the same time to the earth.

In addition to this, the wide range of this worship—in fact, its almost, if not entire, universality—is in favour of my position. In Chaldea, India, Asia Minor, even in Mexico, as well as in Greece, Rome, and Persia, this superstition is known to have prevailed. The sacred fire of Hestia in Greece was never allowed to be extinguished; or if by accident it expired, it was not to be rekindled by ordinary fire, but by that produced by friction, or drawn by burning-glasses from the sun. And the origin of this veneration of fire is not obscurely intimated by the fact, that the goddess Hestia, who presided over it, was also the patroness of sacrifices; and on that account was the first deity invoked during these sacred rites.

Similar opinions prevailed in Rome in connexion with Vesta. Æneas was said to have brought the sacred fire from Troy, along with the images of the Penates. No statue of this goddess stood in her temple; but the eternal fire on the altar was regarded as her living symbol, and was kept up by the Vestal virgins, her priestesses. Every house, indeed, had a fire-altar of its own; and if we may trust Ovid, (Fast. vi,) it is from her name that we derive our term "vestibule,"— that being the place where the sacred fire of the family was continually burning.

All these customs appear to me to have had their origin in one and the same thing,—the infolding fire which stood connected with the primitive cherubim. The worship of the Chaldæans and Persians, as we have seen, was made up of continual allusions to man's primitive history; and the early patriarchs had access to God by some means analogous to the primitive cherubim and the Hebrew sanctuary. Even Balaam, when he went to meet the Lord, "went to meet the appearances in fire." (See my Doctrine of the Cherubim, p. 59.) A traditional regard for the manner of primitive worship, therefore, led men, when they had turned away their hearts from the true God, to adore the several subsidiary elements which had been connected with the appointed way of access unto him; and fire, as one of the principal of these, was thus made the object of worship.

NOTE 54, page 308.—*The Rewards of Heaven, and the Punishments of Hell, according to Zoroaster.*

"Surosh then bore me off to *Kurutaman*, or 'Paradise,' in the light of which I became bewildered in astonishment: I knew none of the precious stones of which it was composed. The angels, by the command of the Almighty, took me round every part of it. I next came to a place where I beheld an illustrious assemblage enveloped in *Khurah*, that is, 'radiance and pomp.' Surúsh Ashú said: 'These are the spirits of the munificent and noble-minded.' After this I saw a great multitude in all magnificence. Surúsh explained to me: 'These are the spirits of all who have observed the *Naú Roz*.' Next them I beheld an assemblage in the enjoyment of all magnificence and happiness. Surúsh observed: 'These are the spirits of just princes.' After this I beheld blessed spirits in boundless joy and power. Surúsh explained: 'These are the Dustúrs and Mobeds: my duty is to convey that class to this honour.' I next beheld a company of women rejoicing in the midst of great pomp. Surúsh Ashú and Ardíbahést observed: 'These are the spirits of women who were obedient to their husbands.' I then beheld a multitude of majestic and beautiful persons, seated along with angels. Surúsh said: 'This class consists of Hírbuds and Mobeds, the attendants on fire temples, and the observers of the *Yasht* and *Yazisht* of the Amshasfands.' After these I saw an armed assemblage in a state of the highest joy. Surúsh informed me: 'These are the spirits of the champions who fought in the ways of God, maintaining their country and the husbandmen in a state of prosperity and tranquillity.' I next beheld a great assemblage in the enjoyment of all delight and gladness. Surúsh observed: 'These are the spirits of the slayers of the *Khurástár* (or noxious animals).' After this, I witnessed a people given up to sporting and happiness. Surúsh observed: 'These are the spirits of the husbandmen, over whom *Safándarmuz* is set; he consequently presides over this class, as they have propitiated him by their acts.' I next beheld a great company surrounded by all the appliances of enjoyment. Surúsh said: 'These are the spirits of shepherds.' After this, I beheld great numbers in a state of repose and joy, and the elemental principles of Paradise standing before them. Surúsh observed: 'These are the heads of families, friends to building, who have improved the world by gardens and water-courses, and held the elements in reverence.' I next came to another class, endowed with prophet-like radiance, of whom Surúsh remarked: 'These are the spirits of *Jádóngóis*.' By *Jádóngóis* is meant one who solicits money from the wealthy to promote the way of the Lord, and who expends it on noble foundations and holy indigent persons.

"What can I say concerning the black-eyed nymphs,—the palaces, offspring, and attendants,—the drinks and viands?—anything like which I know not of in this elemental world.

"After this Surúch and Ardíbehést, taking me out of Paradise, bore me off to behold the punishments inflicted on those in hell. First of all, I beheld a black and gloomy river of fetid water, with weeping multitudes falling in and drowning. Surúsh said: 'This water is collected from the tears shed by relatives on the death of a person; and those who are drowning are they whose relatives after their death, break out into mourning, weeping, and tears.' I next proceeded toward the bridge of judgment, where I beheld a spirit rent from the body, and mourning for its separation: there arose a fetid gale, out of which issued a gloomy figure, with red eye-balls, hooked nose, hideous lips, teeth like columns, a head like the kettle of a minaret, long talons, spear-like fangs, snaky locks, and vomiting out smoke. The alarmed spirit having asked, 'Who art thou?' he answered, 'I am the personification of thy acts and deeds.' On saying this, he threw his hands around the spirit's neck, so that his lamentations came to the bridge of judgment, which is sharper than a razor: on this the spirit having gone a little way with great difficulty, at last fell into the infernal regions. I then followed him, accompanied by Surúch and Ardibehést: our road lay through snow, ice, storms, intense cold, mephitic exhalations, and obscurity, along a region full of pits: into these I looked, and there beheld countless myriads of spirits suffering tortures. They all wailed bitterly, and the darkness was so thick that one was unable to perceive the other, or to distinguish his lamentation: three days' such punishment is equal to nine thousand years, and the same calculation applies to the other pits, in all of which were serpents, scorpions, stinging and noxious creatures: whatever spirit falls into them

> Was stung by one and torn by another,
> Was bit by this, and pierced by that.

"Surúsh having taken me below, I there beheld a spirit with a human head and serpent-like body, surrounded by many demons, who were applying the torture to his feet, and smiting him in every direction with hatchets, daggers, and maces, while noxious creatures were biting him on all sides. Surúsh observed: 'This was a man of vile passions.' I then beheld a man wailing piteously, whose head they were scalping with a poniard. Surúsh said: 'This was a shedder of innocent blood.' I next saw a man who was forced to swallow blood and corrupted mattef, with which they were continually supplying him. The demons in the mean time tortured him, and placed a heavy mountain on his breast. Surúsh stated this to be 'the spirit of a dissolute man, who seduced the wives of other men.' After this, I beheld a spirit weeping through hunger and thirst: so intense was his craving, that he drank his own blood and devoured his own flesh. Surúsh stated: 'This is the spirit of one who observed not the *Báj*, (religious silence,) when partaking of food, and who on the day of Aban partook of water, fruit, and bread, so that the angels *Khurdád* and *Murdád* were displeased with him.' I next beheld a woman suspended by her breasts, and noxious creatures falling on her. Surúsh said: 'This is a woman who deserted her husband, and went after another man.' I then saw a great multitude of spirits, furiously assailed by rapacious animals and noxious creatures. Surúsh stated thus: 'These are persons who adopted not the *Kashti* or sacred cincture, as worn by professors of the excellent faith.' I next beheld a woman hung up, with her tongue protruding from the hind part of her neck. Surúsh observed: 'This is a woman who obeyed not her husband, and replied to him with harsh answers and opposition.' I then saw a man eating with a ladle the most noxious things; of which if he took too small a portion, demons smote him with wooden clubs. Surúsh observed: : This is the spirit of one who betrayed his trust.' I after this beheld a man hung up, surrounded by seventy demons, who were lashing him with serpents instead of scourges; and meanwhile the serpents kept gnawing his flesh with their fangs. Surúsh Ashú said: 'This is a king who extorted money from his subjects by torture.' I next beheld a man with wide-opened mouth and protruding tongue,

> With serpents and scorpions covered all over,
> The one lacerating with fangs, the others lashing with their tails.

Surúsh said: 'This was a tale-bearer, who by his lies caused dissension and strife among mankind.' After this I saw a man, every ligature and joint of whose body they were tearing asunder. Surúsh said: 'This person has slain many four-footed animals.' I next beheld a man exposed to body-rending torture, concerning whom Surúsh said: 'This was a wealthy, avaricious man, who employed not his riches for the useful purposes of either world.' I then saw a person to whom were offered all sorts of noxious creatures, while one foot was free from all kind of suffering. Surúsh said concerning him: 'This is the spirit of a negligent person, who did not in the least attend to the concerns of this world or the world to come. As he once passed along the road, he observed a goat tied up in such a manner that it was unable to get at its food: with that foot he tossed the forage toward the animal; in recompense of which good act that foot is exempt from suffering.' I next beheld a person whose tongue was laid on a stone, and demons kept beating it with another. Concerning him Surúsh observed: 'This person was an habitual slanderer and liar, through whose words people fell into mischief.' I then saw a woman whose breasts the demons were grinding under a millstone. About her Surúsh observed: 'This woman produced abortion by means of drugs.' I next beheld a man in whose seven members worms had fixed themselves. Concerning him Surúsh said: 'This person gave false witness for money, and derived his support from that resource.' After this I saw a man devouring the flesh of a corpse and drinking human gore. Surúsh observed: 'This is the spirit of one who amassed wealth by unlawful means. I afterward beheld a great multitude with pallid faces, fetid bodies, and limbs covered with worms. About these Surúsh Ashú observed: 'These are hypocrites of Satanic qualities, whose hearts were not in accordance with their words, and who led astray the professors of the excellent faith, divesting themselves of all respect for religion and morality.' I next saw a man, the members of whose body hell-hounds were rending asunder. Concerning him Surúsh said: 'This man was in the habit of slaughtering water and land dogs.' I next beheld a woman hurled into snow and smitten by the guardians of fire. About her Surúsh said: 'When this woman combed herself, her hairs fell into the fire.' After this I beheld another woman tearing off with a poniard the flesh of her own body and devouring it. Surúsh said: 'This is an enchantress who used to fascinate men.' Next her I saw a man whom the demons forced by blows to swallow blood, corrupted matter, and human flesh. Concerning him Surúsh said: 'This man was in the habit of casting dead bodies, corrupted matter, nails, and hair into fire and water.' I afterward beheld a person devouring the flesh and skin of a dead body. Surúsh said: 'This person defrauded the labourers of their hire.' I next beheld a man with a mountain on his back, whom with his load they forced through terror into the midst of snows and ice. Surúsh observed: ' This was an adulterer, who took the wife from her husband.' I afterward saw a man, the flesh of whose shoulders and body they were scraping off with a comb of iron. Concerning him Surúsh said: 'This man was an egregious violator of promises and breaker of engagements.' I then beheld a great multitude whose hands and feet they were smiting with bludgeons, iron maces, and such like. Concerning these Surúsh observed: 'This class is composed of promise-breakers and the violators of covenants, who maintained friendship with *Darwands*, or those hostile to the faith.'"—*The Dabistán, or School of Manners, translated from the Persian by Shea and Troyer*, vol. i, pp. 290–301.

NOTE 55, page 319.—*The Argonautic Expedition.*

The substance of this legend in brief is this. Pelias was the reputed son of Neptune by Tyro, who concealed his birth, and was afterward married to Cretheus, King of Iolchis, by whom she had three children, of whom Æso was the eldest. Pelias visited his mother, and was received into her family; and, after the death of the king, expelled the children, and seized the throne. In order to guard as much as possible against losing this prize, he consulted an oracle, which told him to beware of a man who should come to him with only one sandal. When Jason, a son of Æso, arrived at maturity, he came to Iolchis to demand his father's throne, and on his way lost one sandal in crossing a river. This circumstance excited the apprehension of Pelias, who, while appearing disposed to comply, urged Jason first to go to Colchis, and recover the Golden Fleece. This fleece had belonged to Phryxus, a prince of Thebes, who had fled to Colchis, married the daughter of the king, and was murdered by his father-in-law, that he might possess this treasure. Jason, full of youthful ardour, consented, and gathered to himself the most daring spirits of Greece for his companions on the expedition. The details are of the most extravagant and mythological character. The ship Argo, in which they sailed, was built by Argus, the son of Phryxus, directed by the goddess Athene. A piece of the celebrated oak of Dodona was inserted in the prow, and this was endued with the faculty of speech. Among the Argonauts we find the names of the principal demigods and heroes of ancient Greece; namely, Hercules, Theseus, Æsculapius, Castor and Pollux, Telamon and Peleus, Zetes and Calaïs, Nestor, Laërtes, and others. Typhys was the pilot; Idmon the son of Apollo, and Mopsus, attended as prophets; while Orpheus cheered and harmonized his companions with his harp.

The incidents of the voyage are as strange as the equipment of the expedition. Lemnos was the first place at which they touched. Here, it is said, at this time there were no men. The women, maddened by jealousy and ill-treatment, had put to death all their fathers, husbands, and brothers. The Argonauts were, after some difficulty, kindly received, and admitted to such intimacy that they supplied a future population for the island. They then proceeded along the coast of Thrace, up the Hellespont, to the southern coast of the Propontis, inhabited by the Doliones and their king Cyzicus. Here they were hospitably entertained; but afterward in an accidental night-affray, Cyzicus was killed by Jason. The Argonauts thence proceeded along the coast of Mysia, where Hercules was separated from his companions, having gone in search of his friend Hylas. Jason with his crew next stopped in the country of the Bebrycians, where a boxing contest took place between the king Amycus and Pollux.

The Argo then sailed to Bithynia, where the blind prophet Phineus resided. He had been struck blind by Poseidon, because he told Phryxus the way to Colchis: he had, besides, been tormented by harpies. From the latter he was delivered by Zetes and Calaïs, the winged sons of Boreas. Grateful for this deliverance, the prophet forewarned the Argonauts of the dangers which opposed their progress, and informed them of the measures necessary to their safety; by which means they were enabled to effect the terrible passage between the rocks called Simplegades. These rocks alternately opened and shut with great force, so that it was difficult even for a bird to fly through. When the Argo arrived at this dangerous passage, Euphemus let loose a dove, which flew through, and escaped with the loss of a few feathers of her tail. This was regarded by the Argonauts as a happy presage, according to the prediction of Phineus. Encouraged by the omen, they rowed with all their might, Athene aiding them by interposing her powerful arms to retard the closing of the rocks, which came together just in time to crush the ornaments on the stern of the vessel. As the gods had decreed that when a vessel should pass through in safety, the rocks should cease to move, they immediately afterward became fixed in their separate places, and thus in future afforded a safe and easy passage between them.

After a short stay in the country of the Mariandynians, and another in that of the Amazons, they passed by Mount Caucasus,—where they saw the eagle that gnawed the liver of Prometheus, and heard the groans of the sufferer,—and at length arrived at Colchis. Application was immediately made to the king Æetes, that he would grant the Argonauts possession of the Golden Fleece, they promising in return their aid against his enemies. This application was urged on the ground that the Argonauts were heroes of divine parentage, and had been sent forth on this mission by the mandate of the gods. Æetes received this prayer in great anger; but, although he did not absolutely reject it, he clogged his consent with conditions which seemed to render their success impossible. These obstacles were, however, interposed with some show of reason, as tests of their divine origin and mission. Two untameable bulls, which Hephæstos had given to Æetes, were to be yoked; and with these a large field was to be ploughed, and sown with dragons' teeth. Although nothing could be more dreadful than the appearance of these animals, with brazen feet and fiery breath, Jason undertook the task. Hera and Aphrodite greatly aided him: but he is said to have owed his success mainly to the passion with which Medea, the daughter of Æetes, was inspired, when she saw him in audience with her father. This princess had been endowed by Hecate with pre-eminent magical powers, which she exerted to the utmost to promote the success of Jason. By powerful unguents prepared by her, his body was rendered invulnerable; and, thus protected, he yoked the bulls, ploughed the field, and sowed it with dragons' teeth. And when hosts of armed men sprang from the furrows, acting upon the instructions of Medea, he cast a rock into the midst of them; upon which they began to fight with each other, so that he was easily enabled to subdue them all.

Yet although the prescribed conditions were complied with, the king not only refused to give Jason the Golden Fleece, but actually took measures for destroying the Argo, and murdering the Argonauts. The watchful care of Aphrodite prevented him from accomplishing his design; while Medea, having lulled to sleep by a magic potion the dragon who guarded the fleece, placed the prize on board the vessel, and, taking her younger brother with her, accompanied Jason and his companions in their flight.

On hearing of this, Æetes was afflicted and enraged, and immediately put to sea in pursuit. He soon overtook the Argo; but Media again interposed. She slew her brother, and scattered his limbs around on the sea. Æetes stayed to gather up the fragments of his son's body, and meanwhile the Argonauts escaped. The fratricide of Medea, however, was so offensive to Zeus, that he doomed the Argonauts to a long and perilous voyage before they were permitted to return home. The Argo had in consequence to sail up the river Phasis into the ocean, which was supposed to surround the earth as far as its junction with the Nile. By this river they sailed to Egypt, from whence the hero-crew carried the Argo on their shoulders to the Lake Tritonis in Libya. After having been kindly treated here by the god Triton, they departed, being once more on the waters of the Mediterranean. After staying a while with Circe at the Island of Æaea,—where Medea was purified from the murder of her brother,—enduring various vicissitudes at sea, and encountering great danger on the coast of Crete, the ship and crew safely reached Iolchis.

Here Jason was informed that Pelias had put to death the father, mother, and infant brother of Jason during his absence. These crimes he resolved to avenge; but he saw that this could only be done by stratagem. He accordingly remained some short distance from the town, while Medea, as if the victim of his ill-usage, entered the place alone as a fugitive, and soon procured access to the daughters of Pelias, over whose minds she obtained an unlimited ascendency. Bent on the accomplishment of her object, she selected from the flocks of Pelias a ram in the extremity of old age, cut him up, and boiled him in a caldron with herbs, and by her magical powers brought him out in the shape of a young and vigorous lamb. From this the daughters of Pelias were made to believe that their father could in like manner be restored to youth. They accordingly cut him up with their own hands, and placed him in the caldron; upon which Media pretended that she must go to the house-top to offer an invocation to the moon, which she described as a necessary part of the ceremony. When there, she kindled the fire-signal agreed on between herself and the Argonauts, who immediately burst in, and possessed themselves of the place. Satisfied with this revenge on the guilty person, Jason allowed Acastus, the son of Pelias, to rule the principality of Iolchis, and retired with his wife Media to Corinth, where they lived many years in great prosperity.

It seems now to be admitted by scholars that no *basis of fact* can be satisfactorily elicited from the entire mass of these poetical and mythological legends: all that can be given is mere conjecture. That which appears to be most probable has been indicated in the text; to which we now add a brief abstract of the principal opinions propounded by the learned.

Jacob Bryant regards the account as a manifest tradition from the ark of Noah. Sir Isaac Newton traces it to the expedition sent by the Greeks to Amenophis, or Memnon, King of Egypt. Dr. Gillies supposes that it arose out of the wish of the young chieftains of Greece to visit foreign parts, and to retort on the inhabitants the injuries which the Greeks had suffered from strangers. Dr. Hager conjectures that the fleece was raw silk, which often resembles fine threads of gold. Knight regards the whole as a fable, derived, "not from vague traditions of the Deluge, but some symbolical composition of the plastic spirit on the waters, signified in so many various ways in the emblematical language of ancient art." The opinion which we have ventured to express, though it be opposed to all these authorities, is not destitute of ancient and modern support. Strabo, being fully aware of the geographical impossibilities of the narrative, nevertheless believed that the Golden Fleece was typical of the great wealth of Colchis, arising from the gold dust washed down by the river; and that the voyage of Jason was in reality an expedition at the head of an army, with which he plundered the country, and made extensive conquests in the interior. And this surmise has been countenanced by Justin, (xlii, 2, 3,) and Tacitus (Annal. vi, 34). Dr. Leonard Schmitz observes, "The story of the Argonauts probably arose out of accounts of commercial enterprises which the wealthy Minyans made to the coasts of the Euxine." (Strabo, vol. i, p. 45; Smith's Dic. of Greek and Roman Biog. and Myth.; Lempriere's Classical Dic., art. *Argonautæ;* Grote's Hist. of Greece; and Thirlwall's Hist. of Greece.)

NOTE 56, page 319.—*The Theban Legends.*

In the later period of the reign of Cadmus at Thebes, we are told that Dionysus arrived there, in company with a troop of Asiatic females, to obtain divine honours, and establish his peculiar rites in his native city. The venerable Cadmus, his daughters, and the prophet Tiresias, at once acknowledged the god, and joined in the worship which he enjoined. But Pentheus, the grandson of Cadmus, and son of his daughter Agavé, who had married one of the Sparti, and who now reigned at Thebes, violently opposed the new ceremonies, and ill-treated the god who had introduced them. Persisting in this conduct, notwithstanding the miracles wrought by Dionysus, Pentheus followed the female company which had gone to Mount Cithæron, and, in order to witness their sacred solemnities, ascended a tall pine. There he was discovered by the feminine multitude, who, under the influence of the Bacchic frenzy, pulled down the tree, and tore him to pieces. Even his mother joined in this outrage; and, losing all consciousness of maternal relationship under the madness of the excitement, she carried back to Thebes the head of her murdered son. Upon this Cadmus and his wife retired among the Illyrians, and Polydorus and Labdacus successively reigned at Thebes.

The last of these at his death left an infant son, Laius, who was deprived of his throne by Lycus. He also was slain, and was succeeded in the throne by his nephews, Amphion and Zethus. The first of these died of grief for the loss of his wife: the second either killed himself, on the destruction of all his children by Apollo, or was slain by that deity; after which Laius obtained the crown, and married Jocasta, daughter of Menœceus. This king was forewarned by the oracle, that any son whom he might beget would kill him. In consequence of this, on the birth of his son, whom he called Œdipus, he caused him to be exposed on Mount Cithæron, where the child was found by the herdsmen of Polybus, King of Corinth. They took him to their master, who brought him up as his own child. When arrived at manhood, finding himself exposed to taunts in consequence of his unknown parentage, he went to Delphi, and consulted the oracle on the subject. He received in answer an admonition not to return to his country, as, in case he did so, it was his destiny to kill his father, and become the husband of his mother. Knowing no country as his but Corinth, he determined not to return to that city, and departed from Delphi by the way leading to Bœotia and Phocis. On arriving at the spot where the road divided toward those countries, he met Laius in a chariot. The insolence of the king's servant produced a quarrel, in which Œdipus killed Laius, being utterly ignorant that he was his father.

On the death of Laius, Creon, the brother of Queen Jocasta, succeeded to the kingdom of Thebes. At this time time the kingdom was under the displeasure of the gods, and in consequence laid waste by a monster called Sphinx, which had the face of a woman, the wings of a bird, and the tail of a lion. This creature had obtained from the Muses a riddle, which she proposed to the Thebans: and on their being unable to resolve it, she took away one after another of the citizens, and ate him. This continued cruelty reduced the king to such distress, that he offered the crown and the queen to any one who would deliver the country from this monster. At this juncture Œdipus arrived, undertook the task, and solved the riddle; upon which the Sphinx threw herself from the Acropolis, and disappeared. Œdipus thereupon assumed the sovereignty of Thebes, and became the husband of his mother.

On one part of this personal narrative these legends afford conflicting information. It is on all hands admitted that Œdipus had four children,—Eteocles, Polynices, Antigone, and Ismene. The question is, whether they were the children of Jocasta, or of a subsequent wife. Sophocles and other Attic poets adopt the former opinion; and Homer, and an ancient epic called *Œdipodia*, the latter. The gods, it is stated, made known to mankind the relationship existing between Œdipus and Jocasta. According to the Attic tragedians, this was done "quickly" after their marriage: if the opposite opinion is adopted, it must have been revealed only after the lapse of some years. On receiving this information, Jocasta, in an agony of sorrow, hanged herself; and Œdipus suffered a series of miseries, inflicted by the Erinnyes, while a curse of deep and weighty woe rested on his children; and even this appears to have been aggravated by the denunciation of Œdipus on his sons, in consequence of their conduct toward him in his old age.

On the death of their father, the sons of Œdipus quarrelled respecting the succession. Polynices was in consequence obliged to flee from Thebes, upon which he sought refuge at the court of Adrastus, King of Argos. Here he was kindly received, and married to a daughter of the king, who at the same time engaged to establish Polynices on the throne of Thebes by force of arms.

When Adrastus proposed this enterprise to the chieftains of Argos, he found most of them ready to join in the war. Amphiaraus, who had distinguished himself as an Argonaut, and at the Calydonian hunt alone dissented, and denounced the project as unjust and impious: and, being of a prophetic stock, he predicted the failure of the attempt, and the death of the principal parties who undertook it. Full of this conviction, Amphiaraus endeavoured to secrete himself, that he might take no part in the war. But Polynices having bribed his wife by presenting her with the gorgeous robe and necklace given by the gods to Harmonia on her marriage with Cadmus, the sordid wife for this showy prize betrayed the retreat of her husband; and he, after charging his sons to revenge him, accompanied the expedition. It was led by seven noble chiefs, each of whom assailed one of the seven gates of Thebes. The prediction of Amphiaraus was, however, justified: the attempt failed: all the leaders perished, except Adrastus, who escaped by the fleetness of his steed. In this war the two sons of Œdipus killed each other in single combat.

After this, Creon again assumed the reigns of government, and decreed that the Argives who had fallen in the war, and especially Polynices, should remain unburied; and that any one detected in violating this edict should be buried alive. Antignone, sister of Polynices, dared the danger, and attempted to inter her brother; but was detected in the effort, and was buried alive on the spot. Hæmon, the son of Creon, having endeavoured in vain to save her, killed himself on her tomb; in consequence of which, his mother perished by her own hand. Adrastus, moved by the inhumanity which deprived his fallen comrades of the rites of sepulture, applied for aid to Theseus, King of Athens. This hero complied with his request, invaded Thebes, killed Creon, and effected his object.

The calamities of Thebes did not terminate with this war. The sons of the seven chiefs who had been defeated determined to avenge the fate of their sires. Adrastus, who still survived, took the command; Ægialeus, his son, Thersander, son of Polynices, Alcmæon and Amphilochus, sons of Amphiaraus, Diomedes, son of Tydeus, Sthenelus, son of Capaneus, Promachus, son of Parthenopæus, and Euryalus, son of Mecistheus, under the title of *Epigoni*, took part in this assault. They were aided by Corinth and Megara, as well as Messene and Arcadia. On reaching the river Elissas, they were opposed by the Theban army under Laodamas, son of Eteocles, who now ruled in Thebes. Here a battle took place, in which the Theban leader killed Ægialeus, son of Adrastus, but was himself totally routed with his army, and driven within the walls, principally by the valour and energy of Alcmæon. After this defeat, the Thebans consulted the prophet Tiresias, who informed them that the gods had decreed the success of the assailants. By his advice they sent a herald to the Epigoni, offering to surrender the town, while they conveyed away their wives and children, and fled under the command of Laodamas to the Illyrians. The Epigoni then entered Thebes, and established Thersander, son of Polynices, on the throne.

Note 57, page 320.—*The Trojan Wars.*

This, says Mr. Grote, is "the capital and culminating point of the Grecian epic,—the two sieges and capture of Troy, with the destinies of the dispersed heroes." "It would," observes this profound and elegant author, "require a large volume to convey any tolerable idea of the vast extent and expansion of this interesting fable, first handled by so many poets, epic, lyric, and tragic, with their endless additions, transformations, and contradictions,—then purged and recast by historical inquirers, who, under colour of setting aside the exaggerations of the poets, introduced a new vein of prosaic invention,—lastly moralized and allegorized by philosophers."—*Hist. of Greece*, vol. i, p. 386. We can only attempt a brief outline of this in a note.

The Trojan kings reckoned their descent from Dardanus, the son of Zeus by Electra, daughter of Atlas. Tros, the grandson of Dardanus, gave his name to Troy. Zeus, having taken the beautiful son of Tros, Ganymedes, to be his cup-bearer, gave to the father in return a team of immortal horses. Besides Ganymedes, Tros had two sons, Ilus and Assaracus. The first became the father of the Trojan line of kings, Laomedon, Priam, and Hector; the second, of the Dardanian sovereigns, Capys, Anchises, and Æneas. Ilus founded in the plain of Troy the holy city of Ilium. His brother and his descendants remained sovereigns of Dardania.

While Laomedon, son of Ilus, reigned at Troy, Poseidon and Apollo were subjected to a temporary servitude by command of Zeus, during which the former built the walls of the town, and the latter tended the herds. When the stipulated period had expired, they claimed the promised reward; instead of paying which, the king treated the gods with indignity, and threatened to sell them for slaves. To avenge this ill-treatment, Poseidon sent a sea-monster, which ravaged the fields, and destroyed the subjects of Troy. This infliction reduced Laomedon to such straits that he offered the immortal horses as a reward to any one who would destroy the monster. But an oracle declared that a virgin of noble blood must first be given to him; and the lot fell on Hesione, the daughter of Laomedon. Heracles arrived at the moment when the princess stood exposed to destruction; and by the aid of Athene and the Trojans he killed the monster, and delivered both Hesione and the country. Yet Laomedon gave him mortal horses, instead of those which had been promised. Heracles, thus defrauded, equipped six ships, sailed to Troy, stormed the city, and killed Laomedon, giving Hesione to his faithful and brave ally, Telamon, by whom she had Teucros, the celebrated archer.

As Priam was the only one of all the sons of Laomedon who had protested against the injustice of his father, Heracles placed him on the throne of Troy. This king was blessed with a numerous progeny. Among his sons we find Hector, Paris, Deiphobus, Helenus, Troilus, Polites, Polydorus; and among the daughters, Laodice, Creüsa, Polyxena, and Cassandra.

The birth of Paris was accompanied with such terrible omens, that his father consulted the soothsayers on the subject: they informed him that this son would prove fatal to him. Priam in consequence ordered the child to be exposed on Mount Ida, as soon as he was born. The gods, however, preserved him; and he grew up very beautiful in person, fostered by the shepherds, and specially loved by Aphrodite. It was to this prince, while living in this rural solitude, that the three goddesses, Hêrê, Athene, and Aphrodite, were conducted, in order that he might determine the dispute which had arisen between them, at the marriage of Peleus, respecting their comparative beauty. Paris awarded the prize of beauty to Aphrodite, who promised him in return the most beautiful woman of the age,—Helen, the daughter of Zeus, wife of Menelaus, King of Sparta.

The manner in which this promise was fulfilled is too well known to need recitation. Paris went to Greece, and visited Menelaus, who had at that time to leave his home for Crete. During his absence Paris carried off Helen and a large amount of treasure, and safely reached Troy. The injured husband was informed in Crete of the perfidious conduct of Paris, and the infidelity of his wife; and hastened home to consult his brother Agamemnon, King of Mycenæ and Argos, and the venerable Nestor. The result was a determination to assemble the entire strength of the Grecian states, and avenge this outrage on the rites of hospitality. This was the more easily effected, because in her youth Helen had been sought for, on account of her beauty, by thirty-one of the principal chieftains of Greece, who, seeing they had individually a very slender chance of securing the desired prize, bound themselves by a solemn oath to leave Helen to her free, unbiassed choice in respect of her selection of a partner, and, when married, to defend her person and character against any attempts to snatch her from the arms of her husband.

For the accomplishment of this purpose, Nestor, Palamedes, and others went round to solicit the aid of the Greek chiefs. The result is known: eleven hundred and eighty-six ships, and above one hundred thousand men, were at length assembled at Aulis, and sailed for Troy. This expedition contained all the *élite* of the warriors of Greece; foremost among whom stood Palamedes, Ajax, Diomedes, Nestor, Ulysses, and Achilles. The first, although not mentioned by Homer, is celebrated by other early Greek writers as one of the wisest and bravest of his day. He is even supposed on this account to have been treacherously cut off by the envy and malignity of Ulysses and Diomedes.

The Trojans had assembled a great army of auxiliaries, to oppose this invasion; but the attempt to prevent the landing of the Greeks was vain. The Trojans and their allies were routed, mainly by the valour of Achilles, and driven within the walls of the city. But these were invulnerable; great delay was a necessary consequence; a large portion of the invading army was engaged in providing supplies of provision for themselves and their companions: years of siege and casual warfare therefore rolled on.

At length, however, in the tenth year of the siege, the Greeks, having stormed and sacked some towns in the neighbourhood of Troy and in alliance with that city, divided the prisoners among the principal chiefs. Achilles, for his prominence and valour in this exploit, received a beautiful damsel,—the fair Briseïs; while another, a daughter of a priest of Apollo, Chryseïs, was awarded to Agamemnon. The father of the latter lady, distressed by the loss of his daughter, besought the deity to avenge his injury. Apollo complied, and sent a plague among the Greeks. In a great council the cause of the evil was revealed by Calchas the seer. The result was the sending back of Chryseïs to her father; and, to repair his loss, Agamemnon demanded Briseïs from Achilles,—a requirement which so offended that hero, that he immediately withdrew himself and his troops from the Grecian army.

The loss of Achilles subjected the Greek army to terrible reverses. Diomedes, Ulysses, Agamemnon, and other heroes exerted themselves to the utmost, but in vain. Hector led his conquering Trojans to successive victories, until at length he actually set fire to the vessel of Protesilaus, the first Greek who had landed at Troy. The desperate condition to which the Greeks were thus reduced led

Patroclus, the friend of Achilles, to obtain that hero's leave to lead his troops against the Trojans. This reinforcement for a while turned the tide of victory, until Patroclus was slain by Hector. This melancholy event at once diverted the flow of the anger of Achilles, and directed it against the Trojan prince. He accordingly returned to the war, defeated the Trojans, and killed Hector.

The hopes of Troy, which seemed to die with the death of Hector, were revived by the arrival of successive bands of auxiliaries. Penthesilea, Queen of the Amazons, first arrived, at the head of her troop of female warriors. She was the daughter of Ares, and had been hitherto invincible. At first her efforts were successful; but she fell by the hand of Achilles. Memnon next came to sustain the cause of Troy. He was the son of Tithonus and Eos, and the most stately of men. He destroyed great numbers of the Grecian troops, and slew the noble and popular Antilochus. But after a desperate, and, for a long time, doubtful contest, he also perished by the prowess of Achilles.

The fate of this hero now approached. As Achilles was chasing a troop of routed Trojans into the town, he was slain by an arrow from the bow of Paris, which had been guided by Apollo, and struck the mighty Greek in the only vulnerable part of his body,—his heel. The fall of Achilles occasioned still further loss to the Greeks. Ajax and Ulysses having quarrelled as to which should possess the armour of the deceased hero, and the decision having been given in favour of the latter, Ajax slew himself in a frenzy occasioned by grief and disappointment.

The crisis of the war now drew near. Ulysses, having captured Helenus, the son of Priam, who possessed the gift of prophecy, learned from him that Troy could not be taken unless Philoctetes, who held the bow and arrows of Heracles, and Neoptolemus, son of Achilles, could be persuaded to join the Greek army. This was effected by the address of Diomedes and Ulysses. Philoctetes soon after killed Paris in single combat; while Neoptolemus killed Eurypylus, King of Mysia, who had marched an army to the succour of Troy.

But although the Trojans were now so weakened by successive losses that they dared no more to meet their enemies in the field, the city could not be captured while the Palladium—a statue given by Zeus himself to Dardanus—remained in the citadel. Great care had been taken of this statue by the Trojans: they not only did their utmost to conceal this valuable gift, but made many others so like it as to mislead any person who might attempt to steal it. Ulysses, however, the unfailing resource of the Greeks when craft and cunning were required in union with great daring, essayed this difficult task. Disguising himself in miserable clothing and with self-inflicted injuries, he succeeded in entering the city, and carrying off the Palladium. It is said that Helen recognised him, while thus engaged; but that she, now anxious to return to her husband, not only did not betray him, but actually concerted with him the means of capturing the city.

To accomplish this object, the Greeks had recourse to stratagem. At the suggestion of Athene, Epeus made a large wooden horse, sufficiently capacious to contain one hundred men in the inside of it. Here were placed that number of the most celebrated warriors of the Greek army, including Neoptolemus, Ulysses, Menelaus, and others. This being done, and the horse placed before the gates of Troy, the Greek army pretended that they had abandoned the siege, burned their tents, and sailed away,—remaining, however, at Tenedos. The inhabitants of Troy, overjoyed at this deliverance, sallied out, and were amazed at the huge wooden structure which their enemies had left behind them.

Various opinions were propounded respecting it. Some proposed drawing it into the city, and dedicating it to the gods, as a trophy of victory: others distrusted the gift of an enemy. Laocoön, the priest of Neptune, sharing in this feeling, launched a spear against the side of the horse, when the sound revealed the hollowness of the construction. But even this warning was lost on the infatuated Trojans; while Laocoön, with one of his sons, perished by two serpents, which were sent out of the sea expressly to destroy him. The Trojans were seized on by the artifices of Sinon, a perfidious traitor, who had been left by the Greeks to promote their object. He told Priam that he had fled from his countrymen because they had determined to offer him a sacrifice to the gods, in order to insure themselves a safe voyage to Greece. Being favourably received by the kind king, he strongly urged him to bring the wooden horse into the city, and consecrate it to Athene. This advice was followed. A breach was made in the walls, and the horse brought into the city with tumultuous joy, the Trojans devoting the night to riotous festivity. While they were thus engaged, Sinon made the appointed fire-signal, which being seen by the Greeks at Tenedos, they immediately returned. He then unbarred the entrance to the horse, and allowed the Greek heroes to come forth. The city was thus assailed from within and without. The aged Priam perished by the hand of Neoptolemus, having sought refuge in vain at the altar of Zeus. Deiphobus, who, after the death of Paris, had become the husband of Helen, died, after a desperate resistance, by the hands of Ulysses and Menelaus. Antenor and Æneas escaped, as it is said, by the connivance of the Greeks. Thus was the city totally sacked and destroyed. Astyanax, the infant son of Hector, was cast from a high wall, and killed; and Polyxena was immolated on the tomb of Achilles. Helen was restored to her husband, who appears to have received her very cordially. Andromache and Helenus were both given to Neoptolemus; Cassandra was awarded to Agamemnon.

The utter improbability of the legend, especially in the part respecting the wooden horse, led to other versions than that of Homer. The principal of these is that related by the Egyptian priests to Herodotus, to this effect,—that when Paris fled from Greece with Helen, he was driven by adverse winds on the coast of Egypt, where the king, learning the baseness of his conduct, sent him away, detaining Helen; and that consequently, when the Greeks demanded Helen at Troy, the Trojans could not give her up, as she was not there. At the same time they could not convince the Greeks of this truth, the gods having decreed the ruin of Ilium.

The return of the heroes to Greece would require extended notice. We can only observe that Nestor, Diomedes, Neoptolemus, Idomeneus, and Philoctetes soon reached their homes in safety. Agamemnon also reached his palace at Argos, but to perish by the hand of his wife Clytemnestra. The adventures of Ulysses have been fully given by Homer in a separate epic. Every part of Greece, Italy, and of the surrounding countries, bears names, or stands identified with circumstances relating to this war. (Grote's History of Greece; Thirlwall's History of Greece; Homer; Virgil; Herodotus; Thucydides, &c., &c.)

NOTE 58, page 320.—*The Return of the Heraclidæ.*

There is scarcely any portion of the legendary history of Greece which so clearly and so fully develops the peculiar character of its mythology, and at he same time serves as a key to some of the most curious problems in the sub-

APPENDIX. 613

sequent annals of the country, as the account furnished by the poets respecting Heracles and his descendants.

Perseus, son of Zeus and Danaë, having accidentally killed his grandfather, and being unwilling to remain as the sovereign of the country, exchanged the kingdom of Argos with Megapenthes for that of Tiryns; and afterward, fixing on a spot about ten miles from Argos, he founded the famous city of Mycenæ, seating here his descendants as the celebrated Perseid Dynasty. Perseus left a numerous family: of these, Alcæus was father of Amphitryon; Electryon, of Alcmene; and Sthenelos, of Eurystheus. After the death of his grandfather, Amphitryon, in a fit of passion occasioned by a quarrel about some cattle, killed his uncle Electryon. The sons of this chief having been killed by some pirate Taphians, Alcmene was the only surviver of this family. She was engaged to marry Amphitryon, but refused to do so until he had avenged the death of her brothers. Compelled to leave his country on account of the murder of his uncle, Amphitryon sought refuge in Thebes, whither he was accompanied by Alcmene, thus leaving Sthenelos, the only surviving son of Perseus, King of Tiryns. Amphitryon, having obtained the aid of the Cadmeians and others, chastised the Taphians, and returned to claim his wife. On the wedding-night, however, Zeus, having conceived a passion for the bride, had intercourse with her before the husband. The result was that Alcmene bore twins,—Heracles, the son of Zeus, and Iphicles, the offspring of Amphitryon. When the time drew near for delivery, Zeus, who had determined that this offspring of his should be superior to all his other human children,—" a specimen of invincible power both to gods and men,"—boasted in the Olympian assembly, that there was that day to be born on earth a descendant of his who should rule over all his neighbours. Stung with the remark, his wife Hêrê pretended to make light of it, and provoked Zeus to confirm his declaration by an oath. This being done, Hêrê instantly descended to the earth, and, by the aid of the goddesses presiding over parturition, delayed the delivery of Alcmene, and hastened that of the wife of Sthenelos, who was seven months advanced in pregnancy. This feat accomplished, Hêrê returned to Olympus, and announced the fact to Zeus, saying, "The good man Eurystheus is this day born of thy loins, and the sceptre of the Argeians worthily belongs to him." Zeus was intensely astonished and afflicted at the news; but his word had passed, and he could not prevent its accomplishment. Hercules was therefore throughout his life subject to Eurystheus, and compelled to do his bidding.

It will not be necessary to detail the exploits of Heracles, under the designation of his "Twelve Labours." The principal of them are now universally known. It may suffice to say, that he always evinced irresistible power, whether on behalf of friends, or against declared foes and the most savage beasts. His deeds were spread over all parts of the world then known to the Greeks,—from Gades in Spain to the banks of the Euxine, and even to Scythia; while their magnitude was such as to fill the world with their fame, and to vary them into an endless range of poetic myths.

After the death of the hero, and his apotheosis, his son Hyllos, and his other children, were expelled and severely persecuted by Eurystheus. So violent was his animosity, that the Thebans and other neighbouring states feared to afford them refuge. Athens alone evinced sufficient humanity and daring, and protected the refugees. To punish this generous conduct, Eurystheus invaded Attica, and not only failed in the effort, but perished with all his sons in the contest. In consequence, the sons of Heracles became the only representatives of the Perseid family. Hyllos, the eldest son of Heracles, regarding Peloponnesus as his rightful inheritance, gathered together an army, and endeavoured to enforce his claim by arms. This invasion was met by the united troops of Ionia, Achaia, and Arcadia; upon which Hyllos proposed that the contest should be decided by single combat between himself and any hero of the opposing army. The challenge was accepted, and the terms arranged, which provided that in case Hyllos triumphed, the Heracleids should be restored to their possessions; but that, in case he fell, they should abandon all their claims for a given period, which is variously stated by different authors as having been three generations,—fifty years,—and one hundred years. Hyllos was slain in this conflict by Echemos, the Arcadian hero; and the Heracleids in consequence retired, and dismissed their army.

It is said that, in violation of this engagement, Clodæus, son of Hyllos, made an attempt to recover the territory, which was equally unsuccessful; and that his son, in a similar effort, perished on the field of battle.

The time specified in the engagement which issued in the death of Hyllos, at length passed away, and left the Heracleids free to assert their claim to their ancient and rightful patrimony. The manner and means by which this was effected are worthy of attention. It appears that when the Dorian King Ægimius was severely pressed by the Lapithæ, Heracles interposed, defeated the invading force, and killed their King Coronus. In grateful return for this act of heroism, Ægimius assigned to his deliverer one-third part of the whole territory of his state, and adopted Hyllos as his son. Heracles desired that this gift should be retained until his children stood in need of it. After the death of Hyllos, this boon was claimed and allowed. The Heracleids became thus intimately associated with the Dorian race. When, therefore, Hyllos, his son Clodæus, and grandson Aristomachus, were all dead, and the Heracleids were represented by Temenus, Cresphontes, and Aristodemus, they resolved, with the aid of the Dorians, to make another attempt on the peninsula. In this case a new mode of attack was adopted. Instead of a long and hazardous land-march along the coast and through the Isthmus of Corinth, they resolved to prepare vessels, and cross over from Antirrhium on the southern promontory of Ætolia, to Rhium on the north coast of Achaia. This attempt was completely successful. Tisamenes, the grandson of Agamemnon through Orestes, then the great sovereign of the peninsula, and the representative of the Pelopid race, fell in the conflict. Oxylus, who had efficiently served the expedition as a guide, was rewarded with the fertile territory of Elis; while the three Heracleid families cast lots for the remainder of the country. In this distribution Argos fell to Temenus, Messene to Cresphontes, and Sparta to the sons of Aristodemus. It is alleged that Cresphontes obtained his more eligible portion by fraud. As each family offered solemn sacrifices upon this division, it is said that a miraculous sign appeared on each altar,—a toad on that belonging to Argos; a serpent on that of Sparta; and a fox on the altar representing Messene. The prophets, on being consulted, thus explained these omens: The toad, being a creature slow and stationary, imported that Argos would not succeed in enterprises beyond its own limits: the serpent denoted the formidable and aggressive character which Sparta would sustain: and the fox set forth the career of wily and deceitful policy which Messene would pursue. However historical fact may be obscured by ancient legend, it is evident that the entire subjugation of Peloponnesus to the sway of the Heracleids and Dorians must have occupied a very considerable portion of time, during which extended period the vanquished were continually seeking refuge in northern Greece, Asia Minor, or the islands.

Note 59, page 325.—*The Seven Wise Men of Greece.*

Although these Grecian worthies are usually said to have been seven, ancient writers are by no means agreed as to their number or their names. Dicæarchus counted ten; Hermippus, seventeen; and Plato, seven. The names of Solon the Athenian, Thales the Milesian, Pittacus the Mitylenian, and Bias the Prienean, are found in all the lists. The remaining names given by Plato are Cleobulus of Lindus, Myson of Chene, and Chilo of Lacedæmon. (Protagoras, sec. 82.)

It will be necessary to give a brief sketch of these individuals, in order to convey a general idea of their character as the Wise Men of Greece.

Solon in his youth devoted himself to the study of philosophy and political science. In consequence of the reduced state of his family through the prodigality of his father, he was for some time engaged in trade; but he at length devoted his life to the good of his country, and introduced those political and fiscal reforms which laid the foundation for the future glory of Athens. Like all the cultivated Greeks of his day, he studied poetry, and propounded his political reforms in verse.

Thales was born at Miletus, of Phenician parents. Like Solon and others, he travelled in pursuit of knowledge; and visited Crete, Phenicia, Egypt, and the East,—acquiring in his progress a knowledge of geometry, astronomy, and philosophy. He is said to have made additions to the knowledge of the Greeks in mathematical science,—most likely from information he obtained in the East. He is also said to have been the first who insisted on the necessity of scientific proof, and attempted it in philosophy and mathematics. He is known to have predicted the occurrence of an eclipse; but whether he possessed a sufficient knowledge of mathematical astronomy to make the calculation himself, or obtained the result of it in the East, has been doubted. Thales is said to have displayed great political sagacity, and to have used his scientific acquirements in diverting the course of the river Halys at the request of Crœsus. He also instituted a federal council at Teos, to unite and strengthen the Ionians, when threatened by the Persians. He was the founder and father of the Ionic school of philosophy, which produced Anaximander, Anaximenes, Anaxagoras, and Archelaus, the master of Socrates.

Pittacus of Mitylene was highly celebrated as a warrior, a statesman, a philosopher, and a poet. He is first mentioned in history as an opponent of the tyrants who had succeeded in fastening their rule on his country. In conjunction with the sons of Alcæus, he succeeded in delivering the island from this oppression. He afterward appeared at the head of his countrymen, to resist the Athenians, when they made war on Lesbos. In this struggle he challenged the Athenian general to single combat, and slew him. He was afterward made governor of his native city, with unlimited authority. After holding this dignity for ten years, governing with justice and moderation, devising and enforcing salutary laws, and greatly promoting the public good, he voluntarily retired into private life.

Bias of Priene.—Little is known of this sage, except that he appears to have attained his distinguished reputation by the long-continued exercise of his skill as an advocate, and by his uniform and generally successful maintenance of the cause of right and justice. He died at a very advanced age, after pleading successfully in behalf of a friend. Just as the judges gave their decision, the venerable advocate fell dead into the arms of his grandson. The case of Bias is an unquestionable proof that the fame of the Wise Men was derived, not from the possession of abstract science, but from the exercise of practical wisdom and judicious experience in respect of moral and political affairs.

CLEOBULUS of Lindus was remarkable for the beauty of his person. His fame as a Wise Man seems to rest on the success with which he governed Lindus in a season of peculiar difficulty. He is also celebrated for having acquired an acquaintance with the philosophy of Egypt, and for having written some lyric poems, as well as riddles in verse.

MYSON of Chene.—Scarcely anything is known of this person, except that he was in humble circumstances; and that when Anacharsis consulted the oracle at Delphi to know which was the wisest man in Greece, he was told in answer, "He who is now ploughing his fields:" this was Myson. In some of the lists the name of Periander stands instead of Myson.

CHILO of Sparta.—Nothing is known of this person but his name.

NOTE 60, page 326.—*The Amphictyonic Council.*

This institution is one of the most remarkable and influential of ancient Greece. It appears to have arisen, in remote times, out of the very peculiar political disunion and religious unity which prevailed among the Grecian people. Since, from the beginning, it was customary for the several cities and even towns, as well as states, to be self-governing, while they were closely allied together by a national feeling and a common faith, it became necessary to establish some means of communication between these independent bodies, and some efficient mode of adjudication, in the event either of the national interests being infringed, or of the ordinances of the established religion being violated. This was effected by the instrumentality of the Amphictyonic Council. There were consequently several of these confederations in different districts, and among the Grecian settlements in Asia Minor; but the principal, and that which was a model for all the others, was called, by way of eminence, "*the* Amphictyonic League." This body met either in the temple of Demeter in the village of Anthelæ near Thermopylæ, or in that of Apollo at Delphi.

We have but a small amount of information on which reliance can be placed respecting the origin of this institution. That it arose very early, is clear from the fact that neither cities nor states, but tribes, were represented in it. These were originally twelve: Ionians, Dorians, Perrhœbians, Bœotians, Magnesians, Achæans, Phthians, Melians, Dolopians, Ænianians, Delphians, and Phocians. In process of time, cities and states, as they rose into importance, were admitted into the League; so that in the age of Antonius Pius the number of represented tribes was increased to thirty. The primitive nature of this compact, and the simplicity of manners and of means which then obtained, are clearly shown by the terms of the oath which was administered to the members of this League severally, as preserved by Æschines: "We will not destroy any Amphictyonic town: we will not cut off any Amphictyonic town from running water." It seems, at least in later times, that the members sent to this council were of two kinds or grades; which has led to the opinion that two assemblies were held,— one a larger, and the other a smaller, body. This distinction is indicated in the preamble of a decree preserved by Demosthenes: "When Cleinagorus was priest at the spring-meeting, it was resolved by the Pylagoræ and their assessors, and the general body of the Amphictyons," &c. It was this body which decreed those severe and generally cruel crusades which are found in Greek history, under the name of "Sacred Wars."

APPENDIX. 617

It was, in fact, the special function of the Amphictyonic Union to watch over and protect the safety, interests, and treasures of the Delphian temple. This point is set forth in another oath taken by the members of this council, and preserved by Æschines: "If any one shall plunder the property of the god, or shall be cognizant thereof, or shall take treacherous counsel against the things in the temple, we will punish him by foot, and hand, and voice, and every means in our power." At the same time, the truly national character of this council is proved by the fact, that, on the death of Leonidas and his brave companions at Thermopylæ, this council held an extraordinary meeting, and offered a reward for the life of Ephialtes the traitor. They also afterward set up pillars in the Straits to the memory of the Spartans who fell there.

This institution remained, as the last vestige of Hellenic nationality, until the second century of the Christian era; but its power and importance had long been lost. Even in the days of Demosthenes, the great orator complained that it was then only the shadow of its former self.

Note 61, page 327.—*Mortgage Pillars.*

These were stone pillars, which were required to be set up in a field, or some other conspicuous part of the mortgaged property. They served instead of a legal instrument or bond: but they answered this purpose in the most objectionable manner that can be conceived. It was essential that these pillars should bear a legible inscription, stating the amount of the debt with which the property was burdened, and setting forth the name of the creditor to whom the money was owing. These erections were abundantly numerous in Attica at the time referred to, and were so many public advertisements that the former owner of the soil had lost his independence, and was in danger of sinking into a still more degraded and miserable condition.

Note 62, page 329.—*The Judicial Court of Areopagus.*

This celebrated judicial body usually held its sittings in an open, uncovered space on the top of a small eminence at Athens, called Mars' Hill, because Mars was said to have been tried there for the murder of Halirrhothius, the son of Neptune. The origin of this court is lost in remote antiquity: some ascribe its institution to the time of Cecrops. The number of the judges is equally uncertain. But we know that they were for a long period persons of the highest probity and religious character; and that any one of them who was convicted of immorality, had been seen sitting in a tavern, or was known to have used indecent language, was expelled from the assembly. They took cognizance "of murders, impiety, and immoral behaviour; particularly of idleness, the cause of all vice." They possessed power to reward the virtuous, and to punish crime, particularly blasphemy against the gods, and all sins against the national faith. Their authority continued until the time of Pericles. At a later period the Areopagites lost much of their respectability of character,—to such an extent, indeed, that, having censured the conduct of a citizen, they were told that "if they wished to reform, they must begin at home."

Note 63, page 338.—*Banishment by Ostracism.*

This was a peculiar mode of enforcing exile, which obtained in many of the Grecian states, and was several times carried into effect at Athens. Strictly speaking, it was not a punishment, but a precautionary measure, demanded, as was supposed, by the public safety. Ostracism differed from ordinary banishment in that it did not affect the property of the individual exiled; and also, that it always fixed the time when the party would have liberty to return. It was, in fact, a means devised for removing from the republic, for a given time, any individual whose position, energy, wealth, or ambition, might render him an object of envy, distrust, or danger to the government. The mode of carrying it into effect was, by convening the tribes, when each citizen wrote the name of the man whom he wished to have ostracized. The bearer of the name which occurred most frequently, in case it had been written by six thousand citizens, was commanded to leave the state within ten days. The greatest men of Athens were exiled by this means,—Themistocles, Aristides, Cimon, and Alcibiades. Plutarch called ostracism "a good-natured way of allaying envy."

NOTE 64, page 339.—*The curious Mode employed to count the Army of Xerxes.*

The account furnished by Herodotus of this enumeration is so terse and full, that it may be given in the language of his popular translator: "I am not able to specify what number of men each nation supplied, as no one has recorded it. The whole amount of the land-forces was 1,700,000. Their mode of ascertaining the number was this : they drew up in one place a body of ten thousand men: making these stand together as compactly as possible, they drew a circle round them. Dismissing these, they enclosed the circle with a wall breast high: into this they introduced another and another ten thousand, till they thus obtained the precise number of the whole. They afterward ranged each nation apart."— *Polyhymnia*, cap. 9. Yet, notwithstanding the particularity of this account,— coupled with the important fact, that Herodotus might have conversed with those who saw the army numbered,—it is generally believed that the numbers given above are far too great.

NOTE 65, page 344.—*The Rebuilding of the City of Athens and its Fortifications.*

There is scarcely any circumstance in the whole period of the suffering and peril to which Greece was exposed during the Persian invasion which makes a more painful impression on the mind, or produces a conviction more disparaging to Greece, than the mean, the atrocious conduct of Sparta toward Athens. This is sufficiently apparent in the studied delay which abandoned Attica to the merciless ravages of the enemy.

But even this is exceeded by the opposition offered by Sparta to the restoration of Athens. No city or state in Greece had either done or suffered so much to defeat the object of the common enemy as the inhabitants of Athens; and, after this, they persisted in rejecting the most splendid offers of a Persian alliance; and, influenced by a patriotic devotion to the cause of Grecian nationality, they returned, after all their sufferings and losses, to the charred walls and ruins of their temples and their dwellings, to restore and rebuild them by their own efforts and means. On a review of all the circumstances, the reader will fully expect that Sparta and other states—which had suffered nothing by the war but the loss of a few citizens, while they had obtained their share of the booty —would have spontaneously offered liberal aid to restore the capital of Attica to its former condition. Instead of this, however, it is certain that the Æginetans and Spartans were prepared to resist the proper restoration of Athens by a parricidal war, and would, in all probability, have succeeded, had they not been circumvented by the superior policy and craft of Themistocles.

Note 66, page 358.—*The Fulfilment of Scripture Prophecy in the History of Greece.*

The historical events of this country do not fill a very large place in the predictions of Holy Scripture; but the inspired prophecies relating to them are, nevertheless, exceedingly interesting and important.

I. We will notice the reference to this people in the prophetic exposition of Nebuchadnezzar's dream respecting the great image.

Having previously spoken of the head of gold, and the breast and arms of silver, Daniel proceeded to say, "And another third kingdom of brass, which shall bear rule over all the earth." Dan. ii, 39. The position of this passage determines its meaning and application. As the head of gold is explicitly stated to represent the Babylonian power, and the breast and arms of silver to exhibit the Persian monarchy, by which the Babylonian was superseded and followed; so the belly and thighs of brass must refer to the Macedonian Greeks, by whom the Persian empire was subdued, and whose dominion was extended, not only over all the countries formerly subject to Persia, but also over a great part of Europe in addition. On this subject there can be no dispute. Hence Bishop Newton says, "That this third kingdom therefore was the Macedonian, every one allows, and must allow." And the fulfilment of this prophecy will be regarded by every considerate reader as one of the most wonderful displays of the prescient wisdom and almighty power of an overruling and directing Providence. When Nebuchadnezzar, invested with paramount power, and surrounded with every earthly glory, received this prediction, the Grecian states were scarcely known among the nations of the world; and, for centuries afterward, they were so isolated from each other, that any extensive military or political combination among them seemed all but impossible. Yet, just precisely at the time when this prophecy had to be accomplished, a military genius arose, who, with magic celerity, extended his sway over Greece; and then, arming himself with its united power, he went forth and subjected the eastern world to his will. The accomplishment of this prophecy was as circumstantially exact and complete, as the means by which it was effected were unlikely and unexpected.

II. There is further prophetic reference to the Grecian monarchy of Alexander, in Daniel's vision of the four great beasts.

After having symbolized the Babylonian kingdom by a lion with eagle's wings, and the Persian by a bear with three ribs in its mouth, the following, or Macedonian, monarchy is represented as a beast "like a leopard, which had upon the back of it four wings of a fowl; the beast had also four heads; and dominion was given to it." Dan. vii, 6. The principal features of this figurative representation are sufficiently evident, although they have been sometimes applied to an extent which seems rather fanciful than solid.

The leopard form seems very clearly to indicate the daring courage which distinguished the Macedonian conquests. Small as the leopard is, it will sometimes attack even a lion: and when the limited resources of Alexander, and the smallness of his army, are considered, it must be acknowledged that the figure exactly predicted the character of the Greek sovereignty. This leopard had "four wings," —a circumstance that marks with peculiar force the rapidity with which Alexander, in the short space of twelve years, subdued the vast range of territory from Illyricum to the Indies. Again: the beast had "four heads:" these undoubtedly refer to the four great divisions into which the empire of Alexander was divided soon after his death. This interpretation is not arbitrary, but in perfect accordance with inspired authority. So, in the following part of the same chapter, the ten horns of the fourth beast are explained to mean "ten kings that shall arise:" (verse 24:) and here the four heads are four kings who arose after the death of the great founder of the kingdom, and who divided the dominions among them.

III. A third remarkable prediction respecting the Grecian empire is contained in the eighth chapter of Daniel's prophecy, where the Persian power is represented as a ram with two horns, standing on the banks of a river; and the Grecian king as a he-goat with a "notable horn between his eyes." Verse 5. Here also we have an unerring guide to the interpretation of this prophecy; for the angel informed the prophet "that the ram which thou sawest having two horns are the kings of Media and Persia, and the rough goat is the king of Grecia; and the great horn that is between his eyes is the first king." Verses 20, 21. There can, therefore, be no mistake in applying this prophecy to Alexander. While this is undoubted, it is most remarkable that the figurative prediction of Daniel should so exactly represent the conduct of the two kings, and the issue of their first collision. The ram stood on the banks of a river, "pushing westward, and northward, and southward; so that no beasts might stand before him, neither was there any that could deliver out of his hand; but he did according to his will." Verse 4. How graphically these words show the state of Persia, and the unquestioned power of her kings before the Macedonian invasion! The following is equally truthful in description: "A he-goat came from the west on the face of the whole earth, and touched not the ground; and the goat had a notable horn between his eyes. And he came to the ram that had two horns, which I had seen standing before the river, and ran unto him in the fury of his power. And I saw him come close unto the ram, and he was moved with choler against him, and smote the ram, and brake his two horns: and there was no power in the ram to stand before him, but he cast him down to the ground, and stamped upon him, and there was none that could deliver the ram out of his hand." Verses 5–7. How forcefully does this set before us the power of Darius, arrayed on the banks of the Granicus, the impetuous onslaught of the Greeks, and the entire prostration of Persia, from that day, before her irresistible conqueror!

Equally remarkable is the conclusion of this prediction as to the ultimate destiny of the Macedonian monarchy: "Therefore the he-goat waxed very great: and when he was strong, the great horn was broken; and for it came up four notable ones toward the four winds of heaven." Verse 8. Clearly as this teaches the same truth as we found indicated by the four heads of the beast, in this case the interpretation is rendered undoubted by explicit inspired explanation. With reference to this part of the vision the angel said: "The great horn that is between his eyes is the first king. Now, that being broken, whereas four stood up for it, four kingdoms shall stand up out of the nation, but not in his power." Verses 21, 22. We have here a speaking picture of the results of Alexander's death upon the empire which he had created. A few years after the death of the great Macedonian, all his family were cut off, and his dominions divided into four portions. Cassander held Macedon and Greece; Lysimachus had Thrace, Bithynia, and the north; Ptolemy ruled Egypt and the south; and Seleucus governed Syria and the east. So literally did the division into *four* parts stretch toward "the four winds of heaven."

How wonderfully does all this display the prescience and the power of God! Here is a proof that he knows the end from the beginning, and that he can fully accomplish the purpose of his will.

NOTE 67, page 364.—*The Grecian Theogony, a poetic and corrupted Version of primitive History and of the Scenes at Babel.*

The cosmogony of the poet is simply a repetition of the Scripture narrative, with this alteration: here the powerful operating cause is supposed to be the energy of natural elements, and their affinity for one another, in the place of the potency of the Divine Word. With this exception, the Scriptural order is mainly adhered to: first chaos, then the earth, the deep, the heaven, the mountains, and the sea.

Ouranos is unquestionably Noah. This myth gives an extended version of the conduct of Ham toward the arkite patriarch. (See Patriarchal Age, p. 311.)

The principal part of these legends refer to the war of the Titans, and many conflicting views have obtained on this subject. Professor Stoll asserts that this war "represents the struggle between the rough, unbridled powers of nature, and the gods, who introduced order and civilization into the world." The Rev. George Stanley Faber maintains that the Titanic war "relates to the events of the Deluge." And the learned Jacob Bryant supposes it to be the war of the Pentapolis spoken of by Moses, in which Lot was taken prisoner, and rescued by Abraham. The principal ancient authority bearing on this subject is found in a fragment of sibylline poetry, which is referred to by Josephus, and quoted by Athenagoras and Theophilus Antiochenus, and of which Jacob Bryant says, "It is undoubtedly a translation of an ancient record found by some Grecian in an Egyptian temple."—*Bryant's Ancient Mythology,* vol. iv, p. 99. A portion of this was printed in a preceding volume. (Patriarchal Age, p. 325.) The remainder is here given:—

"'T was the tenth age successive, since the Flood
Ruin'd the former world; when foremost far
Amid the tribes of their descendants stood
Cronus, and Titan, and Iapetus,
Offspring of heaven and earth. Hence in return
For their superior excellence they shared
High titles, taken both from earth and heaven.
For they were surely far supreme; and each
Ruled o'er his portion of the vassal world,
Into three parts divided; for the earth
Into three parts had been by Heaven's decree
Sever'd; and each his portion held by lot.
No feuds had yet, no deadly fray arose:
For the good sire with providential care
Had bound them by an oath: and each well knew
That all was done in equity and truth.
But soon the man of justice left the world,
Matured by time, and full of years. He died:
And his three sons, the barrier now removed,
Rise in defiance of all human ties,
Nor heed their plighted faith. To arms they fly,
Eager and fierce: and now, their bands complete,
Cronus and Titan join in horrid fray;
Rule the great object, and the world the prize.

> "This was the first sad overture to blood,
> When war disclosed its horrid front, and men
> Inured their hands to slaughter. From that hour
> The gods wrought evil to the Titan race:
> They never prospered."
>
> *Bryant's Ancient Mythology*, vol. iv, pp. 101–103.

The greatest difficulty which arises in the application of these verses is found in the phrase, "The tenth age successive since the Flood." If the original requires us to understand by this ten generations, as the learned Analyst of Mythology seemed to suppose, then it will be scarcely possible to cite any events which will meet the requirements of the whole case. It would even then be impossible to apply these lines, as he did, to the war of the "four kings against five." For nothing is more evident than that the war here described was between the three primitive postdiluvian *tribes* or *clans*; while this was not the case with the war of the Pentapolis, any more than in the case of the invasion of Judea by Pharaoh-Hophra.

If, however, we are at liberty to construe this phrase less rigidly, as applicable to a decade of stages in the progress of society, of indeterminate periods, or of half-centuries, then we find the other parts of this ancient piece capable of a clear and consistent sense.

In that case we find the three tribes, after the Confusion of Tongues, coming into collision with each other: for one of them, having failed in the proud and irreligious attempt to prevent the appointed dispersion by policy, now endeavours to acquire universal dominion by conquest. It is worthy of observation, that although in general terms the three tribes are spoken of as parties to the war, Cronus and Titan are alone mentioned as mixing in "horrid fray." This is in precise accordance with the Scripture account. For when the purpose of Nimrod was defeated by the Confusion of Tongues, he did not abandon his design, but made "Babel, and Erech, and Accad, and Calneh, in the land of Shinar," the "beginning of his kingdom." Gen. x, 10. Now it is well known that this was in the land assigned to the tribe of Shem, or Titan. It was therefore taken by violence; and Asshur, the head of that house, unable to resist the power of his more martial opponent, was obliged to go forth "out of that land, and builded Nineveh." Verse 11. Thus the sibylline verses and the writings of Moses are in exact accordance.

The humiliation of the Titans, or Shemitic tribe, and the dominant power of Cronus, or the Cuthic, is in equally exact correspondence with every account of the early ages.

At the same time these legends, by showing that the heads of the tribe of Ham, after this triumph, were reverenced as divine, stands in direct confirmation of all that has been said as to the place where idolatry originated, and also as to the profane and idolatrous assumption of Nimrod, whose extravagance in this respect equalled his violence and worldly ambition. (See Patriarchal Age, pp. 395–398.)

Note 68, page 384.—*The Divine Inspiration of Gentile Prophets.*

The conclusion which has been adopted in the text,—that God does on some occasions specially reveal his will to wicked men, and even to idolaters,—may require some further proof, which it has seemed best to give in this note.

First, it may be shown that this divine gift has been communicated to wicked men. The case of Balaam is here fully in point. His wickedness does not require to be detailed: yet his predictions are among the most glorious to be found in the book of God; and, what is specially worthy of note, he was known and recognised as an inspired prophet. Indeed, so fully was this the fact, that his fame had extended from Mesopotamia to Canaan. Balak sent for him from this distant country, that he might come and curse Israel. The objection, *that this instance forms a very special exception to the general rule*, cannot be received as of any weight; for the sacred narrative does not indicate it to be an exception. There, on the contrary, we find the whole affair detailed, as though the inspiration of Balaam had nothing in it of a remarkable character. His access unto the oracle of Jehovah is spoken of as an undoubted fact, and as a privilege which he could exercise at will. Here, then, is one undeniable case of Gentile inspiration, by which undoubted intercourse with Jehovah is maintained, and splendid prophetic revelations uttered, although the prophet is a wicked man, loving the wages of iniquity. The prophecy of Caiaphas might also be mentioned. It was certainly enunciated as a divine prediction; and such, in the highest sense, it certainly was. Then we call attention to the persons spoken of by Micah, (iii, 11,) as "the prophets" that "divine for money." Indeed, our Saviour himself fully bears out this opinion by teaching us that he will say to some who "have prophesied in his name," "I never knew you: depart from me, ye that work iniquity." Matt. vii, 22, 23. Proofs of this point might be multiplied; but they cannot be necessary, it being abundantly manifest that the gift of prophecy has been frequently communicated to very wicked men.

"But then," it is alleged, "not to idolaters." We do not exactly see the force of this objection. On the principle that "to obey is better than sacrifice," we might conclude that a deliberate rebellion against the divine will, as in the case of Balaam, would form as powerful a barrier to the reception of such divine influence as any act of idolatry. Let us, however, pursue our Scriptural inquiry. It cannot be denied that God was pleased to make wonderful revelations from himself to the mind of Nebuchadnezzar. It is true, he required the teaching of the inspired Daniel: but this in no respect affects the truth, that God made direct revelations to the mind of the idolatrous king. The case of the king of Gerar is similar. But what we regard as most important is the fact that the earliest of the Christian Fathers not only saw no difficulty in this matter, but fully recognised the doctrine for which we contend. Justin Martyr, having asked the question, "Since there were true prophets among the Greeks as well as among the Christians, and divinations of future events were given by both parties, by what marks can we distinguish the Christian prophets to be more excellent?" He replies, "All these, the prediction of words as well as the event of things, are of the same God; who both foretold by the holy prophets and apostles what he was about to do, and in like manner foreshadowed future events by those who were strangers to the true worship." After other remarks on the subject, he adds, "In like manner he" (God) "foreshadowed by the Greek prophets whatever was fulfilled by the event."

Without pressing unduly on any branch of the argument, it does appear to be an established verity, that Gentile prophets were sometimes endowed with the divine gift of prophecy; and that this laid a broad and firm foundation of opinion in the Greek mind, that God spake to men by man.

NOTE **69**, page 385.—*The certain Presence of Satanic Energy in Grecian Soothsaying and Oracles.*

Perhaps in no instance is the devout student at the present day called upon to evince a more self-sacrificing devotion to the cause of truth than when discussing the doctrine of the influence of the evil one on the most intellectual and refined of the ancient nations. That which would fain pass for philosophy and rapidly-progressing intelligence, but which is really either a low latitudinarianism or direct neology, cannot endure the presence of supernatural agency. God must, as far as possible, be excluded from the providential government of his own world; and if that cannot be fully effected, there must be no recognition of the existence and energetic influence of Satan. We must, however, endeavour diligently to ascertain the truth, and firmly to declare it.

That the power of evil spirits to work wonders in support of their lying delusions is clearly taught in Holy Scripture, seems plain from the following argument of the learned Cudworth : " Accordingly in the New Testament do we read that our Saviour Christ forewarned his disciples, that 'false prophets and false Christs should arise, and show great signs or wonders, insomuch that, if it were possible, they should seduce the very elect.' And St. Paul foretelleth concerning the Man of Sin, or Antichrist, that 'his coming should be after the working of Satan, with all power, and signs, and wonders' (or 'miracles') 'of a lie.' For we conceive, that by τέρατα ψεύδους in this place are not properly meant 'feigned and counterfeit miracles,' that is, mere cheating and juggling tricks, but 'true wonders and real miracles,' (*viz.*, of the former sort mentioned,) done for the confirmation 'of a lie,' as the doctrine of this Man of Sin is afterward called; for otherwise how could his coming be said to be 'according to the working of Satan with all power?' In like manner also, in St. John's Apocalypse, where the coming of the same Man of Sin, and the mystery of iniquity, is again described, we read (chap. xiii) of a two-horned beast, like a lamb, that he 'shall do great wonders, and deceive those that dwell on the earth, by means of those miracles which he hath power to do in the sight of the beast;' and again, (chap. xvi,) of certain 'unclean spirits like frogs, coming out of the mouth of the dragon, and of the beast, and of the false prophet, which are the spirits of devils working miracles, that go forth to the kings of the earth;' and, lastly, (chap. xix,) of 'the false prophet that wrought miracles before the beast.' All which seems to be understood, not of feigned and counterfeit miracles only, but of true and real also, effected by the working of Satan in confirmation of a lie, that is, of idolatry, false religion, and imposture."—*Cudworth's Intellectual System*, vol. iii, p. 6. And that the same rule applied to the pre-Christian idolatry as to that which afterward arose from the working of Antichrist, is plain from the emphatic command given to the Hebrews : " If there arise among you a prophet, or a dreamer of dreams, and giveth thee a sign or a wonder, and the sign or the wonder come to pass whereof he spake unto thee, saying, Let us go after other gods, which thou has not known, and let us serve them; thou shalt not hearken unto the words of that prophet, or that dreamer of dreams : for the Lord your God proveth you, to know whether ye love the Lord your God with all your heart, and with all your soul." Deut. xiii, 1–3. It is clear from this passage that the reality of some superhuman communication or work is here distinctly assumed. And it is observable that the word here rendered "prophet" (נביא) is precisely the same as that which is applied to Isaiah, Jeremiah, Ezekiel, and the other prophets of God. It cannot, therefore, be maintained that mere jugglery is intended.

From a review of the whole argument, Mosheim admits, "I do not understand how a man is to be refuted who reasons in this manner: With some predictions of the ancients the facts and events corresponded; with others they did not correspond: some oracles were clear and perspicuous; others, again, doubtful and ambiguous: therefore sometimes demons, with the permission of God, predicted, by means of their slaves, the events which were about to happen to nations and individuals; but at others the priests and soothsayers beguiled and imposed upon the unwary vulgar. Those responses of the gods and oracles which were confirmed by the event, I consider to have proceeded from demons; but these which I observe to be of another character, I ascribe to the impostures of men."—*Cudworth's Intellectual System*, vol. iii, p. 21, note.

It is, in fact, freely admitted on all hands, that demons, or evil spirits, superior to man in intellect, agility, the knowledge of recondite causes, and, indeed, of many other things, exist and act; and that, by these means, with the divine permission, they may communicate through their human devotees a knowledge which, in respect of time and space, may be altogether superhuman; although it is equally agreed that they possess neither omnipotence nor omniscience, and therefore cannot, like Jehovah, "see the end from the beginning," and are consequently circumscribed as to the limits of their power and intelligence. The judicious author above quoted finds but one flaw, as he alleges, in the argument; which is this,—that whereas many cases of fraud have been clearly proved, no case of demon agency has, either by argument or example, been made evident. We meet the learned writer on this his chosen ground, and contend that no case of fraud or guile has been more clearly proved than that of demon agency in the soothsaying Pythoness of Philippi. We put our finger on this case, and claim its reception as a type of general demon agency in the heathen world, in accordance with the teaching of Scripture and history.

NOTE **70**, page 389.—*The sacred nocturnal Scenes of the Eleusinian Mysteries.*

The procession on this day was formed after a particular investigation into the claims of each individual; strict care being taken that none joined but those who had been previously initiated, or had at least borne a part in the lesser mysteries, and were therefore called *mystæ*. As these successively passed the barrier which excluded the rejected applicants, their ears were saluted by the sweetest sounds of music and song. Following on by the narrow path, they soon emerged to an open space, where stood a beautiful marble altar, on which lay a slaughtered pregnant sow,—the symbol of fruitfulness and parturition,—the appointed sacrifice to Demeter. This animal had been slain, and lay on the altar consuming with fire, and covered with fragrant herbs. A troop of virgins danced around the altar; while the chief priestess, habited in gorgeous attire, scattered showers of holy water over the crowds of worshippers. Here, amid the smoke of the victim, and the rolling peals of music, a hymn in sweetest strains was chanted to Demeter, while every heart seemed excited to enthusiasm, as libations of wine were poured on the consuming victim.

Engaged in this service of sacrifice and song, the multitude lingered, until the shades of evening gathered over the scene, and each individual prepared to enter upon the nocturnal service, which was at once invested in their thoughts, feelings, and expectations, with the most holy awe and sacred solemnity. Removing from their dress all the appendages suitable to the joyous employments of the morning, with their feet covered with sandals of skins instead of shoes, each passed under the gloomy portal of the sacred temple; and, as he dipped his hand into the bowl of holy water at the entrance, and endeavoured to throw his vision into the darkness of the interior, a shudder of involuntary horror pervaded each individual. Some hesitated a moment; but, gathering strength for the grand occasion, one after another passed into the sacred sanctuary.

At first nothing was seen,—intense darkness reigned; and nothing was heard but the footsteps on the floor. After proceeding a short distance, some glimmering rays of light were observed; but these were scarcely sufficient to afford any idea of the character of the structure. It seemed rather an excavation than a building; green moisture dripped from the walls; an earthy smell affected the atmosphere; creatures like bats or winged lizards flitted to and fro, and sometimes struck the body of the person to be initiated. On each side of this gloomy place were arranged what appeared to be all kinds of beasts, remarkable for excessive ugliness of form, or repulsiveness of manner; while, to add to the horror inspired by these appearances, every conceivable discordant sound echoed in constant succession through the vaulted temple. At one time shrieks were heard; these would be succeeded by yells as of derision; then would come the most strange combination of disagreeable animal sounds; and amid the whole it seemed as if illusory phantoms incessantly glided about.

At length all this ceased, and the novice seemed impelled forward through an aperture, which led into an enormous building. Here were pillars of vast height and size, supporting a concave roof, the interior of which was striped with burnished metal, and adorned with stars and constellations of polished copper. In the far interior of this vast building, the smouldering embers of an almost consumed sacrifice still glowed on the altar, and, when fanned by the breeze, would emit a transient flame, which gave a momentary illumination to the whole structure. By this means the *mystæ* discovered that they stood in the great temple of Demeter. In the centre was the colossal statue of the goddess; around it the worshippers gathered, and knelt in silent awe. Dimly visible amid the gloom were perceived the figures of the sacred servants of this sanctuary,—the torchbearer, with his flambeaux,—the sacred herald, in armour,—the altar-priest, habited in white; while, high above all his assistants, distinguished as much by his lofty bearing as by the elevation of his stature, stood the great hierophant,—the revealer of secrets,—the chief priest of Demeter,—the holiest person in the consecrated assembly. Besides these, other officers and magistrates appeared, engaged in their several peculiar duties, as the expiring flame shot up from the altar; and as it died away, the whole was enveloped in thickest darkness.

As soon as this took place, the sacred herald sent his voice through the building, in the loud and earnest inquiry, "Who is here?" To which the crowd, in a subdued tone, said in reply, "Many, and good." The hierophant immediately added, "Let us pray." No sooner were these words uttered, than a noise like that of a great hurricane shook the building; the floor trembled, as if in agony; the people staggered with overwhelming dread. A silence, like that of death, succeeds for a moment: again the building trembles; thunder rolls in fearful clamour above; vivid lightnings shoot through the fane, and play among the gigantic columns. Amid this unearthly clamour, yells and howlings are heard; and phantom forms of every classic apparition appear in all their savage deformity.—Briareus with his hundred hands, the Centaurs, Hydra, the skeleton of Gyges, the Diræ, Gorgon, and Cerberus; while the Chimæra vomits flaming poison, and Minotaur wildly tramples in every direction.

APPENDIX.   627

Terrible, however, as were these scenes, they were but preludes to what followed. While the crowd stood trembling, the floor divided; a chasm yawned at the feet of the awe-stricken worshippers, revealing all the sights and scenes of the infernal regions. Deep in the vast profound are seen the waters of Phlegethon, washing the foundations of a tower of steel,—the palace of Pluto. There Tisiphone and Rhadamanthus are seen dispensing judgment and ministering punishment to the lost in Tartarus. Here are discernible Cocytus, Lethe, Acheron, and Styx. Charon is seen in his boat; and Pluto, with all the pomp of infernal dominion; and Persephone, as beautiful as when taken from the side of her mother. Thus the multitude, from the edge of the yawning gulf, realized all that their religion had taught,—that their poets had sung,—that their minds had conceived,—of the unseen world, and all its horrors: and while they gazed again and again, the thunders again rolled, the building shook, the disparted floor closed, and all was silence and darkness.

A second time the voice of the hierophant was heard, proclaiming, "Let us pray;" and on the utterance of these magic words, another change comes over the place. The darkness is removed: the gorgeous building is gloriously irradiated with the richest sunlight: from tempestuous night they are translated into a serene and brilliant day. It was at this time that the principal revelations were made to the votaries of Demeter. Here the great divinities were revealed to the spectators, surrounded with a divine radiance, and invested with surpassing glory. Jupiter, Apollo, Neptune, Mars, Mercury, Vulcan, Juno, Minerva, Diana, Demeter, Venus, and Vesta, were seen, each attended by symbols of their power, and visible exponents of their attributes. After these deities had passed in panoramic vision before the crowd, while they stood enraptured at the celestial sight, other inferior deities followed,—the Naiads, Potamides, Oreads, Bacchus, Cupid, and Aurora. During the progress of the visions, revelations were made respecting these divinities, the exact purport of which must always be matter of conjecture. But whether this was eulogistic or derogatory to the characters of these deities,—as the learned have argued on both sides,—it cannot be doubted that it was strongly in support of the great system of national idolatry which these rites tended so greatly to consolidate and conserve. After this was exhibited the story of Demeter and Persephone. Then followed strains of the sweetest music; after which the hierophant ascended a rostrum in front of the pedestal, and read from a sacred book what is supposed to have been condensed, and given at least in substance, by Virgil, as follows:—

> "Know first, that heaven, and earth's compacted frame,
> And flowing waters, and the starry flame,
> And both the radiant lights, one common soul
> Inspires, and feeds, and animates the whole.
> This active mind, infused through all the space,
> Unites and mingles with the mighty mass.
> Hence men and beasts the breath of life obtain;
> And birds of air, and monsters of the main.
> The' ethereal vigour is in all the same,
> And every soul is fill'd with equal flame;
> As much as earthy limbs, and gross allay
> Of mortal members, subject to decay,
> Blunt not the beams of heaven and edge of day.
> From this coarse mixture of terrestrial parts,
> Desire and fear, by turns possess their hearts;

And grief, and joy: nor can the grovelling mind,
In the dark dungeon of the limbs confined,
Assert its native skies, or own its heavenly kind.
Nor death itself can wholly wash their stains;
But long-contracted filth ev'n in the soul remains:
The relics of inveterate vice they wear;
And spots of sin obscene in every face appear.
For this are various penances enjoin'd;
And some are hung to bleach, upon the wind;
Some plunged in waters, others purged in fires,
Till all the dregs are drain'd, and all the rust expires.
All have their *manes*, and those *manes* bear:
The few so cleansed to the' abodes repair,
And breathe, in ample fields, the soft Elysian air.
Then are they happy, when by length of time
The scurf is worn away of each committed crime.
No speck is left of their habitual stains:
But the pure ether of the soul remains.
But when a thousand rolling years are past,
(So long their punishments and penance last,)
Whole droves of minds are, by the driving god,
Compell'd to drink the deep Lethæan flood;
In large forgetful draughts to steep the cares
Of their past labours and their irksome years:
That, unremembering of its former pain,
The soul may suffer mortal flesh again."

Æneid, lib. vi, 724–751, *Dryden's Trans.*

While the people listened in wonder to these revelations, the surrounding sunlight passed away; darkness and thunder succeeded, until, amid its fearful din and the rumbling earthquake, the hierophant gave the word, "Depart;" when they emerged from the grand portal by which they had entered, and found it early morning, with the dew hanging on the green leaves around them.

On no subject connected with the religion of Greece has more labour or more learning been employed than on this; and the above is the substance of what has been thus elicited. Our limits forbid extended comment on a subject so tempting to speculation. Thus much is clear,—that, whatever science and scenery might have done here, or whether anything beyond physical agency was called into requisition, or otherwise, it was found necessary to forbid all discussion of the subject on pain of death. No one was permitted to speak of what took place within the sacred enclosure; and we are told that, as certainly as this law was violated, the body of the criminal might be seen, soon after, hanging dead from one of the neighbouring pinnacles, with an announcement stating that the dead man had perished for divulging the mysterious secrets of the celebration.

For an able, accurate, and eloquent account of the subject sketched in this note, see Blackwood's Magazine, February, 1853; to which we have been to some extent indebted.

NOTE 71, page 398.—*The Doctrines of Plato respecting the Soul and its Transmigration.*

Plato appears to have taken up, and given the sanction of his great name and character to, a notion which prevailed in the most ancient times among the Greeks; namely, that man had two souls: one, the seat and residence of animal life, the senses and desires, *sentient;* the other, partaking of reason and intelligence, or *rational:* the latter, of divine origin, and therefore immortal; the former, of a far inferior nature, and consequently not incapable of utterly perishing. The first was the part which is spoken of as made of the ethereal substance of which the soul of the world is composed; the second, as the immortal emanation from Deity. The opinion received all kinds of modification from the allegorizing tendencies of the poets, and was entertained by the common people in connexion with many gross additions and corruptions.

It is these semi-spiritual and semi-corporeal souls which assume the human figure, and render the departed visible as shades in the regions of Pluto's reign. But one of the most curious results of this doctrine is, the notion that vice deformed, discoloured, and disfigured this external sentient soul, and philosophy and virtue purified and cleansed it. Plutarch states this doctrine: "But the scars and seams remain from the several vices, in some greater, in some less. Now behold those various and diversified colours of souls. The dark and squalid are the taint of illiberality and avarice; the blood-red and fiery, of cruelty and barbarity; the green, of intemperance in pleasures; the violet-coloured and livid, like the ink of the cuttle-fish, of envy and malignity. For there the wickedness of the soul, influenced by the passions, and influencing the body, produces the colours: here it is the end of purification and punishment. When these colours are thoroughly purged away, the soul becomes bright and unsullied." See a poetic version of this in VIRGIL, *Æneid*, lib. vi, 735, quoted in the preceding pages.

Plato fully adopts and uses this doctrine. It is on this ground that he says, "The bodies of the dead, (that is, their outer or more corporeal souls,) we must suppose, are rightly called 'images.'"—*De Legibus*, 11. Plato also agrees with Plutarch in respect of the judgment of the soul: "All things are visible in the soul when it is denuded of the body, both those of nature, and the affections which a man has implanted in the soul by the pursuit of each particular object. When they come, therefore, before the judge, he inspects the soul of each, but knows not to whom it belongs; but oftentimes, taking that of the great and potent king, (of the Persians,) he finds no soundness in it, but sees it lashed all over, and full of scars, through perjuries and injustice, such as the practice of each vice has impressed upon the soul, and all made crooked by falsehood and vanity."—*Gorgias*. These marks of sin it was the province and power of philosophy to remove: hence we read a description by Lucian of the final judgment of a philosopher, a cobbler, and a tyrant. The philosopher being first placed naked before Rhadamanthus, he is considered to be pure, but nevertheless has three or four marks of healed ulcers; and, on seeing these, the judge asks how he had managed to efface the imprints of crime. To this he replies, "Having been formerly depraved and wicked through ignorance, and by that means marked with many spots, as soon as I began to philosophize, I gradually wiped away all stains from the soul." The cobbler is found pure and free from spots. But when the tyrant is stripped, the judge says, "Why, really, this man is all over livid and spotted; nay, is rather black with spots."

Plato, in accordance with all this, observes, "The judge, therefore, having inspected the soul so affected, straightway commits it with ignominy into custody, where it is to undergo the merited punishment." But this sage clearly teaches that this punishment is intended to be meliorative; hence he adds, "Those who profit by the punishment they suffer, both among gods and men, are such as have committed remediable sins; who are benefitted by pains and torments both here and in Orcus; for it is impossible otherwise to be freed from injustice. But whoever are guilty of the worst of crimes, and by reason of such crimes become incurable, of these examples are made, and they no longer are benefitted themselves, as being incurable; but others are benefitted, who behold them suffering for their sins the greatest, and most painful, and most frightful punishments for everlasting, and held up there, in their prison in hell, as examples, and spectacles, and warnings, to the unjust that from time to time come thither."

A peculiar feature in this system was the energetic virtue of philosophy. It not only purged away sin, but insured consummate blessedness. Hence Plato says, "Those who are found to have lived a preëminently pious and holy life, being freed and released from terrestrial places, as from a prison, ascend upward into a pure habitation, and dwell above the earth; and among these whoever have been sufficiently purified by philosophy, live altogether without bodies hereafter, and obtain habitations even more beautiful than the others."—*Phædo*. That is, those who are thus purified lose altogether the lower sentient soul, and live everlastingly in the bliss of perfect intellectuality. To this effect is another passage of our author: "No one is allowed to enter into the family of the gods (after death) but the lover of learning alone, who has devoted himself to philosophy, and died perfectly pure."—*Ibid*.

A part of this remedial punishment was believed to arise from the location of the soul in successive human and animal bodies. But with regard to this doctrine there was an important difference between Pythagoras and Plato. The former thought that the successive transition of the soul into other bodies was physical and necessary, and exclusive of all moral designation whatsoever. But Plato, on the contrary, taught that "these changes and transmissions were the purgations of impure minds, unfit, by reason of the pollutions they had contracted, to reascend to the place from whence they came, and rejoin that substance from whence they were discerped; and consequently that pure, immaculate souls were exempt from this transmigration."

NOTE 72, page 408.—*The Credibility of the earliest Roman Historians.*

In the investigation of history, two opposite errors must be steadily avoided, if we would arrive at a clear and trustworthy knowledge of facts. These are,—general scepticism, on the one hand,—and an indiscriminate reception of reports, on the other. These errors are not imaginary, but have been actually adopted and acted on to a great extent. We have seen the most undoubted historical facts cavilled at and questioned, while the most extravagant legends and idle tales have been received as authentic history.

In order to our maintaining the safe *via media*, in respect of the early Roman historians, it will be necessary to inquire into their means of obtaining accurate information, and their ability and disposition to make an honest and intelligent use of what they secured. This investigation need not be a very extended one. Livy, and Dionysius of Halicarnassus, are the only ancient writers who pretend to give detailed and connected histories of the early ages of Rome. Plutarch, in his biographies of Romulus, Numa, Publicola, Coriolanus, Camillus, and Pyrrhus, affords some information respecting particular periods; while Polybius and Cicero give incidental notices of independent and isolated facts. No other author, living at a period when authentic information was accessible, has handed down his productions to posterity. Of course, poets have been excluded in this summary, as the nature of their productions prevents our relying on them for sober historical detail.

Let us first examine the claims of Livy. He wrote during the reign of Augustus, nearly three hundred years after the close of the period whose annals we question: and this period, be it remembered, ranged over five preceding centuries. Livy must therefore have collected the materials for his history from the several sources of information to which he had access. These were four in number:—the works of preceding authors; inscriptions remaining on ancient monuments; the genealogical records of private families; and, probably, some public registers preserved in the care of officers of state. From such documents this celebrated writer must have gathered his information; and the credibility of his history must depend on the judgment and discretion with which he made his selection. But he has unfortunately left us no means of judging on this head, inasmuch as he very seldom informs his reader whence he has obtained his information, or on what authority he relies.

Our limits forbid an extended examination of the use which Livy made of these several sources of knowledge, as indicated by his works; but it may be briefly observed that Fabius, the most ancient writer and his favourite authority, is very slightingly spoken of by Polybius. Nor does Livy appear to have exercised a sounder judgment in regard to the quoting of other authors. From inscriptions and monuments he could not have obtained much information; the casualities to which Rome was frequently exposed, and the burning of the capitol, must have greatly limited his resources of this kind. Family records are not unfrequently of the greatest assistance to the historian. But then they can only be useful when faithfully drawn up and honestly guarded. Unfortunately there is ample evidence that family vanity had corrupted these records, so as to ascribe exploits and honours entirely fictitious to their ancestors. There is too much reason for believing that even public documents were corrupted from the same motive.

Nor have we any proof that Livy made the best use of the slender materials that lay within his reach. On the contrary, it is evident that, instead of compensating for the scarcity of information by caution in arriving at conclusions, and brevity in the detail of particular incidents, his history is as replete with minute particulars and full-length speeches, as if he had been writing an autobiography, and describing events which came under his personal observation. Nor does he afford better evidence of possessing any correct acquaintance with the state of his country in the early period of its history.

Upon the whole, I quite agree in the judgment which an able writer has pronounced on this subject: "Considering, then, the deficiency of all good materials, the very indifferent character of those which were in his power, and the instances given of his own ignorance, carelessness, and deviation from truth in points of importance, it is not too much to assert, that Livy's evidence, as far as concerns the first ten books of his History, is altogether unworthy of credit. Many of the facts reported by him may be true, and many are probable; but we have no right to admit them as real occurrences on his authority. The story of many well-written novels is highly probable, yet we do not the less regard it as a fiction; and the narrative of Livy, even where its internal evidence is most in its favour, is so destitute of external evidence, that although we would not assert that it is everywhere false, we should act unwisely were we anywhere to argue upon it as if it were true."—*Encyclopædia Metropolitana. art.* "*Credibility of early Roman History.*"

DIONYSIUS OF HALICARNASSUS stands next to Livy as an historian of ancient Rome, and was contemporary with him. His means of information would, therefore, be the same: it will, then, only be necessary to notice his individual abilities. And in this respect we certainly cannot find in him anything of a more trustworthy character than was discovered in Livy.

DIODORUS evinces even greater prolixity, pretending to furnish the minutest details respecting the most remote and obscure periods of history; while his judgment and opinions on subjects that are well known,—such as his criticism on Thucydides,—are even ridiculously absurd; and he confidently quotes authors whom other writers of credit speak of as notoriously untrustworthy. Indeed, Diodorus, as an historian, scarcely equals Livy, whose authority has been found open to very serious exception.

PLUTARCH lived more than a hundred years after these two authors, and was consequently so much further removed from the sources of original information. He appears to have been equally ready with them to adopt and propagate current reports, however distored by personal prejudice, or suggested by national ambition. Reasoning here from the known to the unknown, we can have no confidence in his statements. For, in the compilation of his Grecian biographies, he has certainly used in common the best and the worst authorities, without exercising any sound judgment or careful discrimination.

POLYBIUS presents to the mind a totally different character. Few historical works, of either ancient or modern times, will bear a comparison with his. He prosecuted his preparatory studies with great energy and perseverance. He collected with the utmost care the best accounts of the events which he intended to narrate; investigated with laborious ardour the nature of the Roman constitution, that he might be able to understand its early history; and made long and dangerous voyages and travels, that he might have the best means of knowing the countries of which he had to write. And, above all, he is allowed to have excelled in the greatest of all qualities,—truthfulness. He did not, like many others, write merely to amuse his readers by the strangeness of his facts, or to fascinate them by the elegance of his diction, but to instruct them in the communication of a true exhibition of past history; that a knowledge of the future, and those lessons of practical wisdom which its exigencies required, might thence be deduced. Yet, notwithstanding these great qualities, we cannot expect from Polybius anything like a complete exhibition of early Roman history. He was a foreigner, and was in consequence placed at very considerable disadvantage on that account. But, what is of much greater importance, he does not profess to narrate the events of the early ages of Rome. Of his own time, and the age immediately preceding, he has written ably and fully; but of the antique era of Roman history he only spoke briefly and incidentally. He cannot, therefore, be relied on as furnishing a full and connected account of this period, although in several instances his sagacity and veracity have corrected the popular legendary reports, which earlier and less scrupulous authors incorporated into their narratives.

As an instance, reference may be made to the heroism of Horatius Cocles, recorded by Polybius, lib. vi, cap. 55, and Livy, lib. ii, cap. 10. The former describes this hero as keeping the enemy in check, until the bridge was broken down behind him, when, armed and wounded as he was, he leaped into the river and perished, "having preferred the safety of his country, and the future fame that was sure to follow such an action, to his own present existence." Livy, however, says that he succeeded in swimming across the stream, and that he lived to receive applause and reward. It is in such additions as these, which set all probability at defiance, and convert pretended history into romantic legends, that the real difficulty lies. And such cases abound so frequently in the best accounts of this period, that its incidents, while probably affording a tolerably correct outline, cannot be received as historical detail.

NOTE 73, page 408.—*The Legend of Æneas.*

Perhaps nothing in ancient history is more remarkable than the extent to which traditions have prevailed of settlements being formed in western Europe, by fugitives that had been engaged in the Trojan war. Tacitus mentions the opinions of the Germans, that Ulysses was driven into the Northern Ocean, and built there Asciburgium; and that an altar dedicated to Ulysses, with the name of Laërtes his father, had been found there. Solinus notices a tradition of Ulysses having reached a bay in Caledonia, "which," he adds, "an altar with a Greek inscription shows." A Trojan colony is stated to have founded Trapani in Italy. Virgil intimates that Antenor founded Padua, and led his Trojan followers into Illyria and Liburnia, and to the springs of the Timavus, or into Sclavonia, Croatia, and Friuli. Pliny stations Dardani in Mœsia, which he extends from the Pontus Euxinus to the Danube; and Strabo enumerates the Dardanidæ among the Illyrians; while Pindar ascribes the settlement of Cyrene in Africa also to Antenor. Another tradition connects Ulysses with Lisbon. Livy describes Antenor as likewise founding the Venetian population. Ammianus Marcellinus states that some Trojans, flying from the Greeks, occupied parts of the coast of Gaul which were previously uninhabited; while Nennius, the ancient British historian, says that Brutus, the grandson of Ascanius, driven from Italy and the Tyrrhenian Sea, went to Gaul, and founded Tours, and from thence came to Britain, which he colonized, and gave it his own name, about the time that Eli was judge in Israel. (Turner's History of the Anglo-Saxons, vol. i, pp. 64, 65.)

The legend which teaches the descent of the Romans from Æneas, whatever may be its claims to historical truth, was unquestionably received and believed at Rome at an early period. One thing is certain,—that the preservation of a remnant of the Trojan race, which was ruled over by this hero, is taught by the Homeric poems. But then this teaching goes no further than the existence of this section of the Dardan race in the neighbourhood of Troy, after the departure of the Greeks. But, with respect to the settlement of Æneas and his descendants in Latium, Niebuhr has satisfactorily established two points :—first, that the notion was not imported into Roman history from Grecian literature, but arose among the Roman people themselves in an early age; and, secondly, that, however specious and plausible it may appear, it has not the least historical truth. (History of Rome, vol. i, p. 189.)

It is, however, a question of some interest,—What is the light in which this legend should be regarded? Dr. W. C. Taylor states, that wherever Pelasgic settlements are found, there we find a city named Ænus, which he from hence regards as a generic, rather than an individual, name. From hence it is inferred, that "if any of the Pelasgi on the hills at the south side of the Tiber came from Ænus, they most probably retained their ancient name of Æneadæ; and the signification of that patronymic being forgotten in process of time, it was confounded with another similar name preserved by an independent tradition,— the Æneadæ, or followers of Æneas, who survived the destruction of their country."—*Ancient History*, p. 390. Niebuhr says that this legend and its cognate traditions "may safely be interpreted as designating nothing more than national affinity:" (History of Rome, vol. i, p. 190:) and Dr. L. Schmitz apparently coincides in this judgment; for he observes, that "Æneas himself, such as he appears in his wanderings, and final settlement in Latium, is nothing else but the personified idea of one common origin."—*Smith's Dict. of Greek and Roman Myth.*, &c, art. Æneas.

NOTE 74, page 408.—*The Legend of Alba.*

This is so intimately interwoven with the account of Æneas, that what is elicited respecting the historical character of the one, must be, in great measure, true of the other. On this point Niebuhr observes, "I am not bringing forward an hypothesis, but the plain result of unprejudiced observation, when I remark that Lavinium, as its name implies, was the seat of congress for the Latins, who were also called Lavines, as Panionium was that of the Ionians in Asia. When a legend contains names supposed to belong to individuals, this goes far toward giving it the look of being something more than fiction. Hence many who otherwise might still insist that the Trojan legend ought not to be absolutely rejected, may perhaps change their opinion, when they discern that Lavinia and Turnus are only personifications of two nations, and that Lavinium was a more recent city than Alba."—*History of Rome*, vol. i, p. 201.

NOTE 75, page 409.—*The Legends of Romulus and Remus.*

We cannot do better here than transcribe the brief, accurate, and eloquent summary of these legends, given by Niebuhr:—

"Procas, King of Alba, left two sons. Numitor, the elder, being weak and spiritless, suffered Amulius to wrest the government from him, and reduce him to his father's private estates. In the enjoyment of these he lived rich, and, as he desired nothing more, secure: but the usurper dreaded the claims that might be set up by heirs of a different character. He had Numitor's son murdered, and appointed his daughter Sylvia one of the Vestal virgins.

"Amulius had no children, or at least only one daughter: so that the race of Anchises and Aphrodite seemed on the point of expiring, when the love of a god prolonged it, in despite of the ordinances of man, and gave it a lustre worthy of its origin. Sylvia had gone into the sacred grove, to draw water from the spring for the service of the temple. The sun quenched his rays; the sight of a wolf made her fly into a cave; there Mars overpowered the timid virgin; and then consoled her with the promise of noble children, as Poseidon consoled Tyro, the daughter of Salmoneus. But he did not protect her from the tyrant; nor could her protestations of her innocence save her. Vesta herself seemed to demand the condemnation of the unfortunate priestess; for, at the moment when she was delivered of twins, the image of the goddess hid its eyes, her altar trembled, and her fire died away. Amulius ordered that the mother and her babes should be drowned in the river. In the Anio, Sylvia exchanged her earthly life for that of a goddess. The river carried the hole, or cradle, in which the children were lying, into the Tiber, which had overflowed its banks far and wide, even to the foot of the woody hills. At the root of a wild fig-tree,—the *Ficus Ruminalis*, which was preserved and held sacred for many centuries,—at the foot of the Palatine, the cradle overturned. A she-wolf came to drink of the stream: she heard the whimpering of the children, carried them into her den hard by, made a bed for them, licked and suckled them. When they wanted other food than milk, a woodpecker—the bird sacred to Mars—brought it to them. Other birds consecrated to auguries hovered over them, to drive away insects. This marvellous spectacle was seen by Faustulus, the shepherd of the royal flocks. The she-wolf drew back, and gave up the children to human nurture. Acca Larentia, his wife, became their foster-mother. They grew up, along with her twelve sons, on the Palatine Hill, in straw huts which they built for themselves. That of Romulus was preserved by continual repairs, as a sacred relic, down to the time of Nero. They were the stoutest of the shepherd lads,—fought bravely against wild beasts and robbers, maintaining their right against every one by their might, and turning might into right. Their booty they shared with their comrades.

The followers of Romulus were called Quinctilii; those of Remus, Fabii. The seeds of discord were soon sown among them. Their wantonness engaged them in disputes with the shepherds of the wealthy Numitor, who fed their flocks on Mount Aventine; so that here, as in the story of Evander and Cacus, we find the quarrel between the Palatine and the Aventine in the tales of the remotest times. Remus was taken by a stratagem of these shepherds, and dragged to Alba as a robber. A secret foreboding—the remembrance of his grandsons, awakened by the story of the two brothers—kept Numitor from pronouncing a hasty sentence. The culprit's foster-father hurried with Romulus to the city, and told the old man and the youths of their kindred. They resolved to avenge their own wrong, and that of their house. With their faithful comrades, whom the danger of Remus had brought to the city, they slew the king; and the people of Alba again became subject to Numitor."—*Niebuhr's History of Rome*, vol. i, pp. 220–222.

NOTE 76, page 410.—*The Legend of Tarpeia.*

It is vain to question the allegations of pure poetry and fable, or we might stay to investigate the relative probability of the conflicting versions which are given of this legend. That which is given in the text, although generally received, is sufficiently absurd. That an invading force, just prepared to occupy an important military post, should cast away their shields at the very moment when they would most need them for their personal protection, is manifestly improbable. But it is not more improbable than the version given by Niebuhr, —that the Sabines fulfilled their engagement by throwing on the traitress such an immense quantity of jewelry and gold ornaments, that it was beneath the weight of these that she perished. The fact is, that we have here no approximation to historical *data*.

NOTE 77, page 413.—*The Etruscan Origin of Roman Power and Civilization.*

From this particular incident, taken in connexion with the tenor of the preceding history, it can scarcely be open to reasonable doubt, that Etruria was the real parent of Roman greatness. We have everywhere in the ancient records and legends proofs that, long prior to the foundation of Rome, the Etruscans were a highly civilized and powerful people. In immediate proximity with their country, and copying their political code and religious institutions, Rome grew up to maturity, until sufficiently powerful to assert an independent position, and finally to subdue its former patron.

This fact forms a key to the principal portions of the legendary history of the rising empire. It was to conceal the dependent condition of Rome in the early ages of its career, and to mystify very obvious indications of its Etruscan character and institutions, that facts have been distorted or concealed, and the most puerile fancies have been incorporated into the history. It is deeply to be regretted, that a nation possessing so much real power and greatness should have stooped to such means of misrepresenting its true origin.

Note 78, page 417.—*The Origin and Character of the Dictatorship.*

The frequent appointment of an officer, invested, for a limited time, with absolute power, in a state professedly republican, is an anomaly which merits attention. Niebuhr seems to have shown clearly, that the office was of Latin origin, and was found in some of these states at a very early period. He also places the appointment of the first dictator of Rome ten years after the appointment of the first consuls.

The power of the dictator continued only six months, whether the business which occasioned his election was finished, or not. But usually the office ceased after being held a very short period. Cincinnatus and Mamercus Æmilius resigned their power on the sixteenth day, and Q. Servilius on the eighth. The powers with which the dictator was intrusted were very extensive, and, in certain respects, absolute. He knew no superior, and was not even limited by the laws of the country. He could proclaim war, levy forces, lead them against the enemy, and disband them, at his pleasure. During his sway, all other officers, except the tribunes of the people, were regarded as suspended; and the dictator, with power to punish at his will, with no appeal from his judgment, was master of the republic. While holding this office, he was not allowed to leave Italy, or to ride on horseback, without the permission of the people; and, on retiring from the dignity, he might be called to account for the manner in which he had conducted the government. This was, in fact, the principal check against the abuse of such extended powers.

The object aimed at in the appointment of this officer was, evidently, to afford the Patricians an effective power over the Plebeians, especially in seasons of excitement and turbulence. Hence, we find that the dictator was not appointed by the suffrages of the people, as the other magistrates were; but one of the consuls, by order of the senate, named as dictator whatever person of consular dignity he thought proper. The choice usually took place after a religious reference to the auspices.

Note 79, page 417.—*The first standing Army of Rome.*

In the first efforts of Rome to obtain political existence and territorial sovereignty by martial prowess, the military operations were conducted by the body of the people under the conduct of their hereditary leaders; the troops being supported by their own resources, or by the patriotic aid of their generals. In the war with Veii, the foundation was laid for the future warlike greatness of the mighty republic by the incorporation of a standing army, paid by the state from taxes levied on the people. As this city was well fortified, it could only be reduced by being regularly and permanently invested. And this could not be done by troops who were fed by such precarious means as obtaining provisions from their own homes. For, during the intervals in which they would be obliged to return to obtain fresh supplies, the besieged would not only be able to destroy the works raised against their town, but also to carry ruin and devastation into the Roman territory.

In order to counteract this, the Romans levied an income-tax, and thus provided means for affording regular pay to the soldiers. They were thus enabled to prosecute the war without intermission, and to secure an entire conquest over the devoted city.

NOTE 80, page 418.—*A general View of the legendary History of Rome, to the Capture of the City by the Gauls.*

It is with great reluctance that we are bound to admit, that in the whole of this period we have the few grand separated facts of the history supplemented and adorned by poetry and fable. As such we are compelled to regard the accounts furnished by the most respectable authorities concerning Tullus, and his wars with the Latins and Sabines; Ancus Martius, his legislation and his conquests; the Tarquins, their pride and power, crimes and punishment, together with their allies, and efforts to recover the throne of Rome; Porsenna, and his victory and subjugation of Rome; the wars with the Volscians, Æquians, and Veii; the conquest and abandonment of the latter city; the irruption of the Gauls, their success and departure from Italy. In all these narrations there is an evident *substratum* of historical fact. Most of them refer to events which certainly happened, and the certainty of which is attested by indubitable evidence; while, at the same time, it is as evident that the account furnished by the historians is so distorted by the dictates of national vanity, political artifice, and local partiality, that what we read can only be regarded as a political novel, reared on a basis of historical fact.

NOTE 81, page 418.—*The oppressive Laws of ancient Rome respecting the Poor.*

"It was only when the debt assumed the form of a *nexum*, that a creditor could exact it summarily. Care was taken, however, to protect his right in all other cases, and to afford him the means of converting a common debt into a *nexum*. We meet with a very great variety of instances of such debts, arising out of services performed, out of commercial transactions, out of a settlement of accounts, out of inheritances: it is impossible to enumerate them all. But to these the law likewise added judicial sentences,—not merely those which established debts contracted in any of the afore-mentioned ways, but also those which imposed damages or fines for any crime or trespass. On this head the decemvirs enacted,—what again was probably a mere repetition of an old law,—that for such debts a respite of thirty days should be granted. When this term was over, the creditor was authorized to arrest his debtor and bring him into court. If he did not discharge his debt then, or find some one to be security for him, the creditor was to take him home, and put him in fetters or chains, which were not to weigh less than fifteen pounds, but might be heavier. The prisoner was allowed to provide himself with food: if he did not do so, the creditor was bound to give him a pound of corn a day; which he might increase, if he pleased. This imprisonment lasted sixty days, during which the debtor, or his friends, might take measures for procuring his release. If it was not effected, the prisoner was to be led before the prætor in the *comitium* on three consecutive market-days, and the amount of his debt was to be proclaimed. Should no one take compassion on him even then, his master might put him to death, or sell him on the other side of the Tiber. If there were several creditors, they might share his body among them: nor, if any one chopped off a larger part than was proportionate to his debt, was he punishable for doing so.

"This last provision obviates the difficulty which stood in Shylock's way under a similar legal title: and it shows how completely in earnest the legislators were that the law should be executed. Even in case that among several creditors one was inexorable, his right was secured to him. He was allowed, if not to slay the common debtor at a blow, yet so to mutilate him that death was sure to ensue. Every attempt to explain away the inhumanity of this law is a waste of labour in the cause of falsehood. It was quite as revolting as its literal meaning."—*Niebuhr's History of Rome*, vol. ii, pp. 659, 660.

NOTE 82, page 457.—*The Fulfilment of sacred Prophecy in the History of Rome.*

As all the other great kingdoms were the subjects of divine prophecy, and had their character, prominent events, and ultimate destiny, predicted in the word of God, it might be expected that Rome, the last and the largest empire, and the one which exercised universal sway through the longest period of time, would also be noticed in the prophetic record. This expectation is amply justified. The inspired seer, taught by the Holy Spirit, has placed before us very clear and precise prophecies, which mark out the character, power, and fate of this mighty nation.

I. The first prediction to which we refer is that which has been quoted with regard to the other universal governments,—namely, Daniel's exposition of Nebuchadnezzar's dream of the great image: "His legs of iron, his feet part of iron and part of clay. Thou sawest till that a stone was cut out without hands, which smote the image upon his feet that were of iron and clay, and brake them to pieces. And whereas thou sawest the feet and toes, part of potters' clay, and part of iron, the kingdom shall be divided; but there shall be in it of the strength of the iron, forasmuch as thou sawest the iron mixed with miry clay. And as the toes of the feet were part of iron, and part of clay, so the kingdom shall be partly strong, and partly broken. And whereas thou sawest iron mixed with miry clay, they shall mingle themselves with the seed of men: but they shall not cleave one to another, even as iron is not mixed with clay. And in the days of these kings shall the God of heaven set up a kingdom, which shall never be destroyed: and the kingdom shall not be left to other people, but it shall break in pieces and consume all these kingdoms, and it shall stand forever. Forasmuch as thou sawest that the stone was cut out of the mountain without hands, and that it brake in pieces the iron, the brass, the clay, the silver, and the gold; the great God hath made known to the king what shall come to pass hereafter: and the dream is certain, and the interpretation thereof sure." Dan. ii, 33, 34, 41-45.

This portion of sacred prophecy will be found to convey very important information. It first asserts the unequalled power of this empire: "Strong as iron, forasmuch as iron breaketh in pieces and subdueth all things." The whole history of Rome is a fulfilment of this prophecy. The martial power of this people, unlike the meteor flashings of Macedonian conquest, went forth in aggression on every surrounding state, quietly poising its power against neighbouring nations, and doing this with such daring skill and steady determination that it was seldom forced to relinquish its prey, but persevered in its object, until, after a steady progress in power for five hundred years, it ultimately bent to its rule every other nation, so that it was in fact what the Roman writers delighted to call it, *terrarum orbis imperium*, "the empire of the world."

A second important element of this prophecy is the co-existence of disunion and strength in the Roman government. This was not an accident, affecting any particular period, but rather the character of the national administration. From the days of Romulus and Remus to those of Augustus, Rome was proverbial for intestine disunion and division. Under the sway of the early kings, the Latin and Sabine factions were always in opposition, sometimes one preponderating, and sometimes the other. After the expulsion of the Tarquins, and the abolition of royalty, the appointment of two consuls with equal power perpetuated this division, which was greatly aggravated by other causes. And even when Rome stood forth before the world as on the threshold of universal empire, this singular fatality was more than usually displayed. What other nation ever survived such suicidal contests, proscriptions, and slaughter, as were connected with the factions of Sylla and Marius,—the establishment of the two triumvirates,—the struggles between Pompey and Cæsar, Antony and Brutus and Cassius, and Augustus and Antony? I am not aware of anything in the whole range of sacred prophecy more striking than the continued disunion which reigned in Rome in juxtaposition with boundless power. That which was fatal everywhere else, here rioted with the greatest fury, up to the moment when Rome sat down the queen of the world.

But, strange as was the fact of this internal discord, and remarkable as was its prediction, no less so was the utter failure of the means adopted to prevent it: "They shall mingle themselves with the seed of men." This reads more like literal history than prophecy. How many intermarriages took place in Rome, to cement the heads of the body politic into union; and how fruitless did they prove! Pompey married Julia, the daughter of Julius Cæsar,—Antony, Octavia, sister of Augustus,—and Augustus himself first married, and afterward divorced, Scribonia. Numerous other political alliances might be mentioned; but they invariably failed to secure the object aimed at,—union in the Roman government.

Lastly, this prediction is remarkable for specifying most distinctly, that, under the prevalence of this dominion, the kingdom of God was to be set up in the world: "In the days of these kings shall the God of heaven set up a kingdom." Nothing can exceed in importance the truth enunciated in these words. When Nebuchadnezzar reigned in Babylon,—while Jerusalem was in ruins, and Judea was a desert, and the remnant of Israel were captives, groaning in bondage beneath the rod of the oppressor,—the prescience of God marked out to human observation that chapter of his providential government which was to be evolved during the succeeding six or seven centuries. The fall of Babylon, the rise of Persia, the prowess and conquests of the Macedonian king, with the subversion of the Persian empire,—the progress of the Roman power, and the establishment of its supremacy,—all these great events, arising out of, and connected with, ten thousand remote contingencies, are thus explicitly predicted, as preparing the way for the kingdom of God. We do not speak of this as displaying a wonderful amount of knowledge in the eternal Jehovah. He could as easily have predicted the whole history of the world from its creation to its final conflagration, as have specified this small portion of it. But this text is of grand consequence, as showing the great religious object, for the accomplishment of which the government of this world has always been directed; and proving that, during all these successive revolutions of empires, the kingdom of God was the great institution to which the sympathy and design of Heaven were directed. And how perfect was the fulfilment of this part of the prophecy! Although Rome won universal empire under a republican form of government, it reigned supreme as a monarchy: it was therefore under the "KINGS" of this nation that the kingdom of heaven was founded.

Again, it should be observed, that the changes in Hebrew history during the interval between the publication of this prediction and its fulfilment were no less remarkable than those which took place in the empires of the world. Yet all were made to harmonize, and, during the reign of Tiberius Cæsar, the Messiah's forerunner was heard in the wilderness of Judea, proclaiming, "The kingdom of heaven is at hand: repent ye, and believe the gospel." And soon afterward the glorious announcement was made by the Son of God himself: "The time is fulfilled, and the kingdom of heaven is at hand." Mark i, 15. And Jesus, having died a ransom for the world's sin, and risen again from the dead, commissioned his disciples to preach his gospel under the constant guidance of his own Spirit and power. Thus was the kingdom of God set up in the world.

II. We notice, further, Daniel's prophecy of the fourth beast: "After this I saw in the night visions, and behold a fourth beast, dreadful and terrible, and strong exceedingly; and it had great iron teeth: it devoured and brake in pieces, and stamped the residue with the feet of it: and it was diverse from all the beasts that were before it: and it had ten horns. I considered the horns, and, behold, there came up among them another little horn, before whom there were three of the first horns plucked up by the roots: and, behold, in this horn were eyes like the eyes of man, and a mouth speaking great things. Then I would know the truth of the fourth beast, which was diverse from all the others, exceeding dreadful, whose teeth were of iron, and his nails of brass; which devoured, brake in pieces, and stamped the residue with his feet; and of the ten horns that were in his head, and of the other which came up, and before whom three fell; even of that horn that had eyes, and a mouth that spake very great things, whose look was more stout than his fellows." Dan. vii, 7, 8, 19, 20. In these words we have clearly another important class of predictions of the Roman empire.

In the first instance, it may be observed, that this prediction asserts the peculiar character of this fourth dominion, in respect of the preceding empires. These were so much in the usual order of nature, although remarkable for great power, that they were represented by well-known animal figures, with such additions to their natural conformation as were adapted to mark out their extraordinary qualities. Hence the lion had eagle's wings; the bear had three ribs in its mouth; and the leopard had four wings of a fowl. But, in the case of the fourth beast, it seemed that the monstrous creation defied description, being altogether so unlike everything previously known. This was wonderfully fulfilled in the Roman empire; arising not from an old primitive tribe or family, nor owing its transcendent glory to the genius and energy of a single sovereign. Rome began as a petty minor state, surrounded by many others of greater power, even in the Italian peninsula, and progressed by assimilating these to itself; and thus, either by power or policy, gradually acquired preponderance in Italy. Then, again, another important point of diversity in the Roman state was its republican form of government. Nothing like this had been seen in the preceding great powers: they were monarchies of the most absolute and autocratic character. Rome, diverse from all, arose into power under the legislation of the senate, and through the administration of a succession of pairs of consuls, ruling with equal powers.

Secondly, a very remarkable characteristic of this empire is its amazing strength, fierceness, and implacable disposition. It was "dreadful and terrible, and strong exceedingly; and it had great iron teeth: it devoured and brake in pieces, and stamped the residue with the feet of it." How graphically does this portray the conduct of the Romans toward Carthage, Greece, and many other countries! No reverses quenched their ardour; no success satisfied their ambition. Steady to their purpose, they. endured every disaster, and dared all resistance, until they triumphed over all. The imperishable words, *Delenda est Carthago*, form a striking comment on, and fulfilment of, this prophecy. When the Punic city had renounced all pretensions to supremacy, and even to government, so insatiable was the rabid power of the dreadful and terrible Roman beast, that Carthage was denied even existence. The subdued and powerless "residue" was devoured, broken in pieces, and stamped under the feet of the beast.

The further portion of the prophecy relates to a period later in the world's history than that to which our inquiries refer. But it may be briefly stated, that it was most minutely and circumstantially fulfilled. Rome having accomplished its destiny as a great empire, its dominions were divided into ten kingdoms. These have been differently enumerated by learned men, according to the date to which their inquiries have been directed; but these differences are not important. The following statement may be regarded as substantially correct : 1. The senate of Rome; 2. The Greeks in Ravenna; 3. The Lombards; 4. The Huns; 5. The Alemans in Germany; 6. The Franks; 7. The Burgundians; 8. Spain; 9. The Britons; 10. The Saxons.

But the most striking and important portion of this prediction relates to the little horn. According to the prophecy, one new and separate horn, or power, arose up, as it were, unobserved among these ten horns; and, having attained power, it plucked up three of the horns by the roots, and ruled in their stead,— "having eyes like the eyes of a man, and a mouth speaking great things." Nothing can exceed the exactitude with which this sets forth the rise of the papal power. By successive claims, well covered with humble pretences, the bishops of Rome attained a *status* as possessing temporal rule. They then proceeded onward, until the government of Rome, the exarchate of Ravenna, and the kingdom of Lombardy, were entirely lodged in the hands of the pontiff, in reference to which possessions he to this day wears a *triple* crown, as if to point himself out to the whole world as the subject of this part of the prophecy. As to the greatness of his claims, professions, and requirements, nothing need be said, when it is known that "as God he sits in the temple of God, claiming to be God."

Surely Rome, wonderful in her origin, her power, and her extent of dominion, is no less wonderful as the object of great and glorious Scripture prophecies, which were fulfilled in her history and ruin.

GENERAL CHRONOLOGICAL INDEX.

	B. C.
Creation of the world	5507
Enoch translated to heaven	4020
Noah born	3845
The universal Deluge	3245
Death of Noah	2895
The Dispersion, about	2730
Nimrod established kingly government at Babel	2718
The Misraim settle in Egypt	2613
Job's trial took place about	2350
Kaiomars king in Persia	2253
Abraham born	2113
Isaac born	2013
Esau and Jacob born	1953
The Shepherds expelled from Egypt	1845
Joseph governor in Egypt	1832
Jacob and his family settle in Egypt	1823
Moses born	1688
The Exodus	1608
The spies sent into Canaan	1606
The rebellion of Korah	1588
Ramesis III. (Sesostris) reigns in Egypt	1569
Israelites pass the Jordan	1568
Tabernacle set up at Gilgal	1561
Death of Joshua	1543
Israelites brought into subjection to Mesopotamia	1533
Israelites delivered by Othniel	1525
Sethos king of Egypt	1472
Ehud and Shamgar judges in Israel	1395
Teutames reigns in Assyria	1214
Troy taken and destroyed	1183
Samson and Eli judges in Israel	1152
Return of the Heracleids to Peloponnesus	1103
Saul anointed king over the Hebrews	1099
David king over all Israel	1052
The ark of God placed in the tabernacle of David	1043
Solomon born	1039
The temple begun	1016
The temple finished	1009
Solomon carries out his great scheme of commercial policy and navigation	995
Shishak, king of Egypt, plunders Jerusalem	974
Abijah succeeds Rehoboam in Judah	962
The king of Israel defeated by Abijah	961
Jehoshaphat, King of Judah, provides for the instruction of his people	915
The Philistines and Arabians ravage Judea	887
Arbaces, a Mede, ascends the throne of Assyria	821
Lycurgus legislates in Sparta	817
Jonah prophesies against Nineveh	806
Era of the Olympiads	776
Tiglath-Pileser king of Assyria	753
Era of the building of Rome	—
Era of Nabonassar	747

CHRONOLOGICAL INDEX.

	B. C.
Hezekiah king of Judah	725
Numa king of Rome	716
Sennacherib invades Judah	713
Samaria taken, and the kingdom of Israel destroyed	710
Josiah, King of Judah, slain at Megiddo	630
Tarquinius king of Rome (Sibylline Books)	618
Nineveh taken, and Assyrian empire destroyed	606
Nebuchadnezzar king of Babylon	604
Solon reforms the constitution of Athens	594
Jerusalem taken and destroyed. Captivity of Judah	586
Cyrus king in Persia	560
Belshazzar's feast and death	553
Cyrus subdues Media, and reigns there	551
Cyrus conquers Babylon, and establishes the Medo-Persian empire	536
The first caravan of Hebrews return to Jerusalem	535
The second temple begun	534
Cambyses reigns in Persia	529
Darius Hystaspis king	521
The second temple finished	516
Tarquin expelled, and monarchy abolished at Rome	509
Pythagoras dies	497
The Persians defeated at Marathon	490
Xerxes invades Greece	485
Xerxes is completely defeated	479
Artaxerxes ascends the throne of Persia	464
Artaxerxes sends Ezra to Judea	457
Artaxerxes marries Esther	—
First Peloponnesian War	431
The Romans besiege Veii	405
Joiada, high priest of Jerusalem, murders his brother in the temple	—
Athens taken by the Spartans	404
Death of Socrates	399
Plato and Aristotle flourish at Athens	397
Alexander conquers the Persian empire	333
Alexander dies at Babylon	323
Simon the Just high priest at Jerusalem	300
Septuagint translation made	278
Agis III., attempting the reformation of Sparta, is slain	244
Second Punic War.—Hannibal in Italy	218
Jerusalem sacked, and the temple plundered, by Antiochus	170
Macedonian kingdom destroyed by the Romans	168
Mattathias and his sons resist the Antiochian persecution	167
Carthage destroyed	146
The Jews obtain their independence	143
Tiberius Gracchus slain	133
Idumeans subdued and incorporated with the Jews	129
Caius Gracchus slain	123
Aristobulus assumes the title and state of a king at Jerusalem	106
Julius Cæsar born	100
Civil war in Rome between the factions of Marius and Sylla	88
Civil war in Judea between Alexander Janneus and the Pharisees	86
Pompey the Great triumphs at Rome for his numerous conquests	62
First Roman Triumvirate,—Cæsar, Pompey, and Crassus	60
Julius Cæsar rules supreme at Rome	48
Julius Cæsar slain	44
Herod made king of Judea	40
Octavius, under the title of Augustus, rules the Roman empire	31
The temple of Janus shut at Rome	29
Herod begins the rebuilding of the temple	17
The temple finished	7
Jesus Christ born	4
Vulgar Christian Era	0

INDEX TO SCRIPTURES

WHICH ARE MORE OR LESS ILLUSTRATED.

GENESIS.

Chapter	Verse	Vol.	Page	Chapter	Verse	Vol.	Page
i				vii	2	i,	170
	1, 2	i,	99		11	i,	18
	2–5	i,	101		15, 19, 21	i,	256
	6–8	i,	103	viii	13	i,	298
	9–13	i,	103		14–19	i,	252
	20–25	i,	106		19	i,	299
	26	i,	107		20–22	i,	303
	27, 28	i,	122	ix	3	i,	223
	31	i,	107		3, 4	i,	228
ii	3	i,	108		4	i,	399
	7–9	i,	122		11–17	i,	306
	8–25, 15	i,	141		18, 19	i,	311
	9	i,	142		20–27	i,	309
	10–14	i,	141	x	8–10	i,	330
	19	i,	149		9	i,	329
	21–25	i,	122		11, 12	i,	435
iii		i,	128		21, 24	i,	52
	11	i,	215		25	i,	321
	21	i,	162		30	i,	345
	24	i,	143	xi	1, 2	i,	322
			147		1–9	i,	60
iv	1	i,	200		2	i,	301
	2, 3, 4, 17	i,	162		3–9	i,	324
	3–7	i,	203		4	i,	335
	3–12	i,	213		6	i,	326
	8	i,	233				337
	19–24	i,	168		12	i,	22
	20, 21	i,	177		26, 32	i,	370
	22	i,	178	xii	1, 2	ii,	14
	23, 24	i,	66		6	i,	376
	25	i,	362	xiii	14–17	ii,	15
	26	i,	164	xv	13–21	ii,	15
v	1	i,	56		13, 14, 16	ii,	26
	2–26	i,	18		13–16	iii,	538
	24	i,	214		18	i,	383
			237	xvi	11, 12	i,	388
vi	1, 2	i,	164		13	i,	421
	2	i,	36	xvii	2–8	ii,	15
	3	i,	199		15–21	ii,	16
	4	i,	187	xviii	6, 7	ii,	21
			189	xxi	17–20	i,	389
	5, 7, 12, 13, 17, 19, 20, 22	i,	69	xxiii	17	i,	65
	12, 13	i,	240	xxiv	7	i,	407
	13–21	i,	244	xxv	9	i,	391
vii	1–3	i,	249		16–18	i,	392
	1–5	i,	69		18	i,	499
					22	i,	395

GENESIS.

Chapter.	Verse.	Vol.	Page.
xxvi	9–11	ii,	98
xxvii	1–4	ii,	19
xxviii	13–15	ii,	16
	18, 19	ii,	23
	20, 21	ii,	23
xxx	3	i,	383
xxxi	2	ii,	23
	3, 14–16	ii,	24
xxxii	1, 2	ii,	25
	24–29	ii,	25
xxxv	11, 12	ii,	17
	18	i,	424
xxxvii	3, 4	ii,	26
xli	1–36	iii,	538
xlvii	11	ii,	47
l	29	iii,	62

EXODUS.

i	8	ii,	29
	9, 10	ii,	91
	13, 14	ii,	30
iii	16	ii,	55
iv	30, 31	ii,	35
vii	8, 9	ii,	36
	11, 12	ii,	37
x	22	ii,	44
xii	30, 33, 37, 38	ii,	46
	40	i,	23
	42	ii,	469
xiii	19	ii,	29
	21	ii,	47
xiv	1, 2	ii,	48
xv	1–21	ii,	50
	24	ii,	56
xvi	4, 22, 23, 25–28	i,	220
	9–12	ii,	58
	9, 33, 34	ii,	94
	15	ii,	59
xvii	3, 4	ii,	60
	13	ii,	61
	14	i,	64
xix	3–8	ii,	116
	4–8	ii,	62
xx	2	ii,	466
xxiv	9–11	ii,	63
xxv	1–8	ii,	103
	10–22	i,	146
xxviii	30	ii,	107
xxx	6	ii,	466
xxxiii	8, 9	ii,	96
	16	ii,	115
xxxviii	24–31	ii,	66

LEVITICUS.

ix	23, 24	ii,	67
xvii	7	iii,	18
	11	ii,	111
xxiii	15–20	ii,	112
	34–44	ii,	111

NUMBERS.

Chapter.	Verse.	Vol.	Page.
viii	4	ii,	99
x	2, 3, 7, 8	ii,	245
xi	12, 15, 16, 21, 23	ii,	70
xii	1	ii,	71
xiii	27, 28, 33	ii,	73
xvi	2, 3, 5–7	ii,	75
	28–30	ii,	76
xx	9–12	ii,	77
xxi	4, 6	ii,	79
	13	ii,	79
	28, 29	i,	67
xxiv	21, 22	iii,	549
xxv	4	ii,	81
xxvii	16, 17	ii,	83
xxviii	11, 12	ii,	113
xxxiii	41	ii,	79

DEUTERONOMY.

iv	15	ii,	64
xi	16, 17	ii,	279
xvi	21	i,	130
xvii	2–5	ii,	92
	16, 17	ii,	220
xxvii	4	i,	29
	4–26	ii,	133
xxxi	26	i,	15
xxxii	16, 17	ii,	92
	43	i,	30
xxxiii	8	ii,	108
	passim	i,	91
xxxiv	10	ii,	97

JOSHUA.

i	5	ii,	126
	9–11	ii,	50
vi	3–5	ii,	129
x	8	ii,	131
xiii	1–6	ii,	134
xviii	1, 2	ii,	138
	1	ii,	243
xxiv	14	ii,	92

JUDGES.

i	1, 2	ii,	142
ii	7	ii,	232
iii	7	ii,	235
	12	ii,	147
iv	1	ii,	147
vi	2	ii,	149
	24	ii,	150
	34	ii,	150
xi	9–11	ii,	154
xiii	19, 20	ii,	155
xvi	3	ii,	159
xviii	5, 6, 19, 20	ii,	233
xx	27, 28	ii,	243

INDEX TO SCRIPTURES ILLUSTRATED. 647

1 SAMUEL.

Chapter.	Verse.	Vol.	Page.
ii	7–10	ii,	161
	13	i,	224
v	10	ii,	167
vi	18, 19	ii,	244
	21	ii,	168
vii	1, 2	ii,	244
ix	13	i,	224
x	1	ii,	172
	26, 27	ii,	173
xii	12	ii,	173
xv	28	ii,	177
xvi	5, 11	i,	224
	1, 2	ii,	177
xix	24	ii,	180
xxiii	16–19	ii,	181

2 SAMUEL.

Chapter.	Verse.	Vol.	Page.
v	19	ii,	187
vii	6	ii,	95
x	2	ii,	189
xiv	32	ii,	192
xix	43	ii,	194
xx	25	ii,	244

1 KINGS.

Chapter.	Verse.	Vol.	Page.
ii	15	ii,	197
	28	ii,	205
viii	12–60	ii,	258
ix	17, 18	ii,	212
	26–28	ii,	214
x	6, 7	ii,	216
	16–19	ii,	220
	28	ii,	220
	28, 29	iii,	84
xi	4	ii,	259
	27, 28	ii,	222
	31–38	ii,	222
	38	ii,	271
xii	28, 29	ii,	273
xiv	6	ii,	275
	22–24	ii,	303
xv	17	ii,	276
xvii	1	ii,	279
xix	10, 14, 18	ii,	283
xxi	19, 23	ii,	285
xxii	7, 8	ii,	286

2 KINGS.

Chapter.	Verse.	Vol.	Page.
viii	9	ii,	290
ix	31	ii,	277
xiii	7	ii,	293
xiv	24	ii,	295
xvi	7	iii,	164
	15–18	ii,	330
xvii	4	iii,	89
xviii	4	ii,	332
	32–35	iii,	226
xx	1	ii,	333

1 CHRONICLES.

Chapter.	Verse.	Vol.	Page.
v	1, 2	ii,	243
vi	31–48	ii,	244
xv	2–15	ii,	244
xvi	1	ii,	246
	39	ii,	244
	40	ii,	244
xxi	1	ii,	403
xxviii	12	ii,	208

2 CHRONICLES.

Chapter.	Verse.	Vol.	Page.
i	7–10	ii,	206
v	11–14	ii,	249
vi	1–42	ii,	258
vii	1	ii,	250
viii	17, 18	ii,	217
ix	1–9	ii,	217
	25	ii,	220
x	4, 10, 11	ii,	224
xi	16, 17	ii,	273
xiv	3, 4	ii,	306
xvii	6	ii,	310
	10, 13–19	ii,	311
xx	35–37	ii,	287
xxi	11	ii,	315
xxiv	18	ii,	318
xxv	27	ii,	324
xxvi	16	ii,	323
xxviii	20	ii,	330
xxxii	31	iii,	183
xxxiii	11	iii,	176
	12	ii,	337
xxxiv	14	ii,	339

EZRA.

Chapter.	Verse.	Vol.	Page.
vi	1–12	iii,	268
vii	23	ii,	369

NEHEMIAH.

Chapter.	Verse.	Vol.	Page.
v	8	ii,	372
x	29	ii,	372
	32, 35, 36	ii,	373
xii	27–43	ii,	372
xiii	4, 5	ii,	373

JOB.

Chapter.	Verse.	Vol.	Page.
i	1	i,	357
	5	i,	404
	8	i,	402
v	8, 9	i,	400
vi	4	i,	489
	15–21	i,	485
vii	17	i,	414
ix	4–10	i,	400
xiii	15	i,	411
xiv	10–15	i,	412
xv	8	i,	426

JOB.

Chapter.	Verse.	Vol.	Page.
xvi	12-14	i,	490
xviii		i,	491
xix	23, 24	i,	65
	23-27	i,	409
xx	24	i,	489
xxi	28-30	i,	412
xxiii	10	i,	416
xxvi	5, 22, 26	i,	401
	7, 8	i,	499
xxvii	22	i,	401
xxviii		i,	486
xxxi	13, 14	i,	413
	26, 27	i,	356
	28	ii,	98
xxxiii	23, 24	i,	414
xxxiii	24	i,	416
xxxviii	4-11	i,	403

PSALMS.

viii	5, 6	i,	122
	5	i,	149
xxxiv	22	ii,	254
lvi	10-13	ii,	254
lix	16, 17	ii,	254
lxxviii	60, 67	ii,	244
cx	1	ii,	463

ISAIAH.

i	29	i,	129
iv	5	ii,	331
vii	14	ii,	329
viii	19	iii,	382
ix	6	ii,	463
xiii	17	iii,	576
	19-22	iii,	565
xiv	13, 14	i,	334
	22, 23	iii,	565
xix	2-4	iii,	539
	5-7	iii,	540
xxi	2	iii,	576
xxiii	13	iii,	561
xxxvii	6, 7, 21-23, 28, 29, 33, 34	iii,	550
xli	21-23	iii,	50
xliv	24, 28	ii,	360
		iii,	594
	27	iii,	564
xlv	1-3	iii,	564
	1	iii,	594
	1-5	ii,	360
xlvii	1, 5, 7, 8	iii,	561
	1	iii,	564
liv	9	i,	296
lxiii	9, 10	ii,	97

JEREMIAH.

i	16, 18, 19	ii,	381
vii	12	ii,	243

JEREMIAH.

Chapter.	Verse.	Vol.	Page.
xxiii	18	i,	427
xxv	8-11	iii,	562
	18, 26	iii,	187
	25	iii,	575
xxvi	1-12	iii,	538
xxvii	4-8	iii,	187
			562
	6-8	iii,	194
xxviii	11	iii,	562
xxxii	4	ii,	345
xxxiv	3	ii,	345
xliii	10	iii,	538
xliv	17-25	iii,	213
xlvi	13	iii,	538
xlviii	45, 46	i,	67
l	8-10	iii,	564
	24	iii,	564
li	57	iii,	564
	7, 17	iii,	19
	13, 26, 29, 37, 42, 43	iii,	565
	27	i,	303

EZEKIEL.

viii	7	ii,	383
x	4, 19	ii,	386
	20	i,	146
xi	22, 23	ii,	386
xiv	14, 20	i,	296
xx	7, 8	ii,	92
xxviii	13, 14	i,	148
xxix	14, 15	iii,	539
	18, 19	iii,	538
	18-20	iii,	98
xxx	10, 11	iii,	538
	13	iii,	539
	13-19	iii,	540
xxxviii	2, 15	i,	348

DANIEL.

i	1	ii,	349
	17-20	ii,	352
ii	28-45	ii,	352
			353
	31-45	iii,	563
	33, 34, 41-45	iii,	638
	39	iii,	593
			619
iii	4, 5	iii,	228
iv	7, 8, 19, 20	iii,	640
	25, 30	iii,	229
v	25-28	ii,	357
	31	iii,	198
vi	5	ii,	358
vii	5, 20	iii,	593
	6	iii,	619
	9, 10	i,	427
viii	5-7	iii,	594
xi	2	iii,	274
	14	ii,	415

INDEX TO SCRIPTURES ILLUSTRATED. 649

JOEL.
Chapter.	Verse.	Vol.	Page.
ii	28–32	ii,	392

AMOS.
ix	11, 12	i,	30

MICAH.
v	6	i,	345

NAHUM.
i	8	iii,	552
ii	6, 7	iii,	552
iii	13–15	iii,	552

ZEPHANIAH.
xi	13–15	iii,	553

HAGGAI.
i	6, 8–11	iii,	268
ii	7, 9	ii,	471

ZECHARIAH.
iii	8, 9	ii,	461
vi	12	ii,	462

MALACHI.
i	11	ii,	462
iii	1	ii,	462
iv	5	ii,	462

MATTHEW.
xii	42	ii,	216
xxii	42, 46	ii,	470
xxiv	37, 39	i,	296

LUKE.
iii	35, 36	i,	22
xi	31	ii,	216
xvii	26, 27	i,	296

JOHN.
vi	51, 53–55	i	227

ACTS.
iii	21	i,	216
vii	2–4	i,	370

ACTS.
Chapter.	Verse.	Vol.	Page.
vii	22	ii,	33
xv	16, 17	i,	30
xvi	16	i,	131

1 CORINTHIANS.
viii	10	i,	224

GALATIANS.
iii	17	i,	23

EPHESIANS.
v	2	i,	399

1 THESSALONIANS.
iv	15–17	i,	32

HEBREWS.
ii	9	i,	202
ix	8	ii,	105
	12	i,	202
x	5	i,	30
xi	4	i,	156
	4, 5	ii,	90
	6	i,	197
	7	i,	297
	8–10	i,	405
	9	ii,	26
xiii	10	i,	226

1 PETER.
i	10–12	i,	416

2 PETER.
ii	5	i,	248
iii	2–13	i,	29
	8	i,	97

JUDE.
	14	ii,	474
		i,	66
	14, 15	iii,	143

REVELATION.
iv	6–11	i,	145
xiii	8	i,	202
xvii	5	i,	327
		iii,	19
xviii	3	iii,	19

41°

GENERAL INDEX.

A

Aaron, appointed high-priest, ii, 105—his death, 79.
Abimelech, king in Shechem, ii, 152.
Abraham, history of, i, 369-387—the promises made to him, ii, 14.
Absalom, his rebellion, ii, 192—is defeated and slain, 193—his treason, 554.
Achan, his sin and punishment, ii, 129.
Æneas, legend of, iii, 633.
Ahab, his reign over Israel, ii, 278—his death, and the fulfilment of Elijah's prophecy, 287.
Ahaz succeeds to the throne of Judah, ii, 328—Isaiah's mission to him, 329—his inveterate idolatry, 330—mighty prophetic influence employed to sustain true religion during his reign, 330.
Ahaziah succeeds his father Jehoram as king of Israel, ii, 316.
Ai, the city of, taken, ii, 130.
Alba, legend of, iii, 634.
Alcimus, the apostate high-priest, his remarkable death, ii, 430.
Alexander the Great, his visit to Jerusalem, where he is informed of the prophecies of Daniel, ii, 409.
Alexander Janneus succeeds to the Hebrew throne, ii, 442—saved from ruin by Cleopatra of Egypt, 443—defeated by the combined Pharisees and Syrians, 444—recovers his strength, and completely destroys the rebellious Pharisees, 445.
Alexandra reigns queen in Jerusalem, ii, 446.
Alphabet, its origin discussed, i, 46, *et seq.*—early traditions respecting it, 54—proof of the early knowledge of an, 58—Hartwell Horne's opinion of, 59.
Amalekites, Israelites' conflict with, ii, 61—their origin, 519.
Amaziah, King of Judah, invading Israel, is defeated and taken prisoner, ii, 294—reigns over Judah, 320.
Ammonites tyrannize over Israel, ii, 153.

Amon reigns over Judah, ii, 338.
Amorites resist Israel, and are destroyed ii, 80—two tribes expelled by hornets 545.
Amos prophecies, 296.
Amphictyonic Council, the, iii, 616.
Animal figures, the compound, of Assyria, derived from the cherubim, iii, 218.
Animals, miraculously led into the ark, i, 250—worship of, according to Diodorus, iii, 23.
Anointing of kings, public and private, ii, 551.
Antediluvians, first generation, i, 159—second, 162—third, 163—fourth,163—fifth, 167—sixth, 168—seventh, 168—eighth, 177—ninth, 180—tenth, 180—their religion not destitute of law or revealed truth, 196—were acquainted with the being and government of God, 197—and the fall and depravity of man, 197—had the means of believing on a promised Redeemer, and offered sacrifices typical of his death, 199—believed in a state of future existence, 210—possessed divine laws, 215—observed the Sabbath, 220—intellectual character of, 228-231—addition to their history from the Targums, 233.
Antigonus placed on the Hebrew throne by an anti-Roman party, ii, 455.
Antiochus proscribes the Hebrew faith, and persecutes the faithful to death, ii, 421.
Antipater, his origin and character, ii, 448—he supports Hyrcanus, 448—rules under the nominal direction of Hyrcanus, and extricates Cæsar from great peril in Egypt, 453.
Antony, Marc, appointed executor of Julius Cæsar's will, iii, 452—seduced by Cleopatra, 454—is defeated, and kills himself, 457.
Apostasy of the Hebrews, cause of national ruin, ii, 393.
Apparition of Samuel, ii, 552.

GENERAL INDEX.

Ararat, the ark rested on, i, 300—its geography, 302.
Architectural skill of the patriarchal age, i, 502.
Areopagus, the judicial court of, iii, 617.
Argonautic expedition, the, iii, 603.
Aristobulus wrests the government from his mother, whom he imprisons and starves to death, ii, 441—defeats his brother Hyrcanus, and becomes king of the Hebrews, 447.
Aristotle, his character and doctrine, iii, 399.
Ark of God, taken by the Philistines, ii, 163—wonders wrought before it in Philistia, 167—restored to the Israelites, 167—but not returned to the tabernacle, 243.
Ark of Noah, strange opinions held respecting, i, 246—a wonderful structure, 247.
Army, first standing, of Rome, iii, 636.
Artaxerxes, inscription relating to his reign, iii, 592.
Asa reigns over Judah, ii, 306—effects a religious reformation, 307—induces the Syrians to invade Israel, 308—is reproved by a prophet, whom he casts into prison, 309—the burning for, 387.
Assarac, the great national idol deity of Assyria, iii, 217.
Asshur, his deification in Assyria, importance of, iii, 211.
Assyria, foundation of the kingdom of, i, 435—early history of, 437, 441—the king of, at the instigation of Ahaz, invades Israel, ii, 299—connexion of sacred history with the history of, 578—army of, miraculously destroyed, 579—early intercourse with Egypt, iii, 149—history of, 150—important aid afforded by recovered sculptures of, 150—commencement of connected history, 151—Sardanapalus, his reign and exploits, 151—account furnished by the Obelisk, 154—termination of the old line of kings, 162—Arbaces, a Mede, ascends the throne, 162—reigns of Pul and Tiglath-Pileser, 163—Rawlinson's arrangement of the sculptures which refer to the later period, 164—Sargon (of Isaiah) his reign, 165—account of it from the sculptures, 166—Sennacherib, account of his reign from the sculptures, 168—his own account of his campaign against Hezekiah, 171—Esarhaddon, his reign, 172—conquers Israel, and carries the Ten Tribes into captivity, 176—Nabuchodonosor, his reign, 176—Sarac, his reign, 178—assailed by the Medes, 178—subdued by the Medes and Babylonians, 179—ruling element of its religion, 241—peculiar difficulty of deciphering proper names, 545.
Assyrian sculpture, chronological succession of kings, iii, 546.
Assyrians invade Judah under Holofernes, ii, 338—the general slain by Judith, and the army routed, 338.
Astronomical science, early knowledge of, in China, i, 75—Persia, 75—Chaldea, 76—Bailly's and Brewster's opinion of the early existence of, 77, 78—general view of the evidence respecting the early knowledge of, 80, 81.
Athaliah, daughter of Jezebel, reigns wickedly in Judah, ii, 316—is slain, 317.
Athens, the rebuilding of, iii, 618.
Atonement, great day of, ii, 109—necessity for, believed by the later Hebrews, 488.
Augustus, left heir to his uncle Julius Cæsar, iii, 452—elected consul, 453—with Antony defeats Brutus and Cassius at Philippi, 454—supreme sovereign of the Roman empire, 457.

B

Baal-peor, plague at, ii, 81.
Baasha, his reign over Israel, ii, 276.
Babel, kingdom of Nimrod at, i, 431.
Babylon, kings of, succeeding Nimrod, i, 431—history of, possesses special interest, iii, 181—subject to Assyria, 182—Nabonassar, king of, his reign, 182—Nadius, Chinzirus, Porus, and Jugæus successively reign, 182—Mardocempadus reigns, and resists Assyria, 183—again subdued by Assyria, 184—Nabopolassar king, 184—in conjunction with the Medes, takes Nineveh, 184—Nebuchadnezzar king, 186—his reign, 186-195—Evil-Merodach king, 196—favours the captive king of Judah, 196—Neriglissar, having slain Evil-Merodach, succeeds him, 197—Laborosarchod, the Belshazzar of Daniel, king, 197—his cruelty, profane feast, and death, 198—becomes subject to Media, 199—Labynetus, the governor, revolts, but is subdued, and the city taken by Cyrus, 200—probable state of political relation to Assyria before the reign of Nabopolassar, 553—its magnitude and splendour, 555—chronological succession of kings after Nebuchadnezzar, 556—fulfilment of sacred prophecy in the history of, 561—the type of Papal Antichrist, 570.

GENERAL INDEX.   653

Bacchanalia, infamous rites of, iii, 488.
Balaam, his conduct, ii, 81.
Barak defeats Sisera, King of Canaan, ii, 148.
Bel, the Belus of Assyria, iii, 211—of Babylon, 213.
Belshazzar's feast and death, ii, 357—his case more particularly considered, 582.
Benhadad invades Israel, and is miraculously repulsed, ii, 284—besieges Samaria, and reduces it to great straits; but his army, by the interposition of God, is dispersed, 288—in his sickness consults the prophet Elisha, 290.
Bethel taken, ii, 133.
Beth-shemesh, sin and punishment at, ii, 546.
Bondage of the Israelites in Egypt, ii, 70.
Books, Chaldæan traditions of the early existence of, i, 71—Persian, 71—Indian, 72.
Borrowing by the Israelites from the Egyptians, ii, 514.
Borsippa, where Labynetus took refuge, its geography, iii, 560.
Bows, made of steel or brass, mentioned in Job, i, 489.

C

Cæsar, Julius, policy of, in Egypt and Judea, ii, 453—subdues Gaul, iii, 447—marches on Rome in defiance of the senate, 448—defeats Pompey, and becomes master of the Roman empire, 449—is adored at Rome as a demi-god, 450—is assassinated, 451—his vast designs, 452.
Caleb, his faithful conduct as one of the spies, ii, 74—his brave behaviour, 142.
Calf, the golden, of Aaron, ii, 35—noble and pious conduct of Moses respecting, 65.
Camillus delivers Rome from the Gauls, and restores the city, iii, 418.
Camp, order of the Israelites in their, ii, 68—described, 87.
Canaan, promised to Abraham, ii, 14—to Isaac, 22—to Jacob, 46—thirty-one kingdoms of, subdued, 133—providential preparation for Israelitish invasion of, iii, 535.
Caravans in use in the time of Abraham, i, 484.
Carchemish, route of Pharaoh-Necho to, ii, 581.
Carthage, first war of Rome with, iii, 420—destroyed, 435.
Chaldæan oracles, the information they afford, iii, 207.

Cherubic elements, foundation of animal worship, iii, 24—figures of, origin of animal worship in Egypt, 132.
Cherubim in Paradise, nature of, i, 143; ii, 529—of Ezekiel, their relation to Assyrian sculpture, iii, 568.
China, early history of, i, 442—religion of, 447.
Chronological arrangement of Nebuchadnezzar's dreams, ii, 582.
Chronological position of the lower line of Assyrian kings, iii, 547.
Chronological table of Egyptian history, iii, 126—Assyrian, 180—Babylonian, 201—Median, 250—Persian, 286—Grecian, 359—Roman, 458.
Chronology, importance of a knowledge of, i, 12—of the early ages, discussed, 13—of the Israelites' sojourn in Egypt, ii, 515—of the Judges, 164—of the Hebrew monarchy, 270—of Hebrew history during the Captivity, 376—of Hebrew history from restoration to independence, 433—from independence to time of Christ, 459—of the deliverance of Jerusalem by Judith, 580—of Daniel, 587.
Chushan-Rishathaim, tyranny and defeat of, ii, 146.
Cicero, his exposition of Roman theology, iii, 494.
Circumcision, its divine appointment, ii, 509.
Civilization of first early population of the world, 191, 192.
Clothing, moral effect of its origin, i, 162.
Cloudy pillar, wonderful effect of the, ii, 47.
Coins of Simon Maccabeus, ii, 596.
Commerce, extensive range of ancient, i, 492.
Commercial voyages, early date of Phenician, i, 493—policy of Solomon, effect of, on the conduct of Egypt toward Israel, ii, 560.
Confusion of Tongues, the Mosaic account of, i, 337—the Scriptural account confirmed by learned investigation, 338—a great miracle, 344.
Cosmogony of the Phenicians from Sanchoniatho, i, 109—of the Chaldæans, by Berosus, 110—the Hindus, 111—Persia, 112—Pythagoras, 115—Ovid, 117—review of the Gentile account of, in comparison with the Mosaic, 118.
Council of God, i, 426.
Creation, sublimity of, i, 89—not known by reason, but by revelation, 90—importance of the knowledge of, 91—geological and Scriptural accounts of, considered, 97—state of the case, 97—Mosaic narration of, considered, 100.

Cyrus, Isaiah's prophecy concerning, ii, 359—his tomb, important inscription on, 363—his proclamation of Hebrew emancipation, 363—personal history of, iii, 576—was he acquainted with Daniel's prophecy? 577.

D

Daniel carried to Babylon, and enrolled among the Magi, ii, 352—prophetically declares and explains Nebuchadnezzar's dream, 352—made chief of the Magi and governor of Babylon, 353—delivered from the den of lions, 358—his notation of prophetic time, 590.

Danites, the, prepare the way for idolatry, ii, 232.

Darius Hystaspis, his own account of his wars, iii, 582.

Darius the Mede, who was he? iii, 573.

David, anointed king, ii, 178—builds a tabernacle on Mount Zion for worship, and places the ark there, 244—his religious conduct and experience, 253—kills Goliah, 179—made king of Judah and Israel, 185—takes Jerusalem, and makes it his capital, 186—prosecutes extensive and successful wars, 188—is guilty of murder and adultery, 190—is convinced, and repents, 191—sins by numbering the people, 195—greatness of, displayed in his final arrangements, 198—difficulties in the Scripture narrative of his entrance on public life, 551.

Deborah, prophetess and judge, ii, 148—her noble ode, 238.

Decalogue, proper division of, ii, 527.

Deity, neither the unity nor the purity of, shown by idolatry, iii, 29—language used by the Hebrews when speaking of, ii, 579.

Dejoces, his accession to the Median throne, iii, 572.

Deluge, history of the, i, 241—a punishment for sin, 242—not to be repeated, 399—Scripture narrative of, explained, 242 — peculiar circumstances which preceded it, 251—objection to the Scriptural account of, considered, 254—its universality proved, 256—philosophical refutation of objections, 260—heathen traditions respecting, 267—commemorated in the heathen world, 272—Chaldæan tradition of, 275—Greek, 276—Apamœan medal, 278—Hindu traditions, 279-284—Chinese, 285—Persian, 285—Egyptian, 286—Edda, of the, 286—Jewish, 287—modern traditions found in heathen nations: Peruvians, 289—Cuba, 290—Brazil, 290—Otaheite, 291—Britain, 291, 292—manner of its infliction intended to teach the future races of mankind, 298.

Demon agency, the means by which the magicians of Egypt wrought wonders, ii, 512.

Dictatorship, origin and character of, among the Romans, iii, 636.

Dispersion, history of the, i, 324—the earth, by divine appointment, divided among the sons of Noah, 322—Scriptural account of, attested by heathen traditions, 325—the location of the several tribes, 344—date of the, 479.

Division of Canaan among the tribes, ii, 138—of the Hebrew kingdom, divine purpose in, 570.

Divine influence essential to religious prosperity, ii, 240.

E

Edomites refuse to allow the Israelites to pass through their territory, ii, 78.

Eglon slain by Ehud, ii, 147.

Egypt, early history of, i, 458, 469—religion of, 470-477—the Israelites' sojourn in, ii, 28—monumental proof of, 47—its history, iii, 53—was a nation, not an empire, 54—has not left materials for a complete history, 54—outline of its early state, 56—Eighteenth Dynasty of, its government, 58—advanced state of the arts, 59—warlike operations of Thothmosis III., 64—exodus of Israelites from, 69—Ramses III. ascends the throne, 70—his successful martial career, 71—combination of elegance and excessive cruelty, 76—Nineteenth Dynasty: Rameses, monumental record respecting, 78—Twentieth Dynasty, 79—Twenty-first Dynasty, 81—Tanis or Zoan, 81—contemporary with David and Solomon, 82—Twenty-second Dynasty, 84—Judea invaded by Shishak, 84—Twenty-third Dynasty, 86—Twenty-fourth, 87—Twenty-fifth, 88—Ethiopian power paramount, 89—Twenty-sixth Dynasty, 91—The Dodecarchy, 91—Psammetichus, 92—Pharaoh-Necho defeats Josiah, and exercises the power of appointing a king at Jerusalem, 95—architectural works of great splendour built, 101—Twenty-seventh Dynasty, or rule of Persian kings, 103—cruelty of Cambyses, 104—visit of Herodotus, 107—Twenty-eighth Dynasty, native rule, 107—Twenty-ninth, native kings, 108—Thirtieth Dynasty, native kings, 108—Thirty-first, Persian kings, 111—

Thirty-second, Macedonians, 111—Alexandria built, 111—Thirty-third Dynasty, the Ptolemies, 112—wise government of Ptolemy Soter, 113—a Roman province, 125—great degeneracy of, under the later Ptolemies, 121—its geography and population, 530—chronology of its ancient history, 531—monumental names of its kings, 534.
Egyptian idolatry, progressive development of, iii, 541.
Egyptian sculptures, cruelty exhibited on, iii, 536.
Elah, his reign over Israel, ii, 277.
Eleusinian mysteries, nocturnal scenes of, iii, 625.
Eli judges Israel, ii, 160—his history, 161.
Elijah prophecies, ii, 279—his letter to Jehoram, 577—his conduct and miracle at Carmel, 282—anoints Hazael king of Damascus, and Jehu to succeed to the throne of Israel, 283.
Elim, Israelites arrive at, ii, 57.
Elisha enters upon the prophetic office, ii, 287.
Empires, their origin, i, 481.
Enoch, history and prophecy of, i, 171—piety and end of, 237.
Epicurus, his character and doctrines, iii, 401.
Esau sells his birthright, ii, 510.
Essenes, the origin and character of the sect, ii, 485—were they Christians? 605.
Esther, queen of Persia, ii, 375.
Etruscan origin of Roman power and civilization, iii, 635.
Etruscans, primitive, iii, 460—ancient faith of, 460—theology of, 462—religious doctrines of, 467.
Evil-Merodach succeeds to the throne of Babylon, ii, 356—king of Babylon, iii, 196.
Exodus, wonderful character of the, ii, 46—knowledge and effect of, on surrounding nations, 50—Sir Gardiner Wilkinson on the date of the, iii, 535.

F

Faber, the Rev. G. S., his account of the origin of idolatry, iii, 22.
Faith of the Hebrews, violent aggression on, by Nebuchadnezzar, ii, 396.
Fall of man, Scriptural account of, i, 142—Hindu tradition respecting, 136—Persian, 136—religious consequences of, 149—direct agency of Satan in respect of, 155.
Fetichism, unscripturally and absurdly called "the original religion of mankind," iii, 17.

Fire-worship, Assyrian, iii, 234—origin of, 599.
Fohee, first sovereign of China, whether the same as Noah, i, 480.
Future judgment, believed in Assyria, iii, 240—rewards and punishments according to Zoroaster, 600.
Future rewards and punishments, why mention of them omitted by Moses in the law, ii, 85.
Future state of existence believed by the postdiluvian patriarchs, i, 412.

G

Gauls, the, sack Rome, iii, 417.
Gedaliah appointed governor of Judea after the destruction of Jerusalem, ii, 350.
Gems and precious stones in use in Job's time, i, 487.
Geographical extent of the kingdoms of Judah and Israel, ii, 574.
Geography, knowledge of, in patriarchal times, i, 499.
Geologists, their objections to the Deluge met, i, 294.
Giants, meaning of the term in Genesis, i, 165, 187.
Gibeonites, their craft and doom, ii, 131—their case investigated, 142—their slaughter and its punishment, 554.
Gideon, his call and conduct, ii, 149—his call clearly shown to be of God, 234—following the example of, 234—his ephod, 563.
Glass sent as tribute from Assyria and Babylon to Egypt, iii, 543.
God, manifestation of, in the Mosaic dispensation, ii, 96.
Goliath, his profane challenge and death, ii, 179.
Goodness, compassion, and love of God, believed by postdiluvian patriarchs, i, 403.
Gracchus, Caius, his public conduct and death, iii, 437.
Gracchus, Tiberius, his reforms, iii, 436—his death, 436.
Greece, history of, iii, 313—wonderful character of, 314—geographical outline of, 315—patriarchal origin of, 317—Pelasgians and Hellenes, 317—traditional period, 319—peculiar state of Greece, 320—in early times divided into many and dependent states, religiously united, 320—institutions of Lycurgus at Sparta, 323—of Solon at Athens, 325—the Solonian code in abeyance at Athens while Pisistratus reigned, 329—laws of Solon restored, 330—condition of the states and col-

onies of, 331—first Persian invasion defeated, 336—second, also, at Marathon, 338—third, of Xerxes, vast preparation for, 339—completely repulsed, 344—rapid progress of useful and elegant arts, 345—gained much aid from foreign countries, 346—intellectual elevation of Athens, 347—first Peloponnesian war, 347—Athenian armament against Sicily totally destroyed, 348—second Peloponnesian war, 349—Athens subdued, 349—martial power of Thebes, 351—Philip of Macedon makes himself supreme in Greece, 353—Alexander succeeds his father at Macedon, 354—invades Asia, 354—establishes a mighty empire, and dies, 354—Antipater rules in Greece, 355—Cassander succeeds to the government, 356—the Achæan League under Aratus, 357—the Romans establish their dominion, and make Greece a Roman province, 358.

Greek language, prevalence of, ii, 592.
Groves, sacred, what, ii, 680.

H

Hailstones, miraculous shower of, ii, 541.
Handicraft arts brought to great perfection in patriarchal times, i, 492.
Hannibal invades Italy, iii, 425.
Hazael becomes king of Syria, as predicted by Elisha, ii, 290—his case considered, 573.
Heathens, a knowledge of their religion essential to a sound acquaintance with their history, iii, 15—religion of, not an error, but the work of Satan, iii, 16—history and religion of the ancient nations of, 508.
Heber, house of, ii, 546.
Hebrew community in Egypt, ii, 593.
Hebrew monarchy, general views of, at the death of David, ii, 199.
Hebrew people, remarkable historical account of their origin, ii, 14—their views of Deity, 266—immortality of the soul, 267—faith, peculiar attestation to the truth of, 561—hyssop, figurative import of, 570—several deportations to Babylon, 349—regain their independence, 432—their government, horrid wickedness of, 442—the later, the views they entertained of the promised Redeemer, 463—the effect of their views of the Deity on the doctrine of redemption, 468.
Hebrew religion, historical sketch of, from the time of Israel to Christ, ii, 477—dispensation given of, 493—religion an important development of divine government, 494—a remedial agency, 498—means for carrying out the purposes of redemption, 502.
Heraclidæ, return of the, iii, 612.
Herodotus, value of his testimony respecting the temple of Mylitta, iii, 565.
Herod made king of Judea by the senate of Rome, ii, 545—endeavours to extirpate the Asmonean family, 456—is favoured by Augustus, 457—reigns with great cruelty, 457—domestic cruelty and misery of, 458.
Hezekiah ascends the throne of Judah, ii, 331—labours to abolish idolatry, and refuses to pay tribute to Assyria, 332—his sickness, prayer, and recovery, 333—his vanity, and its punishment, 335.
Hieroglyphics, subsequent to alphabet writing, i, 52, 53.
High places, sacred, their origin and character investigated, ii, 574.
History of the Hebrews, peculiar religious character of, ii, 571.
Hosea prophesies, ii, 296.
Hoshea kills Pekahiah, and reigns over Israel, ii, 299.
Human nature, deification of, a ruling element of heathenism, iii, 22—had its origin in the promised incarnation, iii, 529.
Hunting, referred to by Job, i, 491.
Hyrcanus succeeds his mother Alexandra as king at Jerusalem, ii, 447.

I

Idolatry, antediluvian, i, 234; iii, 525—vast extent of, introduced into the Hebrew temple, ii, 383—its author and character, iii, 17—must have arisen before the Dispersion, 18—postdiluvian, the place of its origin, and principal seat, 19—in Egypt, antitype of its mythology, 22—universal, established in the world, 25—a grand effort to neutralize the scheme of redemption, 26—its ruling agency, 26—affords man no knowledge, 28—reduced to an established form, 205—important passage respecting progress of, 206—of Assyria and Babylon, arose out of patriarchal truth and Elenic representation, directed by him who, as king, aspired to be God, 231—exhibits a gradual, but great, deterioration in the objects of worship, 232—false notions of its origin confuted, 518.
Idumeans subdued, circumcised, and united with the Hebrews, ii, 440.
Immanuel promised, ii, 578.
Intellectual character of the patriarchal

GENERAL INDEX.   657

age, fairly represented in the Book of Job, i, 501.
Isaac, history of, i, 392—the blessing of, ii, 510.
Isaiah, his prophetic ministrations, ii, 327.
Ishmael, history of, i, 392.
Israel and Syria combine to destroy the house of David, ii, 298.
Israelites, national career of, to their passage through the Red Sea, ii, 52—infidelity of, at Kadesh-Barnea, 74—their flagrant rebellion, 74—unfaithful conduct of, 143—lapse into idolatry, 143, 235—number of, who left Egypt, 514—their claims to Canaan, 540—taught and trained by God 562.

J

Jabal and Jubal, their works, i, 177.
Jabin tyrannizes over Israel, ii, 147.
Jacob, his personal history, ii, 19, 28—pottage of, 509—his wrestling with the angel, 511.
Jair, judge of Israel, ii, 153.
Jason purchases the high priesthood, but is deposed and banished, ii, 417—labours to set aside the Mosaic institutions, and to introduce heathen practices and games, 419.
Jehoahaz reigns in Israel, ii, 293—reigns over Judah, 343.
Jehoiachin succeeds to the throne of Judah, and is led into captivity by Nebuchadnezzar, ii, 344.
Jehoiakim reigns over Judah, and becomes tributary to Babylon, ii, 344.
Jehoram succeeds to the throne of Israel, ii, 287—succeeds his father as king of Judah, 315—his cruel fratricide, 315—enforces the practice of idolatry, 315—warned and threatened, and miserably dies as predicted, 316.
Jehoshaphat forms an alliance with Ahab, ii, 286—ascends the throne of Judah, 310—his religious reformation, and system of treating the people, 310—defeats his enemies, 313.
Jehovah, who appeared to the patriarchs a divine person and the promised Messiah, i, 420, 425.
Jehu rebels, kills Jehoram, and reigns in Israel, ii, 291—by craft destroys the supporters of idolatry in Israel, 292.
Jephthah, his history, ii, 154—his vows, 239—his daughter, 565.
Jericho rebuilt by Hiel, ii, 279—the malediction of Joshua, and its accomplishment in Hiel, 572.
Jeroboam, king of Israel, his banishment, ii, 223—becomes king of Israel, 224—his reign over Israel, 271—his religious unfaithfulness, 272—the worship which he establishes, 274—miraculously afflicted and restored, 275—his sin considered, 571.
Jerusalem visited with pestilence, ii, 196—its ruin removed much error from the Hebrew mind, 388—sacked by Ptolemy, who carries one hundred thousand captives to Egypt, 411—stormed by Antiochus, and subjected to horrible cruelty, 420—besieged by Antiochus Sidetes, 439—taken by Herod, aided by a Roman army, 456—taken and destroyed by Nebuchadnezzar, iii, 189.
Jesus Christ condemned to die, not for claiming Messiahship, but for asserting his divinity, ii, 471.
Jethro, his suggestion for the organization and government of the Israelites adopted, ii, 68—his visit to Moses, 520.
Jezebel causes the murder of Naboth, ii, 285—her death, and the fulfilment of prophecy therein, 291.
Joab, his daring energy sustains David, ii, 195.
Joash succeeds his father as king of Israel, ii, 294—reigns piously over Israel, 317.
Job, history of, i, 351, 363—Book of, 364. 368.
John Hyrcanus, alienated from the Pharisees, and favours the Sadducees, ii, 440—subdues the Idumeans, and, on their being circumcised, incorporates them with the Hebrews, 440—dying, bequeaths the government to his wife, 441.
Jonah prophesies, ii, 293—his mission to Nineveh, iii, 236—its great result, 238.
Jonathan, his love for David, ii, 181.
Jones, Sir William, on the Confusion of Tongues, i, 339.
Joseph, his personal history, ii, 27.
Josephus, his testimony, ii, 591.
Joshua succeeds to the government of Israel, ii, 125—leads the Israelites over Jordan, 127—favored with an extraordinary divine revelation, 128.
Josiah, king of Judah, ii, 338—his reformation of religion, 341—resists the progress of the king of Egypt through his dominions, and is slain in battle, 342.
Jotham reigns over Judah, ii, 327.
Jubilee, year of, ii, 113.
Judah, kingdom of, religious character of, ii, 302—relapses into idolatry,

42

303—invaded by Egypt, 304—this event commemorated on Egyptian monuments, 305—placed in danger by an alliance with Israel, 312—threatened by Moab and Ammon, 313—spoiled by the Philistines and Arabians, 315—almost wholly devoted to idolatry, 326—total subversion of the kingdom, 345—the survivors led into captivity, 345—religious view of the ruin of, 378.

Judas Maccabeas, his splendid military career, ii, 424—effects an alliance with Rome, 429—falls in battle, and is succeeded by his brother Jonathan, 429—character of, 429.

Judea, virtually a Roman province, ii, 450.

Judges, their character and power, ii, 146—extent of their authority, 146.

Judgment, future, how represented in the religion of Egypt, iii, 139.

Jugurtha, his character and conduct, iii, 438.

Julius Cæsar. See CÆSAR.

K

Kadesh-Barnea, Israelites at, ii, 71—its geography, 521.

Karaites, the sect of, ii, 604.

King, the Israelites demand a, ii, 170.

Kings of Assyria, regarded as divine, iii, 224—identical with the Sacred Son, 225-227—this proved, 227-230—Babylon, 229—Persia, 291.

Korah, Dathan, and Abiram, their rebellion, ii, 75.

L

Lamech, his history, i, 168.

Languages, three primitive families of, i, 339.

Law, the given, ii, 64.

Legendary history of Rome, general view of, iii, 701.

Literature, the religious, of the Hebrews, ii, 597.

Longevity of early races of mankind proved, i, 184-186.

Lupercalia, infamous rites of, iii, 487.

M

Macedonia subdued by the Romans, iii, 433.

Magi, originally a Median tribe, iii, 290.

Magicians of Egypt, real wonders wrought by them, ii, 511.

Makkedah, Joshua's victory at, over the five kings, ii, 132.

Man, his origin, according to the Chaldæans, i, 120—Hindus, 121—Scandinavians, Romans, and Holy Scripture, 122—his primitive condition, according to Scripture, 122—Jewish tradition, 123—Mohammedan, 124—the Hindus, 124—the ancient Persians, 124—Egyptians, 125—elevated condition of the first, even after the fall, 160—his original condition, iii, 18—the worship of, 528.

Manasseh reigns over Judah, ii, 336—his apostacy and cruelty, 336—is carried into captivity, repents, and is restored, 337.

Manna given to the Israelites, ii, 58—a miracle, 518.

Manoah visited by an angel, ii, 155.

Marah, Israelites arrive at, ii, 56—healing the waters of, 516—laws given at, 517.

Marius appointed consul, iii, 440—and Sylla, their rival factions introduce great disorders at Rome, 444.

Marriage of Solomon with Pharaoh's daughter, ii, 556.

Material elements, worship of, introduced, iii, 25.

Mattathias, his noble resistance of the Antiochian persecution, ii, 422.

Medes, their origin and history, iii, 243—their early character, 244—Dejoces raised to the throne, 245—Phraortes, his reign, 245—is slain in battle, 246—Cyaxares succeeds to the throne, 247—forms an alliance with Babylon, 248—the united army destroys Nineveh, 248—Astyages reigns in Media, 249—is subdued by Cyrus, 250.

Menahem defeats and kills Shallum, and reigns over Israel, ii, 297.

Menelaus outbids Jason, and thus obtains the high priesthood, in which office he promotes heathenish practices still further than his predecessors, ii, 418.

Messiah, a clear apprehension of the prophecies respecting, necessary to a just knowledge of Hebrew faith, ii, 390—teaching of the Old Testament respecting, 468—notwithstanding the explicit teaching of the Old Testament, the later Hebrews did not believe the divinity of, 469—Scripture proof of this, 470.

Metals, working in, common in the days of Job, i, 486.

Micah, his innovation in worship, ii, 143—how far it was corrupt, doubtful, 233.

Midianites, their tyranny over Israel, ii, 149.

Mining, remarkable description of, by Job, i, 486.

Miracle of Joshua, the sun standing still, ii, 542.
Miracles which preceded the Exodus, ii, 32.
Miriam and Aaron resist Moses, ii, 71—her character, 522.
Mithridates makes war on Rome, iii, 441.
Mizpeh, great meeting of Israelites at, ii, 168.
Moab, the plains of, ii, 522.
Moloch, sacrifice of children to, ii, 577.
Monarchy, cause of the Hebrew, ii, 549.
Money, in use in patriarchal times, i, 488.
Monumental inscriptions of Assyria, the, iii, 164—remarkable means by which their reading has been effected, 544.
Morals of ancient Egypt, iii, 134—of Assyria, 240.
Morison, his "Religious History of Man," quoted, i, 43.
Mortgage pillars in Greece, iii, 617.
Mosaic economy, effect of, ii, 124—laws, harmony of, 535.
Moses, his history, ii, 33—his meekness, 521—born, iii, 68.
Murmuring of the Israelites for flesh, ii, 69.
Musical instruments used by the antediluvians, i, 177.
Mylitta, a Babylonian goddess, abominations connected with the worship of, iii, 212.
Mysteries, the heathen, Warburton's views of, iii, 33—refuted by Leland, 34—conflicting opinions respecting, 35—their origin, object, and character, 39, *et seq.*—essential requisites to their celebration, 43—sacred in Greece, 388.

N

Nabonassar, Era of, iii, 553—his reign over Babylon, 182.
Nadab and Abihu, their rebellion and punishment, ii, 67.
Nadab, the son of Jeroboam, reigns over Israel, ii, 276.
Nahash, his cruel threat, ii, 550.
Nahor, account of, i, 368.
Nebuchadnezzar, his impious arrogance, i, 334—destroys Jerusalem, ii, 349—his golden image, 354—terrible infliction on, 355—*rationale* of, 586—reduces Palestine during his father's life, iii, 185—succeeds to the throne of his father, 186—carries away the Hebrews captive, 187—takes Jerusalem, and destroys it, 188—takes Tyre, 189—greatly improves and beautifies Babylon, 190—his dream of the great image, 190—his golden image, 192—his dream of the great tree, 194—its prophetic interpretation and fulfilment, 195—his death, 195—his punishment, and its design, 229—effect of this on the national religion, 239.
Nehemiah goes to Jerusalem as governor, ii, 371—renews the observance of the Sabbath, 373.
New moons, reverence for, ii, 113.
Nimrod, his daring rebellion, i, 328—his profane assumption of religious character, 333—his kingdom at Babel, 431.
Nisroch, the deified Asshur, iii, 211.
Nitocris, the Median princess whom Nebuchadnezzar married, iii, 555.
Noah, prophetic import of his name, i, 240—his mission and ministry, 248—revelation made to him after the Deluge, 306—God's covenant with, 306—his prophecy, and strange circumstances connected therewith, examined, 309—died in Armenia, 320.
Numa, King of Rome, his reign, iii, 411.
Numbering the people, ii, 525—sin of, 555.

O

Obadiah, his faithful conduct, ii, 281.
Omnipotence of Deity, known and believed by the postdiluvian patriarchs, i, 400.
Omniscience, equally recognised, i, 401.
Omri, his reign over Israel, ii, 278—the statutes of, 572.
Onias, the deposed high-priest, murdered at Antioch, ii, 419.
Ophir, geography of, and trade with, ii, 558.
Oracles of Greece, iii, 385—of the heathen, considered, 44—absurd objection to their supernatural character, 45—evidence to show they were sometimes attended by demon agency, 46—result of the inquiry respecting, 50.
Ostracism, banishment by, iii, 617.
Othniel judges Israel, ii, 146.

P

Paradise, heathen reference to the events of, i, 129-133—geographical position of, 141—imitated in the towers and high places of the heathen, 336—imitation of, in the grounds surrounding the palace-temples of the East, iii, 221—the subject further discussed, 569.
Parochial priests, origin of, iii, 483.
Passover, the, instituted, ii, 45—feast of, 112.
Patriarchal age, general view of the history and religion of, i, 505-522—place of worship, ii, 525.

Patriarchs, postdiluvian, history of, to Arphaxad, i, 316—Canaan, 318—Salah, 319—history of, from Dispersion to the death of Isaac, 351–397.

Pekahiah reigns over Israel, ii, 298.

Pekah kills Pekahiah, and reigns in his stead, ii, 298.

Persecutions, wonderful issue of Nebuchadnezzar's, ii, 398.

Persia, early history of, i, 449—religion of, 456—history of, resumed, iii, 251—peculiar interest of, 252—Rawah obtains independence of, 252—annals of early reigns, 253—Cyrus, his early history, 255—his successful war of independence, 256—continued career of success, 258—his conduct to the Hebrews, 259—allows their return to Palestine, 261—his death, 262—Cambyses, King of Persia and Media, 262—invades and subdues Egypt, 263—cruelty and death, 265—Smerdis the Magian reigns, and is slain, 266—Darius Hystaspis reigns, 266—promotes the building of Jerusalem, 268—Babylon revolts, and is subdued, 269—Darius resolves to invade Greece, 271—inscription at Behistun, 273—Xerxes invades Greece, 274—his forces entirely defeated, 276—his diabolical conduct, 277—Artaxerxes, King of Persia, 278—marries Esther the Jewess, 278—Xerxes II. is king, and slain, 279—Darius Ochus secures the crown, 280—demoralized state of the government and court, 280—Artaxerxes III. obtains the throne, 283—Darius Codomannus loses his empire by the invasion of Alexander, 284—deliberation as to mode of government, 580—succession of Xerxes to the throne of, 581—the religion of, 287—difficulty of the subject, 288—essentially the same in its foundation as the Assyrian, 288—divinity of the king fully maintained, 291—in other respects similar to the Assyrian, 291—doctrines held respecting the supreme God, 294—Ahriman, his malignity and power, 296—origin of the sun and fire-worship, 298—antagonism of Ormuzd and Ahriman, 300—account of creation analogous to the Mosaic, 301—nature of the human soul, 302—universal restoration, even of devils, 304—priesthood, 305—their profane claims, 309—festivals, 306—morals, 307—merit, 309—general observations on, 311—probable theology before Zoroaster, 596—predicted invasion of Persia by Greece, 619.

Pharisees and Sadducees become rival sects, ii, 440—origin and character of the sect, 479.

Philistines oppress Israel, ii, 153—defeat the Israelites, 162—miraculously defeated at Mizpeh, 169.

Philosophy, irreligious result of the Grecian systems of, iii, 403.

Plagues of Egypt: water turned into blood, ii, 38—frogs, 38—lice, 39—flies, 40—murrain, 41—boils, 41—thunder and fire, 42—locusts, 43—darkness, and death of the first-born, 46.

Plato, his character, iii, 397—doctrines, 399.

Poetry, beautiful specimen of, in the Song of Moses, ii, 50.

Poisoned arrows in use in Job's time, i, 489.

Pompey interferes in the affairs of Judea, ii, 449—storms Jerusalem, and appoints Hyrcanus high-priest, 450—his military success, iii, 446—rupture with Cæsar, 447—his defeat and death, 449.

Poor, the oppressive laws of Rome respecting the, iii, 637.

Population, progress of, among antediluvians, i, 182—entire postdiluvian, journeyed to Shinar, 326—early postdiluvian, 313.

Prayer, how practised by the Hebrews, ii, 486.

Preaching of Ezra, ii, 475—before and after the time of Ezra, 475.

Priest, the special appointment of Aaron to the office of, ii, 105—Jonathan the high, kills his brother in the court of the temple, 407.

Priesthood, the patriarchal, ii, 523—the Levitical, 533—of Rome, iii, 478.

Profane identification of Jehovah with idolatry, iii, 30.

Prophecy of Ahijah, ii, 222—of Isaiah respecting Cyrus, 359—of Daniel concerning the restoration of the Hebrews, 360—of Ezekiel, 361—of Jeremiah on the doom of Jerusalem, 382—of Ezekiel on the apostasy of Judah, 382—its effect on the Hebrew faith, 391—of the four empires in Nebuchadnezzar's dream, 399—of the precise time of Messiah's coming, and its object, 400—when were the books of sacred, written and collected? 583—the Hebrews returned from captivity, and had their religious economy reconstructed, under the immediate direction of, 460—of Haggai and Zechariah, 461—of Malachi, 462—the divine intention of, frustrated by tradition, 606—fulfilment of, in the history of Egypt, iii, 537—Assyria,

549—Babylon, 561—Media, 575—Persia, 592—Greece, 619—Rome, 638—wonderful influence of, on the policy of Judea, toward the neighbouring nations, 187.
Prophets, schools of the, ii, 170—sons of the, 566—of Greece, iii, 381—Gentile, divine inspiration of, 622.
Providence, views entertained of, by the postdiluvian patriarchs, i, 406—views of the Egyptians on, iii, 143.
Punic war, the second, iii, 425.

Q

Quails given to the Israelites, ii, 71—the wonder explained, 517.

R

Rainbow, conjecture as to its origin, i, 308—deified, 308.
Rationalistic interpretation, its absurdity, ii, 99.
Redeemer, the promised, believed in by the postdiluvian patriarchs, i, 408.
Redemption, primitive promise of, how understood, i, 155.
Red Sea divided for the Israelites, ii, 49.
Rehoboam succeeds his father as king of the Hebrews, and by his folly alienates the Ten Tribes, ii, 224—his conduct considered, 570.
Religion of the antediluvians, i, 362, 404—of the early period of the primitive nations, 431-478—of the postdiluvian patriarchs, 398-430—of the Hebrews in the wilderness, ii, 89-124—while in Egypt, 92-95—important extent and peculiar nature of, 228—undoubted evidence of its truth, 229—of Judah, mighty agencies employed to sustain it during Hezekiah's reign, 334—of the Gentiles, its general uniformity accounted for, iii, 19—promised elements of patriarchal, 20—perverted to idolatrous purposes, 21—of Egypt, general view of, 145—general view of the progress of its declension, 204.
Religious institutions, similarity between Hebrew and heathen, accounted for, ii, 526—doctrines believed in the latter period of Hebrew history, 463.
Repentance recognised as a doctrine of the Hebrew faith, ii, 487.
Rephidim, Israelites at, ii, 60.
Restoration of the Hebrews to their own land, of vast importance as fulfilment of prophecy, ii, 406.
Revelations, special divine, given to Hebrew captives, ii, 394.
Rock, the, smitten at Horeb, ii, 519.

Rod of Moses, miracle of, before Pharaoh, ii, 37.
Rome, legendary history of, iii, 407—the rising power of, 419.
Roman historians, the early, credibility of, iii, 630.
Roman religion complete as an ecclesiastical system, iii, 490—its theology in later periods of its history, 492—its effect on female treatment and manners, 500—countenanced intolerable cruelty, 501—sanctioned the vilest licentiousness, 503—did not prevent the most unnatural impurity, 503.
Romans, their early religion, iii, 470—had no images of God in the time of Numa, 472—their sacred places, 484—worship and sacrifice, 485—offered human sacrifices, 487.
Romulus, his public character, iii, 409—religious education of, 470—and Remus, legend of, 634.
Route of the Israelites from Egypt, ii, 515.

S

Sabbath, the, ii, 113.
Sabbatical Year, ii, 113—computation of, 563.
Sabean worship, its true principle, iii, 566.
Sacrifice, divinely appointed, i, 201—nature of Jewish, 223—flesh of, the only animal food eaten before the Flood, 273, *et seq.*—under the Hebrew law, propitiatory, ii, 261.
Sacrifices, human, of the Egyptians, ii, 514.
Sadducees, the origin and character of the sect, ii, 483.
Samaritans, the sect of, ii, 595—violent party contest between, and the Hebrews in Egypt, 596.
Samson, his history, ii, 156.
Samuel, his birth and character, ii, 161—his judicial circuit, 548—recognised as the prophet and judge, 166—the instrument of a great religious reformation, 168.
Sanhedrim, origin of, ii, 592.
Sargina's wars with Egypt, and the tribute he received thence, iii, 549.
Satan of the Book of Job, i, 427—knowledge of the Hebrews respecting, increased during the Captivity, ii, 403—proof of, 590.
Satanic energy, certain presence of, in Grecian soothsaying and oracles, iii, 624.
Saturnalia, Roman festival of, iii, 489.
Saul, made king of the Hebrews, ii, 173—defeats and destroys the Am

monites, 174—defeats the Philistines and Amalekites, 176—transgresses the divine command, 177—jealous of David, 180—fiercely persecutes him, 181—and his sons defeated and slain, 184.

Scales, alleged discovery of the use of, i, 483.

Schools of the prophets, ii, 548.

Science of patriarchal times, i, 501.

Scipio invades Africa, iii, 429.

Scriptures, the, ought to be regarded by historians, iii, 510.

Scythian domination in Asia, period of, iii, 573.

Semiramis deified, iii, 212.

Sennacherib, his profane and insolent menace, ii, 334.

Septuagint, in some instances corrects the Hebrew, i, 29—chronological testimonies in favour of, 38—version, made by order of Ptolemy Philadelphus, ii, 412.

Serpent, regarded in ancient tradition as the cause of the Flood, i, 138—worship of, 139, 140—miracle of Moses's rod and Egyptian magicians, ii, 37—fiery plague of serpents, 79—the brazen serpent, 522—the form in which Satan seduced mankind into sin, universally worshipped, iii, 27—in Egypt, symbol of dominion, 130—sacred in Assyria, 224.

Serug, history of, i, 368.

Sesostris, his martial career, iii, 535.

Shallum kills Zechariah, king of Israel, and reigns, ii, 297.

Shamgar, his exploits, ii, 147.

Sheba, its geography, ii, 559.

Shekinah, the, ii, 531—of God abandons the temple, ii, 386.

Sibylline Books, iii, 472.

Silk, alleged discovery of its use, i, 483.

Simon the Just, high-priest, ii, 412.

Simon Maccabeus, recognised as sovereign prince of Judea, ii, 433—invested with sovereign power by the people, 437—with two of his sons, basely assassinated, 439.

Socrates, the Grecian philosopher, iii, 393—demon of, its nature, 395.

Solomon ascends the throne, ii, 204—his wisdom, 205—builds the temple, 206—prosecutes other extensive works, 210—his commercial policy, 211—his magnificence and religious declension, 220—his idolatry and death, 223—his piety and inspiration, 259.

Soul, immortality of, believed in Assyria, iii, 215—the, and its transmigration, doctrines of, 628.

Spies sent to survey Canaan, ii, 73—their evil report, 73.

Spiritual religion of patriarchs, reason why not more fully recorded by Moses, ii, 560.

Succoth, halting of the Israelites at, ii, 47.

Synagogues, worship of the later Hebrews in, ii, 475—their origin, 251, 569.

Syria, governors of, oppose the rebuilding of Jerusalem, iii, 579.

T

Tabernacle of Moses, contributions toward, ii, 66—erected, 67—described, 99—filled with the divine glory or Shekinah, 103—important advantages of this manifestation, 103—Mosaic, 528—of David, manner of worship in, 246—typical importance of, 567—importance of its worship to Hebrew religion, 477.

Tabernacles, feast of, ii, 111.

Tages, religious lawgiver of Etruria, iii, 461—institutions of, 466.

Tarpeia, legend of, iii, 635.

Tarquinius, Lucius, King of Rome, his origin, iii, 413.

Tarshish, and its ships, ii, 556.

Temple, the, glorious revelation of God on consecrating, ii, 249—building of the second, commenced, 365—Samaritans oppose its progress, 366—finished, 367—Hebrew worship of the, 472.

Temples, were the royal palaces of the east such? iii, 223.

Terah, account of, i, 369.

Teraphim, Laban's, ii, 510—the, 563.

Theban legends, the, iii, 606.

Theocracy, the Hebrew, ii, 115.

Theogony, the Grecian, iii, 621.

Theology of Egypt, iii, 133—of Assyria and Babylon, 208—outline of, from Col. Rawlinson, 208—Dr. Layard's views respecting, 211—of Greece, 362—of Rome, 474.

Three Hebrew youths, the, nobly refuse to worship the great image, are cast into the fiery furnace, and delivered, iii, 193—religious effect of this divine interposition, 193.

Tola, judge, ii, 152.

Tradition, fatal effects of its adoption on Hebrew faith, ii, 491—unfounded claims of the Mishmaic, 601—patriarchal, special providential provision for perpetuating, iii, 235.

Transmigration of souls, how represented in Egypt, iii, 142.

Tree of life, i, 142.

GENERAL INDEX.

Trees, creation of, i, 104.
Triad of Zoroaster, i, 268—of Egypt, sometimes refers to Noah and his sons, 269—but more generally to the promised Incarnation, iii, 129—changes made in, 542—the Assyrian, 567—its symbol disappears in the later times, 234—its nature and origin, 216—importance of, 217.
Trinity, the doctrine of the, whether known to Plato, i, 266—to what extent understood and believed by the later Hebrews, ii, 464—opinions of Philo respecting the, 464—Targum of Onkelos on, 466—Abraham understood the doctrine of, 467—was the doctrine of, known to the patriarchs? iii, 526—symbol of, in Assyria, 206.
Trojan wars, the, iii, 609.
Trumpets, feast of, ii, 113.
Typical character of Mosaic economy, ii, 123.

U

Urim and Thummim, ii, 107, 533.
Uzziah reigns over Judah, ii, 321—his improvements in exigencies of war, 392—his profane attempt to invade the priest's office punished with leprosy, 323.

V

Valerius, King of Rome, his reign, iii, 415.
Vestal virgins, the, Etruscan, iii, 463.

W

War reduced to a science in the time of Job, i, 490—with Benjamin, chronology of, ii, 145—of six years between the factious Pharisees and the government, 444.
Wise men of Greece, the Seven, iii, 615.
Worship, patriarchal, place of, ii, 525—idolatrous, its vain and corrupt character, iii, 32—of Greece, 377.
Writing, the art of, essential to civilization, i, 46—early origin of, 49—by the early patriarchs, 61, 65—among the antediluvians, 62—employed to give an account of the Flood, 63—first mention of, in the Scriptures, 64—probably used by Noah, 66—Jews had traditions respecting its antiquity, 68.

X

Xerxes, did Jews fight in his army? iii, 590—inscriptions relating to his reign, 591—curious mode of counting his army, 618.

Z

Zechariah reigns in Israel, ii, 297.
Zechariah, the high-priest, martyred at Jerusalem, ii, 319.
Zedekiah placed on the throne of Judah by Nebuchadnezzar, ii, 344—rebels, is subdued, and, having his eyes put out, is led away captive, 345—his punishment, iii, 554.
Zeno, his character and doctrines, iii, 400.
Zerah, his invasion of Judah defeated, ii, 307.
Zimri, his reign over Israel, ii, 277.
Zoroaster, the first, who? iii, 290—the theology of, 293—his creed, 296—conflicting opinions respecting, 595.

THE END.

www.ingramcontent.com/pod-product-compliance
Lightning Source LLC
Chambersburg PA
CBHW021712300426
44114CB00009B/108